# LETTERS OF BASIL BUNTING

# Letters of Basil Bunting

*Selected and edited by*
ALEX NIVEN

OXFORD
UNIVERSITY PRESS

OXFORD
UNIVERSITY PRESS

Great Clarendon Street, Oxford, OX2 6DP,
United Kingdom

Oxford University Press is a department of the University of Oxford.
It furthers the University's objective of excellence in research, scholarship,
and education by publishing worldwide. Oxford is a registered trade mark of
Oxford University Press in the UK and in certain other countries



First Edition published in 2022
Impression: 1



Published in the United States of America by Oxford University Press
198 Madison Avenue, New York, NY 10016, United States of America

British Library Cataloguing in Publication Data
Data available

Library of Congress Control Number: 2021951700

ISBN 978–0–19–875481–7

DOI: 10.1093/oso/9780198754817.001.0001

Printed and bound in the UK by
Clays Ltd, Elcograf S.p.A.

# CONTENTS

# INTRODUCTION

Who cares to remember a name cut in ice
or be remembered?
Wind writes in foam on the sea

*Briggflatts*, Part II, 52–54

On the evening of 22 December 1965, an aging journalist from Newcastle upon Tyne made his way up a battered stone staircase in the city's old medieval walls. When he reached the top, he opened a large wooden door and stepped into a small candlelit room filled with young people.

Over the last eighteen months the Morden Tower, once home to a guild of plumbers, plasterers, and glaziers, had been transformed into an unlikely centre of the global counterculture. From June 1964, a young local couple, Connie and Tom Pickard, had started to use it as a venue for poetry readings. Inspired by American Beat and late-modernist poetry—and nascent scenes in Glasgow, Edinburgh, and Liverpool—the Pickards built up a live venue which breathed life into the culture of a city still searching for a future on the other side of the industrial revolution. In the words of Allen Ginsberg, a notable early headliner, 'the magic enacted in the Tower articulated the unconscious of the entire city slumbering in the mechanic illusions of the century'.[1]

Attracted by its growing international reputation, poets like Ginsberg, Hugh MacDiarmid, Stevie Smith, Robert Creeley, Lawrence Ferlinghetti, Elaine Feinstein, Ed Dorn, Lee Harwood, and J. H. Prynne would make the journey to Newcastle, standing at the centre of the Tower's upstairs room as they intoned their energetic, freewheeling, often highly formally intricate poems. Meanwhile, gathered on the floor around them, and rather in keeping with the demotic mood of the moment, sat an audience which comprised 'half academics, half teenagers, with a sprinkling of thugs'.[2] At times this crowd would include the Pop artist

[1] Allen Ginsberg, 'Allen Ginsberg and Morden Tower', http://www.mordentower.org/allen.html.

[2] See **28/7/64**.

Richard Hamilton (then a Newcastle University lecturer) and future rock musicians Bryan Ferry and Wilko Johnson. But far more important than these soon-to-be-famous figures were the mostly anonymous young women and men who sat on the floor of Modern Tower—people who were, for the most part, experiencing modernist poetry for the first time in a strikingly immediate and vital way. As Tom Pickard would later put it, these members of the audience were 'genuine people'—more to the point, they were 'delinquents' with 'no literary ambitions'.[3] Perhaps this was what Ginsberg meant when he talked about the magic enacted in the Tower.

At the centre of this strange scene was a 65-year-old local journalist, Basil Bunting. A regular attendee of the Morden Tower readings from day one, Bunting had been coaxed back into creativity in recent months, largely through the ambient influence of the Pickards and their friends. In the 1930s, Bunting had been a key figure in a second wave of modernist poetry, which followed in the wake of the earlier, pioneering experiments of Ezra Pound, T. S. Eliot and William Carlos Williams. But since then events had conspired to exile him to the literary margins. Prior to being 'rediscovered' by Tom Pickard in 1964, Bunting had written only a handful of poems since the late 1930s (and none at all since 1951). If he hadn't encountered the Morden Tower and its youthful culture at this point, he would probably have retired from his nondescript job in local journalism the following year, to become a minor footnote in the history of interwar literature.

But the magic of the Tower had rubbed off on Bunting. On this cold evening in the last fortnight of 1965, he would make a belated breakthrough, one that would substantially change not just his own life but also the wider history of modernist verse in English. After climbing the steps of the old city walls and opening the door to a candlelit room smelling of incense and cigarette smoke, Bunting took off his greatcoat and stood in front of the by now familiar throng of teenage delinquents. Then, in a thrumming, melodious voice, he started to read aloud a new modernist long poem for the first time:

> Brag, sweet tenor bull,
> descant on Rawthey's madrigal,
> each pebble its part
> for the fells' late spring.
> Dance tiptoe, bull,
> black against may.

[3] Alex Niven, 'To reach the moon you need a rocket: an interview with Tom Pickard', *3:AM Magazine*, 2 November 2012, http://www.3ammagazine.com/3am/tom-pickard-interview/.

Ridiculous and lovely
chase hurdling shadows
morning into noon.
May on the bull's hide
and through the dale
furrows fill with may,
paving the slowworm's way.[4]

The new work was called *Briggflatts*, and its flight into the air was one of the seminal moments in twentieth-century poetry.

## The Letters

The written record left behind by the author of *Briggflatts* is, however, far from straightforward. Bunting died in his native Northumberland a few weeks after the defeat of the British Miners' Strike in the spring of 1985, just over eighty-five years after he had been born 'amid rejoicings for the relief of Ladysmith in the Boer War'.[5] In between these two historical bookends, he engaged forcibly with two world wars (in two very different ways), worked as a sailor, soldier, journalist, and spy, and played a key role in at least two of the most important poetic movements of the modern era. This extraordinary life, which embodied the modernist century and involved myriad global adventures, was long and dramatic. However, Bunting spent most of it as a relatively unknown figure, without much of a sense that his poetry was being read at all, let alone that his writings were part of an unfolding literary history and might one day be read as meaningful cultural documents.

In appraising Bunting's letters, we must begin by acknowledging this peculiar biographical backdrop. Before his sudden breakthrough with the appearance of *Briggflatts* in the mid 1960s, Bunting experienced several decades of false starts, dead ends, and what might be called serial underachievement. As a result, his correspondence as a whole is wildly uneven and asymmetrical. It is only really in the final, post-*Briggflatts* phase of Bunting's life—the third section in this edition—that his letter writing settles down into the sort of pattern we recognize from the published exchanges of other, more consistently sociable and successful writers.

[4] *Briggflatts*, Part I, 1–13.

[5] See Jonathan Williams, *Descant on Rawthey's Madrigal: Conversations with Basil Bunting* (Lexington, Ky.: Gnomon Press, 1968), no pagination.

Prior to this point, we are faced with a correspondence in fragments of one sort or another. At the time of preparing this edition, the extant material amounted to around 800 letters, of which a little under 200 are presented here. As those familiar with other similar projects will know, this is a comparatively modest body of work to be starting with (though it is, of course, far too large to offer the possibility of a single-volume collected edition). The relative scarcity of Bunting's extant letters is largely a consequence of his marginality for much of the twentieth century. Until his rise to prominence in the mid 1960s, Bunting corresponded with only a handful of notable literary friends. Fortunately for us, those friends were Ezra Pound and Louis Zukofsky (and to a much lesser extent Harriet Monroe, William Carlos Williams, and Dorothy Pound). As a result, though there may be dozens of letters from Bunting's early years to non-literary recipients that have not survived (and are now unlikely to be unearthed), we have in the extensive, well-preserved dialogues with Pound and Zukofsky a relatively comprehensive—and culturally important—written record of Bunting's creative trajectory prior to *Briggflatts* (even if, as we shall see, the biographical record is another matter).

In spite of this fact, however, there are substantial and significant lacunae in the early part of the correspondence, especially in the years before 1930—something of an unknown quantity in terms of Bunting's intellectual and creative development. Biographically, we know very broadly where Bunting was in these years, and what he was doing professionally. However, only around twenty letters have survived from the whole 1920–1930 period (and almost none at all from the preceding two decades). The majority of these are included in this edition—proof of the sparse textual record of Bunting's formative years. Although he was clearly writing poems of a sufficient standard that he corresponded with T. S. Eliot about them (see **10/4/27**), and impressed Pound more generally as something approaching a peer, we do not have a very detailed close-up picture of Bunting prior to 1930 from either poetic manuscripts, of which there are virtually none, or second-hand and retrospective accounts, of which there are very few. Indeed as I suggest in annotations below (see especially **3/12/26** and note), even the basic dating of the poems of this period is sketchy and probably not quite in step with the timeline given in collected editions following Bunting's own later remembered chronology.

The correspondence prior to 1930 does not substantially add to the portrait. Rather, it is a fractured collage of often dazzling and uproarious moments—an aborted trip to Bolshevik Russia in 1920, a first letter to Pound from a Paris jail in 1923, gossipy sketches of W. B. Yeats and Ford Madox Ford—juxtaposed with a handful of more prosaic reflections on the literature of the day and publication prospects. As well as being grateful for the letters to Pound from this interlude deposited in the archives at Yale and Indiana, we must acknowledge the immensely important work carried out in the 1980s and 1990s by Diana Collecott and Richard Caddel at the Basil Bunting Poetry Archive, Durham, in tracking down lesser known recipients like J. J. Adams and Louise Morgan. Given the distance in time, and Bunting's sometimes chaotic existence in the 1920s, it seems unlikely that a much fuller record of the period will emerge, though further accretions to the correspondence are, of course, always a possibility.

After 1930, and especially after Bunting left the Pound-centred expat community of Rapallo for the Canary Islands in late 1933, the picture becomes much less fragmentary. Indeed, after 1931, Bunting's dialogue with Pound becomes subtle, intimate, and frequently compelling. These letters can be exhaustive in both length and subject matter, and so here, for the first time, an editor encounters real problems of selectivity. The 1930s letters to Pound are a seminal document in their own right. They deserve to be published in full, either as a standalone publication or in a more expansive collected edition. In making a representative selection for the present volume, I have tried to preserve the flow of the dialogue, while ensuring that the key points of aesthetic and political debate between Pound and Bunting are included.

Readers familiar with Bunting's narrative may already be aware of the manner in which his 1930s dialogue with Pound ground abruptly to a halt: the explosive letter of December 1938 (**16/12/38**), in which he excoriates Pound's anti-Semitism and seems to put an end to their friendship once and for all. In fact, as we can see from this selection, Bunting and Pound resumed contact fairly soon after the end of World War II, albeit more sporadically and with less intellectual penetration than in the previous decade (and often with legal guardian Dorothy Pound acting as intermediary—letters addressed to Dorothy in this period were typically also intended for Ezra). For the next thirty years or so, Bunting's main prose confidante was Louis Zukofsky, who seems to have acquired this role almost exactly at the same time as the falling out with Pound. These were mostly the years of Bunting's hiatus or middle period—the second section of this volume—a quarter century during which he wrote no poetry at all aside from *The Spoils* (1951) and a handful of short lyrics. As with the first section, the correspondence of these years is erratic at times, with a recession at the height of World War II (for obvious reasons), and a much longer one after 1955, when Bunting abandoned literary work entirely and succumbed to the seemingly interminable 'drudgery' of a desk job at the Newcastle *Journal* and *Evening Chronicle* newspapers.

This is not to say, however, that the letters of these years are uninteresting. Indeed, precisely because Bunting was exiled from literary communities, his exchanges with Zukofsky in the years around 1950 are just as sophisticated and impassioned as the earlier dialogues with Pound. As he confided to Zukofsky in 1949:

> I would hate to have nobody with whom I could be unguarded or even foolish. Perhaps most people reserve such unarmoured self-exposures for conversation: but you mustn't forget that I've been out of reach of conversation now for – how many? – say, with very short intervals, sixteen years. I must be allowed the rather rare outlets; and really there is no one to whom I can write with any hope of being understood except you – so bear with it![6]

As Bunting travelled from America back to Northumberland—and into Italy and the Middle East as the war peaked and reverberated in peacetime—his literary life persisted solely through the medium of his letters, a fact which goes some way toward explaining their great subtlety and depth in this phase.

As well as foregrounding a personal narrative of exile and displacement, the correspondence of the long 1940s is also valuable because it shows modernist poetry entering a strange period. Between relaying news of intrepid adventures in Persia during the war and its aftermath, Bunting's letters to Zukofsky are full of yearning, spiritually inflected asides on the futility of writing verse amid the rubble of the mid twentieth century and its global catastrophes. Even in the 1930s, Bunting had found it difficult to see a way beyond the abstraction and subjectivism of his modernist contemporaries (a position most fully expounded to Pound in 4/1/35). As the events of the 1940s unfolded, he became increasingly convinced that literature itself had come up against an insurmountable dead-end. In 1949, Theodor Adorno famously argued that writing poetry after Auschwitz was barbaric. Bunting would have agreed without a second thought. As he put it to Zukofsky in 1944: 'Our children will never rebuild the Temple: it needs a new race, a new religion; a new heaven and earth.'[7]

*The Spoils*, Bunting's substantial poem of 1951, suggests that in different circumstances he might have responded to the war in less apocalyptic terms. However, just as food rationing in Britain actually became worse in the years after VE Day,

[6] See 6/8/49.
[7] See 25/7/44.

Bunting's most durable depression occurred in the 1950s, after the war and its immediate effects had died down. Though the hardships of these years have sometimes been exaggerated (see my commentary below), it is certainly true that Bunting was entirely creatively inactive following *The Spoils*. Moreover, unlike similar downturns in the 1930s and 1940s, he did not find an escape from his malaise in letter writing. Only a handful of letters are extant from the decade between 1954 and 1964, and those that have survived speak of Bunting's feelings of 'extinction' in terms that are final and indeed on occasion near-suicidal. As he wrote in 1962, in perhaps his darkest letter of all: 'I am ashamed to write to my friends, and they stop writing to me.'[8]

And so we arrive finally at Bunting's late, improbable ascent to major poet status. In 1964 he met the younger poet Tom Pickard and underwent a remarkable upswing in reputation, which goaded him on to write *Briggflatts* and landed him at the centre of the 1960s, their poetry and counterculture. This was, to modify Bunting's earlier metaphor, the rebuilding of the Temple. Suddenly the correspondence becomes more conventionally problematic from an editorial point of view, for being plentiful rather than full of unexplained hiatuses and missing narratives. For a short while after 1964, Zukofsky retained his role as chief confidante, and it is moving to read Bunting trying to communicate to his old friend how abruptly he was turning into a celebrated figure. However, rather sadly, Bunting and Zukofsky seem to have fallen out around the time of *Briggflatts* (as Bunting hints in 30/3/67, jealously seems to have been partly to blame), and the nature of the correspondence changes quite markedly as a result.

Scottish poet Gael Turnbull was by far and away the most frequent correspondent of the post-*Briggflatts* period: he received regular letters from Bunting for much of the 1960s and 1970s (though many of these are short-ish updates handwritten on front and back of airmail envelopes, and their focus is often on Turnbull's own work, which Bunting mentored). Alongside Turnbull, the London poet Denis Goacher was a major interlocutor; and later, when Bunting was geographically separated from his young sidekick Tom Pickard, their relationship was kept up in prose—while more personal news was relayed to his American daughter Roudaba. However, Bunting never quite found a replacement for his near contemporaries Pound and Zukofsky. After the deep, contrapuntal dialogues of earlier years, the final phase of the correspondence is striking in its greater polyphony, but it can also be superficial, with a large number of letters focusing on legal and business matters (arrangements for reading events, letters

8 See 7/8/62.

to publishers, wrangles with poetic antagonists) and a similar number of relatively cursory notes to people Bunting did not know especially well.

In making a selection for this final, 'normative' phase of Bunting's life, I have tried to cut out as much of this sort of material as possible, while mainly preserving letters containing rich, ruminative passages on philosophical, creative, and literary subjects. Even with a much more stringent approach to selection, however, the final section in this edition is by a clear margin the longest. This seemed appropriate given the much greater volume of extant material (around 600 of the 800 letters), but also because I have not yet met a reader of Bunting who does not think that his poetic achievement rests mainly on *Briggflatts*. Even though the final section covers only twenty-one years, it is the *Briggflatts* phase of the correspondence, and therefore, I think, deserving of more sustained treatment than previous sections, in spite of their more intimate and involved exchanges.

## The Significance of the Correspondence

### *Style*

In appraising the style of Bunting's letters, we are faced with incongruous accounts—most immediately those of Bunting himself and certain of his recipients. According to Denis Goacher, a major correspondent for much of the 1960s and 1970s, Bunting was reluctant to send letters in the first place because of his stylistic narcissism:

> His prose style, for example, was absolutely excellent but he was such a vain old devil...he said he wasn't a good letter writer. I was lucky to receive quite a few letters from him. But he didn't write very many letters because he wished—if he *did* write a letter—for it to be, oh, a small prose masterpiece. Now this is vanity.[9]

The psychological inferences here are questionable: self-doubt seems a more likely explanation for Bunting's painstaking creative habits than personal vanity. But Goacher is right that Bunting was often eager to downplay his skill as a prose writer and preclude the idea that his letters were anything other than proxy conversations. As he put it to Louis Zukofsky in 1949:

[9] 'Denis Goacher Talks About Bunting', ed. Diana Collecott, in *Sharp Study and Long Toil: Basil Bunting Special Issue* (Durham: Durham University Journal Supplement, 1995), 205.

> If I wanted to write 'for keeps' I wouldn't have the time, and anyway, never, even when I thought a lot better of myself than I do nowadays, did I write letters intended to be commitments. I write such things at all only because there is nobody with whom I can converse on literary (or most other intelligent) subjects. I forget what I have written: the rejoinder that might make good conversation at the time must necessarily come too late.[10]

Readers will come to their own conclusions about which of these statements is more accurate. But it is probably fair to say that both of the stylistic modes suggested here—one of meticulous care, and another of more offhand familiarity—are present in Bunting's correspondence at different moments in time, and to different recipients.

However, Goacher's notion of the carefully crafted 'small prose masterpiece' is the one that fits with Bunting's wider approach to the written word, and it is this mode that is most often at the forefront in the correspondence. Given Bunting's austere poetic method (embodied in the counsel in *Briggflatts* to 'Take a chisel to write'), it is improbable that he would suddenly have become slapdash and whimsical when he turned to his letters. We must remember that in spite of his non-conformist sensibility and bohemian instincts, Bunting was raised in an early-twentieth-century bourgeois environment and educated in the rigid traditions of the English public school system. Though it is entirely right to emphasize that he often tried to kick against these formative influences, it is also true that his mannerisms were shaped by his strict schooling, and by the formality and punctiliousness we would expect from a doctor's son born in the last year of Victoria's reign.

For the most part, Bunting's letters reflect his post-Victorian beginnings. They are highly eloquent, often densely worded, and always remarkably precise. Bunting rarely made errors, and even the handwritten manuscripts in the correspondence are usually very cleanly executed and mostly free of strikethroughs and other redactions. However, while they are nearly always scrupulous in manner, Bunting's letters are stylistically quite different from those of more conventionally 'English' figures of a similar vintage—W. H. Auden, say, or, from a later period, Philip Larkin. As the letters show quite bluntly (see for example the forthright comments on 'Auden & his friends' in **14/3/51**), Bunting felt a strong and profound antipathy to the centralized culture of the English literary establish-

[10] See **6/8/49**.

ment, its members, and mores. Partly as a result, and even though he never quite abandoned the post-Victorian high style, his prose can be abrupt, colloquial, and sharp-edged in ways that contrast with the smoother, easier tonalities of even supposedly shocking modern and modernist figures, like members of the Bloomsbury Group or the Auden circle.

At times the choppy muscularity of Bunting's diction seems to arise from his status as a transatlantic writer. Though his letters never deteriorate into the chaotic, slang-heavy *parole* of Pound's later correspondence, with Pound and Zukofsky as main recipients the numerous Americanisms (cussed, bullshit, eats) and phonetic spellings (Cawnsoivtifs, corrisponunce, littery, intellecthools) are predictable. And indeed, at times, especially in the 1930s, Bunting does venture to ape Pound's demotic drawl at greater length (as in the first few passages of **11/11/38** and throughout **6/5/35**). In later years, Bunting's transatlantic diction is joined by Arabic and Farsi fragments, in a further deepening of this cosmopolitan modernist texture.

But perhaps a more crucial factor here is Bunting's northernness. Despite being distanced from the proletarian culture of his native north-east by class and schooling, there was a definite Geordie element in Bunting's writing, even before his sometimes arch and exaggerated embrace of Northumbrian cultural identity in the years after *Briggflatts* (see **14/8/76** for an example of his slightly contentious avowal of northern accents). The letters are mostly free from dialect, though here and there words like 'thrang', 'thole', and 'canny' poke through. More generally, as in Bunting's prosody, there is a brusque, end-stopped aspect to his sentences, which to my ear pretty unmistakably betrays his upbringing in the north-east (and, we might add, the fact that he spent the majority of his life among its people, unlike, say, Auden, who eulogized certain uninhabited landscapes of northern England without ever really having lived there).

Bunting's long immersion in the northern English soundscape is surely somewhere behind curt, coal-black formulations like:

> Besides I have got married and my wife eats too. (**2/8/32**)
> What a BORE the hull bloody creation is. (**5/3/35**)
> They have all cut off their own bollocks. (**21/3/34**)
> Auden... showed some signs, if not of life at least of having read something living, but promptly kicked the bucket... (**End of May 1935**)
> No, life is not comfortable often or for long; but fortunately life isnt long either. (**25/5/70**)

Indeed, at several moments, the cultural persona Bunting's diction most recalls is the sardonic, put-upon protagonist of the 1989 BBC sitcom *Blackadder Goes Forth*.

Like Blackadder, a World War I captain played by the north-east actor Rowan Atkinson, Bunting seems to have had an apparently limitless reserve of caustic, world-weary northern remarks to set against the stupidity and rhetorical bombast of his more successful and entitled upper-middle-class peers.[11] In his last years, abetted by elderly grouchiness, this diabolical Geordie mode reached a peak of morbid eloquence, as in the following description of Gregory Corso from 1984:

> The London trip tired me very badly, and the drive home was bad – chiefly because Gregory Corso had wished himself on the journey. He is a clot. He lay in a corner of the backseat, looking at nothing all the way, but keeping his windows wide open to blast the rest of the car; and when we paused for a coffee he complained of the ugliness of the English scenery he hadnt looked at. I'd have liked to piss on him.[12]

It is hard to imagine T. S. Eliot expressing himself in quite this register.

## *Criticism and Biography*

In considering the deeper implications of Bunting's correspondence, there is a limit to how much an editor can or should intrude on the reader's own interpretative experience by providing partial and summary analysis in a paratext. But some sense of the position of this edition in the context of existing writing on Bunting will be helpful—not least to point out the need for further contributions to the field. Criticism of Bunting's poetry continues to develop from the rather humble origins of the late twentieth century, as work by younger researchers like Annabel Haynes, Malachi Black, and Alex Wylie emerges to broaden and complicate the pioneering first-generation accounts of Peter Makin, Victoria Forde, Peter Quartermain, and others.[13] But overall it would be fair to say that there is still much to do where Bunting scholarship is concerned.

[11] Part of the impetus behind Atkinson's portrayal is a comic upending of the stereotype that people from the north-east are clownish boors in comparison with sophisticated, intellectually sharp southerners—an inversion also implied at several moments in Bunting's correspondence.

[12] See **29/5/84**.

[13] See Annabel Haynes, 'Making Beauty: Basil Bunting and the Work of Poetry', PhD thesis, Durham University, 2015; Malachi Black, 'Skeltonic Prosody in Bunting's *Briggflatts*', *Textual Practice*, 28:5, August 2014, 861–879; Alex Wylie, 'Bunting and the Vile Patterns of Expediency', *Essays in Criticism*, 65:3, July 2015, 305–325; Peter Makin, *Bunting: The Shaping of His Verse* (Oxford:

Following Bunting's rise to attention in the wake of *Briggflatts*, and especially as the growth of academic publishing accelerated in the 1970s, a number of critical articles and interviews attempted to shed light on his work. Because he was a poet very clearly in the tradition of Pound, and moreover one who seemed to acquire the mantle of Grand Old Man of Modernism after Pound's death in 1972, these articles tended to be published in Poundian outlets like *Agenda* and *Paideuma*. Indeed both of these journals published comprehensive special issues on Bunting (in 1966 and 1978, and 1980 respectively), with contributions from a reliable cast of modernist critics like Kenneth Cox, Charles Tomlinson, Hugh Kenner, and Donald Davie. Many of these pieces are valuable, though they can be limited by being somewhat partisan in emphasis—unsurprisingly given the coterie setting, and the fact that Bunting was often virtually peering over the shoulders of the authors while they wrote.

After Bunting's death two monographs devoted exclusively to his work appeared (at the time of writing, they remain the only substantial book-length critical studies on his writing, though Julian Stannard's 2012 volume on Bunting for the Writers and their Work series is a useful primer). Both Victoria Forde's *The Poetry of Basil Bunting* (1991) and Peter Makin's *Bunting: The Shaping of His Verse* (1992) benefitted from Bunting's input in their preparation, which helped to ensure they are authoritative and deep-reaching in their biographical summaries and explications of the poetry—even if, like the earlier special issues, they often take Bunting at his own word as a default position. Allowing for this caveat, Makin's study in particular is comprehensive in range, expertly written, and still without question the definitive long-form critical work on Bunting.

As the post- and anti-modernist 1990s and early 2000s progressed, Bunting's reputation began to dwindle, notwithstanding publications appearing via the Durham University Bunting Archive, such as Peter Quartermain's 'Basil Bunting: Poet of the North', Richard Caddel's mini-biography, *Basil Bunting: A Northern Life*, and another *Festschrift* of 1995.[14] As first-generation Pound scholars like Kenner and Davie departed the scene, Bunting was left mostly without scholarly advocates, and he came to be viewed as a rather obscure figure, one without much appeal for either traditionalist critics or ascendant movements like postcolonialism and feminism which often come to the rescue of neglected writers. After the publication of Keith Alldritt's lively but quickly assembled 1998 biography *The*

OUP, 1992); Victoria Forde, *The Poetry of Basil Bunting* (Newcastle: Bloodaxe, 1991); Peter Quartermain, 'Basil Bunting: Poet of the North' (Durham: Basil Bunting Poetry Archive, 1990).

[14] See Richard Caddel and Anthony Flowers, *Basil Bunting: A Northern Life* (Newcastle: Basil Bunting Poetry Archive, 1997) and *Sharp Study and Long Toil*, as above.

*Poet as Spy*, and the 2000 essay collection *The Star You Steer By: Basil Bunting and British Modernism*, almost nothing appeared on Bunting for over a decade.[15]

However, in the 2010s Bunting underwent a slow but significant critical revival. In scholarship there was a growing theorization of British regional poetics, which helped to situate Bunting's marginality in context. Picking up on earlier regionalist appraisals by William Wooten and John Tomaney, both Matthew Hart's *Nations of Nothing But Poetry: Modernism, Transnationalism, and Synthetic Vernacular Writing* (2010) and Neal Alexander's chapter in the essay collection *Regional Modernisms* (2013) did a good job of examining Bunting's geographical orientation and closeness to analogous British-Isles figures like Hugh MacDiarmid and David Jones.[16]

But the two major developments of the last decade were in poetic editing and biography. Published in 2016, Don Share's *The Poems of Basil Bunting* is an exhaustive, milestone edition of Bunting's verse. Share's edition goes way beyond the old Bloodaxe *Complete Poems* (2000), collecting together drafts, variant versions, translations, and juvenilia, and providing copious annotations which situate the poems in their literary and biographical contexts. Indeed, the book's only major limitation is that its encyclopaedic paratexts are so rich in material—amounting to well over half the edition's 600-odd pages—that they can be difficult to navigate in the absence of an index.

Alongside Share's poems, and generating a similar amount of tertiary discussion in settings like the *London Review of Books* and the *Times Literary Supplement* (Share's book also occasioned a feature in the *New Yorker*), the appearance in 2013 of Richard Burton's *A Strong Song Tows Us: The Life of Basil Bunting* ensured that Bunting was finally given full biographical treatment.[17] Burton's book is relatively light on critical explication, but as literary history it is engaging, expansive, and meticulous in its research, with an impressive grasp of the diversity of mater-

[15] See Alldritt, *The Poet as Spy: The Life and Wild Times of Basil Bunting* (London: Aurum Press, 1998) and *The Star You Steer By*, ed. James McGonigal and Richard Price (Amsterdam: Rodopi, 2000).

[16] See William Wooten, 'Basil Bunting, Regional Modernism and the Time of the Nation', *The Star You Steer By*, as above; John Tomaney, 'Keeping a Beat in the Dark: Narratives of Regional Identity in Basil Bunting's *Briggflatts*', *Environment and Planning*, 25:2, April 2007, 355–375; Matthew Hart, *Nations of Nothing But Poetry: Modernism, Transnationalism, and Synthetic Vernacular Writing* (Oxford: OUP, 2010); Neal Alexander, 'The Idea of North: Basil Bunting and Regional Modernism', *Regional Modernisms*, ed. Neal Alexander and James Moran (Edinburgh: Edinburgh UP, 2013).

[17] See Burton, *A Strong Song Tows Us* (Oxford: Infinite Ideas, 2013); Paul Batchelor, 'Follow the Clue' (review of *A Strong Song Tows Us*), *TLS*, 18 July 2014; Michael Hofmann, 'Imagine Tintin' (review of *A Strong Song Tows Us*), *LRB*, 9 January 2014; Christopher Spaide, 'The Improbably Life and Prescient Poetry of Basil Bunting', *New Yorker*, 2 August 2016.

ials relating to Bunting's life and work. It is a hugely useful companion piece to *The Poems of Basil Bunting*, and seems likely to remain the go-to biography for many years to come. At many moments during preparation of this edition, it was a sympathetic and reliable reference text.

However, there are some shortcomings in *A Strong Song Tows Us*, which must be pointed out in the context of this edition of the letters. The first relates to a key facet of Bunting's personal and creative identity. Burton dedicates several pages of his book to a rebuttal of the notion that Bunting was a Quaker poet, arguing that he was an atheist for whom Quakerism functioned 'spiritually, but not religiously'.[18] This is a rather nice distinction, and indeed the whole weight of Burton's argument against Bunting's Quakerism seems to me misplaced, and not really in accordance with the evidence of the letters. Burton quotes, somewhat out of context, Bunting's statement to Zukofsky in **18/12/39** that he was 'fundamentally averse to acts of faith'; however, he might easily have juxtaposed this with Bunting's claim in **5/5/47** that he was 'a kind of Christian', or indeed the long and subtle discourses on Christianity in **21/1/47** and **6/1/51**. Certainly, Burton's claim that Bunting 'was firmly trying to distance himself from the reductive "Quaker poet" tag' is not tenable.[19] Bunting went to Quaker schools, endured a brutal prison experience in 1918–19 for the sake of Quaker principles, and based his poetic autobiography *Briggflatts* on one of the sacred foundational sites of Quakerism—a denomination which is, crucially, well-known for its non-doctrinal inclusiveness. His posthumous 'Note on *Briggflatts*' locates Quaker beliefs and practices at the centre of his imaginative universe, and lest we be tempted to regard this religious impulse as a quirk of old age, we have the evidence of Bunting's first letter to Pound in 1923, in which he states: 'I was born and bred a Quaker.'[20] It is useful to qualify Bunting's religious credentials and apply scepticism to his claims in general. But that he was a self-identifying Quaker poet at several important moments is beyond doubt.

A more general point to emphasize about *A Strong Song Tows Us* is its approach to the overall shape of Bunting's biography. In producing a readable account of Bunting's life, it is of course understandable that a biographer should try to summarize the available materials and pass over undocumented interludes without too much conjecture. However, what is often not apparent from the rather smooth-edged narrative of *A Strong Song Tows Us* is just how much of Bunting's life is a terra incognita as far as the written record is concerned. In the context of

[18] Burton, 394.

[19] Ibid., 391.

[20] See 'A Note on Briggflatts' (Durham: Basil Bunting Poetry Archive, 1989) and **15/10/23**.

an academic appraisal of Bunting's archival legacy, this fact must be stated plainly rather than tidied up for the sake of narrative flow.

As mentioned above, the sources of information about Bunting's final two decades are ample, at least in comparison with the norm for twentieth-century poets (though even in these final years, as I try to stress in my annotations, there are plenty of ambiguities). What must be foregrounded above all, however, is that the vast majority of Bunting's life prior to *Briggflatts* was lived more or less off-radar—a fact which has major implications for both the present edition and a wider consideration of Bunting's biography. While Burton does a good job of ironing-out the narrative of Bunting's life to present a clear portrait in *A Strong Song Tows Us*, for most of the time his account simply progresses from one well-documented interlude to another, without a really clear sense that many undocumented months (and sometimes years) have unfolded in between.

In contrast, in my selections and commentary for the present edition, I have tried to be forthright about the gaps in Bunting's narrative, highlighting the moments (sometimes amounting to entire decades) where, we have to be honest, we still know very little about what Bunting was doing, let alone thinking. This approach will, I hope, ensure that individuals can generate their own conclusions about problematic or unexplained subjects in Bunting's life and work, rather than being led to believe that his narrative has been definitively mapped.

## Editorial Principles

Partly because Bunting's letters have appeared in fragmentary settings prior to this point—for example in quotation form in Makin's *Bunting: The Shaping of His Verse* and in Burton's *A Strong Song Tows Us*—and also to retain the shape and integrity of Bunting's own compositions, I have endeavoured to include all letters as complete documents, rather than incorporating extracts in a 'selected highlights' format.

This means that quite a few interesting shorter passages and *bons mots* do not feature in the selection. However, as the purpose of this edition is to create a comprehensive and readable first edition of Bunting's letters rather than a collage of choice sayings, it seemed important to let the reader get a sense of the materiality and flow of the correspondence *as correspondence*, by heeding the basic principle of including Bunting's whole text from salutation to signature. Accordingly, from the other side, I have tended to omit attached poetic drafts where they are not included within the body of the letter itself, as they seemed to constitute a separate document (and, moreover, Bunting's poems have already been comprehensively dealt with in Don Share's 2016 edition, *The Poems of Basil Bunting*).

The most formidable problem facing an editor of Bunting's letters is his fiercely iconoclastic approach to all manuscripts other than published poems. As he puts it plainly to Denis Goacher in **4/9/65**, 'I disapprove of manuscripts, letters, etc ... alive or dead.' Readers of this edition will note that Bunting's correspondence is littered with similar statements. The most caustic is surely the following note to Roger Guedalla, an early bibliographer of Bunting, who was one of the first people to take on the remorseless task of codifying his written output:

> I am very sorry to hear that you have come across references to collections of my letters. I thought I'd got all my correspondents to burn them up, except a few which Zukofsky sold to the University of Texas a number of years ago which I've no hope of abolishing unless I set fire to the whole place, a task rather beyond my years. If you do lay hands on any, please abolish them as drastically as you can.[21]

The first issue raised by this testimony, and others like it, is one of ethics. It is fairly clear that Bunting did not like editions of writers' correspondence, and that he strongly disapproved of his own letters appearing in public during his lifetime. However, as Bunting half acknowledges here, even before his death in 1985, much of the correspondence was available to interested members of the public in several research archives in Britain and the United States (and thereafter, in extracted quotations published in the critical and biographical texts mentioned above). As almost all of the correspondence was previously accessible—albeit only to those with the means to travel to multiple disparate locations—I felt licensed in preparing this edition to ignore Bunting's desire to keep his letters unpublished, though readers should of course keep this intention in mind when reading them. In cases where personal material ran the risk of negatively affecting Bunting's relatives and other people alive at the time of writing, letters been automatically omitted, at the explicit request of his Estate.

The question then becomes one of *how* rather than *whether* the correspondence should be published. As mentioned, my own response has been to try to present Bunting's own texts as faithfully and extensively as possible given the constraints of a selected edition, with editorial intervention strictly limited to selection, commentary, and notes. On the very rare occasion that Bunting's text itself has been

[21] See **25/10/68**.

amended on the way to presentation here, this was a case of correcting obvious, semantically insignificant typographical errors during transcription and editing (for example, amending 'f rom' to 'from'). I have also standardized some very minor typographical quirks such as dashes, which are presented here as n-dashes unless absolutely necessary. This was for the sake of basic clarity and readability. However, all errors that seemed to bear even the faint possibility of semantic significance have been left as found (for example, variant spellings of Attis/Atthis, and Bunting's extravagantly inconsistent use of contractions, a stylistic trademark which Share discusses in the introduction to his collected poems).[22]

A bigger problem arising out of Bunting's textual iconoclasm relates to the absence of key supporting materials, both by Bunting and, more substantially, his correspondents. If we are to believe Bunting's comments to Zukofsky, he encouraged certain friends to burn his letters, a fact which, if true, would further compound the problems of unevenness and discontinuity discussed above. However, based on my experience of the available materials, I think this claim is almost certainly exaggerated or false. There are very few references to missing correspondents in the texts that have survived, and it is hard to imagine Bunting carrying on a meaningful dialogue and then calling for it to be destroyed without someone somewhere mentioning it over the last several decades. As outlined above, some individual letters—including those to major figures like Eliot and William Carlos Williams—do indeed appear to be missing. However, though the possibility cannot be ruled out, it seems unlikely that either of those figures were sitting on large piles of material that were at some point unloaded onto the fire at Bunting's instigation (partly because Bunting clearly did not make such a request to more obvious candidates like Ezra Pound or Gael Turnbull).

It does however seem almost certain that Bunting did destroy or discard the vast majority of letters sent to *him*. In the 1949 letter to Zukofsky quoted above, indeed, there is clear evidence for this:

> But perhaps I should be blamed for not remembering that you do keep letters, and see in them something more than a rather tired man's turning away from the stupid preoccupations he earns his living by. That, as you remember, has always made me uneasy.

These comments seem unambiguous: keeping letters made Bunting uncomfortable, so, unlike Zukofsky, he didn't do it. The archival record confirms that, in this

[22] See Share, *The Poems of Basil Bunting* (London: Faber & Faber, 2016), xxxvii.

instance, Bunting was probably not exaggerating. Though many letters sent to him have survived, usually in carbon copy or facsimile retained by the sender, the vast majority—including many crucial parts of the other half of the dialogues with Pound and Zukofsky—are missing.

Clearly, this is the right way around in the essential sense: there would be no question at all of an edition like this had Bunting's recipients destroyed *his* half of the correspondence. However, the lack of most of the other side of the dialogue creates obvious interpretative problems when examining Bunting's texts, problems that are not possible to resolve by the usual route of referring to other editions or providing annotations that summarize the gist of the document or passage he is responding to. However, I do not think there are many moments in the correspondence where an intelligent reader with a basic working knowledge of modern poetry cannot infer the essential details of Bunting's account (and probably, such readers will be used to tackling writing that is not always cleanly and immediately knowable if they have ever tried to read the best poems of Bunting, Pound, and Zukofsky).

In providing annotations and commentary to Bunting's text, I have tried to heed the sense that certain basic factual details are necessary to navigate the correspondence, while being mindful about the impossibility of annotating absolutely everything and purposeful about the need to present an engaging first selection of the letters (rather than an exhaustive and impregnable collected works). The gappiness of the correspondence calls for fairly copious editorial intervention at times, but I have tried to simplify matters by assuming that readers will know the very broad outline of Bunting's life and work, and of the wider trajectory of twentieth-century poetry—for example, basic knowledge about seminal works such as Pound's *Cantos* and Eliot's *The Waste Land*. Brief biographies of names are provided in the notes and in the Glossary of Names, though I have assumed that major historical and literary figures (e.g., Dante, Charles I, Swift, Baudelaire, Hart Crane, Eleanor Roosevelt, Churchill, etc.) do not need to be glossed. For ease of reference, less well-known correspondents are given a short footnote, in addition to their entry in the Glossary of Names.

More generally, and again in order to reduce editorial intervention and ensure primacy of place for Bunting's texts, I have tried to be as succinct as possible in my paratexts, and not to digress too often on matters such as the minutiae of Bunting's poems or critical interpretations of his work—though at certain key moments, such as when the letters bear upon a contentious point in Bunting's work, I have intervened at greater length. Readers who wish to follow up on specific poetic references in the letters should do as I did while preparing this edition, and keep a copy of Don Share's authoritative edition of the collected poems beside them at all times.

I have already discussed the broader critical terrain in the previous section, but it bears repeating that there is scope for much more to be published on Bunting—not least, of course, a full, collected edition of the correspondence. I hope this substantial initial selection will join other recent texts in preparing the way for future work in the field, and in provoking more subtle and far-reaching discussion about a writer who really should now be placed—once and for all—in the foreground of twentieth-century poetry.

*Newcastle upon Tyne, 2022*

# NOTE ON REFERENCING

The letters in this edition are held in the following archives, referenced in the text by a short form of their title (usually that of the attached university):

Buffalo—The Poetry Collection, State University of New York at Buffalo
Chicago—Special Collections Research Center, University of Chicago Library
Durham—Basil Bunting Poetry Archive, Durham University Library
Emory—Manuscript and Rare Book Library, Emory University
Essex—Donald Davie Papers, The Albert Slowman Library, University of Essex
LSE—Lionel Robbins Papers, London School of Economics and Political Science
Indiana—The Lilly Library, Indiana University
Scotland—Gael Turnbull Collection, National Library of Scotland
Stanford—Department of Special Collections, Stanford University Libraries
Texas—Harry Ransom Center, University of Texas at Austin
Yale—Beinecke Rare Book and Manuscript Library, Yale University

References to Bunting's poems are to *The Poems of Basil Bunting*, ed. Don Share (London: Faber & Faber, 2016). Line numbers are given in parenthesis, after indication of the containing 'Part' in the case of longer poems such as *The Spoils* and *Briggflatts*. References to the titles of Bunting's shorter poems follow the form in Share (typically the poem's first line), though occasionally, where necessary, these poems are referred to by way of the typology Bunting introduced in post-1950 collected editions (e.g., 'Ode I.15'). Non-poetic parts of Share's text are referenced by way of the shorthand 'Share' and the relevant page number/s.

References to the main Bunting biography, *A Strong Song Tows Us: The Life of Basil Bunting* by Richard Burton, are indicated by the shorthand 'Burton' and the relevant page number/s.

Letters are headed with the date form given by Bunting (or with a reasonable conjecture in the few cases where no date is given). In annotations and other paratexts, letters published in this edition are referenced using the short form of their date in bold type (eg. '**13/12/64**'). Letters by Bunting not included in this edition are referenced by way of the same date form, but in normal type, and with indication of the recipient and holding archive.

Biblical references are to the King James Version. References to Pound's *Cantos* are to the 1996 New Directions edition, with page numbers indicated. References to Shakespeare, Milton, Wordsworth, and Yeats are from *The Riverside Shakespeare* (New York: Houghton Mifflin, 1997), *Paradise Lost*, ed. Alastair Fowler (London: Longman, 1998), *Wordsworth: Complete Poetical Works* (Oxford: OUP, 1936), and *Yeats's Poems*, ed. A. Norman Jeffries (London: Macmillan, 1996).

"Wovon man nicht sprechen kann, darüber muß man schweigen."

—Wittgenstein

# Late Spring
# 1920–1938

Like the second part of his poetic autobiography Briggflatts, Bunting's correspondence begins in early adulthood, with the heady, bewildering events of the 1920s. About the preceding period, a mostly undocumented childhood, we know only the basic outline: birth in Newcastle upon Tyne in 1900, an apparently typical middle-class Tyneside childhood, and schooling at Quaker boarding schools in Yorkshire and Berkshire. A pair of unremarkable juvenile poems has survived (see Share 229–231), but there is little else to speak of Bunting's early personal development (although see Burton 41–64 for a useful summary of moments in his later school years). Aside from the hazily recalled teenage summers which lie somewhere behind the opening lines of *Briggflatts*, the other really key event before 1920 was Bunting's imprisonment in 1918–1919 for conscientious objection to World War I. This traumatic experience seems to have given rise to some of the wildness and dislocation of his student days and the bohemian interludes in early 1920s London and Paris—the period we are thrust into, in medias res, in the first letters below. Bunting's wartime prison ordeal, combined with a much shorter spell in jail in Paris in 1923, certainly fed into his first substantial poem 'Villon', a work of the late 1920s spun out of themes of incarceration.

The rather sparse, partially glimpsed picture that emerges from the earliest letters sets a precedent for the first phase of the correspondence as a whole. As we will see repeatedly in the pages that follow, the record of Bunting's life is dotted with lacunae—professional, personal, and creative. This is more than usually true of the years before 1930, a long apprenticeship during which extended periods of silence are punctuated by articulate (and sometimes very sweet) letters to Ezra Pound and Harriet Monroe. The vast majority of the extant pre-1930 letters are included here, and even so they barely number in double figures, which brings home just how heavily the correspondence is weighted to later years.

In the early 1930s, however, the correspondence springs to life along with Bunting's poetic output (readers in search of a more coherent narrative may wish to skip straight to the letters to Pound beginning around 1930–1931). One of the key facts about Bunting's timeline is its orientation around two alpine peaks: 1930–1933 and 1964–1966. In these two interludes, his creative hesitancy gave way to sudden and energetic bouts of productivity. The first purple patch began with publication of the pamphlet *Redimiculum Matellarum*, which appeared in the same year as 'Villon' (published in Poetry magazine in October 1930). Over the next three years a large number of shorter poems and translations were completed, as well as the longer works 'Attis: Or Something Missing', 'Aus Dem Zweiten Reich', and 'Chomei at Toyama', most of which featured in Pound's *Active Anthology* (1933) and the unpublished putative 'first collection' *Caveat Emptor* (1935).

Underpinning this creative flowering was a personal context of some happiness. Bunting married his first wife Marian Culver in July 1930, and though she features only sporadically in the letters of these years, there is no sign of the animosity that would destroy their relationship in the latter half of the decade. Perhaps more importantly for Bunting's creative life, this was also a great period of fellowship and collaboration, which saw him embedded in the scene that gathered around Ezra Pound and other major literary figures in Rapallo in north-west Italy from the early 1920s. As the letters of the early 1930s show, Bunting was clearly galvanized by contact with this circle. After a busy sojourn to New York in 1930–1931, he also became central to the transatlantic milieu that would shape second-wave modernism; in the States he made contact with William Carlos Williams, Louis Zukofsky, and others, even as he failed to find employment as a journalist. Zukofsky would soon join him in Rapallo and become his most important friend and correspondent.

But when Bunting left Rapallo in the autumn of 1933 to live in the Canary Islands, his confidence faltered—and his great recession began. 'The Well of Lycopolis' emerged in 1935, and work on translation of the Persian epic *Shahnameh* continued for the next couple of years. However, Bunting's sense of isolation on removal from the environment of the Rapallo 'Ezuversity' coincided with creative inertia and increasingly negligible publication prospects, a combination that would stifle his productivity (with the notable exception of *The Spoils* in 1951) until the revival that produced *Briggflatts* almost thirty years later.

Yet the mid 1930s were one of Bunting's most prolific letter-writing periods, a fact which seems to underline just how close he had become to Pound and Zukofsky in Rapallo, and how much he missed them when he moved to Tenerife. The subtlety and sensitivity—not to mention the length—of the exchanges with Pound during this phase are particularly striking. The central discussions of poetry and economics are key to our understanding of modernist literature on the eve of World War II. They show the wheels coming off the Pound project, but also that Bunting was coming to realize that the 'indirect business' of modernism's first iteration had reached an impasse. His intriguing suggestion was that modern poets should respond by concerning themselves with 'telling a story', rather than delving further into interiority and subjective experiments. This impulse would be delayed in implementation until Bunting's own tale of the tribe, *Briggflatts*, emerged much later.

After the fizzing exchanges of the middle of the decade, the letters of the late 1930s narrate the unravelling of Bunting's personal life and the dwindling of his creative practice. Bunting's heated quarrel with Pound at the close of 1938, which temporarily ended their relationship, completes a pre-World War II narrative of broken friendships and disappointed creative schemes—a late spring which never quite blossomed into summer.

The first few—sporadic and elliptical—letters in this section are drawn from Bunting's third decade. On hiatus from undergraduate study at the London School of Economics, he attempted to reach newly communist Russia in late 1920, apparently to study socio-economic conditions there. After leaving LSE without a degree, he mingled with bohemian London, then travelled to Paris in 1923, where he met Pound and Ford Madox Ford, among other notable literati. He joined Pound (and W. B. Yeats) in Rapallo, Italy, on at least three occasions in the mid-to-late 1920s, returning to Britain for periods of itinerant work and unemployment in Newcastle and London.

## To Lionel Robbins[1]

TS LSE

12 October 1920

6 Portland Terrace, Newcastle-upon-Tyne

Dear L.C.R.

I never reached Russia: the police were too efficient for me. First of all in Copenhagen Litvinov[2] wouldnt see me, or more accurately, his secretary wouldnt let me see him. So I went to Stockholm, to see Frederick Ström.[3] He was pleasant and helpful, but when he finally made up his mind to let me thro by Reval, he got instructions from Copenhagen not to. He advised me to try and get to Archangelsk or Alexandrovsk via the Arctic, and I set off by the Lapland train, after infinite passport difficulties with the Norwegian Authorities. It's a wonderful country, and all that, and the Finmark coast is even better: but that's beside the point. I reached Hammerfest, two short days from Russia, and then two detectives came on board, arrested me, and locked me up, with a gaoler who was afraid of me and six or seven selected criminals, mostly drunken Laps. I was deported to Newcastle, no reason assigned. Every port we came to the police had a fresh idea. One lot arrested me, another set me loose, another wanted me put in irons; anon there came more detectives, disguised as Consulate officials, and at N/C were more detectives, dressed up as customs officers. Before I started I was warned by someone that there was an International dossier out against me, but I wouldnt believe it!

By my bargain with my father, I forfeited my right to further education when he financed the Russian adventure. So it became a matter of getting a job: not an easy thing to do on Tyneside and he wouldnt let me go to London. An uncompromisingly truthful advertisement in the Atheneum and the Statesman,[4] brought me two copies of a tract on the Resurrection of the Dead, and a leaflet printed in two colors on The Evils of Drink. There are no jobs to be had in the northern Trades Union world. At present I have two prospects, both very unlikely, one a bi-weekly column on Trades Union Affairs in the local liberal paper, the other a job that Cadbury[5] has been advertising, on their private paper

[1] **Lionel Robbins**: a fellow student of BB's at LSE, and later a notable economist.

[2] Maxim Litvinov (1876–1951), Soviet Bolshevik politician and diplomat. In the late 1910s and early 1920s Litvinov travelled to several European capitals, including Copenhagen, negotiating the release of Soviet prisoners.

[3] Fredrik Ström (1880–1948), Swedish communist politician, in close contact with Soviet Russia in this period.

[4] *The Athenæum* (1828–1921), *New Statesman* (founded 1913): notable London cultural magazines.

[5] Cadbury: British confectionary manufacturer. Based in Birmingham, and best known for its chocolate, it was founded in 1824 by the Quaker Cadbury family, which perhaps explains the appeal of this job to BB.

to keep the workpeople from striking. I dont think I'll get either of them. Yesterday, seeing a picture on which appeared a woman I know, I thought of that. Could Peter or Lawson give me a leg up into that business, thinkyou?

I haven't stopped reading, but Ive had to read some queer stuff lately. My arctic jailer produced two German books for me, a romance about the coming war, written in 1906, and differing from The Riddle of the Sands[6] only in being rather more capable, rather more knowledgeable, rather more frank, and rather duller; and the commanders account of the first voyage of the Deutschland,[7] which, in spite of its technicalities and its very colloquial style, was extremely fascinating. It took my breath like a novel by Defoe, and I read it all at a sitting. Hairrrbrreadth escapes! Daring! Triumph of the legitimate hero, and no women in it!

Since I reached home I have bought a first edition of Swift's poems, without knowing it at the time, for six shillings. They are very good stuff, and there is a translation from the Irish, quite out of Swift's usual style, that I have never seen before, first rate, and as fast a poem as I know. It describes an Irish feast, and I have half a mind to transcribe it at the end of the letter. I read as much German as I can get nowadays, but Russian progresses slowly. Moreover at last I have read La Revolte des Anges, by Anatole France.[8] What a book! I do not think it is equal to Penguin Island, but it is more coherent, and the incidents are delicious. Who else would have materialised the Angel when the hero was in bed with another mans wife, just…

Gibbon says these things are best left in the decent obscurity of a learned language, so I leave you to find the French. Who else would make another Angel earn its living as a "Russian lady"? And who but Anatole France would finish the novel with the triumph of Satan, and his assumption of the exact state just vacated by Ialdabaoth?[9]

[6] *The Riddle of the Sands*, by the Irish writer Erskine Childers (1870–1922): popular spy novel of 1903, set in the Baltic Sea area, in the context of rising geopolitical tensions between Britain and Germany.

[7] *Deutschland*: German passenger boat built in 1866, famously wrecked off the east coast of England in December 1875.

[8] *La Revolte des Anges* ('The Revolt of Angels'), by the French writer Anatole France (1844–1924): satirical novel of 1914 describing the progress of an angel, Arcade, who journeys to earthly Paris, where he loses his virginity and is converted to the cause of Satan. *Penguin Island* (1908) is an earlier novel by France.

[9] In *La Revolte des Anges*, the Gnostic title Ialdabaoth is used as a secret name for God, who is supplanted by Satan at the close of the novel.

Gentle things like Chapmans Homer, Complete Angler, Lambs Letters, Gibbon and Boswell,[10] fulfill my list. The last two have been a standby for years.

The swift Swift poem is long for typing, but here it is.

[...][11]

I type for your convenience, i.e. for legibility, a quality not prominent in my hand.[12] And handwrite this, for courtesy. Isn't that poem Lever's Ireland[13] condensed, & better than the sentimental visions of Yeats & co?

Yours,
Basil C. Bunting

## To Lionel Robbins

MS LSE

1 Mai [1923]

6 Rue Grégoire de Tours, Paris (6°)

"Y-a-t-il un chômage des modèles aujourd'hui?"

"Je n'en sais rien, monsieur. Je n'avais pas eu le temps de m'associer à la féderation."[14]

Unfortunately, Robbins, there is no trades union in this business.[15] Individual bargains, & don't they put it across the poor foreigner! This week I am doing 7 hours a day at one of the most respectable academies, for which I shall touch 80 francs at the end of the week, plus a subscription from the students. In England I could get 15/- a day for the same work. In America, a dollar an hour. Well, anyway, I've got nearly two months of this work, & I hope to learn in that time enough French to get a job on the barges. Paris-Lyons-Marseilles- & then I'll take a summer tramp somewhere or other.

See how cramped my hand is: I've been sitting on it since lunch.

[10] BB refers to canonical English texts commonplace in nineteenth- and early twentieth-century libraries: *Odyssey* and *Iliad* translations by George Chapman (1559–1634), *The Compleat Angler* by Izaak Walton (1593–1983), the correspondence of the Romantic writer Charles Lamb (1775–1834), *The Decline and Fall of the Roman Empire* by Edward Gibbon (1737–1794) and *The Life of Samuel Johnson* by James Boswell (1740–1795).

[11] BB copies out 'The Description of an Irish Feast', a poem of 1720, which Swift worked up from an Irish song translated for him by Hugh MacGuaran.

[12] This last paragraph is handwritten.

[13] Charles Lever (1806–1872), Irish writer famous for his lively, burlesqued novels set in nineteenth-century Ireland.

[14] 'Is there any dole money available for models today?' 'I don't know anything about that, mister. I didn't have time to join the union.' (Fr.)

[15] As becomes apparent in the remainder of the letter, BB's 'business' was life modelling.

Bertrand Russell has some interesting remarks on the French in the Dial[16] (I think) this month. But I've not been here long enough to come to conclusions of my own. Still, there are first impressions.

(a) Women. Nothing to report here. All the famous pretty Parisiennes have taken a holiday to celebrate my coming. At any rate I see nothing but

| | |
|---|---|
| whores | bitches |
| cows | sows |
| dragons | Lesbians |
| wishy-washies | English |
| Americans | Jewesses. |

The little whores in white silk have been being confirmed all the weekend. It was very amusing to see them going out cock-teasing in their confirmation dresses.

There are two brothels in my street, but they look expensive. One has a stained glass window with Venus & Cupid on it.

(b) Cafés. It is very pleasant to eat in the open air, & pleasanter still to drink, not by order, at twelve o'clock, but just when you feel like it. You hear nothing but American (I won't call it English) in the cafés of Montparnasse & Boulevard St Michel. But in my quarter (Vieux Quartier Latin) it is the villainous French of Slavonic people. Slavs & Japanese are the only people in France who don't paint their faces. All the rest are either syphilitic, or else bum-boys & whores.

Good meals, very cheap. Excellent to drink wine. The taximen & cabdrivers who seem to live in the cafés in my quarter wont let you drink vin blanc. They regard it as a confession of impotence, or at least of effeminacy. So I let them have their way & drink red. It is supposed to enlarge the penis.

There is a waitress near the Luxembourg who is fat & good humored. But she comes from the Midi, not Paris.

(c) Language. Parisians are like Manchester men.[17] "Salad'laitue" – to say "Salade de laitue"[18] indicates that you come from the Midi. Normans carry the process of agglutination further, & resolve all the words of the sentence into one continuous grunt. Therefore they are never waiters nor actors nor anything but brutes of peasants. cf Maupassant, who knew them.

[16] *The Dial*: Influential American literary journal responsible for publishing a large number of major modernist works, notably *The Waste Land* in November 1922.

[17] In common with many northern English dialects (though not BB's own North East English), the Manchester dialect has traditionally exhibited a large amount of definite article reduction—for example 'trouble at' mill' for 'trouble at the mill'.

[18] *Salade de laitue*: lettuce salad (Fr.).

I am improving. I shall soon be able to understand a respectable fraction of the conversation that goes on around me. Especially if I think hard of Manchester ("Shut 'door") all the time.

(d) Waiters. Waiters are the true glory of Paris. I set no limit to the admiration that may be legitimately paid to them. They work about twenty hours a day with enormous efficiency, are beautifully polite & even sweet, & will love you for "deux sous de plus". They are always handsome, especially the blondes from Alsace. They smile more cheerfully than anybody else in the world. I abase myself before Parisian waiters.

(e) Architecture. The public buildings of Paris are hideous beyond anything I have ever seen. The Eiffel Tower is rather fine, & has the same effect on the imagination as the dome of St Pauls. Nôtre Dame is indecent. It needs breeches or some such wear to hide its eternal genitals.

Domestic architecture is not so good as English Georgian, but clean, fairly neat, & not at all offensive. The streets become excellent when they have trees in them.

(f) Art. One sees & hears of nothing else. There must be some good art somewhere, & some good artists, but I havent yet seen it or them. The Academies I pose in are infinitely worse than anything of the sort I have seen in London.

(g) Morals. French people appear to be honester than English in money matters. In matters of sex they are wretched charlatans. One may say, or write anything "pour rire",[19] but if I pose before young girls I must wear a pair of striped bathing drawers that stretch from knees to navel. They seem to be astonished that I have been ten days in Paris without securing a French mistress. A friend of mine, having lived for three weeks with ostentatious chastity, was asked tenderly whether he were unfortunately impotent! They sell portraits of cinema stars nude, & on the lavatory, etc. in all the stationer's shops, yet they insist on these beastly drawers.

One café has a splendid Rabelaisian sign. A waiter, nude, is walking between the tables, balancing three trays, one in each hand, & one on the end of his erect penis.

(h) Sanitation. I cannot get used to crouching over a hole in the floor instead of sitting on a seat. The French do it to avoid V.D. infection.

The pissoirs are erected, not by the Ville, but by the Philanthropic Publicity Society Anonyme. They draw a huge revenue from the advertisement of pox-doctors.

[19] *Pour rire*: for fun (Fr.).

That is my impression of Paris –
outdoor cleanliness
pox
vain talk about art
whores

On the whole I like it better than London. French air is worth a lot. So is eatable food. So is wine.

I've temporarily mislaid your letter. If there is anything in it to be answered, I'll do it very soon.

Basil Bunting

The fateful night described in the following letter seems to have involved some form of violent misdemeanour on Bunting's part, leading to a short spell in a Parisian jail. It has been variously and colourfully mythologized, notably by Ford Madox Ford in his 1934 memoir *It Was the Nightingale*, and by Bunting himself in an interview with Carroll Terrell in 1980 (see *Basil Bunting: Man and Poet* (Orono: National Poetry Foundation, 1981), 41–42). Oddly, however, this first-hand account has not featured in previous biographical treatments.

Aside from the burlesque narrative there is a deeper sense in which the embroglio was a symbolic joining of hands: Bunting had clearly made informal contact with Pound prior to this point, but Pound's 'intervention' at this point marks the real beginning of their nearly lifelong friendship.

## To Ezra Pound

MS Indiana

Monday [15 October 1923]

Prison de la Santé, D$^{ou}$9, Cellule 16, Paris

Dear Pound,

Endless thanks for your kind intervention. I was enormously bucked up when I saw you in the court. How did you get to know? From Wyman? Sandford? John?

I saw the advocat Sunday morning, & he says I'll get off with a (how you spell "soorsee"[20] I can't imagine). But I am not sure. The judges of the quatorzième chambre have a reputation for severity. What a bloody mess! There are several things I forgot to tell the procureur that I would like my advocate to say for me in court. I'll write down my whole case systematically here & you can give it to him. Curse the badness of this pen for the ugly writing.

First charge, violence.

Admitted.

I met two friends who were returning to England the next day, & we fêted the occasion. I got very drunk. It is the first time that that has happened to me in France, & it will be the last. I am very sorry. I am ashamed of myself. I remember nothing of all that – nothing until the morning.

Second charge. Carrying arms.

The knife that is scheduled as a prohibited arm was never regarded as an arm by me. I bought it to sharpen my pencils & to cut bread & cheese when I eat my lunch in the Luxembourg or the Tuileries. For that it was necessary to have something larger than the usual penknife. It was sold to me at the Grand Bayar de l'Hôtel de Ville as a "canif",[21] & there was nothing to suggest it was an arm at all, much less a prohibited arm. It certainly wasn't big enough to be dangerous, & I would have expected to find dangerous weapons sold only on the production of a license, as in England.

Lastly, they seem to make a great deal of the fact that I was in prison in England, but that was not for crime. I was born and bred a Quaker. War is forbidden to Quakers & during the last war I was one of the 2000 young Quakers who were imprisoned for refusing to violate the tenets of Quakerism by becoming a soldier. I have never before been arrested for a "delit", nor even, as far as I remember, for a "contravention".[22] That's about all that can be said and I'd rather the lawyer said it than I. I am always nervous in public, & especially when I must speak a foreign language. Thanks again. See you tomorrow.

Basil Bunting

[20] *Sursis*: reprieve (Fr.).
[21] *Canif*: penknife (Fr.).
[22] *Delit, contravention*: both terms for minor or trivial offences (Fr.).

## To J. J. Adams[23]

MS Durham

14 January 1924 — 6 Portland Terrace, Newcastle-upon-Tyne

Dear John J –

New disappointments. My father is very ill and I have to put off my start for London from day to day.[24] I was to have started a week ago – then Monday – then today – now next Monday, unless this accursed malevolent disease intervenes again. The worst of it is that my mother's ill too and cant do much & my sister has her hands full working the practice. What a nuisance! I hold Hamlet's opinion of filial duty – O curséd spite that ever I was born to do this kind of thing.[25] If the old man had any ordinary dismal disease, I believe I'd leave him to his own devices. But its angina, the most painful, I suppose, of all the diseases in these islands, and a particularly persistent & violent form of angina. I couldnt decently leave the old man to that with a chance that there'd be nobody to give him morphia when the attack is at its worst.

He's had angina off and on for a couple of years now, but never much more than "normal clinical angina", but a week ago he furnished me with the most harrowing sight I've yet seen. He was brought home in a taxi by his partner, after a very bad attack. He had another attack on the way home & then he lay on the sofa and had another. His face went a dirty grey colour, almost heliotrope, & it looked as though all the flesh had fallen off it & left just the skull in the skin. His eyes sank back into his head behind perpendicular black cliffs. There were huge deep lines where a normal man of sixty has wrinkles. He stared & stared at the back of the sofa & held tight to it. You know the Greco "Agony in the Garden"?[26] Greco knew how agony manifests itself but he was afraid of exaggerating & so he's very much understated it. My father was like that Christ, only far worse, far more intensely hurt. He couldn't speak – not for weakness, he was no weaker than usual, but for sheer agony. All of him concentrated on that burning pain, & the most dreadful fear in his expression.

[23] **J. J. Adams**: a marginal figure in 1920s London bohemia and a close friend of BB's circa 1923–1926.

[24] BB's father, Thomas Lowe Bunting (1868–1925), was a doctor who practiced in the Scotswood and Jesmond areas of Newcastle. He was originally from Derbyshire.

[25] See *Hamlet* I.5.188–9.

[26] Mannerist painting by El Greco (1541–1614) completed around 1605.

I've seen plenty of bad pain – worked some months in a war hospital[27] & watched men under the probe & so forth – but never anything like this. I was also once locked up in a cell with a homicidal maniac who got a terrible fear at times that shone out of him like a flaming light, but it was not so terrible as the fear I saw in my father. He's been unlucky from his birth, but I fancy fate might have let him off a bit lighter than this (only fate is always such a bloody malignant thing). Most angina patients only have a few minutes at a time of the spasm, but my father has many hours and he had three big & two fairly big dos in one day. The average is one a month.

Well, there's another today, not quite as bad. But you see I cant very well leave him. He knows he's dying & that its only a question of when & how much pain he has to endure first. (If he asked me I think I would fill him up with morphia). But then, Mother had a milder form of the same disease & the shock of his death might finish her off too - & so on & so on & so on.

O cursèd spite!

I hope to cast off my burden on to an ancient aunt, but just at present she's ill too. I have some hope of getting away next week, but not a very lively hope. This is bloody depressing.

Yes, I want any work I can get, Tomlinson or another.[28] I'd work willingly for Old Nick. I loathe Tomlinson's brandy-and-soda-very-weak manner of writing & Koteliansky's religiosity – but there, money must be earned. I loathe Murry, too, & Miss Strachey, & Clifford Sharp & Ford & pretty well every editor in the kingdom. Any devil is good enough to be my devil. Command me to our affable one & a rich one & I will overlook the cloven hoof & the flavours of brimstone – at least, as long as it serves my purpose to do so.

> "He flatters this age that can
> Call Tullia's ape a marmoset
> And Leda's goose a swan".[29]

O, the niggling false pedantry of accuracy & style! Why cant we fly at it like the Elizabethans or translate "Laus Deo semper", as the Tichborne claimant did, "The

[27] BB's father was radiologist at the Northumberland War Hospital in Gosforth 1914–1918, which housed soldiers wounded in fighting on the continent. BB must have helped out there during a school vacation.

[28] BB references a series of the most prominent magazine editors in early-1920s London in this passage. He had briefly worked as an assistant editor to Ford Madox Ford (1873–1939) at the *Transatlantic Review* in Paris at the end of 1923, immediately prior to composition of this letter.

[29] BB slightly misquotes a 1604 madrigal by Elizabethan composer Thomas Weelkes.

Laws of God for ever!" [30] There's fervour & spirit in that, and in the midst of a long cross-examination too.

I want (when I get into the Museum again) to write an essay on Flaubert. As far as I know all the critics have feebly followed Henry James, even Cocteau who disapproves of the sweaty Norman. But as I see it Flaubert was above all an ironist & only really found his vocation in "Bouvard et Pécuchet" (that James thought such an awful example of the Lapses of the Great)[31] I can see nothing in Bovary to boast about, nothing worth doing in Salammbô or Herodias, precious little in St Antoine.[32] We are too precious nowadays, and its Flaubert's fault, and Pater's.[33] And old Sam. Butler wrote finer prose than any of them, really. Read Ulysses descent to Hell in the Odyssey – "Poor feckless ghost!"[34]

Well, well. I yet hope to see you in a few days. I will send you a P-C & take advantage of the offer of a shakedown the first night, which will give me time to pick & choose a decent lodging. Thanks.

Yours
Basil Bunting

## To J. J. Adams

TS Durham

5 December 1924 — 242 Newburn Lane, Newburn, Northumberland

Deceiver!

What devil advised you that Middleton Murry wanted a sub? Know that I spent Time and Trouble composing a seductive, informal, stand-on-your head kind of application addressed to the romantic yearnings of the wretch, a painstaking bit of Bohemianism, built on careful calculation and scheming, plausible psychology. Know that I did well, deceived the detective, seduced the critic, enchanted the Bohemian: and that he wrote back at once to say that I was a delightful fellow

[30] In the late 1860s a man generally identified as Arthur Orton (1834–1898) claimed to be Roger Tichborne, lost heir to the Tichborne estates and baronetcy, leading to a series of prominent London court cases. At one point Orton was cross-examined about Tichborne's schooling at Stonyhurst College, mistranslating a Latin school motto, *Laus Deo Semper* ('Praise God Always'), as 'The Laws of God Forever', provoking derision.

[31] *Bouvard et Pécuchet*: unfinished work by Gustave Flaubert (1821–1880), published posthumously in 1881. Henry James excoriated the novel in an 1893 article for *Macmillan's Magazine*.

[32] *Madame Bovary* (1856), *Salammbô* (1862), 'Herodias' (1877), and *La Tentation de Saint Antoine* (1874): all prose works by Flaubert.

[33] Walter Pater (1839–1894), English essayist famous for his elegant, mannered prose.

[34] A quotation from Samuel Butler's 1900 translation of Homer's *Odyssey*.

and a champion writer and wouldn't I favour his paper with my esteemed contributions? And how admirable were my strictures on Mr Smith![35] But he regretted to inform me that he was, had had and hopes to continue to have the services of an excellent and beloved sub-editor from whom no vile seducer can ever part him.

So I have sent him a bad essay on Villon.[36]

The new Transatlantic contains "Trotter", to my great delight and comfort.[37] Yet I no longer think as I used to that Trotter is the best of the bunch. It was your wonderful, feeling, ironic reading, perhaps, that made me imagine so. But Brainworm and the Bugles in the Brickfields and Diogenes are glorious in themselves. You dont need to imagine the Adams voice and manner to get the most out of them, whereas I fear that Osric at his pitch in Cheapside is not quite the same Osric, not so terrible, nor Lucy quite so enchanting, at this too great distance from your peculiar inflections. The jungle men swinging their beards to the moon are as splendid as ever. So are the High Hills of Hampstead. The garden suburb is almost as tangible as Number seven Park Terrace, solidest Victorian building yet in verse. But after all you know, "A dozen clappers in committee" must someday become part of the regular inheritance of those who write this language. There is nothing so certain and absolute as that in Trotter.

I've been reading Henry James on Flaubert.[38] Quite apart from his jelly-fish prose, I dont like it. He makes out the best case possible for the Bovaryites, but he scarcely dare refer to Bouvard et Pécuchet, so awful a failure does he esteem it. But any man of sense knows that Bouvard is the one book of Flauberts that almost justifies his reputation. There irony delights to begin in a small way and grow and grow and grow, from the Voltaire stage to the Swift stage, until it ends with Rabelaisian howlings and "Ils se remisent a copier."[39] I've not read L'Education Sentimentale, but since James relinquishes it with a sigh as on the way to Bouvard, and since it contains the famous phrase "Il connut alors la melancholie des paquebots,"[40] I intend to get a copy in the hope of finding more irony in it.

[35] Possibly BB wrote some form of excoriation of F. E. Smith, 1st Earl of Birkenhead (1872–1930), a prominent Conservative politician of the period. See **4/1/35** for an aside on Smith's oratory during World War I.

[36] Like the vast majority of BB's prose of the period, this essay has not survived.

[37] Adams contributed a number of poems to *Transatlantic Review* throughout 1924, among them the titles BB mentions in the following passage. His longer poem 'Gongs' had top billing in the December issue (presumably 'Trotter' was an earlier title).

[38] See **14/1/24** and notes.

[39] A precis of *Bouvard et Pécuchet*'s conclusion rather than an exact quotation.

[40] A famous passage near the end of Flaubert's *L'Education Sentimentale* (1869) contains the phrase *Il connut la mélancolie des paquebots*: 'He knew the melancholy of steamboats.'

I must come to London and see you and your new poem somehow. Cant you lie in wait with a hammer for Murry's blackguard of a sub?

Faithfully
Basil Bunting

The following letter is one of the most important summaries we have of the influences and attitudes swirling in BB's formative years. In addition to the intellectual namedropping, note the desire to begin 'at the beginning again', the wide-ranging dismissal of most of the major figures of first-generation modernism, and the use of radical currents in English history ('Cromwell's time') to attack modern English letters.

## To J. J. Adams

MS Durham

19 February 1926 — 242 Newburn Lane, Newburn, Northumberland

Dear J. J. –

I am an even worse correspondent than you, so that no one ever writes to me nowadays. I knew nothing of Christabel's death until I got your letter – exactly a year after my own father died.[41]

It is almost impossible to say anything on these occasions except the common forms of mourning and sympathy. The stress forces us willy-nilly into a ritual…

Christabel was very kind and gentle – too gentle and sympathetic for her own comfort in a world based mostly on callousness. No! She is not likely to be forgotten until we too are all dead. Only ordinary people are forgotten, and Christabel was decidedly out of the ordinary. Ultimately, of course, even ghosts have their dissolution and all memory of us fails; and a good job too. How intolerable it would be if even ones best moments echoed on and on forever! We might be ashamed to live. Even Shakespeare would like to shuffle off some of the coils

[41] Christabel Dennison (1884–1925), sculptor, painter, and lover of J. J. Adams. According to Dennison's diary entries, which were unearthed and published in the 1990s by her daughter Jane Spottiswoode, her relationship with Adams was unhappy and subject to domestic abuse. See Virginia Nicholson, *Among the Bohemians: Experiments in Living 1900–1939* (Harmondsworth: Penguin, 2002), 192–193.

of his immortality. We will remember her from time to time – frequently – while we live, and trust that she and we will find decent oblivion afterwards.

My luck is still out. I thought I had nothing to do but step from the office when I got home from London: but the editor got a fancy to seduce his staff. Once of his papers failed and I was turned off before I had even started work for him. I got a little money out of Middleton Murry, a little more out of the Yorkshire Evening News, for rotten work. I caught a rich man who promised me a job, and lived on his promises for months. Then I became one of the ignoble army of lecturers who pretends to educate adults.[42] I lecture on economics to working men, confuse their minds with the technicalities of the money-market, and get two pounds a week for it. The institution that employs me thus wanted to make me its boss, so I took on a lot of extra, unpaid work – coaching a "Little Theatre", boiling down Frazer[43] and Freud and so on – and then they announced they couldnt raise money enough to pay my salary – a modest item, I'm sure. That's my position.

I don't like the work. For one bright spark there are ten so dull that nothing will bring any expression into their faces. I read extracts from Erewhon and Butler's notebooks to a lot of them.[44] They had to smile, but they struggled not to laugh outright. A lecture is to them too solemn an occasion for laughter.

I found a man of some intelligence and got drunk with him once or twice. Then he tried to rob me, and I had to drop him. The rest are either (a) elementary school-teachers, the stupidest people in the world. (b) secondary trades union officials, far from bright: but some of these have character (c) a hotchpotch of the detestable people who have obtrusive souls and want something for nothing: they have come to be educated, and it is my job to educate them without their help. Terrors. I shock them when I dare.

We have had the hardest of hard winters, and us very poor indeed and mother used to affluence. Bad for the temper, that. I wish I could live on the Mediterranean where it is never cold and a man can content himself with coffee and a little bread and fruit.

I have written one or two short poems, but worries have been too constant and too severe to allow any real work, even reading. A little Dante – too little. Another glance into Wittgenstein – "Die Welt ist alles was der Fall ist", you know,

[42] BB was working during this period at an institution founded by his uncle Andrew Messer: The Adult School in Montague Street, Lemington.

[43] James George Frazer (1854–1941), Scottish author of the hugely influential anthropological survey *The Golden Bough* (1890).

[44] Butler's satirical utopian novel *Erewhon: or, Over the Range* was first published anonymously in 1872; *The Note-Books of Samuel Butler* appeared posthumously in 1912.

leading, after three hundred pages of close reasoning to "Worüber man nicht sprechen kann, darüber muss man schweigen."[45] Eliot's poems. Dryden. Through the Dunciad once more. Eddington: a fallacious and misleading writer who evidently confounds religion with the residue of transcendental metaphysics.[46] After my father died I read the whole of Hardy in about three weeks to quiet my soul.[47] I found that I had never before realized what a command he has over English. Of his contemporaries, Butler alone surpasses him. The stylists, including Conrad and Ford, Flaubert and de Gourmont[48] fall far short of this excellence. Do they become stylists because they are aware of their imperfection, I wonder?

But even the best are too static. Flaubert made a virtue of it, but a series of instantaneous photographs is not literature. We require a verbal cinematograph. The Drama? Who is tempted to go into competition with frauds like Pirandello[49] and the rest? Gertrude Stein? But she is incomprehensible. Joyce is wide, but still static. There is no discharge, no catharsis. Must we begin at the beginning again, before the altar, and rewrite the Prayer-book as Aeschylus did? Should artists be priests and go about in reversed collars and pretend to be chaste? Somewhere we got lost, I think in Cromwell's time, and we have got further & further from the track, and now we are plunging into solitary scribblings, the antithesis of literature, which is essentially public.

I wish I could come and see you or you me. But we have no room for even one visitor in this house, and no money for holidays. We must do what we can with letters. How's Johnny?[50]

Yours
Basil Bunting

[45] The second aphorism BB slightly misquotes here—usually translated 'Whereof one cannot speak, thereof one must be silent'—appears at the end of Wittgenstein's *Tractatus Logico-Philosophicus* (1922) without further elaboration. The phrase seems to have occupied a central place in BB's worldview, acting as a shorthand for his puritan sensibility, an apologia for his poetic style, and indeed an accurate summary of his lifelong relationship with the written word. See **13/7/31** for a later appearance.

[46] Arthur Stanley Eddington (1882–1944), English astronomer, mathematician, physicist, and philosopher. It was probably Eddington's philosophical idealism that BB found so objectionable.

[47] Thomas Hardy (1840–1928), of course, would return at a later date as a key influence on the composition of *Briggflatts* (see **10/11/64**).

[48] Remy de Gourmont (1858–1915), French Symbolist poet, novelist, and critic, notably championed by Pound as a major force in the development of modern literature.

[49] Luigi Pirandello (1867–1936), Italian dramatist whose early-twentieth century plays preempted absurdist theatre.

[50] Presumably **John Collier**, another member of the jobbing literary circle which included Adams and BB.

## To Ezra Pound

MS Yale

29 April 1926 — 242 Newburn Lane, Newburn, Northumberland

Dear Ezra –

Thanks.

I've quoted your honored name as referee. If they should ask you any questions, say I'm in all things excellent but chiefly in respectability, sobriety, persistence, (the school masterly virtues which I lack): above all respectability.

I dont in the least want to go amongst the savages – English, Malay & Chinese-of-the-East, but a descent into Hell is compulsory on all poets & heroes & after the third year I shall rise again from the dead & ascend into the heaven of Italy. Three years is long enough, with judicious neglect of teaching, to compile something saleable: Borrow-ish,[51] I'm afraid, it's bound to be, anecdotes & prejudices, anthropophagi & strange serpents whose tears are wet,[52] the book of a liar. Why not?

I am delighted to write to Rapallo – you, for the moment, are Rapallo. The fact that you are there sanctions my enthusiasm. I should never have left the place if my father hadn't begun to die. I would have starved there sooner than seek a living elsewhere. Rezzo told me I could find work in Naples, but I stayed on the beach – the beach of the third cove eastwards from Rapallo, listening to the sea, the slowest clock on earth. What is the opposite of Accidie, its corresponding virtue? Contented idleness, not sloth: that's Rapallo's air, I think. Just to look at the girls going about their business was Mahomet's paradise. Diogenes contentment in a tub was understandable, there.[53]

All Rapallo's faults are tolerable. A kind of night madness is endemic there. Men sing with guitars; dogs howl. The northern moon is less potent. Has that flea-tortured St. Bernard died yet that used to lie outside the shop where they sell you bread in a heathenish lingo composed of German & gibberish? When I saw him I understood why the pagan hell was guarded by a dog: all anti-canine adjectives were justified in him. Yet he didn't mar the place. He has fed the mullet by now, I expect: a useful burial.

[51] George Borrow (1803–1881), English poet and travel writer, whose style is caricatured here in BB's summary.

[52] See *Antony and Cleopatra*, II.7.48–9.

[53] Diogenes of Sinope (*c.*404–323 BC), Greek Cynic philosopher who reputedly took up residence in bathtub (a wine cask according to some sources) in the marketplace of fourth-century Athens, thereby demonstrating his philosophical asceticism.

There is an old man up in the mountains who came from England in 1870, a newly ordained curate or something, & never went home. I found him pruning an olive tree in a ragged shirt & some things he called trousers. He had almost forgotten English, & was not sorry to see the last of me after he had satisfied my thirst. He has two wives, about half a mile above the ruined monastery – he & the dog were really enjoying life: I suppose that is the real meaning of cynicism?

I've no more to say, except that the north is cold & wet. – I'sono al terzo cerchio della piova Etterna, maladetta, fredda e greve: Regola equalitá mai non l'é nuova. –[54]

By the way, who, from time to time, have been your publishers? My bookseller is a nincompoop and says he cannot discover them.

Yours
Basil Bunting

P.S. If I am sent East may I call on you on my way to join the boat?

## To Ezra Pound

TS Yale

2 December 1926 — 5 Osnaburgh Terrace, London, N.W.1

Dear Ezra –

I am removed from Newcastle and have been unsuccessfully applying myself to journalism. A few evening papers for a while took my article and then of a sudden they all left off and no more dibs are coming in at present. Consequently I was rather gloomy when I opened your letter and correspondingly cheered up when I had read it.

I begin to hate these poems I sent you and think they are rotten.[55] Sorry. They were afterwards slightly improved, but I cant see enough in them myself to justify any discriminating editor in publishing them. I was enthusiastic about them for a time…

[54] BB compares Northumberland to the third circle of Hell in Dante's *Inferno* (see *The Divine Comedy*, trans. C. H. Sisson (Oxford: OUP, 1980), 69).

[55] Possibly among the poems sent to Pound were one or more of the four works later titled 'Odes' and dated 1924–1926 in collected editions of BB's work ('Weeping oaks grieve', 'Farewell ye sequent graces', 'I am agog for foam', and 'After the grimaces of capitulation'). However, it should be noted that these datings are often completely inaccurate. See, for example, **Last of 1928**, which suggests that 'After the grimaces of capitulation' was a composition of that year (BB later dated it to 1926).

I have read E.M. Forster and consider that on the whole he is the best novelist now working, taking the works of Joyce as something over than novels. He is extremely delicate and subtle without being at all precious. "Howards End" seems to be the best, though the fuss was made about "A Passage to India". I think Forster understands England and the English middle class as well as it can ever be understood, it being as mysterious; I dont quite see how he would appeal to an American, except in his comic and exact pictures of Indians and Anglo-Indians in the "Passage".

I knew of two people who have unpublished work which seems to me to have real value.

One is a certain John Collier, something between a pimp and a buffoon in person, but his poems move me even when I have very little idea of what he is driving at. One of them was once published in the Dial, but Thayer[56] edited it and cut out on Bowdleristic grounds certain lines which I would never have suspected of any indecent meaning. He is very young – twenty three or four – and will not work on any account but he has two of three poems which are certainly worth seeing if you are going into the editing business.

The other is J. J. Adams, four of whose poems appeared in the Transatlantic. Ford hated them until they were printed and then inclined to think them amongst the best stuff he had got hold of. He has since written an epic as long as Paradise lost, entitled "The Tower of Babel" which I have not seen, but I understand it is divisible into episodes of reasonable length. He read me a passage about Wordsworth which amused me, though it was partly incomprehensible. He is satiric and parodic in a very individual way and sometimes gets in a patch of really beautiful stuff in a shame-faced manner; but he is diffuse and generally cacophonous. I believe Lewis swears by him.

The only thing I have at present that seems of any value at all is a study, story, what-you-will, of a state of mind engendered by incipient D.T. plus influenza plus a clubbing from the French Police.[57] Eliot has it at present, but I expect he will return it, he is so infernally cautious. Also I know it is immature. Also it ought to be part of a book instead of standing by itself.

[56] Schofield Thayer (1889–1982), publisher and editor of the *Dial* (see **5/5/23** and note).

[57] The comments here seem to indicate that this work, which became 'Villon', was a recent composition. It was clearly not part of the 'rotten' selection BB sent to Pound prior to this letter, and there is no mention of it in other letters of 1926. Importantly, then, BB's dating of 'Villon' to 1925 in later collected editions of his work is probably inaccurate: it seems to have originated in 1926, and was possibly only completed in early 1927 or later given the sketchy description of the poem here.

Finally there is Helen Rowe,[58] who was about to do good work, when she got married, produced three infants and became so taken up with domestic duties that I doubt whether she will ever make time for anything. But if she can be stirred up she might very likely prove worth the trouble. She is certainly a cut above Mary Butts or Djuna Barnes.[59]

In case you care to write to these people yourself I enclose their addresses separately; or if you wish it I will see what they've got and send it on to you. I'd do anything I can to forward any project of yours but am devoid of ideas at present – the inevitable result of trying journalism for the dailies. However I am becoming industrious and am laying the foundations of three books simultaneously (following advice of Valery in Nouvelle Revue)[60] – a book on Dickens as a stylist and a master of form, which badly needs doing. A book on the history of the music halls, not gossipy but treating the thing seriously as it deserves. A book on the Comparative anatomy of Prisons. I have also still a faint desire to accomplish a poem called the Magic Harp in which I wanted to indicate the whole of my own theory of criticism.[61] But that is a labour reserved.

If I do get an idea of any sort I will let you have it at once.

Basil Bunting

Forster, by the way, is not likely to contribute to any new review, being by now fully established and eminently respectable. They even print him at the Hogarth Press.

## To Ezra Pound

TS Yale

10 April 1927

5 Osnaburgh Terrace, London, N.W.1

Dear Ezra,

I intended to send you "The Salad Basket" when you wrote to me about Exiles some months ago,[62] but it was then with Eliot, and letters to him were invariably

[58] Helen Egli (neé Rowe), a model and associate of Wyndham Lewis between 1914 and 1915, and later briefly a writer of prose. Egli and BB had an affair circa 1921 (see Burton, 135–136).

[59] Mary Butts (1890–1937) and Djuna Barnes (1892–1982): prominent modernist prose writers who frequented the same literary circles as BB in 1920s London and Paris.

[60] Major French poet Paul Valéry (1871–1945) was a frequent contributor to *La Nouvelle Revue Française*, a literary magazine founded in 1909.

[61] This poem never materialized, or if it did its final identity is uncertain. The only really plausible candidate for a poem of this period that 'indicates the whole' of BB's 'theory of criticism' is 'The Word' or 'Nothing substance utters' (i.e., Ode 1.15).

[62] Pound's short-lived literary journal *The Exile* appeared in four volumes in 1927.

met with the assertion that he had gone into the country and would be back in a fortnight. However I've got it back at last with various complimentary remarks which may or may not mean that he likes it – I dont find him at all easy to fathom.[63]

Nobody seems to share my opinion that I can write poetry, nevertheless I include four short pieces lately accomplished in case you should incline to be converted to my view. Their merit is simplicity; difficult and rare since modern complications of evidence, thought and technique.

As a journalist I cant say I am a success. I have disposed of a certain amount of tripe in various quarters. But I have not earned more than half of what I have spent, so that I am on the rocks again and may have changed my profession before I hear from you again – may be a busman or a pauper or the Lord knows what. I notice that my spelling is returning to a state of nature and in time, if I remain a vendor of meaningless essays, my style will follow suit.

Why do you allow your works to be published at prohibitive prices, thus insuring that they shall be bought by bibliophiles only, who do not read them and dont allow other people to? Sixpence is the proper price for a book of poetry, and it could be made profitable if the book was short enough and unbound. That, of course, would not include initials by Strater[64] or Gladys Hynes,[65] charmingly pretty, like the children who offer you flowers for soldi, and as useless: appealing specially to the perverted sexuality of the arsetocrats (of commerce included) whom I take to be Rodker's chief customers. Sixpence a canto is what a writing man can pay, and he will go and see the decorations at the Leicester Galleries or the Tate.

Excuse the above impertinence. It is irritating not to get a chance of reading the more respectable output of the age.

Yours
Basil Bunting

[63] For more of this exchange see *The Letters of T.S. Eliot Volume 3: 1926–1927*, edited by Valerie Eliot and John Haffenden (London: Faber and Faber, 2012), 467. Eliot's letter was, as BB says, fairly complimentary, offering BB review work at *The Criterion* and asking to see more in the vein of 'The Salad Basket', apparently a prose work which has not survived.

[64] Henry Strater (1896–1987), American artist who illustrated a number of Pound's *Cantos*.

[65] Gladys Hynes (1888–1958), British artist who also produced illustrations for the *Cantos*. See *A Draft of the Cantos 17–27 of Ezra Pound: with initials in red and black ink by Gladys Hynes* (London: John Rodker, 1928).

## To Ezra Pound

TS Yale

Last of 1928 — 5 Osnaburgh Terrace, London, N.W.1

Dear Ezra,

Is this a poem?[66] Have I found my voice? Everybody says it is exceedingly disagreeable of me to be unpleasant about sunrise and the loud chorus of complaints encourages me to think that I must have done something of my own at last.

I am off for the continent, and I hope to be in Italy sometime in the spring and I hope to visit Rapallo and I hope to see you there. My girl died.[67]

I have been a musical critic for some time now – O but I told you that a year ago. The paper became extinct. The other column was so badly paid that I have no compunction about abandoning it. I am going to hear the orchestras in Berlin and Vienna.

It is good to have a collected volume of your stuff, but I wish Eliot had included Propertius.[68] It is very impressive, all seen together like that, more so – Lord knows why – than in separate little volumes. I knew it all before, some of it by heart, but it calls one to order and refuses to be temporarily overlooked in the new getup. Rodker showed me the new volume of the Cantos, but didnt let me take it away and read it. It is handsome. If he had got as good paper as the Paris lot it would have been the better volume.

Yours
Basil Bunting

## To Louise Morgan[69]

MS Buffalo

11 April 1929 — c/o Ezra Pound, 12 int 5 via Marsala, Rapallo, Italy

Dear Louise_

I have no news of London at all since your letter ages ago, so that I am in serious danger of romanticising the place and even imagining that it may be exempt

[66] A draft version of BB's 'After the grimaces of capitulation' is attached in TS.

[67] This curious elliptical aside—for which I can find absolutely no context—brings home how little we really know of the minutiae of BB's early years.

[68] Pound's first *Selected Poems* appeared via Faber and Gwyer in 1928. Eliot, who compiled the selection, neglected to include Pound's *Homage to Sextus Propertius* (1919), BB's favourite work of Pound's.

[69] **Louise Morgan**: American journalist and editor at *Outlook*, a journal to which BB contributed music journalism in 1927–1928.

from the extraordinary weather that is here – everything short of snow, and there is that too on the mountains.

I have been trying to entertain Margaret's boy[70] for the past ten days or so, with but moderate success. I wasn't prepared for bad weather. He is restless under it, & no wonder. A good lad.

Ezra being away in Venice, W. B. Yeats is the chief fountain of conversation here. Do you know the old boy? He walks about – absent: sees nothing, apparently. But his huge curiosity is busy all the time, & in the evenings there comes upon him an urgent need of conversation and he lets loose metaphysics, mysticism, anecdotes, literary criticism and the history of Ireland all stirred up well together. References to Sligo have the power of making him look almost young again.

And nothing happens, utterly nothing. Except – Ogden[71] appeared to have accepted my proposals for translating a book on Medieval philosophy: but as soon as I had begun to build on that he had to retract because of some difficulty with the French publisher. That was baffling. Much worse, these disappointments, than an immediate refusal. I didn't want to translate philosophy much, but I did want to earn something.

How are things with you? I seized an I. S. D. N. in a café here to read Otto,[72] but it turned out to be an ancient copy, a couple of years old. I suppose the Infant is growing so fast that he is scarcely an Infant any longer but a little boy. Sailing, I remember Jack & Anne & the canoe trip up the river. They would have liked, and livened up, Rapallo.

All the same, I am no longer sure that I will stay here long. I am fond of the place, but after Ezra & Yeats & Antheil are gone it might be as well for me to make a change of scene & avoid being bored in a place where I've never yet made any but good memories. So I don't know where I'll be in June. I don't want to live in London again yet: not before 1930. And France is still forbidden. Perhaps the South of Italy – or Greece –

[70] I.e. one of the sons of **Margaret De Silver** (see 28/8/48 and note), a wealthy American patron of the arts who assisted BB financially from the 1920s to the 1950s.

[71] C. K. Ogden (1889–1957), English linguist, writer, philosopher, and editor at the London publisher Kegan Paul.

[72] I.e. **Otto Theis**, Morgan's husband and also an editor at *Outlook*.

And yet I wish I could step out once a week or so and see you or the Eglis or Bertram Higgins or Nina.[73] That's all the London I really want, & its very hard to do without it.

Love
Basil Bunting

## To Louise Morgan

MS Buffalo

18 October 1929

Santa Caterina, Amalfi

Dear Louise_

Ford

I doubt it's hopeless for me to try to get a photo of F. M. Ford.[74] He's quarrelled with everybody, even Pound, who didn't know his whereabouts this spring. I have a vague idea he is in the States. I have never seen any picture of Ford, except a painting by one of his wives – I think it was in the Salon des Peintres Français of 1923[75] – a very good likeness which would reproduce well if you could find it, but I don't know whether there's any possibility of that. I've even forgotten the lady's surname. Perhaps Ford's publisher, Gerald Duckworth,[76] has a photo, though I don't remember ever seeing one as frontispiece or advert. Ford is too watery-bovine, I think, to want his photo broadcast to his readers in the usual way. I seem to remember quoting to him from Hudibras about "the itch of picture in the front" & him approving.[77] If Duckworth has a photo Nina Hamnett could get it for you: she knows him well. Her address is Thackeray House, Maple Street.

I am sorry I am so little use.

Yeats

[73] Bertram Higgins (1901–1974), Australian poet and critic who edited the journal *Calendar of Modern Letters* 1925–27.

[74] In 1929 Morgan joined the middlebrow weekly *Everyman*. This letter concerns possible contributions by BB to the journal (including, evidently, a photograph of Ford Madox Ford).

[75] Salon des artistes français: annual art exhibition in Paris first launched in 1881. BB refers to the 1923 portrait of Ford by Stella Bowen (1893–1947), an Austrian artist and writer in a relationship with Ford between 1918 and 1927.

[76] Gerald Duckworth (1870–1937), influential British publisher who founded Gerald Duckworth and Company in 1898.

[77] *Hudibras*: mock heroic poem by Samuel Butler (1613–1680) satirizing factions involved in the English Revolution. BB quotes from a passage in Part 1, Canto 1 of the poem, which pokes fun at the vanity of authors who append pictures of themselves to their works.

I don't know his work well enough to tackle it without reference to printed books. I will do an article on him if I can get back to Rapallo next month, say, where I can find all his works on his own shelves.

In the meantime if Ezra or Eliot is any use, I know their work almost by heart & will send in something at once.

I suppose J. J. Adams being practically unpublished is out of the question: but he is really the most characteristic of the lot. He found in "Arden of Feversham" the same sort of hints on prosody that Eliot got from the less excellent Webster & co.[78]

Other modern poets I know little about.

Weather still very warm.

Yrs
Basil Bunting

## To The Editors of *Poetry*

TS Chicago

27 February 1930

Villa Aschieri, piano 2, Rapallo, Italy

Dear Sirs,

In answer to your card of Feb 10: -

I would much rather not have a blurb at all, but if it is the invariable custom of "Poetry" I will conform.[79]

Birthplace, Northumberland, England. Residence, unfixed. Occupation, poetry. Previous publications, journalism. Small book, "Redimiculum Matellarum" about to appear in Milan. (Price 12 lire + postage from me at above address)[80]

I have a strong preference for the greatest possible degree of anonymity and if you could see your way to dispense with the above information I would be very much obliged.

Yours faithfully
Basil Bunting.

[78] *Arden of Feversham/Faversham*: anonymous Elizabethan play of 1592. Its subject matter (the murder of Thomas Arden by his wife Alice) to some extent pre-empts the macabre tendencies of Jacobean dramatists like John Webster (1580–1634), whose work is referenced multiple times in Eliot's *The Waste Land*.

[79] 'Villon' was eventually published in the October 1930 edition of *Poetry*.

[80] This last sentence is a handwritten addition. BB's first pamphlet, *Redimiculum Matellarum* ('a necklace of chamberpots') was, as detailed here, published privately in Milan in 1930. Financed by Margaret De Silver, it contained 'Villon' as well as a handful of the early poems later titled 'Odes' in collected editions. It attracted little attention at the time, aside from a review by Louis Zukofsky in the June 1931 issue of *Poetry*.

## To Ezra Pound

TS Yale

17 June 1930 London ("Damn the place")

Dear E.P.,

Having now got through one of the worst five weeks I ever spent (including nights on the embankment and Primrose Hill) and having apparently landed (but it is not quite sure yet) a commission to translate a substantial part of Lionardo da Vinci for the Mandrake people,[81] two drafts have turned up that have been wandering uselessly about the world for over two months and I am now able to go to the blooming U.S.A.

This I propose to do AT once, since if I delay ten days I am sure to succumb to the temptation of buying a little boat with the money instead.

Will you therefore charitably indite a few LETTERS OF INTRODUCTION, please, please, to any person likely to be either useful or amusing to a man seeking the means of returning to Europe with enough money for a boat and say two quid a week for a year for some not too deadly work?

Lewis's latest is tripe, alas![82] The apes dont gambol satisfactorily. Rodker is in good trim. Mathers is as ever. (i,e, slightly drunk).[83] I have taken to a regime of soda water as the only way of coping with the latest developments of the pub habit. Nina Hamnett is drawing better than ever and why on earth she doesnt make money is a mystery.

The Times was cautious about the Antheil opera. I didnt see any other papers after the event, but the Express[84] published a mucky fore-puff by me, sent in only to ensure that it would be heard of and that somebody would be sent to report it. The subeditor made it even muckier than it was, though I had gone the limit to conciliate the Ex-fucking-press.

[81] Mandrake Press: small, short-lived London imprint founded by Edward Goldston and P. R. Stephensen in 1929.

[82] *The Apes of God* (1930): satire of bohemian London by Wyndham Lewis (1882–1957). Lewis attacked a number of his enemies in the novel, including the Bloomsbury Group and John Rodker, thinly disguising them as fictional characters.

[83] Edward Powys Mathers (1892–1939), English poet best known for translating J. C. Mardrus's French version of the *Thousand and One Nights* (1923).

[84] As BB hints in this passage, the *Daily Express* was then, as now, a Conservative newspaper for a petit-bourgeois readership (and hence looked down on by members of the literary avant-garde).

No one will hear of the game laws, not even the ministry of agriculture.[85] The Herald was very contemptuous.[86] I couldnt get at Lloyd George.

Writing reading and thinking have all been impossible for some time, owing to lack of any sort of a room to myself. Even in the Museum cursed worries chased me.[87] Nevertheless I have read (must surely be the only living reader of) the enormous twentyfive act play of Michelangelo junior and other odds and ends.[88] You must forgive me an incompetent article for the Spectator on Troubadours. They actually asked for it and I wanted the money.

Earnings in five fairly strenuous weeks, 31/6.

Seems there will probably be a second edition of my poems.

Hope all goes well with you in spite of Crowley buying that press.[89] When are the thirty cantoes due? Several people seem anxious to buy them (i.e. at less than five pounds.)

If you know of any works that want translation, mention them for Gods sake. There is a bloke called Brooks who deals with translated novels who is busy for me, but I prefer jobs like the lionardo if poss.

Yrs
B
Basil Bunting
c/o Margaret De Silver
98 Joralemon Street
Brooklyn N.Y.

In the summer of 1930 Bunting travelled to the United States in search of employment as a journalist, and also because he was now married to an American, Marian Culver. It proved

[85] Abolition of the game laws, which regulated the hunting of fish and wild animals in the UK, was a cause about which BB felt some passion. Reflecting on his libertarian-agrarian political outlook in a letter to Dorothy Pound of 11/12/53 (Indiana), he would write: 'I began with a wish to limit my aims (abolish the protection of "game" in England to extend the range of black-faced sheep), and they were still far too abstract and ambitious to do anything but harm if I'd persisted.' See also the suggested 'new program of the T.U.C' in **Summer 1931**.

[86] *The Daily Herald:* left-leaning British newspaper, defunct since 1964.

[87] I.e. the reading room at the British Museum.

[88] Michelangelo Buonarroti the Younger (1568–1646), Florentine poet and grandnephew of his more famous namesake. Buonarroti's twenty-five act comedy *La Fiera* (1618) is likely to have appealed to BB because of its use of demotic dialogue.

[89] Aleister Crowley (1875–1947), English occultist, who led a consortium which unsuccessfully attempted to rescue Mandrake Press from its financial woes in 1930.

a crucial visit. Over the next six months in New York he made contact with members of the 'Objectivist' circle (notably Louis Zukofsky and Williams Carlos Williams) in the months leading up to their breakthrough in the famous February 1931 issue of *Poetry*.

## To Louis Zukofsky

MS Texas

11 July 1930

98 Joralemon Street, Brooklyn

Dear Mr Zukofsky –

Ezra Pound says I ought to look you up. May I? I like the "Henry Adams'.[90]

Yrs
Basil Bunting

## To Ezra Pound

TS Yale

23 July 1930

62 Montague Street, Brooklyn, N.Y.

Dear E.P.,

I hope the Guido hasnt hung fire or been dropped or anything else unpleasant through Crawley's acquisition of that there press.[91] When appears the Cantos?

As to New York, it is hellish noisy and the traffic is the most inefficiently organized I ever saw. The sheer waste of time – hold-ups at crossings where nothing whatever is crossing, for instance – couldnt be tolerated in London or Paris for a minute. It seems to me that their traffic problems are of their own making. Certainly there seems to be less volume of traffic in Fifth Avenue or Broadway than in Oxford Street or the Strand, but it not only goes much slower even in a clear street, but takes ages to wait at every cross street, while nothing, or a few scattered and leisurely taxis one by one emerge and amble across. The elevator is the devils own invention.

On the other hand the restaurant food is edible. That is one up on London.

[90] Zukofsky's essay 'Henry Adams: A Criticism in Autobiography' appeared in instalments in *Hound & Horn* throughout 1930.

[91] Pound's annotated Italian edition of troubadour poet Guido Cavalcanti (*c.*1254–1300) would eventually appear from Genoa in 1932. Presumably an earlier version was offered to Mandrake Press, and so 'Crawley' is Aleister Crowley (see 17/6/30 and notes).

This apt. has a view across the East river of all the big buildings in Lower Manhattan; individually hideous, but undeniably fine as a mass.

As to immigration officials, not only are they pretty foul in themselves, but the disgustingly inefficient organisation causes them to take hours and hours and inflict discomforts utterly unnecessarily. England has pretty strict immigration laws, but it takes about ¾ of an hour to deal with a ship at Southampton against four hours (which it took The Homeric) at New York. An Oxford student on way to Harvard put one of the creatures in a bad temper – going right through the extraordinary list of questions in a scarcely comprehensible gabble he, the official, enquired: "Do you speak English?" (this after a longish interrogatory in that language) "Yes" said the student, "Do you?" After that the rest of us were snapped at.

Impression of huge riches. What I look on as millionaires luxuries in the way of cream, ice, etc etc etc are treated as commonest necessaries. This country in depression is about as poor as Europe at its most booming richest moment. The bums in the Bowery seem to expect as much in the way of comfort as English middleclass people or rich Italians. I thought the sight of a wealthy nation ought to be encouraging, but it is not. On the contrary, it rather appals me to think of the amount of waste that obviously goes on here, the mere getting rid of money. I had also been in the habit of counting it for righteousness to America that some Americans subsidise the arts; but it is clear that the number who could subsidise and dont is about half a million against a few hundred who do.

Zukofsky excellent chap. And this rich land offers him merely $1000 a year to teach in a "progressive" university. i.e. the equivalent, prices allowed for, of about 90 pounds in England. That is disgusting. These first impressions likely to be modified. I am going to see Carlos Williams this week sometime. Prospect arises of a possible job in Colorado for about a year, which I have thoughts of taking. Calling on one Villard at The Nation,[92] with an introduction I was treated somewhat superciliously, like a cub reporter up from the country looking for his first job. I dont expect to be dealt with as a great man or any nonsense of that sort, but the papers I wrote for in England, bad as they are, would not have employed such a stinking charlatan as Macy,[93] Villard's right hand man, and I thought I was entitled to be treated with reasonable respect if that was the best kind of thing

[92] Oswald Garrison Villard (1872–1949), American journalist and contributor to the *Nation*, a major American weekly magazine founded in 1865.

[93] John Macy (1877–1932), poet, critic, and member of the *Nation* editorial board.

they could get in New York. I have very little respect for the English weeklies, but the Nation and the New Republic[94] are more puerile and the impudence of what they think they can get away with vexes me.

Landscape of Connecticut and Rhode Island rather sad. In a country that has been settled for three hundred years there should not be 80 or 90 per cent of virgin waste land. They want a few good wops who know how to get land less rich than Minnesota to yield a crop. It is nonsense to say that wops prefer to stay in the towns. This is because the U.S. doesnt lend them money to start farming as generously as Canada does, where the wops do farm land (I'm told) much rockier, sandier and sourer than New England. Besides, on Cape Cod, where they have Portuguese, the very same soil is made into apparently rich gardens.

The breastless American virgin of twenty is a stupefying phenomenon at first sight. I have not done much investigation yet though!

Certain Fernand Reyher[95] lives in this house, to whom Rodker gave me a letter. He says he knows you. A certain truculence that I have noticed in New Yorkers in Europe pervades his conversation, and still more his tone of voice. That is very provincial. I didnt come here to look down on New York, even if I expected to be made rather uncomfortable and a bit afraid by it. It is not necessary to use violence on me, and violence only makes me suspect that perhaps there is something to look down on after all.

I like niggers.[96]

Is it true that Antheil is writing an opera with a text by that unspeakable professor from Columbia?[97] Why? If Cocteau isnt enough, arent there numbers of quite respectable people ready to write operas? It is up to people of Georges quality to spit on Erskine and Macy (and their nearest English, French and German equivalents) not to lend value to their unspeakable muck by setting it.

Written in haste. Yrs

B

P.S. By the way, I got married to that American girl I was with in Venice.[98] She comes from Eau Claire.

[94] American magazine founded in 1912 (and still in print).

[95] Ferdinand Reyher (1891–1967), American writer, screenwriter, and journalist.

[96] The racist phrasing of this remark is (very partially) contextualized by BB's slightly later comments about the 'black man who runs our elevator' in **21/11/30**.

[97] Antheil's second opera *Helen Retires* appeared in 1931. It was based on *The Private Life of Helen of Troy* by John Erskine (1879–1951), humanities professor at Columbia University.

[98] BB married **Marian Culver** in July 1930.

## To Harriet Monroe

TS Chicago

2 August 1930 — 62 Montague Street, Brooklyn, N.Y.

Dear Miss Munroe

It is now a good many months since you accepted my poem "Villon" which Ezra Pound sent you from Rapallo at the end of last year. Since your acceptance of it I have heard nothing more.

I am now in the United States, and seeing what prices you Americans charge for eats I could very well do with the price of my "Villon". If I were likely to be in Chicago before the end of September I would collect it in person. But I am never likely to reach Chicago at all, nor to get farther than the Brooklyn cemetery unless I can collect it before that.

Besides I have got married and my wife eats too.

Yours faithfully
Basil Bunting

## To Ezra Pound

TS Yale

[August 1930] — 62 Montague Street, Brooklyn, N.Y.

Dear Ezra,

Zukofsky is a good chap, so is Carlos Williams, but they are both out of town now. Liveright[99] is said to be in Los Angeles (publishing talkies with legs in them). Krutch is in Europe.[100]

Gannett; Herald-Tribune,[101] told me your How to Read[102] was huge success, people kept writing in for back numbers with those articles in, and otherwise manifesting interest. I pass on this information, noting also that as far as I can observe the Land of your Birth is far more alive to your merits than England is.

[99] Horace Liveright (1883–1933), American publisher and stage producer. In 1917 he founded two publishing companies with Albert Boni (1892–1981): Liveright and Boni and Modern Library.

[100] Joseph Wood Krutch (1893–1970), American writer, naturalist, and theatre critic at the *Nation* from 1924 to 1952.

[101] Lewis Gannett (1891–1966), book critic at the *New York Herald Tribune*, a conservative broadsheet with literary leanings (active 1924–1966).

[102] Pound's essay series 'How to Read, or Why', was published in the *NYHT* throughout January 1929. It later appeared in book form (as *How to Read*) in 1931 via Harmsworth of London.

Best (Viking Press, with Huebsch)[103] seems about the most intelligent publisher I have met here or at home.

Did you ever hear of a certain Fortune Press, Buckingham Palace Road?[104] They wrote to me to say they heard I had some poems. I wrote and said yeas I had, and they were printed and sold out and Yeats liked them. They have now replied wanting to print them, without so much as having seen them. I am skeptical of their good faith. Somebody – cant identify who – told me they were a rotten grasping lot. I have written them to go to Brooks (agent). But is this wise?

The place swarms with Van Dorens.[105]

Zukofsky's article on twentyseven cantos[106] is exceedingly good to my mind. Wish some wise editor would print it.

Taupin I like.[107] He has good pictures on the walls, too. He talked sense and toured me around a few speakeasies. Hemingway is in Wyoming, McAlmon in Mexico but coming to N.Y. in autumn.

I am so "thrang" with meeting people (I cant really digest above two new people per week) that I havent got round all introductions yet, but am nearing the end of the list.

Journalism, nix. The atmosphere of Irita Van Dorens office at Herald Tribune nearly finished me off – the rows of books of review, the general tiredness of books in everybody, the hatred of the authors who inflict them on them, i.e. – editors. But anyway, besides the same stereotyped replies I used to get in London some years ago looking for work, there does seem to be a genuine determination – not just a reflex action of negation – to keep me out, from which I argue there must be some special depression in the review market lately.

Translations. I remain hopeful, but without good grounds. If I can persuade Huebsch that Moravia's book ought to be done, that would be a good start: but Huebsch seems to be anxious to get it done as nearly gratis as makes no difference and I'm damned if I'll do that.

[103] Marshall A. Best (1900–1982) and B. W. Huebsch (1876–1964) were both editors at the New York publisher Viking Press (founded 1925).

[104] Fortune Press: publisher founded in 1924 by Reginald Ashley Caton (1897–1971).

[105] The Van Dorens (Carl (1885–1950), his brother Mark (1894–1972) and wife Irita (1891–1966)): influential family of critics and editors in mid-twentieth century New York.

[106] I.e. Zukofsky's 1929 essay 'Ezra Pound: The Cantos', which offered an early appraisal of Pound's first 27 *Cantos*.

[107] I.e. **René Taupin**.

Brooks in London has done nothing. Mandrake Press and others refrain from deciding, prefer to keep things hung up. I have tried a cable on the Mandrake and await results.

Good luck be with you.

Yrs
B

## To Ezra Pound

TS Yale

21 November 1930

62 Montague Street, Brooklyn, N.Y.

Dear Ezra,

I've been in correspondance with Zuk. and I went and saw Bandler (not a bad bloke at all – fearfully Oxfordy, but I suppose that's Harvard).[108] But as to getting to Chicago or Boston to see Harriet Munroe or Kirstein, budget forbids. Bandler received me well.

I had a letter from Eliot that has been chasing me from address to address for months apparently, a pleasant letter to get, and at once leapt on the opportunity of pressing all my translating and other schemes on Faber and Faber.

As you say, travel broadens the mind. Travel to U.S.A. also embitters it. Perhaps I ought to have known that what's true of mankind in one place is true in another too, but I really imagined that the enormous wealth of this country might make some slight difference. It does. The respect for Hasgot and the contempt for Hasnt is rather better developed here than elsewhere. And much more universal – the Hasnts share it fully.

Put it, i.e. the present state of affairs, briefly, journalists dislike me because I dont pretend to have much respect for journalism. Also they want docile contributors. Ergo, I cant make a living. On the other hand the demand on me to make a living pressed by facts and still more by the positive hatred that America seems to entertain for those that dont (provided they havent inherited an income) (other lands are content to ignore hardups – here they go out of their way to kick the down and outs.) – this demand is very strong. The impossibility of satisfying

[108] Bernard Bandler (1904/5–1993), physician and psychiatrist from New York. He was co-editor, along with Lincoln Kirstein (1907–1996), of *Hound & Horn*, an American quarterly magazine, which declined to publish the article BB mentions later in this letter.

it fairly paralyses me, and I get nothing done at all, neither living earning, nor anything more interesting.

My allowance, as previously arranged, came to an end in May. Since I got here I have earned about seventy dollars. Prospect seems to be return to London, where, on my last visit I was presented with sleeping room on Primrose Hill and on the Embankment when I couldnt bum a bed from a friend. Earnings in one month in London, one guinea (I think – it may have been one & a half).

I have to leave here Feb 2. The immigration people became quite polite in the end and civil – at a distance. I was nearly packed off to Ellis Island when I went to see them about getting this extension. But I may leave before that.

Smith,[109] now running Liveright and Co, gave me my best yet example of American enterprise. He said: "Why dont you come with a commercial proposition? (the proposition was Moravia's novel) If you want anything like that done you must get it done in London and when its been reviewed we will consider it". He said that was the usual process. I didnt believe it, but conversation with other people confirms him. How a nation can be so rich and spend ALL its savings on Frigidaires beats me. How a nation can get the name of being speculative and be content to have its reading matter selected from the selections of the London publishers beats me. How a nation can get the name of being efficient and maintain such astounding offices as the immigration one, or of being hardworking and yet spread over six people the work that one man and a typist do in London, as in the Herald Tribune office beats me. In short, America beats me. The U.S.A. served up to us in Europe is a bluff – but what the real thing is – Lord save us, it cant be JUST my father-in-laws household? (Eau Claire, Wis.)

I havent looked up all my introductions, and feel a bit guilty about it. But I feel guiltier still when I look em up, eat their dinners and drink their applejack and cant dine or drink them in return.

One George O'Neill seems to be a decent thinking bloke.[110] I havent read his work.

The black man who runs our elevator is the most pleasing person I've run across casually here. He asked me what I wrote, and when I confessed to poetry he earnestly advised me to turn my attention to "theme song lyrics – that's the only poetry a married man can afford to write." However when I was entering him to the credit of U.S.A. he turned out to be a Canadian. Most of the people I meet would despise the writer of theme song lyrics for getting rich by them, and

[109] T. R. Smith: editor-in-chief at Boni and Liveright (see note to **August 1930**).

[110] George O'Neill (1896–1940), American poet, playwright, and screenwriter.

despise the writer of what they are pleased to consider respectable poetry for not getting rich.

(All the same I have found some good things here. But the native population seems very anxious to repudiate them. e.g. the comparative freedom of the American version of English, the vigour of burlesque shows as against the theatre – evidently even more stone dead than in England, and so on.)

Suzanne LaFollette[111] has taken the wrong turning and gone in for Names. The New Republic has recently published two cheering articles – Mike Gold on the fool who wrote the Bridge of San Luis Rey,[112] and somebody called, I think, Soule,[113] on reasons other than gold-shortage for the depression. Mike has been jumped on by the letterwriters for three weeks at three of four columns a week. Soule has been quietly ignored. I had hope of the New Republic, but Bandler, who was going to get me an interview with Cowley and some of the others on it, has not reported and I think its off.

Re Poetry, Chicago. Zuk. seems anxious to publish some of my verses.[114] Doesn't this rather shut out possibility of criticising the number? I am inclined to think that Miss Munroe will not welcome me anyway, whether I thrust or am thrust in. I will do all I can, but think that to write her myself would be error. Zuk. evidently sees symptoms of alarm in her already.

Re Hound and Horn, I gave them an article to read, philosophico-philological-cum-critical,[115] and also sent a carbon to Eliot. If either of them is interested, there is more of the same where that came from, but it takes a long while to get it on paper – its not on tap so to speak. I think its a very good article. It implies that Kaffir has advantages English hasnt as a medium for precise thought. It traces idealism to our syntax. It states that there can be no radical improvement in human affairs without first an overhauling of the language—carried out of course by poets in poetry. However, you may detect flaws in its perfection, and more immediately Eliot or Kirstein may.

[111] Suzanne La Follette (1893–1983), American journalist and editor of the *New Freeman*.

[112] Mike Gold: penname of the American author Itzok Isaac Granich (1894–1967). *The Bridge of San Luis Rey* (1927): novel by the American author Thornton Wilder (1897–1975), which narrates the collapse of an Inca rope bridge in Peru.

[113] George Henry Soule (1887–1970) and Malcolm Cowley (1898–1989) were both editors at the *New Republic*.

[114] The influential February 1931 issue of *Poetry* was guest-edited by Zukofsky and set out the stall of the 'Objectivist' poets. It featured a commentary by Zukofsky introducing Objectivism, as well as the seventh movement of his long poem 'A', BB's 'The Word' (Ode 1.15) and poems by George Oppen, Robert McAlmon, and Charles Reznikoff.

[115] A reference to BB's essay 'Some Limitations of English', which would eventually appear in the journal *The Lion and the Crown* in October 1932.

I cant get up any enthusiasm for Pagany,[116] Williams notwithstanding, the welter of contributions repels me. W.C.W. and McAlmon subtracted, it is impossible to be sure which of the others are schoolboys. Writers on their way to The New Yorker, the Saturday Evening Post, or as the case may be.

Am I justified or merely conceited? I dont know.

All the best to Dorothy.

Yrs

B

P.S. An anonymous poem which arrived here on the subject of Irish censorship – I think a few judicious hints might suffice to father it on Yeats. A pity there isnt a bishop handy, but a senator and nobelprizeman is almost as authoritative. At anyrate such a promising child cant be left to the foundling hospital. I wish I could plausibly lay it at Mr Cosgrave's door.[117]

P.P.S. If Yeats is about, my respects to him. Also Antheil.

## To Harriet Monroe

TS Chicago

30 November 1930

62 Montague Street, Brooklyn, N.Y.

Dear Miss Monroe,

It was very kind of you to speak of me to Mr Bissell of Harper Bros. (Not to speak of publishing "Villon") I have a deep esteem for your feat of keeping Poetry afloat and usually alive and vigorous for so long, and I would very much like to make your acquaintance. Unfortunately I cant come to Chicago, and I will not be in New York very long. If you come to New York before I have to leave it at the end of February it would be kind of you to let me know where I could meet you.

On a postcard which followed me here from Italy you ask me "Why salmon?"[118] It would be easy to answer why not? But though I am shy of giving partial explanations which often seem to mislead people, which is probably

[116] *Pagany*: little magazine (1930–1933) founded by the poet and editor Richard Johns (1904–1970). Its title was derived from the 1928 novel *A Voyage to Pagany* by William Carlos Williams, a regular contributor.

[117] William Thomas Cosgrave (1880–1965), Irish politician who succeeded Michael Collins as chairman of the Irish Provisional Government in August 1922.

[118] A reference to the final couplet of 'Villon' (Part III, 42–3).

worse than leaving them in the dark, I will say that by line 180 odd I have been angling a long time for a very big fish and only landed something for which the Board of Fisheries formula seems an exact and fitting description.

Yours faithfully
Basil Bunting

## To Ezra Pound

TS Yale

26 December 1930

62 Montague Street, Brooklyn, N.Y.

Dear Ezra,

Yes, I think there is more sense in eating macaroni up a hill than in making a new assault on Fleet Street. But I hope there will be no need to come on you for aid in doing it. So far as I can see, if I can get hold of a place fit to live in for about 100 to 150 lire, instead of the 250 I was paying, plus gas and electricity, at Villa Aschieri, we could hold out quite a long time; several months at the least, possibly the greater part of a year. I reckon we can reach Genoa and have from sixty to seventy pounds left, possibly a little more. More if we dont have to buy a table to work on etc.

IF you or Dorothy happen to notice any cottage up Montallegro or Montiwards or in those valleys under the Manico, take it for us, please.[119] We could be there by the middle of February, and an extra month's rent is alright.

There might be a flat at San Michele – there were some on the hill by the church to let a few months ago – or down in the little cove beyond it. Or there might be a cottage at Sant'Ambrogio. I dont want to live in the mainstreet at Rapallo, because of the noise. Quiet and a view are desirables. But dont waste time actually looking for a place (you WONT) because I think if there is anything thereabouts I could find it in the course of a fortnight spent at the Ginetta. [...]

Rapallo or thereabouts because there is no need to multiply the rigours of hardupness by getting somewhere where there is no conversation to be had.

Also it would be nice to be within reach of the sea to swim.

[119] BB gestures in this passage at upland areas in the vicinity of Rapallo (Montallegro, Manico del Lume) and in the following passage at nearby coastal villages (San Michele, Sant'Ambrogio).

Zuk and Taupin helped us to eat a goose yesterday, and Zuk appeared to think the time had come for me to write to H. Monroe with a definite suggestion;[120] which I have done this morning. I mentioned McLeod, Auden, J. J. Adams, Higgins, Collier; footnoted Rickword and Quennell and hoped Eliot might be persuaded to represent the Anglicised American (Z's suggestion). He is printing a poem of mine called The Word; not very exciting. (Z is printing) He sent a few others to Kirstein – I forgot that two of them had been to Kirstein before. Added to my collection of rejection slips one printed on board. Essay on The Limitations of English is also a determined homer.[121] Eliot however may be expected to give it lodging in his desk for at least a year before making up his mind to send it back. H. and H. people, having read it, suddenly dropped all communication with me.

Mother writes that she starts for Rapallo Jan 6th, stopping London, Paris and Turin; so she should arrive on the ninth. Her arm is apparently a good deal better. Maybe she wont need help. If we inhabit an accessible place we could look after her – possibly have her in the house. Dont say so to her: because – well, it doesn't often work...!

My sister has got a permanent pensioned good job now, with not too much work and a very respectable salary; so I'm not worrying about family hardupness.[122]

I dont expect to be in London. May go to Southampton and transfer to the Dutch boat for Genoa; may go to Cherbourg and train it. Leave here first or second of Feb.

Greetings to Mr and Mrs Pound Senr.

Yrs
Basil Bunting

Kitchen, bedroom, workroom. Quiet. View. AND a bog of its own.[123] If you happen to hear of it....

[120] The 'definite suggestion' was for BB's 'English' issue of *Poetry* (see **4/1/31**), which would appear in February 1932, exactly a year after Zukofsky's more celebrated 'Objectivist issue'. Aside from Eliot and Auden, neither of whom featured in the final selection, BB attempted to bring together a group of relatively obscure British poets for this special edition—in addition to bigger names like Ford, Michael Roberts (1902–1948), and **Cecil Day-Lewis**.

[121] BB's essay 'Some Limitations of English' was published in *The Lion and Crown* in October 1932 (see **30/10/32**).

[122] I.e. Joyce Bunting (1902–1992), BB's younger sister.

[123] *Bog*: toilet (Brit. slang).

## To Ezra Pound

TS Yale

4 January 1931

N.Y.

Dear Ezra –

H. Monroe has given me a rather informal commission to collect an English number of "Poetry". I am writing to McLeod, Auden, J. J. Adams, Collier, & Bertram Higgins. If necessary I shall also write to Rickword. The difficulty is going to be getting in touch with some of them of uncertain address. Does Stokes write verse?[124] Is there anybody who ought to be included omitted above? Zuk. thinks I ought to try to get Eliot to figure as the American in England, & I shall try. I expect a few people with longish contributions, rather than many with short ones.

Leave here end of the month, arrive Rapallo about tenth of February: must do everything from there.

Am still sorting ideas about U.S.A. Hope to get starting writing it today. How long does he want the article? I dont think I can run on to any great length.

I figure we shall have about £70 when we reach Rapallo. If we can get an unfurnished cottage or apartmentino I will try to make things myself – buy a saw and a plane & a pot of paint. Probably that is the cheapest way. But I cant make a spring mattress.

My typewriter is phut! Repairers dont know whether it can be repaired. Hoping. Meanwhile it rather delays recopying things I wanted to send out, and accounts for this illegibility.

General gloom froze out Greek for awhile: hope to get a new & better start on it in Italy.

Yrs
Basil Bunting

Don't tell Eliot he's too old. There arent any other Americans in England.

If something of this sort could be done without too frequent losing of tempers, there would be something deserving the name of School – quite unlike the advertising or backscratching rings.

I think the experiment worth making, - much better worth making than what is suggested by Putman's first contents bill (not a NEW but a NOTHER review)[125]

[124] Adrian Stokes (1902–1972), British art critic who contributed to *The Criterion*.

[125] *The New Review*: American magazine founded in 1931 by **Samuel Putnam**, with some involvement from Pound.

No offence.

I conceive this to be merely an elaboration of what you are thinking yourself.

Yrs
Basil Bunting

P.S. Zuk. or you might rewrite a few poems not up to scratch from current decent volumes. Wring 'em dry, so to speak. I can imagine nothing more instructive than confronting the original & the improved version, with reasons for changes given briefly. The poets in question would maybe detest it, but what of that? All the better if there is controversy about it. MacLeish would make a good victim, or Auden. Forced to justify their own readings or accept yours, I imagine they would put up a good show & a heap of valuable little knickknacks of criticism might turn up in the mêlée. But keeping to the point – no philosophizing. (and think how much better their second editions would be!)

## To Ezra Pound

MS Yale

6 January 1931

N.Y.

Dear Ezra –

Got your somewhat mysterious message yesterday and went at once to see Johns.[126] It was the first I heard of his being in N.Y.

He showed me an ad. of "New Review" with your name on it & bill of contents for number one. Said that was all he knew about it, & until he had at least seen a copy he had no opinion, suggestion, or other thing to offer. That seemed reasonable, & is my own case.

Johns said McAlmon was in town, but he had not been able to get hold of him. I went straight down to his hotel & found him getting out of bed after a ten days binge – not very collected at first. He said he had never even heard of the New Review, nor Putnam. However we phoned Johns & went off to a speakeasy. Northing further regarding New Review developed at all. Bob is thinking of issuing one number of a magazine, but apparently cant get even enough stuff for one number – up to his standard. But he said he'd written you about it. You are probably better informed than I.

[126] See 21/11/30 and note.

Williams is due to eat here Friday, so I havent specially troubled him in this matter. Johns, McAlmon & myself are all a bit vague as to what sort of "cooperation" you mean. Johns (as one might gather from contents "Pagany") is not fearfully keen about criticism, which Putnam's leaflet rather stresses; with him I gather it is definitely a case of wait & see. If contributions are intended I should think there'd be no sort of difficulty – that is, if Putnam pays.

No bromides, I hope. H & H is already enough, with the Criterion, of the drugged sleepy review; dosed with academic particularity to the point of having next to nothing of general interest to say. I dont see much fun in pointing out the minor deficiencies and excellences of dead men. Its too late to try & get a corpse, or even an old man, to improve his style. If New Review will point out the weaknesses of you & me, and not pat us on the back at all, not try to act as intermediary between poet & public, it will be doing something thoroughly useful & quite new. There are, or have been, plenty of fairly efficient advertising concerns, & I at any rate would have no enthusiasms for another. Nor is it necessary for people like us to go about deflating say Hart Crane: he will deflate himself surely enough, given time. But to show somebody sufficiently intelligent & un-vain to profit by it why the comma is in the wrong place etc – that is work worth doing. Zukofsky is clearly the man for that (besides you. I am not clearheaded enough to do it really well). Dr Johnson is a good model for criticism. (I've said all this before, but you fair asked for it, so I'm not apologizing. You dont need any comments or such from me, but for all I know Putnam may)

The practice is that a tiny dose of correction is accompanied by a huge one of face-saving blah. That's what I'm objecting to: you too, I gather. If you can really cause Putnam & his contributors to leave out the blah & omit homages to this & that man & personalia & trivia, you will have a very slim review left, but very meaty.

Johns has some poems of mine & will have more. I expect he'll turn them down. Zuk. has rather a good one (I think) in his number. H & H has altogether dropped me, not as the superior Henglishman, but as the dangerous fellow with an idea neither countenanced at Harvard nor directly derived from Pound, Eliot or some other comparatively respectable source.

As to London correspondent, it seems Pagany doesn't want one, especially one domiciled in Italy. The article you didnt like was included because it was written by somebody's girl. So we go on.

Yrs
Basil Bunting

Bunting left New York for Rapallo in early 1931. He would stay in Italy for the next two and a half years, during which time his poetic career reached an early highpoint. Several of his most substantial early poems were written during this final stay in Rapallo, and by this point he was fully integrated into the 'Ezuversity' scene that was beginning to give rise to a second wave of transatlantic modernist verse.

## To Ezra Pound

TS Yale

11 April 1931 Villa Michele Castruccio, Sestiere Borzoli, Rapallo, Italy

Dear E.P.

Auden's volume has reached me.[127] I am considerably impressed with first turning over the pages. He is the first person I have come across who seems to have profited duly by "Mauberley". But he has also his own contributions; and the fourthrate seems to be in definite subdued minority – rare in English poets.

Recommend you to get the pamphlet from Fabers, half a crown. Observe Nos XX XV, XII. I dont like his assonances much. But the syntax is interesting, both where scrupulously of speech and where condensed in defiance of grammar. In short, the poems bear out the impression I got from the Charade of his good points, without emphasizing the bad I saw in it. There is other badness, clearly, but none seems ineradicable nor part of his personal equipment. Very varied badness, but one sort of excellence: that is hopeful, surely. Wish I could do as well.

More perhaps after more careful reading.

I expect send you two or three notes in a couple of days – Mother to be shipped off first. Nothing, however, of much interest.

Yrs
B

[127] Auden's *Poems* appeared in different iterations between 1928 and 1934. BB refers to the best-known version, published in 1930 by Faber & Faber at T. S. Eliot's instigation. It included a series of untitled, numbered lyrics (hence 'XX XV XII'—i.e., 'The stings' excitement, the applauding drum', 'Control of the passes was, he saw, the key', and 'We made all possible preparations') and a play inspired by the struggling mining communities of the North Pennines: 'Paid on Both Sides: A Charade'.

## To Harriet Monroe

TS Chicago

13 July 1931 Villa Michele Castruccio, Sestiere Borzoli, Rapallo, Italy

Dear Miss Monroe,

Herewith two poems – Attis,[128] eleven pages of him, now newly finished: and the short "Fearful Symmetry"[129] that's been on hand for some time.

I hope you like Attis. I am very pleased with the third part.

The poem of Higgins' sent in was, I agree, uninteresting. Adams is always entirely unfinished, but I think one ought to put up with that, since he does get a good deal said, even if he leaves a lot of dead matter about. I am very sorry no one else seems to have sent in anything to you. I thought you would get something from Macleod at least and probably Auden and Rickword as well. Unless you can get something from these young men it hardly seems worth while to have a special English number, since the rest of the existing English poets, so far as I know anything about them, are not worth printing: this is not intended to be fearfully high praise for the abovementioned.

Edgell Rickword, c/o Wishart and Co, 19 Buckingham St
Adelphi, London W.C.2.

Macleod is in the midst of moving, therefore c/o Faber and Faber, Russell Sq. Same for Auden.

Ezra says "Attis" is obscure, from which he deduces that he is getting old. It certainly wouldn't be easy to write a synopsis, but I think its really fairly plain for all that, if the reader doesn't spend time and energy looking for a nice logical syllogistic development which isn't there. I don't like formal logic. There are better ways of connecting things up and anyway Wittgenstein reduced logic logically to the noble conclusion "Worüber man nicht reden kann, darüber musz man schweigen" some years ago and there seems nothing more to be done with that instrument after that.

[128] BB's 'Attis: Or Something Missing' is a long lyric (later termed a 'sonata'), which draws on Lucretius's *De rerum natura* to satirize T. S. Eliot, among other targets. Perhaps agreeing with Pound that the poem was 'obscure', Monroe did not publish it in *Poetry* (its first appearance was in *Poems: 1950*).

[129] 'Fearful Symmetry' (later 'Muzzle and jowl and beastly brow' or Ode 1.13) appeared in the February 1932 issue of *Poetry*. A deadpan rephrasing of Blake's 'The Tyger' in the context of modern British imperialism, it is one of several attempts by BB at this juncture to detourn canonical English poems (see also the Milton parody in Part II of 'Attis' (1–4) and the attempt to rewrite Shakespeare's sonnets announced in this letter).

I have struggled with the business of getting an article out of what I know of current English poetry, but it is a devil of a job. I'll send something along presently.

BY THE WAY I never got any oof out of the poem in Zuks. no. I don't know whether any was supposed to be due. But I've always been against doing something for nothing, and besides, even here, they make me pay for eating. Moreover my wife wont touch spaghettis and altogether it isn't all roses trying to love without earning an honest living.

I am engaged in rewriting Shakespeare's sonnets.[130] They can do with it. After sufficient cutting and straightening out of inversions, rather a nice poem should emerge.

Yours faithfully
Basil Bunting

## To Ezra Pound

TS Yale

[Summer 1931] [Rapallo]

Dear Grain of Salt,

Current number of New Review savourless and borjoy.[131] Bodenheim, Thoma, Perles, why why? No personal prejudice in the matter since Putnam announces my essay that nobody else would print: but I cant be interested.

On the other hand, you publicly talk sense. Why the hell doesnt somebody else take up the tune?

[130] Exclamation mark in pencil added by Monroe on left hand margin. BB's rewriting of Shakespeare's sonnets has been variously misdated. Caddel relates that it first took place at school and was repeated, 'apparently for the benefit of Dorothy Pound', in the late 1920s (see *Sharp Study and Long Toil*, 48); Burton refutes this, arguing that it is 'clearly from the period Bunting spent on the Thistle in the winter of 1937–38' (Burton, 254), an odd claim given that he quotes other passages from this letter, which dates the exercise to 1931 beyond doubt.

[131] BB refers to the August–September–October issue of the *New Review*, which featured contributions by: Maxwell Bodenheim (1892–1954), American poet and writer; Richard Thoma (1902–1974), American writer and associate editor of the *New Review*; and Alfred Perles (1897–1990), Austrian writer who worked for the Paris edition of the *Chicago Tribune*.

The tone of S.P.'s notes to his poem is altogether off.[132] Demand intelligence from the reader, sure, all of it; but learning, if you go beyond what's common in the Sixth Form, leave it to the profs to earn their measly living by pointing it out. I dont object to dice in well or Euclid's square, I mean but to "almost too elementary" and so on which are cheap decorations to award oneself. Let him sign Sam. Put. D.L.S.[133] and save some space.

Atthis, if ever penetrated (if ever printed) is unfair to Eliot. These Bodenh.s and other too-good-for-Americas shd have been slain first, being more indubitably gelded.

If anyone ever says I got out of England for any other reasons than the climate the noise and the impossibility of living on nothing a week, curse his soul. The mere oppressiveness of an organized society of fools is no reason for self-exile. i.e. I dont reckon myself the final judge of fools, and would much rather fight it out with the hacks than go hermit in a populous Thebaid sure of immortality.[134] The exact set of my halo after death seems to me an affair for the survivors. As Milton says, Better to serve in hell than to reign in heaven.[135]

Cant you exert yr authority, import Zuk. (I mean in bulk, not in snippets), W.C.W., McAlmon, none of whom ever hints this exaltation above common men, though further above them than a lot of these clever contributors.

Let these others go back to Chicago, where they will be read by others beside their pals and where the question pro or contra dollars and jobs is likely to be more insistently put than in evertemporary Montparnasse. The function of the New Review ought not to be that of a graduate school preparing for the paying mags. There are too many such. Why not a paper devoted to thinking, (poetry, repetitions of neglected political obviousnesses, showing up of science) instead of to floating a number of nondescripts on an unwilling market?

The hope is that you will pass these on to Putnam in a form more suited to his digestion. It is realised that for you to edit would be a waste of time better spent on Cantos, but for you to bully Samuel, if it doesnt become just as perpetual and exacting a business, that's needed.

These contemporaries? Bloody little con-.

[132] Putnam's poem 'As Browning Would Have Said' appeared in the issue along with the note BB describes.

[133] I.e., Doctor of Liberal Studies: an American research degree title.

[134] Thebaid/Thebais: desert area in Egypt which became a retreat for Christian hermits in the 5th century.

[135] See *Paradise Lost*, Book 1, l. 263 ('Better to reign in Hell, than to serve in Heav'n').

ENGLAND. If Wales and the North dont rise this autumn, there's little hope of anything but extinction.[136] The new program of the T.U.C.[137] should be drawn up quite simply, thus:

1 Hang Rothschild[138] and a select retinue of "merchant bankers".
2 Confine Rothermere in Broadmoor Criminal Lunatic Asylum with public warning to Beaverbook and the Berries.[139]
3 Warn Australia Canada S Africa that if they dont pay up their proportionate share of the cost of the fleet and loosen up a bit on the immigration restrictions, they will be put up for public auction to any buyer who cares to undertake the job of reconquering them, such as Germany or U.S.A.
4 No import dues, and a bloody big supertax.
5 Abolish the game laws
6 Abolish the Home Office
7 Confiscate the church lands and royalties.

After that elect a new house of Commons and omit to summon any of the hereditary peers to parliament.

I think that would almost do the job.

I was trying to think up a way by which it could be made worth while for Russia or Brazil or somebody else with territory to spare to set up an autonomous but allied state, peopled by the million and a half English permanent unemployed. They could pay for the land by carrying out necessary public works, such as road building, in the patron-country. Said country would have to feed them or guarantee a loan for about a year after final settlement, unless the City Shylocks could be persuaded to cough up a few years dole on consideration of

[136] BB's comments on British politics here and in the following passage reflect a pervasive atmosphere of crisis in the summer of 1931. In brief, economic trouble which had been deepening since the Wall Street Crash of 1929, and which would culminate in the departure of the British pound from the Gold Standard in September, led the Labour government under Ramsay MacDonald to introduce austerity measures, sparking high unemployment and widespread social unrest. Despite this fiscal squeeze, foreign investors deserted Britain throughout the summer and the value of the pound plummeted. Though Dorothy Pound worried about the impact of the crisis on their finances, Ezra deemed it 'more intellectually exciting than Aug. 1914'. See David Moody, *Ezra Pound: Poet: Volume II: The Epic Years* (Oxford: OUP, 2014), 125.

[137] The Trades Union Congress (TUC), founded in 1868: federation combining the several trade unions in England and Wales.

[138] Lionel de Rothschild (1882–1942), wealthy British banker and Conservative politician.

[139] Harold Harmsworth, 1st Viscount Rothermere (1868–1940), Max Aitken, 1st Baron Beaverbrook (1879–1964), William Berry, 1st Viscount Camrose (1879–1954) and **Gomer Berry, 1st Viscount Kemsley**: powerful British newspaper owners supportive of the Conservative Party.

getting rid of all those responsibilities. If organised in a more or less military discipline for the first three or four years under energetic leaders, they could make even Kamchatka[140] habitable. If I had the job, I'd make them learn a phonetic spelling, so that they would forget how to read the English newspapers and current dribblings. Simplify the language still more, if necessary, make the bloody native Portugoose or Kamchadale learn it with all existing irregularities removed, thus making a complete break with the bloody British past. The material is good enough. One could elect the stuff to be translated. State agriculture, or at anyrate statesuprintended. (It comes cheaper in labour and material costs). Drain the swamps, put in roads, motorcars; steal the patents if need be. Don't give the Americans any copyright and put a thousand dollar visa on them – Oh yes, there's a lot of things could be done that sort of way. I've even a method of newspaper-debating to shorten & simplify parliamentary procedure!!![141]

The store of cultivatable uninhabited big areas in the world is very considerable. But I dont see how to persuade the Haves to part with any of it, except the Bolshies might, for a contribution of skilled men to their factories. As for taking it without asking, I'd go to the North and collect my migrants in a month if there were any way of getting them guns and ships, but there aint.

Yrs
B

## To Harriet Monroe

TS Chicago

19 January 1932 Villa Michele Castruccio, Sestiere Borzoli, Rapallo, Italy

Dear Miss Monroe,

Enclosed a mitigatory letter, which please print if possible in the same number with my article, [142] if not, in the next. I don't want to call Eliot names, as I almost appear to in the article as it stands.

[140] A remote, sparsely populated region in the far north-east of Russia.
[141] This last sentence is a handwritten addition.
[142] The February 1932 issue of *Poetry* included BB's article 'English Poetry Today', a vitriolic attack on its subject which singled out T. S. Eliot for special opprobrium:

> Mr Eliot's Criterion is an international disaster, since he began to love his gloom, and regretfully, resignedly, to set about perpetuating the causes of it—kings, religion, and formalism…I have nothing to say against his poetry, amongst the finest of the age; but against his influence on the poetry of others, the involuntary extinguisher he applies to every little light, while professing, maybe truly, to hate the dark.

If it is not already too late, please excise from the article the phrase "the involuntary extinguisher he applies to every little light, while professing, maybe truly, to hate the dark." It is alright, but liable to be misread and misunderstood. It is at the end of the eighth paragraph.

There is a man called Becket now having poems printed in the New Review, either English or Irish, by no means devoid of interest.[143] Should have included him in my remarks if I'd known about him soon enough.

I don't know what I ought to say about my prize.[144] It went some way towards paying the expenses of my daughter's birth, arriving the same day. But I am inclined to quarrel with the judges in that they preferred me to Zukofsky, who in my judgment had the better claim on any laurels that were going.

I have heard a rumour that POETRY was to cease publication. That would be a pity. There's nothing to take its place. I hope the rumour's untrue.

Yours faithfully
Basil Bunting

The enclosed may make a group? The material is from the HO JO KI, (in translation)[145] but that is a prose work. I have condensed about half of it into verse, and propose to finish it as opportunity arises.

Please send a copy of the February number to the editors of "Stream" 116 Little Collins Street, Melbourne, Australia.[146]

Postscript.

The omission of the biological hieroglyphic from the fourteenth line of my poem "Fearful Symmetry"[147] rather upsets the cadence. Its function was to set a fact (the animal's maleness) silently before the reader, before going on with the supposedly audible information "Felis Tigris..." etc. The excision by the printer

See *Poetry*, February 1932, 264. Monroe neither included BB's note nor excised the phrase in question.

[143] BB refers, of course, to Samuel Beckett, who had poems published in *The New Review* in 1931–1932, notably 'Return to the Vestry' and 'Text'.

[144] The last nine stanzas of the first part of BB's 'Villon' were republished in the November 1931 issue of *Poetry* after the poem was given the Lyric Prize ($50).

[145] Hōjōki ('an account of my hut'): poetic diary by the Japanese poet Kamo Chōmei (1155–1216) written *c.*1212. It forms the basis of BB's 'Chomei at Toyama', a long poem which experiments with quantitative metres, eventually published by Monroe in excerpts in the September 1933 issue of *Poetry*. In preparing his poem BB worked from Marcello Muccioli's Italian translation of 1930.

[146] *Stream*: short-lived Australian little magazine of the early 1930s, with which Bertram Higgins was involved.

[147] In publishing 'Fearful Symmetry' (see 13/7/31 and note) *Poetry* omitted the male pictogram ♂ from the poem's fifteenth line.

of a pause of this duration destroys the movement and continuity of the rhythm. Alas!

[...]

To the Editor of Poetry

Dear Miss Monroe,

I see from the proofs of my article on English poetry, which arrive at this remoteness too late for revision, that it might appear to a rapid reader that I was making a personal attack on Mr Eliot, whereas I want to have it quite clear that it is only his influence I want to denounce; his influence acting probably far beyond his intentions, maybe even contrary to them. So far as I am aware he has always encouraged whatever decent poetry came his way, independent of its political, religious and so forth aspects. It is the pressure of his phenomenal prestige that extinguishes the sparks, etc. It is all so much weight added to the existing inducements to retrogression in England. If the mournful cadences of The Waste Land have turned out to be as hypnotically effective as the Eat More Fruit advts., it is, of course, Mr Eliot's fault, but in a sense in which one might as justly call it his misfortune.

Yours faithfully
Basil Bunting
Rapallo

## To William Carlos Williams

TS Yale

August the umpth 1932

via Borzoli 39, Rapallo

Dear Bill Williams,

Homer Pound[148] showed me your letter. Glad you like the gent Ezra persists in calling Joe May.[149] Sorry you don't expect to find space for him before say 1934. He wants a little revising (maybe you think: a lot) but I'd like to see him in print. Not that I'm much bothered about Glory or getting an audience, but there are practical advantages in ceasing to be one of the unprinted horde.

In fact, if you want to keep the space for interesting young men, let me tell you I'm an interesting young man. If 32 isnt the prime of youth, at least I'm young in

[148] I.e., Pound's father Homer Lewis Pound (1858–1942), who lived in Rapallo in this period.

[149] I.e., Chomei, BB's 'Chomei at Toyama' (see 19/1/32 and note).

print – about four little poems and my Villon have got into magazines, and the pamphlet[150] was only 100 copies and short at that.

A copy of Chomei is with some bloke who wants to start a magazine,[151] and he may, if he prints it at all, get round to it before you do. I shall continue to try to get it printed, at least by mags that pay for contributions; and if anyone does print it before you find space I'll let you know, and if they don't I'll be duly grateful when you do.

Hope it won't be suspect if I go on to say how much I like the things of yours I've seen lately. Poems, that is, as well as White Mule.[152] Extraordinary limpidity. But nobody can begin that way; you've got to it through many years of hard practise during a good many of which you weren't limpid at all. So if the young fellers are obscure, don't knock em for it; if they're clear while still young, it's probably because they are empty.

It was much more difficult than you imagine to keep Chomei clear, and couldn't have been done if I hadn't had the japs own book (Italian translation) in front of me and kept as closely to it as the condensation of verse would permit. In short it's a collaboration between me and a corpse of sixty-five, and the clarity, such as it is, comes from the corpse.

Best wishes: and to Mrs Williams. I hear McAlmon was jugged but not for anything felonious. Ezra's expression while editing is even benigner than usual.

Yrs
Basil Bunting

## To Louis Zukofsky

TS Texas

2 October 1932 — via Borzoli 39, Rapallo, Italy

Dear Louis,

Current Mare includes following open letter to you:[153] here repeated in English in case you want to reply.

Yrs faithfully
B.
[…]

[150] I.e., *Redimiculum Matellarum* (see 27/2/30 and note).

[151] Perhaps James G. Leippert's *The Lion and Crown* (see 30/10/32).

[152] Williams's novel *White Mule* appeared in instalments in *Pagany* in the early 1930s, before its eventual publication by New Directions in 1937.

[153] BB's letter appeared in *Il Mare* on 1 October 1932. *Il Mare* was a local Rapallo paper to which the 'Ezuversity' circle regularly contributed (see 20/3/85 for a summary of BB's contributions).

OPEN LETTER to Louis Zukofsky
Dear Louis,

Criticism, especially my own, is painful to me. Presumably the poet knows what he meant to do. The detection of fraud and adulteration is necessary police-work, but must keep within the rules of evidence: fact, not hearsay; history, not speculation; all the exhibits there alongside their expert analysis.

There is a purpose in the showcase too; select samples with a sufficient but succinct and unobtrusive ticket, as in "quality" shopwindows. I have very much admired your skill at that job.

But:

If I buy a hat I am content that it should fit, be impermeable, of good texture, and of colour and cut not outrageously out of fashion. If I am a hatmaker I seek instruction in a series of limited practical operations ending in the production of a good hat with the least possible waste of effort and expense. I NEVER want a philosophy of hats, a metaphysical idea of Hat in the abstract, nor in any case a great deal of talk about hats.

The uses of hats are few, definite and practical. Let a doctor call attention to them from time to time for the conversion of the Hatless Brigade, the rest of us will take them for granted.

This is what I would understand by Objectivism, if the word were mine. It seems to me that one passage in your admirable "Recencies" essay in the Objectivist anthology oversteps the limits of useful criticism.[154]

For the reader, an expert's certificate of precision, concision and general good-workmanship; or a warning of their absence. For the state, now and then, a reiteration of the known, definite, limited, practical necessity of poetry. For the poet, technical information as from one good craftsman to another; such as doctors exchange in the medical papers.

For this last, Pound's three items quoted by you are a model (Direct treatment: to use no word that does not contribute to the presentation: to compose in the sequence of the musical phrase, not in sequence of the metronome). His well-known "Don'ts" are as explicit and concrete.

Johnson understood the value of minute examination: there is more to be learned from his Notes on Shakspear and the critical parts of Lives of the Poets

[154] Zukofsky's *An 'Objectivists' Anthology* appeared via To Publishers in 1932. As well as poems by BB, Zukofsky, Pound, Eliot, Kenneth Rexroth, George Oppen, and other members of the group, it featured a preface by Zukofsky ('Recencies'), the subject of BB's criticisms here. As should be clear from BB's comments, he objected to Zukofsky's 'definitions' and indeed *all* writing about poetry on point of principle.

than from almost all the rest of English criticism put together. You have yourself used a similar method both in public and privately correcting my poems, and it has been valuable. Your version of Rexroth's Prolegomena compared with his original, is likewise instructive.[155] I think this is what criticism should be.

But these definitions of A Poem! You are not content to swab up Eliot's mess.

We have a pretty good working notion of a poem. Its marks? They can be recorded in a purely scientific spirit. A naturalist can define a tiger, but his definition fits a wretched, mangy, undergrown, pitiful specimen as well as a Blakean super-tyger. He counts its teeth and vertebrae, measures its skull, observes the structure and disposition of its organs. He does not mention ferocity, barely strength; nothing we un-experts commonly associate with tigers.

I distrust your page 15. "A poem … perfect rest … the desire for what is objectively perfect … the desire for inclusiveness …" (I select what I like least). There is discrimination; but whether the things discriminated between have any bearing on poetry I doubt. If they have it is remote.

I have always supposed you to have a greater care for facts than almost any critic now living; a greater partiality for the particular, for the "very words". But these paragraphs about poetry look to me like flights into darkness, away from ascertained and reascertainable fact to speculative mysticism; to a region I think void of anything permanently valuable.

The mystic purchases a moment of exhilaration with a lifetime of confusion; and the exhilaration is incommunicable but the confusion infectious and destructive. It is confusing and destructive to try and explain anything in terms of anything else, poetry in terms of psychology. And in fact the inclusion of Rexroth's vast vagueness in your anthology is, I think, traceable to the importation of an extraneous standard into your judgement of poetry.

I have no alternative principle. I do not think anything can be simplified. We can only be content to begin at the beginning and remain very near the beginning all our lifetime.

We cannot afford to let a subtle monism obscure the lucidity you have often brought to bear on specific poems, as in your study of the "Cantos".[156] A movement, a religion, is no substitute for clearsight, even if it be a much better religion than those recently current amongst writers.

155 Two versions of Rexroth's long poem 'Prolegomena to a Theodicy' featured in *An 'Objectivists' Anthology* (Rexroth's original and a version edited by Zukofsky).

156 See **August 1930** and note.

Criticism is to poetry what anatomy, histology, physiology are to the living body. You quote Pound's triple distinction: melopoeia, phanopoeia, logopoeia: a contribution to the science.[157] Criticism is concerned with what is written, not with the mind of the writer, as anatomy with man's body, not with the unguessable intentions of an unlikely Creator.

BASIL BUNTING.

[...]

Dodsworth's translation leaves something to be desired: but will do.[158] I would have sent this some while ago to let you prepare any reply you feel like making, but it wasn't certain until a few days ago that the letter was going to appear at all.

Yrs B

## To James G. Leippert[159]

TS Chicago

30 October 1932

via Borzoli 39, Rapallo

Dear Leippert,

I mislaid your letter, hence delay.

MacLeish will no doubt help the circulation. Up to the publication of Conquistador[160] I looked on him as a dark horse, a possibility. No doubt I hadn't read enough of his other stuff to find him out. Now his place is clear, like that of Aldous Huxley and others who have enough of the adolescent talent, imitation, to make a surface not always easy, at any rate for the public, to distinguish from the real thing; but they have no guts of their own, they are, in fact, the public. At its best that class of writers can produce a Tennyson, assimilator of all technical tricks, inventor of a few minor ones of his own, yet vacuous and insipid. In MacLeish's case he is apt to spoil his technical tricks by not fully understanding them. Thus he borrows cadences and phrases from Pound (in Conquistador) but

[157] In a categorization most fully outlined in 'How to Read' (see **August 1930**), Pound distinguished between three essential properties of poetry: melopoeia (broadly, the musical), phanopoeia (the visual), and logopoeia (the semantic and intellectual). See *How to Read* (New York: Haskell House, 1971), 25–26.

[158] Edmond Dodsworth translated BB's open letter into Italian for *Il Mare*.

[159] **James G. Leippert**: American editor of the journal *The Lion and the Crown*, to which BB contributed the essay 'Some Limitations of English' in October 1932.

[160] MacLeish's *Conquistador*, a long poem in terza rima about the Spanish conquest of Mexico, was published in 1932 and awarded the Pulitzer Prize the following year.

usually spoils them in the borrowing by small clumsinesses he seems unaware of. That of course is what the public will always support. The public is genuinely anxious to do what it has been told is its duty by men of genius, but at the same time it wants, and quite reasonably, to be able to understand what it pays for. It is not able to understand the really serious poet, but it can notice his mannerisms, and when it sees these mannerisms reproduced over and around a content it can with care get the hang of, it thinks it has found a genius it can honour and you get those bubble reputations that the next age finds so extraordinarily puzzling.

Poems of self: do what you think fit. I don't hold it against anyone who doesn't want to print my great works, or I'd have a long list of grudges indeed! So far as I know "Chomei" has only two admirers, but they are Pound and Yeats. Eliot is said to have said that it couldn't be good because I had never been in Japan! Which, if true, is an example of whatten years at the head of a dull "heavy" can do to a man. Zukof: pointed out a number of specific failings in it, for which I am much in his debt, but haven't so far been able to correct more than a small proportion of them. It is a long way to send proof across the Atlantic, but if you can do so, I'll see what can be done, especially about the end. If you don't want to print it, very well, but let me know and I will try to wish it on Harriet Monroe, who pays!

"The Body Blazes"[161] has none of my affection. But somehow it has survived numerous holocausts! It has just barely enough life to have prevented me destroying it, and so little I despair of improving it. However, some such have been picked on from time to time and preferred by reasonably competent people to the poems I like best myself.

Taupin: I have just been reading his new "4 essais indifferents pour une esthetique de l'inspiration"[162] and find it so much the best piece of largescale criticism that has been done for many years that I'd advise you to lose all the subscriptions of all the roommates you ever had to print anything of the sort. I am no good at heavy reviewing, but suggest you get someone to do a review of it as early as possible. Williams probably hasn't time. Do you know Morton Zabel of "Poetry"? Farrell ("Young Hooligan" of whatever the sentimental novel was called) is a good philosophic reviewer.[163]

So far in answer to your letter.

[161] Perhaps 'After the grimaces of capitulation'.

[162] Taupin's 4 *Essais Indifferents pour une Esthetique de l'Inspiration*, published in 1932, included the essay 'La Poésie d'Ezra Pound'.

[163] James T. Farrell (1904–1979), American poet and novelist, best known for the Studs Lonigan trilogy, which included *Young Lonigan* (1932).

No copy of the Crown and Lion (both the village publichouses in one phrase?) has yet reached Rapallo.[164] Whether this is the result of 190 proof alcohol or of American optimism in initially estimating the time the printer would take, it is a pity.

I happen to know that Ezra is contemplating getting out a special number of some magazine to exhibit the recent developments of American criticism (with me included as in other publications as the solitary Englishman supposed to be fit to associate with Yanks). He was thinking of "Contempo"[165] but "Contempo" is having troubles, Abernethy and Ibn Battuta not being of one mind as to what constitutes literature. Also "Contempo" is too small. He could fill about sixty pages of the average magazine size, I guess. There would be his remarks on the subject, my letter reprinted from the N. Y. Sun, essays by Zukofsky, Farrell, Mangan,[166] and others. His previous special numbers of various papers, especially "Poetry" years and years ago and the "Little Review" years ago,[167] had effects, which is something magazines don't always have. He was, I know, waiting to see what your mag is like, with the intention, if he approved of it, of proposing to do this job in one, or part of one of your issues, if you like. It is often good editing to let someone else do some of the editing. I am not authorised to make this proposal to you, but I see no reason why your mag. shouldnt satisfy his august requirements, so I'm not wasting time waiting for it.

About Pound and myself? I met him in Paris ten years ago playing a swashbuckling kind of chess. I believed then, as now, that his "Propertius" was the finest of modern poems. Indeed, it was the one that gave me the notion that poetry wasn't altogether impossible in the XX century. So I made friends. I was then digging the roads outside Paris for a living. I got locked up for a colossal drunk. It was Ezra who discovered me, still half blank with something approaching D.T.s, and perjured himself in the courts to try to get me off. When I came out of quod,[168] and was working as barman at the Jockey,[169] he introduced me to Ford Madox Ford and I became sub. and sec. to the Transatlantic Review.

So, afterwards I was chucked out of France and came to Italy, and climbed a mountain, and on the top of the mountain, to my astonishment, Ezra appeared.

[164] I.e., *The Lion and the Crown*, Leippert's/Latimer's magazine.

[165] American little magazine published by Milton A. Abernethy (1991–1991) and Anthony J. Buttitta (1907–2004) between 1931 and 1934.

[166] Sherry Mangan (1904–1961), American poet and journalist.

[167] Pound was foreign editor of (and contributor to) New York little magazine the *Little Review* 1917–1919.

[168] *Quod*: prison (Brit. slang).

[169] Jockey Club de Paris: fashionable Parisian gentleman's club founded in 1834.

So I saw more of him. He was busy writing his first opera and I was busy writing my poems.[170] I am glad no one would print me then. All those poems have been destroyed.

I was some years in England, earning a very meagre living and growing stupid. Then I kicked, decided that I'd rather not earn a living than write any more reviews for weeklies, and have been the better for it ever since. I tried my own North Country for a while, and it wasn't so bad but I got very little done that I wanted to keep, so I took advice and went to Berlin and it was the worst thing I ever did. In the end to save my sanity I went suddenly to the station and bought a ticket for Italy to look up Pound again. And here I've been ever since, with the exception of eight months in the States to get married.

Ezra has a queer flat, like a couple of parallel corridors cut into sections. Unfinished wall decorations. Drawings by Lewis, sculptures by Brzeska, etc.[171] His wife's excellent watercolours everywhere. View of the whole gulf. You go up to tea and talk, very fragmentary, ("politics of literature" J. J. Adams says), but good things in it. He is very quick, I'm slow as the deuce. Small magazines lying about. Not very many books. There is no alternative to the homemade chairs. The ungenteel, lively side of Bloomsbury Bohemia (whatever he says about Bloomsbury), nothing particularly American except his bodily restlessness and sometimes his accent. Alcoholics rare and almost solely for visitors. He bursts with American energy, part of it, I think, truly American, that is, almost objectless; but usually useful and pointed.

His wife is English, mine American, so we balance. And in view of the ultimate AngloAmerican war we have signed a separate peace.

Ezra gives more advice per minute than any other ten men. Most of it is good advice. Some of it is attempts to get things done for which the recipient of the advice is not particularly suited.

I live up the hill, in a peasant's cottage, and see him I suppose about twice a week. There are a few other permanent english speaking residents, an old Indian general, a retired banker, Max Beerbohm. For a while there was Yeats. Ezra knows everybody. I can't be bothered. I liked Yeats very much, but I hate conversation for its own sake. There are also a few intelligent Wops.

[170] Pound's first opera, *Le Testament de Villon* (which has obvious affinities with BB's slightly later poem 'Villon') was first performed in Paris in 1924.

[171] Henri Gaudier Brzeska (1891–1915), French Vorticist painter and sculptor much admired by Pound.

The country is steep and rugged mountains, though not very high on the coast (two thousand to three thousand feet) all terraced as high as things will grow, thick forest of olives and fruit trees. Even just under the summit of a mountain with no path at all and the devil to climb I found a small potato patch someone was cultivating. I sail a small fishing boat in the summer. Ezra plays tennis.

I think that's about all the information. A noise like the statues on the pass to Erewhon is Ezra composing. I work in silence punctuated by curses. The Wops caricature us and Ezra is the pride of the town.

Redimiculum Matellarum isn't obtainable. The hundred copies were sold out long ago. If you know anyone who wants to reprint it without subsequent works (there is now enough for a volume of a hundred pages or so) I'd be pleased to hear of it. I have no special lust for publicity but think I might stand a better chance of getting a decent proportion of my living out of writing if my workses were neatly printed and bound and available.

In fact I hate personal publicity, and if your, I suppose inevitable in U.S., notes on contributors says more than "Basil Bunting is the author of Redimiculum Matellarum" I shall not be pleased.

This is too long, but you brought it on yourself.

Yrs

B

POSTSCRIPT

Hound and Horn has recently published Y Winters disgusting review of Zuks Objectivist anthology. Please read it. If it wont injure yr magazines prospects please spit as publicly and vehemently as possible on Winters. In any case, please run a fair review of that anthology as soon as you can, since that is ultimately the best answer to such patently disappointed spite. I have sent a letter to H & H which if it doesn't get printed will at least make them sit up. You might perhaps also let them know what you think about it. These people are easily intimidated by public opinion and it is therefore up to public opinion to make itself heard.

The following letter amounts to a reader report on the draft of Pound's *ABC of Economics* (the 'pamphlet' Bunting mentions), a somewhat chaotic treatise which would appear the following year. Readers and scholars interested in Pound's book and in the development of both writers' political thinking in this period will doubtless find much that is intriguing in Bunting's detailed report, which if nothing else underlines the growing importance of economic subjects to the Pound–Bunting relationship. It is probably fair to say that Bunting was one of very few people in this period to take Pound's economic views seriously and comment on their particulars (remember that Bunting had studied economics at LSE), a fact which gives them great value. However, the more specific references here will make little sense without some cross-referencing with *ABC of Economics*. Rather than introduce a lengthy 'third text' of byzantine annotations to map Bunting's allusions, I have assumed for the sake of readability that those who wish to explore their deeper implications will do so in consultation with Pound's original text (see *ABC of Economics (London: Faber & Faber, 1933)*).

## To Ezra Pound

TS Yale

[Late 1932] [Rapallo]

Dear E.P.

I like the latter end of yr pamphlet better than the beginning. The whole thing seems to be very uneven, that is, things that you have really got perfectly clear, whether for yourself or others, are jumbled with things that dont seem to be so clear. The clear bits are so good and contain so much that is, if not utterly new, at any rate new in being clear for the first time, that they carry one (me) over the other bits with minimum irritation. I dont think the irritation is due to lack of thinking about it enough while reading. But I don't think anybody is in a position to clear up the whole subject without devoting twenty years to the job, and wouldn't like to encourage you to put yr time to such a use, since I prefer Cantos.

B

Minor points: (forgive repeats. Also things that may seem irrelevant; they dont seem altogether irrelevant to me)

Page 3, first paragraph.

The distinction of property and capital is clear enough as a general proposition, but when you propose a practical distinction, i.e., for purpose of lawmaking or taxing, the line is almost impossible to draw and must be arbitrary and a source of bureaucratic petty tyranny. Compare the history of the attempt to define Income, since it was first taxed.

Page 5 #9

I doubt whether specifically economic thought since 1800 much exceeds that of any previous century. There is a new name for it, a university course and consequently a flood of textbooks: but you cant maintain that say Mill contributed anything, and the contributions of Senior were all merely showing up the fallacies of fools like Malthus.[172] Ricardo[173] and Marx made additions. But there was plenty of economic thought, not segregated as such, in most centuries. The great change is the shift of the centre of contention from usury to wages, that is from an economy of stable prices to one of rising prices. That change followed the discovery of America and was complete by 1640. An exactly similar change followed the Crusades and the Black Death, but was smaller and the stable prices were more rapidly restored. But the statutes and works like Pierce Plowman show that the thought underwent the same change for about a century.

Your main thesis can be reinforced from this: since it is clear that in a time of stable prices, jobs are fairly permanent, there is no great worry and people remain content with their gains or wages, though small. In time of rising prices (rapidly rising, as in the last three centuries) unevenness of distribution are constantly emphasised, and the boom-and-crash rhythm gets everybody worried with consequent encouragement of grab.

Page 5 #10

If you underline "emergency" I think you will forestall many possible objections.

Page 9 last paragraph but one.

"Some fool or skunk plays mean out of stupidity…fear…malice." Usually, surely, out of plain avarice. I think it is as simple, or as complicated if you like, as that. The traditional list of the seven deadly sins is extraordinary able, and avarice comes, I think, second after Pride.

Page 11, price of bar chocolate during and after the war.

They took it out in wrappings. So with cigarettes and other goods sold in enormous quantities in very small parcels, here wrapping is a serious percentage of cost. You got the same chocolate, but less silver paper: it wouldnt keep fresh so long.

Page 16 second paragraph.

Reference to laws of value. This irritates me extremely, since I dont believe there are any such laws, value being a metaphysical nonesuch whose tail nobody ever has salted and about which no two writers have any agreement whatever. There is more unanimity about predestination and freewill!

Page 18. Dumping.

[172] Nassau William Senior (1790–1864): British lawyer and economist. His *Two Lectures on Population* (1829) mounted a critique of Thomas Malthus's (1766–1834) influential theories on population growth.

[173] David Ricardo (1772–1823): influential British liberal economist in the tradition of Mill and Malthus.

I cannot see that dumping does any harm in the end. A few are temporarily deprived of profits, but the public at large gets the goods it presumably wants very cheap. Dumping is of course a symptom of bad organization.

Page 26 last paragraph.

"possible to leave the nominal pay where it is". An administrative detail. What about the real pay, measured in goods? That's where one doesnt see clearly. You would have to have enormous "overproduction" first to insure no decrease in real pay, surely.

Page 27, accelerated movement of money.

The paragraph seems to me very well put. But it is worth noting that it is not only the accumulating of money in richmen's banking accounts that holds things up, there's the stocking-hoard, common in France before the war. The problem is as you observe elsewhere lack of anxiety: on that condition a man will spend what he earns. English judges are said to get rid of their 5000 a year all right. A cross reference to yr remarks on sheep? A distinction between saving, useful objects, and hoarding, mere money?

Same page.

"Prices adjust themselves to the spending power of the general public"... No, but to that of the whole public much poorer. Verbal correction.

Page 29 Chapter 4

Why call it Malthus? He was a stupid old fool who thought what we would eat up all supplies in a few generations, i.e. that we were subject to perpetual inescapable underproduction eternally. There is hardly a word of sense in his two volumes. Call it Colonel Condom, which is nearer your meaning.

Page 36. Government by privilege.

Privilege (as distinguished from its ghost) does seem to breed a sense of responsibility. What it fails to breed is brains enough to make it function. The obvious jealousies of encroachments by men from other classes become obstructions to the use of brains in government. Aristocracies are usually stupid; only rarely, when they lose power and responsibility but retain the more useless privileges, frivolous.

There remain two more important matters, and also this piece of useless but interesting information:

Keynes. He is not a saphead but a crook.[174] He became wealthy by speculation. He then greatly increased the endowments of his Cambridge college by the same

[174] This long passage about the financial dealings of John Maynard Keynes and Geoffrey Pyke (1893–1948) in the interwar years is a mixture of truth, half-truth, and conjecture. Perhaps the best way to read these comments is in light of BB's enduring dislike of the Bloomsbury Group, of which Keynes was a notable member.

means on condition that the funds remained in his hands without enquiries for I forget how long. During the same period he augmented his private fortune considerably. Finally, he was an associate of Geoffrey Pike (another "Cambridge economist") in a company called by a long name which I forget, which turned out to be Bouffon-ic Greek for a kind of Investment Trust. It was going to do Safe Speculation. It underpaid a large staff to collect and collate Stock Exchange hour-to-hour movements for some months, and to get from the British Museum day to day movements over a number of years. All these were charted out very expensively. When it had spent all the subscribers" money the company went bankrupt, the information collected came into the hands of Keynes and Pike (Pike managing director, Keynes "adviser") The company had done nothing else but collect this information. Its only speculation had been a few small dealings in mines (on which it lost) which served as an excuse for keeping the telephone to the Stock Exchange working to get the hour by hour movements.

I am glad to say I never heard of Keynes or Pike getting any special advantage out of the information come by, but they had made the shareholders pay for their little experiment, their data on the technique of speculation. They did not publish these data, it was not scientific curiosity that moved them.

I knew four of the clerks, including one who managed a whole section under Pike, and am pretty certain of the facts. I am not sure whether Pike and Keynes bought the statistics for a few shillings as waste paper or merely walked off with them. I dont think Pike had more than his qualifying shares as a director. I am pretty sure Keynes took up no shares at all. He was the magnanimous famous economist condescending to advise the company for a small honorarium. The investors, of course, were fools attracted by the bait of Safe Speculation.

Stock Exchanges.

I cant see any harm in them. Especially I cant share the popular prejudice against bears. How is a man who sells what he hasn't got, intending to buy it later, worse than one who buys what he cant pay for, intending to sell it later?

But in any case I believe the bulk of Stock exchange business in normal times is exactly what it purports to be, buying and selling securities to keep them. The number of brokers is strictly limited, so that a man can get rich perfectly legitimately on the 1/2% commission, the volume of business being great. He also of course has an intimate knowledge of the market by which to manage his own investments. As to speculation in stocks, I cant see how it hurts anybody but the speculator or the fool who lends him money. He doesnt speculate in gilt-edged or in stolidly dividend paying industrials, which are the chief field for genuine investors, but in companies that havent got round to paying a dividend yet, or those that run a notoriously chancy business like tin mining. But even when he speculates in stocks that are also used to "safe" investment, he doesnt hurt the man who is holding the stuff for an income unless he gets the wind up and sells at the wrong time (which means, unless he ceases to be an investor and becomes a speculator for the nonce).

The fall in prices on the N.Y. exchange in the last panic enriched Rockefeller and associates at the expense of the speculator, at the expense, I mean, of the imbeciles who had been buying on margin for a rise in an obviously inflated market. He didnt get rich on the spoils of genuine investors, at that time. The companies that suffered most were not those paying regular dividends. The investor was it later, but the industrial breakdown – the failure of consumption if you like – that took away both his job and his dividends and finally forced him to sell his investments. That was the further, much slower fall in stockprices which began some months later and still continues and affects serious established concerns more than "recent promotions". None of the responsibility for that can be put on the speculator, bull or bear or stag.

On produce exchanges speculation has a definite insurance-cum-pricesteadying function, though open, in rare instances, to abuses, principally by means of false information. In major products a corner is almost impossible and scarcely ever attempted. The public suffers by large fluctuations in produce prices, which upset the plans of manufacturers; but in everycase the speculator serves as a buffer and takes the worst of the knock. If a few of these knocks are engineered, the commonest and biggest ones are the work of Nature, who spoils a crop or produces an extra huge one.

Overproduction

I am unconvinced. I agree that production is not an urgent problem, because the methods by which most problems of production can be solved are known, but I will not agree that these problems actually are solved in most instances. Consequently I think that the reduction of the workingday, desirable for other reasons besides the distribution of work, ought to go hand in hand with the undertaking of vast improvements planned on a worldwide scale. What Musso is doing here, the Dutch in the Zuydersee, Lord Lloyd in Sind, ought to be done in Australia, China everywhere.[175] Without it you'd get a situation where the present

[175] BB alludes to major irrigation projects of the interwar years: the Zuiderzee Works in the Netherlands, the Sukkur Barrage in the Sindh province of Pakistan, and Italian schemes such as Mussolini's draining of the Pontine Marshes near Rome.

class divisions within nations would become class divisions between nations, far more dangerous to civilization than any number of revolutions.

The test of overproduction in a sane economics is surely not that the product cant be sold for the price the grower or manufacturer wants for it, but that nobody wants it at any price, not even gratis. That is, I believe, the case with coffee, where even the abolition of import duties could not increase the consumption enough to keep Brazil and East Africa prosperous on coffegrowing alone. It has long been the case with opium. But you can only list a few dozen such instances, all in minor products.

Overproduction is common locally, and temporarily, but it is necessary to look at the world as a whole over a period of years. Even the water overabundant in Scotland could be profitably sued if somebody would undertake the not impossible but not within a century remunerative business of building an aqueduct long enough to move it to the Sahara... or even to Spain. I am not suggesting that anything of the sort is in any way urgent, obviously not. But water is not overproduced in Timbuctoo, it has a price, even.

Consequently accuracy of expression requires that you say not that production is a solved problem, but that the methods by which some problems of production have been solved seem likely to solve most of them in time.

Further suggestion: Havent the Insurance Companies been rather lost sight of? Their power is similar to that of the banks, in the field of less "liquid" investments. The power of the Prudential is incalculable. If these companies do not take up a new issue, there is little hope of the "public" absorbing it, to this way they control some branches of production more directly & more absolutely than the banks.

Apparently in search of cheaper living costs, the Buntings relocated to the Canary Islands in the autumn of 1933, where they would remain for the next three years. This was a rather unhappy time for Bunting both personally and creatively. His marriage was beginning to unravel, and his publication prospects were rapidly diminishing. However, perhaps partly because of the troubled backdrop, it was one of his most intense periods of letter writing.

In terms of poetry, Bunting's life in the Canaries was dominated by his deepening obsession with Persian writers, especially **Ferdowsi** (c.940–1020) and **Sadi** (1210–1292). His (ultimately abandoned) translation of Ferdowsi's great epic *Shahnameh*, first conceived in Rapallo, would become his major creative project of the mid 1930s.

## To Ezra Pound

TS Yale

18 November 1933 c/o British Consulate, Santa Cruz de Tenerife, Canary Islands, Spain

Dear EP,

Three weeks on island and still havent been able to get out of this here furnished pair of rooms in the noisiest street I ever inhabited. Ads in the paper are useless – I saw the bus driver taking all the papers for the seventy thousand people on the south of the island – two copies of the Prensa, one of Hoy and one of the Gaceta. Also travelled with a courier, postal, on a camion[176] in the south east corner. At one village he took on a duly locked and sealed empty leather bag. I said: Poco Correos aqui.[177] He said: I have to take this bag backwards and forwards every day for forms sake, but there has never been a letter in the seven years I've been on the job. Nobody in that village can read or write, not even the postmistress.

Therefore I have been going into the villages to try and find a house by word of mouth, very difficult, a thick dialect, and I dont understand even proper Spanish. It seems houses are cheap enough – if you can get one. But practically nobody lets them.

Just got back from a visit to the local Sahara. Seven or eight miles wide and ever so many long, sand covered with loose species of pumice about as big as a man's head. A sort of pale grey thorn scrub, and a few camels eating it. A sort of green shrub is much rarer, and a goat or two eating that. Not even prickly pears, too dry and hot. No communications, except the casual camions that cross it carrying tomatoes to a little port, or a camel not trained to carry human beings but only sacks of potatoes. The camions radiators soon boil, even on the level bits, it is so fiery hot. The port, however, has cool breezes and a fine sand beach, and we may possibly settle there, in spite of remoteness, if we can get a decent house. One well serves the whole village. Fauna, goats, camels, no asses, six dogs, scorpions, spiders. Flora, as described, plus some prickly pear and euphorbia. Five small volcanoes, all perfect cones with craters, surround the village, about a mile way. The courier travels by camion when there is one, and camel when there isnt. Just on the mountainward side of the desert is a very pretty fertile little town, but the difficulty of getting to the sea rather counts against living there.

[176] *Camion*: truck (Sp.).

[177] *Poco Correos aqui*: not much mail here (Sp.).

The evening occupation in all that part of the island is picking the lice out of each others hair. The children go naked.

The north side of the island as far as I have yet seen it is mostly banana plantations, the bananas growing upside down. A fine rich green, a bit too lush. An aroma of tourist about the towns, not much to my liking – too strongly flavoured with German. Mountains huge and very jagged. The very bare ones in the north east are spotty to look at, being dotted with a gigantic euphorbia, very fine and architectural seen close too (it grows about nine feet high, in great clumps).

Alarming busride with a driver just lively drunk, most dangerous road I ever travelled, hairpin bends with precipices beneath every ten or fifteen metres. Took it at thirtyfive miles an hour. Shot the conductor clean out of the bus at one corner, but he wasnt killed. Missed a child by about one inch, and nearly got busted by the only railway engine on the island. Total casualties (twentyminutes ride), one billy-goat, fairly and squarely squashed according to all the rules of the game, after a chase of about fifty metres.

We had a twentyfour hours general strike, owing to four of the policemen supplementing their pay by highway robbery, in the course of which they shot dead the champion wrestler of the island. The governor then suspended them from duty, together with the chief of police and all his deputies. Casualties of the general strike, one chauffeur. Consequently an extra strike of two hours of all chauffeurs the next day, to attend his funeral. Elections tomorrow, the undertakers are working overtime getting the coffins ready.

Harriet writes that I have an Honorable Mention for Chomei. No specie attached. Tennessee Observer publishing the rest of that poem, also Attis, also other things that have been printed elsewhere. The long man from Harvard wrote me, mentioning a lady who wants fifty line poems for a private press. I dont know whether to bite or not. Oglethorpe University wants a harticle on Hobjectivists not by Zuk.[178] I may send them something when I get somewhere where I can write, but probably not. I dont know at all clearly what Zuk means by Objectivists and am not likely to do any good by shoving my oar in. Observer shall be offered your appunti,[179] being the most appreciative as far as I can see.

No Anthology yet arrived here. (The posts seem rather irregular).

[178] BB's review article, 'Carlos Williams's Recent Poetry', appeared in the summer 1934 issue of *Westminster Magazine*. The journal was based at Oglethorpe University, Atlanta, GA, and edited by Robert England.

[179] Pound's 'Appunti': article series for *Il Mare* consisting of 'notes' on a range of political and aesthetic subjects.

Girls in Santa Cruz very pretty, less so in the North. Blondes unexpectedly common.

Wife and child well but worried (owing to unexpected difficulty in finding a house).

I sent the bulk of what we owe Dorothy by International Postal Order, balance to follow when we know how much it is. About a week ago.

Papers have no news in them, except who has married who and who died of what. There aint a bookshop fit to look at on the island.

Live and flourish!

B

## To Ezra Pound

TS Yale

Twentiumpth Jan 34

c/o T.M. Reid, Bankers, Puerto de la Cruz,
Tenerife, Canarias, Spain

Dear Ezra,

Thanks for cuttings. Daily Mirror, as you say, evidence. Zuk informed me of fierce attack by certain J.L.Beevers,[180] which I think should be regarded as first step towards ultimate inevitable canonization of E.P., Mr Beevers being evidently out to become the Sunday Express Douglas of the FUTewer.

Since getting where I can spread out Persian dictionary and Firdusi, havent looked at anything else – damn near forgot there was an Active Anthology. Firdusi is bloody good. Now I can move at a perceptible if insufficient speed expect in two more months to read him without dictionary. Sadi provides:

> Powder and lipstick and lace on their drawers
> Are all very well for young women and whores,
> They look a bit more human in that sort of stuff;
> But for a man, cock and balls are enough.[181]

Which doesnt seem likely to get a place in my collected works but is worth at any rate oral preservation. Literal, nearly: last line word for word.

What textbook? – Have I missed a letter? The post here is instructed, I imagine, to keep all unregistered letters for the archives. Any way, we see very few.

[180] John Beevers (1911–1975) wrote a (mostly disparaging) review of the *Active Anthology* for *New English Weekly* 4.9 (1933).

[181] This letter is the only extant source for this translated fragment from Sadi, which did not appear in editions of BB's poetry prior to Share.

Havent translated any (Firdusi) except a passage of somewhat overlofty eloquence, speech of a prehistoric conscientious objector name of Eeraj. Together with his pore old pa's comments in lower strain. Have got as far as the beginning of the true epic – past the voluminous preliminaries, sort of poetic preface, and the legendary introduction, which contains one really fascinating story, one amusing fairy tale and one circumstantial history of a campaign. Next week, I'll read the Persian of the chap the bird brought up, who was Rustam's father, and be really started.

WM Young unknown to me.[182] Whittaker I think a good man, probably told you so. He's a prof at Glasgow, but none the worse for that, eccentric cove, good conductor, knows almost all Bach by heart, have heard him conduct, at one time or another, over a hundred of the cantatas without the book. Dont know how he would go with a big orchestra, but knows about as much as anyone about choirs and chamber orchestras. His own music extremely lean and learned, but at least some of it satisfactory. I remember a hymn to the virgin for female voices unaccompanied.

The people of this island so unspeakable, and the food so uneatable, they make prolonged residence impossible, in spite of great cash saving – we are spending about ½ what we spent in Rapallo. Marian's people a little better about cash lately, no arrangement, but fifty dollars coming reasonably regularly month by month, which is over two thirds of what we spend here. Also they are paying for the confinement. Unfortunately they are so dumb it never gets here till godknowswhen. However, cant demand everything. But if we have to move we'll be in as deep water again later on. The climate's alright, sky often overcast on this side of the island, but temperature never yet below 20 centigrade except during night: the other side it never rains, no clouds near the sea, positively hot: but there's no accommodation, no houses to rent, futile regulations that in practice prevent a foreigner from renting them if he does find one. The people are also less abominable on the south side. The peak a fine sight, 12 thousand and old feet of it, straight up from the sea, nothing like it as far as I know in the Alps. Everything volcanic. We have three small craters within two miles of us, and there must be several hundred on the island, apart form the upper parts of the peak and its surroundings. Eruptions much more frequent than the guidebook lets on, also floods of

182 William Young (d. 1662): English baroque composer and violist. His collection of sonatas (the first English works to be described as such) were rediscovered and published in 1930 by Newcastle-born composer William G. Whittaker (1876–1944). BB attended rehearsals for the performance of William Byrd's *Great Service* conducted by Whittaker's Newcastle Bach Choir at Newcastle Cathedral in 1924.

boiling water, one of which boiled most of the inhabitants of this valley sometime last century. English and Italian doganas have ruined the banana trade, and since they've given up every inch of fertile soil to bananas, they are all in the soup. Their former gains are still in hand, but wont be for very much longer. They have dug the whole island full of holes and galleries looking for water, to irrigate more bananas. One village on the south hasnt had a drop of rain for over five years now. A lot of the people live in caves, murder each other constantly. Rio de Oro savages peddling sewingcotton and needles also murder solitary walkers.[183] I gather there's a lot more Guanche about the people than is usually supposed,[184] they took Spanish names when they were baptised, but kept quite a lot of stone-age manners. The more Guanche blood the taller and blonder they are. In the mountains east of Santa Cruz they are all tall blonds, and I'm told the same is true on the southwest side. They eat semi-ground wheat dampened with a little water or spittle: and couple of handfuls does them.

Here they don't have the whistling language to any extent, but am assured that on Hierro[185] they can converse quite complicated conversation at four miles and even more distance, whistling. I would like to find out about that. Wonder whether it's a tune, or dots and dashes, so to speak. Guide book says some of the people there hardly use their tongues at all, whistle everything.

Yass, you got patience. Wont try it further now.

Salaam alaik'. And rahmatu'llah etc.[186] Idem Dorothy.

B

## To Ezra Pound

TS Yale

21 March 1934

c/o T.M. Reid, Bankers, Puerto de la Cruz,
Tenerife, Canarias, Spain

Dear E.P.,

Hope I shant be too disconnected: detecting and getting rid of a dipsomaniac servant during last twentyfour hours has left me a bit bewildered. She got dangerous in the end, otherwise I daresay she would have gone on puzzling us some while longer. Its incredible the cunning of that gentry. She took Bourtai out for a

[183] Río de Oro: Spanish territory close to the Canary Islands on the African mainland.
[184] Guanche: the aboriginal culture of the Canary Islands.
[185] El Hierro: a small Canary Island in the far south-west of the archipelago.
[186] *Salaam alaik', rahmatu'llah*: 'Peace be upon you', 'mercy of God' (Ar.).

walk! To the lowest ginshop in the neighborhood, kept her there three and a half hours and finally fell down on the highroad, leaving the kid in the middle of heavy motor traffic all alone. Afterwards she set about making all the trouble she could, the business being beyond further disguise. She's still prowling around us. She was extraordinarily fertile in excuses for being absent, and we knew there was something wrong and had already given her notice to quit because she never got any work done. From what Marian says I think I would have seen what was coming a little earlier in the same day if I hadnt happened to be out. However, not great harm seems to have been done and once she gets back to the other side of the island where she lives we'll sleep in peace again.

(That's not an exaggeration. The actions of people on this island are quite considerably influenced by the fear of being murdered. According to the local paper the epidemic of murder isnt more than a year or two old, but since the juries began to acquit automatically in every case of murder, even, as in one case last week, after the criminals public and detailed confession to a particularly horrific murder and mutilation, anybody who fancies they have a grievance just naturally murders: and since there is practically no way of locking up one's house here, it leaves one a bit uncomfortable after any differences of opinion.)

Yr reproaches on subject of gents, revolutions and prose earnings, dont, on three-days off and on-consideration, seem to me to be justified. I dont know who you think is going to pay me for prose. I have just written a (bad, I fear) review of W.C.W. for England of Georgia, but they wont pay for that two days work.[187] Orage refrained from putting it clearly, but his hold-up of what I did write for an indefinite period and his unencouraging reply to my enquiry about anything more made it pretty clear all the same. As to Eliot, if I had the British Museum round the corner it is just barely possible I might be able to fix up something he would take, but I doubt it. Harriet would probably accept reviews of English poetry, but I havent seen any English poetry for about two years, and dont expect to. Do you think I ought to be one of the honoured contributors to the New Statesman or Time and Tide?[188] I've tried Time and Tide within the last nine months and got a printed rejection slip out of them. I have no doubt it I went to London and hung about a good deal in Fleet Street pubs I'd pick up a little, maybe a pound a week. But it would cost me seven times that to keep my family in

[187] See 18/11/33 and note.

[188] *Time and Tide*: British socialist feminist magazine founded in 1920 by Welsh suffragette Lady Margaret Rhondda (1883–1958).

London, and anyway I dont want to give up my whole time to article-hunting, which is what London journalism as I formerly experienced it means.

As to revolution as you understand it, you know I have no enthusiasm for it. I am not convinced the argument is sound, Douglas's secretary dodged my crucial question:[189] and if it were perfectly proved, I still dont see it as a cure-all but only as one step of a good many necessary, some of them much simpler to carry out and therefore, in my opinion, prior. If I had access to the figures I would write about the land business, and also about the bottling of emigration. But I have not such access, I dont think the chance of publication big enough to warrant me in going to London to dig in files, and the only possible ally is Lloyd George, who is old, unapproachable and discredited.

Or if you are thinking of Fascism, I believe in the personal genius of a chap like Muss. Much as I do in the personal genius of Mr Bonaparte or O. Cromwell Esq. That is, I want it used, but I want an effective check on it, I want to be able to get rid of the great man when the time comes. In the present case I think the time came at the Decennial,[190] what has been done since, other than picking up loose ends that a much smaller man could have picked up just as well, doesnt seem to me to have any relation to the good of either Italy or Europe. The deliberate throwback of diplomatic method to the pre-war style seems to me about as monstrous a thing as has been done since 1914. If the war I still expect actually comes, I shant put the blame on Hitler, nor on the Comite des Forges,[191] for they might both have been kept well in hand, I believe, without Italy's policy of shoving sticks in the spokes. I also suppose that since Balbo was sent to Africa,[192] the last of his original companions is removed and there is no one left in his entourage who can speak to him on even terms. I can see there might be advantages in that, but I think the dangers are much greater. Anyway, the part of Machiavelli he got it from isnt the part that treats of the <u>public</u> good.

[189] The 'crucial question' posed by BB is also mentioned in **Last of 1935**. Though it is not specified, we can infer the gist from BB's various comments about land reform and emigration in the ensuing exchanges with Pound.

[190] In 1926 Mussolini introduced the Era Fascista, an alternative calendar beginning with his accession to power on 29 October 1922. The 'Decennale' or Decennial in October 1932 was a much vaunted tenth anniversary event for the Fascist takeover.

[191] Comité des Forges: organization of French iron and steel industrialists active between 1846 and 1940. During World War I it promoted the commercial interests of the French armaments industry, for which it was heavily criticized in the ensuing peace. Pound's Canto 38, written in 1933, alludes disparagingly to the Comité and its president François de Wendel (1874–1949).

[192] Italo Balbo (1896–1940), Italian Fascist and lieutenant of Mussolini. On 7 November 1933 Mussolini made him Governor-General of Libya, an Italian colony.

And as for gents, it isn't their doing nothing I object to, nor getting a living at the public expense. It's a matter of education and seems to me to be, more than any other single thing, the seeds of destruction for the empire. Its something similar that prevents the people who have to live in Tyne Dock[193] and similar places from shooting a few policemen now and then, which would do more than anything to get their plight remedied. They have all cut off their own bollocks.

Alright. Done now.

If the British Cawnsoivtifs are taking up Douglas you can be pretty sure they intend merely to palm off something near enough to pass for an imitation of it, in order to dish the other parties. Not that the other parties are much better. But generally speaking in England much better not be taken up at all than taken up by the Conservatives. They have sometimes had a few men who meant well, but they were always overwhelmed by the mass that meant nothing but mischief. From Pitt's time on.[194]

The strongest and most sensible, if somewhat clumsy, organisation in England, the Miners Federation of G.B. was busted in 1926.[195] It was a very slow machine, but always open to conviction and very circumspect and levelheaded. If the other big unions had been as slow to make up their minds and as solid in sticking to them, the general strike would have been a revolution. I dont know what may have happened lately, but when I left England, the only sign of life was the Glasgow "Forward", editor Tom Johnson, and it was sucking its life from Russia instead of from the Clyde and Tyne.[196] I expect its either dead or fossilized by now.

I'm not talking through my hat. I knew several miner's leaders at one time and another, from checkweighmen to old William Straker (the chap who had found out in the course of fifty years or so of mining politics that billiards was worse

[193] Tyne Dock: area in the Tyneside conurbation, and a major centre for the export of coal between the late-nineteenth and late-twentieth centuries. In the mid 1930s it suffered badly from the effects of the Depression.

[194] William Pitt the Younger (1759–1806), British Tory statesman and prime minister 1783–1801 and 1804–1806.

[195] The Miners' Federation of Great Britain (MFGB) was formed in Newport, Wales, in 1888 as an umbrella organization for the various regional mining unions. After the 1926 General Strike its membership declined and in 1945 it was reorganized into the National Union of Mineworkers (NUM).

[196] Tom Johnston (1881–1965), Scottish socialist journalist and Labour MP, who founded the journal *Forward* in Glasgow in 1906. Johnston and *Forward* were at the centre of 'Red Clydeside', a period of a radical socialist activity in Glasgow between the 1910s and 1930s (the River Clyde in Glasgow was a shipbuilding and export hub similar to the Tyne in Newcastle). *Forward* was in fact edited from 1924 by Emrys Hughes (1894–1969), the Welsh-born MP for South Ayrshire, who maintained a sporadic dialogue with Russian revolutionary Leon Trotsky (1879–1940).

than booze.)[197] I even talked once or twice to old Charley Fenwick, before he died, a man who had been a Northumberland miners official since the middle of last century and went down the pit to work at the age of nine.[198] Damn it, I was brought up in all that, Joseph Skipsey is said to have dandled me when I was a baby,[199] and he'd been down the pit before the first factory acts touched them. I was on the spot when the View Pit was flooded and forty-five men drowned,[200] I heard what the men had to say about it and whole cursed system when there wasnt any question of politics, mining or otherwise, but just sheer human commonsense. My grandfather, whom I knew pretty well when I was a kid, was a miner, son of a miner. I know the solidity of those people, and I watched it break up in 26, when I was all the time in a miningvillage, took the chair at one of Cook's meetings,[201] stuck a knife in the tyres of a government strikebreaking lorry and tried unsuccessfully nearly every paper in the country to get the scandalous faked benches of magistrates who condemned the strikers to long terms of hard labour shown up. Not even the independent labour party's rag[202] would publish the facts. Jix did that job.[203] He was a perfectly efficient administrator, but you know the quality of his mind. That's what the Tories throw up when they're fairly fortunate.

They live by the votes of the dregs of the country, always have done. Plus of course what they get from the bloody middle-clarses with the gent education and what they can scare with newspaper forgeries. There's been no appreciable change since Castlereagh, except that they dont have the grace to cut their throats

[197] William Straker (1855–1941), British trade unionist and key figure in the Northumberland Miners' Association, BB's local miners' union.

[198] Charles Fenwick (1850–1918), British trade unionist also involved in the NMA. Fenwick was also General Secretary of the TUC (see **Summer 1931** and note) 1890–1894 and Liberal MP for Wansbeck in Northumberland 1885–1918.

[199] **Joseph Skipsey**: nineteenth-century 'pitman poet' from Tyneside.

[200] On 30 March 1925, thirty-eight miners (including many children) were killed when the View Pit at Montagu Colliery in Scotswood flooded due to a burst water seam. Although BB was probably not living in Throckley at this time, he may well have witnessed the fallout from the Montagu tragedy at first-hand (his father had been the colliery doctor, and his uncle Matt worked there). It certainly provided inspiration for a key passage in 'They Say Etna' (39–61), his political poem of 1932–1933.

[201] Arthur James Cook (1883–1931), British trade unionist and secretary of the MFGB.

[202] The Independent Labour Party (ILP): political party separate from, but often integrated with, the mainstream Labour Party. Its history was one of grassroots radicalism in contrast to the more compromised social democracy of the Labour Party proper. *New Leader*: the ILP magazine.

[203] William 'Jix' Joynson-Hicks (1865–1932), British Tory politican who played a central role in the General Strike as a hardline anti-union member of the government.

in the end any longer.[204] You saw England largely from the vantage ground of the nobs who run the show, if you'd seen it from prisons and mining villages, you'd have a pretty good idea that whatever the Tories touch is damned, they spread their dirt over it. The other parties are dumb and corrupt and all that, but they havent that record. Some of them sometimes have done something good.

However – it was always evident, even before Douglas, that Orage wasnt going to see any good in anything other than his scheme of the moment, whole and unimproved. That makes him a good propagandist, but also a damn good ally for anyone who wants to dish the others, intending to drop, dish or ditch Orage too afterwards. He ought to know better, and I shant respect his intellex much if he accepts an alliance with the Conservatives.

Sorry, I dont know what the Musical Times did after sending me the proofs.[205] I havent had any copy of it.

I imagine Whittaker must be over sixty by now, but how much over I cant say.

Haas[206] – No, I'm sick of all the bloody Huns, all alike. Here they all talk Hitler, except the tailor who told me some specific instances of people who had NOT talked Hitler, had gone back to Germany and been instantly sent from the port to the Conzentrazionslager. They all evidently think all the other Germans and an appreciable number of Spaniards and English must be Hitler spies, which makes them extremely enthusiastic Nazis. Some of them probably are genuinely enthusiastic. They are a fairly unpleasant lot. Even Gulde, the painter,[207] when I asked him what he thought about the revolution, gave me a scared look and then uttered a number of noncommittal approbations. Our German landlady tries with clockwork regularly every month to cheat up over the rent and water bill. Her efforts are pitiably inefficient, but thoroughly annoying.

I dont know whether Hitler is any good or not, but its clearly no use asking Germans. I heard one of his speeches over the radio, but only understood a little of it and remained unimpressed. He was evidently shouting very hard, which didnt improve the difficult reception.

204 Robert Stewart, Viscount Castlereagh (1769–1822), leading Tory politician from roughly the same era as Pitt (see above). As Foreign Secretary 1812–1822 he was a hugely unpopular figure partly blamed for the reactionary mood which followed the final defeat of Napoleon in 1815. He committed suicide by cutting his throat in 1822.

205 BB's article 'Musical Notes from Abroad: The Rapallo Manuscripts', a summary of the Rapallo music scene, appeared in British scholarly journal the *Musical Times* in August 1934.

206 Eugen Haas (1891–1968), German artist and member of the Rapallo circle.

207 Gustav Gulde (1906–1953), German expressionist painter who moved to the Canaries in 1932.

I read a book of Frobenius's in English trans.[208] I'll refrain from discussing it here because I think I've differed from you enough for one letter. I suppose it was an early work and the later ones may be infinitely better. They would have to be, to account for you're being impressed, because I dont think you'd be taken in in a matter of that sort, whereas this was – Oh Hell!

Dear EP, I didnt intend to be as grumpy as this letter probably sounds, but I havent the energy today to rewrite it. I may have to begin explaining our dipsomaniac to the police in a language I only know three words of, at any minute; and it worries me. (I loathe the inhabitants of this island so much that I've taken a disgust to the Spanish tongue and succeeded in forgetting the bit I learned in the first few weeks). It's a good island and would be both beautiful and incomparably comfortable in the hands of almost any other people. As it is, its impossible, and we are discussing the means of getting out of it. The neighboring islands are much worse. Gulde spent a week on Lanzarote. The best hotel there furnished him with eggs, cheese, wine and bread. The other hotel gave him a heap of straw, not a bed, and nothing at all to eat. They dont even trouble to import bananas from their more fertile neighbours.

The temporary suspension of work owing to addition to the family is over, but there are arrears to make up. Grrr.

Best to Dorothy.

B

P.S. What do you propose to substitute for fathers in law and similar institutions as a means of subsistence for poets? I never heard of an English poet who didnt have an independent income, or starve, or sponge. I dont know anything about your affairs, but dont believe you get paid enough to keep your family going. My receipts have declined steadily from little to less and now practically to zero since I got sick of lying for a living in Fleet street. Bernard Shaw would say that was a clear indication that poetry is entirely useless since it commands no price. I dont think you take any such view. If my father in law has more money than he needs and does nothing for it but bleed the pore buggers who want offices and houses in a country town in Wisconsin, I dont see why I, who do something I conceive to have a certain degree of use, shouldnt get as much of it as I possibly can, without incurring the suspicion of being a gent. In fact, its hard to think of anything

[208] Leo Frobenius (1873–1938), German ethnologist and archaeologist who was a major influence on Pound in this period.

much more definitely ungentlemanly than systematic sponging on one's father in law. The drawbacks are practical, not moral. Its a fairly difficult job bleeding flints. That's why I would like to substitute something more reliable and less annoying if I could think of anything.

In short, the position isnt that of the useless parasite, but of the fellow who does produce something trying to get something out of the parasite, since its clear he cant get it anywhere else.

The dipsomaniac is said to have marchado.[209]

Alhamdolillah![210]

## To Ezra Pound

TS Yale

19 April 1934

c/o T.M. Reid, Bankers, Puerto de la Cruz,
Tenerife, Canarias, Spain

Dear E.P.,

Chisholm seems pretty dull, afraid you didnt get any fun out of his letter.[211] You were right to open it. I dont think there will be anything urgent from Australia, but it might quite well have had something in it I would have had to repeat to you. The article I sent will do no good in a small arty magazine; was meant for a newspaper.[212] However it may possibly raise some sort of controversy which it would be as well to envenom in the interests of net sales as well as of Australian intellex.

I wasted a lot of time writing a long explain of my political intractabilities, but it went stale on me; being a hopeless case as things stand, probably even with you. Would detail them to Lloyd George or Stalin or to any newspaper with a large circulation, but would probably be assassinated thereupon. Owing to this miscarriage of injustice, letter to you was delayed.

O'Donnell[213] wrote after abyss of silence, wants Appunti and knows of no one but me to translate them. Neither do I. They will have to wait over, owing to inexplicable spurt of Firdusian activity, vide below.

209 *Marchado*: walked, departed (Sp.). These final two exclamations are handwritten.

210 *Alhamdolillah!*: praise be to Allah! (Ar.)

211 Hugh Chisholm (1913–1972), American poet and translator.

212 Possibly BB sent an article to an Australian contact of Bertram Higgins, who had returned to England by this point after editing *Stream* (see **19/1/32**).

213 George Marion O'Donnell (1914–1962), American poet and critic.

Laughlin wrote, wanted 700 lines odd of poems to make a vol with a small press he's setting up. It appeared a very undigested scheme, but he'd written in haste before leaving for Florida, so maybe its better than I suppose. I answered: (very politely and with all consideration for this feelings) (a) Yes, but it was promised first to Zuk if he could do it. (b) If Zuk didnt, he could (c) He'd do better to learn the business devilling for Zuk than setting up on his own with neither experience NOR sufficient capital. Therefore why shouldnt he join forces with Zuk for as many books as they could agree on and afford between them. They could agree on me, maybe on a further Williams, etc etc. The capital or the agreement having been exhausted, they could then part amicably and he, Laughlin, would be the better of the experience when he set up on his own, whereas Zuks exiguous means would be eked out for a while, maybe enough to get him, or give him a chance of getting, established.

I sent a copy of this letter to Zuk, so that he shouldnt be taken by surprise. I dont feel easy about sticking my nose into his affairs, but it wasnt easy not to either, seeing the circumstances, and that Laughlin is certainly going to make no great hit by himself. He proposes to publish in paper backs: now its astonishing how much the public cares about bindings. I want a binding, therefore. I also prefer Zuk as publisher for friendshipsake and for the sake of the exalted company, but dont believe he'll ever have money to publish even one book not paid for by the author, and if he does it ought to be his own. Hence the effort.

However I am also uneasy re you, seeing you're certainly in correspondence with both of them and may have been encouraging quite other schemes. Hence those details. You have time to tell them to treat my communication with contempt if you want to.

Hope to send you a lump of Firdusi before long. Hope you will bluepencil it as severely as you have time for. I cant get rid of translators cramp. Am endeavouring to be as simple both in vocab and syntax as possible, and as idiomatic as poss. Have despaired of rendering any other qualities of the original, save maybe, if I ever find out how its done, a small part of the speed, and variety. As to onomatopoeic accompaniment, which is the marvel of the whole thing, alliterations, internal rhymes, contrapuntal arrangements of stress against ictus against Homer translating Firdusi or Firdusi translating Homer. Minor puzzles, such as what to do about epithets, what to do about expressions that are differentiated in Persian but not in English, how much pointing the moral to leave out. One doesnt want to leave out

"Why does God abandon his nurslings?"

Who are his friends? What's his character?

He brings so many matters for tears to pass"[214]

or other words to that effect. But "You bad tempered reader, see what bad-tempter leads to and reform in time" is, in my opinion, not necessary to the development of the story.

The piece I am doing will be complete in itself, and therefore, if it can be got into presentable shape, usable. It seems likely Firdusi will drive me, not to Persia, but to England and U.S.A. to get the idiom in my ears again. There is no sense in dealing with him other than as idiomatically as possible, I find. A language that has no grammar at all, like Persian, finds itself dealing in much larger units than single words, or words with a preposition attached. It doesnt lend itself in the least to logic or latinisms. That brings in the vocabulary difficulty. Firdusi sticks to Persian words pretty closely, very little Arabic: the effect would be like writing English with scarcely any latin words, IF the pure English vocabulary were about forty times as large as it is. He doesnt use words that the plowman can understand, except maybe a few military technicalities and the like, and yet he is at least as rich as Shakespeare. One is driven, of course, to use the latin words, but unless I just gave up the simplicity, which is the most striking thing, I'll have no chance of getting a tithe of the richness and exactness.

Persian has destroyed what lingering respect I had for grammar: and for avoiding clichés that are clichés of speech rather than of writing. I will never be presentable again in papers that respect respectability.

I read verbatim Charles Ists trial. I think there's nothing there for Cantos. I can use some of it myself I hope in poem now under way but progressing slowly because of activity in Persian.[215] Charles had been reading Shakespeare in jail which maybe accounts for the badness of his speeches. Bradshawe comes out pretty well.[216]

I think you would find Hafiz interesting. He's even abrupter than Horace or La Forgue. He also gets something from juxtaposition of extreme cloudiness, almost Celtic twilight, with observations surprising and exact, even often grotesque. You get, so to speak, Shelley, Catullus, Heine, Donne at his most violent, and Dante at his most exact in five successive couplets.

[214] See Share 209 for this fragment (and *passim* for other sections from *Shahnameh* alluded to here).

[215] Probably 'The Well of Lycopolis' (1935), which contains historical material about the squalor and corruption of London (though nothing in its final version about the 1649 trial of Charles I).

[216] John Bradshaw (1602–1659), President of the High Court at the trial of Charles I.

I want Saadi's Divan[217] when I get richer. I like his poems, which are less arabicised than his prose. If I could read the Arabic without stopping to search the dictionary and construe I would like his prose too, he knows how to tell a story quickly. But his poetry, when it doesnt just dawdle fulsomely round the roses and nightingales, has considerable vigour: in direct statement, much more than Hafiz.

"Many well-known people have been packed away in cemeteries,
There is no longer any evidence that they ever existed, etc etc
"Bas námvár bazér i zamín dáfn kárda and"[218]

Letter too long. Respects to Dorothy.
B

نیست ار خرید کس را رنج همان
"I was terrified nobody would pay me for the poem"
- Firdusi

## To Ezra Pound/Louis Zukofsky

TS Yale

27 April 1934

c/o T.M. Reid, Bankers, Puerto de la Cruz,
Tenerife, Canarias, Spain

Dear Ezra

Please as my friend and Zuk's read the enclosed carbon and do whatever ought to be done and then send it back to me. I am very worried: feel I've got to say it, but Zuk is also one of my best friends and I dont want to hurt him more than necessary. He will know, as soon as he gets the letter now posted, that you have the carbon.

By way of gloss on one sentence near the end: there's a lot of things I dont agree with you about, but since I dont think they have any bearing on the value of your poetry, which is the main thing, I've never argued the point, at any rate with any vehemence or obstinacy: not wanting to risk disturbed relations for anything semi-irrelevant. I've never not told you if I thought there was anything wrong with your actual writing, and I believe if you ever did write anything I thought bad as writing I would go for you just as fiercely as I've gone for Zuk. The worst I remember against you is a certain draggle-tailedness about only a few of the more journalistic scraps, and I know that at least once I made a certain fuss about

[217] *Divân*: collection of shorter poems (Fa.).
[218] See Share 192.

it. I am glad when people do that sort of thing for me, but I know a lot of people are offended at such things, and I dont know at all how Zuk is going to take it.

No news. England wants to put more emphasis on my Williams essay than it will bear, I shall ask him to let it remain a review in the review section. It is not good as an essay, though better than most reviews as a review.

Yrs

B

It seems people have been dunning my mother. Nobody but the landlady has even a ghost of a right to. All debts were paid up before we left; so far as I know, without exception. The landlady has no real right either, but she has, I think, the letter of the law on her side.

Most of my writing is shit, which is one reason why I dont write more. I know that, and dont need to be told. But if you think my poems get shitty, or anything with a reasonable amount of pretence about it gets slipshod, please say so in no mistakable phraseology.

[...]

Dear Louis,

Writing from a snivelling cold, so discount as much as you think it will bear. A cold always makes me half imbecile.

As much of the Apollinaire as has been printed has been read.[219] By Me.

I cant write about it except to you because I have no good to say about it, unless that Parker Tyler in the same mag. is worse, since your abstract polysyllables obscure and protract a statement, his seem meant to conceal the absence of any worth making.

I can see no "curiality" or "just balance of"[220] etc in the language you've used. I dont think Apollinaire would, nor yet Dante. "The quintessence of fifty thousand schoolmen from Scotus to Bellarmin" was said of the Hind and the Panther,[221] which yet is readable if dull. I think it should be a rule to have at least one simple

[219] In 1933–1934 Zukofsky wrote a series of articles on Guillaume Apollinaire (1880–1918), whose abstract, proto-surrealist style is a target of BB's ire in this letter. BB is almost certainly commenting on the installments published in *Westminster Magazine* (see note to 18/11/33) given the reference to Parker Tyler (1904–1974), whose poetry appeared in the Spring 1934 issue.

[220] In the essay 'De vulgari eloquentia' ('On eloquence in the vernacular') (*c.*1302–1305) Dante outlines four essential virtues of vernacular discourse, one of which is 'curiality', a kind of organic pragmatism which, he argues, means vernacular speech is guided by 'the justly balanced rule of things that have to be done'.

[221] This quotation, from Swift's 'A Tale of the Tub' (1704), is a satirical commentary on Dryden's poem 'The Hind and the Panther' (1687).

word used in its usual meaning in every two or three sentences. I am a primitive person with a narrow culture. I cant see the beauty of whole pars. of abstract nouns & co, nor yet, which is worse, can I assign any meaning to them.

I dont believe abstract words correspond to anything except the noises made in pronouncing them. They are a grammatical convenience, but a damn dangerous one, not only because they elude, puzzle, tire readers, and leave millions of microbic ambiguities wherever they go; but they seduce the writer to think in them, which is as much to say, to leave off thinking and give over his mind to verbal quibblings, which I believe to be the root, trunk, leaves, blossom and fruit of seven-eighths of all the blasted philofuckingsophical maunderings that have entreacled the world's surface since Thales.[222]

I prefer any dialect of English or other spoken language to the six-six-sixth generation of bastard latin. Hate to see a friend I admire marrying off his mind to a third cousin of the jargon into which they translate Hegel and other misleaders of mankind. You've seen what the mathematicians have come to from allowing their symbols to bamboozle them into thinking them read. Follow up any abstraction a little way and it will commit suicide.

<u>You</u>'ve no right to any such game of chess, you're wanted IN the world. Its worse than thinking "argyraspides" has an aureole unless of laughter like "Polyphiloprogenitive".[223] The use and origin of language is to be spoken, written symbols only an incident: dont take Fenellosa from THAT end, or he'll lead you effectually into the desert. But your Apollinaire isnt speakable, or isnt hearable, which amounts to the same.

Its not the case of a poem, whose obscurity may arise from the difficulty of a thought never previously expressed, or from abrupt transitions meant to throw off a new force from, so to say, the angle of impact. The obscurity of your Apollinaire arises from the manner in which you choose to express yourself. I have done my best to sound for sunken treasures, but still think it might as well have been written in a manner I could have followed more easily.

In any case, saying a new thing is only half the job, or less. Saying it so that the bum on the bridge can understand it is the ultimate intention, and if its been necessary to explode the notion that all poetry must be as simple as that, that doesnt intend to set up an ideal of obscurity, but merely to say that

[222] Thales of Miletus (*c.*624–*c.*546 BC), pre-Socratic Greek philosopher used here as shorthand for the beginning of Western philosophy.

[223] Argyraspides: soldiers in Alexander the Great's army. BB's suggestion here is that obscure polysyllabic words derived from Latin and Greek sound risible, not refined.

obscurity has to be put up with when it cant be avoided. I think you could have avoided it.

In my worthless opinion the devotion American critics seem to have to the facies of secondrate metaphysics is dangerous not only to themselves, but to the future of American literature that looked pretty bright not so long since. I dont believe many of you will survive a prolonged imitation of death. Must I go back to my teens and go about telling people to read Swift? Maybe Hume would do, not so well.

Or if you like, take this into consideration: nobody not a bloody fool reads anything that has certain symptoms of empty pedantry: your business is to be read by people not fools: ergo, it is wiser not to parody, with whatever intent, a style even more dreadful than that of Haldane's Schopenhauer.[224]

I have a mind to write several articles arising out of this letter: language is no man's private property and I want to keep the right-of-way open.

All this is terribly stiff, and I have to ask you to forgive it on the grounds that I dont think I'd take either the trouble or the liberty with anybody else except Pound if he should ever do anything that I thought likely to be permanently harmful to his genius. In short its my admiration for A and The[225] that makes me ready to express my dislike and distrust of the Apollinaire so fiercely.

I believe not only bad writing but half the evils in the world come from verbalism, i.e. imagining that abstracts have anything more than a grammatical meaning or function. Adjectives, numbers, symbols like the word God, eat away all the sense of reality and land us in every kind of social and economic mess, when people begin to think they correspond to anything genuine. Notation, nothing more. And mostly bad notation. A poet's business is to get a language that wont have to rely on anything so slipshod as algebra.

I think perhaps Pound will have to see this, damn it, I am so uneasy about going for you to this extent. He is our intimate friend, its not proclaiming it to the world. He can soften it and rebuke me, or back it up and excuse me or play Gallio just as it strikes him.[226] I will send him the carbon.

Yours, as ever: more than ever.

224 Richard Haldane (1856–1928), co-translator with J. Kemp of the first English edition of Schopenhauer's *The World as Will and Idea* [*sic*], which appeared in three volumes 1883–1886.

225 I.e., Zukofsky's 'Poem Beginning 'The" (1927), and his life's work "A".

226 Lucius Junius Gallio Annaeanus (*c.*4 BC–AD 65), Roman senator who, in the biblical account, remained impartial in the face of charges brought by the Jews against the Apostle Paul (see Acts 18:2–17).

## To Ezra Pound

TS Yale

July 18 (I think) [1934] c/o T.M. Reid, Bankers, Puerto de la Cruz, Tenerife, Canarias, Spain

Dear E.P.,

Pleased to return your check, having been able to manage without it by the margins of five minutes and five pesetas on catching the boat at Cadia: both because it would probably have been almost impossible to cash in the Peninsular and because I didnt at all like asking for it at a time when I feel pretty sure you are hard up.[227]

Portugal a washout just now, all houses taken for the summer may try again in the autumn, but heaven knows. Its very cheap, the people are cleaner and civiler than the Spaniards a lot, but once out of Lisbon arrangements are amazingly primitive, even Tenerife seems modern beside 'em. Portuguese food admirable, but climate a bit too hot for a family of kids. However, it was unexpected shrinkage in funds that prevented me making some arrangement in the Algarve. Must now hog on here for a while. Temporarily in a pension, hard to do any thing whatever. Hope to move to "the capital" next month.

Met old gent fit for the Cantos in Vila Real de Santo Antonio.[228] Try to translate a little of his conversation later if opportunity. Also the tunny auction held up while a tarantula strolled casually along three rows of buyers desks, one after the other. Some superstition prevented them killing time but they were too afraid of it to attend to business till it took itself off. And the Guadiana, a good river, glad I know it.

ABC here, have read it, but while a big fagged, not attentively enough.[229] For re-reading when rush over. It seems to me pretty good. I take it there's little in the first part that isnt in How to Read shorter, sometimes a bit ambiguous but mostly pithy: here made plain even to English Review.[230] But I cant say whether the soda has drowned any of the whisky or not until I read with my mind awake. The second part for me more interesting. Two or three points of difference:

[227] BB visited Portugal in June/July 1934, where, as described here, he tried unsuccessfully to find accommodation.

[228] Vila Real de Santo António, city in the Algarve, Portugal.

[229] I.e., Pound's *ABC of Reading*, published by Faber in 1934. As BB suggests, *ABC* expanded on many of the literary-critical subjects covered in *How to Read* (see **August 1930**), and contained an abbreviated canon of examples of English poetry, with copious commentary by Pound (this section is titled 'Exhibits', which is what BB means below by the 'second part').

[230] *The English Review*: English literary monthly founded by Ford Madox Ford in 1908. See 12/7/75 for BB's comments on its decline into 'idiocy' after Ford's departure.

1) I think Burns is a serious omission. Maybe he is the only British poet who has contributed something not to be found anywhere else before him, and therefore, I feel, entitled to honourable mention even assuming his works so well known (which they arent, south of the border) that you dont need to print any samples. I mean especially such as:

Beneath these stanes lie Jamie's banes
    O Death, it's ma opinion
Ye ne'er took sic a bletherin bitch
    Into yere dark dominion.[231]

That, I maintain, isnt in Catullus; and if its in the Anthology, Mackail, Aldington and the rest have managed to keep it from leaking out.[232] Also, the cantabile of songs that are have been and will be generally sung by a whole people, is something different from the cantabile of that elegy on Rochester,[233] or of Shakespeare's cantabile.[234] Its less Milanese or Viennese bel canto,[235] more in the genius of this language. That's rare in any language and unique in English.

2) I think Swift's verse is a less important omission, but there's something there very foreign to Butler or Pope. If Swift's best is Gulliver, his second-best is still a good deal above most men's understanding. He was no fumbler, either, with metric, and the drunken bit translated from the Irish is prime singable and Mrs Harris's petition prime gabbleable.[236]

3) The case for Rochester seems to me much overstated. You would have to omit the bulk of his not bulky product, and hide all copies of Denham to get it past a jury.[237] As style of the period, yes, but not as the apex of the period.

[231] BB slightly misquotes Burns's 'Epitaph on a Noisy Polemic' (1784).

[232] *The Greek Anthology*: collection of Greek lyric poetry from antiquity to the Byzantine period which emerged in the later Middle Ages. Samples appeared in *Select Epigrams From The Greek Anthology* (1890) edited by Scottish literary scholar John William Mackail (1859–1945), and multiple works translated by the poet Richard Aldington in the late 1910s.

[233] In ABC Pound quotes extensively (147–150) from an 'anonymous elegy': actually 'Bion. A Pastoral, in imitation of the Greek of Moschus, bewailing the Death of the Earl of Rochester' (1681) by John Oldham (1653–1683).

[234] *Cantabile*: songlike (It.). This term from musical notation is used suggestively here to refer to 'songlike' poetry.

[235] *Bel canto*: beautiful singing (It.). A highly refined vocal style originating in Italy, which became popular in eighteenth-century Europe.

[236] I.e., Swift's poems 'Description of an Irish Feast' (1720) and 'Mrs Frances Harris's Petition' (1700).

[237] John Denham (1615–1669), Anglo-Irish poet best known for 'Cooper's Hill' (1642), an influential poem in heroic couplets describing the topography of the Thames Valley. In a follow-up letter to Pound in October, BB praised the 'slick style' of the poem and urged Pound to read it. See BB to EP, 21/10/34 (Yale).

4) I think Dryden's "Fables" (translations from pretty nearly all the longer latin poets, done in his old age) contain, along with some bits of XVIIc dialect, a good deal of the clearest verse in English, for sense, syntax and sound: not the best, the clearest.[238]

5) As formerly, I miss the merits of Browning. Blindspot, maybe. I cant endure him. Seems to me to fumble around describing things – anything but narrative, which is the claim you make.[239] A novelist, not one of the best novelists. I admit a song or too, with reservations, and a few dramatic shocks. I permit you to attribute to him the revival of the persona, though by Christ, the only importance I'm inclined to allow that is that it gave you a very useful pointer. He reminds me of Ford Madox Ford.

These secondary or tertiary details apart, I believe the reason why I agree with you on all the broad grounds and most of the details has nothing whatever to do with "influence" nor yet with the particular ambience of the generation, but is simply due to the fact that you're right. I arrived at certain conclusions before I came to inhabit Rapallo: some of them you'd already printed in books I hadnt then read.

Mention of me an ad gratis: however, dichten-to condense[240] aint nobody's property unless Hitler wants it for the Reich. But I didnt get it mucking about with a dictionary, but because I have some feeling for words of Indo-European origin which has often been useful: and when it occurred to me that this word might be useful to you, I then looked it up and confirmed what was already my firm belief.

This isnt as egotistic as it sounds. Plenty of How to Read was new to me: but I dont believe I agreed because of your predominant presence.

It seems friends in U.S.A. cant do anything about Roerich Museum: I now go ahead on my own with a long, luvly, well-oiled letter – scrawled already but to be revised: and pray for the help of Tagore and Yeats.[241]

238 Dryden's *Fables, Ancient and Modern*, a collection of translations from Homer, Ovid, Boccaccio, and Chaucer, was published shortly before its author's death in 1700.

239 In *ABC* Pound praises Browning's 'limpidity of narration' (191).

240 Pound uses the maxim 'Dichten = condensare' in *ABC* to argue that 'poetry is the most concentrated form of verbal expression' (36). He credits it to BB who, he suggests, found it when 'fumbling about with a German-Italian dictionary' (36), where he noticed that the German word *dichten* ('to compose a poem') was rendered by the Italian word *condensare* ('to condense')—an account BB modifies here.

241 Pound wrote to Bengali Nobel Laureate Rabindranath Tagore (1861–1941) at around this time to try to assist BB with his application for funding from the Nicholas Roerich Museum in New York: 'Bunting has done what I think a very good condensation of Cho Mei, and writes Persian beautifully (I mean as far as the handwriting goes. I don't know any, so I can't tell whether

Priest at Cacela[242] read me some Camoens.[243] Seems to have very solid indestructible lines and passages mixed up with a lot of Renaissance decoration. Is that right? It's a hard language to follow if you havent the print before you eyes.

Dont think I sent you the first of following two Hafiz's.[244] I still cant read him with any ease, but think you were mistaken in supposing I would find him chiefly "melopoeia". He's extraordinary agile in transition, leaving, for instance, Horace, miles behind: but I cant expect to get that over yet awhile. Sadi seems more melopoeic, supposing my pronunciation is even approximately correct, which isnt certain.

1.

O everlasting self-deluded!
   If there's no love for you there's nothing for it
but to go crazy. Anyway, don't set up for
   a paragon of self-restraint.
Love's dizziness cant invade a head
   dizzy with alcohol.
You're jaundiced, augh! misery-hideous!
   Anybody can read your symptoms.
Give respectability and pride the go-by, Hafiz,
   cadge yourself a drop of booze and get
                                    crapulously drunk.

2.

Isnt it poetical, a chap's mind in the dumps!?
   Of course our cliché's true:
"Your lips the seal on my passport,
   that's a hundred empires in hand.
So, my heart, dont wince when they mock you,
   mockeries rightly regarded are riches –
who doesnt take ghoulish sarcasms thus
   his marble was hacked out in haste.
Wine and tears in a cup, each offers it someone, –
   that's only polite, under Providence:
the routine of the perfumery business,
   one rose crushed, one kept.

it is correct). He has no money, and simply will not melt himself into the vile patterns of expediency.' Quoted in Noel Stock, *The Life of Ezra Pound* (Harmondsworth: Penguin, 1974), 483.

[242] Cacela Velha: village in the Algarve, Portugal.

[243] Luís de Camões/Camoens (*c.*1525–1580), Portugal's national poet.

[244] Both of these Hafiz translations were included in *Caveat Emptor* (see **6/5/35**).

And it's false, the frenzy quitting Hafiz
the durable frenzy warranted to
last ever so long.

He has also the singing stuff: and in his rubayat,[245] when not under Omar's shadow, some very direct stuff:-

You leave nobody else without a bed,
you make everybody else thoroughly at home:
I'm the only one hanged in your halter,
you've driven nobody else mad but me.[246]

I'm not setting this up in competition with anything: but it does seem to me that if my chance-selected specimens of Persian poets are typical, its likely to prove a much larger addition to the literary stock, whenever people begin to learn it, than probably any other single language. There's a long list of celebrities, as far as I can learn all very different from one another. Later I mean to see if Maulana Rumi is up to his reputation, and some of the early blokes.

Best wishes to Dorothy and your parents.

B

P.S., Here its simpler to scribble Cancelled on the cheque than to get a letter registered – Spanish postoffice, endless delay, dozens of forms to fill up.

## To Ezra Pound

TS Yale

August twentysomethingth [1934]

c/o T.M. Reid, Bankers, Puerto de la Cruz, Tenerife, Canarias, Spain

Dear Ezra,

Burns: There does seem to me to be a difference between his epigrams – at least the characteristic ones and such as I know of the greek, or Martial.[247] Maybe the blatherinbitch was an illchosen example, but my Burns is packed up and stored in Santa Cruz and it was the only one I could remember at the moment. Possibly

[245] *Rubāʿiyāt*: plural form of *rubāʿiee*, a quatrain in classical Persian poetry.

[246] A version of this quatrain appeared in *Bozart–Westminster* (a collaboration of 1935 between *Westminster Magazine* and another Georgia journal *Bozart and Contemporary Verse Magazine*, co-edited by Pound, John Drummond, and T. C. Wilson). Later versions introduced a Williams-esque layout and dropped the attribution to Hafez, resulting in Ode 1.28.

[247] This letter continues the discussion of *ABC of Reading* begun in 18/7/34.

Here comes Burns
On Rosinante
He's damn fou
and she's damn canty[248]

is better. I mean, from point of view of form-al distinction. The form is much more violent and less tricky. To class it as sting-in-the-tail or any of its varieties you've got to think of a lizard with a tail longer than its body, very often.

I dont think I'm dazzled by dialect. It doesnt puzzle me nor seem quaint, since its nearly the same as what I speak at home. I find much more of that specious sort of "charm" in old Scottis, such as Douglas wrote,[249] which isnt a dialect but a separate language, and it always, like archaisisms, annoys me because I have to make an effort to understand not the poet but its vocabulary. How-ever!

On the other hand, purely as form, there doesnt seem to be much difference between Omar Khyyam and a lot of the anthology poets. I like Omar better because of his content, his peculiar shade of scorn etc, and maybe because I am better able to appreciate his music, either his own or Fitzgerald's somewhat monotonous substitute, than I can latin, let alone greek, epigram. (There's one odi profanum sort of piece not touched by Fitz because it isnt in rubay form which sings so admirably one would have to include it in almost any lyric anthology – uniting parody and sting-in-the-tail but I wouldnt consider that another form.)

Re Rochester, I mean that Denham was functioning more consistently on a at least nearly equal level thirty years earlier. All these fellows attended to Malherbe's views on diction without remembering that he wrote always and definitely to be sung. As you say, Waller was the last important English poet to bear it well in mind in a part of his work.[250] The nineteenth century fellows tried, but had mostly forgotten how to do it: I think, witness Browning, but perhaps you wont agree.

248 The last couplet of Burns's 'On Himself' is actually 'She's damn'd poor, | But he's damn'd canty!' *Canty*: lively, sprightly (Scots).

249 BB's comments here about Burns and the medieval poet Gavin Douglas (*c.*1474–1522), who wrote in Modern and Early Scots respectively (both languages are derived ultimately from Northumbrian Old English), are a testament to his complex geographical and linguistic identity, which would later play out in his friendship with Hugh MacDiarmid (see especially 27/4/78 and note).

250 In *ABC* Pound wrote: 'The great lyric age lasted while Campion made his own music, while Lawes set Waller's verses, while verses, if not actually sung or set to music, were at least made with the intention of going to music' (60–61). Such theories about the pre-eighteenth-century inseparability of poetry and music, which would feed into the famous climax of Pound's Canto 81, were at the heart of the Pound–Bunting friendship. For a much later elaboration by BB see *Basil Bunting on Poetry*, ed. Peter Makin (London: Johns Hopkins Press, 1999), 35–36.

It all matters very little, seeing there's nobody else capable of putting out as good a guide as yours. Anything like a list is always going to be vulnerable in detail, whoever Homer Firdusi Dante Lurcretius Horace Catullus Burns Villon – no use going on in extenso, my list would differ from yours only in some points and those not at all the chief ones.

News. Check from Eauclaire failing to turn up, irate landlady seized all baggage, down to the babies napkins. We moved to another pension and had to wait in considerable discomfort. A cursed row. Marian said all Spaniards were bad lots, and I was nearly gaoled for this insult to the Republic. We now inhabit with German aristos: Roubada is actually swaddled in napkins from the august arse of an imperial highness. But even since I got my books back I find it very hard to work in a pension that contains 5 infants under five years of age. I am just about ready to give myself out as beaten.

The inhospitable pension possessed bedbugs, lice, mice, fleas (more than the usual large Canary quota) and the worst cook without exception on the entire face of the globe. Sometimes one couldnt swallow his productions, other times one swallowed them and they came back. Here we get excellent food but not enough. Also, it costs more than we can pay and until we can arrange some way of getting off the island or into a house of our own again we will get daily deeper into the hole. However the ex-Hohenzollern's are willing to wait: they are just as hard up as everyone else but not so damn grasping.

Nazi chief here routed an armed brigand by throwing full bottles of whisky at him, about two dozen. They all missed, but were thrown strongly enough to break the planks in the door, as I saw myself. The brigand fired all the shots in his pistol and missed too, then fled. Nazi followed him out, caught him, and gave him six pesetas. Which arouses my admiration.

Drummond hasnt written to me: if however he does want any works of mine he'd better have the Shirazi Blues.[251] Think I sent it you, but repeat it now to make sure. (Itz a roob-eye)

Owing to all this pension fuss, Tagore got in before me. My application to Roerich's should leave today. Dont expect anything from it.

Best to Dorothy.

Yrs
B

[251] I.e., The quatrain from Hafiz destined to become Ode 1.28 (see 18/7/34 and note).

The following two letters to Pound repay close attention, because they contain arguably the most revealing statements about Bunting's literary development in this part of the correspondence. The basis of the discussion is Ferdowsi's *Shahnameh*. Attending to the example of Ferdowsi's great poem, Bunting suggests, is likely to complicate some of the basic aesthetic assumptions made by earlier modernists like Pound. More specifically, Bunting's decisive rejection here of the 'indirect business' at the heart of modern literature since the time of Flaubert and Henry James—and his assertion that he will 'try telling a story' instead—amounts to a key realization on his part. Though it would take him another three decades to work through this impulse, one of Bunting's distinctive contributions to late-modernist poetics (announced tentatively in *The Spoils* and much more emphatically in *Briggflatts)* was an embodiment of the sorts of epic, narrative values he advocates in this letter. If the term 'Objectivism' has any application at all when it comes to Bunting, it should be seen as a way of describing the aesthetic outlined here—'acts' over 'characters', 'story' over 'reflection', and so on.

Perhaps fairly, given the emphasis on heroic action in the Cantos, Pound took umbrage at Bunting's suggestion that he too belonged in modern literature's 'psychological' camp. In an expletive-filled follow-up letter of 27 January 1935 (carbon copy, Yale), Pound cited the examples of Sigismundo Malatesta and Thomas Jefferson in the Cantos as proof of that work's objective basis, prompting Bunting to restate and elaborate his position in **January/February 1935**. All of this seems certain to have fed into Pound's famous claim in 1938 in *Guide to Kulchur* (New York: New Directions, 1970), a work dedicated to Bunting and Louis Zukofsky, that the 'history of a culture is the history of ideas going into action' (44).

## To Ezra Pound

TS Yale

4 January 1935

Tenerife

Dear Ezra,

Card on Firdusi arrived.

A.

I am sorry you sent it to Eliot. It went to you as part of the process of manufacture, rather than as finished product: and incomplete too. However, since he has it, let it take its meager chances.

B.

I am sorry to have bored you, espec. after taking the precaution of attempting to bore Zuk first and failing. If it bores an intelligent bloke, I aint appealing from that verdict, but proclaiming that it isnt by any means right yet and needs altered methods. All of which takes time. And that old baboo Tagore DIDN'T write to the Museum, which has replied to me kindly that times being hard they cant do nuffin but hope somebody else will.[252] Which they wont.

C.

I think you, as you would, hit on the main difficulty of epic poetry in this age, without being possibly quite aware of it or its implications. You say all F's characters (as portrayed by me) bore you. It hadnt occurred to me that you would be sure to think first of the characters, nevertheless I now see you would. But in trying to learn something about epic I was very largely trying to get away from characters and deal with acts instead.

I dont think Homer's characters are very interesting. What fascinates me, at any rate, is what they do. I know that they have been one and all so encrusted with later poetry of a different kind that you cant use the word "Ulysses" or "Achilles" without conjuring up a whole host of ghosts of lines and attributes, in fact the entire recipe for "poetic glamour"; even if its Homer himself that uses the word, the later accretions cant be entirely unstuck unless one is very thoroughly aware of them to begin with: a series of actions, not at all the sort of person you or Browning would chose to make a persona on.

It is true Firdusi's people talk more than Homer's, and write letters, and in the Persian, at least, they do have "characters" of a simple sort (and convincing sort), but what is important is still the act, and the letters are themselves acts, not in the least "arranged" to display character. The whole gamut of them wouldnt keep a Flaubert or a Henry James busy two pages. Nor would Homers, deprived of the later associations.

But the literature of the last – now long? – has all of it been psychological: people talking or thinking about things they didnt do, or would like to do, or why and why not. Even in the Cantos you nearly always prefer to show somebody thinking or writing or telling, and the interest is as much or more in the person as in the deed contemplated. Even your manner of narration where you dont interpose any definitive mask seems to serve a similar end. It is all one manner or another of reflection. (I'm not attempting, Lord forbid, to belittle it: that would be idiotic)

It occurred to me a long time ago that this indirect business had gone about as far as it would go without degenerating. Nobody is going to do it better than you for a hell of a long time, and Zuk can only introduce further complications of method that remove it from the possible reader, step by step, until somebody will

[252] See 18/7/34 and note.

arise who will justify the kind of things the academic nincompoops used to say about you, and be totally unintelligible. Hence "Chomei", to reduce it to such simplicity as I could: which thereupon ended the matter so far as I personally am concerned. I can do nothing with it that will satisfy me. It is much better to leave the field to you, and perhaps to Zuk's elaborations and try telling a story.

This leads to the wretchedly unsuccessful attempt to do a bit of Machiavelli,[253] and consequent considerable thinking.

But a story depends on action. Its elements arent characters. I feel it would be safer to minimize than to emphasise the peculiarities of Firdusi's people. If their names are ever to conjure up "glamours" it must be somebody else's job to do it, not the translators or epic poets. That leaves us at the requirement "Speed" which you have jumped at from the characters instead of the action. I would like to make it faster, but so far cant: havent the technical equipment. At least, a regular, even rhymed, line is faster, of course, but becomes a meaningless gabble very easily.

D.

I dont know Rouse's Ulysses.[254] His Lucretius is pretty bum. My own fancy in Homer translators is Samuel Butler. I dont think he would be yours, though he tells a plain tale rapidly. Yr own Canto One, while excellent poetry of E.P. of a rather specialised sort, doesnt seem to me to have much to do with epic, the anachronistic vocabulary and beautiful vocal decoration belonging to my mind so much to the poetry of associations as to be an exactly adapted beginning to your poem of epic length but philosophic content.[255] Nor is Ovid helpful: for though I get kicks here and there I oftener hear F.E. Smith addressing a war-time house of Commons in favour of something he didnt believe in, and didnt give a damn about.[256] Kipling (prose) somewhat confirms me in the notion that people like to see a machine working more than to know how it works. That is, its not only out of the question to stop to explain, but even to explain as one goes along by means of the twist one gives to the vocabulary: it all de-simplifies too much. And in so doing, abstractifies, ultimately to thinness. Oh, yes, I know you and

[253] Possibly a reference to BB's abortive attempt to translate 'a book on Medieval philosophy' around 1929 for Kegan Paul (see 11/4/29), or else a poetic project of the mid 1930s which has not survived.

[254] Between 1934 and 1940 Pound corresponded with W. H. D. Rouse (1863–1950), who was preparing translations of the *Odyssey* (1937) and *Illiad* (1938). His translation of Lucretius's *De rerum natura* had appeared in 1924.

[255] Pound's Canto 1 is based on an episode in the *Odyssey*; its style and diction are heavily indebted to the influence of Old English alliterative verse.

[256] Frederick Edwin Smith, 1st Earl of Birkenhead (1872–1930), British Conservative politician famous for his pugnacious speeches during World War I.

Ovid have bags of tricks that would enable you to get away with anything you had a mind to. I havent, and must therefore make no attempt to charm the reader over a bad step or round an awkward corner. He must go round on his own unwilling legs. All of which leads back to speed, in the sense of marking the corners well if I cant straighten them out.

E.

"Wm Morris Icelandic Sagas" – merely a measure of my failure.[257] There's the whole gulf between Firdusi and the various Nordic epics. If I dont give you something that suggests (though it probably wont get there by a million miles) something as much alive as Homer, then I'm not getting it across.

F.

Simplest prose statement is easy to talk about but would occupy three times as much paper as my verse. The stuff undergoes various processes, mostly mental. If it isnt simpler than the simplest prose, I'll chew the roller of my typewriter.

X.[258]

[...][259]

Y.

Having sent Louis two shirts value one dollar twentyfive cents apiece for Xmas, the U.S. customs demands from him 5 dollars and 11 cents: though the things were plainly labeled for the customs. A duty of 100% on something they cant make in their own damned trough of a country must help a lot in overcoming hardships of unemployed. Louis cant pay the five dollars and must do without the shirts. Which will probably be eventually auctioned for their keep and sold to some customer swine for ten cents apiece.

Went up in the mountains in a car yesterday, extraordinary views from 8000 feet up, islands like school relief maps, etc. Close view of the cone of the great volcano – last five thousand feet of it sticking up above us – astonishing, many-coloured rocks, ash-heaps white and black, long streamers of lava.[260] Inside the ancient crater the cone now rises from, perpendicular cliffs of the rim, floor mainly gravel, extremely queer vegetation peculiar to the spot, like a compromise between the Sahara and Norway. Clouds over the sea sixty miles away exactly

[257] Morris translated several Icelandic Sagas into English in collaboration with Icelander Euríkur Magnússon (1833–1913).

[258] The jump from 'F' to 'X' here traverses pagination. It is possible therefore that a large middle section of this letter is missing, though more likely BB decided to move quickly to his conclusion.

[259] Paragraph struck through so as to be illegible.

[260] Mount Teide: active volcano in the centre of Tenerife, which probably inspired BB's 'On highest summits dawn comes soonest' (dated 1935).

as though painted on a bowl, lacquer bowl, Jap manner. They are going to build a hotel up there. Queer thing, the only level space large enough for an aerodrome on this island is also within the ancient crater, a circular floor perfectly flat paved with tiny pebbles as though artificially. It is huge, but only a little incident in the crater, which is about fifteen miles across, or some more. There is a bigger one on La Palma, with no new volcano in it.

I recommend the first half of Sir Wm Muir's History of the Caliphate.[261] I cant get his life of Mohammed here, but suppose it to be also worth reading. The Religious Tract Society is the publisher, but dont buy it, get McGeorge[262] to make the library buy it for you. The rulers of Islam paid dividends to all the whole nation of the Arabs, though they taxed the non-Mahometan populations and took a tithe from everybody for the poor. But Muir hasnt much to say about the finance. You might recognise some of your Jewish friends in these kindred Semites: especially in their sexual habits.

Yrs
B

If Eliot should by any chance accept the Firdusi after it has bored you, I will indeed know there is something very wrong with it. Various greetings: Dorothy, Mr & Mrs Pound, Münch.[263]

## To Ezra Pound

TS Yale

[January/February 1935]

c/o T.M. Reid, Bankers, Puerto de la Cruz,
Tenerife, Canarias, Spain

Dear Ezra,

I must be gettin very fuzzy spoken. Youre apparently quite some distance from getting the idear I wuz at. Not that it matters a dam, since bored is bored, and that's that.

Sigismundo was presumably an active lad, but the Cantos dont relate his activities, they allude to them or show him, alluding to them.[264] If I want to know what

[261] Sir William Muir (1819–1905), Scottish scholar of Islamic history, author of *The Caliphate: Its Rise, Decline and Fall* (1891) and *The Life of Mohammed* (1861).

[262] Henry King McGeorge (1865–1940), retired British army colonel who lived near the Pounds in Rapallo.

[263] Gerhart Münch (1907–1988), German pianist and composer, who assisted with the concert series in Rapallo. This postscript is handwritten.

[264] See 4/1/35 and commentary.

Sig did I goter konsult the Encycl. Brit., whose contributor presumably had found out somewhere not in the works of E.P. This doesnt render E.P.s Sig less interesting to me, but he is interesting for something that isnt, and that is only indirectly connected with, anything that Homer of Firdusi would have been likely to set down on paper.

But if I want to know about Nausicaa, Homer will do all I want. Likewise, Firdusi will provide at considerable length all the relevant facts about Faridun.[265] The difference being that reading Homer one is pestered by other peoples lines on his people, and in reading F his people come at one comparatively naked. I think Firdusi really comes off best there, but his people have to make their way from the beginning one isnt predisposed to be interested.

No doubt Freud or E.P., or H James in their several ways could have and communicate quite a lot of fun with Faridun, starting on the Firdusian faults. As with Aedipus or Teresias. By the way, if you can suggest handy colloquial English equivalents for psyche, phrenes, noos, etc,[266] I'll be much obliged, for the Persian language provided F with at least 8 words with distinctions of meaning within that orbit which are, like other embarrasments of the huge Persian vocab, bloody hard to do over. One can dig it out easily enough for people who know Persian, just as the subtleties of the Greek language can be dug out for people who know Greek. But I'm not going to use modico-psychiatrical terms nor invent words a la J Joyce if I can help it. And a series of periphrastical definitions, while interesting to some people, wd somewhat hold up the tale. They are all perfectly colloquial in Persian, and imply no doubt several centuries of science and philosophy considerably different from what we're used to. Which doesnt ease matters.

I take khirad to be a rough equivalent of noos: jan is something between greek psyche and english soul, with a touch of life's-blood or heart. Magz is probably phrenes – originally the physical brain, and thence some of its activities. Andesha includes the reason and the imagination. Hosh is more or less the part of the brain that controls ordinary actions, but it also includes the virtues and understanding. Hunar is virtue and cunning considered as parts of the intelligence. And so on. No use completing the list.

[265] Faridun: mythical Persian king celebrated in *Shahnameh*. The discussion here alludes to drafts BB sent Pound of the translations from *Shahnameh*, which would eventually comprise the sequence 'From 'Faridun's Sons' (see Share 198–211, 454).

[266] *Psyche, phrenes, noos/nous*: ancient Greek words for soul/mind/intellect, with subtle connotations which BB's explores in the list of Persian relatives in the ensuing passage.

The distinctions are fine and invariably very carefully used. Some sorts of thinking are done in the head, some in the heart, but they love and grieve with their livers.

A man is what he does alright, but there are different ways of approaching that nexus: via is and via does, to begin with. With my imperviousness to some respectably vouched for notions, I cant believe Browning knew very much about anything but books; else the gaping gap between you would be a little smaller. The what, quiddity, (chigunagi or how-ness) is intended, I suppose, though I hate to let in even that much abstraction, by all alike. And where's the bellybutton gazer? Not in my Firdusi cantos? surely you cant mean ME, wots been and turned my gaze hon the himmortal Heast simply because I was so bloody sick of myself and couldnt find anything else that so completely excluded me?

It is maybe the ellipses you dont like? They probably are overdone. I realise such often hold up rather than hasten perusal: but I'm thinking more of recitation or chanting, for which I think theyre reasonably adapted.

There arent many fal-lals and furbelows, if you come to look at it. Far fewer than in Chomei: which is, I know, smoother, having been very laboriously constructed upon standard patterns, such as I cant possibly avail myself of here. When everything happened previously, you can pick and choose a lot more freely, rhythms as well as matter.

If its live language and nuts![267] Kundavari, bollockbearing, one of Firdusi's favorite commendations which I cant make use of, such is the age! Well sir, I go flat: but do what I can to keep it alive by using English that is used on the lips as well as on the page so far as that can be done without wholly sacrificing accuracy. A chapter full of medievalisms would put you off quickern effer, even if you was twice as learned, and moreover it would be just as big an anachronism, and ana-space-ism.

This sounds bloody like alibis, but isnt. They are in reserve, when I've got clear what it is that puts you to sleep. You arent tied to tell me, of course. Since re-reading would probably be painful.

Nothing but a tentpeg through the skull could distract me more completely than the sort of life we've had to lead since my departure for Portugal. Returning, we had two months of what would serve very well as a postobit torment for dishonest hotelkeepers. Since then I live amongst a livestock of kids and pension servants, damn rarely get an uninterrupted half hour, and my belly always on and

[267] In the letter of 27 January to which BB is replying (carbon copy, Yale) Pound claimed that 'readability' arises from a combination of 'live language' and 'NUTS' (i.e. balls).

off strike about the incredible island grub. And if Jael would bring me butter (not from New Zealand) in a lordly dish, I'd submit even to the tentpeg.[268] Moreover Firdusi, whom you call kike,[269] was an antisemite, and made very grudging exceptions of the chief Companions of the Prophet. The chief villain in the first part of the book was an Arab domiciled at Jewrusalem. If I did return Rapallo, I wouldnt do a damn thing for the Mare of the Musical Times: however, I think it will probably be cheaper, if less stimulating, to go for England.

You bloody old prohibitionist, if this volcano in the sea bore a single person fit to get drunk with once a month, it would be a lot easier to write poetry here. But the whisky rises to Drerup's[270] lungs and I dont trust any other Tinerfeno acquaintance whatsoever. I had lost sight of the possibility of blinding in company with Gerhart,[271] but now you've reminded me of it, it pretty near turns the scale in favour of Rap.

Sorry to hear Serly missed the boat.[272] My limerick on the other Hun got itself collected some years ago and privately printed in Wien, Wien Stadt deine Träume.[273] But it wouldnt apply in Rapallo.

What a pity that Bela Bartok
Cannot give his smug public a shock
By writing in parts
For the hiccups and farts
And conducting the piece with
yes, obviously.

Sorabji is of the respectable race whose poetry I am murdering,[274] but I agree I would be better on the job: though at present I'd much prefer to do a history of

[268] In the biblical account Jael kills the Canaanite commander Sisera by driving a tentpeg through his skull, having first brought him 'butter in a lordly dish' (Judges 5:25).

[269] BB references one of a series of racist slurs in Pound's 27 January letter (in this case a rather absurd comment about Ferdowsi's religion/ethnicity).

[270] I.e., **Karl Drerup**.

[271] I.e., Gerhart Münch (see **4/1/35** and note).

[272] I.e., **Tibor Serly**.

[273] See Share 465 for a brief discussion of this poem's (appropriately farcical) publication history. Because the Vienna iteration hasn't been traced, and it is unclear whether BB had any involvement in the poem's publication in *Truck* 21 (1979), it would seem to me that the question of how the poem should end remains ambiguous (the final line may or may not be a part of the body of the letter here, and there is no character spacing and full stop after 'with', as seen in later versions).

[274] Kaikhosru Shapurji Sorabji (1892–1988): celebrated Anglo-Iranian composer who regularly wrote music criticism for the likes of *The New Age* and *New English Weekly*.

painting in weekly parts showing why everybody since Cimabue[275] has been no good in the long run, except maybe Rubens.

Three or four weeks would do it.

Poetry ought to be made to print L.Z.'s commentary on his poem, at least if he could be persuaded to excise the three of four numbered refs, which dont apply.

Drummonds[276] postcard to hand, announcing that I aint totally excluded from his anthology. Dont know why. I am certain within myself none of those poems was a tithe as good as the Firdusi which isnt good enough.

I told you the island intellectuals fizzled out with a odour of milk-fed underring N.R.F. cum (faintly) Barcelona surrealisme?[277] One of them is advertised as along with Madariaga chief Spanish authority on English literature. But he aint read nuffin and couldnt, not knowing the language. Where he picked up the names, I dont know. Their faith is that by putting their heads deep enough into a poke and keeping them there they will ultimately attain all knowledge: hence none of them has ever been out of the archipelago.[278]

## To Ezra Pound

TS Yale

5 March 1935

c/o T.M. Reid, Bankers, Puerto de la Cruz,
Tenerife, Canarias, Spain

Dear Ezra

Everything Blunt wrote was a bore.[279] That doesnt prove anything. The Practical Horse Doctor 1835 wasnt.[280] Maybe that does. It wasnt littery work.

You surely got a bloody big bat in the belfry about economics. It seems to me just one of a good number of matters that are all pretty equally wrong. And its not a tithe as strong a moving force as, e.g. morals which also touch human life nearly everywhere instead of only in spots. Or even the left-overs of dead religions.

275 Cimabue (died *c.*1302), influential Florentine painter and mosaicist.

276 I.e., **John Drummond**

277 *N.R.F.*: *La Nouvelle Revue Française* (see 2/12/26 and note).

278 The letter ends at the bottom of the page with no signature, suggesting a missing remainder.

279 Wilfrid Scawen Blunt (1840–1922), English poet and polemicist, with whom Pound was notably acquainted in the 1910s, and who plays a central role in the peroration to Pound's Canto 81. Blunt spent much time travelling in the Middle East (mostly as an owner and breeder of horses), which is probably why Pound recommended him to BB in this exchange.

280 Not an actual publication. BB's point is that Blunt's writings are even less interesting than practical instruction manuals.

I dont speak as one who hasnt considered the matter. Even lectured on it one winter: tough job with a lot of workingmen who had all read pamphlets out of or based on Marx and werent taking anything for granted.[281] Twentyfour lectures on Currency. One hour lecture, one hour and a half answering questions. And I did what I could a long time ago to get a few of the orthodox to read Douglas and have a shot at answering him. But aint it all sort of leisure-time shove-hapenny to a feller like you who can and sometimes does write poetry which in due time and degree and by the usual process of dilutions and popularizations will ultimately affect most English speaking people a lot more fundamentally than any alteration in their financial status?

This NOW business is symptom of impatience. If you want immediate results, you ought to be in politics or its bastard, leader-writing: and the results will result, and they will be worth what Pope What's his name is worth beside Dante. Or rate your political success higher than you are likely to get starting late in life, as Can Grande beside Dante.[282] I'd have thought the Dante business would satisfy a chap, provided he could do without popular acclamations, as I'm certain you can.

Some such idea seems to be eating Louis, but he's got it mixed up with Marx. He says you make him shed tears because the five lines ending "What are you box? I am Hathor?" are perfect, wherease other bits of recently printed Cantos, specifically Mussolini and something I dont follow about Yeats getting his mystic balls wet talking about boys are not, so he says, up to scratch.[283] And he thinks he has the copyright of the Matthias Passion[284] and the game of polo (you were once saying the same about testicles). So he says he wishes you would take care of yourself and get me (by which he really means him) to see there aint no buttons loose and yr tie's straight before you make yr next public appearance. And "there is no need telling him I said so, but no objections if you can do it without hurting his feelings."

[281] See **19/2/26**.

[282] Cangrande della Scala (1291–1329), Italian nobleman and patron of Dante.

[283] The five lines in question are in the middle of Canto 39 (194), published in *Eleven New Cantos* (1934). Canto 41, the final work in *Eleven New Cantos,* contains a panegyric to Mussolini (202–203).

[284] This passage relates to Pound's deepening anti-Semitism and its effects on both Zukofsky and BB. Zukofsky's "A"-1 begins by describing a performance of Bach's oratorio the *St Matthew Passion* (1727) at Carnegie Hall in New York in 1928, while Pound's later poem Canto 35 also contains a more casual allusion to the Mattias Passion (172). In spite of the suggestion of plagiarism here, the real source of Zukofsky's displeasure was probably the anti-Semitic sentiments both in the reference and elsewhere in the Canto. In the thick of this dispute BB attempts to play intermediary. See Rachel Blau DuPlessis, *Purple Passages: Pound, Eliot, Zukofsky, Olson, Creeley, and the Ends of Patriarchal Poetry* (Iowa City: University of Iowa Press, 2012), 71–73.

So I take the responsibility for your feelings, but I cant back Louis up any further than that since I havent seen the new Canto in print. I remember I said I thought a lot of what I saw in type would have to be retrenched sooner or later, and you agreed, and I expect you did retrench as much as you at present see your way to, and it isnt my business anyway. I thought it was getting a bit lopsided. But that might only be because one hasnt the remaining fifty odd before one yet. Louis is much more easily upset than I am. But he also forgets his horror of change pretty quickly. The bloody Yid.

While I'm about it: he also says he's sending a new clean MSS of his poems via Serly, hoping you'll palm em off on the unsuspecting Faber. I trust you will. It wont lessen your credit any to recommend him as strongly as possible, and it really is time something other than Auden and Spender got printed besides the works of yr generation. Particularly in England. He aint asking for no preface, but has a fancy for a blurb on the jacket. I suppose "The greatest Jew since Jesus: signed, Ezra" Or "The psalms of David in 37th Street Verse". The opportunities are unlimited.

We have got a house again, furnished, for six months. This means that the miserable idleness of the last three quarters of a year is over at last and I can get back to work. House very fully furnished, nice garden, bit of land, equivalent of three hundred lire. About eight or nine rooms, plus bath etc. The agent seemed to think we would be impressed to hear the last occupant was an Excellence. It was a German admiral, the only fact about whom that I know for certain is that he wiped his arse on imitation parchment, which shows immense hardiness. Chainmail would be softer. THAT's a fact for the cantos, if you like. Can a man have a rhinoceros-skin bum-gut let into him?

Three weeks before we left the pension the chauffeur here was found in bed with the twelve-year-old housemaid. The other servants rigged up a mirror and then succeeded in taking a photograph of the rape in progress. Next day everything returned to normal, except that the chauffeur was strutting more than usual because everybody knew of his conquests. Our own twelve-year old, Bourtai's nurse, may or may not be a virgin. I wouldnt trust anybody but a surgeon to say.

I have been reading Kipling's Just So Stories to Bourtai and what do you think I found there? All the whole manner of Eliot's Sweeney Agonistes, set as prose, but perfectly recognisable, in a story called How the Kangaroo got his legs.[285] The correspondance is astonishingly close, if a coincidence. The rhythm exactly corresponds, the diction is very similar. Some phrases seem to be perfectly parallel with phrases in the Eliot. I imagine T.S.E. had read it in his childhood, received a

[285] In fact the story from *Just So Stories* (1902) is 'The Sing-Song of Old Man Kangaroo'.

powerful impression, and then forgotten it, and its thrown itself up. On the whole, the Kipling is the better of the two, as poetry. He calls it a sing song or some such word (the copy isnt handy here).

Marian is getting horribly bourgeois, having nobody but the foul English colony to talk to. I cant do anything about it. I dont talk to anybody at all, except very rarely to the two German painters and once a month or so to the aforesaid little nurse-girl. Who has a Luini face and nice legs.[286] And is the only (native) human being on the island. The rest are unbelievable.

German painter number two is going to portray me next.[287] I dont expect anything very startling.

Greetings to Dorothy and Mr and Mrs Homer Pound. Sorry the first half of this letter is so unwelcome. Wish I could step in to tea in-stead.

What a BORE the hull bloody creation is.

Yrs

B

After the quibble over Pound's allusion to Bach's *St Matthew Passion* in the previous letter, Bunting was increasingly caught in the crossfire of Pound's anti-Semitic remarks and Zukofsky's rather patient attempts to rebuff them. The following letter is mostly a defence of Zukofsky on aesthetic, political and religious grounds, in response to a letter of Pound's which hasn't survived, but which seems to have included attacks on Zukofsky (some of which Bunting quotes below).

## To Ezra Pound

TS Yale

[6 May 1935][288]

[Tenerife]

DEAR EZRA,

DO I INTRUDE?

Loooey has sent me a nicely bluepenciled copy of my Faridun, which may help me make it readable even to you.

[286] Bernardino Luini (c.1480/82–1532), Italian Renaissance painter known for his graceful female figures.

[287] I.e., Karl Drerup. The portrait is now in the Basil Bunting Poetry Archive, Durham.

[288] Address and date added in pencil, seemingly in BB's hand.

He has all-so sent in the way of corrisponunce a few extracts from Drummond[289] on 55, upon wh. I desyre to set my ugly oof.[290]

Drd thks it a drawback to publication Engl. that they are "so much outside the trend of modern Eng poetry". If he means the publishers will therefore buck, o.k. But were here to make the damn Ike's[291] buck, Fact, anything outside the current trend in Eng is outside a sure steady down-slide. Or has Drd converted you to Auden? YOU mainly responsible for keeping any life in poetry at all in this century are indicated as likely bloke to aid and superintend attempts to dam the current trend.

Drd opines "form for A dont fit content:" also that said content is elusive and incidental."[292]

I find the Bach bones hard to gnaw, but they dont make holes in the skin, nor elsewhere is there any very lamentable wrinkle in it.

Moreover "a dead poem." Do you agree? If so why urge Zuk on with it? But I find the opening very dead and the rest rapidly livening up and maintaining cawnsiderable interest in 1935.

T witch you choir in that "good poetry will pass a frontier", wh is surely giving Drummond a function no one or ten or fifty can perform. England includes me too. I got a fine bristling frontier out towards U.S.A. Well, 55 gets across to me.

And that Zuk has "wasted my time". But I dont think my time is any more wasted on trying to get 55 given a send off than on writing my own junk, which is surely not noticeably better or more likely to prove palatable in the back alleys off from St Pauls where the stinking publishers live. I daresay "Caveat Emptor" is likely to be a permanent endowment for the Postoffice at three pesetas a time,[293] but why shd I refrain from annoying the publisher's readers if I cant get any wider public? 55 similarly serves.

And that he "hasn't any intention of looking at anything his ma hadnt already told him", wh may for all I know or care be so, but what the hell has it to do with

[289] I.e., **John Drummond**.

[290] Though not published until 1941, Zukofsky's first collection *55 Poems*, which brought together most of his pre-1935 poetry, had been in preparation since the mid 1930s.

[291] *Ike*: a self-important person (US slang).

[292] In addition to *55 Poems*, this passage and the following refer to Zukofsky's "A" (see previous letter and note).

[293] In 1935 BB prepared the manuscript of a book called *Caveat Emptor*. It collected almost all of his poetic output up to this point (very much in the manner of Zukofsky's *55 Poems*) but was never published.

poetry, havent you written that Dante was diablement dans les idees recues?[294] And most of the less men deeper in 'em.

And the "symbol of Zuk's race the wailing wall an obstacle in front not diminished nor removed just there to be wailed at with consciousness of rectitude"?

Seems like a simile made to fit Eliot and that wouldnt be, apart from the racial interjection, out of place on him or even on the fortunately fictitious Mauberley. Zuk seems to do most of his moping in letters not in verses. Also he's a comyounest, wh may not be particularly intelligent, but there's more ways than one of trying to diminish an obstacle. Anyway, is it right for you to be so godalmighty gone on progress? We havent had the chance of observing very much of it. I dont believe in it at all, but if it exists, is it something a poet must take overt notice of? Doesnt he do all his own bit for progress (or the maintenance of the world) by purely linguistic exercises? Public spirit is abused when people try to do what isnt in or pretty close to their own specialty. Aint that Cawnfucian? You and I and Zuk have to keep the language alive, and damn difficult it is, as I am finding more and more, and we dont do any very appreciable good by turning aside to propagate the worthiest causes in economics or politics or patent medicines or quack religions or other subjects we've only a secondary interest in. I dont propose to limit a man's subject matter, but to limit the critics right to judge him on it. What's left of the wailing wall as an objection to Zuk? Progress is for Dutchmen, van Loon,[295] and the wailing waul has a prescriptive right to continue in its family.

I see from Louis' scratchings on the mss fairly closely what must be yr objections to my un-persian. Hope ultimately with my friends' patience to calibrate the bore so as to cause explosions at desired range.

Sent Caveat Emptor (my holy book) to Wishart and HoughtonMifflin.[296] No intention of bothering you with it, since I care less and have less to escape from by publication than Zuk. The book once nearly typed out, I am reasonably free of it. All the same if, when Wishart rejects it, you actually desire to thrust it on

[294] In an essay series on the Italian troubadour-poet Guido Cavalcanti (*c.*1255–1300) first published in 1928–1929, Pound compared his subject favourably to Dante: in Pound's view, Cavalcanti's ideas were radical for his day, while Dante was 'devilishly [stuck] in received ideas' ('diablement dans les idées reçues'). See *Literary Essays of Ezra Pound* (London: Faber and Faber, 1960), 149. BB's basic point here and indeed throughout this letter is that poetry does not have very much to do with political ideas.

[295] Hendrik Willem van Loon (1882–1944), Dutch-American writer famous for his children's book *Story of Mankind* (1921), a history of Western civilization.

[296] Whishart Ltd: London-based left-wing publisher. Houghton Mifflin: a much bigger publisher based in Boston, USA.

Mr Marlow[297] I wont be a stumbling block. If not you need hear no more of it until if ever printed you get a free copy gratis and with no obligation to read it.

It has a section deddykated to yew, as much as you warnt of it, if any. Called First Book of Odes. Forty of em.

Yrs faifully
H.W. Longfellow

P.S. What's Louis race anyway? Half them Rosham jews aint hebrews at all but bloody cossacks and proselytized on mass A.D. I forget the year. It was one of Genghis'successors told them they'd got to worship one god and be jews, Christians or mahometans, and they rationed the tribes out to each.

## To Ezra Pound

TS Yale

End of May [1935]

c/o T.M. Reid, Bankers, Puerto de la Cruz,
Tenerife, Canarias, Spain

Dear Ezra,

Sure. Happy to drop the subject of Zuk's alleged petrifaction if permitted here to observe that you seem still to have missed the practical point (the rest being more interesting but of no urgency to anyone except Zuk if he likes). The practical point is that Faber's (and others) publish annually a number of poems much deader than anything Zuk ever did; they've done, for instance, Macleod, born dead: Auden, who showed some signs, if not of life at least of having read something living, but promptly kicked the bucket: Spender, not dead merely, but putrid. If its argued that Auden and Spender sell, that cant be said, surely, for Macleod. Therefore, if Zuk wants to be published, why shd Fabers be spared the small loss?

Zuk is also hardly in a position to put much life into what he does just now, having all he can do to keep some life in his carcase. I agree the Apollinaire is hopeless, and the dictionary book worse,[298] but dont see they need be his latter end. However.

THE END

297 Probably Charles William Daniel (1871–1955), founder of radical publisher C. W. Daniel Books, and an advocate of C. H. Douglas's Social Credit theory. Under the joint pseudonym 'Mr Marlow', he and his associate W. T. Symons edited the literary quarterly *Purpose*.

298 Between 1932 and 1933 Zukofsky was working on 'Thanks to the Dictionary', a semi-fictional prose work based on the biblical story of David and composed with the aid of an aleatory method. It was eventually published in 1961 in the collection *It Was*.

What about these growing kids you mention? With some of them I thought it was their politics what seduced you. If any of them can write (1) English (2) a rhythm that's four or five feet long, instead of a jerky series of two feet or one foot, plunketty-plunk (3) a skilful image that doesnt look as though it had been sewn on afterwards with embroidery silk (4) an alliteration that doesnt kick the reader diablement dans les idees recues well, I'd be damn glad to see their work and profit by it. Maybe I've missed 'em by living here, but those I saw works by formerly werent any use, except maybe a young chap Williams proposed for the anthology with a sort of pseudo-Elizabethan fancy-work.

I wont believe in Rouse till I see it wiv my own eyes, for his Lucretius is bullshit.[299] Do you know Sam's prose Odessey?[300]

There's a chap called Philip Owen a few years older than me I once saw a couple of poems by,[301] sort of Swinburne subjected to Father Hopkins, but I supposed he was past mending.

They all seemed to me to be writing poetry for the commonest reason, viz, they couldnt write prose. I can, when I've anything worth saying that doesnt seem to be better in verse. So I didnt pay much attention to them.

Williams can write prose. You, ye-es, it would be good if you thought it worth while. Eliot writes Timesese like Aldington. Yeats does the Conrad-Ford purple stuff, but pretty well. I re-read some Ford not very long ago, and thought you were nuts about his prose. Zuk, I regret to say, shows a disposition to write the most awful unreadable stuff and never gets unambiguous except in verse. But that's ambition, not incompetence. Joyce and Stein have a lot to answer for.

Having read all the tecs in the library, I'm now nearly through Gibbon (third time) and more than ever wonder where people got that idea bout progress. Attila is the only respectable person in the book, and he's the least like our contemporaries. I am interested by the account of the quotations from a poet called Claudian (De Belle Getico, etc)[302] Do you know him? Is he any good?

There aren't any other historians except Herodotus, Machiavelli, and Livy. And Gibbon is better than the last two.

[299] See 4/1/35 and note.

[300] See 14/1/24.

[301] Possibly Philip Owens, English poet who featured in the 1930 anthology *European Caravan*, edited by Samuel Putnam.

[302] Claudian (*c.*370–404), Latin poet from Alexandria. In chapter 30 of *Decline and Fall*, Gibbon writes: 'Claudian does not either satisfy or silence our reason... He was endowed with the rare and precious talent of raising the meanest, of adoring the most barren, and of diversifying the most similar topics.' See *The History of the Decline and Fall of the Roman Empire*, Vol. II. ed. David Womersley (London: Allen Lane, 1994), 163.

A chap called Sergius translated the pehlevi histories into greek circ. 500 a.d.[303] Don't think its extant, but if you happen to visit one of the great libraries, please look in the index and see if he's mentioned. He might have a big bearing on Firdusi, the Pehlevi and Arabic versions having disappeared. I take it ALL greek books are translated into English or French?

Work goes very slowly for domestic reasons. Houghton Mifflin printedly acknowledge receipt of "Caveat Emptor", Wishart doesnt waste a stamp on superfluous courtesies. Looking into it, I'm very dissatisfied with the book, standard much too low. But I need a little public encouragement if I'm to get on any faster, also to convince my wife and friends I aint entirely up the pole. Therefore I'll send it out again when it comes home. There seems to me to be also SOME good stuff in it.

Best wishes to you and yours. How much do Fabers (or whoever it is) charge for the new lot of cantos?[304] I shall have finished Gibbon soon, and there aint nothing else to be had from this library. They even have Creighton instead of Ranke for the Papacy.[305]

B

P.S. Satisfy my curiosity by stating, please, whether you think G. Oppen, for whom you wrote an introduction, more alive than L. Zukofsky?[306] It puzzles me.

## To Ezra Pound

TS Yale

11 December 1935 Casa Fortuna, Puerto de la Cruz, Tenerife, Canarias, Spain

Dear Ezra,

Zuk isnt rotting, as far as my contact with him goes. He's hellish busy, semi-editing the poetry for New Masses, conferring with Communist big bugs on what sort of poetry Communists ought to publish, and writing A 8 apparently rapidly, all at the same time as his relief-job, which, judging less by his complaints than by American newspapers quoted in "Lu", must be one hell of a daily ordeal.[307]

303 For 'Sergius' see *Decline and Fall*, 706. Persian works of the first millennium were written in Pahlavi or Middle Persian.

304 I.e., *Eleven New Cantos* (1934).

305 Mandell Creighton's (1843–1901) multi-volume *History of the Papacy During the Period of the Reformation* (1882–1894) would have seemed older and stuffier to Pound and BB than the slightly newer, more reputable *History of the Popes* (1901) by Leopold von Ranke (1795–1886).

306 Pound wrote a short preface to Oppen's first collection *Discrete Series* (1934).

307 Zukofsky was a regular contributor to the American Marxist journal *New Masses* (1926–1948) in this period, though never in any formal advisory sense. He began working

Unless you call it rotting to go Communist. That's a point of view. He seems to think it is a form of rotting, though he doesnt use words to that degree of disrespect for his elders, to go Douglas. It seems to this isolated islander that to spend a great deal of time on these bloody details of politico-economic organisation shows either a misunderstanding, or a weakness of faith in, the essential function of poetry. Let them who can give the pore buggers words, and sooner or later they will use them to think with. In short, an E.P., though not particularly topical news at any time, is more important in the long run than a Douglas, and so one's sorry, in a degree, to see Messrs Pound and Zukofsky submitting themselves to what is much more transient than what they have done and ought to be doing. Especially since it required a good deal of specialised thinking which, since neither of em have any specialised training for it, takes up more time than it ought and stays in the mind longer than it ought, thus colouring things really irrelevant.

Forgive sermon. But my impression is that the political virus, though very visibly at work in Zuk, has affected him rather less than it has you. So I get a bit vexed.

Laughlin got my address from Zuk some time ago, but didnt write: and I've very little he could print, I think. Angold,[308] who doesnt know me nor I him, is another affair, and I'll send what I have, if he's going to print poetry, if you'll let me know where to send it.

I finished a long poem, not very satisfactory, but with bits in it. But dont want to bore you with it until its been revised with the aid of whatever remarks Zuk may make on it. Its longer than Chomei, and I should think, three times less likely to get sold. On "The Well of Lycopolis, cujus potu signa virginitatis eripiuntur."[309] Some lines on the Senussi war may make it unwelcome in your present whereabouts.[310] I like the Senussi's, much better than any other contemporary Moslems.

What was yr tremendous job in Rome? More interviews with the Duce?

No copy of Drummond-Wilson anthology ever came my way, so I deduce my exclusion from the too-many too-bad authors.[311]

for Roosevelt's Works Progress Administration in 1935. *Lu*: *Lu dans la Presse Universelle*, French current affairs journal (1931–1937).

308 I.e., **John Penrose Angold.**

309 BB derived the title and Latin epigraph ('by whose potion the seal of virginity is broken') for 'The Well of Lycopolis' from Gibbon's *Decline and Fall of the Roman Empire* (see Share 297–298).

310 Draft versions of 'The Well of Lycopolis' contained references to the suppression of the Senussis, a Muslim tribe who resisted Italian attempts to conquer Libya in a series of conflicts from the 1910s to the early 1930s (see Share 252).

311 I.e., the *Bozart–Westminster* special issue (see **18/7/34** and note).

Best way to get kept up to date is, lacking converse, to see the papers. But here, daily the local "Prensa",[312] births, deaths and marriages and the Spanish political scandals. Once a month or so, a back number of "Ahora" or "ABC" with a few international snippets. More rarely "Lu" and "Vu", or a copy of the Paris Daily Mail. Two or three times a year a batch of English papers several months old – If you've anything livelier not wanted for Carnevalli, you'd do a serious charity posting them here. I dont mean the Corriere, but something alive, written by people who have heads. Our local Boches[313] sometimes produce a Corriere or Stampa or Italia Letteraria. Or the Frankfurter Zeitung, Hot-dog Daily. And I find the Völkishe Beobachter abandoned in cafes.

BUT and however it seems possible we may move in the early spring and occupy Taupin's liddle 'ouse at Nyack-on-Hudson, which would bring me within reach of occasional intelligences. Anyway, I'm sick to death of this valley with its perpetual clouds and its climate which suits consumptives and heart cases but makes normal people neurotic.

We got a ride round the island last week. That was good. West view of the Teide magnificent, better than prints of Fujiyama, a bit like drawings I've seen of Kluchi, in Kamchatka,[314] more like a spire than a mountain, perfectly conical, white head, only in this case ash instead of snow. The villages in the desert dirty but picturesque. We stayed the night seven thousand feet up amongst huge pine trees that have escaped Spanish rapacity by mere accident. Found an American woman keeping a minute hotel there. The second day it rained, first time in over twelve months in the southern desert: we were sure to choose the one bad day in the year.

We've also had a fine show of waterspout since I last wrote, just as shown in sailors books I used to think were lies, most impressive but wont inflict on you what you've probably read in half a dozen "Voyages". And some more mirages.

I've calculated the rape-rate at one woman in six on Tenerife. Have no data for the seduction rate, but imagine four of the remaining five would barely cover it. An outbreak of Shamanism in the next village might also be chronicled, since the reports of it made it quite clear that all the newspaper men believe in black magic.

Oh yus! I sent a poem to New Masses on Louis' solicitation, but expect it back. All the best to you and yrs.

B

[312] *La Prensa*: Canary Islands daily newspaper founded in 1910. The other titles in this passage are all Spanish, French, Italian, and German newspapers and current affairs magazines of the period.

[313] Boches: a somewhat derogatory British term for German people.

[314] Kluchi/Klyuchi: mountainious area on the Kamchatka Peninsula in north-east Russia.

## To Ezra Pound

TS Yale

Last of 1935 Casa Fortuna, Puerto de la Cruz, Tenerife, Canarias, Spain

Dear Ez,

I agree with that you say about the communists[315] – more or less: and with what others say about the various credit-manipulators, Douglas or not. If you are really thinking out something, first class! Good luck to you and it! But I cant be expected to know that, seeing the only mentions you make of such things are too explosive to convey any meaning at all.

But if you still think that there is enough for everybody, provided it's better distributed, then I maintain that you also are suffering from lack of information, without the excuse of living on a semi-desert island. The figures of the population of India and China are available, somewhere or other. And if you imply, as I dont think you ever soberly did, but Douglas's friends continually have done, that a better distribution, even if it was also a sufficient distribution, for the world's products, would suffice without other very different measures to make the world fairly bearable for civilized people – well, well.

I happen to believe the economic question doesnt take precedence of several others. In that I differ from you and Louis in exactly the same way and to exactly the same extent. You both seem to think what people want and cant get can be expressed in terms of money. That is too single-minded and reminds one of Byrd's setting of the apostle's creed: "I believe in ONE god":[316] I dont. If you had all been as interested during the boom as you were in the first and now in the second depression, I'd still not be convinced that the thinking had gone very deep.

But I am not anxious to counter-argue about economics. I remember your showing me a piece of Wisconsin token-money issued by a lumber company last century, and speaking of it as an ingenious means of meeting a shortage of cash. So it might be. But it would first have occurred to me to see in it a revival of a very old and scandalous method of fleecing the workman, still used in U.S. in some parts, though its been very properly suppressed by law in every other civilised

[315] BB is responding to an undated letter of Pound's which has survived in carbon copy (Yale). In somewhat incoherent prose typical of the period, Pound suggests that Zukofsky's communism—and indeed communism in general—should have evolved beyond its 1918 incarnation and adapted itself to developing economic realities. He also calls BB a 'really BLOODY fool' and defends the link between poetry and ideas BB rejected in 11/12/35, arguing that poets should repeatedly define and analyse until their words are in accordance with 'justice'.

[316] The 'Creed' in Byrd's *Great Service* (see note to 21/3/34) opens with the phrase BB quotes.

country – "truck".[317] Where the initial viewpoint is so different there isnt much hope of useful discussion, so I made no comment then, and only remind you of it now to excuse my lack of interest. Perhaps id better add, though I remember telling you at the time, that a few months before I left Italy I wrote to Douglas, asking three very simple and plain questions. His friend or secretary, Bardsley,[318] answered for him: declined to attempt the last question, shied off the second onto a side-track and misinterpreted the first in way that didnt seen to me wholly due to initial dumbness. After which I concluded Douglas wouldnt bear more investigation on theoretical lines.

BUT I havent concluded that you are therefore dead and done for, even as an economist. And if I think communism looks like daguerreotypes of my grandmother's aunts, it doesnt follow, in my mind, that someone who fancies it is therefore in full decay. A man can even turn Christian and still produce decent poetry. It is a pity if he insists on filling up his poems with Christianity, Communism or Douglasism, but one's reasons for, for instance, not getting terribly enthusiastic over Yeats have nothing to do with Irish political impossibility.

"Poetry" say you "is not the maintenance of ignorance", but it isnt the day-to-day, or year-to-year tug of politics either. Its clear enough that you've been too occupied with other dissociations to make a few that are needed thereabouts. "The poet's job is to define", but what the hell has justice got to do with it? Unless you want to string everything tight together, like a Hegel or a Tommy Aquinas, with a neat knot where the One True God should be? You used to call yourself a polytheist, but I doubt if you've ever considered the implications of polytheism in action. More dissociation.

I asked Zuk how he thought communism agreed with practical possibilities in U.S.A., but he aint answered. I have now, since you ask the parallel, to turn it on you: How can U.S.A. be brought to comparative efficiency on your lines, (not in the abstract, if everybody agreed with you; but now, with the men there are and the notions people entertain?) ARE you any nearer than Zuk to GETTING ANYTHING DONE? Limiting cotton production doesnt help.

But it makes me irritable trying to answer a letter that doesnt say anything. Calling me a bloody fool does me no good unless you attempt to show WHY. Nor does generalised denunciation of Zuk dispose of the pages of A 8 which he sent me the other day: one quarter dull scaffolding, one quarter not very enthralling Marx, and

[317] Truck wages: an alternative form of payment (goods, credit, money substitutes) used in lieu of legal tender. Truck systems were widely used in Britain in the early years of industrialization; as BB describes, they were banned because they were often used to exploit workers.

[318] W. L. Bardsley, Douglas's secretary and a proponent of Social Credit doctrine in several journal articles of the period.

the rest an excellent noise, for another orchestra than yours: not a standstill, not a revolution, and fortunately not dependant on the Matthew Passion or Das Kapital.

I've indicated as afar as is allowed me, from time to time, what seemed to me the next step that should AND COULD be taken. More than that is Calvinism. At present the next step is peopling the empty continents from the full ones, not with men who want to make a fortune in a hurry, but with those who are content to live on what they and their neighbours can grow. Since I dont accompany this dictum with an argument that would have to begin with a complete refutation of whatever may be the exact present form of your own convictions, you will probably dismiss it at once as bloody foolishness. But it's not, and you ultimately cramp yourself by dismissing things inconsiderately.

You turn the blind eye to a good many things, Ezra. Zuk must willy-nilly see certain matters, from certain, not prescribable, aspects. He isnt tied to agree with anyone, nor even to be right, on any particular point. In the things which most interest us, in the long run, he does on the whole agree with both of us. Too much bloody zeal, blast it. Leaves people too busy to think and too intent to see anything outside the microscope.

Hasnt it occurred to you that if it doesnt pay to send Canadian wheat to England, it might pay to send the people who want to eat the wheat to Canada? Alright, I'm not insisting. Say Balls if you like. But IS that as difficult a feat as changing the basis of credit? Is it simpler to make over the Dakotas to mixed farming that people can live on, or to tax the wheat farmer out of his profits in order to relieve a useless crowd in the towns? – one might ask socialists. And that is simpler, because it has some public opinion behind it, than a distribution of dollar bills out of the printing shop, secured on the probability of further improvements in production. I want to show only that there are tenable viewpoints from which you appear to be just as fast asleep as Zuk.

Heinemann's[319] appear to be considering my mss seriously, but not very hopefully.

Thanks for Angold and Wilson's addresses.

Partial analysis of Firdusi's vocabulary begins to show some results, sumupable so far as "beware of the abstract noun".

Prosperous New Year, you, Dorothy, and your parents!

Yrs

B

[319] London-based publisher founded in 1890.

## To Ezra Pound

TS Yale

22 January 1936 Casa Fortuna, Puerto de la Cruz, Tenerife, Canarias, Spain

Dear Ezra,

Waaaal! Fine, I understand that letter, most of it: so anything distrait here must be attributed to the Simoom[320] (they dont call it that but it's a wind of the same nature – thousands of miles of desert, a few hundred of sea, and then at you) which has just given us two days of fury not seen here for a generations, they say. The houses arent built for it, and I had a worrisome night, especially after the neighbours roof rose up and flapped away like a seagull. One of our cedars came down – all I could hear above the gale was a noise like tearing calico – and every tree in the garden lost some of its bigger branches, so that the litter is inconceivable. A huge eucalyptus three yards from our front gallery, and another cedar that leans over the roof and kept banging on it, as though there were half a dozen heavy men fighting in an upper story, were the chief trouble. If either of them had gone, our roof would have gone too, and all the titles dropped on to us. The wind was hot. We were in the lee of twelve thousand feet of mountain. What it must have been like on the other side I cant easily imagine, there were pretty big things floating about in the atmosphere on our side.

The road being covered with fallen trees we are without news from beyond the valley. All wires down, of course. I spoke to the one small cultivator, who had lost above twenty-thousand pesetas in fallen banana-trees, and the manager of one of the big firms told me, after the first five hours of the gale, they had lost every single one of their apple-banana trees (a finer variety) already. Nobody insured – this is Spain. The general mess well increased.

In addition to which there is a general strike in Santa Cruz. Some pistoleros shot three policemen. The Gobernador Civil then came out with the maddest order I ever read[321] – the details dont matter, but it came to this, the soldiers and police were to shoot anybody who didnt instantly do exactly what they told them – this is an island where the police are notoriously the chief brigands. Within twelve hours they shot a taxi-driver dead, and wounded his passengers, three of them, without even calling on them to halt, merely, it seems, for the fun of the thing. So we have a general strike. This is quite the usual type of Gobernador Civil: I am told they are much better now than in the times of the dictatorship. They must have been a pretty foul lot.

320 *Simoom*: a hot, dry, dust-laden wind prevalent in North Africa and the Middle East.
321 *Gobernador Civil*: civil governor (Sp.).

So there are no papers and no mail. Reinforcing the regular fact that a man might have a very large national dividend indeed and still be entirely unable to keep track of anything from this island. I cant get free papers, cant get anything sent, not even Time and Tide[322] more than once in six months. All one can buy is the local births, deaths and marriages, plus a letter from a Madrid correspondent who is the most inaccurate, and the least concerned by his inaccuracy, of any journalist I ever read, and whose only source of information is the French armament press, particularly Le Petit Parisien.[323] Louis is the only person who ever tells me anything in his letters, and consequently the only person besides you I still correspond with. The only way to better my information is to quit Tenerife, and this I propose to do as soon as we can raise the fare. We have taken Taupin's house at Nyack on Hudson. New York will destroy me with noise and very likely starve me, but a word now and then with somebody who has something in his head will do me good.

Angold replied to my letter with a Petition, which I'm not going to sign, because I dont like prerogatives, survived or revived or what, and still less the habit of shoving political responsibilities onto the judges – only a legal mind could imagine the responsibility was a legal one. I am sorry he's too full of examinations to be interested in poetry. He is clearly too decent to snub me, but the effect is similar. I've given him my reasons for not signing up, but doubt if he'll maintain the correspondance. The bloody political narrowness of this age isnt less than the religious ditto two centuries ago, and makes me sick. The poor arent so bad, but the intellecthools, to say nothing of the middle-class and so forth, seem anxious to heave overboard the few small gains they've picked up out of Thirty Years Wars, Commonwealths, and N.Bonapartes. This applies to you and Zuk in a certain degree.

And if you reckon up what people want and are sometimes impeded by others from getting, it includes the freedom not to say "Heil Hitler" or "There is no God but God",[324] or, prospectively, not to acquiesce in particular schemes of economic reform: and take it all round, that's worth more than regular meals (if you dont take my word for it, have another look at the history books, any period). I prefer warders to drill sergeants: couldnt buy the choices in some countries. As for "more liberty under the" Tsar, Soviets, Fascists, or any other exclusive will its been claimed for, nobody who cared a damn about liberty (including economic)

[322] See 21/3/34 and note.

[323] French newspaper in circulation between 1876 and 1944.

[324] The Islamic creed Shahada begins: 'There is no god but God.'

will fall into the illusion. It particularly isnt a function of cash. Why do you ask me to dissociate, if you dont make such simple dissociations yourself? Or rather, if you dont remember them when you begin to get away from their simple terms?

Its not much use my arguing particular points, Loeb charts etc, so long as I'm not within reach of figures.[325] You'll only think I'm ignorant. But on the other hand I'm not going to take on trust assertions of unknown Mr Loeb's which go clean contrary to geographic commonplace until I too, have seen a few convincing figures. I think these fellows, when they're not wholly concerned with manufactures, which are, in the end, a mere bump on globe of production, mix up what saves labour with what produces more: motor plows, for instance, produce less than men and horses, not more. The new cotton picker saves ninety per cent of the wages bill, but doesnt increase the crop one ounce. When we were looking at technocrat trips a few years ago, I found them reckoning the coal-cutter as though it could be used in every pit, instead of in about one twentieth of the mines that exist. Nor is it the slightest use, so far as I can see, to reckon up for one country apart from others, as long as it isnt wholly self-supporting. U.S. cant grow rubber or coffee. Dont know about the British Empire, but doubt if there's any other organisation that can stand three minutes examination from the point of view of men who want it to be self-supporting, however desirable the economic systems that might be applicable if it were. So India and China get let in anyway. Well, if you've written the answers elsewhere, stick a P.S. on your next communiqué to the editor, and I expect he'll send me a copy, that he wouldnt send it I asked for it myself.

Emigration can wait. If I find everybody still in civilized parts as mad as I expect to, I'll be forced to deal with it if I can find a publisher. But I dont want to, its a job for people who cant do something better.

Because if literature dies pretty soon of lack of content (to which proposition or similar I was born adhering) it still isnt for us, you and me, to say WHAT content. The reason it dies, is that the content doesnt interest the chap who's writing it. Lucretius doesnt die of being exploded, nor La Fontaine of being trivial.[326] And if you say I ought to be adding to the discussion of money in my work, I am bound to answer rudely: "Balls! There are other things which seem to me a good deal more important and interesting. Anything I add except the skepticism that

[325] *The Chart of Plenty: A Study of America's Product Capacity Based on the Findings of the National Survey of Potential Product Capacity* (1935) was written by Harold Loeb (1891–1974), an American writer and editor apparently sympathetic to Social Credit.

[326] Jean de La Fontaine (1621–1695), French poet whose anthology of verse *Fables* is a classic of children's literature.

everybody else seems to forget, is bound to be merely academic. I find the curtailment of freedom of speech by means of the law of seditions, blasphemous and indecent libel much more vital: much more like a mortal attack on mankind than the current sabotage is. And I find those who oppose the foolish sabotage at least as inclined as the rest to suppress whatever proposition they dont agree with, in their field."

You doubt if economics was interesting thirty years ago. I wasnt there, but believe they were then busy elaborating Quantity theory and its derivatives,[327] without which you wouldnt have had any of the current discussions. Naturally, mathematical looking tables as repulsive as symbolic logic to the eye dont attract a large public. They dont lend themselves to sensational headlines or simple slogans. They are pretty interesting though. And I'd have thought you'd have looked them up and known, since they certainly bear on your contentions. Of course a good deal of it has been superseded. Still, the velocity business – there was an Austrian whose name I forget[328] did the most of the mathematics, but there's a popular account in Fisher. The crisis that ended in Wilson and the Federal Reserve Board seems to have made the public aware of money for the first time since the eighteen thirties,[329] when there was a good deal of lively discussion both in England and, as you've got in the Cantos, the States.

Sure, if my views coincided with those of a sufficient number of people I'd have an audience. Meanwhile Louis handed over to the American Communists a note on how a working-class paper ought to be organised, which wont do them any good because they arent really communists but just chaps who want to get into journalism and politics by a back door. Your political friends seem to prefer propaganding the intellectuals which at once saves me from having to advise them on the same problem and makes me a bit suspicious of their ultimate motives. I always found workingmen reasonably quick to understand anything

[327] Quantity Theory, which at its simplest states that money supply and price level rise and fall in proportion to one another, was at the heart of mainstream macroeconomics in the early twentieth century. Largely repudiated by Keynesian and other tendencies which emerged in response to the Depression (though revived by neoliberals in the later twentieth century), it relied on mathematical equations such as those formulated by American economist Irving Fisher (1867–1947).

[328] Probably Ludwig von Mises (1881–1973), Austrian economist and key figure in the development of Quantity Theory.

[329] The Federal Reserve System, which presides over the central banking system of the United States, was founded in 1913 by President Woodrow Wilson. Largely a response to the Panic of 1907, a financial crisis which saw bankruptcies throughout the country and subsequent calls for reform of the banking system, the foundation of the Fed was repeatedly excoriated by Pound, who laments the 'dung flow from 1913' in Canto 91 (634).

that was to their benefit if you kept clear of latin words and didnt assume knowledge they havent got. I dont suspect you, of course, but I think some of the Prosperity people are more anxious to avoid a revolution than to bring about heaven-on-earth.

One question I'll bother you with: why this? Here are bananas, tomatoes and potatoes they cant sell to England because of the duties. The English growers chuck them into the sea or use them for manure. The Spanish growers, out of mere indifference, give them to the out-of-work peasants, who eat what they can, feed what they can to the pigs, and lead the rest on their heads to tote them off to another district where they swap bananas for potatoes, and so forth. Why do the English take all that trouble to prevent anybody else using what they cant use themselves? There's no money in it: but its one of the cruxes of the whole situation, not in the Canaries only. No amount of reflection on prices and marginal returns will get you any nearer, as far as I can see. It applies as well to Canadian wheat, Brazilian coffee, and half the rest of the sabotage. The ECONOMIC reasons are secondary. Or maybe dont exist, as reasons.

No, I'm not merely cussed. And if I still dont know about anything that happened at Atlanta since the Civil War, I dont see that the day to day details are large enough to make the difference between knowledge and ignorance. I know geography, and don't know anybody else who does – the late Sir Halford Mackinder did.[330] I had enough sense to know in 1919 that money was the part of economics best worth attending to, I found out what I could about it, got Foxwell to discuss Douglas as well as his then aging brain could, got Orage and Douglas to debate with the most exalted I could catch of the orthodox – one of em's been under-secretary for Foreign Affairs since then.[331] I didnt stick my oar in, having nothing particular to add. I dont think I've missed anything transcendant since then. Douglas brought a few things together, and has since clarified his utterance a little, but I know of no real news since his proposition about accountancy, which seems to be neither provable nor disprovable, and I suspect it will be shown in the end to be verbal – a discussion without factual basis – like the theory-of-value controversies before it. What the rest of you, of all shades, have added has been

[330] Halford Mackinder (1861–1947), British geographer, academic, and politician, who was among the founders of the London School of Economics between 1903 and 1908.

[331] Between 1919 and 1923, BB was a (mostly sporadic) student at the London School of Economics. Herbert Foxwell (1849–1936) was a lecturer at LSE, as was Hugh Dalton (1887–1962), who would later become Under-Secretary of State for Foreign Affairs in the Labour government of 1929–1931, and Chancellor of the Exchequer 1945–1947. In the absence of evidence to the contrary, we have to take BB's word for it that he arranged debates between Orage, Douglas, and Dalton, but his account is possibly exaggerated.

emphasis here, oil there, a cause of friction removed, a further proof of something I, like you, took for proved sixteen years ago, or, I regret to say, a welcome to doubtful evidence, such as the technocratic stuff, which on the whole serves, as I see it, to discredit the party that adopts it. Unterguggenberger[332] or heimer[333] is nothing new. Even Angold's petition is only a variant on what's been done before. Why should I be reproached for not showing excitement? Particularly since I was on the job, in my own fashion, during the boom years when the rest of you seemed to have forgotten there was any economics or monetary anomaly at all: ask Brenton, whom I tried to buy out of his paper,[334] or Biddulph[335] – who, however, on being shown his error in one particular, thereupon changed sides completely instead of merely modifying. Or Prof. Robbins, who was very annoyed by my conversation on his Wages pamphlet.[336] But he was less annoyed by criticism he thought pigheaded than you are.

Bugger intolerance, Ez, even when its you! I think I've guns enough to decommunize Zuk when I get near him, but if he becomes Head Particular Lenin to U.S. I dont see any reason for shelving him. I dont think I could make an agrarian of you, but it doesnt worry me. There are quite a number of policies that can be carried out without irreparably injuring mankind, and some of them might do some good. I've no wish to monopolize.

As for a nurse, I think I'd need a straitwaistcoat to keep me acquiescing in all enthusiasms, especially when you dont tell me what they're about!

As for a shit, whom have I ever compelled to listen or read or answer? I havent informed you that a mutual friend is as good as buried because his politics seem senseless to me. If I took such information from you without protest, that's when I'd be a shit. But I wont.

I am sorry to inflict long letters on you, but it seems I must. I'm perfectly ready to sit down under a good deal of abuse from a man who has done as much for me as you have. I'm even glad of useful abuse, or abuse that clearly intends to

[332] Michael Unterguggenberger (1884–1936), Austrian politician and mayor of Wörgl (Tyrol) 1931–1934. During the Depression Unterguggenberger issued a local currency in Wörgl and introduced an emergency aid programme, thereby decreasing unemployment by 25% in 1933.

[333] Perhaps Hugo Sinzheimer (1875–1945), German legal scholar and author of the Weimar Constitution.

[334] Arthur Brenton, British economic theorist and editor of the *New Age* 1923–1938.

[335] Geoffrey Biddulph (b. *c.*1895), British economist who contributed to Eliot's *Criterion* in the early 1930s.

[336] Probably Lionel Robbins's 1926 pamphlet *Wages: An Introductory Analysis of the Wage System under Modern Capitalism.*

be useful. However! – It is also probably to your interest, though I wouldnt dogmatize on that, to protest sooner or later.

A chap who writes the letters you've been writing lately obviously isnt at his best, no doubt overworked, etc. The remedy is to work less. I havent seen what you have written since I came to this island, but find it hard to think its as good as what you would have written if you'd done half as much. And if you'd done half as much you wouldnt have been so inclined to snap your friends heads off.

Anyway, the net boiling triple distilled is, that I desire to continue profiting by you, but dont get any profit out of mixed abuse and political intolerance. A bad bargain for you? I dont give anything in exchange? That's your affair. If I'm not worth better than what I've got lately I'd rather be dropped. I would lose a good deal, no doubt of it. I've enough confidence in my own abilities to think you'd lose something too.

Glad to hear of new Fenellosa.[337]

Good luck to you and all.

B

## To Ezra Pound

TS Yale

28 March 1936 Casa Fortuna, Puerto de la Cruz, Tenerife, Canarias, Spain

Dear Ezra,

Much thanks suggestion re first lines of Lycopolis, wh. seems likely to be very useful. Don't know how you do it (find the key to weakness). Said excision suggests many emendments.

'Erbert Read[338] writes Heinemann, who's stuck to my CAVEAT EMPTOR for three months, has only been wasting my ti-i-ime and "you might try Stanley Nott, and in that case it would be best to approach him through Pound – though I would support him. Meanwhile I will keep the MS until I hear from you."

Dont suppose he intends that he will support Stanley Nott, whoever that is, but Caveat Emptor if introduced by you. Anyway, I'm going to presume on yr good nature: so's not to waste weeks, I'm going to write Read next post, that is, in three days time, saying E.P. will send a postcard to Nott recommending him to

[337] In 1936 Pound prepared and published a new version of Fenollosa's 'The Chinese Written Character as a Medium for Poetry' for London-based publisher Stanley Nott.

[338] Herbert Read (1893–1968), British poet, art historian, literary critic, and philosopher.

'ave a good look at said great work. Notts address aint supplied. Read's if necessary, is 3 the Maill, Parkhill Rd, London N.W.3.

(In case you dont know Caveat Emptor is my wolume of pomeses: of which you have seen nearly all. Carefully arranged, they do make a book, I think. It has a short pipendicks instead of a preface, in the course of wh. yr useful instruction is recognised, along with that of Swift, Malherbe, Fenellosa and Louis Zuk. Nearly everything in the vilume has been printed somewhere.)

Since Erb readly seems to like the poems, please oblige.

yrs presumptuously
B

P.S. Did Eliot a bad review of a bad book. The Spanish postoffice sent it back here again, suspecting it of being banknotes. Now its gone for the second time, and much good may it do the Criterion. Did you egg him, or did he remember me in his cups or what?

Emigration as ad to be postponed for this season. If the summer's like last I'll have no more life by October than an addled egg.

## To Ezra Pound

TS Yale

3 September 1936 — 6 South Hill Mansions, South Hill Park, N.W.3. [London]

Dear Ez

(And with thanks for p-c[339] with address wh. may poss. become useful, though rather remoter than I can instantly cope with)

IS it criminal to tell you that Hargrave[340] – yes, I've made sure it's the same Hargrave – is the same Fool, footling Fool, he always was, and that far from my enquiring whether such an abject creature could have any use for ME, I'm damned if I'd let anybody so incompetent empty my dustbin. Geoffrey Biddulph the noted halfwit is an altogether saner and healthier person, and if your activities have really led you to Hargrave, I'm convinced there is something fundamentally wrong with your activities.

[339] I.e., postcard.

[340] John Hargrave (1894–1982), British leader of the Kindred of the Kibbo Kift, a youth group established in 1920 which campaigned for world peace. In 1931–1932 Hargrave founded the Green Shirt Movement for Social Credit, a Douglasite tendency which evolved into the Social Credit Party of Great Britain and Northern Ireland in 1935.

Angold accuses you of connections with British Union of Fascists: which I refuse to believe.[341] I had the pleasure of longish intercourse with them eleven years ago, before they had given up trying to include any of the comparative decencies of Fascism (the efficiency, the only thing worth imitation in this country, they never had any idea of). I am not a Left sucker, I dont go mad at the idea of blasphemy against democracy, dont think I'm talking blindly. But they spell Finance with three letters, J E W, and that's all you'll get out of them. And they dont stop at anti-semitism: their services in thus distracting public attention from public matters are recompensed by the police with a degree of freedom from interference which looks to a reasonably observant eye, and not only two eyes, like collusion with pick-pockets. You are too valuable a pearl to go and cast yourself before swine of that sort, and I think, too acute to imagine that an identity of name necessarily indicates any further correspondance whatever with Italian Fascism. If that lot takes up Social Credit, it will complete the discredit which is patently threatening the whole movement.

Yes, Angold incautiously invented this Petition,[342] which was a good publicity device, and the whole bleedin gentry have come in, or as many of them as can see three inches beyond their nose, and clearly propose to use S.C. to defeat nearly everything you and I care about. If only they can stave off the day of reckoning when their more nauseous privileges will be cut off, if only they can prop up Institutional Christianity, Institutional Landowning, and above all keep the upper hand of the people they've had since the Conquest, well, Social Credit is an alternative to tottering present system, wh., having never had any leader of much authority outside crabbed technique, can be grabbed. It looks to me as though you were in danger of finding yourself on the wrong side all round.

That wont prevent me working for Mairet if he can guarantee the quid a week without which I cant possibly afford the time.[343] It is an open paper, as far as I can see, certainly less closed than any other. But I will try to insinuate here and there that the workingman might have some look in other than what amounts to a larger dole: including the man who works at writing poetry, and even though the life said workingman wants is incompatible with nearly every law in the country

[341] Angold was in fact correct about Pound's links to Oswald Mosley's British Union of Fascists (BUF): Pound wrote articles on economics for every issue of the BUF house journal *British Union Quarterly* between January 1937 and April 1939.

[342] See 22/1/36.

[343] Philip Mairet (1886–1975), British designer and translator who assumed the editorship of the *New English Weekly* on A. R. Orage's death in 1934. BB's hostile review of Malcolm Muggeridge's *An Earnest Atheist: A Study of Samuel Butler* was published in *NEW* in October 1936.

and certainly with all those Lord Tankerville and Lady whatshername want to bolster.[344] I'd rather have a revolution, blood and skulls, but since Stalin has reduced himself to a larger Hitler and pretty good imitation of someone else, I doubt whether I could work with communists except for exceedingly strictly limited objects: and there's no other revolutionary party in sight.

Angold's visit was an eyeopener. He is without any judgment, literary or political, though a good chap and a readable writer, and I've got to put it down to Oxford. I've never seen a clearer case of intelligence inhibited and carefully directed into channels useful or at any rate harmless to his class. Not even MacLeod. Have no longer any doubt a degree is merely a certificate that bearer can be trusted not to let down the other gentlemen and ladies. If this brings me thirty years late to an early perception of Old H.G. Wells I cant help it. One up for Wells.

I see no sense in ditching the Yids, together with the Welsh, French, Dutch and ad inf. financiers, in favour of Church and State. In fact, I prefer Mr Morgan[345] to the late Duke of Northumberland, just as I prefer Stalin to the Tsar, Mussolini to nameless anarchy, and nameless anarchy to Alphonso.[346] I've no doubt you, if you would clear up some of the misapprehensions* (*nature of particular organisations, persons, re-actions etc. I'm not speakin' of theories) I think you've fallen into, could do a lot towards pulling the Social Credit movement together. Though its made harder because you are suspect to the brethren, or else I very much misread the signs, because of your pro-Italian propaganda. I expect you know, what I suspected but couldnt confirm till I got here, how high the feeling for war was running here, some of it on the League of Nations grounds, but more on the very real Imperial ones, and that the manoeuvres by which the peace was kept, and for which I am grateful, though not too certain of it, were engaged in patently at the behest of the bankers, who have a lot invested in both Mussolini and Hitler. No doubt if they'd had plenty of millions sunk in Addis Abeba they'd have done a sum to decide whether the sanctions should be successful or not.[347] Anyway, the

[344] Charles Bennet, 8th Earl of Tankerville (1897–1971), Social Credit advocate.

[345] Probably J. P. Morgan (1837–1913), American banker who dominated corporate finance in the late-nineteenth and early-twentieth centuries, and who might be a cipher here for BB's 'ad inf. financiers'.

[346] Alfonso XIII (1886–1941), King of Spain until the proclamation of Republican government in 1931.

[347] Addis Ababa, the capital city of Abyssinia (modern Ethiopia), was invaded by an Italian force in May 1936. The League of Nations imposed sanctions against Italy as a result, but Mussolini ignored them, left the League, and established Abyssinia as an Italian colony.

episode isnt forgotten and isnt likely to be in our lifetime unless Italy should somehow lose all her power first, and you are under the same handicap Houston Stewart Chamberlain would have been under trying to influence English issues in 1913.[348] You are much better equipped than he for overcoming it, and I'd like to see you come plum out for a few things that would put the wind up the oligarchs now laying hands on Social Credit. I dont know whether a chap like Angold can be detached from his class, but it would be worth trying hammer-and-chisel on a few similar cases.

The specific Tinerfeno[349] impotence-of-remoteness being removed, I half-expect to find myself involved in the impotence-of-exclusion. Not that I give a damn, apart from possible sources of income. Let the chaps who dont shoot their landlords go on living in slums. But at least I am no longer dubious by doubts about the quantity of information other people might have. Being on the spot, any spot, has advantages. On the contrary, I get doubts about the quality of the information that is permitted to you by the higher powers. Well, you've been after me for action for a long time. Here it is. You got no right to complain if the first course I try to deflect is yours. It's a high sign of esteem.

News? Angold wants to launch a School. He left a sample of one of the prospective members with me. It will clearly be the School of the Completely Inane that finds Greek names good enough to get its vacuity across. He intends to conscript me, and I dont want to offend him at this stage. I trust common dissension and laziness to prevent it until he can be made to see some difference between platitudes on the Acropolis and doing something other people can make platitudes about later.

Mairet seemed almost as open to conviction as The Daily Worker.[350] He says you have conceived an ill opinion of him, but such files of the paper as I have seen dont seem to disgrace him. There isnt anything better here.

[348] Houston Stewart Chamberlain (1855–1927), British-born philosopher who moved to Germany in the late nineteenth century to become an Anglophobic advocate of German nationalism and culture. His book *The Foundations of the Nineteenth Century* (1899) was a profound influence on the racist theories of German Nazism.

[349] *Tinerfeño*: pertaining to Tenerife (Sp.).

[350] *The Daily Worker* (renamed the *Morning Star* in 1966): house journal of the Communist Party of Great Britain.

Ackerley is bland, like a rabbit shyly toothing a carrot.[351] The carrot is Communism or maybe Mr Auden. I doubt whether I'll be offered any more books after the one Eliot's note almost compelled.

Mother sends remembrances to your parents. I, the best to you and Dorothy: and all that.

B

At the close of 1936, Bunting's wife Marian left him in London, taking their two children Bourtai and Roudaba with her back to Wisconsin (Marian was also pregnant with their third child, Rustam). Bunting's literary career had been in decline since his departure from Rapallo in 1933; now it effectively entered into bankruptcy. The loss of both his family and all hope of even modest literary success was a major personal crisis which thrust Bunting into a kind of vagrant existence. In the short term he returned to Newcastle in 1937, where he enlisted at the Nellist Nautical School in Summerhill Square to train as a sailor. After buying a boat (the *Thistle*) he journeyed from the English south-west to North America, where he worked for a little over a year as a seaman in Los Angeles, then tried (again unsuccessfully) to find writing work in New York, staying at Rene Taupin's apartment in Washington Heights in the autumn/winter of 1938.

The following letter to Pound gives a sense of Bunting's waywardness at this point. If his account is correct, he seems to have somehow waded into the Abdication Crisis of 1936, in which the new King Edward VIII was forced to give up the British throne because of his engagement to Wallis Simpson, an American divorcee. Though it is just about plausible that Bunting would have attempted to occupy Printing House Square, and lead a 'short tail of young men' into the House of Commons as part of an uprising in support of Edward, his involvement with any putative 'King's party' seems somewhat out of character (see, for example, the disparaging comments about the 'nobs who run the show' in **21/3/34**), and this account may be embellished for Pound's benefit. Regardless of its nuances, this letter contains some of Bunting's most eloquent comments about England and the difficulty of challenging its Establishment.

[351] Joe Randolph Ackerley (1896–1967), British writer and literary editor of BBC magazine the *Listener*.

## To Dorothy and Ezra Pound

TS Yale

9 January 1937 6 South Hill Mansions, South Hill Park, N.W.3.

Dear Dorothy, dear Ezra,

It's not incivility that's kept me from writing. The whole mess that's been gathering constantly thicker for now three years broke just at Christmas and Marian and I are separate.

I dont want to go into it. But I'm now able to say clearly that what has prevented me doing any intelligent work during nearly two years has been the utterly miserable situation at home. You cant, or at least I cant, manufacture literature while crisis after crisis at rapidly decreasing intervals keeps you in constant suspense and profound wretchedness. How long it will take me to recover some freedom of spirit I dont know. Things are bad just now. Marian finally kidnapped the children, and I am unhappy about them. Moreover she seems to think that since she has nearly all the money, it is reasonable that I should be left with nearly all the expenses – the lease of this flat, for example. This is the harder, because I doubt whether I can pick up the broken threads of reviewing jobs: I got more than I expected last summer, but after about seven weeks of satisfactorily frequent work, it was suddenly made quite impossible for me to go on – so completely that two or three books for two or three different papers had to be neglected, which will certainly not recommend me to their editors.

The thing that drags most heavily on work is the impossibility of bringing Marian to any durable arrangement on any point whatsoever, so that everything is perpetually in suspense. That is still so. At the best it will be a slow, difficult business for me to make any escape from the financial quagmire I find myself shoved into: the emotional one is likely to be far more tenacious.

Mother is left in considerable difficulties too. And I expect Marian's position isnt very satisfactory, but I've practically no information.

I shall write to Fisher, who is back in Malabar by now, and ask him to let me know of any job going in India.[352] But the expectations arent great. Meanwhile, had a few days as a cinema extra – dull, but endurable – and might get more provided the bankruptcies now taking place dont spread too rapidly. I have so much reluctance to write anyway, and such a disgust for the press, particularly the weeklies, that on the whole I'd rather pretend to be a ham than a journalist.

[352] Probably Warren Fisher (1879–1948), Head of the Civil Service 1919–1939.

Dorothy's cheque helped to provide the children's Christmas, and we were very grateful for it.

I've been in touch with nothing and nobody lately, and can give no news – I dont suppose the casual observation of cinema methods interests you particularly. The only time I broke free from my personal affairs for a bit since September, was during the coup d'état.[353] I got in a round-robin to King Edward at the very start, offering to go "to any length whatsoever" to dish Baldwin,[354] and succeeded in keeping my very short tail of young men together and active during the crisis. The police finally ousted me from the lobby of the House of Commons. The crowd at the Palace didnt respond. But the conspirators managed the whole show very efficiently. Lack of exact information was a huge handicap. The week-end difficulty of getting in touch with Churchill or Wedgwood, and the absence of Lloyd George, made it impossible to put my proposals before anyone of importance until it was clearly too late to carry out my plan (to occupy Printing House Square and prevent the Times appearing unless the Astors and Walters consented to change its policy).[355] I would have had to recruit more men, and couldnt do it without help at a moment when people were actually being gaoled for singing "God Save the King" in the street. The so-called Fascists would do nothing effective, while dishing Edward's chances with the crowd by claiming that he was one of them, the rotten liars.

Nobody any longer has any doubt that the South Wales speech was the clue to the whole business.[356] But at the time the press was so unanimous (Beaverbrook and co didnt support Edward, they merely didnt support Baldwin as heartily as the rest) that the people at large were deceived. They didnt see that there was a coup d'état at the expense of parliament and electorate, they only saw a marriage about

[353] Edward VIII (1894–1972) abdicated the British throne on 11 December 1936, after months of speculation, media furore, and constitutional debate about his planned marriage to Wallis Simpson (1896–1986), an American socialite regarded as unsuitable because she was a divorcee. As noted above, it is very difficult to gauge exactly what BB's role was in this 'coup d'état', more usually called the Abdication Crisis.

[354] Stanley Baldwin (1867–1947), British Conservative Prime Minister during the Abdication Crisis. Along with other politicians and establishment figures (the 'conspirators'), Baldwin pressured Edward to abdicate.

[355] Printing House Square in East London: formerly the home of the *Times* newspaper, of which John Jacob Astor V (1886–1971) and John Walter IV (1873–1968) were proprietors.

[356] On a visit to an abandoned colliery in Dowlais, South Wales, in November 1936, Edward was quoted as saying: 'These works brought all these people here. Something should be done to get them at work again.' The comments were taken by some as a sign of Edward's radical credentials.

which they were divided but the unco- guids[357] who always speak first anyway had the opportunity of making themselves heard, the others hadnt: and that I suppose stampeded parliament in the end. In the North it seems crowds in the cinema were hissing Edward and shouting "She's nowt but a bloody hoor" and so forth.

The success of the wage-parers and purity-fiends is making itself felt already. I'm not clear what it portends, the whole thing is conditioned by the danger of war, which makes everybody chary of going very far against our masters. BUT King George has been publicly hissed.[358] That appearance at the window in Piccadilly a day too early has made people look on him as a usurper.

Now it doesnt seem to me to matter two hoots who is King, but it matters enormously whether we elect a parliament, or merely a cabinet. I dont know whether the unpopularity of the new king can be made to work against the gang, but I hope it will. What seems quite certain is that not only no great change, but not even any substantial alleviation of the lot of the poor in England is going to be possible in future without civil war. That seems to be fairly widely recognised. The owners will play the confidence trick as often as they can – Zinoviev letters,[359] Post Office Savings in peril,[360] League of Nations, Two Living Husbands,[361] – having the whole press in their pocket and an opposition led from Eton and Oxford, that's not very difficult. But they have let it be seen that if the trick doesnt work they will use their police (now officered from the Universities) and their army (with General Gough, the 1914 traitor, restored to full honours).[362] Nobody knows whether they can count on the air force, nobody believes they can count on the navy.

[357] A term derived from Robert Burns's poem 'Address to the Unco Guid, or the Rigidly Righteous' (1786), which pours scorn on self-righteous, puritanical figures.

[358] Edward's brother King George VI (1895–1952) replaced him in December 1936.

[359] Four days before the 1924 General Election, the right-wing *Daily Mail* newspaper published a forged letter purportedly sent by Bolshevik politician Grigory Zinoviev (1883–1936) to the Communist Party of Great Britain, arguing that the Labour government's recognition of the Soviet Union would lead to the radicalization of the British working classes. The forgery and its impact on public opinion helped to contribute to a Conservative landslide.

[360] Immediately prior to the 1931 General Election, Liberal politician Walter Runciman (1870–1949) suggested that the Post Office Savings Bank, where many ordinary British people held accounts, was in danger of collapse under the incumbent Labour government. Runciman's claim was less influential than the Zinoviev letter, but the election result (a decisive Labour defeat) was similar to that of 1924.

[361] Wallis Simpson was twice married prior to her relationship with Edward VIII.

[362] Hubert Gough (1870–1963), senior officer in the British Army in the early twentieth century. Gough was at the centre of the Curragh Incident in 1914, in which a number of British officers threatened to disobey orders instructing them to support the Irish Home Rule Act in the face of likely opposition from the Unionist Ulster Volunteers. He was also heavily criticized for his blunders in the final months of World War I, but by the late 1930s his reputation had been rehabilitated.

Meanwhile, the squeeze out of everything unorthodox or a little liberal in social affairs and in the arts is indicated, and under way. They dont mind communists, at least not the Cambridge kind. They are no danger whatever to the bosses, nor is Mosley. All dragooning is better in their eyes than any freedom or thought or action. One feels the control all the time, if only in the futility of the things people are permitted to do. But the English were always a docile lot.

So long as Europe looks like war, it is my opinion that the bosses can keep their hold on England without difficulty. Partly on that account, I think care will be taken to prevent the situation from stabilizing itself – if indeed it shows any indication of doing so. I think too that the city bankers would be quite ready to subordinate the interests of the empire to what they imagine to be their own advantage in strengthening Hitler, and possibly Mussolini too. What would happen if a reliable peace occurred I dont know. I think England might drift quite rapidly to civil war.

All that's not very concrete nor much use to you. You've probably heard most of it before. Also that Mrs Simpson isnt guaranteed unimpeachably Aryan, which, I am assured, kept Hitler badly puzzled about what his attitude should be for some time.[363]

I havent even read much Persian, I lack heart for anything. Still, I have discovered another poet who ought to be amongst the regularly-read-by-all lot, one Minuchihri, contemporary of William the Conqueror, with a sort of masculine splendor at command in very simple language: but the life amongst the splendour, though energetic, is intermittent, so he doesnt come absolutely up to first-rank standard. Jallaluddin Rumi is disappointing. That is, some pieces in the divan are the best mystical verse I've read, but not enough better than good English and Spanish samples I've seen of Rudaki and other very early poets are very fine indeed, but its next to impossible to find the collections of their fragments.

I'd be glad of letters if you've time to write: but it must be in pure charity, since I've nothing to offer in return just now except my own depression. I dont see anyone, dont feel fit for it: and would certainly bore anyone I did see. Whereas descriptions of the local scenery would be neither pleasing nor useful, though even after that long absence I cant walk along the Lower Marsh or Borough High Street[364] without noticing how much better I know London than

[363] Both Edward VIII and Wallis Simpson were Nazi sympathizers.

[364] Lower Marsh and Borough High Street: areas of London south of the Thames. As BB suggests, they are some distance from the fashionable districts of the West End.

most of the people I meet, who seem to stick strictly to the West End and certain suburbs... There's no money in it.

I hope things are well with you and with the old people. Mother wants me to pass on the news that she hasnt forgotten any of you.

Yours

B

## To Karl Drerup[365]

MS Durham

21 January 1938 Yacht "Thistle", c/o Post Office, Dittisham, S. Devon, England

Caro Carlo –

(Muere Musolini! Abajo Franco! Tenfel strafe Hitler! Etc)[366]

Very glad to hear from you! I didnt answer your previous letter because I was distressed about my kids, & couldnt bring myself to face it. But my own prescription – the yacht – has been working slowly and I am less easily upset now.

You've been having a hard time, I see. I don't know anything about housepainting – all the painting I do is when I get the boat onto the shore and paint her bottom with arsenic or copper, or her topsides white & green. I get more paint on my clothes than on the ship. But I am glad you have contrived to go on painting pictures that partly satisfy you. (Mother seems very pleased with the etching you sent her. Zukofsky also is obviously glad to have the photograph of my portrait.) Pupils are probably almost as annoying as house-painting, but maybe less tiring. I hope you are able to do some pottery – I am sure that is the most hopeful line for you in the States.[367]

I have left off being anything but a sailor. I see nobody but fishermen and naval men, and do scarcely anything but look after the "thistle". Of course, she is a very little yacht. I could not buy the sort of boat I really want. She is very shallow, so that she does not stand up well to the sea: and she has a big open cockpit which makes her dangerous in rough water: and there is very little room in the cabin – only three feet six inches high, and so on. But she is a good ship of her kind and brought me safely about four hundred miles, in conditions she was

[365] Karl Drerup: German artist BB met in the Canaries. He moved to New York in 1937.

[366] *Muere Musolini!*: Death to Musolini! (It.); *Abajo Franco!*: down with Franco! (Sp.); *Tenfel strafe Hitler!*: the Devil punish Hitler! (Ge.).

[367] Drerup's focus was increasingly shifting in this period from painting to ceramics, which would become the basis of his reputation as an artist in future years.

never meant for. I would like a bigger, deeper boat with a different rig, that could face the ocean. Nevertheless "thistle" is a constant pleasure to me, even now, anchored for the winter.

I dont think I had any very remarkable adventures during my cruise. There was a most hospitable yacht-club at Ramsgate.[368] At Dover I met a famous Dutch yachtsman who has been around the world alone in his boat. After I left Dover I got caught in a gale, & when that was over it fell dead calm, so that I was five days at sea practically without sleep, & ran out of food! – This might please you: near Southampton I passed one of the big German liners, I forget which one now, but I think the "Pennland": there was a big group of sailors near the stern doing some work, and when they saw my beard ("Russian") they all ran to the side and gave the clenched fist salute & began to sing the "Internationale". They didnt seem to care what the passengers thought about it – I was a month at Southampton, mostly talking to a remarkable sailor who had been captain of a big sailing ship, captain of a Cunard liner, a Commander in the navy, & is now a whaler. I had become seaman enough by then to be able to enter Lulworth Cove[369] against strong, gusty winds – a tricky business – on a day when, it seems, no other boat could (or would) do it. Finally I sailed to Devonshire, where, after a period of more or less illness and depression at Torquay,[370] I came round into the estuary of the river Dart & anchored for the winter. It is a very beautiful place – a wide, enclosed stretch of water surrounded by high hills covered with forest – mostly oak, beech and elm, but with a good many Mediterranean pines and a few palms and eucalyptuses. There are vines and figs and agaves in the cottage gardens, for this corner of England is nearly as warm as the Riviera, though much rainier.

Of course, this is THE cyder country.[371] The cyder is very cheap and strong and dry: you could get very drunk for a few pence if you wanted to. I go to the pub, but really only to meet the men of the village, who are very kind & good natured. They are nearly all either sailors or shipwrights or fishermen. I get all the news from the three great naval fortresses of southern England! There was great excitement a little before Xmas, when they all expected immediate war & the fleet was very much prepared indeed, but it is all forgotten again now. Though I am not actually enrolled, all the English yachtsmen are considered to be part of the special reserve for the navy, and the ancient laws of "impressment" still stand, though

[368] Seaside town in Kent, in the far south-east corner of England.
[369] Picturesque cove in Dorset, on the Jurassic south-west coast of England.
[370] Port and tourist town in Devon, near the mouth of the Dart river.
[371] The English south-west is famous for its cider, especially the strong 'scrumpy' variety BB describes.

they are never heeded now. So if there were a war, I quite expect I'd have to navigate a trawler or other small coastal vessel.

I have applied for a job in the Colonial Service and am still waiting for news of it. There seems to be some hope, but I do not really expect to get it. If I do, I must get to Singapore, at once, (to censor films!)

I read Firdusi still – except when, as at this moment, there is a gale blowing, so that I have to keep a lookout to see that the ship is safe.

All the best to you and Gertrude![372] I see your English has improved. Do you still swear as much? People dont, in America. But here no one opens his mouth without swearing.

Someday we'll meet again! Meanwhile, take care of yourself, make some nice pots and pictures, and get rich – Do you know, I believe at this time you are my only close friend who is not a Jew? You and I will have to get circumcised. Only the jews have stood by me in real misfortune.

Best of luck
B

## To Ezra Pound

TS Yale

11 November 1938 c/o Rene Taupin, Apartment C 2, 222 Seaman Avenue, New York City

Dear Ole Ezra,

Damn glad to see your phiz on the wrapper, and pleased to find you remember ma name in some however ambiguous connection with the kind of thing your writing of in Kulchur.[373]

When it was rumored to me I wasnt sure I would be pleased, but this here appears to be a good book all right. I havent had time to go wery profoundly into it, but what I perceive on rapid rush through iz that you have come at least near to making what you call your ideogrammic method work in prose: which you'll forgive me thinking wasnt formerly so. Result, for me at least, one is not in the

[372] Gertrude (neé Lifmann) (1907–1977), Karl Drerup's wife, who was Jewish.

[373] This letter is the product of BB's first encounter with *Guide to Kulchur*, Pound's somewhat erratically structured prose work of 1938, which featured a stylized portrait of Pound on the cover. It is dedicated to 'Louis Zukofsky and Basil Bunting, strugglers in the desert.' BB's copy of *Guide to Kulchur* has survived and is currently held along with other of his books in the library at Buffalo. His marginal annotations are strongly critical of Pound's literary and economic arguments.

least annoyed by individual errors; even if they were more numerous, they are of no particular account, the sum is independent of them. And that doesnt mean merely or that I agree necessarily with said sum, but that it exists, isnt a deduction, has substance. And also a large lot of the detail seems to me quite beautiful, or luminous. Anyway, a contribution to thought, not the uneasy premonitions of one.

You save me the trouble of reading "la tua etica" – remembering the Politica etc – But I respect Aristotle on quite other grounds.[374] Isnt it so, wisdom exists, at least appreciably, only in action? And the stag. was tutor to Alexander[375] (truth of history or metaphor of his influence) whose attempt to make a whole civilization failed, but was a bloody good attempt, a real making: and what might have come of the union of polytheism's fluid alertness with the unshakeable availability of the gathas as foundation or ballast,[376] might have saved you the trouble of studying Chinese.

Of course history needs complete rewrite, but not merely or mainly for economic and monetary – the sabotage of the thought-exchange, 600-1200 a.d. is the central damned fact.[377] You have got the moslems upside down somehow. The black curse was Mahommed himself, the rest is very slow mitigation. At least, after the battle of Cadessiya there was a wall between Rome and China, Rome and India, and it took Genghis to pull it down. (Though a few l'il ladders and ratholes had been made before). The crusades meant more than their publicity-agents let on. The Fatimites and Assassins had been to work too. It wasn't Moslem theology, but the curse of the Koran itself, written document, not getting away from it, that baulked them. As to orthodoxy, even the four

[374] BB refers to Aristotle's *Politics* and *Nichomachean Ethics* (in Canto 11 of Dante's *Inferno*, Virgil reminds Dante to read 'your Ethics' ('la tua Etica'), i.e., Aristotle's text). Pound discusses the *Nichomachean Ethics* extensively in *Guide to Kulchur*, with occasional glances at *Politics*.

[375] Aristotle, who was born in the Macedonian city Stagira (hence 'the stag.'), was tutor of Alexander the Great.

[376] The *Gathas*: a collection of seventeen hymns, and a core text of Zoroastrianism, the primary religion of much of the Middle East at the time of Alexander the Great's conquests in the 4th century BC. The holy songs of the prophet Zoroaster/Zarathustra, the *Gathas* are moral and mystical in emphasis, foregrounding essential values such as Truth, the Good-Mind, and the Spirit of Righteousness.

[377] The following passage is a complex mix of historical fact and hypothesis about Islamic history during the Middle Ages. BB's essential point, more extensively outlined in **18/12/39**, is that a cultural schism existed between East and West throughout the early medieval period. However, he argues, during this interlude the possibility of cultural integration or 'thought exchange' was progressively advanced by the heterodoxy of Islamic culture in practice: its several branches and sects moved Islam positively away from the limited orthodoxy of the religion in its original incarnation.

orthodox sects manage to produce as wide a variety as Christianity; when the Ismailiya and Shi-ah get to work, heresy is commoner, wilder than ever in Europe: still is. The Shi'ah are hardly even predominantly monotheistic, in any sense but the one on the lips. Islam made a barrier because it is experessly enjoined to bloodthirsty fanaticism by its founder: it made a desert because he neglected to think beyond Mecca.

Perhaps besides the immediate point to suggest the success of the first Caliphs stems from Justinian's mistakes, leading inevitably to the hundred years war with Persia what destroyed both nations without leaving Amr' and the other general any even military coherence to overcome.[378]

I dont intend to leave contemporaries in ignorance of these matters if I am ever in a position to get anything printed and paid for. It has plenty too much bearing on totalitarianism, commun- or fasc- istic. Both of which seem to me to adopt, deliberately, as their central strength (whatever sidelines of excellence or less they may include) the same barren arrogance that enabled the Koran to block the efforts of the whole world for half a millennium and hamper them for another half. No reform worth paying that for. I wouldnt take a thousand a year to be sterilised, nor should the world be let do so. Efficiency is too easy, much too goddamn easy.

Maybe this is getting a bit far from yr book, though not from Culture itself. One of the Southern States seems to have hit on the admirable idea of a tax on circulations, all the papers very indignant at this attack on liberty of the press: which if they can get it past the Supreme Court may actually introduce something like liberty of the press for the first time since the invention of capital A Ads.[379] There is some integrity in the South: not among the nigger-baiters, but sporadic from Louisiana to Los Angeles (which is the only City, not anthill, I have struck on this continent). The midwest seems to me beyond question the foulest stink heap in the worruld, with New York a pretty close second, neck and neck with Berlin.

[378] Justinian I (*c.*482–565), emperor of the Byzantine Empire from 527 to 565. His reign saw a deepening of the Byzantine–Sassanid war, a prolonged conflict which ultimately weakened both sides. Islamic forces were subsequently able to conquer Persia and make inroads into the Byzantine Empire because of the weakness of these opponents. Amr' is probably Al-Qa'qa' ibn 'Amr ibn Malik al Tamimi, general at the Battle of al-Qādisiyyah, a decisive event in the Islamic conquest of Persia (AD 636).

[379] Possibly a reference to an attempt by Huey Long (1893–1935), governor of Louisiana, to introduce a tax on circulation of newspapers in the early 1930s, though the Supreme Court deemed this unconstitutional in 1936.

NOTHING, from digging to reviewing will yield me a living. I am now lying about imbecile books for cigarette money. Having had two bouts of no eats this year I dont feel particularly worried about another, but wish it could be in a better climate. Moe[380] expresses opinion I am now qualified for Guggenheim, so I've filled up the forms (Firdusi project) and named you, Eliot, Williams, and Bailey-the-Orientalist.[381] I believe you will oblige...Not that I will get the Gugg. but I ought to try. Sailing the Thistle for a year was at least a man's life, not this louse-like writing for money. Not that I court gales, but it is bloody good to have got through a bad one singlehanded in an unseaworthy boat. Good to have learned navigation and seamanship, good to be in the public service even to the infinitesimal amount of an officer of the last and least of the categories of the naval reserve. And the Thistle served her main purpose in getting me through the worst period I've had. I am now beginning to have a little energy to spare from keeping my self in order...Also, a ship proved the least expensive way of living I have yet devised. It was bloody bad to have to sell her.

(The luck doesnt change, however. I had no sooner been mobilized and quit Los Angeles than Fox[382] sent for me for an unspecified but probably well paid temporary job. I missed it by three days.)

Harpooning congers, netting herring, is a good life. If ultimately they wont let me write what I have to write, I'd liefer be a fisherman than another thing.

Meanwhile, I'm glad to have your opus.

All the best to you and Dorothy.

B

The letter from Pound to Zukofsky which provoked the confrontation in the following letter has not survived, but we can infer the gist. Pound's anti-Semitism intensified along with his fascist commitments throughout the 1930s (see **6/5/35** and commentary) so a showdown of this sort was probably inevitable. For all that his language and actions often fell a long way short of today's ethical standards, Bunting certainly thought of himself as a determined anti-racist—and this letter would appear to support that view. In the context

380 Perhaps Harriet Monroe.

381 Harold Walter Bailey (1899–1996), British orientalist and scholar of Persian. BB applied to the John Simon Guggenheim Memorial Foundation in December 1938, having already applied unsuccessfully back in 1932 (in both cases the application related to BB's Ferdowsi project).

382 Possibly Douglas C. Fox (1906–1979), American journalist, scholar and museum curator, who worked alongside Leo Frobenius in the 1930s.

of his historical moment, Bunting's basic philosophical views about race were, to put it mildly, considerably more progressive than Pound's.

## To Ezra Pound

TS Yale

16 December 1938 c/o Rene Taupin, Apartment C 2, 222 Seaman Avenue, New York City

Dear Ezra,

No, I am sorry, and thankyou: but I cant take it. I wish I were not as much indebted to you as I am.

It was not good when you failed to look for the facts about Addis,[383] Padajoz, Guernika.[384] It makes your tirades at others for their willing ignorance of this and that look much worse than silly. But at least one could say: "He does not know. He would take a different stand if somehow the facts – perfectly well known in lands free from censorship – were got across to him".

That does not apply to your anti-semite outbreaks. You know as well as any man that a Jew has the same physique and a similar amount of grey matter as the rest of us. You know as well as any man that to hold one individual guilty of the sins of another is an abomination. You know as well as any man that the non-jews have contributed their fair share, or more than their fair share, of the bankers and other millionaires of doubtful honesty. You have the relevant facts, without any need of information that cannot be found in Italy. I can find no excuse, no way of considering your activities as anything else than willful and thought-out perversion of what you know to be true.

Every anti-semitism, anti-niggerism, anti-moorism, that I can recall in history was base, had its foundations in the meanest kind of envy and in greed. It makes me sick to see you covering yourself with that filth. It is not an arguable question, has not been arguable for at least nineteen centuries. Either you know men to be men, and not something less, or you make yourself an enemy of mankind at large.

[383] See note to **3/9/36**.

[384] Badajoz and Guernica: Fascist atrocities of the Spanish Civil War. At Badajoz, on 14 August 1936, Nationalist forces massacred 4000 civilian supporters of the Republic. On 26 April 1937, German planes allied to the Nationalist cause devastated the Basque town of Guernica during a heavy bombing raid.

To spue out anti-semite bile in a letter to Louis, as I yesterday accidently discovered you to be doing – to Louis who has shown his devotion to you over many years, and who even now insists that you are to be forgiven because after all you are Ezra – to write such a letter is not a mere lapse of taste: it is uncommonly close to what has got to be called the behaviour of a skunk.

I suppose if you devote yourself long enough to licking the arses of blackguards you stand a good chance of becoming a blackguard yourself. Anyway, it is hard to see how you are going to stop the rot of your mind and heart without a pretty thoroughgoing repudiation of what you have spent a lot of work on. You ought to have the courage for that: but I confess I don't expect to see it.

Yours
Basil Bunting

# Midway
# 1939–1963

After the personal and creative crises of the late 1930s, Bunting's life was reset to zero in 1939. As another global war loomed, he washed up in Northumberland again after his transatlantic sailing interlude of 1937–1939. He did not, it should be stressed, 'rush across the United States from California to England to enlist', as William Carlos Williams once put it (see *The Autobiography of William Carlos Williams* (New York: New Directions, 1967), 264). That description passes over both the 1938–1939 spell in New York (summarized in the last letters of the previous section), and the rather cautious comments about the war in the first letters below.

Initially, in the Phoney War of 1939–1940, Bunting tried to acquire government work of a mostly bureaucratic kind (and while that progressed unsuccessfully felt himself 'fortunate' not to be involved). This must have been a strange time. In his fortieth year, Bunting found himself living with his mother in a small Northumberland pit village, as he tried to make sense of a burgeoning global cataclysm and take account of the recent implosion of both his marriage and his writing career. No wonder he took some time to work out a next step.

As he waited for something to happen, Bunting wrote to Louis Zukofsky, who was now clearly his main (and more or less only) correspondent. At first, he relayed historically interesting observations about life in the north-east during an interim period of rationing, evacuation, and blackout. Then, as the war exploded into action, his biography took another intrepid turn. The correspondence of the middle war years is full of gaps—often literally so as a result of censorship—and some of the few extant letters are not included here, largely because they are fairly mundane descriptions of army life. However, we can see from the 1943–1944 letters to Zukofsky that Bunting eventually had a remarkably busy first-hand experience of fighting in the Mediterranean, North Africa, and the Middle East. There is a pressing need to apply more and deeper scrutiny to Bunting's colonial phase than has been evident in previous scholarly and biographical treatments. But whatever its unexamined moral and political complications, Bunting clearly felt his colourful life in the RAF to be a marked improvement from his lonely existence in Throckley at the start of the war.

As the war drew to a close, an even more exalted period began. As we can see from the heading to **18/7/45**, soon after VE Day Bunting found himself asking correspondents to address letters to 'S/Ldr B.Bunting, H.M. Vice-Consul, Isfahan, Persia', a sign that he was now, slightly improbably, somewhere near the top of the British colonial hierarchy in the Middle East. However, the next few years, during which Bunting remained in Iran in various roles, could be precarious as well as prosperous. He found himself back in Throckley when his periods of employment in intelligence and journalism ran out, and in 1952 he was finally 'chucked out' of Iran by the reformist Prime Minister Mohammad Mossadegh (a few months before Mossadegh was himself removed from power in a CIA-backed coup).

At times it is unclear exactly what Bunting was doing in Iran, perhaps inevitably given his army and intelligence roles. What is clear is that this was an unusual period for him, during which he was professionally very active—and politically rather reactionary. Bunting was now at the heart of the Establishment and enjoying it in spite of himself. He met and married his second wife Sima Alladadian in 1948, which finally allowed him to move on from the personal nightmare of the 1930s, even if the age difference of over thirty years was problematic in more ways than one. In letters to Zukofsky—and, after they resumed contact in 1946, to Dorothy and Ezra Pound—Bunting seems mostly fairly content, narrating details of visits to dramatic natural and historical locations in Iran, and continuing the obsession with Persian poetry begun with the earlier attempts to translate *Shahnameh*.

Although the literary discussions with Zukofsky are among the most sophisticated in the correspondence, during this entire phase Bunting was not producing any writing of his own, aside from bureaucratic reports and related forms of journalism. A notable exception is *The Spoils* (which emerged from a short spell in Italy in 1950–1951), a substantial 'sonata' in which Bunting condensed at least some of his experiences of the war years and their aftermath. An edition of his collected poems also finally appeared in 1950, at the instigation of Texas-based Pound acolyte Dallam Flynn. However, Bunting was fairly nonplussed by his first full-length book, and for the most part the letters of this phase are full of unhurried digressions—on literary history, religion and Persian culture—rather than more urgent creative news.

After returning to Northumberland in 1952 following his run-in with Mossadegh, Bunting clearly had a tough time of it, though perhaps not quite as tough as people have sometimes imagined. The evidence of letters such as 27/9/53 seems to suggest a financial crisis of sorts, though we must bear in mind that Bunting often exaggerated his money woes, especially to correspondents like Margaret De Silver and Dorothy Pound, who were to differing extents his patrons.

For a short time in the early 1950s, Bunting earned a scanty wage as an itinerant proofreader, which must have been a humiliating downgrade after the professional successes of the previous decade. However, by 1957 at the latest he found himself with a large suburban house and a steady job on the finance desk of the local daily newspaper. As we can see from the letter to Pound of 11/12/57, Bunting still persisted in maintaining that he was on 'starvation pay', in the same breath as he relayed details of the miniature orchard in his ample garden. This and other examples of pinched bourgeois affluence do not quite fit with the myth of Bunting's pre-*Briggflatts* poverty swallowed by far too many critics and biographers (for a notable example see Share's otherwise excellent introduction to the collected poems, which describes this as a time of 'penury').

What is certain is that Bunting was deeply depressed in this period. Not only had he apparently given up poetry for good, he stopped writing to his friends almost entirely after 1953, apparently leaving many letters from Zukofsky unanswered. Unlike earlier lacunae in the correspondence, this retreat into silence was due to a lack rather than a surplus of activity. The handful of letters that have survived from the late 1950s and early 1960s show Bunting on the verge of retirement—commuting to a hated desk job, trying to look after his young family, and looking forward to nothing so much as his own oblivion.

## To Louis Zukofsky

MS Texas

3 October 1939 — 242 Newburn Road, Throckley, Northumberland

Dear Louis,

I got your letter this morning. And it showed no sign of the censor – why, I don't know.[1] For they stop even French newspapers, according to the "Manchester Guardian".[2] They cannot stop the short-waves, and the stupidity of stopping newspapers under these circumstances should be obvious even to the sort of people who run the Ministry of Information. It is the great scandal of the war, so far. I think I am fortunate not to be in it. An acquaintance of mine and friend of my uncle who is a cabinet minister apparently thought I ought to be in the Ministry of Information, writing articles for America: but when he got round there he found it four times overstaffed with the nephews, daughters, etc of the men in charge. Hardly a journalist amongst them. They have even suppressed the official Foreign Office spokesman. Here in the North the practical work is to be done by a junior school-inspector and an income-tax-collector. Meanwhile the staffs of Reuters, Associated Press, & so on,[3] who know the work, are idle or dismissed.

I would have undertaken such a job, of course: but not too happily. I want to be active & not a parrot. I still believe the admiralty is wonderfully efficient, as departments go, but I am a bit bewildered by the changes in my relations to them – cannot guess their reasons. I am now what I was in U.S.A. last year – "noted for service", but not required "immediately" (twice underlined in their letter.) Whether I have to wait until other officers are killed off, or only until other yachts & trawlers are armed, I don't know. So I've accepted an invitation from the Workmen's Educational Association (W.E.A.) to lecture to pitmen and schoolteachers.[4] A lot of work for very little pay – about 4 bucks a week for a course on history: &, not quite settled, another 4 bucks for one on Art with a capital A, which will take place, if it does take place, at Morpeth, the miner's capital and birthplace of modern trades-unionism, so far as it has a birthplace.[5]

[1] Britain and France declared war on Germany on 3 September 1939. An eight-month 'Phoney War' ensued, until the German invasion of France and the Low Countries on 10 May 1940 ushered in large-scale fighting in Western Europe.

[2] The *Guardian* newspaper was formerly the *Manchester Guardian* (1821–1959).

[3] Reuters and Associated Press: long-standing international news agencies.

[4] The Workers' Educational Association, founded in 1903, provides free educational courses to British adults.

[5] Morpeth, some fifteen miles to the north of Newcastle, is the modern county town of Northumberland. Although Thomas Burt (1837–1922), the radical Liberal MP for Morpeth from

It will buy cigarettes and a new pair of trousers – needed! – and occupy my mind. And the W.E.A. is respectable, fossilized, rheumatic enough to have forgotten that it once really aspired to spread knowledge. By comparison with most of their somnolent and gaseous lecturers I have no doubt I shall shine.

You want to know what the war looks like to an English obscure civilian? I don't think I know anything even our censors can object to, so here goes.

When it began, the weather improved instantly, which of course shows that Jehovah approves. Also the lights went out.[6] It is inconceivably dark without the moon. From my doorstep I should see a largish industrial town & a number of big industrial villages:[7] but an hour after sunset I might as well be looking at a totally uninhabited stretch of country. Occasionally a furnace flares up for a moment, but not often. Even the tramcars which pass the house are so dark that in about a hundred yards they become invisible – though not inaudible.

About the same time a tremendous noise of motors began. The Army does not seem to approve of silencers. Heavy lorries in general have forgotten all about speed limits. A lowering of the quality of gas sold makes private cars speak up too. Unfortunately the noise of a heavy engine is extremely like the first dreary groan-cum-wailing of the sirens that announce an air-raid. At first everybody was exhausted by jumping out of their skins every time a lorry passed, but we are beginning to get used to it.

A lot of the streets as well as parks and waste ground have been dug up to make air-raid shelters. We have none: but I took all the stones from the garden rockery and built a dry wall about a yard from our kitchen windows: and when it is possible to get some sand I shall reinforce it with a few bags. Our house is half tumbling down anyway, because the land sinks into the colliery workings underneath – any bomb fairly near will knock it down. But it is better to take the chance of a bomb than to incur the certainty of pneumonia and rheumatic fever from sheltering in damp, cold holes in winter-time.

We all carry gasmasks – little kids making mud-pies in the gutter & Lord Mayors at public functions. Drunks take their gasmasks to gaol with them, judges have theirs on the desk before them. I don't think gas will be used on England – it

1874 to 1918, was a key figure in the early years of the Northumberland Miners' Association (see note to 21/3/34), BB's claim that the town was the birthplace of the modern union movement is exaggerated.

[6] Blackout regulations, which called for the boarding up of doors and windows and the inoperation of streetlights, were imposed in the UK on 1 September 1939. As BB discusses below, there were similar decrees involving evacuation of children from urban areas (also 1 September), conscription (3 September), and food rationing (8 January 1940).

[7] I.e. Newcastle and its suburbs, including Throckley.

could serve no military purpose whatever: but I am falling in with the government's demand, & carrying my mask: though I have never even tried it on. Without it, I would look singular.

During the first days of the war, the air, which used to be full of planes in training, seemed deserted. Now we see a good many, but a different and altogether more impressive kind – huge machines that seem as steady and stable as battleships. I have never seen anything like it in any country – though I've seen plenty big and advertised planes. These must have been kept quite secret until war began, and their sudden most impressive appearance has given me some confidence in the people responsible for the Air Force. Probably other nations too had better machines than they were willing to show, but it is impossible to believe, seeing these, that anybody has anything more reliable or faster or in such numbers.

You'll have seen pictures of all the A.R.P. people in civilian clothes but tin hats.[8]

What else? Lots of uniforms, of course. Some of the soldiers take their training very seriously – sentry-go in the heel-clicking style of the Coldstream Guards at Buckingham Palace.[9] Others, on motor-bicycles, look more human than soldiers used to, more as though they had, sometimes, to use their own heads a little, if only to repair the bicycle. But I am told that it is harder for a fit young man to get into the army as a volunteer than for a rich man to enter the kingdom of Heaven. I suppose they haven't enough sergeants to train more men than those they call up compulsorily.

We have felt no shortage of anything yet – except stuff for blinds for the blackout. But there will be shortages, I suppose. The coal, gas & electricity rations are a bit slim: about 70 per cent of what we are used to using. That sounds better than it is, as people will find in mid-winter, when it is cold and dark. But there has been no backwardness amongst the profiteers.

Several things have disgusted me again with the English middleclass – a sufficiently disgusting lot at the best of times. The worst was their attitude to the Evacuation. Practically the whole burden has had to be taken over by the workingmen & farmers. In one village near here there are about sixty miners' cottages, two or three farms, a dozen middleclass houses, a big rectory, & two big

[8] ARP (Air Raid Precautions) wardens: designated civilians who dealt with the impact and aftermath of bombing raids.

[9] Coldstream Guards: long-standing regiment in the British Army. With their distinctive red uniforms and black bearskin hats, they play a central role in ceremonial duties at royal residences such as Buckingham Palace.

"country houses". The rector was billeting officer. 92 children were sent. None of the middleclass people would take any. Half a dozen were sent to Sir X. Y.'s house: he promptly shut the house and advertised it to let, to get rid of them. The rector, having fourteen rooms in his own home, did not take a single child. About 80 of the 92 were sent to the cottages, averaging three rooms. The people who have been fined for offences against the Evacuation law have all been middleclass: and they fill the newspapers with abuse of the poor for being poor, ragged, dirty, unused to good furniture, talking dialect, etc. They would be shocked if their dogs were treated as they are treating poor children. There must be plenty of more respectable middleclass people, but they do not protest against the noisy swine. Children on farms are the luckiest and most contented.

Meanwhile the children still in the big cities get no education at all, & those in the country, in the now overcrowded schools, half an education. Even in the "neutral" areas, so many schools have been taken over for billeting soldiers, establishing decontamination centres, & so on, that children have only an hour or two a day of lessons. I don't think they need be any the worse for that if the teachers are intelligent & supple, but a long undisturbed bureaucracy, such as runs our education system, is not very likely to let well alone, or welcome any experiment not dictated from above.

That's about all the war changes actually visible that I can think of.

If Stalin is content to distribute Polish estates amongst the peasants, he may get away with his annexations without much rebellion.[10] But not if he rushes into collectivised farms. No doubt a banker can see the advantages of collective farming without difficulty, but they are more obscure to the countryman; who is also necessarily at the point of friction and discontent in such schemes, and in the best place for observing every mistake of the administration. Besides, peasants who are not actually starving seem to be content under feudalism (– not under absentee landlordism, which is a different problem) and their strong traditionalism makes them averse to any new arrangements, other than that they themselves should own the bit of land they cultivate. I am afraid some of what one hears of the Russian invaders looks just bombastic & silly – the millions of Stalin's portraits are worthy of Dr Goebbels, & Voroshiloff's[11] distribution of medals for gallantry might have been invented by Swift or Butler, its irony is so extreme.

[10] Following the Nazi-Soviet Pact of August 1939, Germany and the USSR simultaneously invaded Poland on 1 September.

[11] Joseph Goebbels (1897–1945), Minister of Propaganda in Nazi Germany; Kliment Voroshilov (1881–1969), People's Commissar for Defense of the Soviet Union between 1925 and 1940.

If such things are typical of the Russian mind, I doubt if Stalin would be an ally much worth having either for us or for Hitler, and whether his system would withstand a long war any better than the Tsar's. But every nation in war seems to give high posts to all its fools.

Here the public already looks on Churchill as Prime Minister, and is, to them, a cypher.[12] Unfortunately he is not yet really a cypher, but there are grounds for trusting Lord Chatfield (one of the greater admirals of the last war) [13] & Gamelin,[14] & if Daladier[15] has only a little resolution, Chamberlain should be unable to do much harm – until Churchill ousts him, &, I hope, at least half his semi-incapable ministers along with him.

– Yes I think the fighting in Lorraine is serious: siege operations, slow, as sieges usually are. We are all impatient; but I don't see any effective alternative while the neutrals remain neutral. Even the fall of Saarbruecken, when it occurs, won't seem a very great success, but it may really mean a good deal.[16] I am not sufficiently "up" in fortifications to feel sure one way or the other.

If Réné was in France when the war began, I imagine he will be in it. He travels on a French passport, & if he tries to assert his Americanism he may be in difficulties. But he will probably want to fight anyway. He is excitable. Tibor[17] should get home with nothing worse than delay. My best to both or either of them when you see them.

And to Carlo. I am still a good deal worried about him and his household.

I hope you & Celia are well settled in your new house. It sounds rather a good place. In future "Dear Louis" at the beginning of a letter must be held to include "Dear Celia" by implication

[...]

disused mediaeval highway I didn't know of. And I have shown[18]

[12] Neville Chamberlain (1869–1940) was replaced by Churchill as Prime Minister when the Phoney War ended in May 1940.

[13] Alfred Chatfield (1873–1967), a Royal Navy officer in World War I, became Minister for Coordination of Defence in early 1939.

[14] Maurice Gustave Gamelin (1872–1958), Commander-in-Chief of the French Army in World War II.

[15] Édouard Daladier (1884–1970), Prime Minister of France between 1938 and 1940.

[16] In September 1939 French forces invaded the German territory of Saarland in response to the Nazi invasion of Poland, but were quickly repelled.

[17] I.e. **Tibor Serly**.

[18] The remainder of the letter has not survived aside from this torn fragment.

## To Louis Zukofsky

MS Texas

18 December 1939 242 Newburn Road, Throckley, Northumberland

Dear Louis,

I like the Catullus translation a lot.[19] Remove a few, very few lapses from spoken – & its all that's wanted. Recast line "kiss what guy" etc. Probably change "miserable" to "poor" – Yes, I like it a lot. Would have been thoroughly pleased if I'd been able to do the like myself. Why on earth not for publication? If only as a reply to Pound's (and my) declaration that you had almost forgotten how English is spoken, its conclusive.

Here there's nothing new. Weeks ago there was a great buzz of planes – reconnaissance machines being chased, I think – but nothing drastic happened in our sight or sound, & I never found out whether anything really happened at all. It was sufficiently exciting for about three minutes – then the whole flock (or bevy, or school, or shoal, or…) was past the other horizon. The balloons float like goldfish in a bowl. I've not heard A. A. guns, except once, very distant, for about thirty seconds, two bursts of firing, also several weeks ago.[20]

Yes, I am fundamentally averse to acts of faith.[21] Faith being belief contrary to the available evidence. But I don't want to labour the point. I was long since convinced that Russia would horribly disappoint the more amiable communists, and so far she's a bit ahead of time with it. – I've wondered whether it might not be wise for me to record my view of American policy 1911–1938, & where it will lead, so as not to be suspected of prophesying after the event – but I don't want to be chased by hornets etc. Briefly, I think American wrongheadedness responsible for most of the mess in Yourrope: which would please neither the U.S. public nor the British Ministry of Information.

I did six very solid, stolid lectures on history. There was nobody competent to challenge me, so I quietly instilled the opposite of what is usually taught. It was not unamusing. If I had a typewriter I would revise & try to publish. Lecture I: Alexander. II & III: Battle of Qadissiyya. IV: Mazdakian communism & its echoes

[19] BB is probably commenting on a version of Zukofsky's translation of Catullus 8, eventually published in the 1946 collection *Anew*.

[20] I.e. anti-aircraft guns.

[21] In his previous letter to LZ, BB had continued—in the vein of 3/10/39—to criticize the conduct of Stalin's Russia in relation to the war: 'You say Stalin has done a lot to stop Hitler. I cannot see how on earth anybody can make that out. Naturally Stalin does & will do all he can to stop anything at all aimed at Russian territory: but in every other respect what he has done has obviously and enormously facilitated Hitler's plans.' BB to Louis Zukofsky, 3/11/39, Texas.

in Islam.[22] V & VI: Siege of Umar. The general theme being that the continuity of civilization was violently broken by the rise of Islam, cutting off East from West, & restored by Jenghis: the interval 623–1219 constituting the Middle Ages. Alexander, by way of introducing the conception of the Civilized World. Mazdak & Co chiefly to reinforce the close resemblance of the sixth & twentieth centuries, partly to define the actual effect of Islam apart from its intention.

I had expected to go on, to the other main event, i.e. Kit Columbus, after the New Year: but seem likely to be sidetracked into things I know little about – American revolution, for example. I had good houses, as W.E.A. classes go, even the day there was an air-raid warning, when we expected everybody would stay at home. There were more people at the last lecture than at the first, & two young pitmen took notes... thirst for knowledge unquenched even by the unspellable, unpronounceable names of the Arabs. Few questions, only one jewel of half-knowledge "Please, what was the connection between this Caliph Omar and 'Omer that wrote the Iliad?"

Firdausi? Nothing written, but have just re-read about the defeat of the Gudarziyân – Bahrâm going back to the battlefield for the whip he had dropped, & bandaging the wounded soldier, & getting killed because his horse ran away when it heard a mare neighing.[23] And Farûd on the mountain top, shooting the horse from under the Persian officers, while all the girls stood on the battlements laughing at the tumbles they got: but when Farûd was killed they all jumped off & killed themselves out of respect for his memory. And Gev swimming the Oxus because the ferryman tried to overcharge him. And the chap who was peacefully eating his dinner when they insulted him, & said he had stolen the joint of venison from a garbage can, & in the ensuing battle he was killed. And Bezhan shooting the spy by the sound of his footsteps on a dark night. All first-rate stuff, bears many readings. This must be my fourth or fifth time through that particular 150 pages, & it is at least as fresh now as the first time I read it. But tranquillity to

[22] BB's lectures were, as he glosses, about the history of the Middle East from the Greek invasions of Alexander the Great (356–323 BC) to the beginning of the spread of Islam in the seventh century AD. The Battle of al-Qādisiyyah (AD 636) was a decisive event in the Islamic conquest of Persia; Mazdak (d. circa 526) was a Persian Zoroastrian leader who advocated communal ownership; the Siege of Jerusalem in 636–637, led by Caliph Umar (584–644), resulted in Islamic control over the city which would last until the First Crusade in the eleventh century. 1219 saw the beginning of Mongol encroachment into the region under Genghis Khan (1162–1227).

[23] The episodes in this passage are all from the second, largest section of Ferdowsi's *Shahnameh*, which recounts events from the 'heroic age' of Persian history (that is, the period preceding the arrival of Alexander the Great in the fourth century BC).

translate it – a secure couple of years – where's that to be had? So I am continuing the useless thing, taping up all the odd words for some faked owlish academism about the Vocabulary of the Persian Epic. If I can actually achieve any such imbecility it will go further than years of real work to get me established.

Salam! Adeus! Hasta la vista! So long! And all the best to Mrs Zuk, & to J. Reisman, Esq.[24] May his what-you-may-call-it flourish! May he flourish his what-you-may-call-it!

Yours
B

## To Louis Zukofsky

MS Texas

19 March 1940 — 242 Newburn Road, Throckley, Northumberland

Dear Louis–

Your letter has somehow got mislaid, but I hope to find it and answer whatever wants answering before I finish this.

My fortunes go from bad to worse rapidly. At the beginning of February I went before a medical board, and was by them rejected totally, not only for the navy but for all the services. They fussed a bit about my eyes, but it was something in my interior that really excited the eleven sawbones, who prodded, pinched, plucked & generally savaged every inch of my intestines so that they ached for a week. They wouldn't say a word to me, but put some hieroglyphics on a form & filed it. Goodbye: don't come again!

That annoyed me, particularly because, though I don't claim to be a model of health, I haven't found it necessary to see a doctor since the last war, when the influenza knocked me flat in about eighty minutes. So I took pains to sort out all I could recollect of their examination, & check up the anatomy I have forgotten in my sister's reference books, & concluded, a little uncertainly, that they suspected my appendix of some naughtiness. Now, during the last week, six or more weeks after the examination, I have indeed been down & out with the symptoms of an abcessed appendix. I cannot possibly afford to be ill just now, so I have been doctoring myself with starvation, rest and Epsom Salts. Today the pain is almost all gone, and I can sit up & write. I suppose the abcess has quickly bust, or subsided.

[24] Jerry Reisman (1913–2000), New York businessman, a close friend and sometime collaborator of Zukofsky.

But I have to expect it to recurr until sometime it will be "acute appendicitis" & I shall have to be operated on or die. My anxiety is to postpone that until I can pay for it, or until I wangle myself into a position where the government will have to pay for it.

I am in no doubt whatever about the appendix & very little about the abcess: but I dare not go to a doctor, because an operation now would put me out of even the few remaining chances of a job, involve my mother in a possible final financial mess, & in short be the end of me quite as certainly as a ruptured appendix would, & involve the old lady too. However, I believe sometimes these abcesses depart for ever, & sometimes recurr without becoming unmanageable, so I am not particular cast down on that score.

The rejection by the medical board is much more serious. Whatever job I try to get, that fact seems to end my chances. I was trying to get taken on as a merchant seaman, & a friendly shipowner actually promised me the first vacancy on one of his boats: but the captains have refused to have me, no doubt partly because they don't want an amateur in the forecastle, but chiefly because I am certified unfit for service... And so on. Even if the other unemployed do get jobs in the end, I seem to be likely to be marooned. Meanwhile, as doesn't need to be demonstrated, the War has reduced the prospects of my true profession, literature, to nothing at all. There is simply no prospect whatever of earning a penny by writing.

So I have been trying to turn my Persian to account with the Intelligence people. I have a certain indirect "pull", for the President of the Board of Education[25] is an acquaintance of mine and a close friend of my uncle, & at the same time bosom pal of the Secretary of State for War, I have done all I could; got De la Warr to put in a word, written in English, written in Persian. But so far the only result has been a form to fill up, an ugly, cramped form on absorbent paper, which looked as though it were hardly fit even to be filed. It did not look as though it meant business. It was not at all like the Admiralty's correspondence – & that came to nothing. I don't expect to hear of it again.

The B.BC doesn't want me for its propaganda organisation. I haven't tried the Ministry of Information yet, but expect much the same from them as from the B.BC They will get their Persian from the School of Oriental Studies.[26] I have no degree...

[25] Herbrand Sackville, 9th Earl De La Warr (1900–1976), British politician who began as a Labour MP in Ramsay MacDonald's Labour government (1929–1930). He served in a number of government roles in the ensuing decade, including the Board of Education presidency (1938–1940).

[26] The School of Oriental Studies (now the School of Oriental and African Studies (SOAS)): Bloomsbury-based constituent college of the University of London.

All this is pretty cheerless. Change the subject. The War? Well, Finland etc is in the newspapers & your guesses will be as good as mine.[27] However, I am well content with the War in spite of that bad setback. While I was trying to become a merchant seaman, or fisherman, or get on the minesweepers by the backdoor some of the fisherman are allowed to use, I had to visit one of our ports, a small one in the navy's eyes, & also to pass through one of the great shipbuilding districts.[28] It was astonishing and exhilarating. I took exactly the same trip one day last summer, & I thought how depressed & dreary it all looked then – empty yards, the harbour asleep. I then noticed one place where the keel & bottom plates of a biggish ship had been laid, & a couple more that seemed to be clearing to begin work. Now, repassing a few days before Churchill spoke about our ship building feats, I saw the ship that was then begun, ready for launching – a big warship: several others almost at the same stage: practically every slip with a ship growing on it: ships in the water having their last fittings put in. Now you know I have lived all the younger part of my life in an air of coal, steel & shipbuilding, & I am not merely being dazzled when I say that nothing like this extraordinary speed & energy has ever been seen in any shipbuilding area before. The Italians are boasting of a ship built at "record" speed, but the nearly complete warship I saw must have been built very much faster, to say nothing of the others. The men who have done this have been out of work for eighteen or twenty years. It has been said that they had become listless and unemployable: but I do not believe for a moment that any similar feat could have been done in Germany, or Italy, or U.S.A. Inherited pride of shipwrights has no doubt something to do with it, but a strong determination, not imposed by the wretched government, but growing from the people themselves, is the effective cause.

My uncle Mat, a colliery manager,[29] was telling me over a glass of whisky he had been looking at the paysheets of his hewers. You know the pay-system of Northumberland miners is extraordinarily complicated, but for a hewer it works out so that he can work or not, as he chooses, & is paid by what he turns out, subject to a minimum working time & a minimum pay. Mat had been struck by the enormous amount of work the men were doing. One had put in 13½ shifts in a period in which, Mat said, in ordinarily prosperous, busy times, the average might be 5 shifts, Mat did not understand, he said, how any human being could have as much energy: but all the men were showing it, in a slightly less degree, &

[27] The Moscow Peace Treaty of 12 March 1940 ended the Winter War of 1939–1940 between Finland and the Soviet Union.

[28] Probably one of the Tyneside shipbuilding areas such as Wallsend or Jarrow.

[29] BB's maternal uncle Matthew Cheesman (1880–1949) was manager of Throckley Colliery.

moreover, the output of coal per shift was not falling off on account of these prodigiously long working weeks, which the men were choosing, of their own volition, without being asked, to impose on themselves. Of course, they earn good money in this way: but at other times when they might have earned as much by similar energy, they never chose to show it.

Finally, the harbour I visited was incredibly busy. No signs of anything "phoney" about the war there. English warships, French warships, minesweepers, merchant-cruisers, merchant ships, furiously busy: sailors in great numbers, working without a pause: the balloons in the harbour mouth & up the coast: in sum, a decaying port had suddenly turned into a naval fortress at least as formidable as in peace time, Portsmouth or Chatham or La Spezia.[30] The same must have happened all round the coast.

To me it seems evident that this tremendous energy – energy of the people themselves – is bound to produce its effect. What is true of shipbuilding coal & the navy, (and of "munitions" too) can hardly be false, I think, of any important part of the nation: & such national energy is quite certain to prevail over however elaborate a "government" efficiency that comes from above, & must lose much of its tautness in the change from paper-schemes to actual muscular effort.

It is true that we are hampered by our miserable Cabinet. But I think if the Cabinet does not display an energy equivalent to that the people are showing, it will simply be overwhelmed & disappear before long. With decent leadership & such a spirit as they are showing now, the English would hardly, I think, be able to stop with merely checking Hitler: they would be bound to impose their hegemony on all Western Europe. There was nothing comparable in the last war. One thinks of the tremendous energy of Rome in Hannibal's time; military genius, superior wealth, & the command of the seas were all helpless against it. And yet nearly all the Roman leaders were mediocrities or worse.

I don't think the prospect is entirely one to rejoice at, though a British hegemony is likely to be much less oppressive to the spirits of other nations than a German or Russian one. But the spectacle is wonderful, as an outpouring of energy: as the spectacle of the French revolution, Russian ditto... It has points of inferiority to the mainly intellectual, mainly "from-above", energy of the first decades of the United States, it is likely to be a damn bad time for artists & writers. But it is worth watching!

[30] BB refers to major naval bases: Portsmouth and Chatham on the south coast of England and La Spezia in Liguria, Italy.

And I am still greatly impressed by our aeroplanes.

I have been reading Toynbee's "Study of History".[31] It is evidently an important book – one you will have to read too, sometime Louis! It is badly written – repetitiously, & ornamentally. But he is very learned, & his ideas, though short of being completely convincing, are evidently much better based than those of any of the other historical philosophers – not excluding Marx. It does not suggest any particular application to the present moment: but if it doesn't illuminate you, as it might, it will at least kaleidoscopically rearrange the ideas you illuminate for yourself.

I still cant find your letter. But may you flourish anyway. Likewise Mrs Z. & Jerry & Carlo & the Frog & so on.[32]

Perhaps I ought to qualify, on re-reading, what I have said about the spirit manifest here:

It may be that I underestimate the degree to which government mismanagement may finally discourage that spirit. It is also noticeable that there is nothing similar in the bureaucratic class which is so much larger & more powerful in England than in most countries. They are commonly plain stupid: often very despondent ("We can't possibly win"): and generally have the air of feeling that their day is done. This feeling spreads to some extent into the professional class too. Again, I don't know how it may be in London, where a mass of clerks & shopkeepers fills the gap that exists between working-man & bureaucrat. The clerks set the tone there, & they naturally usually reflect, rather feebly, what the bureaucrats think. And London is a quarter of the nation.

The Governing Class is obviously & notoriously divided: but so far as my discernment goes, the men of thought & energy are at one with the people: the ones in whom misgivings predominate, though they occupy the government, are really mere Logs – bureaucrats in disguise, or relics petrified long ago: who will not be able to maintain their present position as soon as that demands a positive action on their part to repell the rivals who are really alive. It is not yet possible to name their successors. But, with all allowances for the exceptional risks all

[31] Arnold J. Toynbee (1889–1975), historian and philosopher of history, who achieved enormous popularity in the mid-twentieth century. He is best known for the 12-volume *A Study of History* (1934–1961), which traced the rise and fall of world civilizations. Toynbee was a classic English Liberal, and BB's recommendation to Zukofsky here is a typical (for this period) avowal of liberal centrism in the face of Communism and Fascism. The discussion in this letter of the energy of the English people, and of an etiolated 'Governing Class' redeemed by a minority of creative individuals, shows the influence of key themes in Toynbee's work.

[32] I.e. Celia Zukofsky, Jerry Reisman, Karl Drerup, and René Taupin.

reputations run in wartime, I expect to see Eden, Sinclair, and – probably – Churchill still at work; & to see Chamberlain, Macdonald, Burgin, and – probably – Hoare & Halifax quite forgotten.[33] I don't know when: but I think the first instalment of the change is almost due.

I have no word from Wisconsin.[34]

O! I nearly forgot to tell you our true tale, which has pleased everybody hereabouts since it happened in February.

The skipper of a ship which had just had a gun fired on its forecastle for defence celebrated the occasion with a party on board until he grew so lively that his prudence was overcome by his impatience to play with the new toy, & he fired off his gun. The shell went half a mile down the Tyne & blew the wireless cabin off one of Runciman's ships.[35] Several hundred pounds damage: no lives lost. You can gauge Runciman's popularity in his hometown by the delight everybody in Newcastle takes in this story. I came across it about ten hours after it actually happened, & I think I have heard it from others as often as I have repeated it myself since.

All the best
Basil Bunting.

After his slow start, Bunting finally managed to enter the War as a combatant in the summer of 1940. Joining the RAF Balloon Command after training in Warrington, he spent time at bases in Hull and (for a much longer period between 1940 and 1942) Fife in Scotland. In 1942, after a long sea voyage via the Cape of Good Hope, he arrived in Iran, a posting arising out of his knowledge of Persian. For the remainder of the war, as he rose up the ranks to Squadron Leader (he would eventually become a Wing Commander), his time was divided between the Middle East, North Africa, and Italy.

The correspondence of these years is inevitably scant and fragmentary (and made even more so by censored passages and missing pages), but Bunting provides a decent outline of his movements in the letters below.

[33] BB lists prominent members of the wartime coalition government: Anthony Eden (1897–1977), Samuel Hoare (1880–1959) and Viscount Halifax (Edward Wood) (1881–1959) were all Conservatives; Archibald Sinclair (1890–1970) and Edward Burgin (1887–1945) were Liberals, and Malcolm MacDonald (1901–1981) was a National Labour member.

[34] I.e. Marian Bunting's home after her return to the United States.

[35] In addition to his political career, Walter Runciman (see note to 9/1/37) was heir to a substantial Tyneside shipping business, Runciman Shipping Co Ltd.

## To Louis Zukofsky

MS Texas

20 April 1941 119305 AC1 Bunting R.A.F., The Manse, Methil, Fife, Scotland

Dear Louis,

I suppose torpedoes – or perhaps a forgotten drawer in the censor's office – account for your letters, if you've written any these few last months – never reaching me. And for aught I know, mine may not have reached you. So here goes from the beginning again.

I can't, obviously, tell you much about my work. I am on a small yacht in the North Sea, with a balloon and a machine-gun; & I am kept busy. You must imagine all the rest – there are so many secrets that I can hardly sort out enough non-secret information to be interesting or even coherent.

And I can tell you still less about the situation, because I never see a newspaper & very rarely get time to listen to the radio. You know more about it than I do. That leaves me very little to write about except myself.

Of course, any soldier, sailor, or airman lives in a constant state of exasperation with official stupidities – bullshit, we call it – that hamper our work: & often that's the only mood for days on end. But when there's a chance to meditate and feel at all, I, and probably all who are enough aware of civilised life on the one hand & historical precedents on the other, fall naturally into the tone of Æschylean tragedy.

It seems so certain to me, Louis, that what you and I have stood for – let's call it learning & literature, without implying the commercialised knowledge & castrated rehashes that usurp the phrase – learning & literature are done, now. They were crippled in our generation: but we will find now, however the war turns out, that the life has gone out of them forever, as far as any language we are familiar with is concerned. Oh! I don't mean there'll be no Virgils, even, maybe, Horaces, to plump out the respectabilities of what's to come. But you'll write to please officials, not to put life into a language & a people. There'll be no object to writing, except the making a living by polite toadying.[36]

## To Louis Zukofsky

MS Texas

9 May 1943 1119305 L.A.C. BUNTING, B. 982 Sqdn, R.A.F., M.E.F.

My dear Louis,

Two letters of yours – of October & November – have just reached me, there would be a whole history to write if I tried to bridge the gap since my last – but at

[36] The letter ends at the bottom of the page with no signature, suggesting a missing remainder.

least you know so much of it: that I hope things are going better for you and Celia: that I think of our various friends: that months & months of life in tents is no great fun: and so on.

I don't very often get a chance to write. This afternoon I am out, from the H.Q. where I am, temporarily, attached to the intelligence; and sitting in a bad café in a conquered city of Italian Africa.[37] There is no proper coffee, but I drink what they give me & pay what they ask, so as to have a table to sit at for a few minutes. I don't know whether I have written to you since we first landed in Persia, a long, long time ago. Then, for some months, I was in charge of a large gang of Persian workmen, mostly Bakhtiari tribesmen, and I got on with them famously.[38] My men became the envy of other units. And out of hours (and out of bounds) they entertained me every now and then as Bakhtiari's should, with pipes and drums, dancers and singers, sweetmeats and rice and strong drink, and a man to fan me all evening – very welcome in the terrific heat of Khuzistan.[39] (139° in the shade – it had been 145° a little earlier). I liked Persia and the Persians: a lively, gentle, gay, capable, virile people. I liked their beautiful capital. Teheran has lovely tree-gardens, fine squares & streets, great white mountains to set them off. And everybody who saw an English airman reading a Persian newspaper wanted to talk & buy my drinks for me.

But Iraq – sand, sand, sand: and Baghdad even squalider than Basra:[40] and the sly Arab in place of the magnanimous Persian: and nothing fit to eat but dates. We motored from there to here in lorries – a month's journey, sometimes riding, sometimes driving, always through deserts – stony wildernesses of Arabia, sandy wastes, camel pastures, the unimaginable spring flower garden of Transjordan, the repulsive borders of the Sahara: set off by the teeming beauty of Egypt and the somewhat more restrained fertility of the plain of Jezreel.[41] I would like to have dated a letter to you from Zion, but had no time.

"Sive per Syrte iter aestuosas" – you remember Horace's lines (and Sirte was quite sufficiently aestuosas for me) – "Sive facturos per inhospitalem Caucasum" – we were not actually in the Caucasus, but the Elburz will do[42] – "Vel quae loca

[37] Tripoli in Libya, where BB was posted in the spring of 1943. His journey from Basra to Tripoli is described in Part III of *The Spoils* (54–74).

[38] The Bakhtiari: tribe from south-west Iran. They consider themselves to be the descendants of Shah Fereydun (Feridun) in Ferdowsi's *Shahnameh*.

[39] Khuzestan: province in south-west Iran. Bakhtiari account for half its population.

[40] Basra: second-largest city in Iraq and its main port.

[41] Jezreel: fertile valley in the north of modern Israel.

[42] Elburz: mountain range in northern Iran, which borders on the Caucasus mountains.

fabulosas Lambit Hydaspes" – or at least, the Indus, & the Shatt al Arab.[43] But I wont try to appropriate more of those Sapphics, partly because a fool of a German set a whining tune to them which I can't forget, partly because I am by no mean "Integer vitae, scelerisque purus".[44] All I want is the Horation for "Far & Wide".

Sad to find myself among Italians again, in this guise: but I have had some good evenings with peasant families, Sicilians mostly, singing "Quel mazolin' di fiore" & "Tu sei la stella"[45] etc; as the Fascists used to say, before they went sour, "Canta che ti passa".[46] And anyway, as you quote, from d'Annunzio, "Me ne frego".[47]

All the best. Write. Keep hoping.
Basil

## To Louis Zukofsky

MS Texas

25 July 1944 c/o 242 Newburn Road, Throckley, Northumberland

Dear Louis,

Strange it certainly is, and not easy, to be writing to you after so great an interval: for what changes there must be in you, once so batchelorly and still such a veiled prophet in your writings, I guess uncertainly, knowing only that I must have changed even more under the weight of furnace climates; eternal urgent work; deserts as much mental as geographic; strong feelings, violent in all

[43] BB quotes fragments of the second stanza of Horace's Ode 1.22:

Sive per Syrtis iter aestuosas
sive facturus per inhospitalem
Caucasum vel quae loca fabulosus
lambit Hydaspes
whether his way shall be
through the sweltering Syrtes or the cheerless
Caucasus or the regions that storied
Hydaspes waters……

Sirte/Syrtis is a gulf on the northern coast of Libya; the Hysaspes is river running through Pakistan, as is the Indus, while the Shatt al Arab runs through southern Iraq.

[44] *Integer vitae, scelerisque purus*: 'He who is upright in life and free from sin', the opening line of BB's Ode 1.22.

[45] 'Quel mazolin' di fiore' ('That Bunch of Flowers') and 'Tu sei la stella' ('You Are the Star'): popular Italian songs of the period.

[46] *Canta che ti passa*: approximately 'sing and it will pass': Italian colloquial saying popular in the World War I period.

[47] Gabriele D'Annunzio (1863–1938), Italian poet, playwright and novelist, whose motto *Me ne frego* ('I don't care') was enthusiastically taken up by Italian Fascists in the interwar years.

direction – to see the effects of famine in Persia & Italy; to love as burningly as ever I loved, the Bakhtiari tribesmen, the Lucanian peasants;[48] to note at first hand the malice (really hellish malice, not less but far more than our propaganda allows) of the Germans in Sicily: fear, too, in the last raids on Malta; hatred of the desk-&-pen vermin armies breed so freely, & whom I hold responsible for, for instance, the scurvy we endured in Iran unnecessarily, the thirteen months of unprofitable misemployment I have just finished.

I don't remember when I last wrote. There has been no time, for so long past. No time to write home, no time to read the headlines, no time even to eat or sleep the minimum for health, sometimes. In Sicily, though nominally nothing, I found myself practically in charge of a unit working beyond its strength. The C.O. was in Malta, the Flight-Commander always away. I had to take all responsibility. I've even signed documents as Medical Officer! If I hadn't had a good Flight-Sergeant who undertook the work of the Engineering Officer (though I signed, & was responsible) it could not have been done at all. I planned operations, interpreted ordered from above, ruled everything, without official authority or backing. I even started and regulated a civilian market (not exactly black, but very stripy), caught & punished thieves, traced a spy, instituted liaison with an Italian regiment. Between Xmas day and 1st April I had ten hours of liberty all told. I used them to go up Ætna on a motorbicycle.[49] My other trips beyond the wire round the aerodrome were only to trace the ingenious spy, or to find the bomb-scattered relative of some Maltese nuns who are, I suppose, still praying for me in consequence.

But pressure of work which was just bearable became unbearable when all the initiative was taken away. Since the beginning of May it has often been a twenty hour day for me, without the satisfaction of regulating anything by my own will. And meanwhile invasion flying killed off so many of those I had become attached to that I ceased to feel a part of the Squadron as it is now or to feel any pride in it or loyalty to it. It wasn't mine any longer. What I had done, or had a hand in, for it, was expended over Normandy & exhausted.

In Persia it had been the same as in Sicily: responsibilities far beyond my rank, work beyond that which anyone else undertook in the climate of the Gulf, so far as I saw. Since I left the North Sea my only easy periods have been a month in

[48] Lucania (Basilicata): region in southern Italy. Although there is no record of a spell in Lucania itself, BB spent much time with the RAF in Sicily, Calabria and southern Italy generally in 1943–44. Here as in the letter as a whole (see also 9/5/43) BB poeticizes the landscape of the Mediterranean and Middle East by alluding to archaic and literary toponyms.

[49] Mount Etna: active volcano in Sicily.

Natal,[50] and six weeks in Tripoli behind the VIII Army. Oh yes! The voyage home from Naples, an idle fortnight. And it seemed strange, coming to England, to see windows with glass in them, civilian vehicles (few though they are!), milk from cows instead of tins & soldiers parading instead of working.

Enough for some people to spin books out of all their lifetime. The convoy, for instance: four score lorries, plodding over the desert day after day for a month, from Baghdad to Tripoli. Even now, not so many people have seen Arabia Petraea,[51] or Libya, as close as that. Mostly the motorcoaches cross the Arabian desert in two days to our ten or twelve. Or again, the intimate view of the Sicilian campaign from HQ at Malta.[52] A dozen officers, perhaps, besides the Generals, saw the whole thing so continuously. Or the life with my Bakhtiaris, their tales, legends, songs, dances. A few years ago six months like that was enough capital to set up an Orientalist-cum-Folklorist for life!

Well, I'm done with the Squadron now, finished with Fighter Planes. My disembarkation leave, postponed because of the invasion, has merged with embarkation leave for a second tour in the East – at my own desire, and, I have reason to hope, in the land of my choosing & the capacity I would prefer: the land:- که برکند دل مرد مسافر از وطنش "ki bar kanad dil-e mard-e musafir as vatan-ash" – that is, "which uproots the traveller's heart from his native land": as Hafiz says.[53]

And I haven't written a line of verse or a word for publication for years: nor read anything new of note, for lack of time, though I did manage to steal time, in Iraq, to get through a Persian translation of the best modern Islamic life of Mohammad – originally written in Egyptian Arabic.[54] And that is over a year ago! I have kept pocket editions of Dante & Omar-e Khayyam near me, & I think, fragmentarily, I just got through both in the year and a bit since I reached Malta. My other eastern books are in Cairo, still. I hope to retrieve them on my way to my new job.

I have had no private life.

Residual? I would like a closer view of Sierra Leone, and perhaps of Kenya. I would like to visit the east of Persia & to walk through the Bakhtiari & Kuhgelu

[50] BB spent a month in Durban, in the South African province Natal, in summer 1942.

[51] Arabia Petraea, the Roman province of Arabia, consisted of parts of modern Jordan, the Sinai Peninsula and the north-western Arabian Peninsula.

[52] The Allied Invasion of Sicily ('Operation Husky') unfolded in July–August 1943.

[53] In fact the quotation, accurately translated by BB, is from Saadi's Ghazal 328. I am indebted to Mandana Mashayekhi Ghoyonloo for transcribing this quotation and providing the correct reference.

[54] Probably *Abqariy-yat Muhammad* ('The Genius of Muhammad') (1942) by Egyptian scholar and poet Abbās Mahmūd al-Aqqād (1889–1964).

mountains.[55] I would like to see more of India – not as an officer. I would like to have my land-home in Southern Italy – say, at Agropoli or on the gulf of Policastro,[56] but to live on board a ketch, always mobile & at home everywhere where there is salt water. As to writing – well, perhaps to kill time: but there is no sense in advising a corpse or exhorting a decomposing civilization. They are blowing up the Lung'Arno at Pisa today.[57] We could sing nothing but "as for our own harps we hanged them up... when we remembered Zion... who said 'Let us raze the walls thereof even unto the ground'... Happy is he that avengeth us."[58] Our children will never rebuild the Temple: it needs a new race, a new religion; a new heaven and earth.

They cannot blow up Firdousi or Homer or Minuchihri or Catullus: but they can make the study of them as much an idler's indulgence as cross-word puzzles or chess. It will be a world of ruffians. The Russian officer, who is the square or cube of the Prussian officer (as I have seen him) is the symbol of it, and will grant no passports beyond the "moenia mundi"[59] where his sentries will stand, in small print & cheap binding, proclaiming a more equal slavery, a more complacent ignorance; and all our labours be of no effect, beyond this, that we shall have abolished a nearer, more intimate tyranny – Nazi – in order to establish more distant, less obtrusive, but more tenacious ones; no less opposed to variety & boldness of thought, no less harsh to the unsubmissive. From which I mean to take refuge with Poseidon, if I can save enough money to buy a boat.

I hope your son is still flourishing, & Celia well & content with him. As to your weighty works on Radio, on the whole I hope I shall not come across them. Some Army text-books are well done, but it's not an attractive form of literature. (Do one in rhyme – a "tenzone"[60] between the anode & cathode...) Ugh!

Anyway, Louis, all the best. And after the war? Any hopes of seeing you?

And Drerup?

Yours
Basil Bunting

[55] The Kuhgelu Mountains border those of the Bakhtiari in south-west Iran.

[56] Agropoli and Policastro: coastal towns in southern Italy.

[57] Lung'Arno: riverside of the Arno, which flows through Florence and Pisa.

[58] See Psalm 137: 'By the rivers of Babylon, there we sat down, yea, we wept, when we remembered Zion. We hanged our harps upon the willows in the midst thereof... Remember, O LORD, the children of Edom in the day of Jerusalem; who said, Rase it, rase it, even to the foundation thereof. O daughter of Babylon, who art to be destroyed; happy shall he be, that rewardeth thee as thou hast served us.'

[59] *Moenia mundi*: walls of the world (La.).

[60] Tenzone: medieval Italian poetic form consisting of two debating voices.

## To Louis Zukofsky

TS Texas

21 April 1945 S/Ldr B.Bunting, H.M. Vice-Consul, Isfahan, Persia,

c/o The Foreign Office, London

Dear Louis,

Life's been so busy lately that I don't even know whether I have written to you since I took up this job. It's not one I can tell you much about, obviously. But after four months of it I wouldn't change willingly. Not that an ordinary Vice-Consul's job would interest me, handing out passports and noting down the price of barley; but here there is none of that. The work is all political and one is a kind of little diplomat, all the better off for being more or less out of reach of the big diplomats in the Embassy.

Your letter of last August reached me, I think, in February. With your offspring's portrait, which does you credit.

As you say, my taste for variety has certainly been gratified in this war. I have been on almost every British front worth being on except Dunkirk, travelled through every rank from Aircraftsman First Class to Squadron-Leader (equals Major, to forestall your question), seen huge chunks of the world that I wouldn't otherwise have visited, been sailor, balloon-man, drill instructor, interpreter, truck driver in the desert, intelligence officer of several kinds, operations officer to a busy fighter squadron, recorder of the doings of nomadic tribes, labour manager, and now consul in a more or less crucial post. How I got it I don't know. It's temporary, but I expect to be here till September, anyway.

Isfahan is a good city, with trees and a river that flows all the year round, and the people are all painters and poets and mill-hands, with a nice taste in bribes and a fancy for rioting without killing anybody (yet). There are hardly any English or Russians in the place, still fewer Americans, except for a leave camp that runs through the summer months and of which I see nothing. Such Allied troops as exist under arms, I command – all five of them. The missionaries and bankers treat me with respect and keep away from me. The Persian officials are good fellows (so long as they don't change them, which I fear) and they and the landlords and the chiefs of the Bakhtiari tribe regale me with mounds of rice, acres of mutton, and gallons of vodka at shooting parties, garden parties, receptions, dances and just plain parties without a label. Even the service, the niggardly old Air Force, provides me with a car and a house and four excellent servants, and pays for my drinks and cigarettes, and the Persian army lends me a horse and groom. I keep five large dogs and two sentries in and out of my garden, and altogether you wouldn't recognise the old bum in his present surroundings. But look Isfahan up in Upham Pope's huge book on Persian Art[61] if you want to know what it is like physically, for I am not going to describe it. It is about all there is left of old Persia, before people began to reform and lose their graces.

I am supposed to have distinguished myself to a moderate extent on the job, and on the strength of that I have asked for a permanent job, but I think they will say I am too old.

Naturally there are flies in the ointment, but I don't think I need bother you with them. Except to say that the work is continual and heavy, which must excuse my silences, for it has been that way with me for five years now, so that I have seldom time to write, and when I have I am too tired.

I don't even read literature any longer, let alone write it. The other day I picked up Fakhruddin Gorgani[62] in somebody's house and turned over three or four pages and was astonished to notice once more the pleasure that first rate poetry can give me. I have a row of Persian poets on the shelf, but I never get the opportunity to read them. I write reports; and letters of the kind that begin "Please refer to your F/1905687/G/M2 of 15th Apr."; and lots of telegrams, beautiful cypher telegrams, which, even when translated back into language, must be nearly incomprehensible to anybody whose mind has not been debased to bureaucratic levels. But about half my time is still out of the office, though not as much outdoor as it used to be when I was with the Spitfires or the yachts. I have had to cut down riding horseback lately, but for three months it was pleasant, even though I never felt at home on a saddle, and Persian horses are trained to go straight up what, to my perceptions, appears to be a perpendicular cliff. The car always breaks down in inaccessible mountains or sinks into quicksands in the desert or gets stuck on a hump too high for its road-clearance and has to be dug off it; but so far it's always got home safely in the end. (There is only one road more than a mile or two long in the province – what you would call a dirt track. The rest of the way anywhere is straight across country, streams and marshes included in the rainy weather, small children and ferocious robbers, of which the population outside the city's cultivated fields appears substantially to consist.)

[61] Arthur Upham Pope (1881–1969), American orientalist and expert on Persian architecture, whose six-volume *Survey of Persian Art from Prehistoric Times to the Present* was published in 1938–1939. In a later letter BB describes Pope as: 'three-quarters charlatan, and one quarter enthusiast. Can't speak a word of the Persian he professes to be an expert on, but really does like carpets and tiles' (BB to Louis Zukofsky, 27/10/53, Texas).

[62] Fakhruddin As'ad Gurgani (d. *c.*1054), Persian poet best known for his retelling of the Vis and Rāmin love story.

Anyway, we got ibex and mouflon in the winter, and I expect a lot of rich men in the States would pay a good sum to have the kind of shooting I've had gratis. Now it will get hot, but I know a man who has a fishing rod, and I mean to find out what kind of fish inhabit the Zayandurad river. Somebody said mahseer. Also I want to explore the great river of the Bakhtiari country, the Karun, with a canoe by way of summer holiday, if I can find a canoe. Nobody has ever been right down it; and it will be lazier than walking over the mountains – for even a Persian horse won't face some of them with anything serious on its back.

I want to write to Karl, but don't know his address nowadays and can't find my old diary with it in. You say you see none of our old friends. I'm sorry. If you do run into any of them, give them my greetings. To Celia and Jerry, of course, the best. And let me hear from you even if I'm not a satisfactory correspondent, for I've always found time to read letters, even if not to write them.

I've a lot to tell you when I see you, or when the war is over enough for the censors to go out of business. Good luck to you, Louis!

Basil.

After the war in Europe ended on 8 May 1945, Bunting stayed in Iran for a further year, working for British intelligence in Isfahan.

## To Karl Drerup

TS Durham

18 July 1945 S/Ldr B.Bunting, H.M. Vice-Consul, Isfahan, Persia, c/o The Foreign Office, London

Dear Carlo,

I had lost your address in the course of my many moves about the world, but Louis has sent it me at long last. Now I can ask you to let me know how your fortunes are progressing, and to give my best wishes to Gertrude.

I am sure you would like Isfahan. My lawn is studded with bright flowers, just like a Persian brocade; and the impossible mountains you see in the background of the miniatures actually exist just beyond the town – they are painted realistically, from nature, not from exuberant and El Greco-ish fancy. There are the huge mosques, unique masterpieces of an architecture we dont know at all in the West, and the wall-paintings of the Chihil Sutun,[63] reminding one of Bellini, Gozzoli, and the Chinese all at the same time.[64] I wish I could get photographs for you, but there arent even picture postcards in this uncommunicative land. When you have time to look at the illustrations in Upham Pope's huge book of Persian Art, you will find a rather unsatisfactory selection of photos, but lots of them. And you would like the bazaar – thousands of craftsmen following their trades with a skill and speed and independence such as may have existed in Europe three hundred years ago, but we have lost it and all that goes with it. I love carpets even more than I did since I have seen their splendour in their native land. I wish I could afford them.

My work is ceaseless, as it has been ever since early in the war. I get no time either to read or write. But it is interesting too, and has been all the time, on the North Sea, in the desert, in Malta, Sicily, Italy, and during the invasion of France. Up till a year ago I was always in the thick of it, and now I have one of the busiest posts of its sort. I have to know everybody of any influence in the whole of Central Persia – officials, rich men, tribal chiefs, soldiers – and I spend a fair amount of time travelling about the mountains and deserts in an old Ford as far as it will take me, and then on a horse or on foot. I not only see wonderful places and picturesque people, I get a good view of mens motives, a much more varied view than is possible at home; and I step at will, as it were, from the present into the Middle Ages, from the Middle Ages into the age of the Nomads, and back again.

They make me pretty comfortable. I have a nice Persian house built around a garden, and another garden opening from it, where there are fruit trees, and where I keep my five alarming watchdogs. Beyond, there is a brook, and then more gardens – Isfahan is so full of gardens that from a little distance you would think the minarets rose straight out of a forest. And yet it is a modern manufacturing city of over a quarter of a million people.

I have a good cook to feed my continual guests, a gardener, a butler and a chauffeur – all paid for by the government. They even pay part of my bill for cigarettes and drinks. I have five soldiers all to myself, and nobody within two hundred miles to whom I need account for any of my actions. I would quite like to carry on with a job like this after the end of the Japanese war,[65] but I think they will say I am too old, even though I am good at it and have had quick promotion.

[63] Chehel Sotoun: exquisitely decorated pavilion at the end of a long pool in parkland in central Isfahan. It was commissioned by Shah Abbas II (1632–1666).

[64] Giovanni Bellini (*c.*1430–1516) and Benozzo Gozzoli (*c.*1421–1497): Italian renaissance artists famed for their skill in painting frescoes.

[65] BB is writing after the end of hostilities in Europe on 8 May 1945, but prior to the Japanese surrender on 15 August.

We go hunting – like behind piles of stones near the snow on the mountains while the beaters surround and drive an enormous area of country, and the animals appear all of a sudden, close to you, and they may be deer or mouflon or ibex, or they may be wolf, leopard or bear.

The colours are queer and interesting in Persia, and the outlines very sharp and often jagged. I wish I could paint. I believe I would try, if I had the tools and a bit of time, but neither time nor tools is available.

Now, tell me, what's happened to you? Have you done any more painting as profound as the two big pictures of Teide?[66] Have you got your pots glazed with that depth of blue or green you see on old Chinese and Persian titles? What about your enamels? One of these days I hope to get to America again and see for myself. Have you been able to work, or has the business of earning a living, of keeping well, etc, or the anguish of war, distracted you too much?

I have heard once or twice from Zukofsky. Once from Margaret de Silver a couple of years ago. I have heard nothing from my wife and children, though I write to them whenever I get time. My mother seems to be getting very old now. I saw her for a fortnight last summer – between the Invasion and my second overseas tour – for the first time since 1941. I wish I could do something to make her life a bit easier. But the British government doesnt pay its servants well, and what little I can I must save, because I expect to be very, very out of work as soon as things become what they call "normal" again. If I could get another boat, and say two pounds a week for three or four years! Maybe I could write again: not for the public, but to get said the things I want to say which havent been said before. But I dont fancy my chances, if I have to compete for a living, and at my present age!

Best of luck to you.
Basil Bunting

In 1946 Bunting returned home to Northumberland, where he resumed his correspondence with Dorothy and Ezra Pound. Ezra was imprisoned by Allied forces at the end of the war and spent a traumatic few months in an internment camp near Pisa, where he composed the *Pisan Cantos*. While he awaited trial for treason back in the United States, Pound was admitted to St Elizabeths, a psychiatric hospital in Washington DC, remaining there until the summer of 1958.

[66] Mount Teide (see 4/1/35): subject and backdrop in a number of Drerup's 1930s paintings and drawings, for example *View of Mt. Teide from Puerto de la Cruz* (1934–1937).

## To Dorothy Pound

MS Indiana

22 November 1946 242 Newburn Road, Throckley, Northumberland

Dear Dorothy,

I got your note today. Mother's reached her about 10 days ago. She is in good fettle, considering her age and the difficulties of war & peace. She will write, but is slow about such things – even slower than formerly.

I am very sorry about Ezra's predicament. I didn't see the B.BC monitoring report, but such reports are generally about as accurate as the difficulties permit – less accurate than a good newspaper, but more accurate than the rags most read. (I've had to read hundreds of them picked up from Russian & Arabic stations)

At this stage, I don't think anyone can be expected to listen very attentively to justifications. England & U.S. have avoided "People's Courts", but only just: and there is no doubt that the U.S. public has made up its mind that he is guilty, & must, if possible, be allowed to forget him, before anything effective can be done. The English public generally knows nothing about it & would consequently be more approachable, but not very much more. But after a while it will be possible to set your facts before the authorities with some hope of getting a hearing.

I daresay that doesn't sound very sympathetic, but I really believe it is better advice than might be given by people who want to get indignantly busy right away. I should think Archibald Macleish could be a useful guide – he is a man of affairs as well as a poet, & still must have very useful contacts.

It was a flight of Mitchells that first bombarded Rapallo.[67] They were sent to get the Zoagli viaduct but couldn't get in to it because of weather conditions.[68] One of them landed at Catania[69] where I was, for the moment, in charge, & I had to de-brief the pilot. It was part of the preparation for Anzio: I think.[70] I can't remember de-briefing any other Americans until the invasion of France.

I spent the whole war with the RAF, first as aircraftsman, then as corporal & finally as an officer – finishing up as Squadron Leader. Saw many fronts, North

[67] B-25 Mitchell: American bomber plane introduced in 1941.

[68] Zoagli: small town some three miles from Rapallo, dominated by its railway bridge, a recurrent target of Allied bombing in the last stages of World War II.

[69] BB was based in Catania, Sicily, with the RAF in late 1943 and early 1944.

[70] Battle of Anzio: decisive event in the Italian Campaign, resulting in the Allied capture of Rome. It took place between 22 January 1944 and 5 June 1944.

Sea – protecting convoys in a small yacht: Persia, before Alamein & Stalingrad,[71] when it looked like being the next on the German list: Tripoli, the battle of Wadi Akarit:[72] the last weeks of the Siege of Malta: I arranged the "war-room" for Eisenhower for the Sicilian Invasion, & then went over to Catania with a fighter-squadron: captured Cotrone on my own initiative: in Naples during the fighting north of the City – I just missed being blown up by the delay-action bomb which destroyed the Post Office there: back to England with the squadron to cover the invasion of Normandy: then out again to Persia with the Political Intelligence: lent to the Foreign Office as Vice-Consul at Isfahan – that was a grand job, often amongst the nomadic mountain-tribes, who taught me to ride & to shoot mouflon and ibex: and at last chief of all political intelligence in Persia, Iraq, Saudi Arabia, etc. but I was glad to get out of it at last in July. Baghdad is not an enjoyable city. (Whereas Isfahan is just about the nicest large city I have ever seen)

I have written nothing (except official reports, "appreciations" & such) since Marian walked out on me. She took advantage of the war to get a divorce on her own terms which I would have opposed.

Now, my mind is just beginning to function again. I can form projects of writing, but whether I can carry them out I don't know. I ought to make a connected story of the Isfahan episode, which had some importance, as well as being fun. And after that the Shahnameh still excites me. But I must also earn something. And the Intelligence people think they want me again in the East, but do not make any definite proposals – & if they did, I might not agree to them.

My power to help is very limited indeed. I have very few contacts at all. The best would be Archie Roosevelt, but he is not at present in America: through him, we might ultimately be able to get Eleanor's powerful help, but I think, only after Archie returns & after a longish time for the public to lose interest.[73] I am pretty sure Archie would trust me, & I believe the Roosevelt family think a lot of him. I don't think it would be any use for me to approach Field-Marshall Wilson:[74] he would listen attentively to what I might say about Iraq or Persia, but probably not on any other subject. Eisenhower wouldn't remember me – I only actually met him twice. And I can think of no other power in Washington.

[71] El Alamein (1942) and Stalingrad (1942–1943): decisive battles and turning points in the North African and Russian theatres of World War II respectively.

[72] Battle of Wadi Akarit (6–7 April 1943): Allied offensive in the Tunisia campaign.

[73] Archibald Roosevelt (1894–1979), son of President Theodore Roosevelt, was a distinguished commander and officer in the American Army. He was the uncle of Eleanor Roosevelt.

[74] Field Marshall Henry Maitland Wilson (1881–1964), British Army officer and Commander in Chief of the Middle East from 1943.

But if you think of anything, let me know.

I hope you are not too uncomfortable in Washington with Omar. It looks to me a hell of a place to live in, though I like Annapolis & don't dislike Baltimore.

Forgive the disjointedness of this. I am not yet fully rid of the war, the RAF, delay, red-tape. I am touched that Ezra should have worried about finding me. I would have written years ago if I had any address to write to. You were obviously gone from Via Marsala 12/5.[75] I think of you both with great affection and gratitude.

Yours aye
Basil

I still find Italians the best people – the Neapolitans! the Sicilians! But Bakhtiari & even town Persians run them close.

## To Louis Zukofsky

MS Texas

7 December 1946 — 242 Newburn Road, Throckley, Northumberland

Dear Louis –

So that's that: I'm to have a job when and if the Treasury loosens up; or else if somebody dies or gets bumped off. It hardly suffices –

Meanwhile, a temporary madness (let's hope it's temporary) has seized our Trades Unions, who, while they dare not say in so many words that the men who fought the war may not have a job which could conceivably be filled by a man who didn't, are engaged in bringing about that result wherever possible. Some thousands of dockers have been dismissed in our port the moment they had completed the six months work guaranteed them under the "reinstatement" act,[76] which obliges employers to take back the men who left them to fight. The employer of the dockers is the Government. In place of the ex-soldiers dismissed they are employing those who stepped into the job during the war. This is in response to Union pressure. Something not quite so obvious is happening in the Civil Service. In the mines, some lodges are trying to oblige returning miners to pay up Union dues for the seven years they were in the Army (not drawing union wages nor anything like them). As there are still plenty of complications, this

[75] I.e. the former home of the Pounds in Rapallo.
[76] I.e. the Reinstatement in Civil Employment Act of 1944, glossed here by BB.

issue hasn't yet become clear and obvious to the public, but the British Legion (ex-service men) is beginning to reply to hostile Trades Union resolutions, and I am afraid there may be bad trouble in the end. It is all tied up in the Unions' minds with the effort to oblige doctors, nurses, schoolteachers, lawyers, to pay subscriptions to the Trades Union Congress[77] (i.e., the Labour Party) as a condition of employment. Of course the Government has more sense, but seems afraid to say so. Nor, apparently, dare it defy the Unions so far as to allow Jews, Poles, and miscellaneous refugees to enter England to do the work that needs doing – except as slaves: the Unions don't, apparently, object to the work being done so long as it isn't paid for.

All of which is extremely sickening to me. But alas it greatly reduces my chances of getting a job.

Meanwhile wages are still going up though there are fewer goods than ever before to buy with them. Mr Dalton does not call the result inflation,[78] because, although you cannot buy anything and are not permitted to invest in industry nor to try your hand at trade, you are allowed to lend your money to the Government at 1½ per cent (less the 50 per cent of income tax, leaving a return of ¾ per cent on the money). The very few goods not "controlled" average six to twelve times the pre-war price – I don't know who pockets the profit, for all the trade is licensed to Sir Stafford Cripps, item by item.[79] Naturally, there is an unbelievably huge increase in gambling – the only thing the excess of wages can be used for. A new class of millionaires is being created – bookmakers, pool-operators, totalisator owners, etc. A man who owns one-fifth of one of the thousand greyhound race-courses in the country admitted that his income last year, after payment of taxes, exceeded £200,000. No one whatever in industry received even one-tenth of that, hardly a dozen one-twentieth.

I daresay the Tories might have done no better. The disheartening thing is that they could hardly have done much worse. They are now about to reduce rations, fuel, & train service – all three already below what they were during the worst of the war. Part of the cause is beyond the Government's control, the other part is lack of foresight, lack of organisation, lack of the courage to acknowledge difficulties & limitations.

[77] See note to **Summer 1931**.

[78] See note to **22/1/36**.

[79] Stafford Cripps (1889–1952), British Labour politician, who was President of the Board of Trade 1945–1947 (and Chancellor of the Exchequer thereafter).

Your own country seems also to be enduring Troubles, though not of quite the same kind. What is J. L. Lewis really up to?[80] Our newspapers go no further than outermost surface, about U.S.A. just now. They don't like Truman at all and they appear to despise the Republicans, who, however, must surely have some able men.

Piece on Bill: "Poetry" cannot, of course, print anything so contrary to the pap its readers regard as criticism. If they do continually print hooey about "independent judgment" or "high standards" or being indifferent to the public, it is, naturally, just hooey. So I don't think you need be perturbed or even disappointed. Glad Bill got a new handle to his name, thought it ought to have come from Princetown, not Buffalo.[81]

Eliot wrote. Glad to be in touch again. Said nothing of moment. A scattering of letters falls from ex-subordinates now no longer in the Orient. Not a word from Persia, and I am afraid of compromising friends by writing to them.

All the best for Xmas and New Year
Salaam
B

P. S. Been finding some of Vergil's early poems worth study. Recommend "Copa", & "Moretum" especially.[82] I had no idea he ever did anything genuine & first-rate. There are also youthful imitations of Catullus & Horace, & one or two epigrams of his own. "Moretum" would about fit your anthology of proletarian odds & ends: the peasant's breakfast is wonderfully done.

## To Dorothy Pound

MS Indiana

22 November 1946 — 242 Newburn Road, Throckley, Northumberland

Dear Dorothy –

Just got your letter. I wrote E.P. the other day – by surface mail – but had really nothing to say beyond desultory indication that the War hadn't treated me badly. I am not absolutely certain of the drift of Ezra's note, as it is super-elliptical in form: but I take it he is inciting me to publish or edit a periodical. I had just

[80] John L. Lewis (1880–1969) American union leader and president of United Workers of America 1920–1960. In the immediate post-war period he led strikes denounced by government figures as a threat to national security.

[81] The University of Buffalo awarded William Carlos Williams an honorary doctorate in October 1946.

[82] 'Copa' and 'Moretum': early lyrics by Virgil on demotic, quotidian subjects.

written to Eliot to say that I wasn't particularly anxious to publish anything just now. I gave T.S.E. no reasons, but I see Ez will have to have some –

The first is probably not the root reason, but has its force none the less. I want, if convenient, to earn a living, so as to help my children through their education. Bourtai thinks in terms of the University, Roudaba wants to breed horses (Rustam hasn't yet got any notions, but no doubt he will in a few years.) I don't think Marian can provide all this unaided. Probably I will fail to get a living, but there is a chance: I was sufficiently exalted in the East to make a good many enemies, but also to become known to a certain extent, and I had one foot in the diplomatic service. There have been various proposals which have come to nothing, but I might yet return to Persia, Iraq or thereabouts in some income-earning capacity. To some extent that kind of work attracts me. It is very interesting in itself, and for a while I did, though in a very small degree, succeed in influencing policy, both British and American. Such successes are very satisfying, but such work, done energetically, leaves no leisure whatsoever.

More fundamental: I have changed, and so has the world. As for me, the circumstances under which Marian got first a separation, and then a divorce, so that I was completely cut off from my children, reduced me to a state in which it took all my resolution and ingenuity merely to keep alive and sane. Unexpected success as a soldier and as a minor diplomat set me up again, but did it by bringing out things in me that could hardly have been suspected before, at least by me. In short, it is not merely that I have had more experience, but the experience has been different in kind. I no longer feel, as I did in 1938, that I have nothing to say, but I do not know, except in some details, what it is I want to say, and I don't think I shall know for some time yet to come.

As for the world: the War was itself a revolution, and there is now another revolution in progress in England, which may or may not remain peaceful. Perhaps there are similar revolutions in a number of countries. At any rate, our old preoccupations now seem to me very out-of-date. I cannot go back to them if I wanted to. I do not like what has happened and is happening, but to revive, for instance, Douglas, would seem to me like pretending that nothing had really happened. So that if I were to produce a paper now. I am afraid it would be one of which Ezra would not approve. (I am for threatening the government – all the governments, especially the more powerful and effective ones: and for not reforming backward nations: and for pushing economies out of the limelight for a century or so: and limiting free-compulsory education to reading, writing and 'rithmetic.)

Finally, I am very disappointed with the state of poetry and of communication generally. Leave out the various shams, and the rest all leads to Zukofsky: and nobody can read Zukofsky! Yeats, Ezra & Carlos Williams; Eliot; Marianne Moore; are all in a sense stages on the road to a degree of subjectivity so extreme that, in Zukofsky, it fails to realise that there is an outside world which will necessarily fail to understand. I have no idea what can be done about it, or whether anything can be done about it: but I am clear that somewhere I must find a turning off that road, or else confine myself to calling attention as best I can to Manuchehri & Firdusi and Farrukhi Sistani.[83] I don't think Ezra shares this feeling. His own conspicuous success must convince him that the road is the right one, even for those who go much further along it than he has done. The little magazines in general just wallow in its dusty ditches, without a trace of Ezra's metric skill or Zukofsky's logical consistency. Clearly I am not the right person to rally them.

So far as I have any prospects (but my main prospect is to wait till I see more clearly) they are limited, unambitious, – and not awfully likely to come off. I have thought of a book about Isfahan, mainly the story of trade-unionism there, which is dramatic enough, but including a picture of Persian life, and of the tribal life in the mountains, and some description of the city itself. More remotely, I have a vague project for a full discussion of poetry under the guise of a comparison between Firdusi and Homer: but it would need more reading than I have done and I hope it may be possible for me to write some poetry again someday, or at least to fit together some real translations of the great early Persians. But I am not in a productive state. My skill enables me to write lovely official reports, but I am not definite enough to write on my own account just now.

It is a shame that this is all so negative, for I would have liked to oblige E.P. I may have to write, to try to get money, but that is another matter and an unpleasing one. If there is to be no job, I may stay here: I may go back to living on a boat: or I may establish myself in the South of Italy – I like Policastro and some villages near Reggio, and Cotrone[84] – or, out of political cussedness, in Andalusia or Spanish Morocco.[85] I would go to Sierra Leone very gladly, but think life there would be costly for anyone not "employed". I cannot go to Persia, because of

[83] Farrukhi Sistani (*c.*980–1037/38), Persian poet famous for writing panegyrics for the Ghaznavid dynasty.

[84] For Policastro (see **25/7/44**). Reggio Calabria: city in southern Italy. Crotone: city and comune in Calabria, Italy.

[85] Andalusia: region in the far south of Spain, separated by sea from the Spanish protectorate in Morocco (both were ruled by Franco's Fascist government in this period).

expense, & because the Russians would kick up such a row if the International Reactionary reappeared. It's all very vague, and I get restive when I have to wait around in this way.

I was under the impression Palermo had not been badly bashed, but I had no time to go and see. When I wasn't busy with "warfare" in Sicily I was organising a peasant's market in Catania, tracing lost persons in Randazzo and Enna,[86] or riding a motorbicycle on Etna. Randazzo really was bashed, by artillery, during a big battle. Some Maltese nuns got me to trace their relatives there, & so I am now being prayed for in perpetuity in two convents. I haven't noticed any good effects. Most of the villages on the south side of Etna, as far around as Bronte, are completely uninjured: and they include, I think, the most strikingly picturesque ones, on crags and so on.
Best wishes

Basil

## To Louis Zukofsky

MS Texas

21 January 1947 — 242 Newburn Road, Throckley, Northumberland

Dear Louis

[...]. What is the cause [...][87]

Vergil: my recollection – now vague – of the Georgics is of something prettified: maybe that's wrong. The "Moretum" is not prettified – it includes the clumsiness of the peasant. The other item, about the pub, (name escapes me),[88] has a touch of that identification of the verse with the matter which is so exceedingly satisfactory when it all too rarely happens. Reminds one of Manuchehri, Catullus – only, it has that damned "charm" which makes me distrust some writers: you wonder what they are getting away with – Cocteau, for example. The young Vergil must have had a trace of Cocteau about him. None of that about Manuchehri.

The essay on Poetry for your son.[89] Yes. I enjoyed reading it. However, I am not in touch with what goes on here, if anything goes on under the paper

[86] Palermo, Randazzo, Enna, and Bronte: cities in Sicily.
[87] Most of this short opening passage has been roughly torn out.
[88] I.e. 'Copa', a lyric from the perspective of a woman bartender.
[89] In 1946 Zukofsky wrote an essay addressed to his son Paul entitled 'Poetry For My Son When He Can Read'. It quotes Pound, Williams, Niedecker, Reznikoff, and BB in attempting to objectively define poetry.

ration. I don't know a single magazine nor a single editor. Also, I think if you aim at the magazine public, even the highest browed ones, you must not disdain to repeat and explain, even what you think obvious. Magazines are read at speed or not at all. Nor are references to me, or Lorine Niedecker, likely to mean anything even to the best disposed reader outside your, so to speak, family circle. They puzzle, therefore must be left out unless they will bear discursive explanation – which I doubt. – On a different plane, I'd like to suggest that Science is only another religion, much like many old ones. If its effects are impressive, so were those of Christianity or Islam. I don't admire the contemporary efforts to "reconcile" a scientific outlook with an aesthetic one which is in fact based ultimately on a different religion (nor a moral one; nor, least of all, a hybrid theological one). Science has some affinities with Buddhism, perhaps more with Sunni Islam (not, of course, as Mohammed left it),[90] very few with Catholic Christianity or Shia Islam or Paganism (Greek or Hindu). But a Philo is neither a good philosopher nor a good Jew,[91] a Plotinus[92] corrupts Christianity and Platonism about equally, and becomes the refuge of mystagogues of all sorts. I hate Science. It denies a man's responsibility for his own deeds, abolishes the brotherhood that springs from God's fatherhood. It is a hectoring, dictating expertise, which makes the least lovable of the Church Fathers seem liberal by contrast. It is far easier for a Hitler or a Stalin to find a mock-scientific excuse for persecution than it was for Dominic to find a mock Christian one.

I think we are in such a position as Arsenius or Boethius held[93] – trying to uphold ancient "values" in an age intent on barbarism, whose lever is a religion less humane and civilizable than Christianity, a religion which may produce its Augustine, but probably not its Jerome, certainly not its Francis:[94] a religion, based, no doubt, on a selection of sublime ideas, but whose popular, corrupt,

[90] The two mainstream branches of Islam are Sunni (85% of worldwide adherents) and Shia (10%), with Shia a clear majority in BB's Iran. In the context of BB's remarks here on the 'scientific outlook' the key difference between the two denominations is that Sunnism is arguably more orthodox and literalistic than its counterpart.

[91] Philo of Alexandria (*c.*20 BC—*c.*AD 50), Jewish Hellenistic philosopher who attempted to synthesize Jewish scripture and Greek philosophy.

[92] Plotinus (*c.*AD 204–270), Greek neoplatonist philosopher and a key influence on Pound (for more on this see Peter Liebregts's *Ezra Pound and Neoplatonism* (Madison: Fairleigh Dickinson University Press, 2004)).

[93] Arsenius the Great (*c.*350/54–445) and Boethius (*c.*480–524): authors of instructive philosophies in a period of flux and decline for the (Western) Roman Empire.

[94] BB recruits St Augustine (AD 354–430), St Jerome (*c.*AD 347–420), and St Francis of Assisi (1181–1226) to suggest that twentieth-century rationalism-humanism might allow for the worldly realpolitik of Augustine, but not for the meditative asceticism of Jerome nor the compassionate altruism of Francis.

superstitious version is fairly well represented by the base Communism at present current, whose typical heresy is Nazism –

There is a scientific case for poetry (it will not be heard in this age), but I do not think you are trying to state it. Rather, you are apologising at once, to the scientific Jehovah for going on bowing down in the House of Rimmon, and to Rimmon[95] for diluting his service with that of Jehovah. In short, your essay seems to me to reflect the confusions of our age.

It is ungracious of me to say so, for I've nothing of my own to offer. But I believe you'd rather have me try to grope around the foundations than stand back and admire the cornice or the paint on the front door.

Ezra – in correspondence – seems indomitably out-of-date. Everybody seems out-of-date. It's damned discouraging.

Best to Celia

Yours
BBunting

## To Dorothy Pound

MS Indiana

11 February 1947 242 Newburn Road, Throckley, Northumberland

Dear Dorothy –

I want to ask you to do rather an irritating chore for me; and since I'd rather not have troubled you, I'd better begin by explaining why I am doing so.

I did at last get the Foreign Office's figures of pay for more or less consular jobs in Persia, & they were quite impossible for any one without a largish independent income: so it seemed wise to give up hope of a job and buy this yacht – I think I already said this much in a previous letter. I hope to go on board early in March.

The chief difficulty is to provision the boat, for our rationing scheme is not only severe, but extremely rigid – you cannot anticipate a week or two, for example, so that where a family can to some extent adjust "points", a single person has hardly any hope of obtaining anything storable and must live completely hand to mouth.[96] That won't do if you may be at sea, or at a spot remote from the offices which frank your ration card.

The only supplement allowed is "unsolicited" parcels from abroad. From time to time my children have sent such parcels to my mother, & they have been

[95] In both the Hebrew and Christian Bibles Rimmon is a Syrian cult image or false god.
[96] Rationing in the UK persisted until 1954, with most food still rationed in 1947.

extraordinarily useful to her. Now, if I could get a few such parcels (paying for them in fact, but allowing our authorities to believe they were "unsolicited") I could get over the worst difficulties of provisioning my ship, until the food situation gets a bit easier here.

At this point, I come up against exchange difficulties. I cannot ask Zukofsky, or Marian, etc to do my U.S.A. shopping for me, because there is no way of getting the money to them that is open to me without licences and investigations. But I suppose that you still have an English bank account, & I can dispose of an English cheque through it, without passing through international clearings. I don't know anybody else in U.S.A. who is in that position, & that is why I must come to you.

As the exact regulations about these parcels vary from country to country, you would have to find out just what they are in America. That in itself could be a vexatious business. They have to very solidly packed, & I expect that would be a great nuisance too. So if you don't like the job, say so & I shall not feel let down in any way, because I realise that it is rather a lot to ask of anyone! But in case you can undertake it without too much bother, I am writing a cheque now to save time, & I will also make a list of the things most likely to be useful. When the money is gone, let me know & I will send more if it is still necessary to use such subterfuges.

Things in general are bad, & not improving. We, who live on top of a mine, have been without coal (in very snowy, frosty weather) & with insufficient pressure of gas to boil a kettle.[97] In parts of London, a high proportion of the houses have burst their waterpipes, but since all piping is earmarked for new houses, no repairs can be made, & people have to take a bucket next door, or a few doors farther, to get water. These and worse messes seem to be due to individual incompetence high up (i.e., not the effects of a bad policy) but they are, very properly, discrediting the Government pretty catastrophically. On the other hand, it is presumably policy which is responsible for the inflation, still partly disguised by subsidies in aid of some prices, but which looks as though it would become unmanageable at any minute. And either policy or lack of policy is responsible for the complete overturn of the old "upper classes" – the manager of Newman's yacht yard said that he did not know of one big yacht, of the really expensive sort, that still belonged to a landowner, & very few to old established manufacturers. The large yachts in his own yard now belonged to garagemen, who had presumably

[97] The winter of 1946–1947 was an unusually severe one in much of the UK, resulting in energy shortages, factory closures, and widespread economic hardship.

been working the black market in cars, or to proprietors of football pools & greyhound tracks, or to bookmakers. Betting is a prodigious industry now. There is lots of money, & nothing to spend it on –

But a proportion of people who get fed up with the Labour Party go more or less Communist: and some of the unions, especially the miners, get more unreasonable & more violent (in words) every day. People in the branches say "all the mess is due to sabotage by Tories, & it won't mend until we shoot the lot of them". Others are made bitter by the miners, who have not only got extremely high wages (round £10 a week on the average) and extra rations, but are now seriously threatening new trouble unless a very big share of the beer is earmarked for them. A great many of them will not work more than four shifts a week (30 hours) – they get all the money they need for that. They make it almost impossible for any new recruit to enter the mines & share these privileges. Some unions – dockers, for instance – have been very hostile to demobilized soldiers. A number who were dockers before the war have been prevented from returning to their jobs by strikes designed to keep this now very profitable job for the sons of the men who happened to be dockers when the armistice was signed.

All this is rapidly producing great bitterness. The country is in a much more "revolutionary" posture than it was in 1920 when, I remember, Sidney Webb actually expected a revolution.[98] The most obstreperous are still those who suffered least from the war, but here & there ex-Service organisations are beginning to show resentment. It may all settle down if the various messes are straightened out, but I doubt if many of them will be: in which case there is a hell of a rumpus ahead.

Well! Maybe there'll be something more cheerful to say next time!

Cheerio

Basil Bunting

[…]

Useful items[99]

Dried milk (or condensed)

Soups (Wyler & Co, Chicago: Phenix Pabst-Ett Co: etc: in metal paper packets)

Ready made rice & such (Kitchen Art Foods Inc.)

[98] Sidney Webb (1859–1947), British social democratic economist involved in the foundation of the London School of Economics and the centre-left Fabian Society, both of which were key influences in BB's early political development.

[99] Ticks against some items suggest that Dorothy Pound sent the package, or at least planned to before BB's departure for Persia.

Spam & its relatives
Canned fruit
Jam & honey (not marmalade)
Tea
Cooking fat
Tinned bacon – sardines – etc etc
Tinned butter
Chocolate (specially useful if you cannot leave the tiller)
Soap
Canned vegetables or the like –
Spaghetti (not tinned) Biscuits
and almost anything that will keep

In the spring of 1947 Bunting returned to Iran, arriving in Tehran as British chief of intelligence for the Middle East region. He would remain in the country for the next three years, though after his marriage to Sima Alladadian in late 1948 he left the British Embassy and acquired work as a special correspondent for the *Times* newspaper.

## To Louis Zukofsky

MS Texas

5 May 1947 British Embassy, Teheran, c/o Foreign Office, London, S.W.1

Dear Louis –

It is difficult to write while trying to establish a job likely to require all the astuteness and tact I can now muster, for I find I am likely to be in opposition to most of my Ambassador's advisers. So forgive me if I am over brief. I am glad your job is not oppressive. Mine is likely to be even too exciting & anxious, though less picturesque than the Isfahan Vice-consulate was. Yes, the salary sounds good, & is meant to be good: but this is now the most expensive country in the world, having beaten Venezuela a few years ago. I shall pay, for a tiny house, more than would keep me in comfort in England. At present, my hotel bill is about $150 a week, though I mostly eat elsewhere! If they were to transfer me to, say, Italy, I would be a rich man.

Of course I agree with you about Spinoza. He was a good man. In a sense he was a good Jew, & Spinozism is in a sense the essence of true Judaism, I imagine. But he was not an orthodox Jew, nor, in the ordinary sense, a Jew by religion at all:

which is what I meant. And I can't & don't blame you for standing on principle & not writing Ezra. You will remember I asserted that principle in that way myself, before the War. But I am a kind of Christian. Ezra is no longer a danger to things I hold to be the essence of Christianity, such as the fact that Jews & Christians are all the sons of one father (with Niggers & Hindus as well). All he is now, is an old man in distress, who seems to look to me and Eliot for a kind of help no one else can give him. Omar says his father waits eagerly for letters from me, & is quieter for days after one. Well, how could I hold back? Eliot describes him as the same, except that all the eccentricities have become exaggerated tremendously. Of his two or three letters to me, the greater part was so incoherent as to be incomprehensible. Eliot says he does not realise his situation in the least. He refused peremptorily to let me approach the Roosevelts or Lord Wilson to help in getting his conditions eased a little, at a time when I could have done so with some prospect of success. Omar too, seems to want from me something his father cannot supply. The Foreign Office would be horrified: but I don't think anything I can do for Ezra is done at the expense of (say) Dr Rothschild, a Viennese physician for whose courage in misfortune I have the deepest admiration: nor does it diminish my feeling about the Polish children who used to be under my rule in Isfahan & now, rarely, write to me from Lebanon. I can still distinguish Zion from Zionism & Zionism from the Stern Gang.[100] I can still make my protest against our lack of protests when they hang Qazi Mohammed, & endeavour – probably in vain – to save some of the Iraqi Kurds who were with him.[101] Compassion isn't a command & doesn't need rationing, thank God, & it need not dim one's view of anything. So don't think ill of me for not taking your kind of stand.

Have you read Eliot's "Four Quartets"?[102] I did in Cairo on my way here. In spite of the aggressively Church of England vocabulary, I think the mysticism he expounds might appeal to a Spinozist. The verse is exceedingly skilful – few Eliotisms. I was impressed & am hard to impress nowadays. As by Sadr-ul-Ashraf, in exile at Qazimain,[103] in the house of the mutilated, humbly explaining to me

[100] The Stern Gang: nickname for Lehi, a Zionist paramilitary organization founded in 1940, which mounted a violent campaign against the British in the years leading up to the creation of Israel in 1948.

[101] Qazi Muhammad (1893–1947), Kurdish separatist leader who spearheaded the Republic of Mahabad, a Kurdish self-governing state in Iran that persisted for most of 1946, before Muhammad was executed by the Iranian authorities in March 1947.

[102] For BB's later, disparaging assessment of *Four Quartets*, see 23/5/72.

[103] Mohsen Sadr/Sadr-ul-Ashraf (1871–1962), Prime Minister of Iran from June to October 1945. Qazimain (al-Kāẓimayn) is a northern district of Baghdad, in modern Iraq. BB's sympathy here for Sadr (an arch-conservative) and Shams Sadri (see below note) is in keeping with

what he had tried to do, why he had failed, & how he was finding it difficult to accept the judgment of God on his premiership (and it was in fact by our fault, our failure to back him, that he had failed: but he made no reproach). As by Shamseddin Sadri,[104] selling his house to start a trades-union, with every possible prospect of disastrous failure & his own death, & of being despised by the very fellow-workmen he wanted to help; & with so little egoism that he begged us for any tract, or even rough notes, that could tell him how the English workmen had overcome the difficulties & avoided the pitfalls he knew he was facing. My unbelief is rather shamed by them.

My best to Celia & Son

Yours
B

## To Louis Zukofsky

TS Texas

20 August 1947

British Embassy, Teheran, c/o Foreign Office,
London, S.W.1

Dear Louis,

Yes. A job's a job, and if it provides other amenities besides the minimum of dollar bills, why, it's a good job.[105] With Paul to feed the swans and Celia to play and you to read Wyat, Hamilton can't be a bad place for the present. And another waiting, in the New York you will never allow yourself to be separated from for long. 3600 dollars would be good pay in England. It is less in your expensive land, but must nevertheless be more than ample for your frugalities. I get more, but my frugalities, never insistent, have had to be suppressed altogether, so maybe it seems less.

I hadn't realised your father was ninety. I hope he may go on remembering Zion for a few more years yet with the dignity of his patience. If you think he would welcome my salaams, please tell him I send them. Tell him, truly, though I had hardly recollected it till now, that last time I passed the Jordan, between clouds, in an aeroplane, high enough to see all the ugly wastes it flows between,

the anti-democratic ethos he outlines in the remainder of this letter, a hallmark of his correspondence in this period.

[104] Shams Sadri, anti-communist Iranian labour leader from Isfahan.

[105] In 1947 Zukofsky started teaching in the English Department of the Polytechnic Institute of Brooklyn, where he worked until his retirement in 1965.

I thought of him, as a type of the orthodox, the precarious but durable stream sunk equally deep between the deserts which are all the world sees of their fate.

All the same, the thirst for power, the envy of power, that is the root of what the newspapers call democracy, begins to seem to me almost as idle as the thirst for money. I doubt if it has any satisfactions comparable to those your father and his like find in submission to their god, or the peasant peoples in submission to the toil of their agriculture. It's an old enough notion, and very out of fashion; but I begin to hate reformers, they so rarely learn anything except how to give service to lies in order to profit by lies. The wilderness may be a better place than Pharoah's Egypt, so that we ought to envy the Children of Israel their desert instead of despising it. I used to think I put up with my own wilderness out of fortitude, and that something ought to be done about it, if not by some Moses, then by me. But I see now that I loved my desert, and I know I would have returned to it on board an ex-fishing smack, if I had not deluded myself that I could do something for my children by coming here, to a "position" and a "prosperity" that are, in fact, names for two series of encumbrances and limitations.

St Francis was no fool for wooing poverty. He got his freedom that way. And if we could multiply our power over nature many times, if there were truth in the old nonsense about an age of plenty, we would be the fools to accept that power and plenty at the price we are already paying for the instalment we did accept. I mean, the slavery that began by extending the costly notion of respectability to the masses, and that has, in my lifetime, become a system of documents and regulations that immobilise the bodies of most of us and the minds of nearly all.

I think of the huge armies of teachers (no disrespect to you!) engaged in making whole encyclopedias of statements seem self-evident axioms, to go unquestioned and un-found-out for the future. The fresh discovery a man makes is examined and had meaning: what he learns at school has only purpose, not his own purpose either. The newspapers, the popularisers of all degrees – hateful in their usefulness. You cannot be useful and retain possession of your own mind.

In short, isn't Society a fallacy? Whatever is shared that is worth having is shared amongst a few, because only a few have retained any freedom. What is worthless is doled out by the slaves of power in the name of equality, at the expense – which they count so small – of cutting off men from the essence of their manhood, their mind and soul and freewill. I think I rather envy your father.

That sermon is too elaborate already. I won't go on with it. Since I last wrote to you, I have made a trip to the South which took me through a district new to me – Luristan – and produced one mild adventure, an encounter with highwaymen.[106] Luristan is full of castles inhabited by the same robber barons the history books dilate on. My car broke down in sight of one such castle, and three pretty ruffians came out to collect the spoils. I was alone, but I was able to bluff them. I had in my bag an American insecticide which is sold under pressure in a case very like a hand grenade, and which hisses when you open the valve. I persuaded them it was a sample atomic bomb which I was taking to the Embassy, and that, since I didn't really understand its mechanism, it was liable to go off at any minute. They swallowed enough of that to retreat to a considerable distance, where they watched till the car got under way again. The conversation took about twenty minutes, disagreeable ones, for I had a diplomatic bag with me, and to have lost that to robbers would have been a serious business.

For the rest, mountains, some of them very impressive, valleys very fertile, the piers of ancient bridges over the Kharkheh river.[107] Oh yes! And on the top of a hill the car surprised a young girl having a bath in a puddle. She snatched up her frock to put it on, but the wind filled it and carried it away, and we last saw her chasing downhill like a gazelle stark naked after her only garment. I hope she caught up with it.

The camera was too late, of course; as usual.

The car I have at the moment is mad, and does not know the difference between one gear and another. It also boils. It makes so much steam that after a mile or two it looks like a locomotive. This is not the one that took me South, nor the one that will eventually be mine, but a stop-gap. If it doesn't kill me nothing will.

There is nothing else to say. Goodluck.

B.

## To Dorothy Pound

TS Indiana

17 December 1947 British Embassy, Teheran, c/o Foreign Office, London, S.W.1

Dear Dorothy,

It seems to me ages since I wrote to you. There is no proper excuse, but there are reasons – a further, very unpleasant bout of ex-wife trouble, followed by a very strenuous rush of work. As to work, I am glad it is getting considerable in quantity again. I have very little pleasure in idleness nowadays except on occasions when I have become altogether overtired, and then I do trifle if I can.

[106] Lorestan/Luristan: province in the west of Iran, in the Zagros Mountains.
[107] Karkheh: river in Khuzestan, also in western Iran.

Besides, I can claim a sort of victory in the work. I have really done what was never even attempted before, and done it well enough to astonish my diplomatic bosses into (probably temporary) respectful attention, so that my personal status has improved out of all recognition in the past two months. I hope that I can consider myself secure in what is becoming a pleasant though arduous existence for at least a year.

One of the pleasant consequences is that I am now able to do a certain amount of travelling: not, unfortunately, to any place I don't already know, but I have been down to Isfahan twice since the beginning of November, and enjoyed the welcome I knew I would get there, as well as feeling, when we approached the city, almost the same strong emotion I always feel on re-entering Italy. There they were, the great buildings, the uncountable trees, the delicate, beautifully printed "veils" (but they are more like very large shawls) used far more as instruments of flirtations than of concealment, the courtesy and real kindness of the man-in-the-street, the draped yards and yards of black silk trousers, the bazar where every shop is also a craftsman's workshop, and all the products are beautiful of their kind. In November it was still warm enough to picnic by the Zayandarud river,[108] and at once there came along the life we have banished from Europe – a wolf stepped out of the wood and gazed at us for quite a minute before running away. On the hills I found traces of moufflon, but did not see any. A jerboa ran across the road in front of the car. Gazelle, of course; and a few days ago, a huge vulture, looking larger than life with all his feathers ruffed up against the cold, sitting on the road, which reflects a little warmth from the sun, indifferent to lorries and cars.

One of my old colleagues whom I like very much has settled in Isfahan, a man of some fifty-eight or so who, after a lifetime of Asia cannot face a return to Europe.[109] He has a young Armenian wife whose two younger sisters live with them, a household without a trace of the kind of conventions which we have got so used to that we have forgotten they are merely conventions. I like the whole household. Beds, for instance are places where you sleep, and when you feel like sleeping you get into the nearest one, irrespective of who else may be there already. Clothes are for warmth and for making a show in the street, and when you are at home and the room is very warm, you take off as many of them as

[108] Zayanderud: largest river of the Iranian Plateau. It flows through Isfahan.

[109] Ronald Oakshott (d. *c.*1951), British agent based in Isfahan who as detailed here was responsible for bringing together BB and Sima Alladadian. In a later letter to Zukofsky ('June the New Moonth 1953', Texas), BB describes Oakshott as 'Sima's plus que père, who died drunk a couple of years ago. Banking was his trade, intoxication his calling.'

makes you comfortable, without the least regard to how much of yourself you exhibit. The vodka bottle gets into very strange places. Work is very like Nausicaa's washing day:[110] "What shall we do today? Let's wash the clothes." – a kind of play that never seems to grow stale and become a burden as household chores do in Europe, and that is always mixed up with singing and often interrupted by dancing, and never has to be done on time or against the grain. These girls are peasants, of course, born in a Kurdish village, and perhaps more Kurdish than Armenian in everything except their religion, which sits on them very lightly.[111] Their ambitions are simple and obvious – to see Teheran where there are so many cinemas, to acquire a gold bracelet, to have a ride in my car. It is restful to be among people who are happy and unhampered, who have so few wants and make so few demands on one. I wish I had the sense to marry someone of their sort.

Without the slightest care for natural history or anthropology, I delight in these animals and these peasants, in their beautiful setting, and to be able to get away from the capital for a few days at a time – and it is likely to be every month, I think – will make even the intervening bouts of desk-sitting perfectly endurable. However, even the Embassy is less unpleasant since I came to know a young couple: not very much to them, I daresay, though he writes poetry, and some of it could be made good, and she is very beautiful: but kind and much simpler than the foreign service ever produces, and intelligent and sensitive. Of course, they are on a short contract, and don't appear on the diplomatic list, and never will, I think. The diplomatic wives don't like Flora's beauty and the diplomats themselves, though they are glad of a pretty girl about the place, don't like her husband's determination to do a good job of work when he ought to have instead an earnest determination to adhere to the rules and usages and accept no responsibility which isn't absolutely forced upon him. So I expect they will be got rid of sooner or later, or else corrupted; but at present I am very glad of their company. She's Hungarian; of course she couldn't be English! Amongst the wives of consuls and diplomats, it is almost always the foreigners who succeed in being tolerable. The famous English arrogance comes out strong in almost all the Englishwomen in the East and renders them unbearable to me.

[110] In Book VI of Homer's *Odyssey*, Odysseus is shipwrecked on the island of Scheria, where he encounters the princess Nausicaa washing clothes with her handmaidens.

[111] The Kurds: Iranian people who live mainly in Turkey, Iraq, Iran, Armenia, and Syria. Christianity is a minority religion among the Kurds, but in Sima's Armenian homeland the Orthodox Armenian Apostolic Church is the majority denomination.

All this is very self-centred, I'm afraid; but I have left you so long unwritten to that I hardly know how to approach anything of more interest to you, while my own life is so barren in a sense that there is nothing I can pass on to you except the self-reflecting stuff that comes to one's mind when, being at leisure at last, one is also too weary to use one's brain at all extensively. But I do want to know how Ezra is, and how all your affairs are and what Omar is doing and thinking.

It was circumstances that obliged me to abandon the reflective life for the active one, as seaman and airman and diplomat, and I have no doubt gained something by the change, but I have lost a lot, amongst other things the opportunity of discussing more poetry and such in a way that could interest you. I like to imagine that I will go back to it later, but in fact action is a lust that is hard to abandon. I don't carry arms – that's the cruder idea of action, but it is also a type of it easily understood. Unless he penetrates a little nearer to what adventure really is, a man who has once got used to wearing an automatic will never part from it again; and I am afraid that I shall want to be moving and at grips with people and outwitting them until I die. So I shall probably write nothing, or nothing of interest, until I lose my job and can't get another. And even then I'd be tempted to join the highwaymen near Shiraz, I expect![112] And I bet I could increase their efficiency.

I hope you have as good a Christmas as circumstances permit, and that the new year brings you better fortune than the last ones have.

Yours very affectionately
B Bunting

## To Margaret De Silver

TS Durham

28 August 1948 British Embassy, Teheran, c/o Foreign Office, London, S.W.1

Dear Margaret,

Well I like that! Asking what's become of me and never telling me a word about yourself! But I was glad to see your signature again to deduce that you are alive.

The address, by the way, is nowadays as above, and air mail. Under new arrangements by Foreign Office it takes months for a letter to reach me.

[112] Shiraz: large city in south-west Iran.

I've been working, and the work has got sillier and sillier, more and more futile delays, bureaucracy gone stark mad. In addition I've been illish, not in bed but near it. Besides, I've had no leave, in spite of my contract. Brrr. Grrr. Finally, Sima has changed her mind and doesnt want to marry me after all, which is depressing, even though she may yet change it back again. She was an unexpected stroke of fortune in my middle-age, and now I feel like the chap who hears that he has won the lottery, and then that they have made a mistake over the number and he hasnt after all. I believe I told you about Sima – very young, beautiful, barbarous (Kurd and Armenian), without any of the usual assumptions and inhibitions. She was bound to get tired of me in time, but I'd hoped it might last a few years.

Now therefore the main reasons for doing this job have gone – to help my children, to provide for Sima – and I am left facing the futility of it with no better consolations than that I like Persia and the salary is nominally good (though in fact they juggle with it so wildly that I have actually grown poorer instead of richer during my time here.) I wont make all the complaints of the way they bring ones labours to naught. It isnt any sort of life, and leaves no room for living or even reading and writing. So I am considering not renewing my contract when it falls in next March. If I had just a little more money I'd have no doubts: I'd buy another boat and do a little thinking and reading in comfort, away from these perpetual irritations. But I want to see at least a year ahead when I've paid for the boat, and at present I'm not sure that I can.

I havent had any leave, as I said, but I got a couple of short weekends in the mountains above Teheran, when I took Sima and we were guests of a friend of mine who has put up a couple of tents for the summer, where he catches fish with a handnet and drinks vodka. The vodka is too plentiful, but the river is cold and very fast, just melted snow from the summits. And the fish is fried in batter and tastes excellent.

Well, there you are. That's all the news. I believe I have a few poems inside me, but I'll never get them out unless I stop working for the government. There is also the book about Isfahan. I can do nothing on it now.

It is the kind of world to drive one into the wilderness or onto the top of a pillar. Maybe it would be a good idea to get imprisoned for life. They learned nothing by the war, the politicians didnt. Why dont you stand for President, Margaret? I'll come over and let off crackers at your convention. You dont need a platform – better without one, in fact.

Please give my regards to Harry and Burnie: and to Anne if she will receive them.[113]

[113] Anne (1917–1997), Burnham (1919–2000), and Harrison: children of Margeret de Silver. BB's poem 'Not to thank dogwood' (dated 1938) is dedicated to Anne.

Let me know about yourself. Surely you do something? When am I going to see you again? It seems almost impossible, but I'd like it if it happened.

Love
Basil

## To Louis Zukofsky

TS Texas

3 November 1948 British Embassy, Teheran, c/o Foreign Office, London, S.W.1

Dear Louis,

What an admirable book![114] And having said that, which is the least one can say, what can I add without fear of being misunderstood? I would like to have compiled it myself. I am very glad it has been compiled. I think it will do a lot of good, if it circulates.

But I gather from the quotations on the wrapper that you have heard all that already. What you might want to hear would rather be the doubts and captious remarks that might lead to improvements in any second editions, or the reservations that might set off a train of thoughts useful for the next book. And I have no time to do that sort of thing properly.

I think you, like Ezra (and myself-when-young) look on criticism as a branch of pedagogy, in which your book excels all the others I've seen. I dare not say that you are wrong, nor even that the idea is inadequate; but I think of Longinus[115] (as far as I remember him) or of "Quatre Essais",[116] both of which express or imply general ideas derived from considering, hardly poetry itself, but things only secondarily connected with poetry – its ancient history, its effect on the reader. That is a different thing from the one you have accomplished, and also, I should think, worth your attention.

Secondly, I think you also regard criticism as a means of campaigning for what is good in contemporary writing, and that leads you sometimes to forget more

[114] BB is responding to Zukofsky's *A Test of Poetry*. Published by Objectivist Press in 1948, this was a pedagogical work very much in the vein of Pound's *ABC of Reading* (see 18/7/34 and note), with a similar mix of examples of canonical works and commentary by Zukofsky outlining his aesthetic principles. In the remainder of the letter BB quibbles with Zukofsky's choice of examples.

[115] *On the Sublime*: Roman-era (1st-century AD) Greek work on aesthetics, usually assigned to the author 'Longinus'.

[116] I.e. René Taupin's *4 Essais Indifferents pour une Esthetique de l'Inspiration* (see 20/10/32 and note).

permanent values. When Eliot used to thwack Milton[117] we all applauded, and very well it was; but now that all sorts of people complain of Milton who could neither write Samson[118] nor guess what Samson is about, I think we are both disgusted in the same degree: for it is right to put Milton in his place, and though that is a much lower place than our grandfathers assigned to him, it is still a great one. So I think one or two of your contrasts are not fairly chosen. There is a magnificence that shines suddenly out of the darkness of "The Vanity of Human Wishes" or "The Dunciad",[119] with an effect of controlled splendour such as you find but rarely in the kind of poetry with which you and I are more at home, like the best baroque painting – the less sentimental parts of Rembrandt or Claude, the boldest of Watteau.[120] Horace works wonders with a word order which was crabbed even to his contemporaries, as one may see by reading Lucretius and Ovid on either side of him in time. It is not right to banish such effects, which have their place, one, I think, too much neglected now, even though we and especially I follow Yeats's example of plain diction and plain syntax. I think your own work is apt to have an effect of crabbedness similar in a way to that of Horace, and it is through that that the felicities show up so well. But you only seem to acknowledge it in Browning.

You will say that you want to point a moral, hence the bit out of Laodamia[121] or the most unrepresentative sonnet from Spenser's most awkward translation. But I think such choices (they are few) injure your case by leading the reader to suspect a disingenuousness of which you are not in fact consciously capable. Spenser at least was a master of music matched to his theme, and the real grounds of complaint against him are not that he watered down the sonnet but that he so stubbornly attempted themes which were not his; the whole design of the Faerie Queene is false, so that it lives only in the incidentals. But that is not in general

[117] Eliot's rejection of Milton was a central plank of his critical project. Milton played a central role in Eliot's notion of 'dissociation of sensibility', outlined in his 1921 essay 'The Metaphysical Poets', which held that Milton and Dryden had aggravated a separation of intellect and feeling in seventeenth-century poetry.

[118] Milton's *Samson Agonistes*: dramatic poem in blank verse published in 1671.

[119] I.e. Samuel Johnson's 'The Vanity of Human Wishes' (1748) and Alexander Pope's *The Dunciad* (1728).

[120] Claude Lorrain (Claude) (*c.*1600–1682) and Jean-Antione Watteau (1684–1721): French baroque painters.

[121] 'Laodamia': 1815 narrative poem by Wordsworth based on an episode from the Trojan War. This is the first real engagement with Wordsworth in BB's correspondence. Along with his very cautious praise here of *some of* Wordsworth's shorter lyric works (the 'Lucy poems' of 1798–1801), and the reference to 'Wordsworthian dullness' in **6/7/51**, it seems to cut against BB's claim at the end of **6/5/69** about Wordsworth's towering influence on his early poetic development.

true of his lesser works. And Laodamia is Wordsworth attempting not to be Wordsworth for once. He attempted in Lucy etc the simplicity which is commonly recommended as the nearest road to the sublime, and sometimes came within sight of that distant peak: and he attempted the Lucretian manner, not without successful pages. But Laodamia is an aberration, and therefore, I think, a choice to be avoided, however tempting. Perhaps Cowper might better have filled the place.[122] He excelled in the kind of verse you wish to illustrate.

Indeed, I think all your selections should be from those who excel, for you do not merely want to show the gulf set between a poet and a poetaster, but to match very well with better and best. But even to do that would require only a few alterations, and I've done enough carping for one letter. It is an exhilarating book and has cheered up my present cast-downishness.

However, one misses the Ezra which should be there in so many places...

I have just distinguished myself by smashing my car twice in one month, after never having had an accident of any sort in my life before. The first time I hit a mis-lighted lorry in the dark, the second a wheel came off the car when it was travelling at high speed on a very busy road, and though I failed to kill anyone, the car ultimately turned over and gave me a bang on the head which kept me dazed for three days. I fear the insurance agent has ceased to love me and will buy me no more free drinks.

I have left the Embassy and now represent the Press, capital P.[123] I could stand no more of the Foreign Office. Now I am my own boss, more or less. I am beginning to be able to enjoy my attractive house, of which I've seen so little since I took to going to an office. It was a good office, as they go, but to sit there hour after hour, when maybe there was nothing to do worth doing!

Say "What cheer" to Celia for me, please, and whatever is the appropriate remark to your infant. Insha allah,[124] your book will improve your standing with the University and get you a whacking great salary. Besides a public.

Yours ever
B Bunting

[122] William Cowper (1731–1800), English poet whose work is often located in a transitional phase between eighteenth-century verse like that of Johnson and Pope and the Romanticism of Wordsworth and his contemporaries.

[123] After BB's marriage to Sima in December 1948, he left his job at the Foreign Office and accepted a job as Iran correspondent for the *Times* (see **19/4/49**).

[124] *Insha allah* (more commonly *inshallah*): if God wills (Ar.).

## To Louis Zukofsky

TS Texas

17 June 1949

c/o The Teheran Club, Teheran, Iran

Dear Louis,

What is so strange (about the Cantos, of which Dorothy has sent me a volume) is Ez's persistent praise of maenads and such like wild behavers, whereas he stiffens and is unable to disguise his disgust at even mild or parlour drunkenness in real life.[125] I suppose he never saw (not his fault) a panther except through bars, and until the war began to peter out he had had no experience more violent than a walkingtour or an easy seduction otherwise than filtered through books. He was never even really hard up – never I mean uncertain where and when the next piece of bread would reach his mouth. So the dream has none of the authenticity – or quite another kind of authenticity – of Dante's etc until you get near the end, and then it is only ricordarsi dello tempo felice, done with such skill, but is it necessary to go to such a length?[126] Discursive: the opposite of his own first commandment for poetry, namely, condensation.

That's not to belittle what he's done, which is far less incoherent than a lot of his admirers make out, and shows its coherence better as it nears its close. But one wants to know what the achievement does not consist in, as part of the process of learning what it does. The bees in the bonnet have buzzed away the facts, at any rate they have survived facts properly fatal to them. The vocabulary and imagery of his paganism remain as vague as its philosophic basis if any. They are not real leopards, nor real pictures of leopards, nor any Aphrodite less makebelieve than Botticelli's.[127] Nevertheless the incantation goes on as pleasantly as a summer afternoon, if as meaninglessly, often. I remain puzzled. I "admire" in both the old sense and the modern. There is too much of everything, not only of the pawnshop, and not enough of things, too few items, items of thought or unsuperficial perception, to fill out a volume – of poetry – except by the skill of the recurrences making a kind of music of it. And so back to the old Ez, the Ez

[125] BB's comments in this letter offer a first-hand reading of Pound's *Pisan Cantos*, alluding to several of the key presences in that sequence and in the *Cantos* as a whole. For example, maenads—female followers of Dionysus—feature in Canto 79 under the alias 'bassarids' (508–9), while Pound alludes to his own incarceration in Pisa by mention of a 'caged panther' in Canto 83 (550).

[126] *Ricordarsi del tempo felice*: remember the happy time (It.). A quotation from Dante's *Inferno*, Canto 5, l. 121–3.

[127] Leopards are a recurrent presence in the *Cantos*, notably in Cantos 2 and 79.

ever since his beginnings, an exploiter of music with so little of his own to say that all his themes are borrowed except a few, mostly in Lustra. From whom we have learned a lot, but I think almost all of it technical, how to write poetry, or one kind of poetry, discursive, musical, with in his case little real emotion and that rather stubborn than conclusive, of an irritable sensibility but, at least until lately, a very shallow one. Anyway, it's a great poem.

Here it's hot, and distinguished visitors keep me from my rest, chasing the news about them. Does anybody really care if the Regent of Iran had dinner with the Prime Minister of Iran? Do I owe you a letter or do you owe me? I've lost the last anyway. I shall visit Baghdad next month – a hideous city at an unpleasant time of year, with nothing good about it but the Tigris, though the bad is some of it interesting. I suppose they will put me in the Sindbad hotel with the tall palm trees on the riverbank and the exclusively English wives of officials trying to forget that they have to leave their doors open for air, so that there is only a mosquito screen between their nighties and the passing male.

And the worst of it is I shall have to go by air to save time, no sight of the Senjabi Kurds camped by the Paitak,[128] the flat, long dugs of their old women, perfectly visible, flopping with a loud smack of flesh at every step: no shot at a wolf: no sentimental drinking of sherbet with the kind and pretty Jewish friend at Hamadan[129] (now about to marry a fat young man with a Chrysler and no conscience).

Sima is (uncertainly: these young lasses are unpredictable) set on the road that leads to childbed. She looks lovely but gets cross in the heat. She has learned to swim, very badly so far but a beginning's a beginning, in the tank in our garden, and is going to graduate to the large, deep, Embassy tank this afternoon. I am looking for a new and more powerful car... I am nevertheless broke, the car is a necessary tool of my trade, without which there would be little news from Iran beyond echoes of the local newspapers. Nasr Khan Qashqai[130] turned up at a

[128] Senjabi Kurds: a people from the mountainous border region between Iraq and Iran, where the Paitak Pass is located.

[129] Hamadan: city and province in north-west Iran. It was the site of the ancient Median city of Ecbatana, which features prominently in Pound's *Cantos* as 'Ecbatan' 'the city of Dioce', a metaphor for the ideal city (see especially Cantos 4 and 74). BB had earlier written to Dorothy Pound after visiting Hamadan: 'As for Ecbatana-Hamadan, I can't get up any enthusiasm for it... the modern streets are shabby and the old alleys rather sordid on the whole, though there are fine houses here and there amongst them.' BB to Dorothy Pound, 11/4/48, Indiana.

[130] Naser Khan Qashqai (1899–1983), leader of the Qashqai people, a tribe from the Fars province of Iran comprised of Turks, Kurds, Lurs, and Arabs.

party yesterday: first time I've seen him in four years, looking large as well as cunning and rather goodhumoured, with a hook nose and incongruous brown eyes à la cow and a suit that didn't fit him at all. I forget how many hundred thousand nomads he thinks he governs, but a lot of them go their own way and he has to make the best of it. A few years ago the tribe was really run by his thirteen year old wife, a girl of fierce and indomitable passions, sharing the name of my daughter Roudaba. By now I daresay her children have partially and temporarily subdued her. All south Persia was on tenterhooks till her first twins were born, heirs to a lot of feuds and an enormous number of sheep. Sima wanted to ask him for a horse, but her cheek deserted her at the crucial moment. He would certainly have given her one, or any other person with the remotest claim on his pride, and I am relieved she didn't ask, for I couldn't feed and groom the brute, still less return Nasr's gift in any way. There was also the Governor of the National Bank quarrelling violently with another financier, whom I interrupted, asking after his ulcerated belly, in order to lessen the noise. And the Prime Minister, always the Prime Minister, with his arabesque of whisker, shaking hands all round and wondering each time "Who the devil is this, now? I ought surely to know" and disguising his ignorance with a clever set of politenesses designed to find out whether he ought to ask after the wife or who. I like the upright old Turk, and have more respect for the contents of his skull than I used to.

So anyway, all the best to Celia and Son, and to you.

Yours ever

B

Sima sends salaams.

## To Louis Zukofsky

TS Texas

6 August 1949

c/o The Teheran Club, Teheran, Iran

My dear Louis,

I was very much surprised to find that you attached enough importance to my very casual remarks about Cantos etc to be troubled by them.[131] Don't, please! If I wanted to write "for keeps" I wouldn't have the time, and anyway, never, even when I though a lot better of myself than I do nowadays, did I write letters intended to be commitments. I write such things at all only because there is

[131] See 17/6/49.

nobody with whom I can converse on literary (or most other intelligent) subjects. I forget what I have written: the rejoinder that might make good conversation at the time must necessarily come too late.

But perhaps I should be blamed for not remembering that you do keep letters, and see in them something more than a rather tired man's turning away from the stupid preoccupations he earns his living by. That, as you remember, has always made me uneasy. I would hate to have nobody with whom I could be unguarded or even foolish. Perhaps most people reserve such unarmoured self-exposures for conversation: but you mustn't forget that I've been out of reach of conversation now for – how many? – say, with very short intervals, sixteen years. I must be allowed the rather rare outlets; and really there is no one to whom I can write with any hope of being understood except you – so bear with it!

You could discount most of what I said about "Cantos" by recollecting that I do not like or trust any sort of criticism that starts from or ends in man's biography instead of what he has published. What I had been struck with at the moment of writing was a fact or fancy about Pound's life and psychology, with which in my view the public has no business at all, but which I could remark on to you, since we are both friends of Pound's beyond the likelihood of being thought or at any rate of thinking each other to have undervalued him. I owe him a great deal, and do not need to mention that when I write to you because I know you are very well aware of it. No? Well, anyway, none of what I write in letters is meant in any permanent way, it isn't thought out or deliberated on, it is offered merely in passing, not meant to be dwelt on.

Perhaps I am wrong in supposing that you thought I was running down the Pisan Cantos? I certainly didn't intend to do so, but to track down some sources of weakness in EP's whole output. The Pisan Cantos seem to me Cantos, part of poem which may be great and is certainly there to stay: and to reach a bit further into things than…

But they could be better. What's to hinder it? as Newman asked.[132] If I had time I'd to try to show where and how the tension is lowered or the outline blurred. I haven't, so, speaking only to you and only for the moment, suggest how maybe it is that a poet who comes so near yet apparently misses the bull. In that too – I mean that he misses – I may be wrong. The poem isn't finished yet, and I have nothing to say of it either to the public (supposing they would listen) or to

[132] In a famous passage in *The Idea of the University* (1854), Cardinal John Henry Newman (1801–1890) defined a gentleman as someone who is 'mainly occupied in merely removing the obstacles which hinder the free and unembarrassed action of those about him; and he concurs with their movements rather than takes the initiative himself'.

any friend save you and him, until the last line of it is down in print, and (I hope) the final revision and excisions made.

Or say, for some people whose writings we see, we lower the hurdles on the course and applaud a race which is all very well for that class of runner; but, my dear Louis, in dealing with some other people, of whom Ezra is one and you yourself another, we say "This chap means business: he is entered without handicap against Dante and Lucretius, against Villon and Horace," and we make no allowances at all and if he is beaten we say so: but there is perhaps more credit in it coming even almost last in such a race than in winning the other: at any rate to make a good show in it, to be taken seriously in it, whether you break your neck on the hurdles or not, is nothing discreditable. At least for my part I'd rather have somebody who is thinking of Horace call my poems bloody bad than hear them praised by somebody who is thinking of – who? – Dylan Thomas.[133]

I've a long dreary task in front of me this evening and for days to come. I am desperate for a pause and a chance to let all the nonsense I live by drain out of my mind and make room for something better, but it seems less likely every day. What's the use of a fine car if you only use it to run from the Ministry of Foreign Affairs to the Press Office? What's the use of a pool if you can only get into it once a fortnight? If I didn't have Sima there'd be nothing for me in this life beyond the contact with Persia which helps to clarify Persian poetry here and there. I am not much attached to things money can buy. I can do without them as I did before, and with even less repining . . . if I could exchange them for even moderate leisure. Do you know I've worked seven days every week (except one when I worked six) and twelve to sixteen hours every day since February? That's almost as strenuous as the war, and without any such motive. The prospect of even two or three days break has practically disappeared. Sima suffers by my overwork, too. I have no time to play. I guess I've done enough work of the kind that is more or less paid for during the last ten years to make up for the fourteen or fifteen years when I worked now and then and mostly at what I wanted to do (except for those two and a half damned years in Fleet Street).

(Incidentally, nearly every house here has a pool except the very poorest, though most of them leave their pools too dirty to be swum in. I've had ours cleaned a few times. Its possession doesn't imply Hollywood standards)

[133] It is unclear if BB had actually read anything by the Welsh poet Dylan Thomas (1914–1953) at this point. However, he certainly encountered Thomas's poems within the next couple of years (see **14/3/51**) and it must be said that *Briggflatts* faintly resembles certain of Thomas's works in form, subject and (marginal-British) sense of place.

Well, I dunno if I've cleared up the misunderstandings, if any. This letter is even more hurriedly written than usual, and maybe I've only made new ones…But the Times is bellowing for two long articles, the Abadan Daily News is waiting for its weekly column, there are a dozen shorter items to be sent to Near and Far East Agency, and I have promised a report on local opinion to the Embassy. I have to make up the time we lost by obeying the royal command to be part of a huge crowd having a magnificent supper with King Abdulla of Jordania,[134] which lasted hours and hours at my busiest time: but Sima was pleased because the little King (who comes straight out of Soglow's strip)[135] spoke to her and to no other female, and because there was a good puppet show and some very good Armenian dances, and because she astonished some Kurds by addressing them in their own language. An American newspaper man seemed enormously impressed by the scale and magnificence of the hospitality. The palace gardens are pretty and the fountains were well manipulated and the illumination was mainly by candles and fixed in glasses on trees. I was bored, even by the whisky, but it was Sima's first taste of splendours.

All the best to Celia and her fiddler.

Yours ever

B

## To Margaret De Silver

TS Durham

2 September 1949

c/o The Teheran Club, Teheran, Iran

My dear Margaret,

When shall I get a little leisure again? In a few months now it will be ten years since I had any rest at all except the few months of demobilisation, when I was looking for work. From 40 to 47 I had just over fourteen days leave and worked mostly at tasks far more continuous and often more strenuous than fell to most men. From 47 to today I've had a period when it was necessary to waste a certain amount of time, not to employ it sensibly or for pleasure, and a longer period now growing intolerable of work at a pressure equal to that of the war in its more strenuous phases. Since February this year I have had two days precisely on which I was free to do what I fancied – no Sunday off, no Friday off – and most

[134] Abdullah I bin Al-Hussein (1882–1951): founder and ruler of the Jordanian realm.

[135] Otto Soglow (1900–1975): New York cartoonist best-known for his 'gag-a-day' comic strip series *The Little King*, starring a vaguely Orientalist monarch.

days I have worked more than ten hours, often fourteen or fifteen for weeks together. It is stupefying. When I look back without actually tasking my memory I can remember only the few hours here and there when there was nothing official to be done – walks ashore in Scotland, amongst the bushes by the river at Ahvaz,[136] through the bush at Durban, shooting in the mountains over Isfahan. I remember my years at sea all right; but for the rest I have to think…yes, I spent sixteen hours every day under a sun dispensing 145 Fahrenheit in the shade chasing around driving Bakhtiari workmen to greater efforts…sat for three twelve hour tours and one of seventeen hours every four days at the telephone collating the reports of the Sicilian landings…rose at five and worked until the night raiders came home about midnight or later every day at Catania…worked, as they told me, an average of eighteen hours a day for over six weeks at the beginning of the Invasion of France, until for lack of sleep I nodded off riding my motor-bicycle down the runway of the airfield. Decidedly, whatever liberties I took with my time between 1928 and 1938, I have more than made up for it since! All this may explain why I have been so long without writing to you.

I married my wild girl, and a charming wife she makes. Of course, I say to myself: "The time will come, Basil, when she will perceive that you are old, before you have noticed it yourself, and she will be very young still and may want to swop you for a fresher husband. You must not count on her beyond what is natural to a young human being." But meanwhile she is very pleasant, patient with my lack of time to amuse her and my chronic scramble to make the cash cover the costs, kind when I am tired out with work. There is a baby on the way. What's the answer to a Kurdo-Armenian cross with a northern Englishman?

You know I left the Embassy to marry her, and now I am the Times correspondent here, which I combine with some other newspaper jobs and etceteras. It is harder than Embassy work of course, but lets me get about a bit more instead of sitting forever at a desk. I spend a fortune in petrol and am as handy in the Teheran traffic with a big car as any of the taxidrivers from constant practise. So I get about three times as many interviews into a morning as I could on foot, feeding the afternoon and evening session at the typewriter. But I wish I could rest long enough to get started thinking. I lament the years with nothing written worth the writing – one or two short translations are all the results of real work since well before the war. And now, I think, there would be plenty to say if I had the time to say it.

[136] Ahvaz: city in south-west Iran.

Iran doesnt pall, but I see little of Iran, only a series of government offices and club bars and the telegraph office, the streets that lead to them – or rather, the cars in those streets for there isnt time or space to look aside from driving – and my workroom.

I dont think I ever regret New York, but at odd intervals I think kindly of Los Angeles, one of the very few big cities which, if I hadnt been so desperately broke, I might have liked. Also an orchard behind Annapolis. Not an awfully heavy load of treasure to have brought away from two visits to the United States. There are of course moods when I am fed up with Persia, but all its irritations really add up to very little. Still I like the people, still I wonder at the landscape when I have time to see it, still I find their way of life, with all its little hypocrisies and greeds, a better one in general, in the long run, than those of England and America. What's done well in England is generally something beside the point of life, like the refrigerator in the USA. Here the town has not yet tried to abolish the village as an eyesore and an imposition, or to perceive it as a museum piece. The natural use of leisure here is still to shoot big game or read at home or dance in a circle together where the crop has been taken in. The sea is the only better thing, and by its possession of the sea Italy exceeds Persia.

I'd like to have enough money to live a few years aboard a decent sized yacht, or to sit in a cottage beside the Mediterranean or goodness knows where, and let the things now accumulated in me work themselves out in a bit of respectable writing. However, that seems to be an ambition I must forgo. Here there is such a huge (and growing) cost of living that I cannot save a penny. Two years government service cost me most of my savings, I shall never leave enough to provide for my wife, let alone be able to cease this mankilling overstrenuous style of work.

Did I say a bloke in Texas[137] had undertaken to edit my poems and get them all published by Laughlin of New Directions? I havent had time to do anything at all about it myself and dont know whether it has been dropped. It would be handy to have them in book form, so that I could throw away a mass of mss and stop thinking, as I do once in while, about how much better I ought to make them. I dont suppose there would be many readers, and dont really care. Readers are not what one writes for after one's got rid of the cruder ambitions.

Its getting dark and I must rest a little so as to be able to tackle a long article that must be written tonight after dinner. So goodbye, my dear, for a season.

[137] **Dallam Simpson/Flynn**'s preparation of *Poems: 1950* consisted of collecting together almost all BB's works to date. Many of BB's early works had been published in Pound's *Active Anthology* (1933); *Poems: 1950* featured all the works in that publication, and many more (see Share, 544–545).

Write if you feel like it. I may not be able to answer but I dont want to lose the feel of you entirely.

Love
Basil Bunting

## To Dorothy Pound

TS Indiana

14 May 1950

[Teheran]

Dear Dorothy,

I am leaving Teheran next Sunday, returning for the time being to my mother's house, 242 Newburn Road, Throckley, Northumberland. I lost (chiefly through the sin of not having joined twenty years ago) the job which provided most of my money, and the Times had none worth mentioning, though Hugh Astor swore he would make them at least double my pay.[138] Prices here are so huge that without a commensurably huge job I've no hope of managing.

It will be tough on Sima at first, with so little of the language and the baby to mind.

Goodness knows what sort of a job I shall find. Here I could find two, both well paid by English standards, but I could only have made about two thirds of what it costs me to live. £2000 a year gives you the Persian equivalent of about six hundred at home.

I haven't had the time or the heart to write lately, but will presumably have at least the time in Northumberland. There's been no rest this year. I got one free day to take Astor up into the mountains, but it snowed and blew deadly cold, so we declined into a teahouse and smoked opium until time to go home.

Nearly everything is packed. What a lot of rubbish accumulates in three years.

All the best to you and Ezra until I can write again.

Yours ever
BBunting

[138] Hugh Astor (1920–1999), member of the wealthy Astor dynasty, who was deputy Middle East correspondent for the *Times* in this period (and son of the paper's owner John Jacob Astor V, see note to 9/1/37). As indicated here, BB seems to have blamed Astor for his mistreatment by the *Times*. He later got his revenge by caricaturing Astor as the dung covered 'Cockney hero' Hastor in *Briggflatts*, Part III (28–35).

## To Peter Russell[139]

TS Buffalo

18 May 1950 242 Newburn Road, Throckley, Northumberland

Dear Peter Russell

Returning the pamphlet...

I know nothing of Jung beyond his name: maybe I read some of his stuff in the early twenties when psychoanalysis was necessary to conversation, but I've long forgotten it.

Mr Wertham doesnt seem very inspired, nor even very well informed.[140] But I dont see what harm he can do.

Have you, by the way, considered what might be the effect on Ezra of being released? At present he is free to work and protected from intrusion. If he were let go, isnt it certain that the US press, never willing to drop a story, would see to it that his neighbours always knew that the celebrated traitor was amongst them? I doubt whether he would find much rest. I am assuming that the US wouldnt be likely to give him a passport again, of if they did, other countries would be shy of giving a visa. I would like to see him set free, but mainly for the sake of the USA itself, which ought not, in the future, to have to be ashamed of its treatment of its greatest poet. If there were only Pound to think of I'm not sure that I wouldnt think him better off where he is. Pound is himself too sanguine to be a good judge of that dilemma. But it's a very complicated one, and I'm certainly not capable of coming to any conclusion about it.

German poetry...I gave up trying to like it many years ago. Heine has his own tang, Goethe and Walther von der Vogelweide have an excellent music, Hoelderlin has a barren sort of individuality, there are one or two others:[141] but in the main it seems to me only a repeat of what can be found better done in other languages. Perhaps I'm deaf to it: I've loathed the Germans for so many years that I approach anything of theirs with hostility, their Hegel, their Marx, their Wagner, their

[139] **Peter Russell**: British poet-critic who ran the journal *Nine* from 1949. Russell was in touch with Pound in this period, and spearheaded an 'Ezra Pound Circle' in London.

[140] Frederic Wertham (1895–1981), German-American psychiatrist who argued in 1949 that Pound's award of the Bollingen Prize implied that the worst misdeeds of World War II were being forgotten and brushed over, and that psychiatrists were guilty of allowing Pound to escape justice. See Frederic Wertham, 'The Road to Rapallo: A Psychiatric Study,' *American Journal of Psychotherapy*, III, October, 1949, 585–600.

[141] Heinrich Heine (1797–1856) and Friedrich Hölderlin: German Romantic poets; Walther von der Vogelweide (*c.*1170–*c.*1230): the most celebrated proponent of *Minnesang*, a medieval German tradition of lyric and song-writing.

Beethoven... I've lost my liking, as a young man, for the styles of Schopenhauer[142] and Nietsche, though I still think there is a little more in Nietsche's notions than contemporary disgust with Nazism will allow. He was mad, megalomaniac: but he was impatient with a good many things I detest... including the Germans. Yes, they thought themselves akin to the Scots, but made a mess of translating Burns and were shocked and frightened by Hume. Scots and Scandanvian may be a better combination. But Scots cant be as curtly sufficient as Icelandic, the only Scandanavian language I have any smattering of.

Isnt it possible that a certain clumsiness of utterance, a certain provincialism, common to Scots and German, may attract you because it is immune from the overslick surface of current English, French, etc? But it isn't the identically same clumsiness in both cases. And the absence of an irritating vice is no guarantee of the presence of any virtue whatever. What's become of Celine, by the way?[143] His French wasnt dissolved in copal varnish.

What went on in Paris and Rapallo...? Mainly a comedy. Most of the dramatis personae were comically vain, and the clash of their vanities was funny. Little by little the spectacle reduced my own vanity to manageable proportions, but that didnt appear to be the usual result. Maybe vanity is necessary to perseverance in anything so exacting as an art.

Ezra repeats a former injunction to me to settle in London and play Dr Johnson's part. I have nothing of Johnson except his indolence, and I cant indulge even that until the govt gives me the equivalent of his pension, which wont happen. True, I would like to hear some conversation again instead of the chatter of official cocktail parties, but I hate cities, and the bigger they are the more I hate them. I am not a ready talker, either, nor a very acute listener. So I hope to see London only in transit. But if its at all possible I shall look you up.

Yours faithfully
B Bunting

In late 1950 the Buntings travelled to Italy, where Bunting worked near Rome for the next six months in the employ of the newspaper syndicate Westminster Press (possibly also with some covert intelligence role for the Foreign Office). It was here that he began work

[142] For BB's later praise of Schopenhauer see **4/9/65**.

[143] Louis-Ferdinand Céline (1894–1961), French writer best known in this period for his 1932 novel *Journey to the End of the Night*, set in the aftermath of World War I. Céline's savage pessimism seems to have appealed to BB, and indeed he was a keen reader of Céline's later work in his last years (see **23/6/84**).

on *The Spoils*, his war poem or 'fifth sonata', which was eventually published in *Poetry* in November 1951, after a long and detailed discourse about textual minutiae with Zukofsky (most of which is summarized in Share 306–323).

## To Dorothy Pound

TS Indiana

6 January 1951

Lido di Camaiore

Dear Dorothy,

Ezra's "Letters" coinciding with the first moments of leisure since Lord knows when... (But I wouldn't disturb him, save for the Cantos, of which the remaining ones ought to be as right as possible)

Ez seems to me mistaken when he takes all the good in Xtianity as Greek contribution and denies anything useful of Semitic origin. That is, the three profoundest points made in the gospels seem to me to have no imaginable Greek antecedents, and have never been assimilated by the Church, because of its predominantly Greek outlook: namely

1) The bit about taking no thought for the morrow, and its variant about the lilies.[144]
2) The bit about becoming like little children if you want to get into heaven[145]
3) "Let the dead bury their dead"[146] (which would incidentally dispose of the collectors of laundry-lists of whom he has at times complained)

I can't guarantee that these are Semitic contributions, but I don't know where else to look for them, certainly not Plato, nor the Platonists who have either neglected or misunderstood them and explained them away.

More arguably, I don't know a Greek antecedent for "The Kingdom of Heaven is within you".[147] Sure, it's the essence of all the good mysticism from Plotinus via

[144] See Matthew 6:34: 'Take therefore no thought for the morrow: for the morrow shall take thought for the things of itself', and Matthew 6:28: 'Consider the lilies of the field, how they grow; they toil not, neither do they spin.'

[145] See Matthew 18:3: 'Verily I say unto you, Except ye be converted, and become as little children, ye shall not enter into the kingdom of heaven.'

[146] See Luke 9:6: 'Jesus said unto him, Let the dead bury their dead: but go thou and preach the kingdom of God.'

[147] See Luke 17:21: 'Neither shall they say, Lo here! or, lo there! for, behold, the kingdom of God is within you.'

Teresa or Jelaluddin to TSE, but Plotinus might have had it from his Xtian fellowstudents at Alexandria (Origen, eg).[148] It aint Plato. Maybe Ez disapproves this sentiment, but it's a powerful interesting one all the same, and cracks down pretty heavily on a lot of the mumbo-jumbo that irritates him.

The three points: Francis tried out number one,[149] but it is daily habit in the Arab countries, though anything but Qor'anic. They strain the Qor'an for authority. The children bit having been tearfully sentimentalised is almost past rehabilitating in its existing form. It links closely with the dead burying the dead, which I take to be an exhortation to look at things with one's own eyes and accept no hearsay: history to return to its old status as an art, not pretend to be a bloody science, etc etc. The "children" adds to that a caution against teleology: neither the first cause nor the final cause is relevant. All three make a mesh through which to drain out the damned water of metaphysics et al. They are the antithesis of the Greek position and would, no doubt, destroy the Church. This mesh I take to be the neglected but vital Semitic contribution (though one or all of the points in it might perhaps be shown to have another origin).

Zarathustra anticipated Voltaire and other rationalists: "Digging is better than prayer" is in the Gathas.[150] Voltaire got round to that only at the end of Candide, and without much conviction. Whether it's true or not I don't profess to know, but the old Aryan anti-God prophet deserves his credit.

Finally, Tao, which Ez condemns complete and without giving it a public hearing.[151] The identity of opposites is confusing and a source of confusion. I don't embrace it, but I think there is no guarantee that things are simple and a strong presumption that they aren't (in short, Occam's razor is a misleading principle if taken beyond formal logic).[152] As to the morals of Tao, with which I think Ez is more concerned, Chuang's parable about the butcher who never needs to sharpen his knife because he knows just where to divide the tissues so as to find

[148] For Plotinus see **21/1/47** and note. Saint Teresa of Ávila (1515–1582), Spanish Roman Catholic mystic. 'Jelalludin': the Persian poet and Sufi mystic Rumi. Origen Adamantius (*c.*184/5–253/5), Greek scholar and early Christian theologian.

[149] See **20/8/47** for BB on St Francis.

[150] This axiom, which BB also deployed in a variant version of 'The Well of Lycopolis' (see Share, 250), is possibly drawn from the statement 'movement and activity are better than laziness and inactivity' in Yasna 46, verse 17 of the *Gathas* (see **11/11/38** and note).

[151] In the *Cantos* Pound refers disparagingly to Taoism and it adherents (which he calls 'taozers'), for example throughout Canto 56.

[152] Occam's razor, propounded by William of Ockham (*c.*1287–1347), is a principle which contends that, in solving a problem, we should eliminate unverifiable assumptions and focus on the simplest apparent solution. In contrast, Taoism incorporates a belief in the need to respect the possible truth of apparently irreconcilable opposites.

no resistance to it – it's damned good advice.[153] Maybe it's in others besides the Taoists, but it's there too.

This aint writ in any spirit of contradiction, but only to call attention to some items Ez may have overlooked. In the interests of Cantos to come.

I've nearly finished getting down movement of a new poem, that is, in draft.[154] It's meant to display the Semite, for a contrast, in a later movement with the Aryan also in an Eastern setting. Less subjective than previous "longer" poems. I'd like to get in the bugger dancer with the roses in his hair, as object of desire: but don't know quite how to manage it.

Following ruba'i (Rudaki)[155] contains one word (not an adj.) not in the original:

Came to me-
Who?
She.
When?
In the dawn, afraid.
What of?
Anger.
Whose?
Her father's
Confide!
I kissed her twice.
Where?
On her moist mouth.
Mouth?
No.
What, then?
Cornelian!
How was it?
Sweet.
) - - - - - - - - - - - - e – e

[153] Zhuang Zao (*c.*396–*c.*286 BC), Chinese philosopher and author of the *Zhuangzi*, one of the central texts of Taoism. The *Zhuangzi* contains an allegory about the chef Ting, a 'dexterous butcher' who maintains the sharpness of his knife by cutting his meat skilfully and meticulously rather than hacking away at it.

[154] I.e. *The Spoils*, which begins with a series of monologues by Semitic (Arabic and Jewish) characters, before moving in its second part to a celebration of Persian (Aryan) culture.

[155] This translation of a poem by Rudaki would later feature in slightly altered layout in collected editions of BB's work, beginning with *Loquitor* (1965) (see Share, 146).

Cornelian (grotesque in English?) is apology, possibly mock apology, for indelicately plain language of "mouth". I think it has an impetus, hope I've not lost all of it.

All the best
B

## To Louis Zukofsky

TS Texas

14 March 1951

Lido di Camaiore

Dear Louis,

Your Feb 10 – long-un –: yes. Nothing much more to say on most of those subject(s).

a. I think Joe S. would be disappointed if he got what Russia wants without war. War may not help Communism but it is almost necessary to a despotism that isn't firmly fixed in tradition. As much a Roman-empire sort of despotism as an hereditary one. However, if he got it all without war, that wouldn't help us much. We'd avoid immediate death in convulsions in order to linger it out with cancer...It doesn't much matter where we start. They've apparently made a preliminary pass at Persia (The "Fedayan" aren't, of course, communists: but they have the looney idea that they can make use of Russia for their own ends, with the obvious result that Russia makes use of them.[156] The actual assassins on the last two "Fedayan" occasions turned out to be in fact "Tudeh" – ie Communist – party members who had joined the Fedayan recently without relinquishing their Tudeh membership. Razmara[157] was a good guy and my friend, ready to tackle the extraordinarily difficult job of reforming Persia without defying facts or initiating a new dictatorship. He released the jailed Communists, including the several-times-over murderer Boghrati,[158] and imagined that would ease tension. An error. And I was stopped from advising him, even when he asked it, for fear of "British interference". He took on the PM job just after I left Iran, and he was the man for it, but I'd have liked him to let the Nationalists make a mess of it first and

[156] Fadayān-i-Islam: Iranian Islamic fundamentalist group, which began a long campaign of assassination and targeted killings following its foundation in 1946.

[157] Haj Ali Razmara (1901–1951), Iranian military leader and Prime Minister of Iran from 26 June 1950, until he was assassinated by the Fadayān on 7 March 1951.

[158] Mahmoud Boghrati: founding member and influential figure in the Tudeh Party.

discredit themselves. Now there's no one left with both sense and authority. Even uprightness is none too common among politicians in Persia as elsewhere.)

b. "Russia's next". That sort of remark is universal after wars amongst the unreflecting. After 1918 our own blokes were saying "America's next", not that they either hated or feared America, but just because America seemed to be the most formidable thing in sight and perhaps at that time also the most cock-a-hoop. Nevertheless a farsighted man might, at least by 1946, say without insobriety "Russia's next" because their bad faith in small matters had by then spread to larger ones too. It's not a question of ultimate hopes or maximum aims, so long as they are pursued patiently by what are called and considered legitimate means. It's the contempt of agreements, use of open force and barely concealed fraud, that make peace impossible to maintain. Not that one could rest easy, however the aims were pursued, but they might be countered without war. There would be good hope of it, and at the worst war would be a distant prospect, not for tomorrow. (Incidentally "America's next" was pretty freely said towards the end of this war too. It meant nothing, and I mention it only to say again that such remarks mean nothing.)

c. Korea. I mean, America has been practically, if not in theory, deserted by her Allies and gets only phrases out of the UNO. I think the war there would have been over very quickly but for their drawing-back. Russia can't be ready for a universal conflict yet, must trade on making her conflicts considerably less than universal.

d. Sure, it would be nice to have some less negative aim than to avoid being tyranised over. It would be nice to be back at the beginning of the century. But I am pretty sure that's the most we can hope for, and even that involves a pretty strenuous life without rewards, fighting some with arms and others with arguments, often crude arguments we don't altogether believe ourselves: hoping that someday it may be possible for someone else to be free and at leisure enough to take stock and start afresh with pleasanter things. The consolation – what a word for it! – is that the whole bloody show is stinking dead anyway. Civilisation won't be the worse for a few generations rest; poetry and philosophy and music and what not, all ballsed up by charlatans.

e. Olga Rudge.[159] Seems to me to have become embittered by jealousy of Dorothy, who, of course, has all the honour and glory, besides being infernally unjealous, which must be maddening. Olga presides more or less over the

[159] **Olga Rudge**: Pound's long-term lover. At this point Rudge was somewhat distanced from Pound, as Dorothy became his main partner and guardian in St Elizabeths.

activities of the Accademia Chigiana at Siena:[160] excellent music, annual courses, annual "week". I don't know for sure whether she still fiddles. She was good, and was a lot more than a fingering-machine. Very intelligent. Probably still so. I think she now disapproves of me because I don't take sides in family squabbles which she magnifies until everybody who isn't a partisan of her or at least her point of view is an enemy to be maligned and combatted. It is all damn silly. She goes so far as to assert that Dorothy prevents Ezra being released for fear he should run away to her, Olga. If you will write an article implying something of the sort she will move heaven and earth on your behalf. Old Pea says she's much madder than Ezra, and he ought to know: mad as a hatter himself.[161]

I suggest however that the tricks may not all be there in Tartini:[162] maybe there are twiddly bits in Dvorak or even Greig or who the hell is that – Max Reger:[163] yes, surely there are twiddly bits in Max Reger that can't be found in older music? Chigiana specialises in Vivaldi, Porpora,[164] Tartini et al., moderns, and guitar (They have Segovia teaching).[165] But the entrance standard is arranged to keep out those who are not yet of virtuoso size.

f. Nine aint published anything of mine but some unimportant translations which you've seen anyway.[166] They have also dropped me from their adverts. That's reasonable enough and I'm not grumbling, only explaining that I've no pull. They are, as you say unsatisfactory. When we were young there were Mr Squire and his pals.[167] Then Auden and Spender got hold of the racket, and ran it, I must admit, a trifle more enterprisingly for a while. Now Russell's pals are muscling in. There's a career in fraudulent poetry, jobs in the BBC...I doubt whether it's any worse than the much stiffer more provincial racket in the same

[160] Rudge started working as secretary at the musical institute, Accademia Musicale Chigiane, soon after its foundation in 1932.

[161] Enrico Pea (1881–1958), Italian writer and poet, whose experimental novel *Moscardino* (1922) was translated by Pound in the early 1950s.

[162] Giuseppe Tartini (1692–1770), Italian baroque composer known for his virtuosic compositions for violin.

[163] Antonín Leopold Dvořák (1841–1904), Edvard Grieg (1843–1907), and Max Reger (1873–1916): late-nineteenth century European composers of notable violin sonatas.

[164] Nicola Porpora (1686–1768), Italian baroque composer known for his operatic compositions.

[165] Andrés Segovia (1893–1987), modern Spanish classical guitarist famous for his virtuosic performances.

[166] *Nine*: poetry magazine edited by Peter Russell. It published a handful of BB's Persian translations in the early fifties (see Burton, 338).

[167] J. C. Squire (1884–1958), British writer, poet, and editor (1919–1934) of the literary journal the *London Mercury*.

material run by American English Depts in small universities. So long as they don't make one actually spue they provide a possible page on which to print a poem which maybe somebody will read. They mustn't expect me to scratch their backs out of gratitude, though.

g. Yes, the diplomats would know you aren't one.[168] For one thing diplomats don't often stay long in one post. After a couple of years, three maybe if theyre Ambassadors or Counsellors, they are moved to the end of the earth. The idea is to have chaps of wide experience, not experts in one country, who can always be hired temporarily in case of need (eg me in Persia for two years). Ferdinand might have returned to USA after tours in China, Luxembourg, Egypt and Portugal. He wouldn't have stayed there. There are exceptions, few, mostly Turks.

h. Eliot, though a good fellow, wouldn't regard my recommendation. I think he likes me, not my poetry nor taste in lit. Of that he probably thinks that it ought to be published, but he doesn't very much want to press Fabers about it. That at least is my guess. I haven't read Nightwood,[169] never read novels, really. The odd one now and then, when I'm off colour and sick of detectives.

i. Music and dance, certainly. Firdosi conducting while his ravi sings and the mimes are dancing, as in the ancient miniature in an mss of the Shahnameh. The giullar in the piazza.[170] Malherbe complaining he was handicapped by rheumatism, so that he couldn't finger his lute: couldn't compose odes any other way. That's poetry, every time we get back to it. Ezra knows, but broke off half-way, or maybe he wasn't entirely conscious of knowing. TSE has a compromise, and that's why he wont last at his present level of quasi-universal appeal. (Nothing to do with his subject matter – poetry never has in the long run). You know it in your bones, but your god-damned intellect keeps getting in the way with little ifs and buts: and besides (forgive me if it seems uncourteous) your ear is tuned to a different set of noises to our English ones – an advantage in some ways, leaving your cadences, when we get them, fresh: and when we don't, a nuisance. What can I say as rude, if I ever want to insult you?

j. There is no question about your merits: I'd like them to be more obvious and maybe greater even than they are.

[168] This passage refers to Zukofsky's novella *Ferdinand* (written in the early 1940s), set among the embassies and emigrés of interwar Europe. It appeared in two instalments (May and November) of the *Quarterly Review of Literature* in 1950.

[169] Djuna Barnes's *Nightwood* (1936) was published in 1936 by Faber & Faber, with an enthusiastic preface by Eliot. In style and premise it is not dissimilar to Zukofsky's *Ferdinand*.

[170] *Giullar*: jester (It.).

k. Dahlberg.[171] Yessir, good work. I think, dated: ad imagists. But good for all that. I never heard of him before and am glad to do so now. Would he despise my felicitations? What's his seniority? Fifty, you say, in years, but as a poet? God defend me from ever becoming a man of letters but, as a shabby ex-diplomat, as a soldier, as a sailor, who has written a few poems, as a God-cursed journialist, as a man of a fair number of misfortunes and some good fortunes, as the husband of a wild and frequently startling girl, would Mr Dahlberg care for the acquaintance?

l. Bard College[172] opines that my "breadth would embarrass other members of the faculty", so USA isn't an immediate prospect. Cash has eased a little, not enough, the TIMES is wondering again whether it can afford the frightful cost of a correspondent ("own correspondent" next time I hope) in Teheran. That would be better for Sima and by no means unwelcome to me in spite of the prospect of having to pack and flee suddenly. In short I don't in the least know what next.

m. Feeling I'd maybe been over severe on too little acquaintance I recently bought a collection of Auden & his friends.[173] I was wrong. I was far too indulgent. They are a useless set of cunts, even if rather less abject than their immediate predecessors. And Auden, who has or who had an ear, can't reasonably be excused. If Russell has to kowtow to the rowdy Roy Campbell[174] to get someone to batter Auden, well, ok. The boy-scout shorts and the incubus of the daily good deed, the – well, the opposite of Gongorism[175] – which I take to be too elaborate a treatment of uninteresting matter. Theirs is too crude a treatment of what they had to hand, which wasn't after all, worse matter than we all get. There's a horrid female in one of EM Forster's novels who gets all hysterical over the wrongs of the underdog when what is really the matter is an unrubbed clitoris:[176] her diatribes closely resemble those of Auden and Day Lewis in the 30s. Pseudo-sincere!

171 **Edward Dahlberg**: American poet and a good friend of Zukofsky's in this period.

172 Bard College: private liberal arts college in New York, founded in 1860. BB appears to have made enquiries about working there in 1951.

173 This was probably the anthology *Twelve Modern Poets*, published by Zephyr Books in 1946, which included selections from Auden, Spender, Day Lewis, MacNeice, Dylan Thomas, Pound, Eliot and others. A copy is held in BB's library at Buffalo.

174 Roy Campbell (1901–1957), South African poet known for his controversial right-wing politics and visceral verse style. Campbell coined the composite nickname 'MacSpaunday' to refer to the Auden circle in his satirical 1946 poem 'Talking Bronco'.

175 Gongorism: florid, pun-heavy literary style following the example of Spanish baroque poet Luis de Góngora (1561–1627).

176 Possibly Margaret Schlegel, the idealistic protagonist of Forster's *Howards End*.

n. I write to Ezra and Dorothy, and they write to me, fairly frequently. I invented a project for the bilingual series of Oriental classics, chiefly to give EP something to think about. Nothing can come of it. At present he's rushing after it most magnificently. Especially since I revealed that Arabic historians aren't totally blind to economic and currency problems. I foresee that the leaden coinage of pre-Islamic Bokhara[177] will make an appearance in the Cantos. Letter before me is the sanest in years, and might well not be from an asylum. He says he is trying to get a little sense of prosody into a few blokes who know Greek…Chinese vowel sequence…etc etc. Praises Ethel Merman (Taj and Moluk-e Zarrabi may be forestalled!)[178] "voice like a slide-trombone and sings like a bleeding BAND without needing an accompaniment to lie down on"

He doesn't get anti-Semitic very often, and has announced that the only sane historian of the USA was a Jew (Del Mar).[179] I doubt whether Del Mar was a Jew, but once bitten they see mad dogs everywhere. I would still say, write to him! Why stand on your dignity or ceremony or what-have-you? If he leaps down your throat, well, he's NOT sane: but sane enough to finish the Cantos sooner or later I hope. And, a side remark, no cat ever liked butter more than he does. Spread intelligently but thick…I don't need to, perhaps you don't: we're old friends. Dorothy says letters make almost his only fun, and though he chases everything that chimes with his politics etc, it's the letters of old friends, of TSE, BB, Bill Williams, that really cheer him. Of course, he cherishes the Protocols of the Elders of Zion[180] somewhere or other, but he hasn't said so to me. Think of Mr Dick[181] and King Charles's head. I don't reply to the wilder currency sallies, anti-bankerisms etc, and it doesn't seem to matter.

Sima, with no regard for the local priests, is burning a huge candle with Gregorian ceremonies in Pisa cathedral to persuade God to make Truman let EP out. EP says that's a sound idea, evviva Sima! The time is coming for her annual theft of the Host, to slip it surreptitiously into my wine or coffee and so get me to

[177] Bukhara: ancient city in modern Uzbekistan with a coinage dating back to the 4th century AD.

[178] Ethel Merman (1908–1984), American singer and actress known for her roles in Broadway musicals. As with the reference to Bokhara/Bukhara, in alluding to the Persian characters Taj and Moluk-e Zarrabi, BB is nodding at Part III of *The Spoils*, which Zukofsky was helping to edit at this time.

[179] Alexander del Mar (1836–1926), American economic historian of Jewish-Spanish descent.

[180] *The Protocol of the Elders of Zion*: notorious fabricated anti-Semitic text of 1903, which describes a plan for Jewish world domination.

[181] Possibly a reference to Richard Brandon (d. 1649), executioner of King Charles I.

heaven in spite of myself. Daughter is now walking. Weather is still abominable, phenomenal, catastrophic, etc etc. The best to you and yours

B

Large excisions in Fifth Sonata taking place, which I suspect you'll anyway recommend.[182]

## To Alan Neame[183]

TS Buffalo

16 April 1951

Lido di Camaiore

Dear Mr Neame,

I do not like the idea of a commentary on the Cantos. I do not see why people should want to "understand" everything in a poem. Presumably they are misled, because it is set down in writing, into supposing it to be some sort of statement, about something. They do not want to understand every line in a drawing or every note in a fugue, though there is no essential difference between these and a poem, such as there is between any of them and a record or argument. A poem appears to me to be an object made by a craftsman or artist, to be liked or otherwise for its own sake, and not for anything he may have had in his mind when he wrote it. Otherwise we should have nothing but ridicule for the puerile fables of, let's say, Ovid, and those of us who are not catholics could derive little pleasure from Dante.

In the second place, if there really is a need for a commentary (and in the Cantos case I doubt it), that is surely a weakness in the poem. If it cannot stand without scaffolding it is probably best to let it fall at once. What Pound wants in the Cantos is in them, I think. There is no need to call attention to what is not in them, namely, further information about things or people which have been mentioned for a particular purpose and not for what may be found out about them elsewhere by the diligent. "If Basil sing of Shahnameh . . . etc"[184] obviously implies

[182] In a letter sent to Zukofsky dated the previous day, BB had written with long notes on the development of *The Spoils* (i.e. the 'Fifth Sonata').

[183] Alan Neame: writer and translator who was part of the neo-fascist circle centering on Oswald Mosley's Union Movement in the late 1940s and early 1950s. He corresponded with Pound in St Elizabeths and wrote several apologias for Pound's work, beginning with the article which probably occasioned this exchange with BB: 'Ezra Pound Reconsidered', *New Blackfriars* 32:371 (1951).

[184] This allusion to BB appears in Pound's Canto 77 (494), along with a Farsi rendering of Ferdowsi's name. As BB argues here, there is nothing especially suggestive or arcane about this fragment: like much of the *Pisan Cantos*, it is simply one of Pound's reminiscences about his pre-war friends, though it fits with a general theme of internationalism, translation, and cultural exchange.

somebody concerning himself with an outlandish-sounding poem: it is also a nice noise: it adds nothing whatever to know that Basil is my name, and very little to know that Shahnameh is the name of Firdosi's epic. IF Pound has anything more in mind than this (and I don't think he has), it could only be on the assumption that my name would convey more to a reader at some other time than it does now. I think this or something like this is true of all the names that occur: everything is in the poem that the poem needs, or else Pound believes that time will put there whatever he has, for the moment, omitted. More is irrelevant, and can only diminish the effect of the verse.

So much for general principle! In this particular case there is, however, a further strong reason why a commentator should not come to me and my like for information, namely, that the author of the poem is alive and perfectly capable of explaining to the public or to the commentator what he means by any particular phrase. He knows, where I can only guess, and however probable my guess there must always still be some doubt about it. Maybe he has not time or energy to spare for explanations which he would otherwise give (I don't think he would!) but he might find time later. The Cantos will be finished, and, I hope, revised someday, and then there might be leisure to dot i's and so forth. Until all hope of that is removed by Pound's death – long be it delayed! – I should feel I was committing an impertinence by hazarding any explanation whatever.

There is yet another consideration which makes me loth to comment. Pound (who is my oldest friend) is a great poet, almost certainly the greatest of our time: That will be acknowledged in time, I am sure: but meanwhile we can do no good either to Pound himself or to literature by claiming for him very much more than the public is disposed to grant. A commentary would seem to the public to be setting Pound, a living man, alongside the immemorial classics, and they would resent the claim: rightly, I think, since all such judgments must be matured over a long period and in the light of what follows, as well as what precedes a man's work. Those who are exalted too much by one generation are generally denigrated by the next: a man's work is usually more effective in the long run when his reputation is of slow growth than when it has to be revived after a reaction (commonly as a stick with which to beat his successors rather than for its own sake). Pound's personal position is a miserable one, but his public reputation has grown very steadily throughout my lifetime: I should be sorry to see it bound forward now, for that would seem to me to foretell a coming reaction. A commentary is "asking for it".

With all this, since it is evident that you will write your commentary whatever I may say, it would be churlish of me to refuse to give you such help as I can – very little, I think. Unfortunately I am extremely pressed just now, and I cannot be certain of seeing you. I will do my best to come on Friday or Tuesday, but cannot promise – I have to be in Rome meanwhile.

Yours faithfully
Basil Bunting

## To T. S. Eliot

TS Texas[185]

2 May 1951

Lido di Camaiore

Dear TSE,

Salamun, in the first place, alekum! I take it that you have got back safe from the States, richer, more learned than ever, and (I hope) somewhat wickeder.

I am oppressed by the uniformity of virtue amongst my admittedly few acquaintances.

But business. Louis Zukofsky is anxious that you should see his little novel, "Ferdinand" and I have therefore cut it out of the Quarterly Review of Literature (the Annandale on Hudson one)[186] and am sending it either with this letter or simultaneously with it. Obviously he hopes Fabers will publish it, and I think they might do worse. They wouldn't, I imagine, make money on it, but it wouldn't disgrace their list. I hate novels almost always, but read this one with interest and thought that in spite of some asperity of structure and a lack of nearly all the customary clothing it was capable of interesting other people. It would at least be nice to see the ordinary canons defied again as they were sometimes in the days of my youth by you and Ep and Jj, and those who then published you.

I would much rather have canvassed you on behalf of Zukofsky's poems, which really are necessary, not merely a change. There ought to be a collected edition, since there's only a couple of privately printed thin volumes, and he is the only bloke besides you and Ezra who has added anything to the poetic stock: others have played variations very prettily. However, it's the novel he is interested in at present.

Secondly, it seems that some of Ezra's friends here and in England have got impatient at his long incarceration and are planning in a vague and restless way some move which, I fear, might only make things worse by setting up the backs of the Great American People and perhaps also of their rulers. To keep these folk quiet, and not out of hope of other betterment, I've undertaken to recommend EP

185 This letter survives in a carbon copy sent to Louis Zukofsky.

186 See 14/3/51 and note.

and DP to consult another lawyer, namely George Richards of Wall Street, if he will be consulted: but they distrust Wall Street, do the Pounds, and I may find I've only made myself a nuisance.

Meanwhile I am told (for I haven't seen her) that Gabriela Mistral[187] wants to make a letter, manifesto, petition or something of that nature to be signed by all the literary Nobel Prize winners and a few others of similar standing. If it were very tactfully drafted such a performance might do no harm, even conceivably a very little good: and it seems to me that you, American by birth and much experience, would be the obvious bloke to do the drafting: besides your successful caution, as manifested in the Criterion etc etc. so I want you to be aware of the proposal. Miss Mistral is now Chilean (I think) consul at Santa Margherita Ligure, Italy.[188] Her contact with Ezra is through D. D. Paige, Casella 30, Rapallo,[189] whom I suppose you already know since Fabers have done his edition of EP's letters.

That's really all the business. As for my own poems, they are said to have sold twelve copies in the United States, so I wont persist in suggesting that Fabers should do them in England without the preposterous preface.[190] Even a philanthropic concern might be discouraged by those statistics. Getting a living is going very badly and my job may stop anytime now. I would like permission to use your name as a reference if I have to apply for jobs of a kind where it would be useful – teaching jobs, for instance. Now, going grey, I'm a bit cast down at the lack of security, not so much for me, since I don't care much what I eat etc, but for my wife and infant.

Italy seems to me useless for any purpose just now. The people haven't any spirit at all, are ready to submit to anyone or anything that will leave them merely alive. Turbulent ignorance, as in Persia, is less dispiriting.

Yours faithfully[191]

[187] Gabriela Mistral (1889–1957), Chilean poet, diplomat, and winner of the Nobel Prize for Literature in 1945. As BB describes, she organized a petition in 1951–1952 calling for Pound's release from St Elizabeths.

[188] Santa Margherita Ligure: north-west Italian town very close to Rapallo.

[189] Douglass D. Paige (1917/18–1983), American editor and translator responsible for the Faber & Faber publication *The Letters of Ezra Pound 1907–41* (1951).

[190] BB's *Poems: 1950* (see **14/5/49** and note) featured a highly opinionated preface by Dallam Flynn/Simpson, which mounted a splenetic attack on a number of contemporary targets (including Eliot).

[191] No signature (carbon copy).

## To Louis Zukofsky

TS Texas

22 June 1951 242 Newburn Road, Throckley, Northumberland

Dear Louis,

As you see, the job ended, and I am here looking for work.

A letter from Eliot at last yesterday: he has been in Spain as well as USA, and had a cold – a serious matter I imagine, for he's got a very fragile look about him these days.

He says: "I turned over the Zukofsky story to our fiction people, and will find out what decision they have come to. I have not yet read it myself, but I fear that it is too short to fit in with our list, unless, of course, it is a work of very exceptional genius." – I imagine that is to be read as meaning that the chances are very small.

As to me, he says that he "had long deliberations and mental wrestlings over your book, and I have had to take several opinions from different points of view. I think the poetry is good, some of it very good indeed, and the writing is clean and workmanlike, with no fluff, but the trouble is that we are now having to restrict our poetry list, and to submit every newcomer to study from the point of view of a restricted list which must make every item tell. What I feel about your poems, and one or two others feel as well, is that they are still too much under the influence of Pound, for the stage which you have reached. They ought to have been published some time ago, I feel, as that might have helped you to assimilate this influence, and let your original talent emerge more clearly" and a little more in the same strain. I haven't reminded him that they were offered to him for publication some time ago![192] And I find it difficult to understand how, let's say, Ronald Duncan gets by…But TSE no doubt took some care over them, and that's that.

Our ride from Italy was damned strenuous but not uninteresting. Took an unusual route through eastern France. In England the Festival of Mr Morrison has filled all the hotels,[193] we had to drive continuously from Dover to Throckley, a hell of a trip.

I'd like to have sent Dahlberg my poems, but I haven't a spare copy – only my own one, and one to show to publishers, and Simpson seems stuck in the binding-paste.

[192] See, for example, 2/12/26, 21/11/30, and 30/10/32.

[193] The 1951 Festival of Britain, spearheaded by Labour minister Herbert Morrison (1888–1965): major London exhibition showcasing British design, engineering, art, architecture, etc.

He's taken so much trouble with so little result to comfort himself with that I can't nag him for more.

Maria seems to like Throckley. Various quite biggish boys talk to her, and she likes boys. Also the garden is safe for babies, and her Granny spoils her. Sima is having to work too hard, and I don't see how to mitigate that until I get a new income somewhere. She has put up with our recent bad luck extremely patiently, good girl that she is. Mother is older...

I've nothing to expand about and no time to expand at the moment, therefore, with the best of luck to you and household

yours ever
BBunting

## To Louis Zukofsky

TS Texas

6 July 1951 242 Newburn Road, Throckley, Northumberland

Dear Louis,

Dahlberg's missionary fervour is a grand spectacle. It must get him disliked, which is a pity. I suppose it has some effect.

Glad Shapiro will print his poem:[194] and that may also do some good.

Approximately fifty letters re jobs to be written, so not much energy to spare for friendly intercourse: and the damned thing is, getting a job is likely to mean no time to spare... There are faint indications of a return to Persia, once more for the Times. The Times is generous and helpful, but I've got to find something to supplement the inadequate amount it can pay.

I imagine New York is no spa for the rheumatic. But you are glued to it. You wouldn't be happy in California, would you? Or pack up and come to Teheran... should be able to get something with the American cultural or what do you call it people: even with the missionaries, who run a school, grade and high, with merits and without much godliness. Of course, you might have to pack and run from Brother Stalin: but I risk that, with trimmings. Teheran is very unrheumatic. So dry you can leave your penknife in the garden for a week or two without engendering any rust at all.

[194] Karl Shapiro (1913–2000), American poet and essayist, who edited *Poetry* 1950–55. Dahlberg's poem 'For Louis Zukofsky' was published in *Poetry* 78.5 (August 1951).

I hope Old Lyme answers summers needs reasonably adequately.[195] That Paul fiddles with pleasure. By the way (or have you deduced it from Spoils?) I think Euramerican music could profit by Persian same more promptly than poetry by poetry or painting by miniature or even architecture by Isfahan. I think it could easily be as rich an addition and as strict a purge as Russian music was last century (and most of the best of Russian was Persian at third hand via the Caucasus). This is brought back to my mind by Sima, yesterday exclaiming "That's Persian, keep that on" when the radio more or less accidentally produced some early and more than ordinarily fierce Sibelius.[196] She also enjoys Schönberg and Stravinski, but is bored by Mozart and is maddened by Beethoven. On the other hand, Monteverde is also Persian...[197]

A preference for the uncompromising: and a huge reservoir for melody and rhythm.

Yeats? His Platonism respects Plotinus as yours does Spinoza or Ezra's his misunderstanding of Scotus.[198] All three abominations to my empiricism. I don't think his aura is any wronger than that. The doll poem, the weak worm, "when this soul, its body off, naked to naked goes" and some others put him high.[199] All this judging is very difficult. TSE has got through largely because his metric is crude and violent, easily felt. But is that something that will fail him in the long run? I doubt it. What he says isn't obvious, his diction is admirable, and the capacity for feeling a movement not wide-spread. There is Kipling to be reckoned with as well as Hardy. Neither of them has had the slightest influence on people

[195] Between 1948 and 1953 the Zukofskys spent summers in Old Lyme, Connecticut.

[196] Jean Sibelius (1865–1957), Finnish Romantic composer, who mostly lived during Russian rule of Finland.

[197] Claudio Monteverdi (1567–1643), Italian composer best known for his polyphonic vocal works.

[198] Johannes Scottus Eriugena (*c.*815–*c.*877), Irish neoplatonist philosopher who became a major intellectual influence on Pound—and a key presence in the *Cantos*—from the late 1920s. For more on this see Mark Byron, *Ezra Pound's Eriugena* (London: Bloomsbury, 2014). For Plotinus see 21/1/47 and note and 6/1/51.

[199] BB refers to well known poems by Yeats from different phases of his literary career. The quotation here is from 'A Last Confession' (1933) and the 'doll poem' is 'The Dolls' (1914). In alluding to the 'weak worm', BB is nodding at a passage from 'To the Rose upon the Rood of Time' (1893), which seems a more plausible literary antecedent for the slowworm figure in *Briggflatts* than those suggested in Share (333):

> Lest I no more hear common things that crave;
> The weak worm hiding down in its small cave,
> The field-mouse running by me in the grass,
> And heavy mortal hopes that toil and pass; (ll. 15–18)

capable of profiting by it, but that's probably only delayed action... No, Hardy isn't as crabbed as LZ often is, though harsh, harsher: and both capable of quite Wordsworthian dullness once in while and quite indefensible philosophies – Schopenhauer, Hegel. But I've no place in this list. My excellence, if I have one, isn't new or striking. I suppose that's what TSE misses. I'd say I remember the musical origin of poetry, the singing side of it, better than anybody except Ezra and Carlos Williams; and that the process of association or contrast or what you will I think I derive from Horace, Hafez, and the symphonic composers, differs from Ez's "ideogram" or the Waste Land manner, being at once less arbitrary and more under control... but if so, that won't be perceived in this generation. I've added nothing much. But I think I've done the job quite well; skilfully, unrepetitively. I hope so, anyway.

You know Cole, "Imagi"?[200] Seems intelligent. Paper clearly well-edited. Doesn't pay however. Has he had a chance of whatever you've got that the paying mags wont print? (1019 S 47th St Philadelphia 43)

EP's reply characteristic. He doesn't seem to have the capacity for more than three consecutive sentences, except very intermittently. Who Krim is I've no idea.[201] He undoubtedly thinks you know or ought to know. He has several unheard of objects of enthusiasm. DDPaige might be able to enlighten you – he's wonderfully persistent in tracking them down. Ez being consciously and conscientiously Confucian according to his own interpretation of the sage isn't aware how very Platonic he is too. The coexistence of such metrical and so-on craftiness, such a feeling of some items of history with such naïve (even credulous) conscious history and politics is deceptive. The difficulty is how to avoid being involved in the network of fallacies while profiting by his illuminate faculty for verse and enjoying his energy and kindness.

I don't give a damn what you say to him, so long as you are available, an occasional correspondent. Amongst the cryptic scribbles you'll get in reply, there will be some good bits. And he won't feel that you're one of the lost or hostile.

Maria, Sima, well. Hope you can say the same of Celia and Paul.

Yours
BBunting

[200] Thomas J. Cole (1921/22–2013), American poet and editor of the magazine *Imagi* (1947–1960). Cole published Pound and visited him regularly in St Elizabeths.

[201] Possibly Seymour Krim (1922–1989), New York-based writer and journalist later associated with the Beat Generation.

In late 1951 Bunting returned to Tehran for a final short spell as *Times* correspondent in Iran. However, the political situation in the country grew increasingly parlous over the next few months, as the nationalization of the Anglo-Iranian Oil Company by radical Prime Minister Mohammad Mosaddegh led to tension between the British and Iranian governments. As Bunting describes in the following letters, he was eventually expelled from the country by Mossadegh in May 1952. After escaping from Iran, apparently at gun-point, he was forced to embark on an epic drive home across Europe to Northumberland, with a pregnant Sima and their infant daughter Sima-Maria in the passenger seat.

## To Louis Zukofsky

TS Texas

17 June 1952 — 242 Newburn Road, Throckley, Northumberland

Dear Louis,

There's a great gap in correspondence to be closed somehow. From the beginning of October till the end of April we were in Persia again, for the Times, and it was an all-day and nearly all-night job. I used to begin reading the local press as soon as I was shaved, by say 6.30, and I'd never have a pause in the work until it was too late to telegraph for the next day's paper, about nine at night. I hardly saw Sima or Maria unless it was Friday, and even the Friday picnics were few. In a way exciting, in a way dull; Mosaddeq kept doing silly things that had to be reported more shrewdly than the agencies and other papers could do it, and I was under threat of expulsion from the beginning of December. Some of the correspondents got the wind up and thought they were going to be imprisoned, and one by one they left, often at their own request. By February I was practically alone, and having to intrigue to prevent the police serving an expulsion order on me. But there was no chance of getting away from work or seeing anything worth seeing for its own sake. At first I didn't even have a car, and had to walk or get taxis – a damned physically tiring business when the whole day is a series of calls, always in a hurry.

The British Chargé d'Affaires, Middleton,[202] and one of his commercial staff turned out to be readers of poetry, both careful students of EP and able to quote

[202] George Middleton (1910–1998): British diplomat and Chief Political Resident in the Persian Gulf Residency at the time of the rise and fall of Mossadegh.

my own stuff from the Active Anthology, but there was never time to talk about anything but politics or finance. And if there had been I'd have been too tired. All I had energy for was to play with young girls, of whom the house always seemed to be full, cousins and friends of Sima. They needed no mental effort and were always at hand when there was a pause in the work. Our heavy luggage with the books in it never reached us – it was held up in the Persian customs, waiting while they considered whether to leave me alone or chuck me out. For nearly twelve weeks I had no papers at all – passport and identity card impounded by the cops.

Then, as you maybe know, they heaved me out for the absurdist set of reasons imaginable (had been a vice-consul, knew Persian, had a Persian wife – all very suspicious circumstances in Mosaddeq's eyes) and I found myself notorious for a few weeks. Some politician had told the police to make trouble about Sima's exit visa, and there was a beastly period of cross-examinations and efforts to persuade her to leave me and remain in Persia. They even announced that Maria was to be regarded as a Persian subject and kept there by force. Makki managed to get it straightened out for us in the end.[203]

Thereupon we set out for England by car. It is done from time to time – about one car a year gets through, mostly starting from the west, and about five or six fail. We managed pretty well – a month's journey, during which I was driving nineteen days, mostly for about ten or eleven hours. The Persian roads were flooded by a freak downpour, so that you couldn't see the holes in them, and we broke a spring just as we reached the frontier. We passed through Iraq, Jordan, Syria, Turkey, Greece, Yugoslavia, Italy, Switzerland and France. The Greek roads were even worse than the Asiatic ones, quite probably the worst in the world, but we didn't begin to have serious trouble with the car until we reached the excellent surfaces of Italy. By then, the damage done earlier was making itself felt.

Well, it was interesting, of course, as well as tiring. Turkey, Greece and Yugoslavia were new to me, and to see the other Middle Eastern countries on our route in sequence, instead of by separate aeroplane journeys, suggested some ideas that hadn't occurred to me before: contrasts and comparisons. The letter would grow far too long for me to write it now if I tried to exemplify. Turkey was unexpectedly pleasant, Yugoslavia not unexpectedly pretty unpleasant (the peasants seemed much as peasants are everywhere, allowance made for different temperaments prevailing, but the townspeople seemed thoroughly oppressed, with an air of shabby unhappiness that weighed us down.) The first quick impression –

[203] Hossein Makki (1911–1999): leading Iranian politician of the late 1940s and early 1950s.

all we got – suggested that Tito was much nearer to being an inferior Mussolini that the patriotic "sincere communist" we are told he is.[204]

There were a couple of pleasant days in Italy, at Sirmione, where the hotel people knew us: and all the way I found some advantage in my temporary notoriety – we were treated well by frontier officials, consuls, press clubs and so on. But I noticed that cleanliness, kindness and hospitality declined fairly steadily the further west we got. The Swiss hotel at Brig, a good enough place in its way, took far less trouble and was far less pleasant, for all its scores of travellers per day, than a Turkish inn in the little town of Gerede where we were the first foreigners who had ever spent the night.

Well, now we've to look for another job: not likely to be an easy task. I'm on half pay until October, and would be sent back to Persia for the Times if Mossadeq should fall and be succeeded by someone likely to reverse his expulsion: but I think he's likely to rule either in person or through a deputy for a good many more months. We'll cease to have an income just about the time we are due to have another baby. So, if you hear of any possibilities, let me know.

Let us hear how you and your family are, and what is in your mind. I'll have time to write letters now for a while, I suppose, and even perhaps to reflect. Best of wishes.

Yours
BBunting

## To Ezra Pound

TS Indiana

17 March 1953 — 242 Newburn Road, Throckley, Northumberland

Dear Ezra,

Whatever determines one's fate in modern society, it's neither sense nor sensibility. I've been silent these many months because I've been too ashamed of the way I've been treated – Oh, quite impersonally! – to grumble about it very actively. It must depress decent people. But I can't stay silent with old friends, and can only apologise in advance for adding to the gloom about.

[204] Josip Tito (1892–1980): Communist revolutionary who spearheaded the Yugoslav resistance to the Nazis and became president of Yugoslavia from 1945. Notably, he quarrelled with Stalin and forestalled Yugoslav membership of the Soviet-controlled 'Eastern Bloc', and was therefore looked on with (relative) sympathy by Western powers.

Very well. Mosaddeq chucked me out. He said it was because I had once been a vice-consul in Persia, which he regards as a heinous offence. But I'd been under threat for several months, and during that time I had several messages from Mossy and his pals, hinting strongly that if I would modify the news (I was the only foreigner reporting it) he'd see what could be done for me. Instead I kept on telling the truth, which is reputed to be a virtue, and imagined that the Times, (which had previously promised to back me up if I got expelled) would impute it to me for merit.

Not a bit of it. When I got to London they found they had no suitable post to offer. They paid me half-screw for a while, then dropped me altogether. I suppose I might have made a stink, but I thought it wouldn't encourage the many other newspaper correspondents who are resisting pressure in various countries.

But now see the final result. Every job that I have applied for that has consented to see me has asked "Why did the Times drop you?", and every one has refused to believe that a newspaper would drop a man merely because a petty tyrant had expelled him from his post. The Times must, they conclude, have something against me which they cover with decent reticence. So the short list is as far as I get or have any prospect of getting.

In fact the Times isn't the only similar offender. Reuters dropped Hermann in exactly the same way, but more shamefully, since he'd been doing good work for them for ten years: and Reuters again abandoned and even disavowed Mackertichian when Mossadeq locked him up.[205] His children would have starved altogether but for a distant relative who paid up for them. In short, it is extremely costly to tell the truth and the beneficiaries – the newspapers – decline to bear any part of the cost.

Maybe that's no news to you. Many newspapers don't want the truth and couldn't be blamed for refusing to pay for it. But the Times, curiously, does: and where it has an intelligent bloke to gather news, it usually gets something as near the truth as can be guessed. I don't know who runs the foreign correspondance since Deakin died,[206] but it doesn't show any obvious falling off.

I found the British government (or rather, the officials more directly responsible to the government than I was) didn't like the truth at all, and tried every way short of direct suppression to hinder me telling it to them. My service to them cost me all the savings I made during the war. My service to the Times was neither

[205] As BB describes, Leopold Herman and Keghan Mekertichian were both Reuters journalists expelled from Iran by Mosaddegh.

[206] Charles Deakin: foreign editor at the *Times* in the late 1940s.

profitable nor a direct loss until my expulsion. Now I find it's deprived me of any way of making a living for my family (increasing now – son Thomas Faramarz born in November).

The Manchester Guardian professed to be horrified by the Times' attitude, but didn't offer anything except the prospect of selling them an occasional article which would cost more to collect than they are prepared to pay. I can't afford either the time or the expenses to work for them.

As to other jobs – well, there are few I have any qualifications for, and the few are either those you get by knowing somebody I don't know or else those which pay nearly nothing. A House of Commons answer yesterday says that £400 in 1914 or £600 in 1939 is the equivalent of £1450 today. On that basis, the £200 I scraped together from the Outlook, etc, in the late twenties would be £600–£700 now. That is precisely the amount the Central Office of Information[207] is not willing to pay me as an "expert" on Middle East affairs. My £2400 in Teheran (£650 in 1914?) wasn't extravagant in such a country: but it was worth a good deal more than a quarter of that amount in England. Hereabouts a miner thinks himself badly used with less than £800 a year, and a dustman gets £500 or more. But I see universities advertising lectureships at £400. (£2 per week in 1914.) Gateshead[208] excelled them all a few years ago by combining in one advertisement vacancies for a dustman and an assistant Borough Architect, who was to get exactly four-fifths of the dustman's pay.

I thought of various ways of getting a living by "enterprise". I'd have had to try and borrow the capital. But every trade is so fenced about with licences it is hardly possible for any new competitor to enter. I cannot, for instance, sell foreign and classical books to the students etc at the university here. It is hard for established booksellers to get foreign books into the country and licences just aren't granted to anybody else. Not by law: by the practise of that part of the civil service responsible.

The BBC expressed lack of interest in me whether as a littery gent or as a Persian expert. Instead it has been broadcasting utter nonsense about Persia to Great Britain, and is still carrying on the programmes to Persia which I (then an

[207] Central Office of Information: UK government marketing and communications agency 1946–2011.

[208] Gateshead: urban district to the south of the Tyne, practically (though not technically) a part of Newcastle.

"expert" in government service) condemned in a long statistical and carefully argued report six years ago.

Poverty on the scale we've now to face (none of us is eligible for any of the benefits of the welfare state except free medical attention)[209] means no leisure for anything. I must spend nearly all of nearly everyday in household chores – Mother is past them and Sima can't manage the whole house with a baby to be nursed. One suit is carefully kept to be interviewed in – the rest are practically rags. So far we have eaten enough, though with such a restriction of variety that it is sometimes almost too disheartening to face a meal: but even eating is going to be difficult from now on.

I thought I'd done with the particular kind of endurance test a good many years ago. I had plenty of it from time to time when I was young enough to expect it to end someday. Besides, I'd to some extent courted it then: at any rate deliberately risked it. But now I'm back at the same or a worse place on account of doing what we are all continually exhorted to do, and which I really thought would have enhanced my value as a journalist at least.

My books caught me up at last a month or two ago, after a year and a half of wandering about the seas or resting in customshouses. They are battered but still readable. I've returned to the Shahnameh and reread the Siyavash story: newly impressed.[210] I still wish I could do it in English, though I think I'd now try prose.

No intelligent or intellectual interests – the previous pages explain why.

I've heard nothing from Omar since we left Persia.

I've hardly seen anybody or heard from anybody. I've not looked them up or written to them, because being poor looks so damned like begging and I am so thoroughly sick of it. Besides, what have I to say to anyone?

Sima is getting the worst of it: exiled from her own country as well as penniless.

And the day of sitting down to write a second more workmanlike volume of poems looks about as near as the millennium.

Yours ever

B Bunting

209 Given the universalism of the British Welfare State at this point, this claim seems unlikely, and indeed BB suggests to Zukofsky in a letter of 27/10/53 (Texas) that he was receiving unemployment benefit payments ('the dole') in the autumn of 1953.

210 Siyâvash: legendary Persian prince who plays a major role in *Shahnameh*.

## To Louis Zukofsky

TS Texas

29 March 1953 242 Newburn Road, Throckley, Northumberland

Dear Louis,

I took your advice and wrote to Read (Sir Herbert now). In three weeks he hasn't answered. Since I sent a copy of "Poems", signed to him, it seems uncivil. The packet was registered and its hardly likely he hasn't got it.

I said you'd advised me to write him: mentioned two mutual friends now, I believe, dead, referred to the bulk and solidity of his work, and to my lack of product: that Eliot thought my poems too Pound, but I believed the influence much less than TSE imagined: didn't know what Z's idea was in bidding me write, but thought might be referring to my difficulties earning a living: my recent jobs in Persia & expulsion: didn't see what he could do about it. Maybe his firm could print poems: Ferdosi – but who on earth could or would finance that? Kegan Paul used to be interested in Oriental languages, what about a Persian anthology or even grammar? His own early work on Persian poets would render my interest in Persia intelligible: anything at all I could do for Routledge? Any advice?

Reread it seems to me a civil and even in parts entertaining letter. Maybe anyone who is hard up seems to be a begging-letter-writer, I dunno.

We've now had a year of continual misfortune. It can go only a little further, for our debts can't be increased and there are no "welfare state" benefits for unpatriotic capitalistic colony-exploiters who have worked abroad. The other newspapers wont give me work because the Times didn't; therefore, they argue, there must be something against me, because it would be too bad to be credible if I had been dropped merely because of my expulsion. Nevertheless that is what happened. If I had agreed with Mosaddeq to doctor the news, the Times wouldn't have known any better, for there was no other correspondent, English or American, capable of checking my news. I preferred to go on telling the truth and have been left to pay the whole extravagant cost of that luxury myself. Reuters had set the example by treating their man Herman the same way. The American papers whose correspondents were expelled did exactly the opposite – promoted them. So did the gutter-press here.

I've been too ashamed of all this to write to anybody. And to find myself back in 1922 at my age – well, why did I ever compromise with the idiotic age by doing its work in Persia and exposing myself first to the meannesses of bureaucracy and then to this unmitigated disaster? I might have stuck to my intention after the war, bought my boat, and sailed in destitution but independence and written poetry. Of course, that way I'd have missed Sima and a lot of very good things in Persia...

Margaret[211] has a genius for getting details wrong. I told her you had praised Rustam, not that you gave me the news of his death. That came from Roudaba: but I have had no letter, not a word since her telegram, no reply to my letters. No doubt my daughters are preoccupied with their children, and I don't want to hear from Marian. You do well to avoid her. But do as is convenient to you. She has given me several years respite from mischief now, and I have no right to assume that she is still as vindictive as ever.

Maria at three is a beautiful child. Thomas Faramarz, now four months, is lively, but has had bronchitis. Sima puts up with our horrible situation partly from courage and loyalty, and partly because she doesn't fully grasp it. But if nothing better comes, I will have to let her family take her back to Persia. After that, I don't know what there will be to live for.

Why should I prefer England? The post-war revolution, which has resolved itself into a post-war inflation with privileges for the three strong trade-unions, has stripped us of the old advantages. Officials here aren't as arrogant as they are in Syria, but no less arrogant than in Turkey. Public illiberality is possibly less than what's reported from your land of the free, and certainly directed to different objects, but it is far worse than in any of the Islamic lands. My very considerable services to the state haven't entitled me to anything whatever. They are even, by the workings of the Official Secrets Act, sometimes a handicap – I mustn't satisfy the perfectly legitimate curiosity of prospective employers about what I did in such and such a post. Penalty, fourteen years in jug. No, apart from a wish to relax for a few years, which would be easier, I suppose, in one's native land than elsewhere, I've no reason to prefer England. But I won't write to Payne. He is too fantastic a fool and too unblushing a charlatan for me to be indebted to him. I wish I had the effrontery to get jobs as he does, though.

I would like to hear from you about yourself. But it may be difficult to answer, since my days are filled with domestic chores: mother aged and ailing, wife cluttered up with babies. No hope of writing anything that takes time or thought.

Yours faithfully
BBunting

[211] I.e. Margaret de Silver.

## To Louis Zukofsky

TS Texas

10 May 1953 — 242 Newburn Road, Throckley, Northumberland

Dear Louis,

Yes, Read wrote at last, but with no useful comfort. The situation is as the situation was, only with even less hope of escape. I am making what seems the last attempt I am likely to have the ingenuity to contrive to get some sort of work from the Times. Suggested the Litt Supp.[212] Small hope, it used to be a racket in Richmond's day,[213] and though Richmond is now far in the past, a dimmish figure in the History of the Times, I've no reason to suppose it's changed: as the main office undoubtedly has.

Sir Bruce Richmond, contriver of sentences that didn't say anything. Still, even Richmond was used to feed some people not entirely unworthy of their grub.

You are probably wise to teach Paul at home if you can find the time. At this distance, knowing nothing about it, it looks sensible. And his fiddling is obviously good. Presumably he's committed to it. That's the less good side, but he at least wouldn't agree, I suppose. (I wonder what's the anthropobumfical connection (or what) between the many western Jewish virtuosos and the ancient Islamic tradition of the Jewish musicians. To this day. Even the two-man band I found earning its living by playing for the Bakhtiari wild men to dance, with one flute and one biscuit-box-drum beaten with an old umbrella handle). (They combine music with weaving amongst the Kurds, and lovely trousers they do weave for them).

I am sorry to hear you've parted with your hut, cottage, Old Lyme. At least one sucking root outside the city seems necessary to mental health. I hate cities worse than ever. Though Throckley is being absorbed into the suburbs of Newcastle with the damned modern spread I can still stroll up the river and if the otters have moved away there are still kingfishers to brighten the banks. It costs nothing to look at them, one thing one can do even in England on the same economic plane as most of what an Arab does.

Which is the case when you and I write poetry nobody wants to pay for and nobody will give us glory for. I enjoyed Spook's Sabbath:[214] high spirits and fireworks, not without an occasional flick of the wrist that shows the master's dexterity. But a reservation against the first item of it which to me suggests that

[212] I.e. the *Times Literary Supplement* (TLS).

[213] Bruce Richmond (1871–1964), British journalist and editor of the TLS 1902–1937.

[214] I.e. Zukofsky's 'Spooks' Sabbath, Five Bowings', written 1952.

horrible earnest trying characteristic of USA small magazines. Why it should I don't quite know. Obviously you aren't one of them there... maybe the unnecessarily farfetched ice-cream scooper, maybe the arbitrary grotesque conclusion. Hard objects far too vague to become buttocks, the general expression and the particular don't go together...I dunno...something not right. The remaining poems excellent and I hope, like Anew and 55, permanent. You have a singing voice that floats off most of the odd syntactical things you often do: a deeper voice than the others one hears: and an absence of moral fervour which is refreshing. As the years go on I find my Zukofsky far more in these lyrics than in the larger more ambitious stuff which seems to claim importance for people and ideas I don't find important and sometimes for tortuous metricalities which aren't necessary because you have the sleight of hand to dispense with them – which would lighten the product. I am not sure about Gubin's gamps:[215] maybe insisting on writing something that ought to be painted?

I'd like very much to see A 12 but don't care to undertake responsibility for a manuscript in our present utterly unsettled condition. I might be anywhere (jail or poorhouse or jungle or desert) at a moment's notice and haven't been able to keep track of all my own books and papers in recent years. It would be unfair to accept your offer of a loan of the mss until I've a prospect, time to handle it discreetly and return it before the next earthquake, etc. and the damned thing is, ten to one I wouldn't get time to read it reflectively anyway. (That was the trouble with the last slab: you can't hold down the politics of a complex region with one hand and read poetry with the other. Except for a while in Italy, which I used to write The Spoils, I've been at work all my waking hours for years now except odd days off. This last year its been not real work but household chores (sick mother, pregnant wife, young baby) plus work-seeking plus anxiety.)

No New Directions within a hundred miles of Throckley.

And supposing a poem is neither a tool nor a vessel nor a remedy for anything but only and just a poem: for at any rate that's what it survives by – we don't read Lucretius for a concourse of atoms, no fear! nor even Dante for catholic philosophy though he did it so well he's still usable by converts, im told; and I'm damned if I really know what the Ode on the Imitations of Immorality is really driving at, but I can still get a lot of pleasure from it.[216] OK. Haven't we all, poets, been riding

[215] I.e. Zukofsky's 'Selma Gubin's Umbrellas' (written 1953), inspired by a painting by Selma Gubin (1903–1974) a Russian American artist who was a friend of Zukofsky.

[216] I.e. Wordsworth's 'Ode: Imitations of Immortality', first published in 1807.

much too high a horse for a long time? A bit of the Yeatsian Grecian goldsmith[217] or just plain potter (not for teacups though) or the guy who paints the Sicilian carts and British canal boats. Without anonymity you can't have a healthy art nicht wahr? Nobody's stripes are daubed on the circus caravans, nobody knows who tiles the Masjed-e Shah, Durham cathedral exhorts nobody.[218] Sure, we've all said it repeatedly: but we haven't drawn the conclusion. Poets still act as though they thought they had some special claim. A skill worth preserving, with possibly some rather tenuous uses from the economic-social point of view: but if nobody buys my pots I don't accuse the customers of anything but poor taste, if nobody buys my poems what's the difference? The old millionaire ferryman at Baghdad still poled his ferry because Salman the Persian earned his living weaving baskets when he was viceroy of Syria for the Emir-ol-Momenin,[219] and the shepherds make their pipes for the fun of it. The fowler could get a better living in another occupation. Poetry is overrun with guys who want to tickle their own vanity, and I don't like it Louis! That's what falsifies everything. If we'd had the sense to be anonymous among these, when you were Objectivising, and to stay anonymous, maybe we'd have had more effect so that more people would have had pleasure in reading us and more people would have written in a way to give them pleasure.

Reverting to the West has made me more convinced than before that we've got to learn almost everything from the East (which, to the measure of my limited experience is the lands of Islam) before there's a chance of any peace of mind or dignity for most of us. And that's a way of saying To hell with material welfare, and, logically, of all the laws and reforms and adages designed to procure it.

And still one must eat!

Yours

B

All the best to yours

[217] The final stanza of Yeats's 'Sailing to Byzantium' (1928) is a famous instance of the pure aestheticism BB advocates here, imagining a perfect form 'such . . . as Grecian goldsmiths make | Of hammered gold and gold enamelling'.

[218] The Shah Mosque in Isfahan: masterpiece of Islamic architecture, built between 1611 and 1629 during the reign of Shah Abbas (1571–1629). Durham Cathedral: masterpiece of early-twelfth century Romanesque architecture, which BB described to Zukofsky in a letter of 12/11/50 (Texas) as the 'finest cathedral north of the Alps'.

[219] In some accounts Salman the Persian, a companion of Muhammad, was appointed to the governorship of Al-Mada'in in modern Iraq in his last years, at the behest of Ali, cousin of Muhammad and Amir al-Mu'minin ('Commander of the Faithful'). Mindful of the importance of not wasting a God-given talent—and of the value of labour-for-its-own-sake—he spent his last days crafting and selling wicker baskets.

## To Ezra Pound

TS Yale

9 July 1953 242 Newburn Road, Throckley, Northumberland

Dear Ez,

Not totally extinct, yet, but hardly more than flickering. I can get no work, have nearly reached the limit of the debts I can make, and now seem to be in for a period of illhealth into the bargain. I daresay an end of anxieties would also end ill-health: but meanwhile I've been ordered to take a whole pantryfull of drugs. The longer it goes on the sicker I am with a system of govt or enterprise or what you will that allows Mossadeq to take it out of me for declining to lie in public. The Times and the British Govt both benefited by my abstention from making a good thing out of my job in Persia, and might have been expected to see to it that I didnt lose my whole livelihood as a result.

I dont know that I'd be very much use to anybody in USA. Could be, but in fact the standard of "up-to-the-minute" is technically very high there, even if the standards of accuracy and penetration are low, and that's the bit I'm weakest on – it didnt matter in Persia if I was behind the news-agencies, since I was the only person whose views were likely to be attended to at all, but in USA I'd have to be ready with the interpretation within half an hour of hearing the fact. I know much better when I've slept on it.

But as to persuading newspaper magnates – once you've exhibited some understanding of the Middle East, you're a Middle East expert only and merely forever. Thus the Manchester Guardian, the New York Times, Kemsley and others. The Times would have sent me to Sudan or E. Africa, but their rule is strictly the best man for the job, and guys with long experience of both places turned up, so I was left…

Secundo. As to Jews, out of the large number I've met scarcely any were rich or even moderately well off: and out of the bankers I've met only one was a Jew. Usury seems to me to be at a very low ebb just now owing to the prevalence of inflation. Inflation pleases the tradesunions and some of the manufacturers, and is in essence a means of making all money-lenders pay for the war. As most moneylenders are merely people with some savings to invest, they and the big usurers suffer together. My mother's annuity buys about one third of what it did when she bought it, which is nice for the insurance company, ie. the borrower. All the other borrowers have profited similarly at the expense of the lenders – I mean here and in other places where money has been inflated. So, whatever may be the theoretical objections to usury, in which I am not fearfully interested, it seems that its not one of the urgent abuses of this decade. (Not much use prohibiting the scale of raincoats in the Sahara, plenty of prior matters)

More I've seen of govts and the people who run them, more certain I've become that ANY govt is evil and only to be tolerated when the other evils it can obviate are absolutely proved by long trial of them to be of perfectly satanic dimensions. There would be very few laws in my Utopia and hardly any govt to enforce them. Sure, we'd have to pay dearly for freedom: but we pay even more dearly for daily petty oppression. The most tolerable habitats I've surveyed are those where the govt is least efficient. Which give most scandal to the moralist – any systematic moralist, not just the kind lately in fashion. The desert Arab, the Afghan, the Persian provincial, get on pretty comfortably where govt consists solely in extracting bribes from those who can afford them. The usurers of Golpaygan who oppress the Fereidani[220] peasant are subject to unavenged murder (by the way, they are mostly Georgians like Papa Stalin, not Jews). It works pretty well. If the usurers werent there the peasants would be oppressed by landlords instead, better able to avoid knives and hammers.

Which brings us to Winston. Why judge him or any of these coves by some absolute standard? So long as somebody is going to govern us, better a lively intelligent body than a stultified clerk. Both Winston and Truman were at least aware that quite half the services under them were prepared to warp information; both took some pains to get round the heads of their abominable civil services and a little nearer to facts. A whole cabinet of Winstons or Trumans might circumvent the professional obstructors and, even if they served their own interests, allow the fog to clear a bit. If Truman had been less curious or more "correct" the Russkies would probably have had Azerbaijan.[221] Heaven save us rather from the Attlees,[222] in the dark and content to remain in the dark, until some bloody catastrophe lights it up.

I dont want to exaggerate: the civil service is too much for Winston to tackle alone and he's getting old. I hear, unreliably, he was in the dark about Farouk[223]

[220] Golpāyegān: city in Isfahan province, close to the Fereydan region and its large ethnic Georgian population.

[221] In 1946 the Soviet Union refused to leave Iranian territory. Stalin proclaimed the Azerbaijan People's Government in Iranian Azerbaijan, before being pressured to withdraw by the United States.

[222] Clement Attlee (1883–1967), British Prime Minister 1945–1951, and leader of the reforming Labour government responsible for creation of the Welfare State. After defeat in the 1951 general election Attlee was succeeded by Churchill.

[223] Farouk I (1920–1965), last king of Egypt, overthrown in a 1952 military coup.

and still is about the feelings in Iraq.[224] But he is less at the mercy of the "permanent heads" than most "statesmen". Whereas Attlee, told of the Persian nationalisation demand, wrung his hands, wept and cried: "Why wasnt I told?" He wasnt told because Sir John le Rougetel[225] wouldnt forward my reports, and when they were sent another way, Sir William Strang[226] sat on them. Then he let them send Stokes[227] – thus making certain that no agreement wd be reached – out of pure ignorance, deliberately unenlightened by the blokes who are paid to enlighten him. That might have happened to Winston or Truman, but there'd be a good chance it wouldnt, they have too much contempt for these officials. I'm not talking about the absolute ultimate moral thises and thats of the Persian business, but about preferring facts to fiction in a wicked world. Winston does, to the limit of his not negligible energy.

If you tell me who Seaton[228] is and where, I'd cheerfully do whatever I can and he wants to enlighten him about Manuchehri and so on.

But oh Ez I am disheartened to such an extent I doubt if I can do anything at all. You say, with whatever proportion of irony, that I can speak with authority (what about?), but in fact if there were anybody willing to print anything I could say, I still couldnt say it. You have to have a handle to your name before you can flout the Official Secrets Act without getting 14 years hard. I cant get a job at seven quid a week (no experience) let alone get listened to. What they mean by experience Lord knows. Last board that interviewed me simply refused to believe my record. Wouldnt even take the trouble to check up and find it true. "You mean to say a former GSO2[229] and Counsellor is applying for a piddling little job like this? Make your claims more modest next time."

Proved efficiency is a disqualification.

I hope all this isnt too boring. I haven't anything real or interesting to report at all, and feel I shouldnt be writing to a bloke who dislikes being bored quite as much as I do.

224 Following World War II Britain occupied Iraq until 1947 and retained military bases in the country thereafter, provoking anti-imperialist sentiment which climaxed in the proclamation of the Iraqi Republic in 1958.

225 John Le Rougetel (1894–1975), British ambassador in Iran during BB's time there.

226 William Strang (1893–1978), British diplomat and Permanent Under-Secretary at the Foreign Office 1949–1953.

227 Richard Stokes (1897–1957), British Labour politician and Lord Privy Seal in 1951.

228 Pound corresponded with the Belfast poet Allan Seaton (1916–2007) in the early 1950s. Seaton stayed with the Buntings in Throckley in the summer of 1954.

229 In the British Army, General Staff Officer Grade 2 amounts to Major (in BB's RAF it was Squadron Leader), a high-ranking position.

I would like very much to know (a) how your problems are altering. Any chance of being set free since the change of party in power? (b) what are you writing and publishing? There's no means at all of finding these things out here if you or Dorothy doesnt tell me. (c) news of Omar, who's completely disappeared from my horizon since I left Persia.

If I had joined in snubbing the people well disposed to Britain and produced false evidence to support the silly despatches or a fool of an ambassador: OR if I'd taken quite handsome bribes to pretend Mosaddeq was other than he is, I'd have had a secure job and little, very little, influence now. I have neither. Am disgruntled. Am therefore a bore. Sorry.

All the best
B Bunting

P.S. Le Rougetel was promoted – High Commissioner in S. Africa, where he can & probably does go on misinforming the Govt.

## To Louis Zukofsky

TS Texas

9 July 1953 — 242 Newburn Road, Throckley, Northumberland

Dear Louis,

I can't remember what I said in my last, but think I remember having some sort of afterthought about Art of Fugue[230] and ramming it in without over-meticulous regard for the context, so you're probably right. Anyway, the instrumental half of any classical Persian ghazal is a serious thing,[231] often as long as a movement from a symphony at the beginning and of quite respectable dimensions every now and then when the singer gets out of breath or whatever the criterion is for setting the tar and drums and nay to work again.

Anyway, no oblique reflection on your poem.

An unexpected note from EP. After silence. He thinks the Kikes are terrifying the Americans and seems to want me to go there and reveal this horrible business to the world. They have made schoolteachers afraid of expressing anti-Semitism.

[230] *The Art of Fugue* (*Die Kunst der Fuge*): incomplete work by Bach of the 1740s which experiments with contrapuntal and fugue structures.

[231] Ghazal: poetic form of the Middle East, somewhat analogous to the Petrarchan sonnet, which is often recited in a musical setting.

Well, if you're an anti-semite that may be a distressing state of affairs. The Jews I've met were a depressingly poverty-stricken lot on the whole. I did know one of the Sassoons[232] and he was good for nothing – I got him transferred from my unit for incorrigible idleness, which doesn't seem to make him very dangerous, nor even very powerful, for the job was a desirable one and the one he went to far from it. However it may be otherwise in the States. There are certainly lots of most offensive Jews in NY, but they are even there outnumbered by the offensive Irish and offensive miscellaneous.

I can easily understand the thoughtless type of anti-Semite who dislikes certain habits that are thrust to some extent on all more or less oppressed minorities – on Armenians, Assyrians, Christian Arabs, for example, and even to a less obvious extent, on Quakers. A kind of Masonic playing into one another's hands, a degree of slyness, etc etc, uncomfortable to those who don't benefit. But the wild mythology which turns the rather irritating small free-masonic power and privilege into power of an altogether different scale and attributes all sorts of evils to Jewish machinations, thinks them formidable, even THE enemy, – it looks so crazy to me, so much at variance with what it's in everybody's power to observe for himself, I am discouraged from argument. It is beyond argument.

And when Ez keeps on about usury – What the hell? Theres an inflation going on almost everywhere which must have hit usurers pretty hard along with all other lenders, such as annuitants and pensioners. Whatever can be said about usury seems to me at best academic, almost metaphysical, unrelated to the commonsense of getting on with the job of keeping the world in existence. It isn't by making more laws that we'll make life tolerable but by repealing nearly all the laws we've got and letting civil servants earn a living instead of "administering". If a fool makes a bad bargain with a usurer, that's his own look out, whether he's a manufacturer or a sharecropper. If governments make bad bargains of that sort, there are electors who chose those governments, and if electors WILL choose bad governments, all the more reason for having no government at all or very little.

The Marquis de Sade wanted a law to compel everybody to submit to being fucked when and how anybody else fancied: the more intelligent Retif thought it would be sufficient to repeal the laws that sought to restrain people from fucking, if they'd a mind to.[233] All turning back to love of power? And in those who

[232] The Sassoons: wealthy Baghdadi Jewish family. The British poet Siegfried Sassoon (1886–1967) was perhaps their most famous member (see 6/8/53).

[233] Nicolas-Edmé Retif (1734–1806), French writer and rival of Sade, responsible for the term 'retifism' (shoe fetishism).

have hardly any, envy of the mainly imaginary power of Jews, Free-masons, Priests, or whatever class your attention is first called to?

All the attempts to better the world by constraint that ever I heard of have ended in worsening it, and most of those that wanted to better it by nothing more lethal than precept were nearly as objectionable. Still, Jesus and Spinoza and so on have done less direct damage than lawgivers.

Excuse all this impatience. I wish I could see Ez's translations of Kung's Odes,[234] I'd feel less jaded.

Yrs ever
BBunting

## To Louis Zukofsky

TS Texas

6 August 1953

242 Newburn Road, Throckley, Northumberland

Dear Louis,

First, your questions:

A tar is a stringed instrument played both with a bow and pizzicato, the basis of Persian classical music as the fiddle is of ours. Borrowed by the Arabs, it was modified into the lute. Reduced to three strings (se tar) it re-evolved into zither and guitar by different roads. The word tar originally meant merely a gut string, but the present instrument must be at least as old as Hafez and probably a few centuries more.

A nay is a flute (nose-flute) cut from a can (nay) and is at least as old as the tar. Both are in use, apart and together, in unison and in a kind of counterpoint, as solo instruments, as accompaniment to dancing and as the preface and coda and intermezzos of classical singing. The voice itself is usually, but not always, accompanied by the drum alone, and almost always begins, after a rather long rest, without even drums. But when the singer pauses the instruments get going again. I have, however, sometimes heard the instruments accompanying the voice, quietly, the nay making a kind of subdued descant, very florid.

I remember escaping, vexed, from an overcrowded illtempered hotel in Shiraz into its lovely garden, and there, under the huge chenars (oriental plane trees) whose shadows were making a dance of sun-dapples on the ground, I found

[234] Pound's translations of works by Kǒng Fūzǐ/Kung or Confucius, were first published in 1954 as *The Confucian Odes, the Classic Anthology Defined by Confucius.*

Naystani,[235] the chief virtuoso, just taking his flute from his pocket, and he played most beautifully for a couple of hours, the flute music as kaleidoscopic as the shadow pattern, getting in a single line that feeling of extreme multiplicity that Byrd gets in many parts, and that is nearer reflecting life than any simpler art. Nobody joined us, Naystani said nothing beyond "Salaam", it was unlike the same thing over the radio: not addressed to an audience, but almost as though addressed to the trees and the sun. The great player celebrating the first of spring in his own natural talent.

Saasoon: I'm not sure, maybe it is Hebrew, but in Baghdad, where the family fortune was founded, it is thought to be the common Persian pronunciation of Sassan. That was the name of the father of Ardeshir Babakan,[236] and consequently of his dynasty, the Sassanian. It is not an unlikely name for a Persian Jew to take, and most of the Baghdad Jews reckoned themselves Persians. Sure enough, Siegfried Sassoon, foxhunting man, was Jewish (or is it is?), a nephew of the multi-millionaire head of the family, whose father had settled in England, and another of whose sons, Siegfried's uncle, was Lloyd George's great financial backer and politician of parts.[237] They are not, I believe, practising Jews any longer, but I'm not sure. There was a sojourn in Bombay between the Baghdadi origins and the settlement in Sussex, with Parsee connections there. There is also some connection with the Moslem Persian millionaire firms of Isfahani (tea monopolists in Calcutta now) and Sheikhzadeh-Herati. The present head of the Sheikhzadeh-Herati family married one of the Seven Deadly Sins, ie. the seven daughters of Prince Ismail Kajar, whom I knew fairly well in Isfahan. She took a young cotton-spinner for her lover and put such spirit into him that he became a really useful trade-union leader, first in harmony and then in strife with the Communists. When he was more than half murdered she threw up respectability to sit by his bedside in the hospital and was for a while a popular heroine (and a target for Communist pistollers) with ballads written about her. Her name, Iran, helped the legend. That was the same time when the Persian govt insisted on providing me with a guard of soldiers (I was vice-consul and credited locally with the most hairraising anticommunist performances) which I found a nuisance.

[235] The musician Naystani is celebrated in Part II of *The Spoils*, along with Taj and Moluk-e Zarrabi (see 14/3/51 and note).

[236] Ardashir I (AD 180–242), founder of the Sasanian Empire (see 11/11/38).

[237] Siegfried Sassoon's (see 9/7/53 and note) account of his World War I experience was titled *Memoirs of a Fox-Hunting Man* (1928). His cousin Philip Sassoon (1888–1939) was Parliamentary Private Secretary to Lloyd George in 1920.

An English newspaper (Reynold's) without even Tass to inspire it[238] creditted me with an attempt to burn down the city of Yazd and massacre the inhabitants. Yazd is the ancient stronghold of the Sheikhzadeh-Herati family.

That's strayed a bit from the point. Well, well.

Sometimes the soldiers didn't recognise me and I had trouble getting into my own house: and there was dismay when I fetched a Russian consul home to dinner. The danger (of me being assassinated) was, I think, imaginary, though they did have a shot at one of my colleagues (Communists did). I wore a pistol after dark for a week or two, out of deference to the Chief of Police.

Shakespeare: I seem to remember pointing out to somebody some Lucretius in him long ago. But I don't think I've read a word of Shakespeare for well over twenty years. I am maybe too impatient of bombast. I can do nothing with Marlowe either, and the only Elizabethans I seem to get on happily with are the unknown bloke who did Arden of Feversham[239] and Spenser (Donne in moderation). Your observations on Old Bill sound interesting.[240] Where are they to be found?

And where had these drum-bangers and trumpeters mislaid Wyat's lute? Had they no ear for Dowland? Whenever a bit of loud-mouthed slapdash from the Elizabethan stage comes my way I remember Shakespeare was a contemporary of Malherbe, the man who never forgot music for a moment and who, for all his determination to eat more toads than the next fellow, ate 'em with such a clean melody and so little mumbo-jumbo that he stands inspection still without any allowances for period etc.

I've been thinking when worries let me about how and where I got whatever I know and feel about poetry, and the more I think the bigger Malherbe's part in it seems. Wordsworth, when I was a small kid, showed me what it was; Rossetti's translations from the Dolce Stil people,[241] in my teens, and Whitman at the same time, enlarged the scope. Horace gave the first inkling of how it was done (odes). Malherbe produced all I afterwards found in Ez's writing except what I'd already got from Horace. Ez and Spenser, great galleries of technical accomplishment. Lucretius. Dante. And after that, Hafez for what I got from Horace (and Ez from

[238] *Reynold's News*: left-leaning British Sunday newspaper active 1850–1967; TASS (Telegraph Agency of the Soviet Union): major Russian news agency.

[239] See **18/10/29** and note.

[240] I.e. Zukofsky's critical work on Shakespeare, written between 1947 and 1960, and published as *Bottom: On Shakespeare* (1963).

[241] Dolce Stil Novo (sweet, new style): the poetry of Dante and his associates. The British Pre-Raphaelite painter and poet Dante Gabriel Rossetti (1828–1882) produced popular translations of this group in *The Early Italian Poets* (1861) (later republished as *Dante and His Circle* (1874)).

Chinese,) only more, taken further: Manuchehri, greater and more splendid gallery than Ez and Spenser: Wyat: the Mo'allaqat: and for sheer pleasure, when I am not out to learn or have my mind fixed, for diversion, for mere living, Homer and Ferdosi. Could one make a kind of "Education of X?" out of these reflections I wonder?[242] Would it have any sort of interest?

And here's a book on Welsh poetry, from the library, mine for a fortnight, with at least some lines of Aneirin and Taliesin that belong with the best and straightest.[243]

No luck yet. And we've all been more or less out of sorts. Tom stays strong, crawls now. Maria stays pretty and lively. Sima always dear.

All the best to you and yours
B

## To Margaret De Silver

TS Durham

27 September 1953 — 242 Newburn Road, Throckley, Northumberland

My dear Margaret,

Things here – I mean our personal affairs – seem to be very close to a climax. We spent the last few days entirely without money and with very little to eat, though we managed to feed the babies. Mother has run her overdraft to the limit the bank will allow: it is secured on her house, and she is being pressed to sell the house to pay the bank its five hundred pounds. Meanwhile I've been applying for "National Assistance" – the new name for outdoor relief.[244] They are not polite, and I doubt whether we will get it. We have not sold Sima's engagement ring nor any irreplaceable Persian or Arabic books, and I am still nominally owner of a car, or the rusty remains of one, which the customs will not let me sell; and they cannot even make up their minds how much duty they mean to charge on it. It is clear that the car will not fetch even the minimum they can charge – they have

[242] This list of poetic influences corresponds almost exactly to the one given in BB's preface to his 1968 Fulcrum Press *Collected Poems* (see Share, 554–545).

[243] Aneirin and Taliesin: 6th-century poets, probably from areas now in northern England and southern Scotland (i.e. BB's 'Northumbria'); however, they wrote in the Brythonic language and are revered as founding fathers of Welsh literature. They are both mentioned at the start of Part IV of *Briggflatts*, where Aneirin's poem *Y Gododdin*—about a 6th-century battle in northern England—forms the basis of a passage lamenting the destruction and aftermath of war.

[244] The National Assistance Act 1948 extended the universal welfare programme of the Labour government.

caused it to lie rusting for over a year. Unfortunately our National Assistance area is the Marxist stronghold hereabouts – Blaydon[245] – and we are bourgeois parasites, or so I gather.

I had been led to believe several times during the past ten years that I had deserved well of my country in a small way, and eighteen months ago half the papers in the country were praising me for my work in Persia – just after Mosaddeq chucked me out. But in that time I have earned only about ten pounds. The Manchester Guardian keeps consulting me about the Middle East, but they have paid only for a leading article I wrote them, and that at so low a rate I wonder how they manage to get writers at all. The Times, under its new editor has dropped the policy I gave them and now seems to have none, except to repeat in softened terms what the Anglo-Iranian Oil company says roughly – in short, what I fought, not without some success, in one position after another for five years: so that I think the Times would not employ me again in the East even if I succeeded in getting the Persian government to annul Mosaddeq's expulsion. They did not even publish a short letter to the editor about Persian affairs – and that is a grave discourtesy to a former staff-correspondent.

My borrowings amount to one hundred and fifty pounds, but I am also really responsible for more than half Mother's overdraft, and for various taxes which might have been waived but have not been. So even if I found a job – and so many have turned me down so unceremoniously I despair of getting one at all – we'd be in great difficulties for a longish time. You might suppose the BBC, which pays so poorly, would have a use for me: their correspondents are rarely of my standing. But they have turned me down now seven or eight times, not only for more of less journalistic work, but even for summarising monitors reports from the Middle East – work my junior officers did for me six years ago. You might suppose the British Council could use me – but I suspect the qualification there is to be a bugger: any other talent is subordinate to that. You might suppose the many "press relations" jobs under the Colonial Office would leave some place for me: but I've been turned down three times. Maybe they dont like the Foreign Office – I dont know. The Foreign Office itself doesnt approve of Sima: you may have a German or a Russian wife, but not a Persian – that's low or something. And the newspapers suspect me because the Times didnt keep me on when I was expelled from Persia. Outside that range I stand no chance – too old to be a clerk, too

[245] Blaydon: mining district just across the Tyne from Throckley. It incorporates the famously militant village of Chopwell (nicknamed 'Little Moscow'), which has streets named after Marx and Lenin.

ignorant – save the mark – to be a schoolteacher or a librarian. Least chance of all out-of-doors. A labourer is expected to be a man of experience with plenty of good references. I am not even plausible enough to get a job selling vacuumcleaners from door to door.

If I'd had a small capital I might have tried any one of several things – the north of England badly needs a paper of the Economist or New Statesman kind to deal with politics from the very neglected northern point of view and remind the north that literature etc exist. There is a real, though so far unformulated and inarticulate desire for federalizing Great Britain, (after the style of the now old and forgotten "New Heptarchy" move of about 1910),[246] distinct from the hare-brained romanticism of the Scotch and Welsh nationalists, which could nevertheless use their fire: and much uneasiness in the North over what is increasingly a Southern monopoly of senior jobs in politics and administration. It is all somewhat less than incipient, but I agree with it and would have liked to try to give it some direction. I suppose, once started, I could have hoped for subsidies from some of the Northern rich. But I would have had to have something to start on, and there has been never a penny.

I could even have dropped to the shabby toil of literary freelancing if I'd had money to set us up in London for the first few months: but I hate London anyway, and its worse with children: and I dont think I could ever have got more than a pittance in exchange for such humiliating work. Outside London there's no hope in anything of the sort.

I would have very gladly set about three acres of land, with bees and chickens and vegetables, but could not hope to live by it, only to eke out some other living that way.

If I could have bought a suitable boat and still had funds for a summer I'd have tried to live as several now do from cruise books – I've a good camera (although it wants mending) supplemented by other literary work. It might very likely have failed, but there'd have been a chance, and meanwhile a healthy life for the children.

[246] *New Heptarchy Series*: series of tracts proposing the reorganization of Britain into regional governments, published by the Fabian Society 1905–1910 (see 11/2/47 and note). Its title recalled the division of Anglo-Saxon England into seven kingdoms (including Northumbria). BB refers more generally to the push for regionalism in post-war Britain, culminating in the Redcliffe–Maud Report of 1966–1969, which recommended division of England into eight regional provinces (not unlike those of the Heptarchy). These radical proposals to break Britain's London-centrism faltered in the reactionary climate of the Thatcher years, and they remain unimplemented.

But all these possibilities depended on having something fairly substantial in hand, and I had nothing at all.

What is to happen now I dont know. Perhaps the bank will insist on Mother selling her house: if so, she will have to go and live with my sister, who does not want her and with whom she quarrels terribly, frequently and bitterly. My sister is generous in an overcalculated way, without any apparent kindness, and it would be a wretched life for the old lady, who is happy with Sima. Mother would have only just enough to keep herself (and she has nothing to leave). I suppose I would have to beg whatever balance remained from the sale of the house to send Sima and my children to their relatives in Persia – if the Persians would allow it. They could manage there for some years, declining little by little into the helpless starvation of the Armenian poor in Teheran. Then I would be left alone, with no place even for my few books, no money, no prospect of reuniting the family. Such an outlook seems to me worse than undeserved. Goodness knows I have worked hard – many hours a day longer than any other correspondent I've met – and before that, far longer than anyone except, in times of crisis, the Ambassador, in our Embassy. I have done far more than my "task", and done it exceedingly well. Not many people have my knowledge of Islam, hardly any have anything like my knowledge of Persia. Those who have some real knowledge are devoid of the skill to set it out simply on paper. That field is now to be covered by the ignorant and the muddled, and there is to be no other field for me. I am to be insulted by relieving officers who treat all applicants as some sort of thief, and if I get money out of them in the end, the maximum the law allows is (on the figures given to Parliament last summer) less than the unemployed got in the nineteen-thirties: less even than their unemployed pay (dole) which was augmented by in those days by relief. Such is the Welfare State. I mean, of course, less in purchasing power: in mere pounds it is a lot more.

Try again, Margaret please, to see if there isnt something I can do – in America, or for an American paper, or firm, or even the American government – though I think they dont use foreigners in your State Dept. I think the break-up of my family would be the end of me. I must get money somehow, and the work I can give in exchange is good work, worth their paying for. But something I must do, immediately. Or there is no hope at all.

HELP! Try anyone you know and anything you can think of. Goodness knows I've been an unsatisfactory sort of friend, often silent, often absorbed in things that dont interest you and yours: still, within my limitations I've counted you amongst the chief of my friends for a good many years, with Zukofksy, who hears rather oftener from me, and Pound, who hears rather less often. Please, Margaret, chivvy the newspaper folk or anybody else I can earn pay from.

Yours rather desperately
B Bunting

## To Ezra Pound

TS Yale

21 March 1954 242 Newburn Road, Throckley, Northumberland

Dear Ezra,

Thank you (or Dorothy) for Deianira and her bloke.[247] The one spot of intelligence for a long time past. How much is uninterpreted Sophocles? If most, then he's a better poet than I took him for. Is the "It all coheres" your contribution (I mean, one of your contributions)?[248] I feel the Soph. with whom I had a meager acquaintance at school would have been likely to mean no more than that the various oracles were not inconsistent with each other if suitably explained. Maybe I do him injustice. Anyway, I havent read that play in greek or any other version than yours, so I'm only guessing. Aeschylus was the one I'd always intended to get a proper look at some day, but maybe I've been wrong... Though all your generation preferred the Odyssey to the Iliad, and I still believe that was a mistake. The thing done solider than the idea intuited, the sharp eye surer than the sympathetic guts, the deed seen without the trick lighting charm. I'd like to see your version of the catalogue of ships – parallel with Ferdosi's catalogue of coats of arms –, but maybe that's the real reading of your Chinese emperors in the Cantos if one could exorcise the strangeness. So I've maintained, anyway.

I have only just found time to write. I do not think I can endure this job much longer, but whenever I get ready to ask the foreman for my cards I think how

[247] A reference to Pound's translation of Sophocles' *Women of Trachis*, first published in 1954, which narrates the marital strife of Daianeira and Herakles.

[248] 'SPLENDOUR | IT ALL COHERES' is a phrase uttered by Herakles at the climax of *Women of Trachis*, which Pound argued in his notes was the 'key phrase, for which the play exists' (see *Sophocles: Women of Trachis* (London: Faber, 1969), 66). He also quotes the original phrase in Canto 109 (792), and refers to it more indirectly in Canto 116 (817).

hungry the children can be and swallow some more of the filth I am halfdrowned in. But I think I will die of it in the end.

I have written to the Persians, having waited long for a time when they might be disposed to revoke Mossy Dick's expulsion. But even if they do, I'll have the devil's own work trying to get a job there again. The Times seems to be in the oil co's waistcoat pocket. The Guardian hasn't the cash. I havent the knack for such a paper as the Express.[249]

Well, I suppose I am still better off than you, old friend, though without the consolations of being audible and being solvent. My companions are not actually mad, only crass; and I can get out any time I am willing to let the family starve. But it's a sorry outcome of long hard work for all that. And even if I were free of it, its hard to write when you know there'll be no one to read.

This is Persian New Year's Day. We have a bottle of very cheap sherry, and the sun is shining. A season Dante considers propitious to hope...I have answered an advertisement – not a very nice one, but there's not often one that can be answered at all.

Granny is pretty well. Sima well. Children very well. I'm losing weight fairly drastically after a lifetime of invariable ponderosity.

There is no means of sending any more interesting news, because if there were any I couldnt learn of it.

Yours ever

B

After a very gloomy couple of years during which Bunting tried unsuccessfully to find writing work and eventually accepted piecemeal work as a proof-reader, in 1954 he secured a more permanent post as a sub-editor at his local daily newspaper the Newcastle *Journal* (switching to its evening edition, the *Chronicle*, a couple of years later). Although he was deeply unhappy during this period, he would remain at the *Journal/Chronicle* for twelve years—by far his longest and most stable period of employment.

[249] See 17/6/30 and note.

## To Ezra Pound

MS Yale

28 November 1954 — 242 Newburn Road, Throckley, Northumberland

Dear Ez –

More oats arrived.[250] Thankyou.

This past aeon leisure's been rarer than ever: that's mainly why I've not written, though I believe I'd have found time forcibly if there'd been anything to say likely to interest you.

I improved life to a small extent by getting away from that printer. Now I subedit at the table of a provincial morning paper for Kemsley. 5 p.m. to 2 a.m., or later. With bicycling time, it doesnt leave much of the day: I am usually in bed by 3.30, but sometimes not till 4 or later, and I have to read several papers in the time between getting up and getting on the bicycle again.

Still, the work, though monotonous, is less monotonous, and though stupid, less stupid, than what I was doing: and I get more notes in the pay-packet – not enough to begin repaying my debts, but enough not to make new ones, if we are rigidly thrifty.

There is nothing to be said for the Newcastle Daily Journal except that it has kept going since 1711 and is therefore, by about half a century, the oldest newspaper in – the world, I think: maybe its only in Britain.[251]

Bridson did some of my poems on The Third Programme.[252] Not my selection. It was interesting to me to hear what the readers made of them. I havent heard that anybody else was interested. The cheque provided Sima with a superfine sewing-machine, which will of course contribute to the family budget as long as she and the children need clothes.

Gladys Hynes[253] wrote, via Bridson, after the Broadcast. I hadnt heard from her directly for about 17 years.

Typewriter is bust. May be repairable. But its almost old enough for a museum. The prospect of reading my fist isnt likely to attract you. Sorry.

[250] Probably a reference to *odes*, i.e. Pound's translation of the *Book of Odes* by Confucius (see **9/7/53** and note).

[251] The first daily British newspaper was in fact the London *Daily Courant* (1702). BB is probably referring to the *Newcastle Courant* (1711), absorbed by the *Journal* in 1876.

[252] A selection of BB's poems was broadcast on the BBC Third Programme on 9 November 1954. They were introduced by the producer **D. G. Bridson** (who would become a correspondent of BB's) and recited by actors.

[253] See **10/4/27** and note.

Nothing read, nothing seen, nothing done but unnecessary silly toil. While the autumn was still tolerable I used to be able to reflect a little during the ride home at night, but now that is often a struggle against a gale.

Still hoping I shall see your Confucius someday somewhere, but even the library subscription had to be dropped more than a year ago, so the prospect is not good. Omar said you were busy with Cantos again. Excellent.

What a pleasure it would be to see you and Dorothy again. I am tired of fools.

Yours ever
B Bunting

## To D. G. Bridson

MS Indiana

23 August 1955 — 242 Newburn Road, Throckley, Northumberland

Dear Bridson,

I have just applied for a job with the BBC – reporter, advert no 1155 – and into the space for references within the BBC I've written your name. I am above the age they mention, but please endeavour to earthquake them into taking me nevertheless, for I am perishing in the swamp still where Mosaddeq threw me and The Times left me.

I can do the job: and if they had the window to use me in the Islamic countries, I would do it a good deal better then the next man you might meet.

I wish I had had time to write to you. I wanted to say things (pleasant) about Gilgamesh,[254] but couldnt, and cant, find an hour. We have kept alive, but it has taken all our leisure and all our energy to accomplish it.

Yours ever
B Bunting

## To Ezra Pound

TS Yale

11 December 1957 — Shadingfield, Wylam, Northumberland

Dear Ezra,

It would be cruelty to bore you with letters when I havent time to use my head for anything but living-earning, but it seems so long now since I greeted you or heard from you you might think I didnt think of you. I do.

[254] Bridson's *The Quest of Gilgamesh*, a loose poetic adaptation of the ancient Mesopotamian *Epic of Gilgamesh*, was eventually published in 1972, but portions were performed in radio-play format on the BBC Third Programme throughout the 1950s.

I think a great deal about you and Dorothy when I have a break in the miserable scrawling I do to live. I work now for a newspaper, one of the Kemsley lot, at starvation pay, but a trifle better than the printer gave me. For a long time it was night work, very long hours, and hardly time to see my children. At last I got transferred to the evening paper and can work normal office hours (on the long side), but I am still without free time. We brought my wife's nephew over from Persia for an education,[255] and I go out in the evenings coaching him in things the Persians havent bothered with such as algebra.

Meanwhile an old aunt died. She led such a starveling existence I supposed her to be penniless, but she left several thousand pounds and my share enabled me to send Sima and the children for a holiday in Persia with my mother-in-law and to buy a house.[256] Luck was with me for once. I bought at the very bottom of the market, and though I have an uncomfortable mortgage to satisfy I have also a good place to live, with space enough – Edwardian, not a modern dog-kennel – and about half an acre of garden where the children get strong playing and I cultivate cabbages. The view is very pleasant, down the garden to the river, across the cricket field to the village jammed around its church, and up the hill to the Roman Wall. There is a miniature orchard – seven appletrees and a lot of good red currants – enough lawn for the less exacting games, and air as good as you are likely to get within commuting distance of industries as smoky as those of Newcastle. Throckley had gradually ceased to be a village and been absorbed into the city, and the huge new power station two miles away had filled the air there with sulphuric acid which made me and my son cough. The acid doesnt get here, and most of the builders are kept away by our steep, sharp-cornered lanes and the rickety bridge which is closed to anything bigger than a private car and may tumble into the Tyne any day. The village, 1,600 souls including outlying farms and hamlets, has six pubs and an eccentric squire, last of a family living on the same plot for now 900 years. The house is hideous outside (but without pretension) but the rooms are well-shaped, high and big enough for moving around. We can put up a guest.

255 Presumably Rubik (see 1/12/59).

256 BB's Shadingfield home was—and still is—a large suburban house in one of the most affluent postcodes in the north-east. In 2019 its approximate market value was almost three times the national and four times the regional average.

Dogs eat too much at English prices, but the children have a cat, Mithradates,[257] who is lively as well as handsome. A very familiar magpie lives in the garden, and two preternaturally cheeky robins from the beech hedge will perch on the hoe if you pause, watching for worms.

The Zukofsky family stayed three days with us during their tour of Europe. I was very glad to see Louis again and hear his deep growl of a voice. The time was too short to talk intelligently. He just made his number and sailed on.

I have often wished something could be done to get you your freedom, but I cant think of no steps open to me and my like that would not make it more difficult.[258] Even celebrated literati, like TSE, can only annoy the Americans and make them stubborn. Eisenhower could do it, no doubt, for the public, I'm sure, dont give a damn – if they remember you at all; but there seems to be no way of reaching Eisenhower without setting off the press batteries which would inhibit him. People still suggest petitions and I still try to dissuade them – I am sure that sort of thing, especially from England, could only confirm your captivity. It is a great disgrace to America. But it would be hard to persuade the contemporary voter of that.

Dorothy will be glad to hear my mother is well and still, at 83, trots off for her afternoon struggle in the shopping crowds a couple of times a week: but all her many sisters but one have died. She lives with us, in the room with the best view, so deaf I cant make her hear even with wires and microphones: but Sima can converse with her all right. She sends her greetings.

Here it ends. The children are back from a play in the Women's Institute, and I must be a parent. I wish you both exceedingly well. You are my oldest friends and about my closest, silence notwithstanding.

Yours truly, B

[257] Mithradates ('given by the deity Mithras'): the name of several rulers in the Persian region in antiquity. There is a notable Mithraic temple on Hadrian's Wall in Northumberland (which BB knew), so it seems likely that the cat Mithradates was named to honour his family's mixed Persian/Northumbrian heritage.

[258] Pound was in fact released from St Elizabeths shortly after this letter, in April 1958.

## To Ezra Pound

TS Yale

1 December 1959 Shadingfield, Wylam, Northumberland

Ala ya dust qadim![259] Ol Ez,

What's this balm among the disconsolate? I've not seen your typing so long I swear I thought it was the rates. Its a break in the slave routine, anyway. You've no notion how welcome.

Vondel? No, never heard of him. But something was tranṣlated into Dutch about 1930, I don't know what: I thought it was that article I wrote for an Australian magazine. Maybe I'm wrong. And then I think I remember something about The Well of Lycopolis being dutched or daned or something like that, but I never saw the results. That would be less remotely gone.

I have no letters. I ad some of yours once, in spite of conscientious objections to such documents, but they disappeared like almost everything else during the war. If any I wrote have not been put to cloacal uses yet and are wanted to elucidate yours, why, use 'em: they're no good to me. Remuneration nihil. Johnson was wrong about money, it poisons writing.[260]

Whitman on Emerson, no. But I've had a liking for Walt since I was fifteen and am glad to hear him kindly spoken of. I'd not heard that he did any criticism. I liked the great long poems with the great long rhythms and I think I would still like them if I had Walt in the house; but not the pieces the anthologists choose because they hate him.

Oh Ez! What the anthologies will do to you!

Dutch looks alright, its when you hear it spoken. It whines, and Afrikaans whines worse, though you'd think a dose of kaffir klicks would have given it some snap.

I wonder how English dodged the clumsiness of the other Germanic languages. The Scandanavian ones are not so bad, of course, but there's English in Beowulf, before the Norse came along, and a few lines of it are worth all the Germans ever did. The best bits of Sir Gawain are short (norse?), right way up, and telling. Also they sound, not so say resound.

My slavery has lasted near seven years and I dont think it will ever end. Kemsley has gone: he had the paste watered till it wouldnt stick and provided

[259] *Ala ya dust qadim!*: o my old friend! (Ar.)

[260] BB was fond of repudiating Johnson's axiom ('No man but a blockhead ever wrote, except for money') from James Boswell's *The Life of Samuel Johnson.*

one blue pencil per annum, so I thought the change couldnt help being an improvement: but the new man[261] has stopped subscriptions to other papers and having given us each one one shilling ballpen, expects it to last us till our dying day. I dont think there will be many newspaper proprietors in heaven. The Astors and the Kemsleys and Beaverbrook are tied up close to Mammon's tail and stink accordingly. I toil over lists of shares that go up and down and ships that go in and out, too overworked even to read the drivel I put printers marks on; too overworked to get any lunch several days a week; too underpaid to take a days holiday, let alone get out of debt. I have a roomy house (rates owing) a fairly patient wife (with hardly any clothes), nephew to keep at an expensive school (but the government pays four fifths of his fees) daughter at equally expensive school (government wont help with her fees for another two years) son ready to be sent to an expensive school... granny stubbornly extravagant to be kept for what was a reasonable keep for granny twenty years ago... student lodger, quiet decent Persian architectural bloke, who has a friend with a good reciting voice for Hafez. The onions I grew were useful, but the slugs had most of the lettuce. We can keep the house full of roses and sweet peas in the summer and still have plenty in the garden and I'm told I'd get the village flowershow prize if I had time to arrange my delphiniums for it. The garden takes up all the time on days off nearly all the year round, but provides enough exercise to prevent the newspaper killing me at once. Children's home work, when I'm not too tired to help with it, five evenings a week. So I'm not likely to revive you with correspondence. I am almost always too depressed to write to anybody. I'd be an infliction.

Tom decided to be Robin Hood and was given a bow for his birthday, and has shot an arrow through the panel of the kitchen door. The cat survives, by nimbleness... As Tom is usually to be found at the top of the sycamore tree with any impediments he has a fancy for the range is wide, and I think I ought to have taken out third party insurance before stringing that bow.

Rubik's main distinction is that he plays Rugby football quite well, the only Persian, so far as we can learn who ever played Rugby football. All the schoolgirls in Newcastle cherish his photograph: he has them printed by the gross, and I think it would save time if he had "To my only girl" printed on the lot of them at

[261] Roy Thomson (1894–1976), Canadian newspaper proprietor, who became BB's employer in 1959 when he bought the Newcastle *Journal* and *Chronicle*. Both newspapers were based in Thomson House in central Newcastle until 2018.

the same time. They used to come in droves on Sundays and eat a week's victuals at a sitting, but he has been persuaded to get them to take him to the pictures instead. How they make their fathers drive him home in Rolls Royces I cant imagine.

Maria has got as far as her first school anthology and remarked: "I dont understand why all the nicest poems have this funny word Shakespeare written after them". I dont think her teachers quite approve of her enthusiasm for Autolycus's songs and Full fathom five:[262] it would be so much nicer, dont you think, if little girls thought about gnomes and elves you know. Perhaps I do them injustice, but the blasted gnomes keep cropping up.

Sima is tired, like me, but so not tired as me. Her lamb coat is the sensation of prize-givings and pantomimes. You'd guess her husband's salary as a good few thousands, which gives us a laugh. It attracts charity organisers at any distance and it takes quite a time to persuade them that I work for the Chronicle at a weekly wage, not as a director.

Granny, at eightyfive, still trots off to town down the hill to the station so long as it isnt iced over, about three times a week. But I cannot make her hear any more and have to carry on conversation through the medium of Sima.

So long, Ez: give my love to Dorothy.

B

## To Louis Zukofsky

TS Texas

7 August 1962 — Shadingfield, Wylam, Northumberland

Dear Louis,

Now, half the annual twelve days of comparative freedom past, though cold and wet as Iceland, and without a grain of cheer, I can begin to read again, a page or two at a time: so I thank you, and whoever abets you, for Origin.[263] It will last my few days out – with much left over for next summer's catch of breath. I would say something about this and that if you were here; but it wouldn't be right, for I have heard not one word of conversation since you visited Shadingfield. I would

[262] Autolycus: character in *The Winter's Tale* who sings several songs, perhaps most famously 'When daffodils begin to peer' (IV.3.1–12). 'Full Fathom Five' is sung by Ariel in *The Tempest* (I.2.397–405).

[263] *Origin*: Cid Corman's magazine.

be labouring or silly. There is no help, you must put up with silence. That is not ingratitude but helplessness...

One Sunday I picked up Firdausi and reread the story of Bizhan and Manizhe:[264] but I could not go with the power of it, only look on. These are things for men of another class, not ridden by poverty and debt and all the poisoned strife they breed. I saw the words rushing on, I did not miss the skill, but I could not, as it were, lift my limbs for the weight of the chains. Our income is now well below the AVERAGE income of British people – including the pensioners and labourers – and out of it we try to buy the children an education. It is astonishing that one act of tyranny – when Mossadeq expelled us from Persia – and one of faithlessness—when the Times abandoned us – should have such an enduring effect. There has never been even a remote chance of escape: and year by year as the value of money falls and others get their pay raised, mine stays as it was because the wretched who employ me know I cannot get away from them.

So I am ashamed to write to my friends, and they stop writing to me.

Margaret de Silver is dead. Her sons wrote to me. I will not say I wish it were me. Because who then would care for my children: but if they were safe, I would wish it.

I think sometimes of Paul, and his astonishing skill. I hope he is flourishing. And I like to think of recognition, late and sporadic, but yet recognition, coming to you. Your short poems – is lyrics the right name for them? – are the best I know from our long generation – the best since Yeats – so that the future will take care of itself: but there ought to be more present recognition. Your young Scots disciple, Finlay,[265] must be almost the only one this side of the ocean. Sometimes I hate the English.

I think it must be some time since TSE ceased to exist. Letters over his name are printed in the Times, but they seem to be written by aldermen. A zombie: as also my long-ago friend Lionel Robbins, now a big, self-important bogeyman with a bellyful of senseless phrases. I hear only saddening things of Ezra. I hope I can write to him before this week is ended, but I fear I will not find the spirit.

Sima sends her love to you and Celia, and says she is looking forward to seeing you again. The raspberries were big and many this year, and we get many lovely red gooseberries now from the bushes I planted; but the red and black currants died of a plant disease, and there has been no money to replace them.

[264] The story of Bizhan and Manizhe is a *Romeo and Juliet*-style love story in *Shahnameh*.

[265] I.e. Ian Hamilton Finlay.

Jean Richardson[266] still asks after Paul. She finished school a few weeks ago and goes to the local university presently. My Tom collects coins: he has a silver penny of King Edward I, and two of the first bronze coins (William III) as well as pennies from every mint year since 1860. Maria is pretty at 12. Both are good at school.

Salve!
BBunting

## To Jonathan Williams

MS Buffalo

22 February 1963

Shadingfield, Wylam, Northumberland

Dear Jonathan Williams –

It seems best, if you can, to stay the nights of March 17 and 18 with us at Shadingfield. We have plenty of room – about the only thing we do have a surplus of. Wylam is 20 minutes by train from Newcastle, and we are quite close to the station. If, after inspecting us, you care to stay longer, we'd be pleased. Any conversation is a rarity and a luxury to us: and anyway, a friend of Zuk's is bound to be welcome in my house.

But you must be warned that the drudgery by which I feed my family will probably make it impossible for me to be at home on a Monday before 5:30 p.m. I shall try to get off for the day, but havent much hope of it. That doesnt mean that you must waste your time at Wylam. Sima, my Persian wife, is not a reader even in her own language, but she is lively, and entertaining: and if you prefer to write, there's a room for it. Also, Wylam is a pleasant place. The children dont get home from school till late afternoon, so their inquisitiveness and noise need not interrupt you much.

I havent seen the Satis bloke[267] since he came out (once and only once) to see me: and, I think, borrowed my copy of Pound's collected poems – the U.S. edition. At any rate it has disappeared from my shelves. If you see it in his, please jog his memory.

Read ought to be interesting.[268] I think I saw him only once, maybe twice, about 1920 or 1921, but he seems to have kept his mind active. I've thought again

[266] Jean Richardson (b. 1943), a neighbor of the Buntings in Wylam, and latterly Professor Emerita of Natural Resources, Environmental Studies and Geography at the University of Vermont.

[267] Matthew Mead (1924–2009), editor of the journal *Satis*, based in Jesmond, Newcastle.

[268] I.e. Herbert Read (see **28/3/36**), who lived at Stonegrave House, near York.

and again of going to see him, but even York is quite out of reach to a man trying to do what I do on my income.

No, it wasn't that I wouldn't have liked you to do an edition of my poems: but (a) I had little to offer you beyond what Flynn printed – only, in effect, "The Spoils". (b) I didn't, and dont, know what became of Flynn and his edition: there must have been complications (c) I thought you were better occupied in printing Zuk, who is still a poet, and in encouraging the young, than in reviving an extinct man. You will see for yourself how my instruments prevent correspondence: dust I could write would be too depressing.

Yours faithfully
B Bunting

# Revival
# 1964–1985

As we have seen, Bunting felt himself to be 'extinct' in February 1963. But over the next three years a dramatic revival occurred, at the centre of which was *Briggflatts* (published in early 1966, but begun in late 1964), the work on which his reputation very largely rests. The first letters of this final section convey the excitement of the period which gave rise to Bunting's masterpiece, though they suggest a more nuanced portrait of the 1964–1966 years than is sometimes assumed. Bunting's first meeting with Tom Pickard, the ascendancy of Morden Tower as an international poetry venue, and the composition and publication of *Briggflatts* did not coincide exactly; rather, these events unfolded across an interval of two years, during which time Bunting felt lingering feelings of depression and obsolescence alongside a growing awareness that his career was finally taking off (in late 1964 he was still looking forward to a 'posthumous volume someone is sure to do about 2064').

But by 1966 Bunting had decisively broken away from the stagnation of his middle years. How had he managed it? A clue is contained in the letter to Jonathan Williams at the close of the previous section. After many decades without the sort of creative community he enjoyed in the earlier 1930–1933 purple patch, the link-up with Williams was a sign that Bunting was again connecting with a transatlantic scene that was—in Poundian terms—'live'. The cultural high watermark of the mid 1960s was looming, and the late-modernist networks extending outwards from figures like Williams, Gael Turnbull, Michael Shayer, and Stuart Montgomery (and later Allen Ginsberg and Robert Creeley) would give Bunting the boost he needed in terms of publication and reception. When it finally appeared in the first month of 1966—the time lag was crucial—*Briggflatts* was fully in step with the literary scene of the day, a work admired by the countercultural young just as much as modernist veterans. For a while this incredible composition—the poem of Bunting's life in every sense—put him somewhere near the centre of international poetry.

But appropriately for a poet who now identified more and more with forms of northern English regionalism (see especially 21/9/68), the really key event of these years occurred closer to home. Bunting's meeting with Tom Pickard in May 1964 has acquired a fabular aspect over the years, and understandably so. It is difficult to read the letters of 1964–1965 after what preceded them without marvelling at the extraordinary mix of luck and poetic symbolism at the heart of this intergenerational encounter. Pickard rescued Bunting when he was utterly at sea, transporting him from a miserable Newcastle desk job to the vibrant candlelit happenings just a couple of streets away at Morden Tower. This was, truly, the beach beneath the paving stones. As Bunting makes clear in his correspondence more than once, *Briggflatts* was written directly because of Pickard and the young people who attended the Morden Tower readings: it could not have happened without them, and we can imagine an alternate history in which he made contact with Jonathan Williams and Gael Turnbull and enjoyed a moderate revival of reputation (perhaps based on republication of *The Spoils*), but did not connect with Pickard and the Newcastle young, and so was not spurred on to write his passionate Northumbrian epic.

After this high renaissance, the final phase of Bunting's life—from *Briggflatts* to his death in 1985—was marked by frustration and personal crisis as well as professional success. The letters of these years relay details of the many visiting lectureships and reading tours Bunting underwent following his mid-1960s revival. On the one hand, he clearly enjoyed being 'pickled in Bourbon' in Texas and eating wedges of Wensleydale in between tutoring students at Durham University. But the constant travelling could also be enervating for a man now venturing deep into retirement age. Rather pointless squabbles—with Ian Hamilton Finlay in 1969, and Robin Skelton during a year in Canada in 1971–1972—brought out Bunting's cantankerous side, for all that he seems to have been essentially right in both cases.

Above all, we must note the absence of references to new creative material in this final phase of the correspondence. The success of *Briggflatts* conspicuously failed to initiate a new chapter in Bunting's poetic development; rather, that all-inclusive autobiography seemed to use up his creative reserves and ensure that his last years were taken up with writing lectures and preparing editions rather than drafting original poems. There were occasional hints that new thoughts might grow, notably the 'New Moon' fragment summarized below in letters of 1972. But while the later correspondence contains many revealing comments about past works and literary history, there is very little suggestion that Bunting was thinking seriously about a follow-up to *Briggflatts*.

Personally, the final period of Bunting's life can be divided roughly in two. His most professionally successful interval, by some distance, was 1964–1976, and during this time he also seems to have been pretty comfortable in his home life. In spite of the frequent travelling, Bunting could always count on returning to Shadingfield, his handsome Edwardian house overlooking the Tyne in suburban Wylam. He was a celebrated figure, increasingly financially secure (in spite of his grumbles to the contrary) and blessed with a growing brood of children and grandchildren on both sides of the Atlantic, with whom he seems to have maintained mostly very good relations. But in 1977 Bunting separated from Sima, his wife of thirty years, and his Augustan period came abruptly to an end, at roughly the same time as he began to feel the Briggflatts Effect draining away. From this point until his death in 1985 his life was itinerant, often lonely, and at times somewhat opaque.

Ultimately, for all Bunting's deserved luck in pulling off the crossover success of *Briggflatts*, there is a sense in which his overall career as a poet was one of unfulfilled potential, largely for reasons of generational misfortune, regional marginality and, it has to be said, low self-esteem (the latter hardly helped by external factors such as the prison experience of 1918–1919 and repeated rejections by Eliot and the Auden circle). In this respect, the rather melancholy outro to Bunting's life is in keeping with his wider narrative. By the mid 1980s when he died, his reputation had fallen back into relative obscurity after the radical breakthrough of the 1960s. And there, for the most part, it has remained.

A full exploration of the reasons why Bunting's non-conformist Northumbrian modernism has never quite made its way into the mainstream of English cultural life lies far beyond the remit of this edition. However, readers of the letters in this edition will see plainly that in spite of his chronic pessimism, Bunting did at least hope that younger generations would be able to rise above the peculiar mix of indifference and disdain so often shown to challenging, centrifugal literary examples like his. As he advised his young 'apprentice' Tom Pickard in 24/5/77, who was then awaiting a probable lengthy jail term: 'You can endure whatever they are likely to inflict on you, and it wont last for ever! It need not embitter you, let alone demolish you.' This determination to survive—and occasionally flourish—in the face of adversity and internal exile is the moral at the heart of *Briggflatts*. It might also be Bunting's epitaph.

## To Louis Zukofsky

TS Texas

13 June 1964 Shadingfield, Wylam, Northumberland

Dear Louis,

Nothing pains me more than the long silence between us, for which I am responsible: yet it would pain me more to have to write of myself from the grave that has engulfed me so long. I hear of you sometimes, I see work of yours in magazines which I think you have had sent to me. I wish I knew more and saw more.

But I am writing, not to beg for news of you which I cannot pay in news of me, but because there is a boy here you can help, who seems to deserve help.[1]

He looked me up. Jonathan Williams seems to have mentioned me. His name is Tom Pickard, his age is 18, and he is a poet.

He showed me a bundle of poems, mostly a boy showing off, but amongst them a certain number of passages, even whole poems, written with a simplicity and originality which seem quite beyond what adolescence so often produces. Enough to convince me, and to make me want to do whatever I can to help him on his way to being a poet indeed. I dont think there is anything that ought to be published yet, and nobody would publish them anyway except maybe some of the beats.

He thinks of himself as a beat, but the poems he shows an insatiable appetite for are yours, and to a less extent Carlos Williams'. He has no education to speak of, needless to say no money, and yet a wife and a baby. On this capital he has set up a poetry bookshop in a mediaeval tower of the city wall of Newcastle, which he has somehow persuaded the city council to rent to him for 10 shillings a week.[2] He has advertised readings (I have promised to read) and means to print a magazine[3] (I have told him he can use anything of mine that isnt already printed in England – The Spoils, for instance). Where the money is coming from to run

[1] Following a recommendation in a letter from Jonathan Williams of 17 April, Tom Pickard met BB in Wylam at the start of May 1964.

[2] Morden Tower in Back Stowell Street, Newcastle: part of the town wall constructed circa 1200 to repel Scottish invaders. From 1964 Tom and Connie Pickard rented the Tower's upstairs room from the city council and it became a major poetry venue and epicentre of the Anglo-American counterculture. Notable early readers included Robert Creeley and Allen Ginsberg.

[3] Pickard's magazine, *King Ida's Watch Chain: A Moving Anthology*, would eventually appear in the summer of 1965. The first and only issue was dedicated to BB and featured contributions from Zukofsky, Hugh Kenner, and Denis Goacher, as well as several of BB's own poems. **Richard Hamilton** designed its experimental packaging. For BB's summary of the contents see **4/9/65**.

the magazine I cant imagine, but a boy who can hire a mediaeval tower from the Philistines may be able to spoil them in other ways too.

What you can do is to let him print some of your poems. He cant pay, of course, but you get nothing from England anyway, and he'd be happy to reprint those which have appeared in America only. I mean "happy." Perhaps I should say delighted. The company would be mixed, no doubt. Some of his friends dont strike me as living beings at all, and his taste is so unsure it hardly exists. But I've asked Goacher for verse, and suggested that if Pound is fit enough to be asked, he might be asked to give a few lines. He – Tom – himself fancies Patchen and certain eminent beats[4] whom he either has written to or is about to write to.

You were 18 yourself once, Louis, and you'd managed to get to a university. This lad has to sustain his belief in his vocation on nothing at all but inner certainty. His seems to me the only spark of talent I've come across in my own country, and I would hate the spark to go out or go smoky for lack of whatever encouragement I can give. Perhaps I'm wrong; but even so, his enterprise is something gay in a grim world, and what helps it is not wasted. Please can he have some poems?

The children are half-grown, Sima is the mainstay of Wylam tennis club, the garden is more than halfway back to the wilderness you saw, after an interval of good cultivation. Even my mother, just short of 90, is healthy and fairly active. My slavery is worse than it was, and my pay worse. Enough!

Please give my love to Celia, and everyone's to Paul.

Yours
B

## To Louis Zukofsky

TS Texas

28 July 1964 — Shadingfield, Wylam, Northumberland

Dear Louis,

Tardy: but now, with the family packed off for its holiday, I have something that seems like a little leisure for the first time in years.

[4] Kenneth Patchen (1911–1972), American poet published by New Directions. Although not part of the Objectivist group, Patchen corresponded with Zukofsky and was a close friend of Kenneth Rexroth.

Our postal strike probably accounts for the non-arrival of the books you said you were sending. They are getting the parcels sorted at last, and if they've been lying in a pile at Southampton they'll turn up shortly.

Still, I'd have managed something to reply sooner if I hadnt stirred Tom Pickard to write on his own account, so that you knew your kindness was appreciated. He is engaged in trying to find the minimum for which he can get a printer to start on the job of producing his magazine. It can hardly be done, directly, for I dont suppose he sells three books a day. But he is attracting the attention of those who have funds to provide. With luck he may make it. He started readings in his tower. The first was done by one Pete Brown whom I had never heard of. Apparently from his lair in some sordid dosshouse in Liverpool he delights the young of that tough city with a brand of "pop" surrealism founded on a mixture of Lewis Carol and gross words. At least this enabled me to get the Morden Tower into the local papers on quite a scale, and about fifty, half academics, half teenagers, with a sprinkling of thugs, turned up to listen. I read a month later. The academics had gone on their holidays, but a much larger number of teenagers and some of the miscellaneous provincials who seek self-approbation in that sort of thing filled the place, showed something approaching enthusiasm, and queued up for my signature at five bob a time. The Manchester Guardian gave six or seven inches of approval and congratulated Newcastle City Council (which must have been astonished, for it knew nothing about it) on having found such an inexpensive way of keeping its young thugs out of mischief. That should make the tower secure against Aldermen who might want to get "an economic rent" for it.[5] Now Denis Goacher says he is coming north to see me, and I think I'll try to get him to do the August reading.

This has apparently stirred the conscience of the North-Eastern Council for the Arts, which recently turned over some £15,000 of civic funds to theatres and a much smaller sum to our local orchestra.[6] It hasnt done anything about poetry yet; but one of the members has been indoctrinated and the chairman has at least apologized for his absence from the readings (He's electioneering). If I can get a

[5] Prior to 1974, Newcastle City Council was presided over by councillors (elected by popular vote) and aldermen (elected by members of the council).

[6] The organization BB mentions is the North Eastern Association for the Arts, founded in 1961, which would later evolve into Northern Arts, the most energetic of the regional branches of the state-funded Arts Council. It played a central role in BB's revival period: he would become Northern Arts Fellow at Newcastle and Durham universities in 1969–1970, and its president in 1974 (serving until 1977). For more on the institutional backdrop to the north-east arts scene in this period see Natasha Vall, *Cultural Region: North East England, 1945–2000* (Manchester: Manchester UP, 2011).

few more readings noticed by the Press, I think the council might fund Tom's first printer's bill or something of the sort.

Apart from all this rather parochial manoeuvring, it was a curious experience, reading to these youngsters. They were not hindered by the difficulties that annoy their elders. They took poetry as poetry – a nice noise – without questions about its "meaning." They laughed at the comic bits, they were rapt at passages of intricate metric that nobody ever took any notice of before – not that they understood what was attracting them, but it certainly did attract – and the piece about the sick child[7] made at least one girl cry. I found it all very encouraging.

I'm told that something like this is happening all over England, and that in Liverpool and Bristol the local poets (all quite unknown to me) get nearly as much juvenile adulation as the Beatles and more than Elvis Presley. If so, its admirable; but I can hardly believe it. (Even if the poetry is thin)

I am at once glad that Paul has managed, in spite of the almost insurmountable economic difficulties, to make his career in music, and sorry that he hasnt been able to set off on the virtuoso life of fame etc for which he was fitted. I am a little surprised that America hasnt used the radio to make such beginnings easier. Here undoubtedly the BBC leaves few fit performers without a thorough hearing. Perhaps if you could have settled here it would have been easier for him to take off. I sometimes play the tape he made for me when he was thirteen. I know no better bit of Bach playing.

Give him and Celia my love; and believe me, I'd write more at length and oftener, if I could do it without depressing you.

Yours ever
B Bunting

## To Louis Zukofsky

TS Texas

7 September 1964

Shadingfield, Wylam, Northumberland

Dear Louis

Still I put off saying anything about the rich gift you sent me except how much I have enjoyed poems I had not seen before. But perhaps it is enough to say that between you and Tom Pickard and Denis Goacher, somehow the old machine

[7] I.e. BB's 'Search under every veil.'

has been set to work again, and I have actually been writing. Therefore I send you the firstfruits.[8]

It is hard for me to estimate how much, if any, of the old skill is left, and whether a decade of foul drudgery after a decade of absorbing action has reduced me to imbecility. Moreover, facing at last the death of my elder son, I have courted the risk of platitude and even cliche by trying to banish "literature" as far as I can from the statement of what I feel, or felt: for you will say I am as slow as Malherbe, whose ode on the death of somebody's wife was not ready until the man had been remarried several years and was rearing a new family.[9]

It has made me very sad, unwrapping this, and I hope I have clipped something out of it that has shape and grace: but I feel incompetent to judge. So I send it to you, for your strictures. Tell me the truth, surgeon. I can hold my tongue under sentence.

All the best to you and yours.

B Bunting

## To Louis Zukofsky

TS Texas

16 September 1964 — Shadingfield, Wylam, Northumberland

Dear Louis,

Many thanks: and my apologies for pestering you. It takes, of course, time to consider amendments, especially fairly drastic ones, and time is what I am shortest of: so no definite remarks here, no argument.[10] I am not cast down – couldnt be by honest skilled criticism, whether I come to agree with it or not – as you must have seen on innumerable previous occasions when I've been indebted to you for strictures of which, I reckon, I must have adopted more than half, either at once or on consideration.

At a guess, I'm unlikely to go the whole way with you. Your amended version is an LZ poem, I think. Some things puzzle me: you keep the line "lost, late, dumb," where in my copy the word "dumb" is ringed to be changed, IF I can do it, because it seems too cerebral a defiance of "words." A bit mechanical. Some others are expected, and partly discounted: you reject easily recognisable rhet-

[8] 'A Song for Rustam', is attached in TS. It is BB's elegy for his son Rustam (see note to 15/5/37). The comments here are significant because they confirm that this was BB's first original work since the completion of *The Spoils* in 1951, thirteen years earlier.

[9] Perhaps Malherbe's 'Consolation à Monsieur du Périer' (1599).

[10] BB is responding to Zukofsky's suggested edits to 'A Song for Rustam' (see 7/9/64).

orical figures, because they suggest a bloke posing for a "public relations" photograph. I am ready to risk that, if the devices bequeathed to us seem useful.

Anyway, its all for long consideration, I suppose. That "long" is the trouble. I've a feeling that there isnt so long to write what I want to write. I'll die or petrify, or my disgusting drudgery will make me an imbecile. Still, better silence than rubbish.

In the grave's narrow slot
they lie: we rot.[11]

The we doesnt mean you, whose work for a living is merely dull, not stultifying. Worms dont eat you alive.

I owe poems to Rustam – part paid; – to Cooper Stephenson, who was killed in the great battle of March 1918, the closest of all the friends I've had; and to Peggy Greenbank and her whole ambience,[12] the Rawthey valley, the fells of Lunedale,[13] the Viking inheritance all spent save the faint smell of it, the ancient Quaker life accepted without thought and without suspicion that it might seem eccentric: and what happens when one deliberately thrusts love aside, as I then did – it has its revenge. That must be a longish poem. Presumably the effort will breed little poems too. And then I'll be ready to write a great hymn to death that cleanses the world and puts an end to its stench. Well, that looks like the programme of an old man revisiting the scenes of his youth, casting up with his accounts, as my father did in the few months before he died. I have no means to carry it out, but I must try.

We are all very little more than turds. I've said more here than I ever said to anybody, Louis, at least since I grew up. YOU wont dive after useless salvage, but chuck this flotsam back into the ocean to sink. And having no even approximate equal to talk to, it's a relief to write it to you.

Yours
B.

[11] An amended version of this couplet ('In the grave's slot|he lies. We rot.') appears in the final version of *Briggflatts* (Part I, 25–26).

[12] Ernest Cooper Apperly Stephenson (*c.*1900–1918), friend and classmate of BB at Ackworth School in the early 1910s, at around the time he met Peggy Greenbank.

[13] The Rawthey and Lune: rivers in the North Pennines. Brigflatts, where BB spent summer holidays as a teenager and met Peggy Greenbank, is in the Rawthey Valley; Lunesdale/Lonsdale (not to be confused with Lunedale, also in the North Pennines but further to the north-east in County Durham) is a much bigger adjacent valley.

The first material products of BB's revival were his contributions to *King Ida's Watch Chain* and the book version of *The Spoils* that appeared in June 1965. Although it was published by the Morden Tower Book Room, this edition, which featured minimalist artwork by Richard Hamilton, was distributed by Gael Turnbull's Migrant Press (Turnbull had met and briefly corresponded with BB in the late 1950s).

## To Gael Turnbull

TS Scotland

24 September 1964 Shadingfield, Wylam, Northumberland

Dear Gael Turnbull,

I'm glad to hear from you, and will certainly be pleased to hear your voice and, I hope, feed and bed you when you come north.

Dont forget that Tom Pickard is a mercurial youngster, inapt to distinguish between hopes and facts. That enables him to get things done that might never otherwise be attempted, but it doesnt make him a very reliable business guide. I think he has led you to believe that I have a number of poems waiting to be printed: but in truth there is only "The Spoils," which was printed by Poetry, Chicago, a dozen years ago and has been read on the Third Programme,[14] so that it isnt a novelty – though it is even harder to get in England than my Texas volume.[15] That is to say, something less than 350 lines, already known to at least part of your clientele. Eventually, if the horrors of earning a living dont quench me altogether, there should be other poems, but so far none exist, only drafts for a couple of short ones, still unpruned and ungerminated, and two or three little translations, not worth putting even in a magazine by themselves.

It is true I would like to see the Spoils in getatable form. If you really want to do it, I'm grateful to you. If you dont, well, its waited so long that no doubt it can wait for the posthumous volume someone is sure to do about 2064.

An English edition of the whole extant works would be the ideal thing, but that would be an expensive luxury, for a commercial publisher mad enough to believe he could get enough prestige from publishing unwanted poetry to compensate for the shelf room it would take up for ages to come.

[14] A reading of *The Spoils* was broadcast on the BBC Third Programme on 24 July 1957.
[15] I.e. *Poems: 1950*, published from Galveston, Texas.

You speak of agreements. But my only stipulations are that the copyright remains mine: you have a licence (or whatever the legal term is) to publish so-many copies; and that the look of the thing shall be respectable – a tolerable fount of type, paper not too shabby, etc. I dont think poetry is a commodity. Nobody ever made any money out of it except Byron and Pope, and for my part I have always maintained that copyright should merely ensure that the author has a supervisory right not to be misrepresented by incomplete or altered copies. Letting him charge for his work only invites the mob of prostitutes of the press to multiply. I would like a rather larger handfull of copies of my work than publishers usually give the author, but I dont give a damn about royalties, advances and so forth, even if they were anything but empty words so far as poetry is concerned.

I've been pleased by what I've seen of your efforts to keep poetry in existence on this side of the Atlantic. It is difficult to give the young men a chance to be heard, and well worth doing even when they turn out duds. Young Tom Pickard is worth encouraging for the spark of poetry in him, struggling to get out of the schoolboy showing off which still surrounds it, and Tom, with Connie Watson, is being damn useful to Newcastle with the readings he is running at the Morden Tower.

The county court judge came round the other day and borrowed the only spare copy of my poems (and stood me two tumblers of whisky, so that poetry is not totally devoid of material reward). I hope it may stand me in good stead when I am sued for my rates or the gas bill – both imminent. The copy in the local library, unread for year, seems to be always out now. All this is owing to Tom and Connie.

If you know any rich, foolish person, easily parted from his money, what's wanted most is a solid edition of Zukofsky (complete, or complete excluding "A") in England. That would have a far greater readership than I can hope for, and his austerity is obvious enough to do far more than my verse ever can to curb the follies poets are apt to lose their way in.

I imagine – perhaps too hopefully – that by now there are people willing to see that Z and myself are/were not copies of Pound, Eliot and Carlos Williams, however glad we were to adopt what we could from their discoveries. Or is the distinction too subtle for people brought up on pre-1910 writings?

Yours ever
BBunting

## To Louis Zukofsky

TS Texas

23 November 1964 Shadingfield, Wylam, Northumberland

Dear Louis,

I hasten – I hope I havent given you the impression that I think your work too staccato. You use staccato properly, where the effect you are after is enhanced by it, and, as you say, you also show your ability to write in (musical and syntactical) phrases of great length when that's the intention. Also A is more of a piece by far-sighted planning of the form than any of the other "poems of length" undertaken in these times. But I have the impression that some of the poets who profess your influence have taken over the staccato where it isnt wanted, and perhaps even mistaken the short lines for an indication of staccato utterance. Hence I tell 'em to read Williams's To Elsie, where all but the last few lines is a single sentence and a single musical mouthful.[16] It would be no good referring them to EP. They feel that's the past.

Yes, Creeley stayed at Shadingfield and talked, all the time, very well. We liked him. He has set a bloke named Hall on my tail, who seems to think he can get commercial publishers to do a collected BB.[17] Good luck to him! But I'm not putting much of my money on such an unlikely horse. I've not been near a publisher for more than a decade, and the last certainly made it clear he didnt think much of me either as an investment or as a prestige item in the list.[18] When I'm well and truly dead someone will do a collection.

They never read you? Tom Pickard is reading you voraciously, not once, but over and over again. Though the magazine, King Ida's Watch Chain hasnt started yet (it's a little nearer) he proposes to bring out the whole poetical works of LZ loose-leaf, little by little, to fit into a couple of ring files. Tom is very much attached to me, but I'm mistaken if he doesnt think you the better poet. He is doing little bits he calls hokkus which have some resemblances to some of your early stuff. Also both Turnbull and Shayer appear to have quite a lot of Zukofsky by heart.

[16] 'To Elsie': largely unpunctuated 66-line poem first published in Williams's *Spring and All* (1923).

[17] Donald Hall (1928–2018), American poet, critic, and anthologist, highly influential in the Anglo-American poetry scene of the 1950s and 1960s. He did not ultimately have any hand in publishing BB.

[18] Seemingly a reference to **Dallam Flynn/Simpson**.

Yes. Maria is said to be a good painter, but she keeps the stuff at school. What I have seen is good, and not altogether in the manner that happens to be fashionable. A shell in black and deep blue, making a shape on the board that looks right without looking contorted or forced, and yet isnt at all familiar. But I say nothing. If she can still do it when she's eighteen in another three years it will be worth thinking about. Tom (Bunting) is now working for the exam called Common Entrance which opens the doors of the Public Schools, if you can pay for them. We cant, and what's to become of him I dont know. Sima stands up to our mounting difficulties with courage. They've cut off the gas. Water and electricity are yelling for money I havent got. There's neither coal nor oil left, the mortgage and the rates to be paid, and I hear that my employer will give all his serfs a rise after Christmas, except those over 60.

All the best to you and yours

B Bunting

P.S. Granny, now just on 90, sends her love.

## To Denis Goacher[19]

TS Durham

13 December 1964

Shadingfield, Wylam, Northumberland

Dear Denis,

I do not know what to say. Now there is a fire burning, thanks to you.[20] But that was not why I told you we were short of this and that, but to let you know that there were limits not set by us to the kind of hospitality we would like to offer you. It is miserable to be back in the same sort of predicament I endured more than thirty years ago, but it is nothing my friends can mend, and it is rather shameful to tell them of it all. Thankyou.

Things go on much the same. Tom Pickard is to have £10 from the NE council for the Arts for each reading, but he has had to close the Tower except for the readings, having run through all he and Connie can raise. I doubt whether they have enough to eat. But it was always the same story with the man who tried to write poetry without a private income or an academic half-job. Poetry Chicago

[19] **Denis Goacher**: British poet, actor, and Poundian acolyte. After first meeting in the 1950s, BB and Goacher corresponded regularly from the 1960s on.

[20] Although BB gave Goacher some credit for his return to form in these months (see 7/9/64) the reference here is to a literal rather than a metaphorical fire: Goacher seems to have given (or lent) BB money to alleviate financial difficulties.

has accepted a few of Tom's poems,[21] so he will soon have something to show, and he will soon be at the end of the little I can do to send him on his way.

Poetry has also put in its claim, which I had already conceded in my mind, to publish Briggflatts when it is done.[22] Did I tell you one Donald Hall, prompted I think by Creeley, is attempting to get publishers for a collected BB?

No, I dont think wordplays, however neat, should stand if they hamper the rhythmic movement. Goodness knows it is difficult enough to move at all. I despair of keeping any life in the verses sometimes. Perhaps it would be easier for me never to try anything longer than a dozen lines or so; but I am impelled by love of a larger shape, more architectural, which has been so much neglected. The first two movements of The Spoils have it just as I want it, but the third is lopsided and shored up confusedly. The Well of Lycopolis begins and ends as I intended, but the middle movements fail to fill out the shape as they should. No doubt some similar fate will overtake Briggflatts: meanwhile I struggle with words, to keep them from sagging. Out with it! It catches attention, but in the wrong place. It is clever, but slows down the flow. Etc etc. Chomei has the shape, but at the cost of some pretty dull brickwork. No one else but Eliot seems to care about the plan – they all get engrossed in detail – and Eliot is apt to make the plan too plain – council houses where we want temples. ("Quando flautos, pitos")[23]

Yours ever
B Bunting

## To Gael Turnbull

TS Scotland

4 January 1965 — Shadingfield, Wylam, Northumberland

Dear Gael,

Of course I would like to come and see you. Of course I would like to read to people who want to hear.[24] And I am very much moved by your kindness. Sometime soon the newspaper will arrange a spring week-off, and there will be a

[21] Three poems by Pickard ('Street Cleaner with His 18th Cent. Muck Cart' and two untitled lyrics) were published in the March 1965 edition of *Poetry*.

[22] *Briggflatts* was published for the first time in the January 1966 edition of *Poetry*.

[23] Literally 'when flutes, whistles': part of the final couplet of 'Quando pitos flautos' by Spanish Baroque poet Luis de Góngora (see **14/3/51** and note), which works here as a paraphrase of BB's 'council houses when we want temples'.

[24] Turnbull arranged a series of readings for BB in the English Midlands in April 1965. As well as public readings at Leicester and Nottingham, he organized a private reading of the draft of *Briggflatts* in Worcester for a small literary audience including Michael Shayer and Roy Fisher.

limited choice of when it will happen: but once fixed it is fixed for good. So if I know when you will want me, I may be able to fix my week for that date, but if I dont know, we will just have to see if you can fit in with whatever date has been allotted here.

Your letter chanced to come at a moment of dejection. It would be useless to spread that disease by enlarging the causes, which are all ultimately one – poverty – which obliges one to fall short of one's responsibilities and to leave chances untaken, and brings so many unforseen humiliations besides the daily ignoble drudgery among foul people. I curse Mossadeq and the Astor family every day. None of it should concern you, except as an excuse for the poor response I must seem to be making to your kindness. I just havent got it in me at the moment to be cheerful.

The poem Briggflatts has reached the end of its second part in fairly satisfactory draft (though no doubt there will have to be very considerable cutting and patching later on); but there I am stuck. Part Three wont come, perhaps because I find it impossible to abandon my lifelong reserve about myself, which I must do if the poem is to have the simplicity which must alternate with more complicated mental states to give it its shape.

I was never troubled by physical modesty, but I am unwilling to stand emotionally naked. I could not write, for instance, as Creeley does. I dont put this forward as a virtue, but as a limitation which may or may not have good reason, I mean good literary reason. Perhaps it is only that I am too commonplace a person to be exposed to critical examination. The proper course would be to find things which reflect the simplicity I want indirectly. The bull is right. The cart ride to Bainbridge is probably right.[25] But I can find nothing to do the same for the matter that should go into part three. And without that, the plan for part four would be no more than pornographic. I thought I had found part of what I want in a little piece by Meendiño (Gallegan troubadour) but it turned out to depend so intimately on the exceedingly cunning form he gave it that it couldnt be annexed.[26] I stay stuck.

[25] Bainbridge: village in Wensleydale, some twenty miles east of Brigflatts. Part I of *Briggflatts* (40–60) describes a cart travelling through the landscape of the Pennines, carrying the stone of the mason and the young couple (BB and Peggy) as stowaways.

[26] Mendinho: probably a Galician ('Gallegan') poet writing in the early 13th century. In a notebook in the BB holdings at Buffalo, there are several fragments which seem to have fed into versions of *Briggflatts*: one of these is a pastiche of Mendinho's sole surviving work, the densely formal lyric 'Sediam'eu na ermida de San Simión,' with 'Briggflatts' standing in for references in the original to the Galician shrine San Simión. The 'exceedingly cunning form' of Mendinho's poem involves a complex parellistic technique with an intricate, interwoven rhyme scheme.

As to reading, public reading is one thing (and Tom's Tower is singular – it lacks that obituary feeling natural to assemblies of people who feel they have a duty to be cultured) and private gatherings of poets quite another. It might be good if those who are alive, not mere zombies, met from time to time, not to hear one now antiquated man, but to listen to each other. However, they are a touchy brood. I dont think many have the humility to learn from their contemporaries. They aspire to some individual inspiration called genius which I never encountered, instead of the good craftsmanship Bertran de Born[27] or Wyat or Malherbe cultivated. It was once suggested to the young W.H. Auden that he should come for a week or two to Rapallo because EP, BB and WBY thought he had something in his first book, but it seemed too diffused and they thought that might be remedied.[28] He replied that he preferred teaching boys to play rugby; and he became more diffuse with every piece he wrote.

I think I read you Part One of Briggflatts. It has been modified, but not much altered, and there are still weak places and bad lines to be dealt with. Part Two is too long for me to face the labour of copying it out, or I would send it along. Your reactions would help to determine its final shape. It is built rather like part two of the Spoils (or Eliot's Quartets) in panels hinged on short lyrics. One or two of these are detachable, and I will try to find time to type one or two to add to this letter. I think you and Shayer have a kind of right to see what is going on, and I am vain enough to suppose you may be interested. If you're not, nothing's lost but a little labour. You are not required to comment unless you have something you want to say, and blame is at least as welcome as praise.

Please give Shayer my best wishes. I hope you and yours are well, and that you are producing. Sima sends her regards.

Yours
BBunting

## To Denis Goacher

TS Durham

20 January 1965 Shadingfield, Wylam, Northumberland

Dear Denis

Again I'm slow answering. Work is half the excuse and children making the room useless for anything but their television pop orgies the other half.

[27] Bertran de Born (*c.*1145–1210), Occitan troubadour much admired by Pound.
[28] See 11/4/31.

Thanks for your curious litany on TSE's demise.[29] The process of death is too continuous for me to feel any longer much interest in its completion. Plainly, Churchill was mainly dead a few years ago, and EP seems to be at least a good deal dead now. I feel that all these salutes from the young and preparations for complete editions etc are the first steps of my funeral, which isnt yet overdue only because the corpse has recently sat up and uttered a few words.

I said hard words about TSE from time to time.[30] I thought he surrendered too easily to the damned orthodoxies he had no real need of. But he was a kindly man, affectations and all; and people of my age remember how much Prufrock and the Waste Land did for English taste and understanding. Even persistence in what everyone said was a foolish marriage was a fault of kindness, though it was there he first put his foot in the grave, I think. As for "royalist, classicist, anglican," well, Yeats believed in witchcraft, or tried to persuade himself that he did, and EP beheld the devil before Confucius taught him better. Nihilism is hard work for some chaps, and I dont hold it much against them.

It would interest me more, I think, to know what you are doing. Is the leg well? How is your lady? Does the BBC keep you occupied? The Dante?[31] What about your friend/enemy Wigham?[32] I suggested him to Tom for a reading, but it could only happen on a visit to England, though the Northern Council for the Arts has been bullied into giving Tom a minute subsidy which will at least prevent him losing much money on the Tower.

He has your mss, getting bits ready for the first number of his magazine which will now, I think, probably really appear. He also has plans for a bout of readings to coincide with the City-University "festival of the arts," bless them, which I think happens in February. I dont quite know what he is up to. I am too self-centred till Briggflatts gets finished to keep track. I think he had some intention of asking you to take part. I believe I am to read again, with a guy tickling the lute in between poems.

Sima sends her regards. I must hurry to get my hair cut – local TV interviewed me last night ("a major poet," said the dumb journalist announcer) and my family was outraged by my unreassuring appearance.

Yours ever

B

[29] Eliot died on 4 January 1965, as did Churchill a few days later on 24 January.

[30] BB's record of anti-Eliot invective was long (see especially **19/1/32** and note).

[31] Goacher was translating Dante's *Inferno* for a BBC Third Programme broadcast.

[32] Goacher edited Pound's *Women of Trachis* (see **21/3/54**) with British poet and translator **Peter Whigham** in the early 1950s.

## To Denis Goacher

TS Buffalo

28 February 1965 Shadingfield, Wylam, Northumberland

Dear Denis,

Slow, this answer – drudgery and the kids radio and TV in the only room warm enough to sit in at this season.

Tom Pickard showed the file for number one of King Ida's Watch Chain to some poets here for the idiot festival (more later). All were struck by your work in it. Hugh MacDiarmid spoke to me about it, much impressed. Gael Turnbull had had no idea that you were a poet of such strength and accomplishment; he was short of time, but expanded quite a bit on "Carousel." Others, less likely to carry weight with you, the same. So I wasnt codding you along. The stuff is there and you have no reason to get glum about it.

Dont be misled by my severity. I do that to make what's good better, and do the same to anyone whose work is worth it. When I say something anodyne, begin to suspect the worst, not when I demand reform and retrenchment. I've never been anything but rough with EP and LZ, nor they with me. And if your manner is quite out of the current fashion, regard that as a guarantee that it isnt mere apestuff or the easy way into print.

Squalid little festival. The fools on the City council and the dupes in the University think that by spending a very small amount for a week they can persuade the reluctant business men that Newcastle is a centre of Art, Art, Art. So by arranging concerts, plays and poetry readings all for the same night they make sure that nobody has a respectable audience; and just to clinch matters they put on a few floodlit football matches to take a few more away from the other doings. Finally, they allow the chief constable to close down the cinema that was to have put on some films worth seeing, because it couldnt afford to do this till late in the evening and he "will not have a lot of people on the streets after 11 p.m." – except, of course, the drunken drivers for the clip joints.

Hugh MacDiarmid stayed with me. I was warned that he ate nothing but whiskey, and he justified the warning. As near as I can calculate he drank 3½ bottles during his 36 hours on Tyneside, which he ballasted with two boiled eggs, a small spoonful of curry, and a piece of toast. Leaving for Manchester, he complained of stomach qualms, which he attributed to the curry – "rich oriental food I'm not used to." Turnbull and I put him to bed at 3.30 a.m. the first night. The second he was capable and coherent at midnight. But I liked the old guy very well, though somewhat disconcerted when he kissed all the girls in the tower and all the waitresses and barmaids he encountered, making some very startling improper proposals meanwhile in a loud, clear voice. He believes women have no brain, and that it is his duty to cheer them up with the only kind of talk they understand; and I must admit none of them seemed much put out, though they were all scandalised. They didnt withdraw their ears or run away or scream.

I am going to Worcester, Nottingham, and Leicester at beginning of April. If there's a few quid in hand I intend to come to London, maybe two nights, to show my daughter pictures in the National Gallery and the Tate – she wants to be a painter. I think it is more likely than not to fall through – short of time as well as money – but if it works there might be a moment to see you. If not, come up here when the weather loses some of its chill. With Sima at home there will bc some baqala pilau or chilao kebab or similar – anyway, not the queer scramble we had in the summer. I can be ill for two days without having to get a doctor to certify it. With a weekly day off that might make three, or even, if Sunday coincides, four days.

Yours ever
B.

## To D. G. Bridson

TS Indiana

20 April 1965

Shadingfield, Wylam, Northumberland

Dear Bridson,

I promised to send you the draft of Briggflatts, incomplete and not even touched by revision. Here it is. I cant record it instantly as the kids and their pop stars have put our tape recorder out of action.

First aid? You will not need it. It is about love, in all senses, beginning with a kind of Daphnis and Chloe[33] and ending with St Cuthbert[34] in love with all

[33] *Daphnis and Chloe:* romance by the Greek writer Longus (2nd century AD). The protagonists are abandoned at birth, but rescued and nurtured by shepherds; they meet, fall in love, and after a series of separations and hardships, are reunited and married. The parallels with the central narrative of *Briggflatts* are obvious.

[34] BB repeatedly stressed the central role in *Briggflatts* of Saint Cuthbert—a positive mirror-image to the brutal, controlling Eric Bloodaxe.

creation. Alexander's journey[35] is central to it. Bloodaxe, Pasiphae,[36] the turd-bakers[37] and the little imitation of Scarlatti[38] have functions fairly easily divined, and need not trouble the reader.

I know there are very weak passages, and some awkward lines, and have laid my plans for eliminating them – it will take some time. It reads aloud better than on the page.

Let me know how it strikes you. If it seems all rot, say so, I am not offended by drastic opinions and consider them carefully when they come from people I trust.

Meanwhile, what about Gilgamesh?[39] A pamphlet? I daresay Turnbull would do it for Migrant Press or perhaps Tom Pickard for his enterprise, unless you prefer proper publishers and all their rigmarole. I assure you, I really have waited for it and expected it this several years.

Or what about your Gilgamesh and Turnbull's both in one pamphlet? Two interpretations, a rounder sight in the epic? I will try to remember to suggest it to him when I write.

Thankyou for your hospitality. Maria was much impressed, and you cannot imagine what a change it is for me to be able to talk and listen over my victuals.

Yours ever
B Bunting

In the summer of 1965, after some fifty years without contact, Bunting was reacquainted with the dedicatee of *Briggflatts*, Peggy Greenbank. Following some go-between work by Gael Turnbull, Bunting and Peggy met at her home in Hope, Shropshire (out of view of Peggy's husband), subsequently at their primal scene Brigflatts, and then sporadically for the next few years.

In placing this episode in the context of Bunting's life and work, we must bear two things in mind. First, although the final lines of *Briggflatts* make reference to BB's realization that Peggy was still alive and contactable (as detailed in the following letter to Turnbull), the first

[35] Part III of *Briggflatts* is based on a retelling of a narrative from the Persian epic *Shahnameh*, in which Alexander the Great experiences a vision of the angel Israfel at the 'top of the world'—the summit of the mountains Gog and Magog.

[36] The myth of Pasiphaë, who gave birth to the Minotaur after coupling with a white bull sent by Poseidon, features at the close of Part II of *Briggflatts*.

[37] The turd bakers appear in Part III of *Briggflatts* as a metaphor for meretricious members of the English literary establishment (journalists, poets, academics).

[38] After a brief encomium to Domenico Scarlatti's aesthetic virtues, the conclusion to Part IV of *Briggflatts* echoes Scarlattian musical structures, though not exactly in a way that is 'easy to divine,' as BB suggests here.

[39] Bridson continued to work on his *Gilgamesh* translations throughout the 1950s and 1960s (see 23/8/55 and note).

draft was in place by this point (see 20/4/65), and the reunion itself certainly took place after *Briggflatts* was finished. There is therefore little evidence to suggest that renewed contact with Peggy had any substantial impact on Bunting's creative output at this point. Second, although there is no doubting the sincerity of both BB and Peggy in this interlude (Peggy's devoted letters to BB, held at Buffalo, mirror BB's heartfelt comments in the letters here), we should note that there are very few references to Peggy in BB's letters either before or after the 1964–1966 period. For all the poetic realism of the 1965 reunion, then, Bunting's correspondence taken as a whole suggests that the relationship with Peggy was not quite the central biographical drama he claimed; rather, the *idea* of Peggy seems to have acted as a powerful and relatively short-lived afflatus in his imaginative life during composition of *Briggflatts*.

## To Gael Turnbull

TS Scotland

13 May 1965 — Shadingfield, Wylam, Northumberland

Dear Gael,

I stole time from Lord Thomson to write this, neglecting his stocks and shares. I type it to be legible.

You knew of course that your report on Briggflatts would strike very deep.[40] Yet what you tell me is no more than I foresaw and expected before I began to write the poem. I suppose I had refused to draw the inferences for what's to be done.

But first I must be sure. I dont doubt that the old woman you didn't meet was the little girl of the poem. Her elder sister had no health. Still, unexpected things happen, the weakling often survives. And I must be sure she has no living husband to hurt. For if she is she, and alone, I must obviously see her. It would be cruel to leave her to hear of the poem from anyone else. And even if she is quite indifferent, it would be discourteous.

On thing I wrote wrongly to you. I dont really think there is any need to take warning by Flora Finch.[41] The girl at Briggflatts had so much life and character she could never become a fool.

I am too much moved to be sure of anything just now: but it seems at the moment that, if she and circumstances permit it, the poem must keep the name

[40] BB is responding to Turnbull's report of a visit to Brigflatts. during which he met Peggy's elder sister Sissie and learned that she was alive and living in Shropshire.

[41] Flora Finching is a character in Dickens's *Little Dorrit*. After a twenty-year absence she is reunited with her fiancé, the novel's protagonist Arthur Clennam, who finds his youthful sweetheart transformed into a 'diffuse and silly' middle-aged widow. See *Little Dorrit* (Oxford: OUP, 1999), 125.

Briggflatts and be dedicated to her. She has been with me all this half century, often when nobody else was. I must acknowledge it.

Yours

B

Peculiar recesses there are in a man that he knows very little about. I went into a pub at lunch time, thinking about your letter. While I was drinking my beer a middle-aged man came up and said: Why Grandad, whatever is the matter? And only then I became aware that the tears were running down my face as they havent done since I was a little boy.

So you know why Briggflatts was written, and why it will probably have to keep its "irrelevant" name.

## To Denis Goacher

TS Durham

26 May 1965

Shadingfield, Wylam, Northumberland

Dear Denis,

Well anyway we're glad to hear from you. I was afraid we must somehow have offended you, and there was no knowing how. Yes, the time was too short: on the other hand, if you were feeling glum of temperament, what else is change of place and company for but to cure that? Come when you can. We are always waiting.

As for having nothing to show – to a man who writes nothing at all for a dozen years – how could that trouble you? You have a good deal done, mostly excellent stuff. I am sorry we are so slow about getting it into print. The Spoils isnt ready yet, though daily expected. On the other hand, Briggflatts was completed on May 15, and the revision is going rapidly, with far fewer cuts than I expected, though part five may yet need reconstruction. I've begun to type out the final (let's hope) version.

Let me know if you hear anything from Ezra, though he wont be pleased with my writing: partly for sound reasons, I expect, but partly because Olga has him persuaded that I (and probably TSE) wouldnt cooperate in getting him out of the madhouse, whereas we merely wouldnt cooperate with her in publicity which seemed likely to make it harder than ever to get him set loose.[42]

Allen Ginsberg was here last weekend – read to a full house for four hours.[43] He looks like an owl in a bunch of ivy and carries excentricity quite a distance,

[42] See 14/3/51.

[43] For Ginsberg's colourful account of his reading at Morden Tower, see 'Allen Ginsberg and Morden Tower'. Morden Tower website, http://www.mordentower.org/allen.htmlo.

but is amusing and very likeable. His work far too diffuse – all prime-sautier, he hasnt learned to cut nor even the respectably ancient art of the pumice. But there is quite a lot there, if it could be sewn together. Whitmanesque. I dont know what Tom Pickard has next in store.

Bridson says Newby[44] offered half an hour for Briggflatts, to include explanation. Since it takes about an hour to read and isnt really dismemberable, I've said, Thankyou, lets wait. You'll want to do it sooner or later whole, and I am in no hurry. There is a caricature of the same view of things going on here, where Tyne Tees Television thinks it is conferring an inestimable benefit on the Modern Tower and on me by offering to do a bit on us, and is very huffy because we dont want the kind of bit it proposes to do. The producer rashly broached the matter after a reading and everybody in the place rose up and smote him verbally. He seems to be revising his views, so I have rubbed some salt in the bruises, and am waiting to see what happens.

On the other hand, the editor of the Sunday Sun printed a picture of Ginsberg and me on the front page, very large, and is preening himself on the March of Culture – the first popular Sunday paper ever to admit on the front page that such a thing as poetry exists.[45]

Yes. Come North at the first opportunity. As I said, we're always waiting.

Yrs
B

## To Dorothy Pound

TS Indiana

11 June 1965 Shadingfield, Wylam, Northumberland

Dear Dorothy,

How glad I am to hear from you at last. My own fault, for writing so rarely, but there was never any good to report. Now there is.

I wrote to Ezra last autumn, but got no reply. Whether that is general lassitude or whether he thinks ill of me because I thought some of the efforts to get him

[44] P. H. Newby (1918–1997), British author and managing director of BBC Radio.

[45] On 23 May 1965 Allen Armstrong, editor of Newcastle's weekly *Sunday Sun*, published an article on Ginsberg's Morden Tower reading, with the accompanying picture BB mentions, and the caption: 'Mr Bunting, a Newcastle journalist, and one of Britain's foremost modern poets, was sitting at the time, on the settee next to Ginsberg. America's original "Angel-headed hipster" flopped forward and lay with his head in Bunting's lap. He giggled. Bunting smiled. The young admirers laughed.' Quoted in Richard Caddel and Anthony Flowers, *Basil Bunting: A Northern Life* (Newcastle: Newcastle Libraries and Information Service, 1997), 49.

out of St Elizabeth's tended rather to prolong his stay there I dont know. What the hell difference does it make? If he doesnt want to write, why should he? Perhaps he is as gloomy as I was till recently and doesnt want to pass it on. It's catching.

But I'd imagined you would see the letter, and was disappointed not to hear from you. Evidently you didnt. Your drawing of a denuded palm tree is hanging in my study here, and I count you surely among the chief of my friends, with Ez and Zuk, and wish I could see and hear you now and again, or oftener than that.

My own news, for now nearly a year, is a series of small miracles, or things as unexpected and welcome. I am still tied to my deadly drudgery, make no mistake, with hardly any leisure and a mere pittance to feed the family on, but everything else seems changed.

First, about a year ago, somebody rang me up on the phone and asked if I would like to read some poetry. It turned out that the voice thought it belonged to a poet of sorts, so I said: Come out. He took the next train and turned up inside an hour, a boy of 18, long-haired and fairly ragged, with a fist full of manuscript. He said: I heard you were the greatest living poet, so I brought my poems. Are they any good? Naturally I expected drivel, but thought it only kind to have a look. Well, there was a good deal of drivel, a good deal of useless violence, and a good deal of rather helpless filling out of lines: but not very deeply buried there was poetry such as one is lucky to see from time to time, and such as I had never seen from a young man, let alone a boy. I told him surgery was required, took a pen, and crossed out a lot that was encumbering the stuff. He watched, then grabbed up his manuscripts and disappeared. I thought he was gone for good, offended. Not a bit of it. In two days he was back, and he had done for the rest of his work what I had done for two or three poems. That is my chief pleasure, the discovery of a new poet, a good one, young enough to grow a great deal. Since then three short bits have been in Poetry, Chicago, and four in another American small, making their neighbours look stuffed, though one set of neighbours includes Gael Turnbull, Mike Shayer and BB.

Well, I thought, if poetry really has the power to renew itself, I'd better write something for these younger chaps to read: and with the boy, Tom Pickard, and Gael Turnbull each urging me on I planned a longish poem about 750 lines, which I finished about a month ago and have just revised and sent off to Poetry Chicago today. I believe it is the best thing I've done. I read it, not yet complete, to a couple of dozen miscellaneous poets and what not in London and they certainly seemed more impressed than I could have imagined.

Tom Pickard has a girl and a baby, and she, an enterprising lass, has found a derelict tower on Newcastle city wall, which the town let to her for ten bob a week. There the two of them started poetry readings, and with energy and the telephone they got a remarkable series of readers. On my advice, they put in no chairs. The audience sits on the floor. It is quite astonishing how this abolishes the platform-and-audience atmosphere and produces an intimacy in which it is possible to get over much subtler effects than an audience on chairs seems able to get. Every reader has had the same astonishment, and the place has become famous with extraordinary speed – letters turn up from San Francisco and from Tokyo, asking Tom for advice.

As this went on, it gradually became clear that there were a number of respectable people who had a higher opinion of BB than I thought anybody shared except Ez and Zuk. Rumours of this got about the town, and recently the Northern newspapers and television people have been treating me with exaggerated respect as "The North's great poet," all very stupid, but an echo of what seems to be a real feeling in the very young. School children spending a whole week's pocket money to get in and hear me read touch my heart.

So! I shouted at the Northern Council for the Arts, and after some huffy replies they decided to quiet me by guaranteeing Tom's readings against losses, up to a very modest sum. Then a painter of parts, on the university staff,[46] got that august body to stand a lot of the cost of printing The Spoils as a pamphlet (out this month, I think) Then a guy I'd never heard of in London, but who had heard of Tom's tower as well as of me, proposed to reprint Dallam Flynn's Texan volume with a few excisions and editions, which is to appear in my native land at last, under the title Loquitur, later in the summer.[47] Finally, Gael Turnbull without asking me proposed me to the Arts Council of Great Britain for a grant, and they are to part with £300, which will stave off a lot of duns.

Also publishers of the strictly commercial sort are inquiring about a possible collected works.

This must seem like a lot of boasting to you. In fact, spread over a year, I find it very hard to believe myself. I keep waiting for the bubble to burst. But even if it does, I will have had a lively year after all the deadliness.

Mr Cookson, whom you mention, was one of those who heard me read Briggflatts in London. I am vaguely in touch with him, but have nothing short. He has sent me Agenda faithfully for a long time.

[46] I.e. Richard Hamilton.

[47] In summer 1965 Stuart Montgomery's London-based Fulcrum Press published BB's *Loquitur*, a collected works very similar in content to *Poems: 1950*.

Gael Turnbull has been a great acquisition since he returned to settle in England. Do you know his work? He writes too much, but much of it is good, some very good.

The safeguard is, that it is the teenagers who like me the best. They wont mince their words if I write slop.

Yes, after all, I think I can see how St Elizabeth's might give Ezra an unreasoning hate of everything associated with it. It is rather horrible, but not quite beyond understanding. I have said to myself in the past that I would not come near Tirolo.[48] I did not want to see the hulk of what was so fine a ship as EP. And I loathe the hangers-on. Some of them came around me in Rome and Viareggio in 1950, some gossipers, some looking for a reflected notoriety, and they made me sick. They didnt think of Ezra as a man: some sort of institution to help them to admire themselves.

But now I think I must come, if ever my poverty will let me, to see you, Dorothy, and put up with the alien atmosphere long enough to refresh friendship.

Affectionately
B Bunting

In early 1965 Gael Turnbull recommended BB for an Arts Council Poetry Bursary. Although he was unsuccessful in securing a bursary (£750), he was one of four poets to receive an award of £300. While BB's account of the meeting with Day-Lewis in London is partial and somewhat embittered, the fact that he was so publicly ranked below two younger, more pedestrian poets—Bursary winners Elizabeth Jennings (1926–2001) and John Heath-Stubbs (1918–2006)—shows that his low opinion of the English literary establishment and its systems of patronage was probably justified.

## To Gael Turnbull

TS Scotland

17 June 1965 — Shadingfield, Wylam, Northumberland

Dear Gael,

I scrawled this on copy paper while I ate my sandwich, for sheer lack of time: but now there is a spare half-hour I can make it legible.

[48] Between 1958 and 1962 Pound lived with his partner Olga Rudge and daughter Mary de Rachewiltz in Schloss Brunnenberg, a thirteenth-century castle in South Tyrol (Tirolo), Italy.

FIRST, Holiday. Some fuss, but they did at last yield half way. I can start my holiday on August 1, actually July 31 because that happens to be my day off, to August 14. This overlaps the fortnight you have by a week, and if you cant or dont like to wangle the week's difference, well, we cant help it. We still overlap and must make the best of that.

SECOND, current events. Corso and Ferlinghetti[49] are here. They read. I am not much impressed. Corso seems to do pop less well than Pete (whatever the priorities may be). Ferlinghetti sometimes shows signs of care, but most of what I heard was just plain lazy writing. Not a bit like Ginsberg, whose improvisation almost seems to be forced on him by his temperament, alas!

Tyne Tees Television[50] was shooting while they read and their newsmen with cameras – not a help. The TV producer, Tyrrell, called out to his camera man "Cut!" while Corso was reading. Kids near me, who had already terrified Tyrrell when he seemed arrogant, shouted "Cut his throat." I believe Tyrrell thought them capable of it. He stood looking white while Corso lectured him on manners. But the evening ended without hostilities. Now I hear Ferlinghetti is off to Oxford, taking Tom along. They have found the violent "Geordie" poems and persuaded him to read them . . . unwise till he knows far better where and what he is and has a surer foundation of technique.[51] But reading at all should help him.

Cookson is angling for Briggflatts. So is Clark. But the poem went safely off to Chicago on Friday. I want, timorously, to visit its onlie begetter this weekend if the gods permit. But British Railways have surpassed all other excentricity on those lines, and it seems harder to get to Sedbergh by rail than to Bordeaux and about as long. I may funk it, too. Maria is in my confidence, Sima not yet. Life is damnably difficult.

THIRD, the hard part, report on London. But first I say again, I was deeply touched by your devotion, doing all that work for a surly old man, to get me an incredible grant from the Arts Council. I never dreamt it would succeed or even go near (or I might have discouraged you more energetically, for timeo Danaos,[52] to say nothing of hybris). And of course the money will be a blessing (when I get

[49] Lawrence Ferlinghetti (b. 1919), American Beat poet and founder of City Lights, a seminal San Francisco bookstore-publisher responsible for publishing Ginsberg's *Howl and Other Poems* (1956), among other major works of the 1950s and 1960s.

[50] Tyne Tees: local independent television network for the north-east. Founded in 1959 and based in Newcastle, it was a branch of ITV, one of only three TV channels available to British viewers between 1959 and 1982.

[51] Pickard's first collection *High on the Walls* (1967) featured a handful of lyrics (notably 'Scrap' and 'Rape') written in a demotic style with phonetic spellings of Geordie dialect words.

[52] Part of a famous axiom from Virgil's *Aeneid*, the full version of which translates to 'I fear the Greeks, even those bearing gifts.'

it – it seems that it takes several weeks to sign a cheque in that office). I am extremely grateful, however it may seem to you.

This is what happened.

I turned up twenty minutes early, thinking White[53] might have some instructions to give me about the procedure. He seemed embarrassed to see me and pretended to be surprised, though he had rung me up at the Chronicle to make sure I was coming. A man from Manchester, Massingham,[54] also turned up, and at the last moment a third, from London, strolled in to enquire whether it was in order for him to be present. No more. We were left to kick our heels in an exhibition of bookbindings for a good while, then called into the conference room. White met me and took my arm, saying: "I must introduce you to our chairman, Day Lewis." Lewis was standing alone, looking rather like a mummy that has come unwrapped. I intended to say "The last time we met was in 1930," but I didnt get the chance. Introduced, I put out my hand. Lewis looked at if for some time, as though it were pretty filthy, and his mouth tightened very hard. Finally he just touched it, and instantly turned round, full back to me, and began talking to White about "dear Wystan" and "dear Stephen," who had been doing something to celebrate the memory of TSE. White looked more embarrassed than ever, then walked round Lewis and led me, and the astonished Massingham, to the whisky, and left us there. Nobody offered us a seat, but I took one, across the table from Lewis. Presently White got down to business and told the reporters about some mss the Council has been buying before he called on Lewis to announce the awards.

Lewis treated it as a competition. He said: "The vote was quite conclusive. There was an overwhelming majority for the two winners. They were by far the best. They were the only ones of the quality we are looking for. The others were just also-rans." He repeated this three times in all in not very varied phrases, for fear the reporters wouldnt get it. Then he went on: "We had some money over, and it was decided to pass some of it on to the unsuccessful competitors – not for any particular reason." They were on the short list, and the Council had not chosen the short list – and so on. Then: "Mr Bunting is a very peculiar case. No English publisher has ever been found willing to publish what he writes. Who (he didnt say whoever, but made it sound like that) Who was it nominated him? Oh, yes; a Dr Turnbull." He mentioned Massingham's name without comment, but

[53] Eric Walter White (1905–1985), British musicologist and arts administrator, who was assistant secretary and later Literature Director of the Arts Council.

[54] Harold Massingham (1932–2011), British poet from Manchester (hence a northerner like BB), who also received a £300 award from the Arts Council in 1965.

had to be prompted by White for the rest. "Of course the real bursary winners are quite a different matter. There are no conditions to these grants. (looking at me -) You may go out to the next pub and blue the lot on booze for all we care." And after a few commonplaces he pointed us out to the reporters: "I think you will like to ask Mr Bunting a lot of questions."

It was, in its way, quite clever. Nothing that could not be attributed to a rather unfortunate choice of words. I dont think the reporters noticed anything, but White did, and kept looking more and more confused and a great deal less unctuous than usual, but also determined firmly to believe that nothing so nasty was happening in his dear Arts Council. While the reporters, fools to a man and woman, were being satisfied I swallowed down my fury or drunk enough not to have noticed. So when the time came to go I went up innocently to shake hands. Lewis looked at my hand quite a time, then turned his back without touching it or speaking.

So I am glad you werent there, Gael. It looked very much as though I had been brought to London (with Massingham merely to keep me company in a semi-anonymous way) purely to be systematically insulted. No one else seems to have been pressed to come. So this letter, unlike any other letter of mine, is for the record if there ever is a record. There is of course neither need nor use in doing or saying more about it now. I never thought Lewis worth notice, and it cost him £300 of the Government's money to play his funny little game, so we'll let him alone, I hope. But I thought, he has had his fun rather cheaply. I was not reluctant to take the money any more. I put myself down for all the expenses I seemed likely to get, and wished I could think of a number to multiply it by. But no more grants or competitions for me... The Northern Council for the Arts has a competition up its sleeve and has been asking me to enter, with hints that its in the bag; but more than half the members are sheep and two or three detest me. Moreover, they mean to appoint judges, who might easily include Lewis or one of his pals. No. Let Jon Silkin have the prize. Since he is not even a northerner, he is almost bound to get it. If they want to help me, they can read my works without exacting preliminary prostrations. I will give them no excuse for treating my lifetime of work as an "entry" to be depreciated in competition with nincompoops.

I got to London late on Sunday, declined to be read in public, but read for Ginsberg at Stuart Montgomery's house; and said goodbye to that good man and diffuse poet with real affection. I blessed him "now and forever," and he took it as it was meant, from the older man and harsher poet, and I hope the blessing works.

Now Mr Lucie Smith[55] has got the editor of the Sunday Times to send him to Wylam to interview me at length. Next weekend. He met me at the Arts Council and fed me expensively. Golly, what a BOUNDER. The old word fits perfectly. His remarks revealed that he hasn't read (though he may have glanced through) any of my work, but he is clearly convinced that I am the coming thing and he means to be in on it. Local press surpassing itself. I enclose the Chronicle's effort before the news of the grant reached them. And both local TVs did interviews, one of them quite well.

Too much to say. Goodbye for the time, dear Gael.

Yrs ever

B

## To Dorothy Pound

TS Indiana

11 July 1965 Shadingfield, Wylam, Northumberland

Dear Dorothy,

I've forgotten what I did write to you, now. Turmoil everywhere around. Perhaps good, for otherwise I'd be overcome by the world's sadness. I told you I find myself in the last chapters of a Hardy novel? Approaching the denouement, with no idea what it is to be, but a strong premonition of something tragic. Turnbull could tell you the story. He knows most of it. The rest is between myself and her. I never told you about her in the old days. I was too ashamed to speak. But the poem Briggflatts has exploded the past into the present, and I am largely living in 1915 in the remotest dale country, whatever seems to be going on around me. No, a happy ending is not out of the question, only very unlikely.

This makes me very self-centred. All the interest seems to be there. Still, I have enough left of common humanity to feel sad about you too. Why must people visit their common misfortunes on one another? You were always one of the kindest of my friends, Dorothy dear, and you must know, I'm sure, how much affection I feel for you. Saying so doesnt show it, but sometimes it is not quite worthless to be told in so many words that you are loved.

Send Omar and his lady to see us. We have room to put them up. All we ask is a telephone call, to make sure we're at home. Sima talks of his time in Teheran sometimes. We failed to corrupt his morals, but we wont hold that against him.

[55] Edward Lucie-Smith (b. 1933), British poet, editor, and art critic, who sat on the Arts Council literature panel.

Cape and New Directions are the latest recruits to the queue of publishers enquiring after my collected poems. There are so many I dont know where to begin, and can afford to tread a bit cavalierly. What an extraordinary change! It even makes me wonder if there isnt something wrong with what I write. People never liked good stuff even a generation ago.

The Beats, apparently are among my admirers: and though they seem to me mere improvisers, they are amusing company. I am also informed, perhaps wrongly, that the Beatles, no less, spent a lot of money on getting secondhand copies of Poems 1950 and carry them around.[56]

Tell Omar to forgive silence and look us up. There is heaps of room in this house and always a bed of some sort for a few nights, though there may be shortage of drinks etc.

Denis seems to be in very temperamental states. You probably know I like a lot of his poems and try to encourage him. I like him a lot, a kind man and a good companion.

My children are pleasant to have about. Maria is a painter, her school says, and though I have only been permitted to see one painting, it was good and strange, in sombre colours. At 15 she has plenty of time to forget how; but I've the impression she really is an artist of sorts, and we must try to help her along that very thorny road. Lately she has begun to take an interest in poetry and a pride in her dad. She went to London with me and made an impression, chiefly I think by her prettiness. The boy, Tom Bunting, after lethargic beginnings, has astonished his prep school, is a year ahead of others of his age, and, after failing his exam at 11, passed into the Royal Grammar School here at 12 as one of two admissions out of more than 300 trying for it. He likes mathematics, but does best in Latin: surprising tastes some people have.

Sima is still all I ever hoped, dear lass, though there are traces in her temper of the hard times we have had to get through together. We quarrel, but not for long.

So Dorothy dear, there is lots of news for you. Now send me some. Do you ever come to England? Is Northumberland too far?

And tell Ezra, my silence never meant any diminution in my love, and I dont believe his silence is any more sinister than mine was.

Love

B.

[56] This intriguing claim is unsubstantiated, so perhaps BB was right to couch it in scepticism. However, there were certainly connections that would have made it possible (notably Allen Ginsberg, who first met The Beatles in London on 9 May 1965, less than a fortnight before he met BB in Newcastle on 22 May).

## To Denis Goacher

TS Buffalo

17 July 1965 Shadingfield, Wylam, Northumberland

Dear Denis,

The squirrel poem, though a bit puzzling and apparently uneven, seems to me very nice. Third line of second stanza seems wrong – dunno just how. Look at it again after your German adventures.

We are sorry to miss you again. I expect to be away August 1–10 or thereabouts. After that it will be work again and the usual routine: in London Sept 11 to read at Better Books.[57]

Life still plagued with televisionaries and journalists. However, they let me write my own blurb for The Viewer (North-East Edition)[58] It might mildly amuse you, but isnt worth chasing – nothing new in it. July 31.

I've had the first copies of The Spoils, but only five of the expensive edition, which have gone to Pound, Zukofsky, Peggy Greenbank and my own shelves. Twenty of the other edition are due to me during the coming week, and one of these will be for you. It may take a few days before I can address and despatch, so dont blame the post if there is delay. The cover photograph has come out well and makes an effective design, besides being the building described in part two.

You sound more cheerful. That's good. As you know, you're welcome here anytime when you are fed up with London. If you can stand my egotism, now much inflated by publicity, Wylam should be an acceptable change.

Sorry this is so snippety. I am writing in the midst of the clamour of my daughter's end of term party – twenty each of boys and girls, aged fourteen to twenty, and six guitars, all strumming different tunes. I like to see the absurd creatures, holding hands and disappearing into our jungle garden; and anyway, they grow up before very long and give us peace – more than we want, no doubt.

The extra-ordinary effects that have flowed from Briggflatts are still in full spate. Peggy has her copy of her poem, and has written to her sister, obviously proud and excited, but worried to death about the jealous husband. I am full of hope and delight. Clearly, she will see me, as soon as she can contrive to. Clearly, she will leave her name on the poem and risk scandalising her neighbours if she has the least reason to hope her husband will not see it. She is minimising the past suddenly served up to her, perhaps only because she is writing to her sister;

[57] Countercultural bookshop on New Compton Street in London founded by Tony Godwin (1920–1976). Barry Miles (b. 1943), co-organizer of the International Poetry Incarnation in London on 11 June 1965, also worked at the shop.

[58] The listings magazine for Tyne Tees (see **17/6/65** and note).

but she certainly does not reject it. Can I make it become the present? Her letter was so alive and vivid, it was like having her with me.

There goes the egotist again. What do you care about my antique love affairs?

Maria sends her best wishes. She got an extraordinary high mark in her art exam and is confirmed in her intention of becoming a painter. Turner is still the favourite.

All the best to you,
B.

## To Denis Goacher

TS Durham

8 August 1965 — Shadingfield, Wylam, Northumberland

Dear Denis,

Briggflatts (the place and its people) and then the Turnbulls in force here have kept me from answering your letter promptly.

Bridson is welcome to record away, as far as I am concerned. I suppose the Better Books man might have something to say about it,[59] but I dont see why he should mind. However, I dont know what I shall be reading. Rago[60] has written, Briggflatts will be in Poetry, but he had been away and hadnt had time to think out when. I dont like to anticipate him too much by reading it in London. So the programme might be merely stuff Bridson's audience has heard before.

As to reading Cantos, am I competent?[61] I doubt it. Also I dont know whether I could get away to do it; probably not. And you might not care for a mere recording. What about reading the lines on the fly-leaf of Pound's Cantos, which Cookson has just annexed for his birthday issue of Agenda?[62] They would make a good tail-piece for such a programme.

My few days in Briggflatts were a delight. Turnbull's visit here made a holiday of what might have been a mere change of drudgery. The BBC radio interview and the Tyne Tees Television TV interview were both pretty fair, unobjectionable. My voice comes over with a grand growl on both. My mug looks solid, grim and

[59] Either Tony Godwin or Barry Miles (see 17/7/65).

[60] Henry Rago (1915–1969), American poet and editor at *Poetry* between 1955 and 1969.

[61] BB read Cantos 2, 4, and 81 as part of a BBC Third Programme celebration of Pound's eightieth birthday (produced by Goacher) in late 1965.

[62] BB's 'On the Fly-Leaf of Pound's Cantos' was first published in the October–November 1965 issue of *Agenda* (a special edition in honour of Pound's birthday).

mobile on TV. By chance I heard Robert Graves[63] on Spike Milligan's TV show the next night, and by comparison his voice seemed characterless and his face pretty usual (I say nothing about the stuff read).

We are still waiting hopefully to see you. I am free still next Sunday.

The best to you and your lady

B

## To Denis Goacher

TS Durham

4 September 1965

Shadingfield, Wylam, Northumberland

Dear Denis,

Yes, Tom's envelope is a peculiar product, and he has noticed that for himself.[64] The idea was that all the bits and pieces should be one size, so that they could be filed by anyone who thought fit and used for arsewipes by the rest: but Richard Hamilton's passion for designing things ran away with him. Never mind. It's entertaining.

I tried to persuade him not to devote his first number (or any number) solely to me, but he was determined, and I do not want to act as anything more than occasional adviser to him or anyone. As you say, let the children do as they please.

The desnudismo snapshop was a joke of Eugen Haas more than thirty years ago.[65] The mock mss of the Thrush was a surprise to me.[66] Tom knows I disapprove of manuscripts, letters, etc... alive or dead.

Zukofsky's prose – well, I'm not going to embark on critical exposition. Its faults are obvious, but its merits are real and considerable. Tom's mistake is to use dead and gone reviews at all. Or am I vain, thinking I don't need anybody's commendations?

Morals: yes, I've always been happy to sap the pervading prison walls. And its more effective than using a battering ram. As for pessimism, no, though I'm a lot

[63] Goacher was a mutual acquaintance of both BB and Robert Graves, moving to Deia, Mallorca, to be near the latter in 1984.

[64] I.e. *King Ida's Watch Chain*, see note to 13/6/64.

[65] *KIWC* contained a photograph of BB during an excursion to Portugal with Eugen Haas in 1934 (see 7/18/34 and note). In a walking cane and suit, BB stands next to a poster featuring two naked women and the slogan 'DENUDISMO'.

[66] BB's short poem 'A thrush in the syringa sings', probably written in 1964 (see Share, 407), was first published in the *Paris Review* (Summer 1965) and more or less simultaneously in the Newcastle *Journal* (17 July 1965). *King Ida's Watch Chain* contained an autographed MS of the poem.

more at home with Timon or Schopenhauer[67] than with Leibniz or the passing Pippa,[68] but nihilist if you like. Yeats was perturbed by that in my very earliest published poems. But the last lines of The Well of Lycopolis and the Spoils are hopeful; even if Briggflatts closes in darkness. Those are the "thoughtful" poems. It's only humanists who must find the world hopeless. It's a good enough world for stars or mushrooms, and why assume that it was meant for us? I've said I hope Briggflatts may have a cheerful sequel, but that doesnt mean a sequel that is any more complacent about the human race. Desperately wicked, I believe Cranmer calls it in his Prayer book.[69] Incurably crass, he might have added.

Phone me at Montgomery's flat on Saturday afternoon, please. I wont know what arrangements I can make until I get to London. But I'd certainly like to see you, long enough to talk. Not about Peggy. Who knows where we are going? Who cares?

Lord Thomson[70] will give me a better job when I marry the Queen's sister. Since that will involve Princess Margaret in a divorce,[71] as well as me, unless I turn Moslem meanwhile, I think it is likely to be somewhat delayed. The Archbishop of Canterbury could give me a better job too. He is legally entitled to confer the degree of DD[72] on me at any time he sees fit, and he had a lot of good livings in his gift. But after what you have said about my morals, he might hesitate to entrust any parish to my care.

You continue to write good stuff. Wish I could say the same of myself. What I have by me will probably go to the dustbin.

A new small magazine called Gnomon reached me. Formidably pious; but the verse in it seems tight. I say seems, because I am not yet certain that that isnt an illusion. At least its different from the slithering mass of its contemporaries.

[67] Timon of Phlius (*c.*320–235 BC), Greek philosopher, poet, and playwright. His sarcasm, satire, and philosophical scepticism would have appealed to BB, as would the pessimistic strain in Schopenhauer, though BB felt little affinity with the German post-Kantian tradition in general (see 27/4/34 and note).

[68] Gottfried Wilhelm Liebniz (1646–1716), German philosopher and polymath, who subscribed to the 'best of all possible worlds' axiom; Robert Browning's Pippa, the kindly, virtuous protagonist of *Pippa Passes*, a verse drama of 1841. Both names function here as ciphers for philosophical optimism.

[69] In fact a quotation from Jeremiah 17.9: 'The heart is deceitful above all things, and desperately wicked.'

[70] See 1/12/59.

[71] Princess Margaret (1930–2002), Queen Elizabeth II's sister, who married Anthony Armstrong Jones in 1960.

[72] I.e. Doctor of Divinity.

An ingenious version of Arnaut's L'aura amara.[73] Pious pedantry – as good a foundation for poetry as any other, I suppose. Had Eliot any more?

And I, the Quaker-atheist? I write about commonplaces. In a commonplace way. That is what makes this century of paradox and ingenuity find me so odd.

Yours ever

B Bunting

The following letter marks the long delayed reunion between Bunting and his daughter Roudaba (we also learn that he had made contact with his elder daughter Bourtai immediately beforehand). Another of the poignant consequences of *Briggflatts* and its success was that it gave Bunting the means and the opportunity to travel widely again. From 1966—and for much of next decade—he spent much time in North America on reading tours and visiting fellowships, putting him back in touch with his American family. Although Roudaba was in Hawaii at this point, the prospect of a reunion after some thirty years apart seems to have excited both father and daughter, and after a series of subsequent meetings, Roudaba developed into one of Bunting's most intimate correspondents.

## To Roudaba Bunting Davido

MS Durham

14 April 1966 — Shadingfield, Wylam, Northumberland

Roudaba dear –

Bourtai's address came to me almost by chance, and she has given me yours. I am very thankful for this chance to end the long silence between us. For far too long I never had anything to tell my daughter – or my friends – except what must depress them. I am still poor – and old now – but life has become full of hopeful things, and I would like to share my hopes with all my children, and to have some way, even only by letter, of telling you of my affection and learning what has happened and is happening to you. I hope we shall never lose track of each other again.

My own history, for years, were drudgery; until about a year and a half ago, an extraordinary boy, a boy without education, called on me and showed me some poems, full of mess, but always with a core of deeply original poetry. I showed him (it took only a hint) how to pull his work together; and he, in turn, with his

[73] Pound translated 'L'aura amara,' a poem by the twelfth-century Occitan troubadour Arnaut Daniel, in *The Spirit of Romance* (1910).

energy and his hero-worship set me writing again, after so many years when it had not seemed worthwhile. I wrote in trains and at odd moments in the beastly newspaper office, and in less than a year I had finished a long poem, "Briggflatts," which seems to have stunned nearly everybody who has seen it. At the same time a young publisher appeared; so there were three books, which I will send you (they'll travel slowly). You know almost all the contents of "Loquitur" and "The Spoils." I will let "Briggflatts" speak for itself.

Briggflatts has brought me friends, and an invitation to lecture at Buffalo this summer.[74] I wonder whether I can meet Bourtai there?[75] But a more wonderful thing happened too. When I was very young I met, at the hamlet of Brigflatts in the mountains of Westmorland, a girl four years younger than myself, and loved her. The story of that love is the skeleton of the poem. As the poem grew, I understood that I have never stopped loving the girl, and that our parting (my fault) was foolish as well as wrong. I felt certain that she and I were so much one that she must feel the same, still be in love with me, after forty-five years of separation. So I took my courage in both hands and went in search of her with the finished poem in my hand. It was a slow search; but I found her, found her exactly as I had felt she must be. So I have a love again, one that has survived a lifetime's separation and will surely last till Peggy and I die. There are great difficulties: we are both married, both have children, are both poor. But there is also, now and then, when we can meet, great happiness, such as I have not known since I was a boy.

Granny is still vigorous at 91, and lives with us in this large, old, tumbledown, house with a pretty view. Sima puts up with the rest of us with difficulty. Her mother too is here at present. Maria is taking to painting as a profession (two poster commissions so far). She has still more than two years of school to do, and probably the university after that, if I can go on feeding her. Tom has got himself into the best school in the North and seems to be doing well. He plays much chess, very well.

I shall be reading some of my poems between the symphonies at a Northern Sinfonia Orchestra concert at the beginning of June – first concert of the sort ever, they say.[76] I have also read "Briggflatts" for the B.B.C. Third Programme, and they are lacing the tape with harpsichord sonatas I have chosen by Scarlatti – the

[74] Throughout the summer of 1966, and coinciding with his retirement from the Newcastle *Evening Chronicle* in August, BB was visiting fellow at the State University of New York, Buffalo.

[75] Bourtai lived in Wisconsin, a (long) day's drive from Buffalo.

[76] Northern Sinfonia, based at Newcastle City Hall, was founded in 1958 as the first permanent professional resident chamber orchestra in Britain outside London. For a more detailed summary of BB's collaboration with NS in June 1966, see **7/9/66**.

longest poetry reading they have ever done: the poem itself takes an hour.[77] The "Collected Poems" look like coming out next year.[78]

I must end here to keep the weight of the letter down. Please send me your news, dear daughter. I love you and Bourtai dearly.

Your father,
B Bunting.

## To Denis Goacher

TS Durham

5 June 1966

Shadingfield, Wylam, Northumberland

Dear Denis

I'll be in London June 14 to June 20, when I leave for USA. I can be found through Montgomery. It would be a great pleasure to see you.

Concert went well and I am for a moment content. The fool journalists etc who might have been there and werent missed something rather striking. Audience some 700, no highbrows whatever (university conspicuously absent) sat still and seemed to seize the point of it, or the points, rather. Better publicity would have brought two or three hundred more, and the thing would have paid its way. Sandwiched between Vivaldi and Corelli,[79] the structure of Briggflatts IV was so evidently the same that at least half the musicians, unprompted, remarked on it. Also, having their ears opened by Albinoni, the audience listened for the sound instead of perplexing itself about meanings, and obviously enjoyed the verse on the same footing as the music. Noticeable, when Bergman speculated about the possibility of bringing in audience by more popular music, Mozart, for example, Brott instantly answered that it wouldnt do,[80] Mozart was too repetitive, didnt pack his music with thematic stuff as these others did, and so would not parallel and reflect the poetry. Perception... and Brott knew nothing whatever about poetry before the rehearsals.

Some talk of doing similar concert with Tudor music, to show similarity of texture, as this showed similarity of structure.

[77] This reading was eventually broadcast in February 1967.

[78] In fact the Fulcrum Press *Collected Poems* would appear a year later, in 1968.

[79] Arcangelo Corelli (1653–1713), Tomaso Albinoni (1671–1751) and Antonio Vivaldi (1678–1741): Italian Baroque composers. All three were favourites of BB.

[80] Tom Bergman (1920–1992) handled PR for Northern Sinfonia; Boris Brott (b. 1944) was its precocious leader and conductor.

Wanted, a millionaire to buy the Theatre Royal Newcastle from Howard and Wyndham,[81] who want to pull it down, and hand over the running of it to you…

Hasta la vista

B.

## To Roudaba Bunting Davido

TS Durham

7 September 1966 Shadingfield, Wylam, Northumberland

Darling Rou – Your dear, touching letter came this morning. It was written before you can have seen the letter I sent to Ulupaina,[82] telling you about my job at Santa Barbara and asking you to join me there. I'll repeat the essence of that, since you may not have received it. I have been offered and have accepted a post for nine months at the University of California at Santa Barbara. If there are no snags about visas, etc, I will be there at the beginning of October (address c/o English department) and I will take my daughter Maria with me. She is sixteen and an art student. I suggested that it might be possible for you to transfer your nursing course to Santa Barbara and join us there. I shall have just about enough pay to send you all or most of your fare from Hawaii and to provide house and, I hope, food. I dont think it will extend to fees and clothes etc, though you'd be welcome to them if it did. You need not feel at all dependent on me, partly because I think your mother would go on helping you, partly because I am now almost half-blind, cannot drive a car, and would be a prisoner on the campus if I could not find somebody to drive for me from time to time – you'd do that, wouldn't you? – in any old wrecked jalopy I can buy. Monica, of course, would be a delight to me, and probably to Maria too. Is this feasible? Bourtai hopes to visit us at Christmas, and we to visit Madison on our way home next summer. – Poor Sima stays at Wylam to look after Tom, who cannot be spared from school just now; and poor Peggy stays lonely at Hope, in Shropshire, without visits and with too few letters. It is a shame that the people I love are scattered. Would like to have them all around me in some village up the North Tyne in Northumberland. – Daphne is a dear: she just wanted to play and be tickled and kissed a bit. I think she liked her grandfather pretty well. Your mother – peace is established. Much is forgotten and all forgiven. I know the difficulties she found, better than she knew them when she chose to face her awful family rather than poverty. Eau Claire has

[81] Theatrical company founded in 1895, which owned the Theatre Royal, an elegant neoclassical building in Newcastle city centre.

[82] I.e. Roudaba's home in Hawaii.

left a fearful mark on her, and it would be false to pretend that I am not glad she divorced me, for I could not endure long contact with her as she now is. But there would have been no divorce, no separation, if I could have prevented it, for I loved my two daughters beyond anything else in the world. I would have put up with anything to have kept you with me. Dear girl, you tell me that when you were a little girl you wrote to ask me to take you; believe me, I never received any such letters. What happened to them I cannot guess. Perhaps your mother prevented them – Often I was too poor to do anything effective, but my home was always open to you, poor as it was. Later, in your early teens, you did write, dear letters that I tried to reply to as gently and wisely as I could, but at such a distance it was difficult to know what was happening to you. When I had an income for a while, I asked for Bourtai, not because I didnt want you, but because I had no hope that your mother would part with you. Bourtai was old enough to help to look after herself. You, at eleven or twelve, could hardly have been left alone or with some embassy acquaintance every time I had to go away for a week. Yes, I think it was wrong of your mother to keep Bourtai then, but she had her family to contend with. I do not know whether she was free to let Bou go. Later I was very poor again, powerless to help. I suppose you lost faith in me, and that is why you stopped writing and I lost touch with you. You cannot guess how glad I as when chance put Bourtai's address into my hands at last. – My dear! You "stand in awe of my knowledge"! But I am an ignorant man; and what little I do know is at your service, just as I hope what you know and I dont will be at my service when I need it. All I really know is that there is a handful of people whom I love, and you are one of them. How could I have any "contempt" of you? I will laugh at your mistakes and naiveties if I want to, and you shall laugh at mine. It's one of the privileges of love and has nothing to do with contempt. – Bourtai has told me nothing but good of you, though you must sometimes have been very rash, and often unfortunate. Marian talked to me of her own woes, of which you are, of course, one; but she wasnt speaking objectively and I took no notice beyond letting her feel that I was listening with sympathy. All I heard made me sure that you are like the rest of the people I love best – free of humbug, free of greed, very open, I should think, to love: which is almost all I have to offer. Surely we shall meet soon, even if you cannot move to California. I long to see you, and will do all I can to bring it about. – My children? Maria is very pretty, or at least all the boys seem to think so. She is not very industrious, but has a real talent for drawing and painting, according to her school and to Richard Hamilton (well-known painter, sort of heir of Marcel Duchamp). I've seen little of her work, but some I saw was very good indeed, she likes the sound of you and Bou. She seems to like a tall young man who is just going to Cambridge.[83] She makes far too bloody much noise about the house and runs up huge telephone bills for me. Tom is a tidy boy – an unusual quality in boys – and works hard at school. He is small for his age, curly headed, likes bicycles, chemistry, chess and rugby football. Other boys seem to like him, but he keeps mainly to himself. He likes Mike Shayer's daughter Sigrid but does not want to be seen associating with a girl (inferior creatures, girls) so Sigrid has to put up with a lot of snubs. Both good kids. No obvious complications. They are luckier than you were. – Poems? Dont try to understand, just listen. I'll bring or send a tape, if I can get it copied. Briggflatts is, as you've guessed, the best.

There is at the moment a hitch about our visas for America, but it will soon be cleared. However, it might make us a week late in Santa Barbara, where we are due on October 3. Meanwhile I've an enormous lot to do, so that I am not likely to write again till I teach the university; and unless you write immediately you get this, dont write here, for we'll be in California, or on the way, before your letter could arrive. – I've just this moment opened a heart-broken letter from Peggy, desolate because I am going away so long, yet still unable to face the crisis of conscience required to leave her husband and join me. I could so easily oblige her to do so, but it would hurt her now and for a long time; and so I try only to reassure her. That's a bit hard on me, of course; to find my love again after a lifetime and have to leave her committed, to all intents and purposes, to another man; and yet feel that at any moment some crisis may cause her to change her mind, perhaps when I cannot help effectively. – Sima fortunately, is not a jealous woman, and I could easily make some amiable agreement with her. Anyway, it's not absolutely impossible, though unlikely, that Peggy too might join us in California. Since all my friends seem to love her, that prospect need not trouble you.

What else can I say to my dear daughter now? Only, I think, that I hope very earnestly that you can come to Santa Barbara: that I love you: that writing poetry is a skill like weaving carpets or shaping bowls on the potter's wheel and is not an intellectual exercise to make people afraid of the poet. Bourtai felt that she needed a father, and I that I needed a daughter even more. I think it will be the same with you and me.

Sun is shining here. All omens good! (except the rheumatism!) Goodbye for now, dear Roudaba, and let us meet and kiss soon, soon.

Love from your stranger father

B

[83] I.e. John Halliday.

As detailed in the previous letter, in late 1966 Bunting began a visiting lectureship at the University of California, Santa Barbara (partly with the assistance of English faculty member Hugh Kenner, who would become a firm friend). He would ultimately remain in California for the best part of two years. Though relatively little happened during this interlude, it seems to have been a pleasant time; Bunting's money worries were now in abeyance, and he could finally savour the achievement of *Briggflatts*—and the international esteem it brought him—in the comfort of the sun-soaked West Coast. A capstone of this period was the publication of the *Collected Poems* by Fulcrum in 1968, which presented Bunting's canon in more-or-less final form.

## To Tom Pickard

MS Buffalo

30 March 1967

839a Embarcadero del Norte, Isla Vista –
Goleta – California USA 93017

Dear Tom – Stuart gave me a copy of "High on the Walls" and it seems very nice.[84] Congratulations. I left a copy at Harvard where it had impressed some students, and I have just read parts of it to a graduate class here, two of whom went off to order it from the bookshop down the street. As soon as I get a spare I'll send one to Ezra.

Thanks for your letter. Sure, the country is the best place;[85] but I wish we could think of some way for you to live. It would be a bad business if you put poetry aside: (By the way, I've not seen any new poems for quite a time). But I am damned if I can think of anything except harrying Dunbar,[86] and that's not been very fruitful in the past. A hind works long hours, hard, and skilled. I doubt it! What does Connie think? (And Matthew)

It seems a long time since I wrote to you. Not neglect – I was ill in February and found the rest of the term pretty stiff going. My daughter Roudaba came over from Hawaii for Christmas, bringing my youngest (half-Chinese) granddaughter,

[84] Pickard's first poetry collection *High on the Walls* was published by Fulcrum in 1967, with a preface by BB.

[85] In the mid 1960s Pickard lived temporarily in a remote house in the Allen Valley, a former lead mining area in the Northumberland portion of the North Pennines. The area is famously eulogized in the 1995 volume *Pearl* by Newcastle poet Barry MacSweeney (1948–2000), also a member of the Morden Tower milieu.

[86] Alexander Dunbar (1930–2012), founding head of the North Eastern Association for the Arts/Northern Arts (see 28/7/64).

very pretty at three. They got on famously with Maria, and delighted and scandalised the English Faculty by getting the professors drunk at New Year.

I'm just back from a trip, reading in Texas; New York; and Harvard. In Texas they try to pickle you in Bourbon whiskey, and in New York they all talk at once and give you no chance to rest; but the kids at Harvard were nice, really nice, and I got, not peace, of course, but an easier passage there. In New York Allen Ginsberg asked after you; and Gregory Corso. Ginsberg was very hospitable, friendly, kind and useful – and enthusiastic. Corso, drunk, gave an amusing account of the animals before the Ice Age – a toad as big as ten elephants, for one. He was less wacky than in Newcastle. Creeley came down from Buffalo to be chairman at the reading, and he also asked for news of you and Connie. But he has too many friends. Their chatter was tiresome. I met Denise Levertov and disliked her heartily.[87] I also called on Zukofsky, but he seemed very bitter and, strangely, very jealous. A painful hour. He did not go to the reading because of "drafts." Yet I rank as his oldest friend. Stuart was a great help. Alan Power was in N.Y. too; and fed us.[88] Robert Payne, an acquaintance from Teheran days, met by accident, has grown rich. He presented me with a copy of the almost priceless "Survey of Persian Art."

Luck and Ginsberg between them found a "saqi"[89] to pour my wine while I read – a really beautiful girl, with big eyes and a long solemn face, who sat on a cushion by my chair, still as a rock, and kissed me unexpectedly at the end of "Briggflatts." I had a saqi at Harvard too, a twelve-year-old enthusiast who wanted me to take her back to California with me.

A boy called Andrew Wylie looked after me at Harvard. He writes competent poetry, and I like him a lot. Aged 19, he and his girl took me up the coast to Gloucester, and up-state to Concord. Nervous, a bit wild, gentle and intelligent. I think you would like him. His Christina looked after me like a daughter.

I think both those readings went well. Ginsberg stamped and yelled in New York, and the rest do what he does. At Harvard they clapped steadily for a very long time, and one man said to me: "It's a good many years since we saw a GREAT poet at Harvard." Hm! Both readings were recorded; each time "Briggflatts," with the Scarlatti sonatas on tape.

[87] Denise Levertov (1923–1997), British-American modernist poet associated in this period with Creeley's Black Mountain milieu.

[88] Alan Power was the son of E. J. Power (1899–1993), one of the most prominent arts patrons in post-war Britain. Alan continued his father's philanthropic activities.

[89] In this period BB revived the ancient Persian tradition of having a *sāqi* or cupbearer on hand during recitals to pour wine for the poet. The reliance on a servile 'beautiful girl' for this practice as a matter of course appears to have been BB's own innovation.

Today's my busy day. I registered students, talked about Eliot, and read "The Waste Land" this morning. This afternoon I argued with three times as many students as I am supposed to have and read from Carlos Williams and Tom Pickard. This lot are all graduates.

I've left little space to send my greetings and my love to Connie, dear lass, and Matthew, who must have forgotten me by now. Whether I'll see you this summer or not I dont know. I may have to stay here to keep my family going at home. However it is, Tom, dont lose touch. And better luck to you (a published poet now)

Yours ever
B Bunting
Maria sends her affections.

## To Ted Hughes

MS Emory

16 April 1967

839a Embarcadero del Norte, Isla Vista – Goleta – California USA 93017

Dear Mr Hughes –

I'm sorry, I thought I'd replied to your invitation.[90] I shall not be in England in July, nor indeed until July 1968 – I have to stay here to keep my family fed and educated at home.

But I'd have asked you to excuse me anyway. I don't like these great poetic jamborees – snippets of everything, with no coherent programme. No one would arrange a concert as haphazardly. It's the tradition, of course – a new one, a ragged one, and one that I hope will be revised.

Thankyou, however, for the invitation and your flattering words. I wish you every success.

I've just been hearing a tape made of my reading at Harvard – not too bad, needs improving. But it's a feat to be performed in solitude, not in competition, I think.

Yours faithfully
Basil Bunting

[90] In July 1967, Ted Hughes coordinated the first 'Poetry International' event at the Southbank Centre, London. The first of these yearly jamborees was somewhat in the vein of the 1965 International Poetry Incarnation at Royal Albert Hall, though less radical, with cameos by Hughes, Ginsberg, MacDiarmid, Auden, Spender, William Empson (1906–1984), Anne Sexton (1928–1974), John Berryman (1914–1972), and Pablo Neruda (1904–1973).

## To Allen Ginsberg

TS Stanford

18 February 1968 6798a del Playa, Goleta California USA 93017

Dear Allen,

Delighted with the Piccadilly poem;[91] and no less pleased to hear living news of Ezra. May his depression ease further! I do remember speaking (rather writing) to him in the sense you report, but it can hardly have been less than thirty years ago – a long time for a friendly criticism to ferment in a man's head.[92]

Forgive the inelegant and possibly illegible typing of this note. I am still recovering from a cataract operation and it will be some time yet before I can read and write in anything approaching normal style. I return to Wylam in june and must have the other eye butchered at once so as not to interfere with earning some sort of living from the northern universities. Your letter was a charming break in the boredom of not-quite blindness which is just beginning to disperse.

I don't think you'll mind if I show the EP part of it to Hugh Kenner, who is busy with another book on Ezra, and to whom it may therefore be a handy signpost.

Good luck always

Affectionately

BBunting

## To Denis Goacher

TS Buffalo

16 September 1968 Shadingfield, Wylam, Northumberland

Dear Denis,

No news yet of those prior engagements. It may be that I wont be able to go to Paris, though I certainly want to. A few days will show.

My own forties were largely spent in war, discovering, to my satisfaction, that when it came to doing instead of contemplating I was faster and more efficient

[91] Possibly Ginsberg's 'Who Be Kind To', written in London prior to the International Poetry Incarnation in June 1965, which alludes to his Newcastle trip (see **26/5/65**).

[92] In October 1967 Ginsberg visited Pound in Venice. According to one account of the meeting, Pound admitted that his 'worst mistake was the stupid suburban prejudice of anti-Semitism', and received Ginsberg's 'blessing' in return (see Michael Reck, 'A Conversation between Ezra Pound and Allen Ginsberg', *Evergreen Review* 55 (June 1968), 29). Reck's narrative makes no mention of a discussion about BB's earlier attempt to challenge Pound's anti-Semitism (see **16/12/38**), though BB's comments here underline that it remained a point of contention in his relationship with Pound.

than most men. Other things may have happened then, but to disentangle them from that pleasing discovery is not easy. Still, I fancy that many people about that age perceive a gap between what they are and do and what's officially expected of them by the public, the clergy, their friends, their wives, what have you. No doubt some reject themselves. I preferred to reject the others. Perhaps I was fortunate, because my friend from 1940 to 1942 was an Australian who followed the profession of tramp.[93] He was a man of great curiosity about the world with enough resource to master anything he found worth mastering. (He learned, successively, Hindustani and Italian, with no help from education, of which he had none whatever, because he wanted to talk to people in India and Tripoli) He had no moral preconceptions and judged everything as it arose, in its circumstances, giving full weight to his own desires. Precedents didnt interest him, though he considered consequences, thus differing from the courts of equity. Perhaps his example helped me to be candid with myself, however cautious and disingenuous I might find it prudent to be with other people. My work towards the end of the war may have reinforced the tramp's example; I had to be most exact with a very few people, while deceiving and observing nearly everyone else. So reserve, natural to me, stopped tripping me up. I wasnt reserved with myself any more. Eventually I expect most people emerge "jenseits von Gut and Böse"[94] or at any rate, beyond the normal representations of good and evil. And there is no need to make the fuss about it that Nietsche made. It's easy enough in theory; nothing new about it; there's Butler and Lawrence and any number of people besides Nietsche who've produced plausible arguments against public morality. But it's not really easy for young men. They dont see themselves, only their reflections in other people's lookingglasses; or they fear to. I wonder what an intelligent homosexual, say, a Gide for example,[95] feels when he first has to admit to himself: "I'm an incorrigible bugger" and hasnt yet the nerve to add: "and the buggery is very pleasant too." Not that I imagine you to be, any more than me, tied up with sexual mores in particular, but what applies to them applies to morals in general, including what is modestly called "behaving decently."

That's probably what Shaw meant when he said every man of forty was a scoundrel.[96] It's the last stage of growing up, except for (what must seem unbeliev-

[93] This is the only extant reference in BB's writing to this anonymous character, presumably a fellow serviceman encountered at the RAF base in Methil, Scotland, where BB was based 1940–1942.

[94] *Jenseits von Gut and Böse* ('Beyond Good and Evil'): philosophical work of 1886 by Friedrich Nietzsche, which argues for the destruction of traditional Western morality.

[95] André Gide (1869–1951) was openly gay.

[96] See 21/3/34.

able to the young) the acceptance and welcoming of the idea of dying, which I think most people manage sooner or later. The prayerbook says we are all "desperately wicked"[97] and I see no reason either to doubt it or to be put out be sharing in the wickedness of men in general. If, as I suppose, you also are desperately wicked, or feckless, or otherwise unsatisfactory from the point of view of your educators, and the view taken for granted in general conversation, I dont see that you need repine. I remember Edward Pease, secretary to the Fabian Society in its great days,[98] telling me, when I was too young to understand, that smothering his conscience was the act he was proudest of. It made great demands on his resolution to murder it completely.

If what worries you is a notion of failure, it makes no difference. Modern public morals require you to be a success, but there is no other reason why you should want to be. You write the poetry you want to write, with a considerable degree of skill, and what does it matter whether anybody notices it? In fact, I, and now Corman, have noticed, and others have noticed in passing, though it is too unlike their own more conventional stuff to keep a place in the front on their minds. It is a very long time since I left off caring whether anybody liked my poetry or not, and that isnt altered by my late success. In fact, success may be dangerous to peace and selfapproval if you begin to want to prolong it.

Bread and butter is a source of worry; but if that's approximately taken care of, use your leisure to perfect your skill with words and you'll find you dont need much more to enjoy life moderately. And if that doesnt work, play chess or golf or Don Juan or anything which doesnt lead too directly to destruction like opium or whiskey.

Forgive the sermon. You asked for it.

Yours ever
B

The following letter contains one of Bunting's most eloquent defences of northern regionalism, a cause that was increasingly dear to him in his later years. In brief summary, Bunting's litany of historical oppression against the north by 'southrons' was as follows: 1) The Norman Conquest of the 1060s, which saw up to 100,000 northerners massacred by William the Conqueror in the 'Harrying of the North' as retaliation for a rebellion of 1069; 2) The subsequent foundation of fortresses at Newcastle and Carlisle as centres for Norman

[97] See note to **4/9/65**.

[98] Edward Reynolds Pease (1857–1955), British radical writer, among the founding members of the Fabian Society.

control of the region; 3) The defeat of the rebellious son of the Earl of Northumberland, Henry 'Hotspur' Percy, by Henry IV at the Battle of Shrewsbury in 1403 (as dramatized in Shakespeare's *Henry IV, Part 1*); 4) The Battle of Hexham in 1464, a skirmish in the Wars of the Roses which put an end to Lancastrian resistance in the north against the Yorkist King Edward IV; 5) Henry VIII's suppression of the Pilgrimage of Grace, a pro-Catholic northern uprising of 1536 against Henry's Dissolution of the Monasteries, which resulted in around 200 executions; and 6) The Rising of the North, an uprising against Elizabeth I in 1569 led by northern Catholic nobles, which resulted in around 700 executions, largely focused on commoners. In spite of all this, Bunting suggests, the traditions of Northumbrian art were maintained, and stand as a continual reminder of the possibility of revival.

## To Gael Turnbull

TS Scotland

21 September 1968 — Shadingfield, Wylam, Northumberland

Dear Gael,

Thanks. I've been enjoying it, just read it through.[99] Cape have done it handsomely. I'm not going to lie and say that I found all of it firstrate, but I did find more than enough to justify my exacerbated belief that there is an essential Turnbull, a possible Turnbull, a Turnbull to be dug up and dusted, but who not infrequently does the dusting and digging himself. Best the short ones, usually: the knot in the wood, the metronome and mousetrap; though I find a good deal in Twenty Words. Some I might have liked to see aren't there.

You know, if you sail, that when you've set up the halliards and swung on them and sweated down the last inch, they still slack off a trifle as the day goes, and the boat sags away from the wind unless you take an extra swig at those damned ropes from time to time; till at last, after many hours, you've really got the better of the lay of the cable, stretched it as hard as it will go, or at any rate harder than the wind can tease it. Then the boat will point up and do all its hull permits.

Its good, seeing what gets written by others, to find nothing pretentious or portentous, no putting on airs. And that's something I've always valued you for. Yet there is something muffled about it all, as though you moved out with an intention of candour and then drew back with an impulse of reserve or distrust. It must sound as though I were getting personal and abandoning my usual criteria, but in fact such appearances are fundamentally effects of style, of getting

[99] Turnbull's *A Trampoline: Poems 1952–1964* was published by Cape Goliard in 1968.

the words right, and therefore few, and the rhythms definite, however delicate. Approximations may be all the facts allow; yet one bull is more convincing than a whole series of inners. Sometimes indeed you seem to aim for the inner rather than the bull. Some current cant seems to encourage that, but look at all the ammunition some people waste shooting rings around the target.

This is written, of course, with a view to what you will do in time to come, long time and fruitful I hope. It would be easier, but I hope not more welcome, to say only the smooth, pleasing things, and of course that's the custom. I'd rather say the harsh ones when writing to my friend whose work I value. Well, I enjoyed it anyway; and I hope the book does well and that you reap all the grain of it.

My temporary glasses – till March or April – make reading and writing easy, almost normal, though my eyes refuse to cooperate with each other with the distance glasses, so that I see two of most things.[100] Two glasses of beer, but there's only one to drink. I've begun sorting my books again and the study is knee deep in them, though the bulk of those from California havent arrived yet. But I've also been reading bits of the county history (the 14 volumes cover less than half the county) and a remarkable collection of letters, official reports, et al. about the Rising of the North,[101] glad to find that dislike of the southron domination had more to do with it than disbelief in southron religion. How Elizabeth's soldiers hanged the northerners! Roughly half the muster roll of each village, diminished to about one-in-four in the bigger villages. This was only thirty years after her father's soldiers had done the like, after the Pilgrimage of Grace. The population of the Borders of England diminished during the 16th century, and the historians speculate why. These papers show why. They'd been slaughtered. (The muster rolls profess to show all the males between 14 and 55, though some probably managed to dodge them). Say a fifth of one generation and a fifth of the next hanged – a drastic check on overpopulation. Also, much land went out of cultivation: economic pressures? No, hanging.

The Conqueror had tried to exterminate them too, and Rufus established southron colonies in Carlisle and Newcastle. I cant find out what happened after the Shrewsbury fight, but I don't suppose it was merciful. And after Hexham the

[100] In 1968 BB was recovering from a series of recent eye operations, which largely restored his vision (with the aid of glasses and lenses) after years of poor eyesight.

[101] The history BB mentions is probably the 15-volume *A History of Northumberland* (1893) by the Northumberland county history committee. According to Peter Quartermain, the history of the Rising of the North BB consulted is Cuthbert Sharp's *The Rising in the North: The 1569 Rebellion* (1840). See Quartermain, 'Basil Bunting: Poet of the North' (Durham: Basil Bunting Poetry Archive, 1990), 7.

Yorkists made a mess of the north. There were the Scottish wars in between everything. No wonder we've no great array of painters and poets.

Yet in Hexham there's a tomb, called the tomb of one of the last Northumbrian kings, but, say the experts, probably 12th century, on which some mason made the tree of life with a clean, abstract intricacy that recalls Lindisfarne and Bewcastle.[102] It is very beautiful, and if it really is as late as 12th century, it shows how the life goes on, underneath all the suppressions and oppressions. I like this, and the Corbridge lion. They are my kind of art: the firm line, the counterpoint, the essence, not the illusion, the intricacy, not the confusion. I want more of it, a Northumberland as fertile as any land you can mention.

We had the (Harvard) Wylies for two days and a half and drove them about: one day the North Tyne and Rothbury and Alnwick, one day Hartside and Briggflatts and Stainmore and Blanchland.[103] I think they enjoyed it. Since then no adventures. A visit to the theatre to see one of Sid Chaplin's stories turned into a play rather crudely.[104] Tom Pickard and Stuart Montgomery are planning a joint raid on New York two weeks from now. Tom's Matthew is now a very pretty and attractive little boy. The baby looks fine.

Dunbar fed me, badly, in a pub. We drank Tom Bergman's coffee one night. I've done no work.

I've still to meet the professors and arrange my work with them. If that can be done without eating up all the time till term starts, I mean to descend on you, but I can get nothing made definite enough to know where I am. California seems very far away and a long time ago, and perhaps it never existed. A hole in my life.

Give my love to Johnnie and the children, please. Sima's out and I must eat, which will take time. So goodbye and good luck and may that Trampoline shoot you up very high.

Ever

B

[102] BB compares the (late-13th century) 'Tree of Life' carving in the North Choir Aisle of Hexham Abbey to earlier examples of Northumbrian art: the Lindisfarne Gospels (c.AD 715), the 7th–8th century Bewcastle Cross (see 1/12/81 and note) and the Corbridge Lion, a 2nd–3rd century sculpture at Coria, a Roman fort on Hadrian's Wall near modern Corbridge in the Tyne Valley.

[103] Rothbury and Alnwick: picturesque country towns in north Northumberland; the Hartside Pass, Brigflatts, Stainmore, and Blanchland are further to the south and west, in the remoter landscape of the North Pennines.

[104] Sid Chaplin (1916–1986), north-east novelist who worked as a miner in County Durham before establishing his writing career. In spite of the lukewarm comments here about *Close the Coalhouse Door* (Alex Glasgow's celebrated 1968 musical based on Chaplin's short stories), BB and Chaplin were good friends.

## To Roudaba Bunting Davido

TS Durham

11 October 1968 Shadingfield, Wylam, Northumberland

Dear Rou,

I've persuaded the two northern universities to put my days of duty close together, so that I'll make two appearances in one week and then have ten days with no official work to do.[105] I daresay you'd like a job of that sort. It's true they've managed to shove in a few extras which will postpone my comparative freedom for a few weeks, but I cant grumble. Meanwhile my eyes are all right for most things but useless for billiards – I cant see the end of the cue properly. I made some queer shots.

Maria has become secretary of her school's Arts Society and has compelled me to face it – in a couple of days time. I dont think the headmistress will consider my poems exactly right for the younger ones. All that about untying the tape of drawers might put ideas into their heads.[106] I'm still very uncertain how to deal with this engagement. Maria is full of life, tearing around, running everything and everybody. She's going to grow up bossy. You ought to be here to cure her. Poor John has a hell of a life when he isnt safe at Cambridge, and she's hunting him down in his lair there at half-term. She's a lot of fun.

Sima is doing less to her cottage at Frosterley.[107] It's got a tenant for the moment – a Siamese friend of ours. I dont much like the place. It has a good view and is halfway up to the fells, but its on a fairly busy road and near a municipal dump haunted by hosts of large rats. And its too near the busy little tourist town of Stanhope. She's been pleasant and easy to deal with since I got home. She looks well, too.

[105] BB was Northern Arts Literary Fellow in Poetry at Durham and Newcastle universities between 1968 and 1970. Durham, founded in 1832, is an elite institution in a small city some twenty miles to the south of Newcastle; since 1988 it has housed the Basil Bunting Poetry Archive. Newcastle University was attached to Durham as a subsidiary college between 1883 and 1963. Its students (though not its administration) played a key role in the success of nearby Morden Tower. See **10/6/69** for BB's own comments on the two institutions. BB's lectures at Newcastle in the first semester of 1969–1970 are transcribed and collected (by Peter Makin) in *Basil Bunting on Poetry* (Baltimore: Johns Hopkins UP, 2003); taken together, they amount to his most substantial critical statement on poetics and literary history.

[106] See *Briggflatts*, Part I (99–100).

[107] Sima had recently bought a property in Frosterley, a picturesque village in Weardale, County Durham; Stanhope, a larger Weardale market town, is close by.

Tom is rather silent, and I dont think he is doing well at school this year. He needs to, the big O-level exams come in June.[108] Perhaps its because he wont wear his glasses. He spends his time in his own room, where perhaps he works. I hope so, he swims a lot and still enjoys the naval cadets.

Thanks for your news of Bourtai – she hasnt written, of course. I'd like to see Daphne and Monica. I'm glad Rustam is pleasing you and sorry Finn is proving remote. I like Finn and wish I'd been able to see more of him.

Myself, I got one week off: but in London I had to labour signing sheets of my book, satisfying the record company, coping with journalists who want to write about me, etc. It was too busy. But I got out to Harrow to see David Jones and try to persuade him to visit London next February when there's a jamboree of sorts at which I've promised – conditionally – to appear. Ezra Pound is being asked, and Hugh MacDiarmid.

Jones was as amusing and interesting as ever. He needed only a word here and there to keep him talking, and I thought he was never going to let me go. His life in a hotel room must be very lonely. He showed me his latest treasure, a book of which I am sure he is the only reader, which speculates for 600 pages of small type on the exact pronunciation of three diphthongs in the language the Britons spoke before the Romans came to Britain. Since not one word of the language has been preserved the ingenuity required for the books is extreme, and just the kind to keep Jones happy. But I was glad to escape from London and spend a couple of days with Gael Turnbull and his children. The middle one, Julie, is my delight. She's twelve and a half, very pretty, thickly embroidered with freckles, and unable to sit still for thirty seconds. I've seldom seen a child so full of life, and I enjoy her company immensely. Gael and I went off one day and had a look at Gloucester cathedral, a strange building that looks like lace from outside, but inside it has lacy parts and also austere Norman parts. There is some very fine lively sculpture in it from about 1620, and one fine tomb from about 1100. It is far from being so impressive as our great northern cathedrals, Durham, York and Lincoln, but it is an amusing and rather charming building and I'm glad I've seen it at last. And we went on into a steep deep valley of the Cotswold Hills to visit Charles Tomlinson, who was much more likeable than his poetry.[109] His wife gave us a good tea and the whole family collected my autograph in their albums.

[108] O levels: standard examinations taken by British schoolchildren (usually at the age of 15–16), replaced by the modern GSCE system in 1988.

[109] Charles Tomlinson (1927–2015), British poet and academic associated with the Anglo-American modernist scene. Tomlinson taught at Bristol University, which put him in (relatively) close contact with Turnbull, who lived on the other side of the Malvern Hills.

I got only a day and two nights with Peggy, but well worthwhile. At last I begin to feel close to her again. But what a journey home from Shrewsbury! Four changes of train in two hundred miles, four hours of waiting on chill railway platforms, a walk right across Manchester in the rain. The railways have gone mad and we will soon be obliged to have a car apiece, like you Americans.

Yes, I'll send you book and records when I can.[110] They should be out in about three weeks or a month.

It's raining this afternoon, but we've had a pretty good summer and a late autumn so far. I'm sure in town tonight, and must stop writing this.

Dear lass, let me hear from you. My love to the children, and to you.

Your father

B

## To Roger Guedalla[111]

TS Durham

25 October 1968

Shadingfield, Wylam, Northumberland

Dear Mr Guedalla

I am very sorry to hear that you have come across references to collections of my letters. I thought I'd got all my correspondents to burn them up, except a few which Zukofsky sold to the University of Texas a number of years ago which I've no hope of abolishing unless I set fire to the whole place, a task rather beyond my years. If you do lay hands on any, please abolish them as drastically as you can.

I keep no letters whatever, except receipts from the income tax people and such things. I believe the writers of some letters I havent kept are a little dismayed, but I really do dislike all that letters and incomplete mss and such like stand for.

I was born in 1900, and I am notoriously a Quaker of sorts, though the Quakers are very uneasy about it and handle me with long tongs. The rest is all in the poems.

At present there is no hope of a new poem. But I am getting very tired of the poems I have written in the past, and will soon have to write a new one to escape from them.

Yours ever

B Bunting

[110] As well as publication of the Fulcrum *Collected Poems*, 1968 also saw the release of a recording of BB reading *Briggflatts* (via Stream Records).

[111] **Roger Guedalla**: British scholar and editor who compiled a BB bibliography (eventually published in 1973).

On 3 February 1969 Bunting read at the Poetry Society's diamond jubilee at the Royal Festival Hall in London, which also featured readings by Hugh MacDiarmid, Ted Hughes, Stevie Smith, William Plomer, Christopher Logue, Spike Hawkins, Brian Patten, and Tom Pickard. Plomer (1903–1973) was an elderly establishment editor who wrote orthodox neo-Georgian verse; Logue (1926–2011) a much younger and more progressive poet associated with the British Poetry Revival, as were Patten (b. 1946) and Hawkins (b. 1943), both of whom were attached to the Liverpool scene (see **28/7/64**).

Overall, the event caught the mood of the British poetry scene of the very late 1960s, presenting an interesting clash of traditional Poetry Society types (Plomer, Hughes) and the younger, edgier 'Children of Albion' (Pickard, Logue, Patten, Hawkins) who would briefly gain control of the organization some five years later in a radical 'coup' (see **11/5/75** *and note*). MacDiarmid, Smith, and Bunting stood somewhere in the middle—radicals grown respectable in old age.

## To Denis Goacher

TS Durham

10 February 1969

Shadingfield, Wylam, Northumberland

Dear Denis

Aye aye. You cant get them to plan or to rehearse. They dont know how.

Stevie Smith certainly got all there was to get out of her smaller stuff.[112] I admire anything that is done with such meticulous care as her reading, and have told the Poetry Society so. But McDiarmid reads well too. It sounds dry, because he wants to keep all the clarity of good prose, different from the verse clarity; but he leaves no point unmade. Perhaps you miss the mysteriousness that is a part, though not a necessary part, of at any rate romantic verse. And Tom Pickard, less deliberately, happened to read well too.

Plomer and Logue were beneath any degree of contempt that I can express. Ted Hughes was partly unfortunate – he was nervous to a pathological degree and he didnt seem to know what a microphone is for or how it works and they were chivvying him because they were short of time: but I didnt think he would have done much better in better circumstances. The chivvying of Spike Hawkins was quite shameful, and since he was even more nervous than Stevie Smith or

112 Stevie Smith (1902–1971), British poet and novelist who rose to prominence after the publication of her first collection *A Good Time Was Had By All* in 1937.

Hughes, I'm not surprised that he went to pieces completely. He can, and sometimes does, read well. I didnt hear Patten.

I am sure you misjudge the pace (or paces) for Canto 1.[113] You are familiar with it, its difficulties for an audience that isnt are pretty formidable. In fact I read most of it about the same pace as Ez used to, but I vary the pace more in the later part of it and read faster than Ez. The second part of The Spoils is equally difficult, no doubt, but it fitted the time and has a sufficiently lyrical movement from about the middle on. If I'd been out for glory I'd have chosen something or things other and simpler, but that would have been playing down to the entertainers who end by doing nothing but cheap jests or cheap pathos. What the Chairman told Tom was very carefully picked, to loosen up the audience without debauching it.

Auden and Graves had been invited but didnt accept. Graves reads as badly as anybody. I havent heard Auden. They might have made the list more acceptable to the Great public, but I doubt if they would have improved the quality of the poetry. Auden is just as longwinded as Hughes.

The Times account of the proceedings was written by a man who had asked Montgomery for a job a few weeks back and been refused. No other paper seems to have been displeased. Either the Times man wasnt there at all (that happens) or he's a liar for his praise goes to the inaudible Hughes, not possible to anyone who had tried to hear him; and he makes fun of me for fooling with a despatch case, an object I've never even possessed. Perhaps he mistook one of the others for me, but that seems less likely than lying.

Enough! I'd not have been there but for the prospect of meeting Ezra. Last time I heard you read your own stuff, it was well done, very: yet I'd like to say, dont let the actor gain on the poet. They "cry out on top of the question"[114] or some such thing – anyway, they all seem to read poetry too fast to give any chance to rhythmic variation, and they're apt not to trust the words but to try to supply what they believe is the right emotion by other means. I'd trust Tom Pickard, in a sober mood, much further than Gielgud.[115] Yeats read almost as wrongly as a parson, yet he was right about that – I mean, not acting the poem. Some of your remarks made me uneasy about your orthodoxy on this, hence the inquisition tone of my letter.

Flourish. Thanks for the Corbiere. And to all yours, respects.

B

Montgomery once said I read Spenser as though I'd just finished composing it myself. That's what I'd like to do with other men's verse, and my own.

[113] Pound did not appear at the Poetry Society event, so BB read his Canto 1 in tribute.
[114] See *Hamlet*, II.2.340.
[115] John Gielgud (1904–2000), eminent British Shakespearian actor.

## To Roger Guedalla

MS Durham

6 May 1969

Shadingfield, Wylam, Northumberland

Dear Mr Guedalla,

I shall be at Wylam in July and August, probably also in the latter end of June, and would of course be pleased to see you there. We can usually put somebody up for a night or two, but since we've one guest already for most of that time, don't count on it without telephoning in advance.

Redimiculum Matellarum is practically unobtainable. The rare book people ask a millionaire's price for it, but I believe the British Museum copy is still legible. There's nothing in Poems 1950 for you or anyone that isnt in Collected Poems.

I am sorry you've dug out so much dead journalism. As for a letter in the New York Sun, I dont remember it. Distrust anything of such a date, for I wrote with one eye on EP then, partly because it seemed to me that the only undeniable poet of the time wasnt getting a fair deal from the papers, partly because I wanted to please him, to go on learning what I could from him. I imagine I'd repudiate lot of what was written then now that neither of those motives operate.

There's a lot of such cautions needed: other people might have given similar ones in other ages if they'd thought anybody was going to notice their incidentals. I think, for instance, Ode I 3, might mislead.[116] Everytime it's been reprinted I've wondered whether to drop it. I kept it, I suppose, mainly because Yeats liked it, but he liked it because it was so clearly the attempt to assimilate Mallarmé (not Coup de Dés, but Las du triste hôpital), or so I imagine. In the same way I 13 repeats a trick Ezra invented about 1912 and Eliot used (when I dont remember) with the numbers; and I 30 annexes what I could of WCW's technique at the time – very cleverly no doubt, since his technique got more and more like that afterwards, but it's a young man's cleverness, not something with which you can probe into my mind. So with several others, though what I pick from Horace or Manuchehri may be less obvious to the contemporary observer.

Music? Chopin, J.S. Bach from 1914. Scarlatti from about 1916 or 17, Byrd, 1919, I think. Monteverdi two or three years later. Among contemporaries, Schönberg almost alone. I dunno when I came on Corelli, the tersest of the lot. But obviously no one who writes poetry can pass by Dowland or Campion; nor did Yeats and Pound, though I think they were less than half aware of it.

[116] BB's 'I am agog for foam' is unusual in his oeuvre for being stylistically very free, somewhat in the symbolistic manner of Mallarmé, as BB goes on to point out. Yeats recited the poem by heart in front of BB at a dinner in Rapallo around 1930.

Well to renew the dates: Hopkins wasnt available till about 1929: it's delusive to imagine his influence.[117] He hadnt any on Pound, Yeats, self or L. Zukofsky. No decent edition of Wyat was available until the late 20's,[118] I think: so what might seem to be Wyat in E.P. and specially Yeats just isnt. But I probably got something there. I was young enough still, and his ear worked something like mine.

But repeat, Wordsworth first:[119] Wordsworth never out of sight: Wordsworth most durable of all, most persuasive of all: Dante: Lucretius. My contemporaries come after those, perhaps after Spenser too. And I dont want to play down my dept to E.P. It's great. Just to keep the proportions.

Yours ever
B

## To Hugh Kenner

TS Texas

28 April 1969

Shadingfield, Wylam, Northumberland

Dear Hugh Kenner

First, before I forget: Pound, Canto IV, "No wind is the king's wind/Let every cow have her calf." Have you, or has anybody, noticed that theunderscored here is the famous sentence delivered at Tara by King Diarmuid in the lawsuit between St Columba (Columcille) and St Finnian?[120] Keating reported it from the Black Book of Molaga as "le gach biuno a boinín," and I get from Hyde's Literary History of Ireland, 1899 – certain to have been among Yeats's paraphernalia. The suit was about copyright: Colum had transcribed part of the psalter of St Jerome from a copy belonging to Finnian, secretly while the book was lent to him, and Finnian sued and won his case. The copy was the book's calf. Colum's copy was saved as a relic, and part of it still exists.

[117] Although Robert Bridges's first edition of Gerard Manley Hopkins's (1844–1889) *Poems* had appeared in 1918, BB is (nearly) right that it was only after publication of the updated version of 1930, with additions by Charles Williams (1886–1945) that Hopkins's work was really widely read.

[118] The first widely available modern edition of Thomas Wyatt's poetry was E. M. W. Tillyard's *The Poetry of Sir Thomas Wyatt, A Selection and a Study* (1929).

[119] See **3/11/48** and **6/8/53** and notes for context on BB's late interest in Wordsworth.

[120] Hill of Tara, in County Meath: ancient seat of the High Kings of Ireland. Around AD 560 it was the site of the quarrel BB describes.

My interest in Columcille is that I regard him, pride apart, as the forerunner, the foreshadowing of St Cuthbert;[121] but it struck me that you might care for the reference to Pound (and were the man best qualified to use it) if by any chance you hadnt come across it already.

I had another oddity for you, but I didnt write it down at once and have lost it, though no doubt it will come back into my head at some moment when it's no use at all.

Many discoveries in Wordsworth's letters, not noticed, it seems, by those who write about him, all confirming my view of the poems – in fact the Quaker influence is far stronger than I would have been willing to claim. So is the musical element – a most conscious and deliberate music, though inaudible if a southron reads the poems aloud. But I go very slowly, making few notes, for I read this at the university in Newcastle, and dont get there very often and am sometimes very busy with students when I do.

I must admit that I find one serious inconvenience in Leaving California – I am out of reach of your ingenious learned mind and have nothing in the least equivalent here to make up for it. Sure, plenty of professors: but some are not curious and some are not learned. No man can be called learned who doesnt know twice as much as I do and twice as accurately: perhaps they have other virtues. Industry, for instance; or prudence, or some such damned irrelevance.

My eyes are now in excellent shape and I hope to be driving a car again before the summer is over. That makes a big difference to my spirits, though after a year almost without exercise because of my sight I've also had a long winter without exercise because of vile weather, and that certainly contributes to make me lethargic. I trust you've been well. And I think kindly of your household, at moderate intervals.

I'd not have written just now, for I'm for behind with my letters, but for the little discovery I began with: but now I'm at it I'd better say now that I'd like to return to Santa Barbara in September 1970 if Santa Barbara would like to have me. There's no prospect of anything more to do here (I mean, paid for) and I still have my family to provide for for several years yet. Will you sound them? It will be lonely, no doubt, but I can think of worse misfortunes than that. And I dont

[121] BB's comments here and throughout this letter bear out his interest in the distinctive 'Northumbrian Celto-Anglic' culture of the northern British Isles. Around AD 563, Saint Columba/Colmcille (521–597) migrated from his home in northern Ireland to found an important monastery on the island of Iona in western Scotland. The Northumbrian King Oswald (*c.*604–*c.*642) grew up in exile on Iona and, after claiming the Northumbrian throne in 633/644, used Ionan missionaries to establish Lindisfarne, the religious centre that would eventually nurture Saint Cuthbert.

think I'll be past giving the kids something to think about for quite a while to come.

My notoriety here chafes me a bit – too many reporters, too many TV people, I'm too much cast into a part it's hard not to play. I cant afford to dodge it, though.

Paper's done and I must finish. All the best to you and yours. Gael Turnbull asked me to call him to your mind.

Yours ever
B.

## To Roudaba Bunting Davido

TS Durham

10 June 1969

Shadingfield, Wylam, Northumberland

My dear pet daughter

You've had to wait an awful long time for this letter. I mean to answer everything, but so many letters come, some of them so irritating: and so many visitors or engagements: that everything gets cast onto a great pile and it's only now and then that I manage to get going on the task of cutting the pile down.

We had a lousy spring – rain and cold long past the proper time – but now the sun is out and the temperature about 75 and the garden full of flowers and lots of people coming from town to litter the little river-beach opposite our windows. I've begun to take a little exercise, walking by disused footpaths about the district, watching the fishes jump and the bulls getting frisky and the lambs fattening and the kids at the weekends undressing as much as they dare (which is sometimes a great deal more then they would in USA).

I'm nearly finished the year's work at the two universities. All the students are busy with exams and packing up for the summer. My room at Durham is still a delight, opening above the river Wear, with the steep rock opposite on which they've perched certain colleges in fine XVIII c. houses, and over their chimneys I see the main tower of the great cathedral and a corner of the castle. The racing boats pass just beneath me, practicing for the annual regatta. I like walking across Durham from the station too, the narrow streets, steep and twisting, the American tourists in despair at the madness of the traffic system that results from streets often only wide enough for one car at a time, or turning so sharply that cars cant turn the corner at all; and the girl students and girl shop-assistants on their way to work in the most ridiculous frills of miniskirts (quite unbelievable on your side of the Atlantic, I should think).

I get a good lunch at Durham too. Either I walk up to "my" college, a mile and a half with splendid city views, the cathedral on its rock dominating everything, and eat well for very little money, or, if time is short or weather rough, I cross the road to a pub where I can get a great hunk of crisp bread, a formidable lump of Wensleydale cheese, an onion, an apple and a pint of bitter beer. I like that.

Newcastle University has none of these attractions. My room is open, but looks out only onto our biggest hospital, and as for food! Decent food cant be had in the whole city. However, I get to Newcastle easily in 20 minutes, whereas Durham, though it's only about 23 miles away as the crow flies, has been so isolated by the follies of our latest railway system that it takes hours to get there or back.

The surgeons have kept putting off the moment when my eyes would be altogether my own again, but at least they've measured me up for contact lenses and I expect to see nearly as well as anyone in another two or three weeks. I'd like to buy a car, but I'm afraid I probably wont be able to afford it. Being tied down has been the biggest curse for several years. There are so many things I love within range of a moderate car drive. Sometimes I get out – Sima driving one of Edmond's cars, or a television company determined to make a film of me. In this way I've been out a couple of times on the bare wilds of Spadeadam Waste, up into the forest where they have to put up notices about not running into deer, over into Scottish Liddesdale, where no tourists seem to go, or to Lunesdale, with its abrupt mountains (and no tourists) and solitary river and bridges barely as wide as a car or even to Briggflatts.[122] We had tea in Liddesdale a week ago at the Douglas Arms in the little town of Newcastleton. They have us loads of sandwiches, chicken and ham, three kinds of scone in piles, grand homemade raspberry jam, enough butter for an army, and several kinds of cake at about 40 cents each person; and when I tried to tip the waitress she didnt understand and thought I'd made a mistake counting out the money. But she accepted the equivalent of a quarter when we'd explained to her.

Maria is swallowed up by exams at this moment, the last ones at school. Tom will be engulfed next week in the O-levels (with two years of school yet to come). John Halliday spends all his holidays with us now that he and Maria are "engaged" and I expect he'll be here in a fortnight for almost all the summer. He's a good

[122] Spadeadam Waste: remote moorland area on the border between Cumbria and Northumberland, and location of an RAF base; Liddesdale is a little to the north of Spadeadam, but on the Scottish side of the border. Both are in the wild frontier terrain subject to clan warfare in the later Middle Ages (BB became increasingly fond of this locale in his last years). For Lunesdale see note to **16/9/64**.

enough lad, but a bit of a stick, I think. He's just sat his finals at Cambridge and another year, studying in chambers, will qualify him as a barrister – the higher but often less prosperous branch of the law, which leads on to being a judge if you're lucky. Maria has a travel scholarship for the summer, but a very stingy one: it will just about pay her fares to Cornwall and Brittany for three weeks to look at stone-age bits and pieces; and I'm afraid I'll have to find what she needs to eat and sleep. Tom has found means to get two holidays instead of one out of the Navy, at least one of them afloat on a smallish ship. It is cunning of the Navy to treat the kids so well – Tom is at least flirting with the idea of becoming a Naval officer. Year after year, in return for an hour of drill and seamanship on Friday evenings in term time, they've taken him to sea and to camps and given him his share of dinghy sailing on a lake as well, any fine weekend. You should see the care he takes of his uniform – the webbing all whitened, the brass all polished, the bell-button trousers folded justso, and his shoes polished three times over. He always was a rather tidy boy. And those cadet uniforms certainly fetch the girls. I thought he'd have been bored with it long since, but he carries on. He has borrowed nearly all my books on seamanship and navigation and a chart or two to practise working out courses on. I think the only thing he respects his father for is that I am expert at knots and splices.

Dorothy Pound, now about 84, will be with us through most of July and August. Her son is off to Canada to see his wife's family. Sima and Maria intend camping in Scotland in September, but Tom's dates dont fit, so I think I'll take him down to London then.

I've done no writing. Far too many fools plague me with their bad poetry. But I still hope to get something done someday.

It seems more and more as though I shall see you all a bit over a year from now. There's nothing for me to earn here after that, I must earn, and Santa Barbara says it would be glad to have me back. Other places have also enquired – Stony Brook and Vancouver, for two. But I like the climate of California. Certainly I wish I could see you all. Finn will have grown up, and Daphne will have passed the most enchanting stage of her adolescence before I can get to Wisconsin. Rustam has a long way to go yet, and Monica will be a delight for years. Give them all my love, please.

I dont know just what to say to you, dear girl. I hope you dont have to work too damn hard, but I fear you probably do. I'd like to cuddle you a bit and somehow give you a long rest. I havent forgotten the dear, loving baby you were long ago.

Give my best wishes to your mother.

Love from your father

B

## To Bruce Berlind

TS Durham

14 July 1969

Shadingfield, Wylam, Northumberland

Dear Mr Berlind

My fee for reading is eighty guineas.[123] In the United States I usually receive 750 dollars. I am continually astonished at the arrogance of institutions which offer a poet sums which they would be ashamed to pay a railway porter. If I were to read for you I would have two days of travelling, one on which to read, and one at least to prepare the reading – four days at £2-10-0 per day. This is about 2/3 of the usual pay of a builder's labourer in this country. Yet you would be ashamed to ask a secondrate pianist to play to you for less than £100.

No wonder readings are generally perfunctory and even squalid. A beggar's pittance can buy nothing but a beggar's antics. Here there are schools so squeezed for money that they can do no better: but your university is a wealthy one, and whether the sum you mention expresses your opinion of poetry or your opinion of Englishmen, it is an insolence which I resent.

Yours truly
B Bunting

The following two letters detail a complicated quarrel involving the American poet Ronald Johnson, the Scottish poet Ian Hamilton Finlay, Stuart Montgomery, Bunting, and several others. The fallout from Bunting's intrusion into it is somewhat exhaustively detailed in multiple letters (original and carbon-copied) in archives in Durham and Indiana. But a very brief summary will communicate the gist.

In 1969 Bunting's publisher, Stuart Montgomery's Fulcrum Press, released *The Dancers Inherit the Party* by Ian Hamilton Finlay. The collection was billed by Fulcrum as a 'first edition', but it had in fact appeared in a previous iteration (separate British and American versions published in 1960 by Gael Turnbull's Migrant Press), though the Fulcrum edition was bigger by about 50 per cent due to the addition of new material. Taking umbrage at this apparent false advertising, Finlay fought an extensive legal campaign against Montgomery, which ended in Finlay's victory and, ultimately, the bankruptcy of Fulcrum. Bunting waded into the dispute with this letter to Johnson, responding to an open letter he had received from Johnson attacking Montgomery. Bunting then received a torrent of letters

[123] Guinea: old British currency unit worth slightly more than the pound (thus 80 guineas was a little over 80 pounds, equivalent to about £1200 in the early 2020s). Even prior to being rendered obsolete by decimalization in 1971, the guinea had archaic, rarefied connotations, which are perhaps being invoked by BB here.

from Finlay and his defenders objecting to Bunting's caricature of Finlay in the letter to Johnson, along with threats of legal action from Finlay, which were eventually dropped.

## To Ronald Johnson

TS Durham

August 7 [1969]

Shadingfield, Wylam, Northumberland

Dear Ronald Johnson,

I am sorry indeed that you have chosen to address to me a copy of your very wild, and, in my opinion, very vile letter to Stuart Montgomery, since the other people to whom you have sent copies might imagine that I approved of it in some degree unless I take the trouble to answer it, a most disagreeable task.

You are, I suppose, championing Mr Ian Hamilton Finlay, who had, I gather complained to you about some of this transactions with Fulcrum Press. There is no sign that you have enquired whether Mr Finlay's complaints are justified. Neither do you take the pains to set out clearly what those complaints are, and I, for one, do not know (nor much care) in what he thinks himself aggrieved.

I do not know Mr Finlay personally, but only by his books. I have, perhaps, heard anecdotes about him, for he is reputed to be an eccentric; but I have paid no attention to them and cannot at present remember even one. I must judge him solely by his poetry. On that alone, I would regard him as an unreliable witness. My Finlay used to write verses teeming with whimsy and with what seemed to be self-regarding sentimentality: but since he is, I conclude, no fool, he took a leaf out of E.E. Cummings book and disguised the essentially trivial nature of his work under tricks of typography. Naïve people take such gimmicks for originality.

This riffling with type is characteristic of advertisers (Cummings was, at first an advertiser) and is designed to prevent the reader, or beholder, from paying too much attention to what the text is saying. It may be an art of a sort, but hardly a literary art, certainly not poetry. What is offered is a usual trick and if there is anything at all behind the trick, what's behind it is irrelevant, or at any rate is not connected with the trick in any but a purely accidental way.

Of course Mr Findlay is entitled to play his game, and to persuade people, if he can, that it is an art. I would never have written down what I think about it if your letter had not forced me to do so. But you have made it necessary to consider what induces a man to deploy such gimmicks as Mr Findlay uses. It may be unjust of me to imagine that Mr Findlay did not find that the reputation of a purveyor of whimsy could satisfy his vanity. Perhaps he deceives himself as well as his readers by hiding the nullity of his verses behind a noisy blast of ballyhoo he calls "concrete poetry." But whether he deceives his readers or himself, I would be very cautious indeed about accepting any statement of his. I would suspect it of being warped.

You see, the first of the many evil effects of your letter is to cause me to make an enemy of a man who has done me no harm and about whom I need never have said a word.

Then you write about "double dealing lies" which, you say, Stuart Montgomery told in order to make profit out of publishing my verses. In fact Stuart Montgomery tried to get me to give them to Oxford University Press.

I rejected Cape because either Mr Maschler[124] or some less conspicuous employee of Cape's tried to get me to sign a contract which gave Cape, in the small type clauses, all the rights which I had specifically reserved to myself in the preliminary letters, and for terms considerably less advantageous than those which had been agreed. It seemed to me dishonest, and I thought that a business relationship which began in such a way could never be comfortable. I rejected the O.U.P. because on long consideration it seemed to me that Stuart Montgomery would give me better service, if I could induce/convince him to take the book on. Till then, he had not contemplated publishing any but short books, & he took a severe risk in undertaking a longer one. All the time Stuart Montgomery minimized Cape's undeniable shortcomings & tried to influence me in favour of O.U.P.

"Double-tongued lies," then, is false. (I wonder what lies, & whose, brought you to believe it true if you do believe it true). It is also, of course, unmistakably libelous, and sending your letter to almost a dozen addresses constitutes publication. If you had any money I would advise Stuart Montgomery to prosecute you for it, but I imagine you to be what the lawyers call "a man of straw" who can make his poverty a shield for blackguardism.

I don't think I need correct your funny account of my own imagined feelings about Stuart Montgomery's publication of my work, at any rate here and now. My present notoriety has given me both amusement and annoyance. I was quite content without it. But, for whatever it is worth, I do not think I would have become notorious without Stuart's hard work. None of the many other people who were aware of my existence ever bothered even to write a paragraph.

I do not doubt that your own motives are generous, naively, to help a friend in distress; but I hope you are ashamed already of your very silly accusations of theft

[124] Tom Maschler (b. 1933), influential literary director (later chairman) of major London publishing house Jonathan Cape.

and of the violence with which you condemn the "shoddiness" of a book you have not seen. So far, I havent seen any shoddy books from Fulcrum, and though various people have criticized Stuart Montgomery or quarreled with him, their complaints so far as I have heard them, boil down to one: he dislikes writing letters, so that those who are fidgety endure a kind of torment between acceptance of the book and its printing. I am not fidgety myself, though I think I am at least as finicky about proofs and corrections as any but the most intransigent writers. I daresay Mr Finlay has worried himself silly about his book, and if so I sympathise with him, though it was foolish of him to pass on his worries to you, with all the inevitable exaggeration & one-sidedness, especially since you seem to have enhanced the hysteria.

Yours faithfully
Basil Bunting

## To Ian Hamilton Finlay

[TS Indiana?]

26 August 1969 — Shadingfield, Wylam, Northumberland

Dear Mr Finlay

I am glad you have written to me at last.

Yes, of course I wanted my letter to Johnson to remain private. It was intended only for those to whom he had addressed the letter which insinuated that I was somehow a party to his infamous charges against Montgomery (theft and fraud). Of course I did not imagine that a dozen people, most of them unknown to me, would all be perfectly discreet, but I did not expect any of them to be spiteful enough to send on to you what was bound to anger you. As to those who have been circulating it since, it is hard to tell whether they are more concerned to humiliate you or to exhibit me as a monster; but I think we can both afford to take no notice of such vermin.

You know that I have told your wife already that I would have worded my letter differently if it had not seemed necessary to reply to Johnson instantly before his charges could do much damage. It may be that a different way of putting it would have seemed less offensive to you. I doubt it, though. If, however, you think I need not have mentioned you at all in my reply to Johnson, you have an arguable case, though I would not agree. I think you were to some extent present behind Johnson, though I do not credit you with his extravagences.

You see that I am being candid with you. Will you be equally candid with me? Some of the people who have written to me say that you instigated them.

Is that true? Others had been sent my letter, but not Johnson's, and left to infer that my remarks were practically unprovoked. Are you responsible? And was that honest?

For the rest, it is quite possible for people to tolerate each other, and even to be friendly, in spite of extreme and violent differences. I regard Edgar Bowers as a friend though my poetry seems to him as false as his does to me.[125] I dont see why you and I should not go each his own way without more collisions, if no new Johnson chooses to cause them.

Yours Faithfully
B Bunting

## To Hugh Kenner

TS Texas

7 November 1969 Shadingfield, Wylam, Northumberland

Dear Hugh K.

After several weeks struggle with a virus which kept me only just not in bed and forbade any use of what passes for my brain except perfunctory ones, I'm behind again with all letters. How are you? And how are your family?

I'm concocting lectures for Newcastle University and soothing students at Durham with anodyne noises about their verses. Next to nothing written, little read. For a while I was besieged by letters, anonymous or from quasi-nameless people, inspired by Ian Hamilton Finlay who is displeased because I said (in a letter, not in print) that his productions were trivial. I was astonished – thought I'd seen all kinds – by the number and baselessness of the lies he put about, and I wasted quite a lot of time trying to put people straight. He took to lawyers – several successive lawyers – thus obliging me to waste money as well as time before the last lawyer told him to belt up.

Dorothy Pound was with us for seven weeks of summer, and we enjoyed showing her the north and making her aware of Northumberland as a land uneasily asleep, but by no means absorbed in London's England. No real news of Ezra.

I've just had a letter from Guss,[126] saying the department is broke, or near broke, and probably cant take me on again in September. This leaves me floating

[125] Edgar Bowers (1924–2000), American poet with a somewhat refined style quite unlike BB's sinewy modernism. BB must have met him during his 1966–1968 fellowship at UC Santa Barbara, where Bowers was a professor.

[126] Donald L. Guss (d. 2013), English professor at UC Santa Barbara.

just a little above Niagara, with the plunge over the falls imminent. I must write to other universities without delay, and wonder whether you have any ideas. May I, in any case, use you as a reference? Here, Durham is trying to get my job made permanent, but the Northern Arts Association, which puts up a third of the money is humming and hawing and I've no idea what the New Broom at Newcastle intends. On the whole, I think they will save their money for postage or coffee instead of poetry. It is uncomfortable, for I must keep my family going for a good while yet, and cannot see any means of doing it without a job of this kind. I'll be seventy in March. With nothing but the Old Age Pension (£3.10.0) after June.

MacDiarmid was with us for a few days, and sober part of the time. He seemed to have aged a great deal since last year. He mumbles more, and his suitcase was obviously too heavy for him. You know he had a bad bout of pneumonia in Canada and a less violent one immediately after his return to Scotland. His brain seems at least lively as ever, but I'm not confident about this flesh and bone, though he still doesnt look 77. How good his stuff is, and how unlike everything else since Langland.

Montgomery's final version of Circe is out, and reads very well indeed.[127] He's talking about a long poem Tchaka the Zulu, not the kind of hero to get him loved by the naive Left, still less by the Rhodesian Right.

No answer yet to my last letter to Gael Turnbull. He's busy doctoring, I know, and may have been ill or had a rush of patients.

All good wishes to you and yours.

B Bunting

## To Denis Goacher

TS Durham

16 December 1969 — Shadingfield, Wylam, Northumberland

Dear Denis,

I get round to it at last, feeling a bit guilty for too much silence. You should see my desk, deep in unanswered letters. And outside its snowy and beastly cold, and I've got to chatter for Tyne Tees television in about twenty minutes, and there are bills to pay if I can find them in the file of paper.

[127] Stuart Montgomery's *Circe*, a translation of books X and XI of *The Odyssey*, appeared via Fulcrum in November 1969.

Not much to report. The term at Durham has been very quiet indeed, but at Newcastle I've had to lecture, because the professor died and they were short-handed, and thinking out lectures has taken a lot of time. It caused me to do a good deal of rereading too – Beowulf and Green Knight and Wyat and Spenser and Swinburne amongst others. I'm also overdue with an essay on McDiarmid for Agenda, promised and not done, and an essay on Wordsworth ditto.[128] I read The Brothers,[129] not very well, for the BBC's Wordsworth celebrations next spring. Macbeth and someone a bit like Lady Macbeth gave me lunch in the worst pub in Newcastle because it is handy to the BBC studio and they knew no better.[130] I'd tried to persuade them that Norman Nicholson, being a Cumbrian, was better qualified to read Wordsworth than I am, but McB said they'd had Nicholson, and he didnt sound enthusiastic.[131]

Else, I've done nothing and been nowhere. I got to Shrewsbury for two days to see Peggy, very satisfactory. And resumed driving, now that I see better than any time since I was 12, with an aging Ford Zodiac, heavy on petrol, but I knew the car and it was in prime condition. No fines yet. But its hard to park in Newcastle, so I still have a use for the train. I daresay I could do my shopping in Hexham, but I dont want to transfer my bank account there, because they've treated me well in Newcastle and goodness knows what another manager might be like.[132]

Eheu fugaces – well, trying to make Horace sound human.[133] As for popes and pontifexes, any translation at all must commit anachronism either to the author or to the reader, and popes are highly respectable wealthy gentlemen who presumably drink firstclass wine. They'll do. Cardinal wouldnt have suited the line, and priest is anglo-catholic and teetotal too often.

[128] BB's MacDiarmid essay 'Thanks to the Guinea Worm', would appear in *Agenda* VIII (Autumn–Winter 1970); the Wordsworth piece is probably the introduction to the 7 April 1970 BBC broadcast subsequently detailed, which was reproduced in *The Listener*, 8 October 1970, 484.

[129] This long narrative poem, published in the second volume of *Lyrical Ballads* (1800), was a favourite of BB's.

[130] George Macbeth (1932–1992), Scottish poet and novelist. Between 1955 and 1976 Macbeth produced radio broadcasts on poetry for the BBC, including the 1970 Wordsworth bicentenary BB mentions here.

[131] Norman Nicholson (1914–1987), British poet from Millom, Cumbria. BB's introduction to the BBC reading stressed the importance of Wordsworth's Cumbrian accent for understanding his poetry, a strongly held belief (see 14/8/76).

[132] Hexham: large market town and 'capital' of the rural Tynedale district. As BB aged and moved to remoter Tynedale homes, Hexham would increasingly replace Newcastle as his local centre.

[133] 'Eheu fugaces': part of the first line of Horace's Ode II. 14, which BB rendered 'You can't grip years', in a translation eventually included in the 'Overdrafts' section of his 1978 OUP *Collected Poems*. The final line ('fit wine for a pope') is the subject of discussion in this passage.

Which reminds me to assure you that I liked a number of poems you sent me. I dont think I've anything to say about them, except that I liked them. If I were paid to lecture on the subject no doubt I could find some bloody nonsense to fill the time with; but I've nothing to say about good or goodish poetry, really, or merely "read it."

I'm glad you're enjoying Devonshire and scrumpy.[134] I dont think malic acid on the grand scale would agree with my guts any longer, though it did once. I find Peter Whigham a disagreeable subject, though he has certain somewhat academic virtues in his verse; and industry, which I lack. He had an agreeable looking little daughter, but between such parents I dont think she has much chance of staying agreeable as she ages.

Please give my best wishes to Mrs G and the boy, and the rest of your family. There doesnt seem much prospect of my getting to Devon, and I'm so rarely in London that I cant guess when we'll meet unless something brings you north. But you know, or ought to know, my affection for you, so I wont elaborate.

Oh yes! And Merry Xmas.

Yours ever
B

## To Michael Shayer

TS Durham

2 April 1970 — Shadingfield, Wylam, Northumberland

Dear Michael

The handwriting did require study, but didnt entirely disguise your words; and they also seem to require study and I'm not certain I've decoded them correctly.

I dont know a damn thing about Zen but gather that it boils down to kindness and unassumingness, both pleasant characteristics which mitigate life for your friends and neighbours; but like Buddhism and Humanism in general it misses out god completely, so that nothing is ad maiorem gloriam[135] any more; only to the comfort of your race and your conscience. (The "you" is impersonal).

Now if I am ever kind it is because I am too lazy to be disagreeable, not because of virtues I havent got. For the same reason I like other people to be kind. When they spare their fleas, it is very gratifying for the fleas. I admire fleas. They are athletic, bold and very resolute creatures, marvelous under the microscope, etc., but I dont propose to let them bite me. And a tiger would be unkind to me, and none the worse a tiger for that.

[134] Goacher had recently moved to Devon, where scrumpy is a local delicacy (see 21/1/38).
[135] Latin for 'to the greater glory of God', the motto of the Jesuit Order.

In short I find the whole business of morals, mores, habits, manners, more or less irrelevant. Whether you plump for original sin or original innocence, we are all of us pretty wicked by the time we are forty (I am, anyway) and, on a longer view than our present comfort, what does it matter? But if you write the Iliad or design the mosaics in Sant'Apollinare[136] or put notes together as skillfully as Corelli or do a number of other things that will bring you neither ready cash nor peace of mind nor make people like you nor serve any useful purpose whatsoever you can add a trifle to the sum of things, and thus go partners with god (whoever or whatever he or it may be); share the spoils and the responsibility.

That's what I once thought you and Gael were up to; but I now think that you articulately and he inarticulately are in fact struggling to make head or tail or some less definite thing of morals, the useful or useless habits of humanity. To a man who thinks mankind unimportant that is disappointing, though usual.

Gael is a good, kind chap, and I value him. You too. I am glad you are pleased with him again. I hope to see him presently (When he was here a week or two or three ago there was no real contact, I dont know why. Maybe I'm too much of an egotist to keep any contact close for long. Maybe there is some underlying resentment of my uninterest in groups and such. Maybe he feels I'm conceited.) I wish he got on with Stuart M. I wish he were better pleased with life.

News? I've got myself a rodent ulcer which they've burned, and forbidden me to wash the north-west corner of my face for the next three months. I'll look the opposite of Chirgwin the White Eyed Kaffir by that time.[137] Tom Pickard looks like being chased out of his comfortable house in Ovingham and homeless again.[138] Jonathan Williams is trying to make his whiskers conform to the pattern of the late Lord Henry Cavendish Bentinck who used to own the land thereabouts (Dent),[139] The Prime Minister has put me on the Civil List for £250 a year less income tax.[140] It's cold, but not wet.

[136] The Basilica of Sant'Apollinare Nuovo in Ravenna, Italy, built by the Ostrogoth King Theodoric the Great in the sixth century, is decorated with exquisite Hellenistic-Christian and Byzantine mosaics, which were much admired by Pound and Yeats.

[137] G. H. Chirgwin (1854–1922), aka 'The White-Eyed Kaffir', British music-hall comedian known for his black-face minstrel act featuring a white diamond shape around one of his eyes.

[138] Ovingham: next village westward from Wylam.

[139] Lord Henry Cavendish-Bentinck (1863–1931) British Conservative politician who was part of a wealthy aristocratic family in possession of large tracts of land throughout the British Isles.

[140] Notable British cultural and scientific figures can be added to the Civil List at the discretion of the sovereign/government, thereby gaining entitlement to an extra yearly pension allowance.

I like the poem (the noise of it) but dont altogether get its bearings. All the definite articles in it seem redundant, but that's a small matter. I hope to be at Cradley[141] a week today for a couple of days and will call on your family if there's a chance.

Good luck, Mike.

Yours

B

## To Rodger Kingston[142]

TS Durham

May Day 1970

Shadingfield, Wylam, Northumberland

Dear Rodger Kingston

You think I'm an ungrateful correspondent. I've just seen the deck of my desk again through the papers and letters waiting for attention, and though its partly lethargy its partly harassment too. I am sorry.

You wrote in February, if you've forgotten.

I am glad to hear you are getting on with your writing and hope your schemes succeed.

I think Laughlin will always say anything that sounds agreeable. As for his negotiation with my publisher in the forties, I hadnt a publisher in the forties: but in that decade Laughlin turned down my work for the second (or was it third) time. Montgomery tried to interest him a few years ago and he hummed and hawed a bit and wouldnt hear of it. He came to my reading in New York in 1967, oozing the oil of public relations, and practically pushing Ginsberg, who had done all the chores, aside; but shied off when I suggested he might handle my stuff in America. Literature owes Laughlin some respect for what he has done (fairly profitably) for Ezra; but he has the distinction of having turned down both Zukofsky and BB time and again in spite of Ezra's advocacy. He is not a serious character, only a big bank balance.

It is possible I may be in Canada this autumn, but only possible. 45 Canadian and US universities have no use for me. My appointment here ends in June and when it ends I must endeavour to live on my old age pension – about £6 a week – and a Civil List pension which has just been awarded me of £5 a week less

141 Gael Turnbull lived in Cradley, Herefordshire.

142 **Rodger Kingston**: apparently a young American poet, who seems to have proposed a critical work on BB in 1970.

income tax! Not much for a man and wife and two university age children in a country where £25 a week is considered too little for a bricklayer's hodman. Here, there seems to be a new dead set against all the arts, a triumph of the administrators and academic teachers over everything living. The police are chivvying Tom Pickard, the Beatles, anything handy, in a panic fear of novelty.

As you'll gather, I'm depressed. Perhaps its only due to the long winter, longest for many years; but I do see a general resurgence of everything unscrupulous, illiberal and brutal in Great Britain. Lord Chief Justice Parker, the worst LCJ in fifty years, is in favour of abolishing the rules of evidence because they hamper the police.[143] Lesser lights advocate police perjury – the police are so honest they would never perjure themselves except to convict someone whom they know to be guilty. Besides, even when the prisoner isnt guilty, his conviction is a warning to those who are. We had better send all the Pakistanis in England home for fear the sight of them annoys the South African cricket team.[144]

And so on.

Good luck. Yours faithfully
B Bunting

## To Rodger Kingston

TS Durham

25 May 1970 — Shadingfield, Wylam, Northumberland

Dear Roger Kingston

You are right, I dont like the notion of books about me. If people want to write about my poetry, o.k., though it's a waste of time to write about any art. But I dont like going on show in my own person. As for pestering people to write testimonials to my work – please dont.

No, life is not comfortable often or for long; but fortunately life isnt long either.

It's a sunny day and I want to be out, so forgive my brevity

Yours faithfully
B Bunting

143 Hubert Parker (1900–1972), Lord Chief Justice of England 1958–1971.

144 After a concerted campaign by anti-apartheid activists, the South African cricket team abandoned plans to tour England in the summer of 1970.

## To Cid Corman

TS Indiana

27 May 1970

Shadingfield, Wylam, Northumberland

Dear Cid Corman

Thanks for the volume; or rather, for its contents.[145] They are not uniformly what I seek, of course, but there are several so lucid and round that they do set up a social standard. They become conduct.

That, I suppose, was the aim of much Japanese poetry, and there are traces of something similar here and there in Greek and even Latin. Certainly it is something to respect. Yeats would have liked it, raising a kind of screen between behaviour and its motives; a mask everybody can wear at the same time at the cost of some discipline; and a great deal of circumscription.

Fan, tea, cherry blossom, assume man is the measure. Since I dont think so, I cannot write that way, cannot expect to be neat or seamless. But just as I like Dante without being a catholic I can like your kind of work without being a humanist (under whatever disguise...Buddhist?). You do it well, often exceedingly well, and it is not only honest, it seems so. Much pleasure, then, for a reader. Thankyou

B Bunting

## To Tom Pickard

MS Buffalo

4 October 1970

care of English Department, University of British Columbia, Vancouver 8, B.C., Canada

Dear Tom – I'm glad the house is pleasing you.[146] Long may it do so, particularly if it leads to more poems, as you expect. I agree, without some such anchor for a family, writing isnt easy. Now does Connie like it? Are there schools at hand for the bairns?

Your description of the N/c Festival tallies pretty well with what I would expect. Why the hell havent they sense enough to get a Northerner to run it instead of an Irish advertiser?

[145] Corman's output was prolific in this period (eighteen publications between 1964 and 1970) so it is difficult to determine the volume referred to here without any identifying detail from BB. His translation of Kusano Shimpei's *Frogs and Others* seems a likely candidate, as it had been published fairly recently in 1969.

[146] Pickard had recently moved to Gateshead (see note to 17/3/53).

I was a bit cheered up by a bunch of letters last week, just after yours: Tom B. full of good news at school and navy, Maria cheerful, and a surprise letter from Ezra Pound. First time I've seen his fist for years. Concise – he wastes no energy on superfluities. "Dear Basil, Thanks for your note from Vancouver. If I had your eye for detail I might have done something decent. Yours E.P." What it means I'm not sure. I thought he had demonstrated fairly often that he had at least as good an eye for detail as anyone whatever. However, it's a fine compliment and I'm not disposed to quarrel with it. Else, I dont enjoy myself. The students are like oxen, but they dont even moo.[147] The staff, polite, kind, at least in intention, but dull, dull. The city – its incredible how a place so beautifully sited can be so damned uninteresting. I visited Simon Fraser University, [148] the other end of Vancouver, and hated it: a monstrous building that covers all the top of a mountain: stairs and stairs, wider than the M1,[149] and a central room you could drill a couple of regiments in. Everything calculated to impress by mere size – The very essence of a bully's architecture. There are fine views, but there are finer ones at my end of the Town. The few staff I met were bores. I would hate to have to teach there.

I am thinning. No appetite at all.

It was sunny for a good while, but now it drizzles steadily, very like home. The mountains are hidden in the drizzle.

My love to Connie and both offspring.

All the best

B.

## To Alexander Nelson[150]

MS Durham

25 November 1970

care of English Department, University of British Columbia, Vancouver 8, BC, Canada

Dear Mr Nelson

I am not inclined to figure in Mr Quasha's anthology,[151] for several reasons.

[147] BB taught briefly at the University of British Columbia, Vancouver in late 1970.

[148] Simon Fraser University, founded in 1965, was housed in a daring Brutalist structure designed by Canadian architect Arthur Erickson (1924–2009).

[149] M1: British motorway between London and Leeds.

[150] **Alexander Nelson**: probably an editor at Sumac Press, publisher of the anthology discussed in this letter.

[151] George Quasha (b. 1942), American avant-garde poet and artist who edited *An Active Anthology* (the experimentally inclined collection discussed here) for Sumac Press in 1974.

If you have examined "Briggflatts" Part 3 you must have seen that it needs what goes before and what follows. By itself it would have no excuse, either as sense or as music.

Secondly, my publisher, who is also my agent,[152] would think the terms you offer funny. I am not a young man anxious to get into print, and the fee I expect for a piece of that length would certainly exceed $1,000.

Again, you set a date just ahead as though you hoped to hustle the poets you are approaching. I wonder why; and I think any experienced person would distrust such an approach.

Finally, Mr Quasha must have noticed, and very many people could have told you, that my work is at the furthest possible distance from "Found Poetry," "Concrete Poetry," "Mixed Media Poetry," "Protest Poetry," etc. I prefer to work at the job and make so good a poem as I can without looking for short cuts to notoriety.

Your own letter is courteous. I would not have troubled to answer Mr Quasha's if it had come by itself. I do not think he can have considered what he is asking.

Yours faithfully
B Bunting

## To Karl Drerup

MS Durham

9 January 1971 [Shadingfield, Wylam, Northumberland]

Dear Don Carlos –

Your excellent early portrait of me dominates this room, as the small preliminary study dominates my room at home.[153] But nobody believes it is me – I'm pretty ancient now, you know. I am writing because, for the first time in these many, many years, I shall be within reasonable distance of you for more than three months. It may be difficult to meet, but it wont be altogether impossible, as it always has been hitherto. I shall be teaching at a branch of the State University of New York at Binghamton. So long as the show lasts there is probably nothing to be done: but when it relents I'll have a car and might be able to get off long enough to drive over to you. I got back to England late in may to be given an honorary degree by one of the universities. – I'd like to see you and Gertrude again: a

[152] I.e. Stuart Montgomery.

[153] BB was writing from Vancouver, just prior to taking up a short-term teaching post at SUNY Binghampton. For Drerup's portrait of BB see 21/10/34.

breath from Chinerfe at its least disagreeable.[154] The last time must have been in New York in 1938. These years have made plenty of changes. I suppose I'd be called "well-known" nowadays, but it doesnt help much financially. I have to work at teaching far from home, though I am 71. At home, at Wylam, in Northumberland, my second family is almost grown-up – Maria will marry this year, and Tom will go to university. You'd like Wylam: pleasant views, near the moorlands, near little towns full of relics of the Dark Ages. – For a short while, three years ago, I was blind, but cataract operations and contact lenses have made me see the world more clearly and more vividly than any time since I was twelve years old. Brilliant colours, since there's now no lens to absorb the light. – Are you painting? Potting? – My address from January will be: c/o English Department, S.U.N.Y. at Binghamton, New York. –

My daughter Roudaba sends her love.

Yours always
B Bunting

## To Dorothy Pound

MS Indiana

28 March 1971

c/o English Department, S.U.N.Y at Binghamton,
N.Y. – U.S.A.

Dear Dorothy –

Your letter pleased me, of course. There is no sinister meaning behind my delay in answering. I've just had lots to do.

Nothing could please me and Sima more than to have you at Wylam again, as long as you please. I shall be home by early June, and though I may have to go on my travels again, that wont be before September. I've been thinking off and on that it is a long time since I saw Omar; and his book is good;[155] so I hope he will come north while I'm at home.

Here the snow seems to be melting at last. I've seen nothing but snow on a lifeless landscape since early in December, and all that time I've been housebound, which is irritating. With such winters to bear I wonder how the Americans have preserved even a fraction of civilisation.

154 *Chinerfe*: archaic name for Tenerife in the Canary Islands, where BB and Drerup lived in the 1930s.

155 BB contributed a preface to Omar Pound's *Arabic & Persian Poems*, published by Fulcrum in 1970.

Not much sign of intelligence among students or staff here. Some are kind, but that is almost embarrassing when you have to despise their heads. I am very bored with teaching, and it inhibits writing: though I've made a selection of F.M. Ford's poems and put a preface to them for the Pym-Randall press of Boston.[156] Pym, by the way, was a cat. Randall took him into partnership to satisfy the law about how many shareholders a limited company has to have. The firm is now in mourning for its senior partner, dead, of old age at sixteen or so. Penguin wanted me to do a selection and preface too to some poet, but from a list which did not include any poet I cared enough about. I'd have tacked Wordsworth or Spencer or Wyat on merit; or Swinburne or Churchill (Charles) etc on undue neglect, but I couldnt undertake to read Tennyson for any money they could offer.

Affection doesnt diminish, my dear.

Yours
B.

## To Ronald Duncan

TS Texas

23 July 1971 — Shadingfield, Wylam, Northumberland

Dear Ronald Duncan

Thankyou again. Of course I havent had time to read the book yet,[157] but I've turned over the pages and hope there'll be time when I get to Canada in another month.

Your difficulty will be to avoid turning science into a new metaphysics. There's no virtue in abstractions, wherever they spring from. But the basis of science is using your eyes (etc), and that is what most "poets" dont do. As to the vocabulary, there must certainly be a good deal worth annexing; but I dont forget that there are notions in both logic and theology that are useful, and shouldnt be lost sight of. Grace and original sin are instruments as powerful in their way as Occam's razor, and as void of explorable foundations. But they, like the algebra, only work on organising what you've seen for yourself, and it is the seeing rather than the principle of organisation that can be passed over to a hearer of poetry.

[156] Pym-Randall would publish this edition of Ford Madox Ford's *Selected Poems*, with BB's preface, in 1971.

[157] Duncan's *Man*, a long poem preoccupied with themes of science and human evolution, was published in four parts by Rebel Press between 1970 and 1974.

WCW's clinical training gave him a head start over Ezra and Eliot. His confused metrics and naive American chauvinism are all the critics notice (and applaud), silly academics. In fact, these are what ultimately reduced him to something less memorable than the other two, in spite of an inborn mastery of syntax which they didnt have so fully. And Ezra at least used his eyes too.

Keep at it. All the best

B.

Bunting's short year of teaching at the University of Victoria 1971–1972 was unhappy, largely because of a quarrel with his colleague Robin Skelton. As with the Ian Hamilton Finlay dispute two years earlier (see 7/8/69 and commentary), exhaustive accounts of the episode are available (see Burton 443–451), but the important details can be briefly summarized.

Part of Bunting's job at Victoria involved teaching a creative writing course, but in an interview with a local paper following a poetry reading on his arrival, he ridiculed the notion of creative writing as academic discipline. As an advocate of the new subject, Skelton took offence, and wrote a furious letter to Bunting questioning his professional conduct. Because Skelton also copied the letter and sent it to other faculty members, Bunting threatened to sue and refused to begin work until the matter was settled. Eventually Skelton apologized, and Bunting assumed his teaching duties. But relations with his colleagues had been irretrievably soured, and he passed a lonely few months in Victoria until his return to the UK in May 1972.

## To Jonathan Williams

MS Buffalo

14 November 1971 Care of English Department, The University, Victoria B.C., Canada

Dear Jonathan –

Your letter was perhaps more welcome than you'd expect. Letters dont pour in on me (not the sort of letters I want to read) and this university is full of the most repugnant people you can imagine. Those who are not blackguards are bores. I'll look up your friend Atchley:[158] but I think he is a man I was introduced to the first

[158] Dana Atchley (1941–2000), American photographer and designer who collaborated with Williams on the print series *Six Rusticated, Wall-Eyed Poems* (1969). He taught in the art department at Victoria between 1969 and 1971.

day I was here, who asked if I knew you, but who was off the same week for several months in U.S.

If I see the libraries I'll try to get in a word about your papers. The "special collections" man has asked to see me, but I am wary of everybody here. None of them seem to mean any good and my situation is very precarious.

Look in on Sima at Shadingfield if you are visiting Newcastle: she's always pleased to see you, and I think she is a bit short of company now that both children are at the university. I'm sorry you're "out" with Tom Pickard. He is thorny, yes. However, I find it possible – no, necessary – to laugh at all my friends and I presume, or hope, they laugh at me. How else we are to thole[159] the ridiculous burden of human oddity I dont know. Tom is also young – raw.

The industrious but possibly thick headed young man in Toulouse who has been writing to you also plagues me.[160] I dont know of anyone in Fort Worth. There are too or three more. I expect they'll get on your track sooner or later because of the interview – pamphlet.

The "brief exotic poem" amused me. Hope you keep busy and manage to dodge financial compulsions.

And if you see Mary Dawson, say I asked after her.

I've had to bring a libel action against Skelton, an outrageous attack, without provocation, calling me all sorts of cheat. Stuart Montgomery has the details. Here, where there's a smell of blackmail pervading the campus like a whole tribe of skunks, and public scandals in every department, it's no news. I'm told it was really aimed to discredit the man who got me invited here.[161] But they are all terrified of Skelton, especially the senior authorities. No one speaks to me any more, since he declared hostility. The strain is a bit much for an old man, and if I could feed my family any other way I'd walk out.

Meanwhile all good fortune to you (and Tom)

Yours

B.

[159] *Thole*: endure, tolerate (Northern English).

[160] Anthony Suter's article 'Time and the Literary past in the Poetry of Basil Bunting' was published in *Contemporary Literature*, Vol. 12, No. 4 (Autumn 1971). Suter was a graduate student (later lecturer) at the University of Toulouse.

[161] Mike Doyle (b. 1928), Anglo-Irish poet, academic, and a long-running antagonist of Skelton. He was responsible for inviting BB to Victoria.

## To Sister Victoria Forde[162]

MS Durham

1 January 1972

Care of English Department, The University,
Victoria B.C., Canada

Dear Miss Forde –

Surely, Sister Pitz may use lines from Briggflatts for her etchings:[163] and surely too, I would be honoured to be given a set. I suppose she had the customers she needs. It is possible that the Laing Art Gallery, Newcastle-on-Tyne, or the gallery at the university there might be interested,[164] but they would want to see the etchings, and that might be a fussy business.

Thankyou for the information about your Persian friends.

I dont think there is likely to be any other reading in Victoria; and it is clear that I shall have no chance of travelling elsewhere on the continent to read, unless it were at Vancouver or Seattle, presumably too far away for you; but even these are not likely. My fees are Enormous, so it may be just as well!

Please give Sister Pitz my compliments. Is she allowed to pray for heretics? There is a convent in Sicily where I'm told they still pray for me because of some trifling politeness I was able to show them during the war. It is something to value. And I in turn will think of her in meeting (I'm a Quaker) or next time I visit St. Cuthbert's tomb at Durham.[165]

Yours faithfully
B Bunting

The following two letters show Bunting in a rare (for this period) mood of creative excitement. Returning from his torrid short year in Victoria by boat via the Panama Canal, he

[162] **Sister Victoria Forde**: literary critic and nun who corresponded with BB from the early 1970s, after making enquiries relating to her doctoral thesis at the University of Notre Dame.

[163] Sister Pitz: presumably a contemporary of Forde at the University of Notre Dame.

[164] In the 1970s the two main art galleries in Newcastle were the Laing (a traditional municipal gallery built during the city's Edwardian heyday, which contains *The Destruction of Sodom and Gomorrah* by John Martin (1789–1854) and a handful of pre-Raphaelite works) and the Hatton (a more modern university gallery which contains Kurt Schwitters's third and final *Merzbau*, and which hosted Richard Hamilton's seminal 'Man, Machine and Motion' exhibition in 1955).

[165] Under threat of Viking invasion in the late 9th century Saint Cuthbert's remains were exhumed by the monks of Lindisfarne. After being carried to various locations throughout the north-east they were eventually deposited in Durham, giving rise to a shrine around which the cathedral and city developed. Cuthbert's shrine remains a centrepiece of Durham Cathedral (see **10/5/53** and note).

had an epiphany inspired by the simultaneous sight of a young girl and the appearance of a new moon. However, in spite of Bunting's hope that this might lead to a new 'sonata', no such work was forthcoming, and even the fragments sometimes associated with the episode seem to bear little or no relation to it (see below note).

## To Hugh Kenner

TS Texas

9 May 1972 Shadingfield, Wylam, Northumberland

Dear Hugh K

The long voyage is over and I've not finished reading The Pound Era, though nearly.[166] It was very kind of you to send it, and it's clear that it will bear rereading more than once. You've a wonderful skill to keep it lively and a Sherlock Holmes touch that would be fascinating even if the reader didnt agree with your deductions: but this reader almost always does. It must not go among the ruck of criticism out of reach on my top shelves, but have a handy place of its own. I forsee much showing it to visitors.

(Two years divorce from my typewriter accounts for the eccentric spelling I commit and will commit for a week or two: but I found more than FIFTY letters waiting at Wylam to be answered, among them some of real importance. Yet this is the second I've written. You must put up with the bad typing in view of the priority.)

My year at Victoria was a nasty mess. However, I've almost forgotten the place already. There are no new jobs in sight and perhaps they are not very likely to loom over the horizon any more for a man of my age, however he needs them. It's time I wrote something new, and I think that may just possibly happen, for ideas I've had in my head which would not hold together seem to have found a keystone in the most astonishing way,[167] round a very young girl noticed on the boat,

[166] *The Pound Era*: Kenner's monumental 1971 study of Pound and his modernist coevals (Joyce, Eliot, Lewis).

[167] An untitled poem of 1978 included in Share is subtitled 'opening of "A New Moon"?' apparently at Peter Quartermain's suggestion. Even if this is a fragment of a destroyed or unfinished longer work, it does not seem to relate to the experiences described here and in the following letter other than in use of a (highly generalized) nautical setting. The canonical ode 'Such syllables flicker out of grass' has a more plausible connection: a draft version was attached to 23/5/72, and BB described another version sent to Peter Quartermain as a 'working draft of the opening lines of "A New Moon"' (Share, 448). However Quartermain maintains that a variant version of this poem (also included in Share) was composed much earlier, in

who seems to be the new moon in person and is, by ancestry and name, goddess of the flowers too, for she's a descendant of Linnaeus.[168] Very remote the moon is. No use crying for it. Fragments of Leda's egg still hang on her down.[169] And I watched the occultation of Jupiter off the coast of Baja California and its end, the silver seed of her father dripping from the new moon's flank. Oh, very complex, no doubt, and the willows that bury the pitheap are in it too, and the emptiness where the coal was that they call the goaf. But how do you make the mythology vanish into what it implies? And still hold the thing together? I wait for the sounds.

I've hardly set my feet firmly on Wylam soil yet or nodded to my family, so if I neglect the proper ceremonies of letter writing you'll allow me to. At least I can, with genuine interest, ask after your daughters and sons and Mrs Kenner, all of whom have supplied me with nice memories that seem permanent.

I need hardly wish you success. You have it.

Yours gratefully
B Bunting

## To Sister Victoria Forde

TS Durham

23 May 1972 Shadingfield, Wylam, Northumberland

Dear Sister Victoria

Your letter came this morning, thankyou. Yes, the month of sea and sun did me a great deal of good. I am clearing up a great heap of chores that were waiting for me at a reasonable speed and hope to get down to work before long.

1969–1970 (Share, 472), and indeed none of the versions seem to contain any reference to the boat journey of 1972 (though one does allude to 'the emptiness where the coal was that they call the goaf' mentioned to Kenner here). Even if 'Linnaea' did offer a 'keystone' around which to organize prior ideas, she does not seem to feature even indirectly in any of the surviving fragments of BB's final years—and so ultimately the possibility of a tantalizing 'lost work' with an evocative Gravesian title must be set beside the more banal reality that only a handful of very short works have survived from the entire post-*Briggflatts* period, none of which explicitly mention the 'New Moon' conceit or its apparent inspiration.

[168] Carl Linnaeus (1707–1778), Swedish botanist who formalized the modern two-part Latin naming system for living organisms.

[169] BB's treatment of mythological sources here and in the following letter is, as he says, complex, recalling Pound's practice in the *Cantos* of building up elaborate patterns of allusion around a central image (and possibly inspired by BB's concurrent reading of Kenner's *The Pound Era*). According to one line of argument, Helen of Troy, who is said to have emerged from an egg born of the encounter between Leda and Zeus/Jupiter, is an iteration of the moon goddess Selene (Selanna).

I dont suppose I can be very much help to you. Small things first. "Archipiada" is a mysterious person mentioned in Villon's Ballade des Dames etc.[170] Guesses are no use – most editors tell you that St Thomas made some confusion and thought that Alcibiades was a woman, but I think that is based on a misreading of St Thomas's text, and anyway that Villon, who was far from profound in his theological studies, probably never read St Thomas with sufficient attention to remember such a minute detail. So for me she is any product of the imagination. As for the author of more plays than Shakespeare, he was Gerhard Hauptmann.[171] He and his entourage are perfectly recognizable, but not, of course, from acquaintance with his writings only.

For sonatas, Kenneth Cox's study of my "Villon" in "Stony Brook," 1969 issue, might clear up some difficulties.[172] It is no use pushing any analogy too far, and the analogy of poetry and music has some obvious limitations. The most fundamental is that poetry can carry only one line of sound at a time, music many. Pound, I think, and certainly Zukofsky, tries to get some of the effect of many voices by letting them work, not simultaneously, but in quick succession, much as Bach managed to give an illusion of fugal writing on an unaccompanied violin, each voice implying what went on while it was overlaid (or suspended) by a different one. I have never been happy with that. I prefer to let the poem be shaped by the fact that only one voice is ever really audible at a time. That is part of the reason for returning from Beethoven to Scarlatti – Scarlatti generally lets one voice predominate decisively. His sonatas are, as you say, single, except a few written late in his career, but it was an obvious development to link two or three or four of them together in an age that was making so much of the dance suite. Something very like that had already been done by Corelli in his Concerti Grossi.[173] And that is, of course, what happened in J.C. Bach and others. The dance suite origin is made plain by the final movements, mostly minuets, rondos, etc. The thematic links in the earlier dance suites were attenuated or dropped: but 19th century composers often brought them back again in their sonatas. I wanted something not rigid, but capable of a kind of hidden continuity, and a string of movements made like Scarlatti's but unobtrusively linked seems what was wanted. It is perhaps fortunate that though I knew Scarlatti well I did not then know much of

[170] Archipiada: angelic figure who comforts the speaker in BB's 'Villon' (Part III, 21) during a dark night of the soul in a prison environment.

[171] BB knew the German dramatist and novelist Gerhart Hauptmann (1862–1946) from his time in Rapallo.

[172] See Cox's 'A Commentary on Basil Bunting's "Villon",' *Stony Brook Poetry Journal* III–IV (Fall 1969), 59–69.

[173] Corelli's *Twelve Concerti Grossi* were published posthumously in 1714.

Corelli, or I would have tried to emulate his aetherial largos and the way he makes the angels dance jigs, and I would have failed utterly instead of only relatively.

I dont want to challenge comparison with Eliot. His mind and mine were exceedingly different. I've never wanted to be precise in his sense of precision. Now to follow anything very closely, as the young Eliot followed certain verse forms – Jacobean blank verse, for instance – is to some extent to be controlled by the model instead of controlling it. Music has suggested certain forms and certain details to me, but I have not tried to be consistent about it. Rather, I've felt the spirit of form, or of a procedure, without trying to reproduce it in any way that could be demonstrated on a blackboard. (There's no "one-one" relationship between my movements and any of Scarlattis) You could say the same of the detail of sound. Eliot – and Kipling – show prodigious skill in fitting words to a prearranged pattern, very admirable: yet they dont do it without losing some suppleness. To my ear their beats seem to be trodden out too heavily. In the same way, the Four Quartets, with their reproduction of the architecture of The Waste Land, and the deliberate emphasis on the musical parallel which, in the Waste Land, was an accidental result of Pound's cutting, seem stiff to me. Critical notions are in control from outside so that the poem is constrained to fit them, as though it had never been conceived in the form it wears. Well, I fail too, perhaps from lack of just the kind of skill I am attributing to Eliot and Kipling. But I never have, on the one hand, something I want to say, and on the other, a form I want to say it in. My matter is born of the form – or the form of the matter, if you care to think that I just conceive things musically. There's no fitting, at least consciously. Whatever you think I am saying is something I could not have said in any other way.

Always the complete architecture of the poem is implied in every line; and when that has to be abandoned, the poem is lamed, as The Spoils is lamed. Or should I say, lopsided.

I've nothing on tape except Briggflatts; and no tape recorder available. If Quatermain cannot get you a copy of the Briggflatts from UBC I'll have my own tape copied for you. There's a young man who wants to record the lot, but he's not very persistent and I dont think it will ever get done.

Hafez: If I'd thought there was very much of Hafez left in the product I'd have put it with the other translations.

Pym-Randall Press: 361 Harvard Street, Cambridge, Mass.

It may illuminate what I've said about sonata form or any other form if I tell you what happened on the voyage home.[174] I'd had a number of themes in my

[174] See 9/5/72 and notes.

head for at least three years, some longer, but could do nothing with them because they didnt seem to join together or oppose each other in any way that suggested their proper shape. Then one night I saw the new moon, the very first new moon, emerging from the old moon as Helen, Selanna, the new moon, must have emerged from Leda's egg; and the next night I watched Jupiter occulted by the then invisible old moon reappear as a drop of molten silver sliding down the flank of the new moon. And as I turned away from this marvelous sight I caught a glimpse of a very young girl who seemed obviously the new moon in flesh, slim, graceful, blond; and instantly many old themes began to assemble themselves as though this were the keystone enabling them to form an arch, themes of renewal, mainly, closely bound, though I had never perceived it. And this was wonderfully reinforced when I spoke to the girl and found her name was Linnaea and she a descendant of Linnaeus who named all the flowers, as though she were Persephone as well as Selanna. There was even the germ of an anti-theme ready to fit in, though that needs more perception before I can use it. I cannot say more yet: but it seems to me that I shall soon be able to begin work on a sonata, or what is more likely to prove a sonata than not, with the transformations of the first theme all worked out though those of the second may delay me.

Perhaps I expect more of myself than an old man can carry out; but I feel more confident and gayer than I've felt for years, and at least there is an example for you of how the matter fits itself together, with no intervention from the conscious me: whereas I think TSE did much of his work very cerebrally. My difficulty may be to hide the myths in something more ready to the contemporary mind. Corelli would have seen in them types of the resurrected God, but he wouldnt have underlined that. It would have been hidden in jigs and long, long notes that you can take merely as delights.

Yours faithfully
B Bunting

## To Denis Goacher

TS Buffalo

12 June 1972

Shadingfield, Wylam, Northumberland

Dear Dennis

This is, again, a long delay. Stupid chores needed my attention, and broken contact lense made it difficult to attend for long together. Besides, I'm lazy, disinclined to do anything but idle for a time. I'm stationary too, since the old car has expired of rust and age and the new one, the smallest I can sit in, isnt yet here. And when I've done whatever needs doing, and looked about me and said hallo to the people I like – those within reach – I've a poem half-formed in my head, but nothing yet on paper. All causes of delay.

I am sorry you're so deep in gloom. It's a state of affairs I've plenty of experience of. Money in your pocket and tolerable wine in your belly go a long way to cure it, but may be hard to come by. Of course I'll recommend you to Sheffield or any other rookery if I'm ever asked. It is more wearing than you seem to suppose: easier to lecture than to sit improvising answers to the questions the young ask. Six or seven hours of that takes a full day to recover from. "WHY dont you like what Stephen Spender writes?" "If you like Charles d'Orleans,[175] how can you possibly like Carlos Williams too?" "Why didnt Whitman write in rhyme?" "You say sound is what matters, and then you tell us to read Spenser's Fowre Hymnes and note how he improved on Pico.[176] Can you reconcile that?" – And so on. Theseus couldnt have got to the centre of such a maze as they set up. The effort to get there is exhausting.

No, I wouldnt want to write, or even read, the life of Sir Michael Ansell ABC DEF GH.[177] But then, I didnt want to write or read comments on the Stock Exchange List, but I did it for some years without expiring of it. I'm sorry you have to bother with such things, and they are always horribly obtrusive; but the damage can be limited to the loss of time so long as you dont get interested in it, or in making it pay.

I've no cure to offer for middle age. Patience. When it begins to turn into old age there are consolations. You get kissed by pretty girls who think antiques are safe, and you dont have to dig the garden any more. I like children more and more, and if you've got some around you'll find they too seem to think old men are safe playmates, where middleaged ones are potentially savage.

I cant suggest how to "get on." I don't think you'd ever have stooped to the university rings which, as you observe, enable their members to live by mutual back-scratching or by a sort of free-mason slyness (such as I associate more

[175] Charles of Orléans (1394–1465), medieval French poet.

[176] Spenser's *Fowre Hymnes* (published in 1596 but begun much earlier) drew on the courtly, neo-Platonic tradition of Italian poets such as Girolamo Benivieni (1453–1542), whose work inspired the *Commento sopra una canzone d'amore di Girolamo Benivieni* by Giovanni Pico della Mirandola (1470–1533), a famous Renaissance treatise on love.

[177] Michael Ansell (1905–1994), British soldier, show-jumping administrator and polo player. Goacher was ghostwriter of two autobiographies for Ansell: *Soldier On* (1973) and *Riding High* (1974).

closely with the Winchester tie).[178] No doubt there are others like Kipling who idealize such arrangements without apparently ever suspecting how ninetenths of the eligible exploit them for gain, but they are in fact shabby dodges to profit at the expense of the public. Better to endure poverty and insignificance.

By the way, that was a good "Playboy" on BBC1 last night.[179] An excellent Christy Mahon and a good Da, though I didnt think much of Pegeen Mike turned into a screecher. Not all the current actors are scum!

Log Book is not on my shelves.[180] It may be hovering around British Columbia. Faber wont risk anything, I'm sure. Cape might, conceivably, but the smaller presses are a likelier bet. Fulcrum is still hard up for cash flow, I think, and though that will mend, it may mean longish waiting. So Rosamund must hang around like a High Court litigant. Ever think of trying Jonathan Williams? He does books too handsomely to make profits and therefore not many books, but he's open-minded.

I dont want to read unnecessarily. I read for Tom's Tower the other day, with BBC cameras turning. They were surprised and pleased by my saqi, a pretty lass of fourteen to keep my wine glass filled, so they focussed on her and paid her five quid and took her with us to dinner after. Is the Beaford Centre that place tied up with Dartington?[181] I dont know why I've conceived a distaste for Dartington. Perhaps because they are rich, perhaps because they seem so selfsatisfied. I like Wennington, where they've no money, no patrons, and no reputation, but just run a school without rules because they like kids.[182] They get no space in Time and Life, no time on TV, and the teachers work for about half-pay, but the kids are happy, dirty, rather ragged, and delightful. About half of them are sent there by county councils who think their homes arent fit to live in, and they arrive sulky, sometimes suicidal and almost unmanageable. Then after a month or two of roaming about the woods with and without clothes on and sleeping where they

[178] Winchester College: public school in Hampshire. Its distinctive red-and-blue-striped tie connotes the elitism of the 'old boy network', a web of friendships between male former members of the major public schools, which dominated—arguably still dominates—English political and cultural life. See also **17/6/78**.

[179] BBC adaptation of *The Playboy of the Western World* by John Millington Synge (1871–1909), directed by Alan Gibson.

[180] Goacher's *Logbook*, which contained translations of Aeschylus, Euripides, Dante, Corbiere, Rimbaud, and others, was published by Grosseteste Press in 1972.

[181] Dartington: village in Devon, south-west England. It was the location of a progressive boarding school (Dartington Hall School) between 1926 and 1987, and the Beaford Centre (now Beaford Arts), a rural arts organization.

[182] Wennington Hall: progressive, Quaker-inspired institution founded in 1940 in Lonsdale, Lancashire.

choose singly or together, they begin to turn up at lessons and eventually pass their A and o levels very efficiently.[183] I enjoyed my weekend there a couple of years ago, and some of the kids are still writing to me from time to time. The young lady whom I met crossing a meadow on her way to the swimming bath clothed in a bangle, all fourteen years of her, stays in my memory too. But nobody suggests or encourages odd behaviour to them. They arent told they are better or more cultured or more liberal than the rest of us, and I suspect that at Dartington they are. There are no fees at Wennington – most of the kids couldnt pay anyway: only, a few rich parents are pressurised to pay a lot.

My long voyage home put Victoria out of my mind. I liked the forest ground around the Panama Canal, and I liked the blacks in Jamaica; and there was a day at Lisbon, beautiful city, seen again after forty years, and remembered in detail enough to pick out an excellent cheap feeding shop, with huge trout and lashings of green wine. I stayed aboard at the more offensively Americanised places. A shipload of horrors, of course, redeemed by a very pleasant New England doctor and a most beautiful young Finnish-American girl, like the new moon, but, alas, almost as remote. A descendant of Linnaeus, and called after him.

I'll be mobile shortly, and will try to reach Devonshire: but it is a long way.

Yours ever
B

## To Gordon Browne

TS Durham

7 September 1972 Shadingfield, Wylam, Northumberland

Dear Gordon Browne

I've no idea just when your Benedict Biscop festival takes place; but in any case I could only read once. I've not enough stuff to read more.

In this case I'm not concerned with a fee. You probably know that nowadays I get £100, but its as certain as can be that your festival cannot afford anything like that, so I'd be content merely to have comfortable arrangements for transport and my own idea of how to arrange the hall for reading in it. Benedict and Bede, Cuthbert and Wilfrid,[184] are entitled to be remembered without pay.

[183] A levels (the Advanced Level of the General Certificate of Educations): standard British school leaving qualification. For O levels see note to **11/10/68**.

[184] BB alludes to Northumbrian saints associated with Benedict Biscop (*c.*628 – 690), founder of the twin monasteries Monkwearmouth–Jarrow, both in County Durham. Saint Wilfrid (*c.*633–*c.*709), a friend of Benedict, was the founder of Hexham Abbey and a major figure in the

I'm in pretty good condition, only hampered by chores, one of which is letter-writing; so I wont prolong this.

I hope you're well.

Yours

B

## To Denis Goacher

TS Durham

6 November 1972

Shadingfield, Wylam, Northumberland

Dear Denis

I think I wrote to you shortly after I got home from Devon, but I'm not quite sure – I find no note of it. If it got overlooked in a heap of other things, I'm sorry. There has been a heap of things, more and more troublesome, the worst just over, but I'm not writing now to bother you with my troubles.

I've just been in Newcastle with Tom Pickard (Morden Tower), Philip Bomford (Northern Arts) and the head respectively of the English Department and the university theatre and its resident rep. company, and the Northern Sinfonia Orchestra, planning a memorial concert for Ezra.[185] I was too upset to do it last week. The notion is this: we can have the theatre on Sunday November 16 – it holds 449 audience – at 8 p.m., besides rehearsals during the previous week. There I will speak for about four minutes to get going: the sinfonia will play Vivaldi's "Seasons," ending with "Spring," EP having been the chief reviver of Vivaldi. Between these pieces I will read an early Canto, Tom Pickard a stretch from the Pisans, Jon Silkin and Tony Harrison bits from Propertius and Cathay respectively (Cathay for those of the audience who cant grasp anything more complicated), and when "Spring" ends, the actors will do a part, what there's time for, of The Women of Trachis, probably the last ¾ hour of it or thereabouts.[186] They want you, as a friend of EP's, to play Herakles.

introduction of Roman Christianity to Northumbria, as was Cuthbert. Bede's (672/3–735) *Ecclesiastical History of the English People* was written from his monastic home in Jarrow.

[185] Pound died on 1 November 1972. BB's memorial concert brought together the Newcastle literary community in a concert held at the recently opened University Theatre (now Northern Stage) at Newcastle University, with a programme as described here.

[186] See note to 20/1/65.

Of course there is no cash in it. Everybody is doing it for nothing or bare expenses except the orchestra which is debarred by its subsidy from doing anything gratis but is making a very low price indeed. If you will be Herakles you'd get your fare, and you'd stay, I hope, with us at Wylam for the few days necessary. On the other hand, this seems likely to be much the most elaborate wake for EP in England and will be advertised in London, so that the audience will be worth playing to, besides the pious satisfaction of doing something Ezra might have liked.

I think the idea is to do the play in lounge suits or the like, but I'm not sure. Production of the whole affair is in the hands of Gareth Morgan,[187] who will let you know what he has in mind. Organisation and programme are being done by Tom Pickard.

So if you are willing to help us, since the time is very short for organizing and advertising, will you please phone at once:

Me 066-14-3255
Morgan 0632-27184 (or his home, 0632-34335)
Pickard 0632-29460 (Home 0632-74430)

Of course I would pass on your message: but we are all so busy it might be overlooked, and anyway not a single one of us can either ask all the proper questions or answer all the questions you'll need to ask, so if possible please phone all three. Reverse charges, at least as far as I am concerned – I forgot to ask the others that. When you know about rehearsals, come to Wylam at the appropriate time and from there on things are easy to arrange.

Please do it if you possibly can.

I dont suppose I've remembered all I ought to write, but I lack time if I'm to catch tonight's post. Therefore I'll sonly send my love to your wife and children.

Yours ever
B

Deficit if any met by Northern Arts & University

Surplus if any worth mentioning, an E.P. prize or the like; if small, Morden Tower, for readings

[187] Gareth Morgan (d. 2008), actor and theatrical director in charge of the Gulbenkian Theatre, a smaller studio venue within the larger University Theatre building.

## To George Oppen

TS Buffalo

16 January 1973

Shadingfield, Wylam, Northumberland

Dear Mr Oppen

Thankyou for the book.[188]

I do not think that I am qualified to say anything about it. It is, to begin with, American and I am not; and it seems, secondly, to be written by someone who knows what's going on amongst poets, and I dont.

You have, you Americans, tasks – creating a language, inventing a history – which we escape in England. That leaves our poets a freedom they dont know what to do with, so that they seem and usually are aimless. On the other hand it leaves some of yours unaware that skill and patience are wanted.

I've wondered lately whether intelligence and reading are not handicaps, very poor substitutes for a sharp eye or an attentive ear. All my generation, which isnt so much older than yours, were too bookish, except WCW. Yet I'm disgusted by the crowd of writers who have read only Time or some less durable antagonist of Time. Perhaps a poet's training should be in biology or physics. Too many of us live in echo chambers.

Now I see I've written too much for civility and perhaps too little for the something more than civility I wanted to show. I'd better end.

Yours faithfully
B Bunting

## To George Oppen

TS Buffalo

6 February 1973

Shadingfield, Wylam, Northumberland

Dear George Oppen

Yes of course I've not forgotten we met in Rapallo, and for a moment in San Francisco. But you are taking me far too seriously. I've no longer any idea what I wrote to you; but, whatever I said, I dont write letters for posterity but for pulp, and probably my only intention was to indicate that I was pleased to have your book, to be reminded of you, and that I'd given it some preliminary attention. Certainly I havent "read" it in any way that implies close attention. I've little time and many distractions. But I've noted it as a book worth attention when there's

[188] Oppen's *Seascape: Needle's Eye* was published by Sumac Press in 1972.

leisure for it. All the same, I did read rapidly every page, which I dont always do with the books that reach me. I read little that hasnt been in print for several centuries.

I may also have been considering that most of the people who write to me or whose names I notice are parts of what is called "the world of letters." They often know each other and read others books and articles, and have done so for many years. But I vanished to the Canaries, the high seas, and ultimately Persia long, long ago, so that I've read very little of what has been read between 1932 and 1970. There are advantages in that, but there is also the disadvantage that I cannot take part in current literary conversation and therefore must give people the impression of either being an ignoramus or thinking myself too lofty to share their concerns. It doesnt worry me in the least, but it needs explaining because it sometimes worries other people.

I think all our generation – Ezra to Oppen – were too bookish in letting too much of their reading escape onto the page: bad enough when they were learned, too bad when, like me, they werent. This will tell against us all one of these days. (Exception, WCW) Yet its better than the lazy ignorance of a lot of our contemporaries. Care and attention, surely! Long labour. Complexity and what asses call obscurity. But sentence by sentence, phrase by phase, we ought to have been more perspicuous than any of us are. If I use, for instance, three words from one of Aldhelm's letters[189] I ought not to expect the reader to recognise the quotation and supply the possible associations. He, the reader, probably hasnt read Aldhelm and may not even know who he was. But worse still to borrow from one's private past words and references nobody can conceivably dig out. I think I was probably trying to say to you that WCW's clinical training, of the eyes, of the precise reporting of what's seen, has somehow to be incorporated into the practise of the more complex poets before we get where we all set out to go.

Yet I admit that I feel far surer of Hugh McDiarmid, with all his parade of learning, and even David Jones, whose footnotes are an encyclopedia of odd knowledge, than I do of anybody left over since Ezra's death (bar LZ, whose stubbornness is a virtue outweighing some things I dont like).

What you say of Briggflatts overvalues it.[190] A nice noise, but not faultless even as noise. The books are not fearfully obtrusive, but there's more evidence than should have been left of the means by which effects are reached.

[189] Saint Aldhelm (*c.*639–709), Anglo-Saxon priest, scholar, and poet praised by Bede in the *Ecclessiastical History*. Much of Aldhelm's correspondence survives.

[190] Oppen was an admirer of *Briggflatts*, writing on its publication to his sister June Oppen Degnan: 'Basil Bunting appears in the Jan Poetry with a long poem. Unforgettable; Creeley told

Did you ever read Goethe's Italienishe Reisebuch?[191] Now and then he forgets to be smug and just describes something at which he is still wondering, and it stays in your mind.

If all this puzzles you as much as the previous letter, I'm sorry. It would take months to make myself clear.

Anyway, all the best

Yours

B.

## To Jonathan Williams

TS Buffalo

26 February 1973

Shadingfield, Wylam, Northumberland

Dear Jonathan

Glad to get your card and to think that you'll be at Dent again by May. You've been missed, though I find the winter has kept me in in a way it never used to.

News is so little and so unimportant it can keep a few months. I read at Cardiff the other day – Wales paid me decently, and the people I met were pleasant; and next morning I had two hours before my train to look at Cardiff. Once you've lost sight of the mean railway station it is a very attractive city, new to me, and looks alive too. All in one, docks and castle and shops, all one concord. Do you know it?

But they told me the speculators have persuaded it to get rebuilt in huge flat-sided towers of offices. To no useful end whatever, merely to fill the pockets of fools who are too rich already. However the bulldozers havent got there yet, and I hope some general bankruptcy of all the greedy idiots may yet save Cardiff and what's left of Newcastle. There's a smell of bankruptcy in the air, something like, say, 1928; and a stench of repression of such as I dont remember even in 1926. It's hard to compare depths of stupidity and baseness, yet I've a suspicion that I'm watching the worst bout of misgovernment there's been in my lifetime, and not only in England. I'm not usually a revolutionary, too aware of what's rightly permanent, but I'd welcome a 1789 or 1917 rather than another decade of this.

you rightly...I'd been finding the poetry which is current impossible if not ridiculous until the Bunting arrived to make such undertaking seem ponderable again.' See George Oppen, *The Selected Letters of George Oppen*, edited by Rachel Blau DuPlessis (Durham: Duke University Press, 1990), 129–30.

[191] Goethe's *Italienische Reise* (*Italian Journey*), a diaristic account of his travels in Italy in 1786–1788, published 1816–1817.

Also I think that unless financial incompetence destroys the system first, as it almost did in 1930, some revolution, whether from the people or from a lot of wouldbe Diocletians and Mussolinis, is sure in much less than a generation.

I dont often bother you with politics. Overlook it.

Yours faithfully
B.

## To Denis Goacher

TS Durham

8 April 1973

Shadingfield, Wylam, Northumberland

Dear Denis

Poetry International, which is the mask of the Poetry book Society, which is Charles Osborne, has asked me to do an hour and a quarter, more or less, of Pound at the Institute of Contemporary Arts on June 27; and has suggested that I might like someone else to help.[192] I've said I'd like you to, and that if that suits them, they must offer you not only return fare to London, but a fee what would make the formidable work involved worth doing. They should be writing to you once they've got my letter, sent at the same time as this, and I hope to goodness they forget the parsimony they usually display – I myself get either nothing (tribute to EP) or something ludicrously tiny. But that's my affair, and I intend them to deal at least reasonably with you. If you dont hear from them pretty soon, I imagine it means that they cant bear to fork out.

Their intentions for the reading seem the usual vague thing – reminiscences, snippets. But I've told them we'll read Cantos only, in such a way as to display the structure of the poem. (The people who still take refuge from EP in Mauberly or Propertius are out of date). I'll go into details in a minute, and want your help to sort them out. I think I would not talk at all, or no more than two or three sentences, read "On the Flyleaf of Pound's Cantos" as an introduction, and then go straight ahead.

[192] In contrast to the Newcastle Pound memorial concert (see 6/11/72), the event described here was the work of London establishment organizations, which explains BB's mildly contemptuous tone (see also 4/7/73). The Poetry Book Society was founded by T. S. Eliot in 1953; it serves as a vehicle for the promotional culture of mainstream British verse, administering the annual T. S. Eliot Prize and announcing a quarterly series of 'recommended purchases'. In the late 1960s it initiated the Poetry International events (see 16/4/67 and note). Charles Osborne (1927–2017), Australian poet, critic, and Arts Council of Great Britain president 1971–1986, directed the PI programme from 1970. The Institute of Contemporary Arts (ICA): gallery and arts venue with countercultural leanings near Trafalgar Square in London.

I would not want to do the usual daisy picking with Usura and Pity and other chrysanthemums[193] – nor, of course, the long, often dull cantos in which the materials are dug up, but the cantos in which they are mixed with some freedom and fine results. There are alternatives. Either we begin with Cantos 1 & two, which set forth the scheme of the whole, and then select cantos or longish sections of the cantos in which the scheme is seen at work. (That needs no comment – those capable of poetry will see the bearings without any pointer). Or, if you want to take a chance of offending everybody except a few who really understand the poem, we could simply read Canto 74, the first of the Pisans, straight through. It is a very long canto, and would fill the time: but mainly, it is almost selfcontained, and in it, for the first time, all the assembled material mingles freely, fluidly, and makes something of its own that everybody can feel, even if they cant understand or explain.

You perceive that that is what I would like to do – you and I taking turns – but it would anger a lot of people I think, and I shrink from controversy at present. If you prefer the other way, then Canto One (you), Canto Two (me) and the rest selected from among the following: 4: 39: 47: 49: 79, from "O Lynx my love, my lovely lynx" to the end: 80, from 'Nancy where art thou? To the end: 81, from "What counts is the cultural level" to the end: 90: 91: 106: 114. That list, of course, is about three times as much as we have time for. I reckon we could do about 700 lines, maybe a trifle less. I think you read faster than I do, but I'm not sure. If this second way pleases you, let me know at once which bits you think should be in, keeping (if your conscience will let you) within the fairly wide field I've set down. Then I'll say again, and we can get it down to size pretty quickly. Let me know, too, which ones you especially like to read yourself.

Perhaps it will be possible to arrange a meeting in London a day or two before the reading, when we could make some sort of rehearsal. Montgomery or Mottram, who lives fairly near, might have room for us.

I hope this attracts you. If not, I'll shoulder the whole bloody affair myself, for I cant think of any other reader I want to trust with the Cantos.

Let's hear. All the best

B

193 As BB intimates, 'Usura' (a section from Pound's Canto 45) and 'Pity' (from Canto 30) are often anthologized as easily digestible fragments of an otherwise far more difficult work. They are both simple anaphoric passages listing the vices and virtues of money-lending and pathos respectively, and as such are not especially representative of the sorts of historical and structural complexities BB admired in the *Cantos*.

## To Denis Goacher

TS Durham

12 April 1973

Shadingfield, Wylam, Northumberland

Dear Denis

Thanks for "Transversions."[194] There are some nice things there. O saisons, o chateaux[195] comes out well, for instance.

I'd write to the Arts Council and try to cadge whatever sums are going nowadays if I thought it would be the slightest use. However, since I myself am left in the dryest of deserts without even the mirage of a job or an income, I dont think I cut much ice. The hullaballoo about "Briggflatts" died away some time ago. Now half of them would want to know who I am and the other half would resent my existence.

Sudden appearance of winter, which has been missing this year, has upset hopes of getting about. Half April, so far, the Pennine passes have been closed and several times my daughter and son-in-law have been stuck in their cottage on the Roman Wall, unable to get the landrover through the drifts.

A local poet, James Kirkup, had spent many years in Japan.[196] As he was well-spoken of, I thought I'd have a look at his work with the notion of making him welcome; but my God! how can such stuff be printed, let alone read and praised. There's been a great heave back again of all the stupidest men in England, in the arts to match in politics. The hangers, black-kickers, censors, fatuous writers, squalid journalists, all intent on diverting attention from the plethora of super-spivs. It is wicked to strike because you havent enough to eat – the strikers, not the employers, are responsible for all the public inconvenience: and I think there is a strong inclination to regard any kind of art as waste, any acre of grass as a building site, any accidental moment of honesty as an affront to the advertisers.

Sorry. My love to your children. All the best to your wife and you.

Yours

B

[194] *Transversions,* containing more of Goacher's translations, was published by Grosseteste Press in 1973.

[195] 'Ô saisons, ô chateaux': poem from Rimbaud's *Illuminations* (1886).

[196] James Kirkup (1918–2009), poet and travel writer from South Shields (near Newcastle), who lectured at several Japanese universities in the late twentieth century.

## To Denis Goacher

TS Durham

4 July 1973 Shadingfield, Wylam, Northumberland

Dear Denis

I too met Auden, and was baffled by a sort of heaviness and dullness of mind. However, next morning I saw in the Sunday Times a few quotes from him about how lousy it is to publish people's letters, alive or dead, of which I approve so heartily that I wrote to him to say I'd have been more cordial if I'd known of them before.

And I agree, I think the reading made an impression:[197] but I am best pleased to have given an example of how to commemorate a poet with proper reserve and without indulging one's own vanity. I dont suppose that will have much effect, but it might have some.

Olga Rudge interrupted Shayer's explanation of what the ICA is: "Isee. The Apes of God."[198] For myself, I saw that even the typists have been taught to condescend to mere poets – almost more so than at the insufferable Arts Council. Probably the poets have brought it on themselves by toadying, which is the necessary consequence of public patronage for men who prefer not to starve.

I cant help about Cornish, since I keep no notes and dont know where I got the information – maybe somewhere unreliable, but there's an excellent book about composers and poets in that century, and I did note it's title somewhere – if I can ever find the note.[199]

So. Thanks indeed for your cooperation. I dont think I could have found the same skill with the same intelligence elsewhere, and I do think the piece would have been too long for me to tackle it as successfully alone. I hope my introductory remarks didnt diminish the effect too much.

Affection to the family.

Yours

B

[197] I.e. the Poetry International tribute to Pound (see 8/4/73 and notes).

[198] Rudge's pun alludes to Wyndham Lewis's caricatures of bohemian London in *The Apes of God* (see 17/6/30).

[199] A handwritten note by BB reads 'Bruce Pattison (the author)'. Pattison (1908–1996) published *Music and Poetry of the English Renaissance* in 1948; William Cornysh (1465–1523) was an English composer of the Henrician court.

## To Jonathan Williams

TS Buffalo

1 September 1973

Shadingfield, Wylam, Northumberland

Dear Jonathan

The spite of fate has frustrated all my attempts to get to Sedbergh this year.[200] Now, I have to turn up at hospital on the sixth to have my cancerous tendencies checked up – an annual, unproductive feast since they X-rayed away a rodent ulcer on my forehead some years ago. Also Henshaw is due on an unspecified day early in the month to fight the great Camlann final battle[201] of his war against the income tax ogres on my behalf, and I must be on hand to feed him Glen Fiddich and persuade Sima to provide him with a bed: not so easy as usual as the house is full of Persians.

I am sorry about Finlay: but not really.[202] You are better rid of him. I hope Stuart is not in for another strenuous pestering; but if he is, now that he spends all his time calming down very similar lunatics for University College Hospital he may know how to handle it.

I like the notion of Ginsberg singing to the sheep, but I myself find his music so dismally platitudinous that I dont think even my friendly feelings towards him will ever get me to sit out another hour of it.

I worked hard at Sligo amongst dull people – a lecture, two readings, and five seminars (where the students were all university lecturers) in a week – to earn a total of fees and alleged expenses which together came to just a pound or two short of real expenses; but I got a glimpse of preposterous Ulster and two days wandering about Connemara, a place worth seeing.[203] Witnessed a fight of tinkers, thirty of them, men and women, fighting each against all; and saw the same thirty an hour later sitting in a line by the church wall looking crestfallen and silent. I suppose all defeated each, a fairly satisfactory result. As picturesque as Spaniards were 40 years ago. All Irish cars have bent front fenders, and are driven at night without lights on the wrong side of the road. Bulls, rams, donkeys etc obstruct all roads, dead dogs and cats litter them anywhere near a town. Perhaps you know the place.

Yours, still anxious to see you,
B.

[200] Sedbergh: small town in the North Pennines near both Brigflatts and Williams's Dentdale cottage.

[201] Camlann: according to legend the site of King Arthur's last battle.

[202] I.e. Ian Hamilton Finlay (see **7/8/69** and commentary).

[203] BB was invited to speak at the annual Yeats International Summer School at Sligo in north-west Ireland in 1973. His lecture was published as 'Yeats Recollected', in *Agenda* 12/2 (Summer 1974). Connemara: remote, mountainous region of western Ireland.

## To Jonathan Williams

TS Buffalo

23 November 1973 oShadingfield, Wylam, Northumberland

Dear Jonathan,

Remiss and lethargic, I am, but I don't really intend to leave your letters unanswered or half answered. I am too depressed by the utter pennilessness now close ahead to stir myself in any way that might be agreeable.

I might just possibly skid over to Dentdale about December 13 or 14, if the weather isnt too tough for an old man; but if so I'll phone nearer the time, to see if you are free.

There are not many chores, but vexing ones, lectures I dont want to give and such, and always the enormous, unnecessary mass of stupid correspondence with fools who think I can somehow turn their silly verses into poetry. Even to say just "No" takes some minutes, and envelope and a stamp.

Your adventures in Cambridge dont surprise me. Never a year goes by but I am invited to Cambridge in terms which, at their extreme, reached: "Of course we cannot offer to pay any fee, but we will make sure you get a good meal." I answer roughly. Oxford doesnt quite treat me as a beggarman, still, it's much the same. Poorer universities have more sense, but yet one's usually out of pocket by going to them. London institutions are worse, if you allow for the extra expense. So far as my experience goes only Cardiff and Newcastle try to make a reading worthwhile.

I think I prefer your version of Catullus to LZ's.[204]

Glad, as you know, to hear that Mary Dawson is flourishing. I'm sorry the government is freezing her at meeting. As you say, Harrods is warm enough, and so are the cinemas and the striptease clubs.[205]

Childish Jon Silkin is trying to involve me in a scheme to make libraries pay authors per borrowing. I hope you arent taken in. First, however you juggle it, it's a tax on reading, bad for all writers and for the whole population. Second, the books borrowed by those who can pay a few pence are written by Micky Spillane,[206] or at least by people with purely commercial motives for pandering.

[204] Probably a reference to Williams's pamphlet *A Wee Tot for Catullus*, published by Moschatel Press in 1974.

[205] BB refers to the fallout from the 1973 Oil Crisis, which saw an embargo from the Organization of Arab Petroleum Exporting Countries (OPEC) cause severe energy shortages in the UK (though he hints here that wealthy establishments like the London department store Harrods were unaffected).

[206] Mickey Spillane (1918–2006), bestselling American crime novelist.

Good books are borrowed almost exclusively by the young, in process of education or self-education, who havent got the pence and will just have to give up reading. So the effect, at its first level, would be to encourage bad writing at the expense of good. Thirdly, these too will be disappointed, for whatever they get from such a scheme will soon be absorbed by the publishers, who will be able to offer even smaller advances and royalties than they do now. I cant imagine any more disastrous plan. There might be some sense in abolishing royalties altogether. Nobody would write then for gain, and there would be room for decent books. How few have ever earned money by writing well.

As for the arts councils...they have wonderfully multiplied the number of parasites on poets, composers and painters. The new National Poetry Secretariat[207] is very helpfully trying to fix a minimum (ie maximum) fee for readings at £12 plus third class fare, but hints that there are exceptions who might take less. Feed and lodge yourself. A decent reading is three days work at least, so if you do two a week you will earn a lump less than an agricultural labourer, but a bit more than a forestry labourer.

I am selling my miniscule investments – at the very worst moment – because there is no other way of going on living. They may last till early spring. I will not throw away the proceeds on giving readings, least of all to people who do not realise that it is not themselves giving alms.

Yours ever
B.

## To Jonathan Williams

TS Buffalo

7 August 1974 — Shadingfield, Wylam, Northumberland

Dear Jonathan

I'm afraid there are a number of things not acknowledged and notes unanswered. I get less like a civil servant every day. However, I must say something to your last letter.

I lost a contact lens, in a jam-packed train, and cant drive till I get a replacement (due now), when I shall go to your hospitable close if it's anyway possible. I am sorry Mary Dawson is leaving Sedbergh, and I would certainly like to see her again. And I'd like to make some contribution to the tercentenary of the meeting

[207] A subdivision of the Arts Council founded in 1973 to act as an agency for poets undertaking public reading engagements.

house, though you know I'm not much good at that kind of thing. I hope I'm there for your first sermon, and wager you'll be an elder in another ten years.

I've nothing much to tell you, though. The authorities (cunning) sent us an invitation to the Garden Party addressed to Sima, so that I had no chance to decline.[208] Sima, looking very elegant for the first time in her life, had a conversation with the queen, which made her next neighbour in the crowd faint with envy. She tackled the Chinese embassy contingent too. Enough to exalt her at Wylam Tennis Club for a long time to come.

But as Yahweh asked Iyyob "Why yammer?"[209] Enough, hasta la vista.

Yours ever

B.

## To Louis Zukofsky

TS Texas

2 October 1974

Shadingfield, Wylam, Northumberland

Dear Louis

Out of this jumble of years – where I've no business to be – I cannot sort even a rag to send you. So read, if you will, Wordsworth's "Complaint," to Coleridge, and all I find to say is said.[210]

Yours ever

B.

## To Roudaba Bunting Davido

TS Durham

14 October 1974

Shadingfield, Wylam, Northumberland

My dear daughter

Yes, it's a long time since I wrote, chiefly because I sink deeper and deeper into gloom, wondering how on earth I am to complete my responsibilities – get Tom

[208] Following a practice established by Queen Victoria, every summer the British monarch holds formal garden parties in the grounds of Buckingham Palace, to which those involved in some notable form of public service are invited. As the guest list can run into the several thousands, the chances of speaking directly to the queen, as Sima did, are slight.

[209] A quotation from Zukofsky's 'A'-15, which references the Book of Job (Iyyob).

[210] Wordsworth's 'A Complaint' (1807) mourns the decline of his relationship with Coleridge, with whom he became increasingly estranged in the first decade of the 1800s. The poem's expression of regret at a fading friendship echoes BB's sadness at his own estrangement from Zukofsky (for which see **30/3/67**). Zukofsky died four years later, in May 1978.

through college and provide something for Sima. It is terribly difficult to keep just short of final bankruptcy. There was a rather vague suggestion that I should dodge around New England during the winter, a week here, a month there, but it came to nothing, partly, I daresay, because of my lack of enthusiasm. I am glad it did, for I dont think I could face another North America winter and I'd be very unwilling to set about housekeeping for myself again now. Do you realise I'll soon be 75? Anyway, I like America less each time I go there. American men (if they're halfway prosperous) with gross bellies, American women like a field of cows, chewing, chewing, and pretending to have bigger udders than any cow has a right to. There's a rush to accept the easy way and pretend that it's the right way – of course, you find a similar disposition everywhere, but in America it is standard. O, I didnt intend to bellyache like that when I started this letter, but I certainly ought to tell you that I dont think I am very likely to be in the United States again.

But I'd like to see you. I wonder whether it will ever be possible to have you over here for a few months – or even weeks? I never forget what a loving baby you were, holding tight to me on Hampstead Heath, or going to sleep on my lap.

Your questions! Maria has no baby about yet. No, she got fed up with her house on the Roman Wall because the proprietors of Vindolanda have been trying to make a ballyhooed tourist trap of their excavations and have taken to unloading buses full of tourists almost on her doorstep.[211] I dont think I would mind tourists in season, and after all they only arrive in large numbers in the summer months: still, I recollect that in the course of about an hour and a half while I was left alone in the cottage in July no less than seven different people knocked and asked for water, what's the way to the Roman Wall?, do you do teas?, etc etc. So she's sold up (negotiations not quite complete yet) and bought a ruinous farmhouse high on the fellside by Allenheads,[212] which it will take ages to reconstruct sufficiently to keep a baby in it.

The views are very fine, the barn most picturesque. There's no fear of any tourists turning up there. But I wonder very much whether they will ever get it put to rights. Also, some of its virtues – quiet, a little chunk of usable land for ducks, geese, a pig, goats, a garden, – have corresponding vices: it's a long way to work in Hexham; it is part of two or three villages which are the highest and also the

[211] Vindolanda: Roman military fort *c.*AD 85–370. It is in west Northumberland, close to—but not part of—Hadrian's Wall. Since the 1930s the Birley family have conducted substantial excavations of the site—from 1970 opening up their work to the public by way of a museum and visitors' centre.

[212] Allenheads: small village in the Allen Valley (see **30/3/67**).

snowiest in the island, on a narrow lane where the district snowplow will be in no hurry to come, so that they may be cut off for a week or two in the winter; it is approached by a ford, with a stream subject to sudden floods, otherwise a long roundabout route in very narrow lanes indeed. There arent any neighbours – or yes, a couple of cottages a mile away across the ford. Still, I admit I'd like to live there if it were once straightened up. And John has discovered in some ancient deeds that possession of this farm gives him the right to run 92 sheep and six cows on the great common (not what you probably think of as a common, but a big stretch of exceedingly wild heather and bent grass on the top of the mountain.) By hiring this right out to local farmers he might be able to get enough to pay the rates – local taxes. They intend to live in a caravan during the first stage of rebuilding, but I think their baby, intended for next year, is postponed again. Maria is still teaching in her school for rich children. She likes it. The classes are very small. John is still telling the Hexham magistrates what they are entitled to do to the drunks and pilferers who come before them.

Tom went back to Durham, for his final year, ten days ago. Though he keeps to himself very severely and hardly says a word, I miss him. I see some real qualities in that lad, though I cant imagine how he will ever earn a living. He cut down the fuzzy-wuzzy bush on the top of his head some while since, but when he buys a new pair of jeans he carefully rubs a hole or two in them before he will put them on. Everything is dyed black. I tell him he looks like a bloody clergyman. Sima is as energetic as ever, playing tennis, running the tennis club, plastering, carpentering, even bricklaying, mixing and pouring concrete. As for me, I've still to go on responding to students at the university here, though less than lately. The other day I lectured, and was then taken by a handful of students to eat a curry violently hot, which may have contributed to the exhaustion I felt for four days afterwards. Tomorrow I go to London, to read at a largish gathering. Then back and to Durham, to open the annual meeting of Northern Arts, the government patronage body up here.[213] Then back to London to discuss some project I dont understand with a dozen people invited by the prime minster's chief wangler, Lord Goodman.[214] After that I may have a chance to look at some of my own business.

Is Bourtai still in Denver? Do you think she is reasonably happy? I sometimes worry about her, but dont know anything to do about it, nor even what sort of thing I could say to her. How is Saul? Has he grown more amenable and a bit

[213] BB's three-year term as president of Northern Arts began in 1974.
[214] Arnold Goodman (1915–1995), British lawyer and Arts Council chairman 1965–1972.

more sensible? Tod and Colin no doubt are much as one expects youngsters to be. What of Fenris and Gideon?

Finn wrote to me, and I cant remember whether I answered. I certainly intended to, for I like Finn a good deal, but it is very possible that the damned business of dealing with students and bad poets and the income tax and other botherations may have made me forget to. Give him my best wishes anyway. I'm glad your pretty Daphne is doing well, and Rustam to be a doctor, eh?

I'd have liked to look in on you and Monica at the nudist camp in Canada; but it's a long way from here. I hope you had fun there. Were there any decent looking young lasses, or were they all tough old women and fidgety old men? I've never been in a nudist camp. Maybe I've been missing my opportunities. Anyway, it would be a change from nursing dafties for you. Are you still interested in your job? Does it pay reasonably?

And Marian is bicycling about the dry lands, you say. I wonder how she keeps her vigour. I dont get actually ill, but I cant walk more than a short way, and that with a stick. I drive when I've time and the price of petrol, or else I end my journey at the nearest pub, or the next, and then go home.

I get nothing much written. "Agenda" printed an essay on Yeats a few weeks ago, really a lecture I gave last year at Sligo in the wild west of Ireland.[215] Two books are half done, but if they ever do get finished they wont be me at all – a selection of Skipsey's poems with an introduction, and a queer kind of anthology.[216] The young, who got excited in the years after "Briggflatts," have forgotten me again, and the old respectable dull institutions try to make use of me, but I'm not very forthcoming to them.

Tom Pickard is in London now – he and Connie parted – so I dont get him livening me up now and then as I used to. Stuart Montgomery (still terrified of you) is mad-doctoring, taking an exam this week which, if he passes, should open a lot of very well-paid positions to him. I don't remember who else you know. I hear nothing from Hugh Kenner, nor from the people (I forget the name but you'll remember them) who had two pretty young daughters and a son and kept a pet king-snake and sang lustily, at Santa Barbara.

[215] See 1/9/73 and note.

[216] BB edited a selection of Joseph Skipsey's poems for Ceolfrith Press (1976), a small, Sunderland publisher based in the city's art gallery. In the last years of his life he was also preparing—apparently with no concrete publication plans in mind—a historical anthology of poetry, including works by Homer, Aneirin, Heledd, Ferdowsi, Manuchehri, Hafiz, Dante, Wyatt, Malherbe, Spenser, Sidney, Wordsworth, Darwin, Pickard, Zukofsky, Yeats, Eliot, The Beatles, Ben Jonson, and others.

That's all, my dear. It's no good covering more paper with nothing more to tell you, though I'd like to hug you a bit and stroke your cheek. Useless and silent as I am, I still love my daughters.

B

I daresay I ought to add: Merry Christmas, for its as likely as not that I'll not be able to write again before then.

## To Roger Guedalla

TS Durham

25 November 1974 Shadingfield, Wylam, Northumberland

Dear Roger Guedalla

Flu, and subsequent depression have kept me from answering your Guy Fawkesday note; and thank you for it.

Your audience did less than justice to McDiarmid; and it was hard on Gael Turnbull to be sandwiched in between McDiarmid, a great poet in great form, and myself, a very good reader.[217] Gael shows up better in more average company. But it was a good evening, all the same.

Nevertheless, that visit, and the immediately subsequent one to be talked at by Lord Goodman, deepened my antipathy to London enough to make me resolve not to venture there again without very solid reason. How can a city which once was more than half civilized have become so barbarous within my lifetime? There used to be teashops in no hurry, restaurants where half a bottle of tolerable claret cost less than a shilling, a Café Royale where you were sure to meet someone worth talking to,[218] and reasonable efficient cheap public transport. There was a madam – what was her name? – in Jermyn Street[219] whom any personable young man could count on when his pockets were empty for a guinea, tea and toast, and chatter; and Harold Monro feeding poor poets while he listened;[220] and the shop in the Red Lion Street[221] where pork and pease pudding cost one penny, take it away, or a halfpenny more for the use of a plate.

[217] BB read alongside Turnbull and MacDiarmid at a 'Modern British Poetry' conference held at the Polytechnic of Central London, 18–20 October 1974.

[218] Café Royal in Piccadilly: famous hangout for artists and celebrities in the late-nineteenth and early-twentieth centuries.

[219] Jermyn Street (also in Piccadilly) is famous for its upmarket gentlemen's clothing.

[220] Harold Monro (1879–1932), owner of the Poetry Bookshop in Bloomsbury from 1912 to 1927. He published Pound's 1914 anthology *Des Imagistes*.

[221] Red Lion Street: small thoroughfare in Camden.

No, I wont put in a claim for expenses. They are heavy, and in any reasonable system they would be included in the fee. It's not as though they were hard to reckon up. Part of the intolerable airs of "administration," like the County Council who duplicate all the inquisitions of the inland revenue before they will pay up for my son at the university or calculate my rate rebate. A phone call to the tax inspector would do their business in ten seconds, but they must make work for themselves, whatever inconvenience it puts the public to. The huge new trade of "art administration" ought to be discouraged. I wont visit the Arts Council since, some years ago, I suffered the insolence of their junior staff, who have learned from their seniors that there is no need to be polite to poets. Even at Northern Arts, where I am president, I dont like the receptionists' manners.

Mule bile: take no notice.

Yours ever

B

## To Sister Victoria Forde

TS Durham

11 May 1975 Shadingfield, Wylam, Northumberland

Dear Sister Victoria

I am very sorry to have left your letter so long unanswered. I am not going to try to explain that, because it would be a long complicated list of dull things you dont need to take any notice of.

I am always glad to hear from you, so your letter gave me pleasure. I did what I could to prevent 75th birthday celebrations, and succeeded in Newcastle, but I couldnt dodge the Poetry Society of which I am still president for a final year, so I had to turn up in London for two days of what seemed to me suspiciously like a rehearsal for my funeral.[222] All sorts of unexpected people turned up; and I must admit they seemed to enjoy having Briggflatts read to them yet again.

Yes, it is still difficult to get my Collected Poems in the United States, and they even seem to have vanished from the bookshops here. I had a letter a few days ago from a man in New York who wanted my permission to look for a publisher for them, but I am confident nothing will come of it; for the publishers over there

[222] In March 1975 the Poetry Society held a two-day event in honour of BB's 75th birthday. BB had become president of the society in 1972, at the invitation of a radical tendency spear-headed by Eric Mottram (the ensuing struggle between radicals and conservatives for control of the society is extensively summarized in Burton, 458–468).

wanted nothing to do with me a few years ago, and the economic situation will hardly have encouraged them to take on new poets. If anyone is interested, I am sure Fulcrum Press would do whatever negotiations etc might be wanted. However, I'm not anxious to thrust myself on readers, so I dont worry.

I hope you have luck with turning your dissertation into a book.[223] I am sure a lot of university libraries would buy it at any rate. O.U.P. ought to be hospitable to it.

I've written almost nothing for a long time. You will easily imagine that inflation on the scale we are enduring leaves no peace to a man whose income is fixed and very small. More and more has to be done without. I never know two months in advance how we shall live. That is not a circumstance favourable to reflection, let alone steady craftsmanship. But I'll put a little bit into the envelope that I concocted for the tercentenary of Briggflatts meeting house, which is being celebrated this spring.[224] It is not easy to write "religious" poetry without falling into a dozen traps: but perhaps I have avoided most of them.

I am of course glad that your youngsters enjoyed the noise of my tapes and records. I think more of them, I suppose, than of any other class of reader. A little boy up the road here came to me a few weeks ago to present me with a copy of his first poem, dedicated to me. He is about ten, I think, and the poem just what you would expect at that age, but I was touched and delighted.

My wife Sima is away in Persia for a month, to see her mother who either is, or believes she is, ailing. Such a trip is disastrously expensive, but it would be a bad job if Sima did not see her mother again before she dies, and she is a bit older than I am. My daughter Maria, the youngest, is looking after me, with her husband – and expecting a baby at the same time. My son finishes with the university of Durham next month, and goodness knows what he can or will do then. The combination of mathematics, philosophy and psychology doesnt suggest any profitable occupation to me.

Herr Mueller has sent me a copy of his long dissertation, done by offset printing for the university of Freiburg in Breisgau. I believe he wrote to you a year or two ago.[225] He has some pretty wild errors in it, but why not? I am inclined rather to encourage than to correct errors in such contexts!

[223] Forde's University of Notre Dame thesis, *Music and Meaning in the Poetry of Basil Bunting*, was completed in 1973. A revised version would eventually appear via Bloodaxe Books in 1991 (see note to **16/3/83**).

[224] BB's 'At Briggflatts Meetinghouse', a short lyric meditation on the Quaker ethos, was written for the 1975 tercentenary of Brigflatts.

[225] Karl Müller was writing a PhD thesis on BB at the University of Freiburg.

I have quite a lot of work to do in the next few weeks, and am glad to have found time for this letter, since it might have had to wait a good deal longer if I hadnt. That would have belied the very warm feeling I have for you, dear Sister.

Yours
B Bunting

## To Tom Pickard

TS Buffalo

12 July 1975 Shadingfield, Wylam, Northumberland

Dear Tom

I think I'd better send a carbon of this letter to Connie, merely because I've not been able to see her, and wont be able for some days yet for fear of carrying the infection of your kids' german measles to the five weeks old baby now in this house, and because part of it concerns what is largely bothering her just now.

I dont think it is worth shedding many tears for the loss of the Morden Tower.[226] I said at the start that it would exhaust its impulse in a couple of years: it took a good deal longer, but (as you can see easily by the change in the audience) the life went out of it some time ago. I think that baffles Connie. She does not see that even the most fruitful notions can only stay fertile a shortish while with a narrowish scope. The Mermaid had gone barren long before Ben Jonson died.[227] The Wordsworth–Coleridge partnership was really exhausted before the second edition of Lyrical Ballads – within about two years, though the pair didnt realise it for four or five years longer. The good days of the English Review and the transatlantic review lasted a year and 18 months respectively, and Ford had to watch the English Review becoming steadily more idiotic in the hands of his successor.[228] There's only so-much in an idea; if you spin it out it dies on you. No doubt it is more satisfactory, when the time comes, to wring the thing's neck yourself and have done with it; but that's seldom easy, and when you depend, as Connie did, on it for a part of your income it may become practically impossible. So you have successors, and they go from mediocre to bad and then worse; but you can perfectly well turn your face away from them. In fact you both got a great deal out of

[226] Morden Tower was going through one of its perennial funding crises in 1975. In spite of BB's premature eulogy here, Connie Pickard continued to maintain the venue successfully for several decades.

[227] The Mermaid, on Cheapside, London: tavern frequented by many of the leading literary figures of early-Jacobean England, including Jonson and John Donne.

[228] For the *English Review* see 7/18/34 and note; for the *Transatlantic Review* see note to 14/1/24.

the Morden Tower; acquaintance, experience, practice, an important part of your education in poetry, and no less useful, a measure of the meanness and ingratitude, not of particular individuals, but of most of mankind. It will not be difficult for Tom to put the whole thing behind him, but Connie may find it harder because she has nothing actually in hand to fill the place in her mind.

If you want to do a Brechtian musical, as you say, you must, I think, up-date it.[229] You werent around in the 1930's, and if you had been you'd have edited your memories by this time enough to distort the picture. But no writer knows the current NAB[230] scene better than you. I'm not trying to prevent you earning a fee from the BBC; even the BBC prefers something living to the stuffed skin of a dead menagerie. Life was even worse for the working man in the 1840's, but it would be no good using the facts for a play or a poem. We cant get them right, so far away (though there are no survivors lurking to contradict us) and if we could get the facts right, we'd get the feelings wrong, so much has happened since. The 30's have been distorted beyond recognition long since, nothing's written about them without some kind of propaganda purpose. The people who keep talking about Jarrow are really talking about the best piece of advertising done at that time: Jarrow wasnt the extremest case nor a specially typical one; and the whole mess of the depression has to be seen in the light of the fact that England had then far and away the worst government in every respect for more than a hundred years before, as stupid and disastrous in foreign affairs, in defence, in education, as it was in economics, and that it had been chosen by the people in more than one election and went on being chosen till the war (and would probably have been chosen again if there'd been an election when Chamberlain fell, instead of Churchill taking over without one.) Other countries had it even worse, though I think we only just dodged the Hitler business here. Almost the same is happening now, so far as economics politically run, and Wilson is performing all sorts of gymnastic wriggles to try and avoid the fate of Ramsay McDonald while doing almost the same things.[231] However, not to do it would tend towards civil strife on a big scale, and it is usually the fascists who win in such cases. (My name being

[229] Pickard produced a documentary for BBC Radio 3 (broadcast November 1976), to mark the 40th anniversary of the Jarrow March. This tribute to a 1936 protest march by 200 unemployed men from Jarrow (South Tyneside) featured testimonies, journalistic accounts, music (by Alan Hull), and original poems by Pickard. Much of the material would eventually be published in book form by Allison & Busby in 1981.

[230] I.e. Northern Arts Britain.

[231] Harold Wilson (1916–1995) had returned to power as leader of a Labour government in March 1974 (he had previously been Prime Minister 1964–70). He was a largely unpopular figure during this economically turbulent interlude and resigned in April 1976, making way for his colleague James Callaghan (1912–2005).

in Who's Who I've had letters from organisations beseeching me to pledge the use of my car for strike-breaking purposes)[232] If you write about Now, you can be true and moving; and even supposing the BBC turns down the product you'll have made something effective and durable. I dont think you can with the 30's, where you're bound in the nature of things to get too much wrong.

My broadcast?[233] I didnt hear it and dont know what the BBC may have done in editing it; but when it was made my impression was that it was no good; Eric asked the wrong questions and asked them in a muddled way, and I was tired and fed up with London. (He too is trying to carry on too long, at the Poetry Review. He is afraid of something worse to follow him (correctly, perhaps) without realising that he had done all there really was to be done in the first two years.) The ACGB[234] has decided that nothing can be helped in future unless it has "professional administration" thus making salaries for clerks out of the money the taxpayers meant for artists. I suppose Northern Arts is under pressure to go in the same direction. I'm inclined to resign my presidency, but dont want the fuss, and anyway they havent gone quite that far yet, though towards it.

Yours
B.

## To Donald Davie

TS Essex

25 September 1975

Shadingfield, Wylam, Northumberland

Dear Mr Davie

Thankyou for getting Mr Woodings to send me your Fontana book on Pound.[235] I've enjoyed reading it.

Concerning a sentence or two about me: I would not repudiate anything you say there about Briggflatts; yet I think you and other critics sometimes forget that other poets besides Dante can bundle two or three different meanings into a sentence on occasion. The meanings you have read were in my mind, but were not

[232] BB's entry in *Who's Who*, an influential biographical reference aid featuring notable British public figures, first appeared in 1975.

[233] Eric Mottram's BBC radio interview with BB marking his 75th birthday was broadcast on 7 March 1975.

[234] I.e. Arts Council of Great Britain.

[235] Davie's *Pound*, an introductory guide to Pound's work in the Fontana Modern Masters Series, was published in 1975. Robert Woodings (b. 1942) was an editor at Fontana.

those which determined the choice of words. That doesnt matter, and I'm sorry to have felt obliged to say even that little about myself.

There is another paragraph which I have failed to understand. Perhaps age makes me dense. You seem to have written that it might be said of large-scale and small-scale rhythms that "none of them come home to us."[236] Rhythm is surely a perfectly concrete phenomenon, however evanescent – air, waves of it, bumping one's ear-drum – and must come home to anyone within hearing distance who had his ears open.

But for the book as whole, it is certainly one of the best about Pound: and possibly because you are a skilful poet yourself you do perceive and may make some of your readers perceive that the essence of the Cantos, at least, lies in their rhythms. Perhaps they are combined on musical models rather more consciously than you seem to allow. He and I discussed such matters a good deal about 1930, and I have no doubt at all that Walt Whitman's practice in a few poems such as "Out of the cradle, endlessly rocking" first set Pound to combine, repeat, modify, rhythmic themes much as a good XIXc composer does.

I wont make points. No doubt the employees of what you call the Pound industry, which I detest, are hurrying to tell you all the errors and omissions, particularly those which are quite irrelevant to what you have to say. There's no stopping them. However, towards the end of the book you advance the notion that the excuse for poetry and the reason for writing it is the pleasure it gives. That's a much more general proposition, and one I dont want to let pass without dissent.

Artists of any kind whose work is worth considering dont spend much time wondering why they do it, and a great many of them havent the kind of clarity which would enable them to discern their own motives. Not greed or gain, of course, nor vanity of reputation, still less the youthful exhibitionism most of those who write to us display – and not the rather sycophantic desire to give pleasure. What keeps a man at it in spite of bitter poverty, general indifference, public distaste and so on? I do not think there is any contemporary expression for what holds him to difficult work such as his, but a few centuries ago, when the world still had an admitted meaning, they might have said he did it for the glory of God.

Pound wrote too much to keep this motive steadily in view, and he would certainly have found or tried to find some other way of expressing it if he had paused

[236] One of the chapters in Davie's book ('Rhythms in the *Cantos*') examines Pound's prosody in light of a comparison with the rhythms of *Briggflatts*. Davie quotes *Briggflatts* Part II (93–96) to support his argument that the rhythms in the *Cantos* 'ride through' but do not 'bind together' (90), by which he seems to mean that Pound's sense of rhythm is free-flowing and not easily discernible.

long enough to figure it out; nevertheless I am sure that was his mainspring at least in the main part of his life, when he had outgrown his initial vanity.

Thankyou again for the book.

Yours faithfully
B Bunting

## To Donald Davie

TS Essex

9 October 1975

Shadingfield, Wylam, Northumberland

Dear Donald Davie

What shall I say? Christian? No, if that were to imply, as it usually did in the chief Christian centuries, a literal belief in the gospel myth; but yes, in so far as all we who live in Western lands are bound by the habits of our ancestors and cannot altogether escape them at least in our ethics, even when our intellect would like to reject them. Myth to me is myth, and I distrust the Sermon on the Mount, but I know I cannot cast off the habits of nearly two thousand years completely.

Quaker? It's an exceedingly elastic belief of habit, in which I was educated. The earliest Quakers were far freer than their children became when Fox, with the help of Penn and Barclay decided to make them respectable.[237] Some of the Ranters, and many of the first Quakers must have thought much as I do, allowing for the change in vocabulary between their day and ours. I find a similar disposition here and there in the Divan-e-Shans-e-Tabriz of Jelel ad Din ar Rumi.[238] Or say, as some mediaeval theologians did, imitating Arab philosophers, "God is that of which nothing whatever can be predicated" – then I would want to modify it, since God must include his creation (or you become a Manichaean) and say that the scientists perform a kind of histology on the bit of God we can get at, but how much more there may be we cant guess.[239] Contemporary Quakers are

[237] Robert Barclay (1648–1690) and William Penn (1644–1718) were both followers of George Fox (1624–1691), founder of Quakerism.

[238] *Dīvān-e Kabīr/Dīvān-e Šams-e Tabrīzī* (The Works of Šams Tabrīzī), collection by Rumi consisting of lyric poems mostly in New Persian.

[239] BB is, perhaps, referring to Irish neoplatonist John Scotus Eriugena (*c.*800–*c.*877) (see 6/7/51 and note) who held that the universe proceeds from an infinite, transcendent, and unknowable God; BB accepts that we mostly know nothing of God, but claims that we can know a 'bit' of him, by scientifically examining the tangible products of his creation (without this caveat, he suggests, we would be left with a form of Manichaeism, which holds that life is a struggle between unfathomable good and evil forces).

mostly respectable dissenters with a minimum of beliefs, but ethically so humane that I think they are in danger of making Mankind into God. Still, they put up with me, and some of them probably think much as I do. They differ from the rest of "Christians" in allowing no interpreter whatever between God and the single person (in the last resort they reject the Bible, Gospels and all.) At any rate, I am much nearer the Quakers than to any other organised body of thought.

Snyder[240] wanted to consider me a Buddhist, presumably because I dont want to separate men from animals or trees or stones, any more than Wordsworth did in his youth. St Cuthbert preached to the birds and the seals, and I daresay he'd have preached to the pebbles if it had occurred to him. Buddhists might sympathise: but their contempt for their own life revolts me. It's a good life we lead, crime and disease and war and all, and when they put us through the meat chopper at the end of it we go to supply the materials of more life (but without the Buddhist or Christian notion of some enduring consciousness).

So that Briggflatts is a Quaker poem, the centre of which – Alexander's meeting with the angel on the mountain top – is the rejection of what is usually reckoned as success and as consistency. But it's not a piece of theology or philosophy. Its reason for existence is only to be a poem.

I must apologise for thrusting all this on you. You must blame your own lack of caution in asking the question.

For the rest, your letter is most courteous and even flattering. Thankyou

Yours faithfully
B Bunting

## To Hugh Kenner

TS Texas

14 August 1976 — Shadingfield, Wylam, Northumberland

Dear Hugh

Pleasant it is to hear from you.

The chief evidence for Wordsworth's pronunciation is that neither Hazlitt (his own account) nor Keats (I'm not sure now whether it's in one of his letters or somebody else's description of their meeting at a dinner in London – maybe

[240] Gary Snyder (b. 1930), American poet who emerged from the San Francisco Renaissance of the post-war years. After studying anthropology at university, Snyder developed an interest in Asian culture and religion (especially Zen Buddhism) which he subsequently introduced into Beat and late-modernist poetry circles.

Lamb) could make out what on earth Wordsworth was saying, he was so very northern.[241] (And Hazlitt met him in Somersetshire). Somewhere Coleridge too is said to have explained Wordsworth's return to the north: "It was the language difficulty."

I thought I had a note of some of the rhymes, but cant find it. Never mind. Enough in itself to clinch the argument is the last couplet of the first stanza of Resolution and Independence, where "waters" rhymes with "chatters."[242] Glancing at the volume, in three minutes I find: "devil" and "evil" in The Idiot Boy; "warm" and "arm" in Her Eyes are Wild.[243] Very typical. I'm pretty sure that somewhere you'll find "out" rhymed "hoot" and "laugh" with some such word as "chaff," but it would take time to find them.[244] All these are excellent precise rhymes anywhere near the Border.

I think Wordsworth knew what he was doing, but it's not certain, for he avoided dialect words deliberately. It's rather astonishing that the northern vowels survived his years in Cambridge, London, France and Somerset, to say nothing of his intercourse with the Beaumonts who must have been, as their descendents still are, rather la-di-da.[245] However, Grasmere[246] would soon resurrect them. I've lived longer away from home, but no one would take me for anything but a northerner.

Two or three years ago I read several times for the BBC poems by Wordsworth,[247] and lots of people wrote in, pleased, some of them saying they'd never guessed that Wordsworth wrote musically till they heard him read with broad vowels.

[241] The quotation BB has in mind is perhaps that in Hazlitt's 'My First Acquaintance with Poets': '[Wordsworth] sat down and talked very naturally and freely, with a mixture of clear, gushing accents in his voice, a deep guttural intonation, and a strong tincture of the northern burr, like the crust on wine [...] Wordsworth read us the story of Peter Bell in the open air; and the comment made upon it by his face and voice was very different from that of some later critics!' Quoted in *The Broadview Anthology of Literature of the Revolutionary Period 1770–1832*, ed. D. L. Macdonald and Anne Whir (London: Broadview, 2010), 897.

[242] See Wordsworth's 'Resolution and Independence', ll. 6–7.

[243] See 'The Idiot Boy', ll. 343–346 and 'Her Eyes Are Wild', ll. 5–10.

[244] I can find no example of out/hoot in Wordsworth, and indeed there are many cases (out/rout in 'The Kitten and Falling Leaves', ll. 67–68, out/sprout in 'A Wren's Nest', ll. 34–36) that contradict BB's claim. He is on firmer ground, however, with 'chaff', which is rhymed with 'staff' in 'A Poet's Epitaph', ll. 14–16.

[245] Sir George Howland Beaumont, 7th Baronet (1753–1827), wealthy arts patron and friend of Wordsworth and other of the Lake Poets. In referring to Beaumont's descendants, BB is perhaps mistakenly referring to the (not closely related) Beaumonts who, as Viscounts of Allendale and Hexham, were a powerful presence in BB's locality.

[246] After some years living in southern England and abroad, Wordsworth settled at Dove Cottage in Grasmere, Cumbria, in 1799. From 1891 the cottage became a major tourist site and, more recently, a venue for literary events.

[247] See 16/12/69.

I was at Grasmere last week, first time since my boyhood. It's changed. Slow bumper-to-bumper processions of cars, queues for everything, the Waggoner's Swan poshed up and selling bad sandwiches and indifferent beer at high prices to swarms of tourists. A civilised young woman was in charge at Dove Cottage, whom I thought I recognised for the poet's great-great-granddaughter (once met), but I'm not sure. I didnt care to interrupt her very busy explanations to other tourists.

I was sorry too that we didnt meet during my United States tour, but perhaps it was as well: I was harassed, tired and kept very busy, so there might have been no satisfaction in meeting.[248] I didnt see Louis either – didnt expect to, but I'm sorry. I'm glad you enjoy Johns Hopkins, and hope your family enjoys Baltimore, a pleasant looking city when last I saw it, 35 years ago. If not, there are refuges within reach on the Chesapeake.

Did the publisher, Ceolfrith send you my "Selections from Skipsey"? He didnt send it to some who were on the list. If not, you dont miss much, though I like Skipsey, what there is of him, for his simplicity and spontaneity. Swinburne next, if they ever pay up for the Skipsey.

I'm too old to enjoy travelling now, even as far as Kent. And too old to earn anything, so that the Lord knows what we'll be doing when the profits of the American tour run out. Universities here have not learned to pay poets.

Cheerio

B.

## To Jonathan Williams

TS Buffalo

27 September 1976

Shadingfield, Wylam, Northumberland

Dear Jonathan

Disappointing: for I'd intended to seek your hospitality for a few days, maybe a few days longer than usual, as soon as I'd got a reading at Stone out of the way on October 1.[249] And for you too, in spite of water shortage, I imagine. You've had no time to enjoy your garden, though I'm glad you got your walk, wet or fine. The last two times I've seen you you've been too busy with visitors or professors to produce much of the wit and sense I enjoy, and I'd hoped to elicit some.

[248] At the instigation of Jonathan Williams, BB undertook a commercial-style tour of east-coast USA in the spring of 1976, reading to mostly packed houses at Harvard, Yale, the Poetry Center in New York, and several other locations.

[249] Stone: market town in Staffordshire.

Wont they all be electioneering too hard to pay proper attention to the business of your papers?[250]

Sima is away in Persia, lured there by what seem to me patently false appeals from her mother, who has been dying, in her own estimation, though remarkably tough in everybody else's, for the last 28 years. The journey costs me very dear, of course. Besides, Tom B. is temporarily at home while he hunts out a new quasi permanent place at Durham, and he is hard to please about food and such like. I can cook, but it's certainly not my business by choice. All the same, I'm glad to have Tom at hand for a while, taciturn though he is.

Thanks for the proof of the Hamilton drawing. I like it well. The original hangs in my study, against the outer wall to dodge the sunlight which might fade it.

I believe I stirred up Northern Arts a bit more deeply than usual this year by opening their annual general meeting with an attack on Lord Redcliffe-Maud's long dull report on the arts.[251] Some of them looked seriously uneasy, and I hope they may, for once, reflect. Doing such things and still keeping one's phrases "diplomatic" is at least good exercise. They seem determined to keep me presidenting for them as long as I can stand on my feet and talk.

There's a new excellent poem by Tom Pickard in "Montemora," a review run largely by ex-pupils of mine from British Columbia.[252] I dont know whether they've put you on their mailing list. It seems to me a good deal better than most of its sort. Even the Japanese obsession the editor has seems more thoughtful than most such obsessions; and they are paying due attention to late Reznikoff. Montemora Foundation, Box 336, Cooper Station, NY NY.

I've had enough of Calvin, though I'm glad I've read a bit of him at last. He had a gift for words, unlike John Knox, who had none at all but only a Lenin-like competence in revolution. Calvin's French is admirably terse and clear, and his Latin at least free of the Renaissance affectations you'd expect him to have picked up from Erasmus. And there is more sense in his doctrines, or some of them, than his followers let you find out. (My standard of late Latin is Bede, not EPs assorted Renaissance figures).

[250] The United States presidential election, held on Tuesday, 2 November 1976, sent Democrat Jimmy Carter (b. 1924) to the White House. Carter came to Newcastle on his first foreign trip as president in May 1977, also visiting nearby Washington, ancestral seat of the first American president's family and soon to become BB's home.

[251] Lord John Redcliffe-Maud, (1906–1982), British civil servant and diplomat.

[252] *Montemora*: New York-based poetry magazine edited by Eliot Weinberger (b. 1949) and Geoffrey O'Brien (b. 1948), which ran for eight issues between 1975 and 1981. The summer 1976 issue contained BB's 'At Briggflatts Meeting House' and the spring 1977 issue featured an interview with BB by Dale Reagan.

Saw Woof for a few minutes, who said it was a pity that we didnt warn him we were visiting Dove Cottage, as all the most interesting things are not on show, but he'd have instructed them to bring them out for us.[253] But I dont really have more than the most superficial curiosity about mss and such – what Wordsworth wanted printed he printed, and I think his judgment was pretty middling good. To hell with the first drafts of stanzas that werent good enough and had to be reworked.

My compliments to the North Carolinans I met in April, please. And salute the mocking birds next time they start performing.

Also, all my best to Tom.

Yours ever

B.

## To Jonathan Williams

MS Buffalo

12 January 1977 Shadingfield, Wylam, Northumberland

Dear Jonathan

Of course I am glad to hear that the sale of your archives seems to be going forward: but I wont congratulate you yet because there have been so many ships already between that particular cup and lip. And something not quite dissimilar for the last festschrift.

Whitney Jones wrote to me a little time since about his expedition to London.[254] I'd have been pleased to see him (them): however things have come to a fearful crisis at Wylam, so that he wont find me there.

I dont want to dwell too much on that, but cant avoid saying at least a minimum. Sima has been behaving as though she were actually mad, though I fancy it is only an exaggerated form of the "change of life" troubles women undergo. She finally drove me out (after miscellaneous violence and what seemed to be a try at strangling me) into a snowstorm. I had nowhere whatever to go. At Hexham the snow was thick: up the Hexham Rothbury road it became very dangerous driving with lots of skids, next to no visibility and some drifts. When I stopped in a lay-by to smoke a cigarette and rest, a lorry driver told me the road was impassible on the

[253] Robert Woof (1931–2005), literary scholar who lectured at Newcastle University and directed the Wordsworth Trust and Wordsworth Museum at Dove Cottage.

[254] F. Whitney Jones (b. 1944), American academic and president of the Board of Directors at Jargon Society, the small press founded by Williams.

high ground beyond Wallington.[255] I had to turn back a long way before I could find a side-road to Morpeth that seemed to be open (only just) and so reached the Great North Road, which was not too difficult, though uncomfortable. But by the time I got to Belford I was exhausted – only about 60 miles direct, though twice as much at least the way I had to go, in more than four hours; so I put up at the Bluebell, still a very good inn, though expensive now. There they told me of a man with a furnished cottage to let "cheap" in the winter, so I hurried to see, was taken to look at the cottage, and agreed to move in the next morning. That was very nearly impossible, because they had to have a gang of men to dig the cars out in front of the hotel. The top of mine was up above the snow, but another near it was buried. It's a cold place, fixed for summer visitors only, I suppose, and in this weather thoroughly forbidding. I am sitting almost on top of an electric fire, with a car blanket round my head and shoulders, and still shivering. For the first time in my life I've had to thaw out my fountain pen – not very completely, it seems – by toasting it in front of the fire. But the typewriter has not enjoyed its journey and is not co-operating. Besides, I'd have had to go to the table and freeze myself to use it.

The address is 4 Fenwick Village – Fenwick – Beal – Northumberland (under the top corner of the Kyloe Hills), but I am not sure that I shall stay more than the month I've paid in advance, so use the address cautiously. I think letters to Wylam will be re-addressed. Of course I cant afford to live so for many weeks, eating the tail end of my savings: but what happens then I cant guess. Not, at any rate "Old People's Home" or "Geriatric Ward" or some other meally-mouthed version of the old Workhouse. Nor can I live on my friends – very few of them would be happy if I proposed to stay with them for a whole week, and I, I hate other people's houses, though they must be visited to talk in.

Pity Simms only got you by phone. He is interesting on his own subjects (pole-cats lately, I think).

Next door – old Scotsman – has just been in with the cheerful news that two old people, one in this village, one in the next, died of cold last night. "Hypothermia" the coroners call it now, for fear people should get the notion that the Old Age Pension ought to be increased. But at least the pen seems to have thawed out fully at last.

And good luck be with you; whenever, if ever, I see you, as well as now.

Yours ever

B.

[255] Wallington Hall: country house once owned by the Trevelyan family, on the border between the populous south-east and remote north-west of Northumberland. Morpeth is on the Great North Road (the old road between London and Edinburgh, most of which forms the modern A1). Belford and Beal are much further to the north, near the crossing to Lindisfarne.

## To William Cookson

MS Yale

12 May 1977

Shadingfield, Wylam, Northumberland

Dear Cookson –

(I write from Dentdale, for I've no real address of my own any more, though letters to Wylam will still reach me for a while – delayed)[256]

Your summer number will surely turn into an argument about what the devil does "myth" mean.[257] Since it does not seem to mean anything very particular, I fancy that will prove unprofitable.

The function Homer performed for Greek poets was performed for 3 centuries for English poets by the Bible. But since the Church of E. has now translated it from English into journalese, and since nobody reads it any more (audiences dont even seem to be familiar with the adventures of King David), there doesnt seem to be anything tangible we could attach the word "myth" to.

I've no new poem, even yet: sorry.

Wish you well!
B Bunting

In the winter of 1976/77, Tom Pickard was arrested and charged for his role in a marijuana smuggling operation in London the previous year. Though his involvement was real enough (as detailed in the 2010 memoir *More Pricks Than Prizes*), the charges were inflated and Pickard faced a lengthy jail sentence. Bunting appeared at the trial in autumn 1977 as a character witness. Introduced as 'Ex Wing Commander Bunting', and dressed accordingly in full RAF uniform, he was asked by the prosecution if he was aware that Pickard took drugs. Bunting replied that he 'would be surprised if a young man of his generation didn't'. Though his accomplices were given eight-year prison sentences, Pickard was acquitted by a majority jury verdict.

[256] BB was staying at Jonathan Williams's home in Dentdale.

[257] The summer/autumn 1977 issue of *Agenda* (15.2–3) explored the presence of mythological motifs in the work of a series of writers.

## To Tom Pickard

MS Buffalo

24 May 1977

Shadingfield, Wylam, Northumberland

From Corn Close

Dear Tom –

Never mind about my expenses. Who cares?

What matters is your despondency. There's not the least need to despair. I dont mean to suggest that there's much to mitigate the misery of waiting, waiting, for a trial which will be a serious ordeal however it turns out. But put it at its worst, for a moment: say you are sent to prison. No doubt such places have changed since my day. The changes were meant for the better, and probably most of them are for the better, though there is something to be said in favour of solitude and silence. Anyway, hardship and humiliation, though severe, didnt give me any cause for despair. Yet I was a boy, 18, with nothing I could look back on to bolster my self-esteem or my courage. You have solid accomplishments to stiffen you – you invented and ran the Morden Tower, with very little support from outside; you have written at least one first-class poem, not likely to be forgotten, and a lot of excellent, lively work besides. You can endure whatever they are likely to inflict on you, and it wont last for ever! It need not embitter you, let alone demolish you. Afterwards, freedom, with a deepened experience and perhaps a more accurate measure of your self; and no less pride, though perhaps a less truculent pride.

Moreover, there is an excellent chance that they will not send you to prison. You are innocent, half-innocent, or a first offender. The publicity will bring difficulties and perhaps amputate a few friendships not worth having, but that's no reason for despair.

As for Joanna, nobody but yourself can know what she means to you, and even you cannot know what she will mean at some later time.[258] Much, or perhaps nothing. Love, in the sense of "falling in love" is a transient emotion. Sometimes it leads to the lasting love, more worth having, which grows from habit, but often it does not. In your case, having no common language almost rules out long love (but not quite). You know the fable of the man with a dumb wife? [259] It's in the Gesta Romanorum that a monk wrote at Tilburg 700 years ago. The man saved

[258] Pickard met Joanna Voit during a Poetry Society sponsored trip to the International Poetry Festival in Warsaw in the spring of 1976.

[259] BB relates a well-known misogynist folk tale, with antecedents in the English ballad tradition and a farce by Rabelais. It does not seem to feature in the *Gesta Romanorum* (an anonymous Latin collection written *c.*1300).

and travelled, till he found a doctor who could cure her; but a few weeks later he was back asking the doctor to make her dumb again. When Joanna knows more English or you learn Polish, she will seem another woman to you, and you another man to her. Whether love can survive that is a toss-up. You dont like seeing that written just now, especially when you have just parted with her: but it is worth bearing in mind.

The Lake District Festival reading is, I believe, on June 7, Jubilee Day, a Tuesday. But I wouldnt voyage north for it if I were you. You've heard me before! And I shall be untangled with the organisers and not even at Corn Close –

All bright sunshine here, with an east wind, but not too chilly. The field is taken over by a bull and his eleven fiancées, all maiden heifers. Great fun to watch their girlish capers.

Yours ever
B

After his separation from Sima, Bunting eventually found a home in Washington with the help of Northern Arts. In the wake of the New Towns Act of 1946, several new towns were built in the United Kingdom, including Washington—in effect a suburb of Sunderland, a former shipbuilding city some fifteen miles to the south of Newcastle. The legacy of the post-war new towns has been fiercely debated: they were initially seen as desirable alternatives to the inner-city Victorian slums, but from the later 1970s they became symbols of social decline and were repudiated along with much of the social-democratic inheritance by neoliberals. More recently, their idealistic basis and modernist design have been championed. Given his hatred of institutions and love of the countryside, it is predictable that Bunting would have resented living in this 'huge slave barracks designed by a team of lunatics'.

## To Roudaba Bunting Davido

TS Durham

5 July 1977

107 Stridingedge, Blackfell, Washington,
County Durham, NE37 1HJ

Dear Daughter Rou

That's where I can be found for the next few months, perhaps for a whole year. It's the result of upheavals which have lasted six months now and are not finished yet, I daresay. I think I was unwilling to write about them at all, but perhaps I did write to you. There has been such confusion that I do not know.

Briefly, and jumping the details, Sima, who is about the "change of life" seemed last autumn to be going more or less out of her mind. She pretty well drove me out of the house at the beginning of January, in the midst of the worst blizzard we have had for years. I had a terrible day backing the car out of snowdrifts, but at last I found a ramshackle cottage where I stayed for a month. Sima knew she was a bit off her head, and I stayed with her a few days again before going to occupy Jonathan William's cottage in Dentdale while he was away. Now she's come back: but it happens that Northern Arts has a house, given to them by Washington New Town as a kind of advertisement for some artist or novelist or what not to live in. They have never found anyone willing to put up with Washington for more than the minimum six months. It's not a nice place (I wonder what President Carter thought of the village his capital takes its name from. He was here a few weeks ago.) rather a huge slave-barracks designed by a team of lunatics. Inside, however, the house is reasonably convenient.

I had given Shadingfield to Sima, and did not want to make any dispute about it. I am sorry for her. She has sold it and bought a bungalow in the next village, where I hope she will be able to be content and get back her balance. And also, she has divorced me – after 29 years of marriage.

Dentdale was a pleasant place, though solitary. There I conversed with sheep, but could not settle to anything purposeful, in somebody else's house, and only temporarily there.

At Washington I expect to be driven back on myself – there's certainly nothing to do out of doors. Maybe, perhaps, I wonder, I might even get some work done.

Thankyou for your news of everyone. I got Finn's card in time to send off a message to the pair – only a message: the old age pension is not calculated to include wedding presents. I am glad that Daphne and Monica are flourishing and Rustam and Fenris coming on. I'm glad too to hear of Lloyd's good fortune (or whatever it ought to be called) and hope he does go on to Washington (not this one) and make the kind of career I think he wants. (I like Lloyd, you know, – making the quite obvious but quite superficial reservations.) Gideon, Tod, Colin – I wish them all well.

If you do get over the ocean this summer, I have a spare bed – just one – and though I cant recommend Washington nor its neighborhood, we could drive out of it onto the Northumberland moors or into the Pennine dales, besides looking at things like Durham cathedral and Hermitage castle.[260] I wont guarantee good

[260] Hermitage Castle: imposing border fortress in Liddesdale (see note to 10/6/69). In the sixteenth century it was famously a residence of Lord Bothwell (1534–1578), third and final husband of Mary, Queen of Scots (1542–1587).

cooking, but I can dish up some sort of meal. Let me know. I'll have a telephone soon, but not in the book; but if I havent sent you the number you could get it from Northern Arts (Newcastle) if you told them you were my daughter.

Oxford University Press is issuing the third edition of my Collected Poems this autumn.[261] Till then, they are out of print, only to be got at high prices second hand.

Not Seattle for me, my darling. I have got to get what living I can, not sponge on my children.

Love
B

## To Tom Pickard

MS Buffalo

[September 1977]

107 Stridingedge, Blackfell, Washington, County Durham, NE37 1HJ

Dear Tom –

I dont know whether they leave you on bail or back you up during your trial, so it may be that this is the last chance I'll have of addressing you before the verdict. I have of course assured your solicitors that I will bear witness to your good character, and I'll go to Henshaw's nearer the time I'm wanted, for I dont like to burden him and his wife too long.

Of course I hope you'll be "not guilty," and on the whole that is what I expect; but it would be foolish not to consider the possibility that you will be convicted.

What I chiefly want to say is that conviction and imprisonment would not be the end of your career by any means, nor would it alienate your friends. Prison is hard to bear, but it is not unbearable, and if you keep your eyes open to what is around you (as I'm pretty sure you will) you'll pile up a stock of experience you can make good use of in poetry eventually. Keep objective. Your own happiness is no capital stock, but what your eyes see and your ears hear is.

In my day there were no letters at all for writers, and then only one a quarter. That may have been changed a bit, but I quite expect neither to hear from you nor to be able to write to you if you are sentenced. You'll need your letters for more intimate folk, children, ex-wife, girl etc. Bearing my age in mind, I may not be around if you are released after a long time; so let me say now that I've always

[261] OUP would publish BB's *Collected Poems*, a corrected and expanded version of the 1968 Fulcrum edition, in March 1978.

admired your courage against odds, your readiness to learn whatever there was to learn, your goodwill even to people who have earned no goodwill; and I value your ear for rhythm, your readiness to cut down to what's essential, the way you evoke and emotion without a word that isnt concrete and factual. When I am gone and probably McDiarmid, you'll have to carry the main weight of real poetry in English. Bear that in mind and it may help.

And, for the present, keep your chin up: and good luck if luck is needed.

Yrs
B.

## To Roudaba Bunting Davido

TS Durham

27 February 1978

107 Stridingedge, Blackfell,
Washington, County Durham, NE37 1HJ

Roudaba my dear

I am ashamed of my long silence. I find it difficult, very difficult indeed, to write in a simple, reasonable way about the misadventures that have upset my old age. However, I daresay there is nothing that you should worry about.

Firstly I must say that I am very pleased to hear the news about the wedding you intend. I wish you happiness, and Robert too. If it depends on you, I'm sure you'll find it. And if, as you suggest, you are both coming to England this summer, please come to me a little of the time. Washington is a lousy place, but my car is still running and I can take you to many beautiful and interesting places that "tourists" have never heard of... mountains NOT beset by touts, solitary moorlands, castles not exploited, villages as old as old that no one ever took photographs of: some of the oldest things in northern Europe. And I've a spare room, not at present arranged for two but it could be, if I had notice.

I must write to Bourtai later this week, if my energy holds out.

As to me, last summer I had what the doctor describes as the ghost of a stroke. It hasnt disabled me, only all my right side is numb. My hand does what it's told, but it doesnt feel things – light things not at all – so that I cannot pick up a needle anyhow and my handwriting has become very laborious and more illegible than ever. Also it affects the corner of my mouth so that once in a while a word is slurred, which rather hampers my public reading though I can control it with an effort. And now and then I stumble, not feeling the ground quickly enough with my right foot. It hasnt prevented me driving, though I take care now not to slip into my old habit of driving very fast. No hundred miles an hour any more. To my amusement, the doctors seem to have changed their notion of how to avoid a stroke. When I was young, you got a stroke out of the rum bottle. Now it seems cigarettes are more to blame, and alcohol improves your chances of dodging them. So I "waste" some money on wine and whisky.

What I live on isnt easy to explain. I have an old age pension, a good deal less than the usual one because I spent so many years abroad, and a very small pension from the Queen, supposed to help out distinguished persons who have fallen into poverty,[262] which just brings my income up to the average old age pensions standard. Then I have the use of this house rent free – a big help, though I wish the house were in a more endurable place. Besides, I usually get a few small cheques for royalties on books and records and another small cheque or two for little broadcasting or TV jobs – not enough to make much difference, but they come in handy for a new pair of shoes or repairs to the typewriter and so on. This year there is a special bonus – the Arts Council of Great Britain has given me a grant which was meant to be enough to see me through the year frugally. However, the Inland Revenue has suddenly decided that all grants, fellowships, prizes and so on must pay full income tax. They used to be looked on as capital windfalls. This will take away two-fifths of my grant, so that I am not sure of having anything left in the bank by autumn. But I may be wrong. Oxford University Press is just bringing out a new edition of my poems, and it may be, just possibly, that it will sell enough to bring in some small royalties. The publication is in New York as well as London, and that's where I hope there may be sales worth counting up.

The London publication is on March 16, and they want me to go down to London to read, drink bad sherry, and sign copies. I dont want to, but suppose I must. When the New York publication happens I dont know, but no doubt soon. The magazine Agenda, the best known of the "heavy" literary magazines over here, is also devoting its March number entirely to me.[263] What it will say I've no idea, but at the worst it will be publicity for the book. When all that is over I mean to go to Dentdale, to Jonathan Williams's cottage there, to spend a week or two out of sight of industrial towns, enjoying the sheep, the many birds, the weasels and hares which abound there. We'll go and look at the place if you come here. It is close to Briggflatts and a beautiful dale.

[262] See 2/4/70 and note.

[263] In the spring of 1978 *Agenda* produced a special issue (16.1) dedicated to BB. For a discussion of its contents see 12/4/78.

A fortnight ago I was down in London too, and in Kent for a week, staying with Stuart Montgomery and his wife. But the weather was so snowy and cold I was tied to the house and as much a prisoner as I am here. The Montgomeries were too busy with a crisis in their research to spend much time talking. The journey took it out of me too. The train I went down on had to be dug out of a snow drift, which injured the heating apparatus, and it was two hours late. Brrr! But now the snow has melting enough to show cabbages where you could never have guessed at them a few days ago.

I see Sima once in ten days or so – drive over to her bungalow at Ovingham, near Wylam, and drink a cup of tea or eat a curry. I think whatever was wrong with her a year ago has pretty well cleared up, and I even get the impression that she would like to remarry me, but it would be very hard to arrange now everything is dispersed and no real room for me in her bungalow. I dont really know what goes on in her head now. I see Maria now and then. I went out to see her this morning. She lives in a very remote, little known village, with her husband John Halliday and their little boy Jonathan. Jonathan is just beginning to talk, very late. John's clients are the farmers and landowners of the beautiful North Tyne valley, or of Allendale (with its pagan survival new year fire dance),[264] so he's often out of the office at Hexham with clients in the forest or the moorlands, or shooting roe deer with them to keep in touch. Jonathan is a pretty child, as round faced as Maria was when she was young. I see less of Tom, who is living in Durham but not on the phone, and yet I feel closer to him than to the others. He's out of a job again but doesnt seem to worry. He has a girl in tow, another Maria, Irish, just finished as a student at Durham.

Our Maria's house is only a few hundred years old, but she told me this morning that when they were doing some repairs at the house opposite recently they found a whole Roman hypocaust system in the cellars. Their written records only go back to 1602, but the foundations are huge blocks of stone, six feet by four, roughly cut, and their walls are six or seven feet thick. The pub, which I've known for years, has made no alterations since 1580 except to put in a small rickety bar into one of the rooms. The chief barn in the village looks like a fortress, and the smithy, no longer a smithy, has archives of extreme antiquity. It is odd that no one seems to know the place, even in Newcastle, for the village is extremely ancient even by Northumberland's standards. There's a Roman paved road under the grass running south.

[264] Allendale (a larger village to the north of Maria and John Halliday's home near Allenheads) is the site of an annual New Year's Eve procession in which local men carry barrels of burning tar through its central marketplace.

I'm glad you had Marian with you for a while, and sorry that her memory is erratic. Mine is too, but only for names. I hope Finn and Paula are doing well, and am sure that Daphne is – she's the sort who would always do well, I think. Pretty girl. I'm glad of your news of Rustam and Monica too. What is Lloyd up to nowadays? Finished with the Wisconsin Assembly?

Did Jonathan Williams call on you during his visit to Seattle? He was going to, but I gather he has mislaid some papers, and maybe your address was amongst them.

I have a bit of a poem done: and I think it will be completed slowly, but it is hard to believe that a man my age – 78 the day after tomorrow – can write as well as he did before.

Dear daughter, forgive the rarity of my letters and dont forget me altogether, even in a happy marriage.

Love
B

## To William Cookson

TS Yale

17 April 1978 — 107 Stridingedge, Blackfell, Washington, County Durham, NE37 1HJ

Dear Cookson

I dont <u>think</u> I've written. If I have, my apologies for repeating myself.

I owe you thanks for a very unexpected, very welcome cheque; and for untold numbers of copies of <u>Agenda</u>.[265] I know what to do with the cheque, but I'm not at all sure what to do with the magazines. I am much more isolated than you may imagine – might almost as well be back in Isfahan or in the Canaries – seldom see friends and have very little to say to them when I do see them. And I would be embarrassed to present copies to others who are less than friends. Still, I daresay they'll disappear one at a time, slowly.

[265] Among the contents of *Agenda*'s Spring 1978 Bunting issue were a version of BB's last original canonical poem ('Perche no spero') and an interview from 1970 conducted by Peter Quartermain and Warren Tallman. Kenneth Cox's essay 'A Commentary on Basil Bunting's *Villon*' had originally appeared in *Stony Brook Poetry Journal* in 1969. Also included were new essays by Anthony Suter, Peter Makin, Jeffrey Wainwright (b. 1944), Roland John (b. 1940) and Peter Dale (b. 1938). The last of these was titled 'Basil Bunting and the Quonk and Groggle School of Poetry'; as BB describes, it was an attempt by Dale (*Agenda*'s co-editor) to challenge BB's emphasis on the importance of sound in poetry.

I own to being a bit disappointed – not with your efforts, but with the fact that so little new has shown up. Cox and the Vancouver interview and Hamburger are all reprints – old news. (And I dont like the interview anyway, too much guff about what's nobody's business but my own). Suter is too academic, and Makin too though he has a new observation or two. Wainwright has a point I havent seen made – I wouldnt myself have picked Tintern Abbey to illustrate my debt to Wordsworth, but it certainly serves. That leaves me with Peter Dale.

But Dale disappoints me too. It would, I think, be quite possible to make out a plausible case against my view of poetry, one that might stir me to argue at least with myself. Unfortunately Dale takes the easier (and well-trodden) path of setting out to refute something I have never maintained. I do believe that music is the essential feature of poetry, without which there isnt any poetry, and beside which other elements are relatively insignificant; but I would have to be very perverse to deny that words have meanings, or that didactic works like De Rerum Natura[266] or passages in Dante fail to convey meaning. All the same, Dante's verse expositions are less perspicuous than the prose of St Thomas which he takes them from, and though we've no one to compare Lucretius to, I'd be surprised if Epicurus hadnt managed to be clearer than his disciple. And yet, Lucretius was probably the more persuasive, thanks to his sometimes very subtle sonorities. In short, it wasnt the prose, or prosable, argument that was effective, but the convincing sound.

I think it is also a pity that he bolsters his theme with a number of what can only be called "carps." It is absurd for Dale (it would not be for an American) to pretend that he is unfamiliar with the word "girdle." It's a piece of kitchen machinery everywhere north of Leicester or west or Reading, and even he must have eaten girdle cakes in what amounts to four fifths of England, though I allow that an entirely untravelled Kentishman, or perhaps even Cockney, might not know them.

He is, of course, entitled not to like my poetry, and to say so, with or without gibes, and I've no complaint of that, only of the dullness he has involved himself in by answering a thesis never maintained … and attributing elaborations of it to me. (By the way, since he writes poetry himself, I think he might be wise to look into the business of quantity in the English language. It is not by any means as simple a matter as people – even Makin – seem to imagine. With that, and maybe some consideration of Welsh prosody of about 1200 ad, he might even begin to develop an ear.)

[266] *De Rerum Natura*: 1st-century BC didactic poem by Lucretius.

Sorry to bore you with all this; but I imagine you are curious to know my reactions. They dont need any sort of comment, and I am grateful to you for the efforts you have made.

Yours ever
B.

Much amused at Rowland John's notion that lack of a philosophy prevents me being a major poet. What philosophy had Chaucer? Or Shakespeare? Catullus? Etc. Think of the comedy of Wordsworth, who proposed to write a long philosophical poem, but having no philosophy he intended to borrow one from Coleridge, who gave him the slip, leaving him with a Prelude, and Excursion away from the subject, but not a line of philosophical poem.

## To Gael Turnbull

TS Scotland

27 April 1978

107 Stridingedge, Blackfell, Washington, County Durham, NE37 1HJ

Dear Gael,

Darent go out for fear of getting drowned by the pelting rain. I hope it's less violent at Malvern.[267]

I went up to Biggar on Tuesday and saw McDiarmid.[268] I'd been warned that he'd probably not be fit for more than ten minutes talk, but in fact he was very reluctant to let me go after more than four and a half hours, and Valda said it had done him enormous good – he hasnt seen anyone he calls a friend (bar his sons) for a very long time.

He was sitting rather slumped by the kitchen fire, his face a good deal more shrivelled and a general air of having shrunk a bit (there wasnt so very much to shrink anyway) but delighted to see the bottle of Glen Fiddich I was armed with. With some help from Valda we drank the lot.

I didnt succeed in catching the doctor but Valda told me, in another room, that the trouble was cancer of the colon and she had been warned that "it was only a matter of time."[269] McDiarmid doesnt know. He is puzzled because the doctors cant stop the frequent severe pain and yet cant say what it is that is wrong with

267 For much of the 1970s Turnbull lived in Malvern, a spa town in Worcestershire.

268 MacDiarmid's last home was Brownsbank, a cottage just outside Biggar in Lanarkshire. His wife was the writer Valda Trevlyn Grieve (1906–1989).

269 MacDiarmid died on 9 September 1978.

him. He is making plans. There's an honorary degree at Dublin due in July and he not only expects to go there and get through the ceremony but to have a proper binge – it's a long time since the last one – and show the Irish how to drink whisky. And there is some further plan for next spring, though I forget what. Also he wants to do another round of readings – the last was the one where he and I read at Warwick, ages ago.

He mentioned getting a letter from you and was obviously very pleased by it. But most of his talk was of the far past. He and I, he said, were the only survivors of Orage's set of likely young men in the early twenties. But then he remembered Ruth Pitter, in her nineties now.[270] But she wasnt a young man, I said. "No, but she might as well have been, she was such a Lesbian." We recollected Edward Pease[271] and other worthies, so far in the past you may never have heard of them: E.D.Morrell etc.[272] But he couldnt match my (insignificant) memory of Annie Besant,[273] and was fidgety for a moment about that.

He spoke of my collected poems, and of his own which are due out next month. "They'll boycott us two in the end," he said. "We're not gentlemen."

That's my report: better than I thought, but clearly not likely to survive many months. He'll be a loss to me, and to a good few other people who perhaps dont realise it yet.

I drove back by Broughton and over the big fells to Moffat, but there was so much snow on the hills and it was so cold that I funked the long tour I'd planned from Moffat to Selkirk and Hawick,[274] and even so I was glad enough to call on Maria for a cup of tea and an hour's rest before finishing the drive. I'm sorry to have missed the big fells round St Mary's loch yet again. I've not seen them since I was a boy except from the back.

All good wishes
B

[270] Ruth Pitter (1897–1992), British LGBT poet, whose work was first published by A. R. Orage in the *New Age*.

[271] See **16/9/68** and note.

[272] E. D. Morel (1873–1924), British pacifist campaigner and journalist who defeated Winston Churchill to become the Labour MP for Dundee in 1922.

[273] Annie Besant (1847–1933), British socialist feminist campaigner and orator who played a major role in the union movement and other radical struggles in the late-nineteenth and early-twentieth centuries.

[274] BB attempted to drive back from Biggar to Washington through the Southern Upland towns of Selkirk and Hawick, but then took a more moderate route via his daughter's house in the Allen Valley, on the English side of the border. St Mary's Loch is a large natural loch between Selkirk and Moffat. This landscape was the Border Country which united BB and MacDiarmid, in spite of their different nationalities.

## To Tom Pickard

TS Buffalo

3 June 1978

107 Stridingedge, Blackfell, Washington,
County Durham, NE37 1HJ

Dear Tom

Good that Ruskin College has seen the light – or at least some distant reflection of a spark of it.[275] I hope Sussex bites and can be landed – they made Raworth[276] an MA after a year there and he's living on it still in USA, I believe. But I fancy you'll find my recommendation a heavy handicap to overcome. To most of these blighters I am still the Enemy, and moreover no gentleman. To put in a recommendation from me is practically an act of defiance.

They only deal with dead writers and Philip Larkin.[277] It isnt so easy to tell Larkin from a corpse.

You can supplement Ruskin's language lectures by (a) some commercial language course (b) gramophone records etc etc. They are bound to have some "language laboratory" fitted out with recorders. It's up to you, if you're willing to put the time in.

Three days ago I learned, from Jonathan W. by letter, that Louis Zukofsky had died.[278] That thins the population of good poets rather drastically. I hope McDiarmid can make a fool of the doctors, but I fear that, bar road accidents and strokes of lightning, I'll soon be the only survivor of what was rightly a famous generation. Louis had finished "A," and maybe it seemed to him that his business in this world had been completed.

W.B. YEATS

| | |
|---|---|
| EZRA POUND | W.C. WILLIAMS |
| T.S. ELIOT | LOUIS ZUKOFSKY |
| DAVID JONES | HUGH MCDIARMID |

[275] Ruskin College: independent educational institution in Oxford established in 1899. Affiliated to, but not absorbed by, the University of Oxford, it has a record of supporting adult and working-class learners. Pickard studied there in 1977–1978.

[276] Tom Raworth (1938–2017), Anglo-Irish poet central to Pickard's late-modernist milieu.

[277] Philip Larkin (1922–1985), hard-right British poetaster and trad jazz critic. His neo-Georgian light verse was the antithesis of BB's non-conformist modernism.

[278] Zukofsky died on 3 May. The first complete edition of his magnum opus "A" was in press at the time of his death and would appear via the University of California Press in December 1978.

and a lot of pretty good secondaries, such as Marianne Moore, Mina Loy, Hilda Doolittle, and what not, besides, rather isolated, yet part of it, Lorine Niedecker.[279] All these, except H.D., were among my friends; and I think there have been a great many generations that could not match them. Perhaps I could claim, like WBY, that my best epitaph would be "He had such friends."[280]

You'll have to be patient with English faculties for a while if you intend to exploit the universities; but of course you are right, they hate and fear literature, even the work of writers long since dead unless they can turn attention away from the poetry onto the footnotes.

If your friends Alison and Busby hang on to the Pious Cat for another week or two I intend to recall it and offer it to Ceolfrith – they've no distribution, but they like doing coloured pictures.[281] Or forgetting it, which would be very little loss.

Good poem. Yes, end it at the moustache.

Do you think if I made my tea with whisky instead of water I would find Washington more endurable? Come and have a look at it. The New Slum Development Corporation has made a splendid job of it. All we need is a large Borstal and a big annex to Durham Gaol.

Best to you and Joanna

Yrs
B.

## To Hugh Kenner

TS Texas

17 June 1978 107 Stridingedge, Blackfell, Washington, County Durham, NE37 1HJ

Dear Hugh Kenner

(It's a pleasure to hear from you. But first – you ask me to expand what I said of Zukofsky and Pound in the preface of my Collected Poems.[282] Here you are:)

[279] Lorine Niedecker (1903–1970), American modernist poet who became involved with the Objectivist group in the 1930s. A close friend of Louis Zukofsky, Niedecker met BB—who much admired her work—following his 1960s revival.

[280] See the final couplet of Yeats's 'The Municipal Gallery Revisited' (1937): 'Think where man's glory most begins and ends, | And say my glory was I had such friends.'

[281] *The Pious Cat*, BB's loose translation of a Persian children's story by Ubayd Zakani (*c.*1300–1371), was begun in 1937 but prepared for publication in BB's last years. In spite of the sorts of attempts demonstrated here, the poem was not published until 1986, when it appeared in a limited edition via Bertram Rota. Allison and Busby was Pickard's publisher in the 1970s and 1980s. For Ceolfrith Press see 14/10/74.

[282] In the preface to the 1978 OUP collected poems, BB acknowledged the influence of 'two living men... Ezra Pound and in his sterner, stonier way, Louis Zukofsky'.

Pound's conversation was as full as his writings of genial maxims about making poetry, with the advantage that you could sometimes ask him to exemplify. His maxims were by no means always compatible with one another and still less with his own practice, yet they were never negligible. You thought about them – at any rate I did – and might profit from them.

Zukofsky, about 1929 or 30, had selected a few of Pound's more cogent maxims and rephrased them (alas! in what I took to be the more obscure dialect of pedants) and he lived up to them and seemed to apply them to all he wrote in verse.

Pound made a few verbal strictures on my early poems, and he also did for my "Villon," at lightning speed, much what he had done far more momentously for Eliot's "Waste Land"; he struck out much, amended a little, and told me to amend more. Later he retrieved some discards of mine from my wastepaper basket and insisted on having them published.[283] I am not sure whether I am pleased about that.

Zukofsky however went through poems I sent him very meticulously, word by word, making suggestions here, fierce strictures there and sometimes recommending the wastepaper basket. (He would also sometimes express enthusiasm for particular lines or passages.) This he did when, as in the early thirties, I think his admiration for my work was very tepid indeed; and he kept it up later, after he had changed his mind. Even after the war he helped greatly with "The Spoils" and still took pains, though less lavishly, with the manuscript of "Briggflatts."

A systematic man might possibly have derived all Zukofsky's critical help from Pound's obiter dicta, but I am even less systematic than Pound, so that Zukofsky's patience and severity were very valuable to me...as they were to Carlos Williams – so WCW told me long ago.

It took more than two thousand years of violent opposition to make the Jews as stubborn as many of the best of them are. Sometimes I dont like it; but everyone admires and even loves that stubbornness in Spinoza, Zukofsky's favourite amongst philosophers; and the stubbornness L.Z. used in his verse and in his detailed criticism is just as admirable.

Pound was volatile, malleable and acute. Zukofsky was relatively unchanging, if somewhat slower to perceive.

(I hope that will suffice you.

No newspaper in this country, so far as I can learn, took any notice of Louis' death. It seems to me disgraceful. They were not, cannot have been, unaware of

283 Included in Pound's substantial selection of BB's work in *Active Anthology* (1933) were several poems BB disavowed in his later years: for example the ballad poems 'Gin the Goodwife Stint' and 'The Complaint of the Morpethshire Farmer.'

the estimate American poets made of him; but they are as helpless in the grip of a lot of contemporary dullards as they were sixty years ago in the grip of the "Georgians," and will stifle any rival reputation if they can. Of course, he wasnt a "gentleman" (neither am I) and to be a gentleman, particularly one from Winchester, is still far more important in England than to have talent, or candour.

I am interested to hear that you intend to review my poems. I wonder how you will see them on a second reading – which stand up to time and which have wilted.)

Yours ever
B

## To Sister Victoria Forde

TS Durham

[Late 1979] 107 Stridingedge, Blackfell, Washington, County Durham, NE37 1HJ

Dear Sister Victoria

Before I say anything else, let me tell you that I have talked to Colin Simms on the telephone (with some delay because of public holidays) and he has no objection at all to having bits of your book printed in Terrill's publication or in Loyd's and neither have I of course.[284] I think there has been some confusion. Simms probably said you'd have to consult me or some such nonsense, but of course there is no need for anything of the sort. It is your book, not mine. I think it will be useful publicity if chapters do appear elsewhere before your own publication.

Of course I am delighted that your labours are not being wasted entirely on the dusty shelves of theses in some university. I hope somebody will notice how able you are at such work – I've told people, but very few of them have ever taken any notice.

I hope that you are well and happy. Do they let you have any rest, any change, any travel? I know some literary nuns are allowed to roam about, because I have met more than one in the United States. I suppose it might depend on whether their convent was rich or poor.

I am sure I would like to meet you. I am to go to a sort of miscellaneous jamboree at Orono, Maine, in August. It is partly concerned with Pound, partly with me,

[284] Sections from Forde's doctoral thesis on BB (see 11/5/75) found their way into Caroll Terrell's essay collection *Basil Bunting: Man and Poet* (Orono, ME: National Poetry Foundation, 1981). Like the BB special issues of *Agenda*, *Paideuma*, and *Poetry Information*, though much longer, it featured the now typical mix of critical articles, memoirs, and bibliographies by the likes of Kenner, Davie, and Mottram.

and partly just a general (pointless) gathering, but it is organized by Terrill who is, you must have discovered, rather a vague man and it would not astonish me very much if something went wrong at the last minute. After that, I'll be finished with public reading, except for the two local universities and the Morden Tower, to which I feel some obligations: but first I may possibly read in Paris where my French translator, Jacques Darras seems to be arranging something.[285] Darras keeps his intentions dark till the time comes, so that too is uncertain and vague.

I have lived ten years too long. It is cheating the Bible to keep on after three score and ten; and so all my surviving friends of the past have died and I sometimes feel very much alone. MacDiarmid died, Zukofsky died; Tibor Serly gave me the hardest blow, because he was on his way to see to see me. He telephoned about his journey from London, stepped out of the telephone kiosk and was knocked over by a bus and killed – within a minute of talking to me about our old, dead friends.

Old men talk nonsense and write silly stuff, so I dont write any more – rarely even letters as, I'm afraid, you know. My children and grandchildren are resigned to getting no reply – and now that I'm a great-grandfather the next generation will have to put up with it too.

But I wish I had written oftener to you, since it is such a pleasure to open a letter from you.

Anyway, my dear, believe me I have much affection for you, even though I have never seen you.

Yours ever
B Bunting

## To Denis Goacher

TS Durham

29 April 1980

107 Stridingedge, Blackfell, Washington,
County Durham, NE37 1HJ

Dear Denis

No, no, no, no: things are much less usual than you are thinking.[286] To begin with, this celebration or whatever it should be called was not organised by the

[285] Jacques Darras (b. 1939), French poet and translator, whose French edition of BB's poems (*Briggflatts et autres poems*) was published in 1987.

[286] A celebration to mark BB's 80th birthday was organized by Tom Pickard at the University of Warwick on 26–27 April 1980. The programme was as BB describes below, though we

university, the English department, or some poetry society, but by the students' union and most of it had to be done while Tom Pickard, nominally in charge, was in fact in Warsaw. Nobody seems to have thought for a moment about the National Poetry Secretariat (no wonder, for Tom dislikes it even more than I do) and though they raised a little help from the Midlands Arts organization and a little from some other sources, practically the whole expense fell on the students' union, fortunately an unusually prosperous one. It was the students who insisted on making it a kind of congress (I am well known to detest such affairs) and some at least of the poets invited were picked by the students against Tom's advice. He hadnt a free hand. The only invitees present whom I had suggested were Turnbull and Roy Fisher; and one or two had been brought against my express wishes. I think perhaps a lot of the students would have been quite happy to have me omitted if I hadnt been the excuse for the jamboree. In part they would have been right – the one thing they all really enjoyed turned out to be Bob Cobbing's parlour games. That you were missing seems to be due almost entirely to Tom's absence in Warsaw at the convenient time for asking people, and partly to the Foreign Office who tried to deny Tom's Joanna a visa, misinterpreting Margaret Thatcher's new immigration laws which were aimed at the wretched Pakistanis but seem to be affecting all foreign-born wives of Englishmen, even, I hear, some Americans.[287] It took Tom three weeks of haggling with officials to get his wife admitted, and that certainly interfered very seriously with his general supervision of the students' efforts at organization.

I dont blame you for being thoroughly fed up and bitter, seeing how you have been treated for years; but it is a pity to single out a man who would have helped if he had known how. It is ultimately my fault for encouraging you to rely on writing; but indeed I dont think I had ever imagined you would lose or abandon other sources of cash meanwhile. Some people might think I had had an even rougher time, editing stock exchange prices and football results for years, and even a year correcting the proofs of bus timetables; and though I certainly resented the way the Times had treated me, on the whole I felt no grudge against

should note that Goacher was evidently upset not to have been invited, which might account for BB's consolingly downbeat retelling.

[287] Margaret Thatcher (1925–2013) led the British Conservatives to power in May 1970. Her eleven-year premiership saw a sharp turn to the right in British domestic and foreign policy, including the tightening of immigration BB mentions here. Prior to her election Thatcher had famously commented: 'If we went on as we are then, by the end of the century, there would be four million people of the new Commonwealth or Pakistan here. Now, that is an awful lot and I think it means that people are really rather afraid that this country might be rather swamped by people with a different culture.' Margaret Thatcher, TV Interview for Granada *World in Action*, 27 January 1978.

the poetry establishment, let alone against other strugglers. Tom Pickard has never had any help at all until this year (bar a partial subsidy for the Morden Tower when he was running it). His efforts as a labourer and his extremely unpleasant relations with the public assistance people have left him a bit bitter too. Life in Washington is not really like life in gaol, but it has some resemblance to it – I am not enjoying my old age – but I cannot really blame anybody for even a part of it, since I chose the path I have followed with my eyes open. If I'm very poor and very uncomfortable and decidedly lonely, I foresaw it all when I took to poetry. And yet I dont kick myself. I know I was right to do so.

The Poetry Secretariat, even more than the Poetry Society seems to me to have damaged the position of poets quite seriously, first by fixing minimum fees (which soon become maximums) at a rate even lower than that of the crudest entertainers in workingmen's clubs,[288] and second by exercising no discrimination between serious poets, would-be poets, and mere frauds. Of course I know that if they had tried to discriminate, I'd have been left out altogether; yet it would have been something to grade fees by some standard or other. The flood of readers who give poetry a thoroughly bad name might have been less overwhelming. The regional arts organisations are better, but they are moving fairly fast towards the standards of Women's Institutes and of the more imbecile Youth Workers – always away from art. No wonder the greater part of the nation, including most of the working class, despise us. Some of them even hate us.

The Warwick jamboree went much as I'd expected. They crowded into Tom's little rooms and ate and drank everything they found there without consulting him or Joanna. They talked alternatively bawdy with little point to it and the politics of their calling. One section seceded to some other room to devise means of ridding the Arts Council of Mr Osborne, pointless because his successor, whoever he might be would soon be up to the same tricks and manipulations. Others insisted on disorganising the programme that had been fixed by exceeding their allotted time, usually by about 60 per cent. Many read so badly they couldnt be heard – a dreary drone: yet perhaps it was as well they werent heard, for there was no sense or point in their stuff. Roy Fisher was excellent and Gael Turnbull up to standard, and I liked a very quiet modest fellow called Clark whom I'd never heard before, reading sly ironies a bit like those of Jonathan Williams. Wives and such like hovered around. Ken Smith[289] brought his son, an exceedingly pretty boy of 14 or 15 who would have driven Allen Ginsberg wild with lust if he had

[288] See 23/11/73 and note.

[289] Ken Smith (1938–2003), British poet who assisted John Silkin as co-editor of the Newcastle-based magazine *Stand* from 1963 to 1972.

been present, but Tom had sensibly left his equally pretty son in Gateshead. The musicians were not to my liking – an alleged "folk" singer from the group called Lindisfarne, hitting a guitar the way these people do, as though it were a banjo or ukulele.[290] No "folk" I can imagine had ever had anything to do with his words, which he'd doubtless concocted himself, and his tunes can hardly be said to have existed, as flat and dreary as the so-called cowboy stuff you hear at times. The universities own music man played the harpsichord, but did not understand how to phrase the Scarlatti sonatas he had practiced for the occasion. So you missed nothing much except your fee. I'm told the Times Literary Supplement had sent a reporter to abuse my performance. Maybe we'll see when they print it if they ever do.

I feel a little responsible for raising your hopes and then disappointing them; and perhaps you ought to have a small fraction of my fee, not as compensation – I cant give that – but to buy a few glasses of ouzo to sweeten life for an hour.

Yours ever
B

The Claudian excellent[291]

The latest review OUP has sent me treats me and Zukofsky with the utmost contempt. Bear up! Perhaps they'll think it worthwhile to abuse you before long!

## To Carolyn Burke

TS Yale

3 July 1980

107 Stridingedge, Blackfell, Washington,
County Durham, NE37 1HJ

Dear Carolyn Burke

Yours is the first letter for a long time to catch my interest.

As to Mina Loy, I cant help you in any way that would be of interest to your ultimate readers. I never knew anything about her since even then I didnt like to concern myself with the private lives of my friends. I knew her only a very short time; and not at all well, since she must have been nearly twice my age which set a narrow limit to intimacy. And in the second place, memory is, I believe, a chronic liar, not very far from fiction (think of any novelist you know – all liars), so that what I think I recollect is certainly not to be relied on. Take it with a great many grains of salt.

[290] Alan Hull (1945–1995), close friend of Tom Pickard and lead singer of Lindisfarne, a popular Newcastle folk-rock band.

[291] Presumably a translation by Goacher of the Roman poet Claudian (c.AD 370–c.404).

The poem you mention was itself a product of memory, and was not even addressed to recording facts.[292] Nothing in it is more than metaphor except the description of her face, which you have already noted, and which may easily have been distorted by the eight years or so which already stood between me and my last sight of her. I was sorry that I had never tried to make love to her, though I expect she would have laughed at me.

I cant remember how I met her. There's a very vague suggestion in my mind that I was in company with Brancusi,[293] the only one of the great artists of that time with whom I had more than a nodding acquaintance; but perhaps it is more likely that I was introduced by Ford Madox Ford, who introduced me to so many people. I was enormously struck by her beauty, a dark, melancholy beauty that didnt sentimentalise itself as so much female beauty does. Somehow I got invited to tea and cakes where she lived and then took every chance I got of calling on her or of sitting by her in the cafe, watching her face rather than talking; though probably I chattered as sillily as very young men do. She put up with it. She even let me imagine that she liked it, though she was probably amused at my pretensions to poetry, yet seemed to treat me seriously. So I was at least half in love with her – the only time I have ever had such feelings for a woman older than myself.

I dont know what she talked about, though it must have been in some sense encouraging. I dont remember who else she saw, though I am sure that sometimes Robert McAlmon was about and nearly sure that Berenice Abbot also appeared,[294] though I like Berenice so much I may merely have associated her in my memory with someone else I liked. She too deserved to be remembered and recorded.

After a few months of this curious friendship, never seeing much of her, Ford told me one day that Mina's daughter was coming from Italy and sent me to greet her with a bouquet. Joella was beautiful too[295] (and very conscious of it, I think) so that I found myself split as it were, between mother and daughter. I even imagine, looking back, though I cant have guessed it at the time, that the errand with the bouquet had been planned by Ford and Mina together as a likely way to rid Mina of my altogether too young attentions. I felt as much attached to her as

[292] BB's 'Now that sea's over that island', apparently written in 1930, is dedicated to Mina Loy.

[293] Constantin Brâncusi (1876–1957), Romanian artist who moved to Paris in 1903 and thereafter became one of the pioneers of modern sculpture. Loy's 1919 poem 'Brancusi's Golden Bird' is a tribute to him.

[294] Berenice Abbott (1898–1991), American photographer based in Paris in the 1920s.

[295] Loy's daughter Joella (1907–2004) would go on to marry the Bauhaus architect Herbert Bayer (1900–1985).

ever, but it was Joella I now wanted to make up to. I think Mrs Bayer must remember me, perhaps with tolerance, perhaps only with amusement.

Then Ford gave a great party, which served to return a great deal of hospitality offered him and to gather many of the contributors to the Transatlantic Review, but which he also intended to be a chance for me to dance with Joella all the evening. Unfortunately Ford didnt know that the very old-fashioned Quaker school at which I had been brought up regarded dancing as a sin, or almost a sin, so that I never learned how, but had to watch Joella dancing most of the evening with Tristan Tsara.[296] I never spoke to Tsara again, though we had been good cafe companions for a while. Mina tried to make up for this by a little intimate party where I could show off, and it was suggested that Joella should teach me to dance. I dont think anything came of the suggestion, but am not sure.

I went on seeing them for a while; but I was due to leave Paris soon. Then there was a great party when all the Americans gathered together – an embassy affair or something else semi-official, and Mina Loy got me invited to it. I had had enough drink already to set free my taste for mischief, then very active. When I came in some American lady, goodness knows who, introduced me to a very august looking female sitting with another like her in full evening regalia with a very cutaway bodice. She was said to be the wife of the missionary bishop of somewhere or other. As she held out her hand for it to be kissed in the French fashion I reached beyond it and scooped her exuberant bosom out of its corsage. Scandal. She, however, seemed to like it, set about drinking a great deal, and was presently doing cartwheels on the dancing floor. The scandal of the bishopess (or whatever you call her) was at its worst just as Mina Loy and Joella arrived. Joella ordered me home and I went off in disgrace. I have seen this incident described in some reminiscence of the time, but without names. It gave great pleasure to the cafes, but when I thought how angry Mina and Joella must be, I was in despair, so that I put forward my departure from Paris and left at once.

That was a mistake; for the very first letter that was forwarded after me was Joella's invitation to tea. I suppose I was forgiven. But I never saw either mother or daughter again, and I am not sure that I even wrote to them. Seven or eight years later I sent them each a copy of Redimiculum Matellarum, my first pamphlet, but again I cant remember whether or not either of them acknowledged it.

[296] Tristan Tzara (1896–1963) Romanian-French poet, performance artist, essayist, and one of the founders of the Dada movement in Zürich and Paris in the 1910s and 1920s.

That is the whole of my acquaintance with Mina Loy and her daughter. I can tell you no more and I dont think telephoned questions would be likely to stir any more memories.

Of course I read many of her poems. I still have the Lunar Baedeker McAlmon printed.[297] But they have largely faded from my memory and I dont think I can profitably say anything about them now. I thought very highly of them at the time.

I am afraid this is all about me and hardly at all about Mina Loy. For that I must apologise; but I hope it may at least entertain you for a moment and give an impression of some of the environs of her life.

I would be very pleased to see your biography when it is done. Let me know of it. I suppose you are already in touch with Jonathan Williams (Corn Close, Dentdale, Sedbergh, Cumbria) who is very interested in Mina Loy and all that concerns her.

Yours faithfully
B Bunting.

Forgive senile typing, senile irrelevance.

## To Kenneth Cox

TS Buffalo

19 December 1980

107 Stridingedge, Blackfell, Washington,
County Durham, NE37 1HJ

Dear Kenneth Cox

(Merry Christmas) (and a happy New Year)

I have just been looking through Montemora and I daresay you guess what pleasure your three reviews in it have given me.[298] I take pleasure, malevolently, in watching you trounce Geoffrey Hill, who deserves every word of it besides a lot more for the now common stupidity of imagining that 1980 is more or less 1630 in everything but industrial technology.

[297] Loy's first collection of poetry, *Lunar Baedecker* (corrected to 'Baedeker' in later editions) was published in 1923 by Robert McAlmon's Contact Editions.

[298] *Montemora* 8 featured articles by Cox on August Kleinzahler and Tom Pickard, and a forcible critique of the work of Geoffrey Hill (1932–2016).

And I am very pleased to see you praising Kleinzahler, one of the three pupils I believe may do something memorable sooner or later. Brent Mackay hasnt published a book yet:[299] when he does I hope it falls into your hands.

And then there is Tom Pickard. Somehow everybody else who has written about him seems to be deaf, or never to speak verse aloud, and they all slight him in one way or another. But you seem aware of the delicacy of rhythm which first caught my attention when I read his mss in his teens: even, though you dont use the word, his employment of syncopation in the sense in which you notice it in Dowland's music and Wyat's poetry. That's almost unique in his age. There seems too to be an implication that you have seen more coherence in Hero Dust than I have yet disentangled, though I dont doubt it's there. But you pass by Dancing Under Fire[300] – perhaps you wrote about it before, but I've forgotten? At the risk of sounding silly I'll tell you how it strikes me. I have just been listening to Beethoven's quartet Op 130 – the one that ends, or ought to end, with the Gross Fugue.[301] There again and again, especially in the first movement, I find themes set end to end which anybody going by the usual canons of music would say were entirely incompatible, and yet they are exactly right. That's what made Stravinsky call the work contemporary forever. The succession of themes in Dancing Under Fire strikes me in exactly the same way. Again and again you'd say: "This is impossible," but it isnt. Almost, once it's happened, you think it was inevitable. Very notably the long sequence of "dissolve," made, I should think, on a vague recollection of my description of one of the Taliesin's poems, has no logical line with the rest of the poem, and looks as if it went on far too long: but it doesnt.[302] It fulfils its part, no more. And again, the sudden unprepared appearance of Marta, the shell-shocked man – but the poem is about love, in some sense, and the poor wretch, shown through the mockery of children's voices, is an object of love, or something similar. He is in his place to a nicety. Moreover the whole poem holds together with a music which is never repetitive or mechanical and could hardly be deprived of even one line without damage. Everytime I see it again or it is

299 Like Kleinzahler, Brent MacKay was a student of BB's at Victoria University in 1970. His collection *The King of Bean* was published by Brick Books 1981.

300 Pickard's sequence 'Dancing Under Fire' was published by Middle Earth Books in 1973. A slightly adapted version is included in *Hero Dust: New and Selected Poems*, published by Allison and Busby in October 1979.

301 Beethoven's String Quartet No. 13 (1825), which originally incorporated the *Große Fuge* as its final movement, is a subtle, technically difficult work from Beethoven's intellectually daring late phase. For many years regarded as an aberration, the Quartet was championed by twentieth-century composers like Stravinsky, who celebrated its proto-modernist qualities.

302 BB refers in this passage to sections from 'Dancing Under Fire.' See Tom Pickard, *Hoyoot* (Manchester: Carcanet, 2014), 56–57.

brought to my mind I admire more. Four Quartets is far less consistent; Pound is sometimes as astonishing, but very rarely with such an economy of words and rhythms. I cant come near it. Only The Waste Land, amongst modern poems, fits together such contrasts convincingly, though you might treat Joyce as a long-winded poet and say that he does it too in many chapters of Ulysses. I'd go on, but I fear you've me down as absurd already. Nevertheless, I am sure that if Tom's poems escape the oblivion to which most reviewers seem to have assigned them, they will last an extremely long time, and Dancing Under Fire will be moving readers centuries hence. Nobody has said that publicly. I cant, because it is known that Tom is my "apprentice," and it would be discounted at once; but I want to see it said – and believed.

You are a patient man, Mr Cox, putting up with me ("in his second childhood")[303] even explaining when I misunderstand. So forgive this. It's main object is to thank you for three essays which get an awful lot into very few words.

Yours ever
B

## To Sister Victoria Forde

TS Durham

2 June 1981 The Cottage, Greystead, Tarset, Hexham, NE48 1LE

Dear Sister Victoria

How kind of you to write to me! People ought to have forgotten me by now, old enough to be of no interest to anybody and not old enough to be matter for archaeology.

But first let me call your attention to my new address. It signifies that I have at last escaped from Washington, a place I detested, and am just settling in to a little house, pretty nearly where I've wanted to be for many years. I look out over a big garden (not mine but I can use it) to the hills of the dale of the North Tyne, covered with sheep, and lambs too at this season, with a glimpse of the river and quiet all around. Very big trees shelter me from most winds – an enormous ash grows right up against my chimney, and an owls lives in it which never fails to a say goodnight to me. I'll miss the children who were the only good things about

[303] See *As You Like It*, II.7.165.

Washington, since the population of Tarset is only about 30, and no doubt I'll find shopping awkward, for the nearest shop is six miles away and for anything more than basic needs I'll have to drive 25 miles into Hexham, down an exceedingly twisty road, which makes it nearly an hour's drive. But the place is so lovely nothing of that sort matters.

So I'm very pleased to hear that you are enjoying the dramatic sight of the Rockies. The mentally retarded adults may not be pleasing, of course, but the mountains will be some consolation.

I'm afraid I stay more or less indifferent to things like Terrell's book, as also to the film Derek Smith intends to make of me this summer.[304] But I am not indifferent to your thesis.[305] It turned up when I began to unpack books, and I looked through it again. I hope Colin Simms gets on with it. However I noticed a lot of inadvertent slips, slight misquotes and one or two errors of fact in the typescript, so I'd be willing, if you approve, to go through the proofs when there are any before Colin sends them on to you to remove a few such blemishes (but not of course to modify any of your interpretations or opinions). If this seems desirable to you, please write to Colin. I wont approach him unless you do so first.

I am sorry you have had the ordeal of your father's death to disturb you. However as you describe it death seems to have taken him fairly gently, so that the hurt to you will mend before too long.

I dont expect to write any more. What a man of my age writes can seldom be any good. Nevertheless in such a splendid place, if there are no nagging worries, something might happen to get down on paper at last – even perhaps "The New Moon."[306] There are sure to be visitors in the summer (this is a "beautyspot," thronged on public holidays) but I dont expect any at all in the winter so that I may write out of boredom!

I think all my friends know that I love your gentle intelligence. Probably you know it yourself in spite of the letters I rarely write. So now –

Love

B

[304] Derek Smith (1927–2015), British television producer. He co-wrote the film *Basil Bunting: An Introduction to the Work and the Poet* with director Peter Bell.

[305] Forde's thesis on BB would eventually be published as *The Poetry of Basil Bunting* (see **16/3/83** and note)

[306] See **9/5/72** and notes.

## To William Cookson

TS Yale

5 October 1981 The Cottage, Greystead, Tarset, Hexham, NE48 1LE

Dear William Cookson

Thankyou for the David Jones book[307] and the current Agenda.[308] I am even more isolated than ever in this remote place, and though that doesnt worry me at all I'm pleased to hear what's going on now and again.

It's quite an interesting number of Agenda, though to me discussion of poetic drama is as far away as the speculations of the Gnostics. There's been nothing of the sort in English since about 1640, only an affectation which has withered steadily since Dryden's day through stage after stage of irrelevance and pretence. And since the theatre is dead anyway, slaughtered first by the musichall and then by television, poets who fancy action had better investigate what form television has room for – not a vain attempt to force poetic drama on it, but something that fits into regular needs (not usually self-consciously arty). I cant read Mr Dale's dramas and though I did at one time oblige myself to read Eliot's, because I thought he must surely know what he was doing, I didnt enjoy them. Ibsen wrote plays; I wonder whether any have been written since he died. Chekov? Not a bit of it. Bar a few short farces, he has nothing that emerges from a very narrow middleclass gossipy mirrorgazing. Becket? Good lord no! Those are case histories. You can find the like in the textbooks of indifferent psychologists.

The last inventive theatrical maker was Charlie Chaplin, and his outlet is closed now too. But a bit of clowning wouldnt hurt, and might suggest possibilities, if there were poets less concerned with their personal dignity than those I hear of.

Agenda's editor was wise to invest heavily in Ezra Pound and then in David Jones, and there is still room to write about them; but time is narrowing that space quickly. The Pound people get more and more pedantic. As for Jones – I am annoyed and scared to see a volume full of verbiage, which might have become poetry if it had had strength enough to force Jones to work on it and boil out the slops. If you like his peculiar erudition, there are paragraphs of some interest, but nothing essential. He had done the job in Anathemata, thoroughly, once for all. I said, when asked about the subsequent bits and pieces, that there couldnt be any more David Jones, because he was too old to rid himself of a great task that had

[307] The descriptions below seem to indicate that Cookson sent BB a copy of Jones's *The Sleeping Lord*, a work of poetic fragments published prior to Jones's death in 1974.

[308] *Agenda* 18.4–19.1 (Winter–Spring 1981) was a double issue dedicated to verse drama, which included Peter Dale's play *Sephe*.

been accomplished; more Anathemata only obscured what he'd done already like needless outhouses tacked onto a splendid building, there was no new notion to be worked on and shaped. But this isnt even new Anathemata, just discarded material, builder's rubble. Oh, if people would only use their waste paper baskets!

Glad so see Michael Alexander busy.[309] If you are writing to him, please relay my respects.

I am sorry to hear of marital trouble and of your concussion. I do hope it wont interfere with your work any longer. Here I'm as content as I need be, delighted with the countryside and I think healthier than for some years past. But nothing to write comes into my mind, and perhaps it had better not, for most old men seem to be fools and I dont claim any right to be thought an exception.

All the best
B.

## To Sister Victoria Forde

TS Durham

1 December 1981 — The Cottage, Greystead, Tarset, Hexham, NE48 1LE

Dear Sister Victoria

I was just sitting down to answer your previous letter (at last) when your letter of November 21 was delivered.

First let me say how pleased I am to hear that you will be visiting England and that there may be a chance to see you, in spite of the very limited time your job will leave you.[310] More about that presently.

I had great difficulty in getting in touch with Colin Simms, but on Saturday 29 November he suddenly tapped at my door and walked in. He has been in Siberia, where I imagine no letters followed him. I told him you were worried about your thesis-book. I cannot say that he explained clearly what was going on, but he assured me that all was well – there had been difficulties but things were going ahead now. I couldnt press him hard because there was a young woman with him, a stranger to me, and I was also busy trying to get tea for them – I'd nothing

[309] Michael Alexander (b. 1941), British literary scholar who wrote *The Poetic Achievement of Ezra Pound* (1981), and later co-edited a collection of essays titled *Sons of Ezra: British Poets and Ezra Pound* (1995), which featured James McGonigal's 'An XYZ of Reading: Basil Bunting in the British Tradition.'

[310] Forde visited BB in March 1982.

much in the house – so I cannot give you any definite news. However he wasnt worried, so I suppose it is all right.

You will be in London, with intervals, from 6 January till 8 May. One of your sisters will be there during your February break and another in March. I may be in London for two or three days, but it is not certain, and I dont know the date, to do a reading or two readings, which you (and perhaps your pupils) might like to hear. I will let you know what is arranged when it IS arranged. In addition, you want to show them something of the North Country, and indeed that is worth doing. I think everybody ought to see Durham, one of the most beautiful cities in northern Europe and the most splendid Norman cathedral of all – the most impressive cathedral this side of the Alps. I dont think you will find that hard to arrange through whoever handles your travel schemes. Perhaps the university might put me up for a couple of nights so that I could meet you there – I've a standing invitation to Grey College.[311] Then, all Americans and a great many European tourists want to see the Roman Wall, which is quite near me. It's a bad time of year for it, since the usual thing is to walk along the top of the Wall from Housesteads to the Twice Brewed, in very bleak exposed country; but there are diggings to look at for those who dont like the hardier task.[312] Maybe, if your flock is gathered in some hostel, you could spend the night in my spare room here, only 20 or 30 miles from them. The train journey from London is costly; but if their purses run to it, there are also castles to be seen – the showy ones at Alnwick and Bamburgh, the less known the enormously impressive one at Hermitage.[313] It is possible to visit Holy Island (Lindisfarne) where Aidan[314] and Cuthbert settled down to turn the Angles into Christians, and very picturesque it is, though the tides bar the road twice a day for a few hours. And there is Bewcastle Cross, standing where it has stood for at least 1300 years, with its Runes, its carvings and its crisscross patterns looking as though they had been cut yesterday in spite of all that exposure to our roughest weather.[315] Finally, almost all Americans

[311] Grey College: constituent college of Durham University.

[312] As BB describes, the best preserved and most visited section of Hadrian's Wall is in south-west Northumberland, between the auxiliary fort Housesteads (Vercovicium) and Milecastle 39 near the Twice Brewed Inn.

[313] Alnwick Castle, latterly famous for its role as a location in the *Harry Potter* film franchise, is a medieval castle in north Northumberland, and the seat of the duchy of Northumberland; Bamburgh, the ancient seat of the Kings of Northumbria, is a coastal fortress much renovated in the nineteenth century; for Hermitage Castle see 5/7/77.

[314] St Aidan (d. 651) founded the monastic settlement on Lindisfarne at the behest of King Oswald (see note to 28/4/69).

[315] Bewcastle Cross: well-preserved Anglo-Saxon cross with runic inscriptions in Bewcastle, Cumbria, near Spadeadam (see 10/6/69).

and a great many other people like Edinburgh, which has much variety and as much dignity. But Edinburgh is a bit out of my range.

I'm afraid all these are rather "cultural" shows, not always what youngsters want to see, though it is surprising what they will digest. Take them to a football match in London. Years ago I would have said take them to the pantomime at the Elephant,[316] but they pulled down the Elephant long since, and though there may still be theatres in the suburbs or in south London where they keep up the Old Victorian pantomime, the lush ones in Central London are just what you might see anywhere – no real fun.

I am not sure whom you know in London. Tell me, and I'll see if there are others to introduce you to. Stuart Montgomery? Gael Turnbull? etc etc

I dont think Oxford University Press is likely to be any use to you about publishing the thesis. I fancy they dont take much stock in me and correspondingly little in anything about me.

Perhaps Agenda might tackle it – I doubt it, but it might be worth trying, and Cookson knows you since he printed part of it. (Didn't he? Or am I getting confused in my old age?)

I'm in excellent health (for my age), much better since I came out here. Every morning when I look out of the window I still tell myself how lucky I am to have found this cottage, after seven months of it! I dont mind that it is rather cold or that shopping is troublesome so far from the shops – that's nothing set against the beauty of the place and its quietness. The only thing I miss is the society of children; there arent any here at all, after the crowds of them in Washington. My daughter Maria comes to see me now and then, and other visitors turn up on occasion. I'm out of reach of libraries, so I'm rereading Shakespeare, enjoying a lot of it, though not all. But just keeping the house going takes a lot of my time.

What you tell me about Tom Gunn is surprising and reassuring. I had supposed his lot were indifferent when they were not hostile.[317] Though I'm not ambitious, I like to hear that people enjoy what I've written.

[316] The Elephant and Castle Theatre in south-west London flourished 1879–1932. It was famous for its Christmas pantomimes,

[317] Thom Gunn (1929–2004), Anglo-American writer originally associated with the Movement poets of the 1950s, who were usually regarded as a separate and opposing tendency to BB's late-modernist milieu. On 17 November 1981 Gunn delivered a lecture on BB's work at the University of Cincinnati (close to Forde's home at Mount St. Joseph University), in which he effusively praised *Briggflatts*, stating: 'I am not in the business of assigning positions in a literary hierarchy, but I would guess that *Briggflatts* will someday be recognised as being as rich and important a poem as either *The Waste Land* or "Canto 67"—I am certain that no living writer has composed a poem that means more to me.' Recording at https://drc.libraries.uc.edu/handle/2374.UC/697042.

Meanwhile, you are busy getting ready for your trip; and I must light a fire and cook a meal, so here I stop writing.

Good luck to you; and you know you have my love.

B

## To Sister Victoria Forde

TS Durham

16 March 1983 The Cottage, Greystead, Tarset, Hexham, NE48 1LE

Dear Sister Victoria

Disappointed? Good gracious me, what nonsense. Like everybody else who met you I was delighted with you. I wonder how I could have given you the wrong impression. Of course it is true I was very tired – that's just a part of growing old, and I have been even more tired this year, having been nearly three weeks in the South judging that silly poetry competition: I was quite exhausted for more than a week after it and am very far from being my usual self again even yet.[318] Or perhaps it is because I havent written. But you must know by now that I very seldom write letters, even business letters. I am not good at it. I am getting worse, and lazier and perhaps I will lose all my friends by never writing. No, my dear, I am very fond of you and took great pleasure in your society, though I was a bit harassed by my inability to offer you a better stay and show you more.

I am sorry Anvil Press[319] isnt more enthusiastic about your book. As for Neil Astley,[320] I dont know him, though I must have met him. I have the impression that he is very ambitious and quite serious. His "Bloodaxe Books" did that flimsy disk of me reading Briggflatts, and I didnt think much of that: but I didnt expect to.[321] I dont think I have seen any of the books he puts out, but I have been told they are quite decently done.

[318] BB spent three weeks in February 1983 as one of the judges of the Arvon International Poetry Competition, run by the Devon-based Arvon Foundation and chaired by Ted Hughes.

[319] London-based poetry publisher founded in 1968 and absorbed by the larger Carcanet Press in 2015.

[320] Neil Astley (b. 1953), Hampshire-born graduate of Newcastle University, who founded the publisher Bloodaxe Books (named after BB's *Briggflatts* character) in Newcastle in 1978. Bloodaxe eventually became an orthodox poetry imprint best known for its commercial anthologies, but in its younger days it published adventurously in disparate genres and forms—see for example Sirkka-Liisa Konttinen's photographic survey *Byker* (1983) and Tom Paulin's apologia for Irish Republicanism, *Ireland and the English Crisis* (1984). As such it would have seemed a fitting home for Forde's monograph, which eventually appeared via Bloodaxe (as *The Poetry of Basil Bunting*) in 1991.

[321] In 1980 Bloodaxe issued an LP, 'Basil Bunting reads Briggflatts.'

Silkin's fame is for selling copies of "Stand" to everyone he meets. He plods on, issue after issue, never livening up: honest work, I think, but misconceived. His real interest is something between rather raw politics and even rawer ethics. Nevertheless he once wrote a few pleasant nature poems. I know nothing about Mr Gunn except what you tell me. However I think well of Tony Harrison. He translates good plays well for the stage.

I am a bit limited these days because the car is even more decrepit than I am. Often I cannot go shopping but have to depend on the van that comes round twice a week or bother my daughter Maria to shop for me and bring the stuff all the way up here. She will get sick of me sooner or later.

In the South I spent several days with six other poets in Devonshire, as guests of Ted Hughes, finishing the judging of 33,000 poems! Three of them had first of all reduced the number to 1,800 or so by throwing out those they thought the very worst. Adrian Mitchell[322] lightened his share (11,000) by making a private collection of the most preposterous entries. He read us a few of them for fun. A poem about the soldiers who were killed by a bomb while parading through Hyde Park[323] began: "Klip-klop, klip-klop, klip-klop, BANG!" but then, I'm afraid, fell off into maudling. I read all my 1,800 poems without finding one good one, or more than three or four that were excusable. That was exhausting if you like! One of the judges was a tiresome fool, who spent half a day reading entries aloud in order to tell us why he didnt recommend that one. That might have gone on for ever, if I hadnt made an alliance with Stephen Spender to reverse the procedure and get them to exhibit only the poems they did recommend for the main prizes, and in that way we polished the poems off at a good pace and finished with half a day to spare. They were all so bad that I didnt care what the result was, yet three of the first five prizes were poems I had chosen. After the choice, we were told the names of the authors, and not one of the 35 prizewinners was anybody we had ever heard of. Earlier, I had recognized, from the style, one poetess, but her poem was bad and I chucked it out, and nobody else mentioned it.

Ted and his wife were very hospitable and very attentive. I liked them both.

Now I've enough money to be sure of one, probably two years before I get into difficulties. But I'm sure I'm a lot older for the experience.

I had a day with Richard Hamilton, the painter, too, and enjoyed it a lot.

Stuart and Deidre Montgomery had a little party for my birthday; much wine, much laughter, going home at 2.30 a.m. I stayed at Henshaw's house by Regent's

322 Adrian Mitchell (1932–2008), British poet associated with socialist and pacifist causes.

323 In July 1982 the Irish Republican Army (IRA) detonated two bombs during military processions in Hyde Park, London, killing eleven.

Park, but I have aged enough to prevent me going out into the streets of London even once.

Your flowers are further on than ours. Our daffodils are only promising to blossom, though we have out usual early profusion of snowdrops, thousands of them, amongst the trees and by the path.

We've a very fine fox about, astonishingly big and astonishingly bold. He often comes to raid our rubbish bins. Sometimes he brings his lady friend with him, so that we could reconstruct what they were up to from their tracks in the snow while there was snow. The fox goes and peeps through the pub window to see who is there, and the vixen goes every night to a house at the Eals where they put out food for her.[324] She is partial to bread and marmalade. No one will help the Tynedale hunt to get either of those two.[325] We are really proud of the dog-fox, who walks amongst the flocks of an afternoon, scared of no one and nothing.

Oh! While I remember... will you please tell me the name of the sister who did those colour etchings for Briggflatts?[326] I have forgotten it, and I want to find a home for the etchings, but cant until I can at least say who they are by. I cant show them myself – no space – though they deserve to be shown.

Thankyou for your card. The writing on the picture is so small that I haven't been able to identify the two on the throne, but maybe I will one day.

Meanwhile, love to you. Flourish.

God bless you
B

## To Tom Pickard

TS Buffalo

19 March 1983 — The Cottage, Greystead, Tarset, Hexham, NE48 1LE

Dear Tom

No guilt. The history of most poets not born rich is much the same, and if, like me, you fail to get more prosperous later on, the discomfort is that you have so little chance of helping your juniors. But that competition has put a tiny balance

[324] Eals Lodge: former coaching inn a few hundred yards from BB's house at Greystead.

[325] Tynedale Hunt: foxhunting organization based at Stagshaw Bank near Hexham. Although BB sympathized profoundly with rural labourers, he was less keen on the squirearchal figures who directed Northumberland field sports. In one of the most abstract passages in Part IV of *Briggflatts*, he finds a metaphor for his late middle age in the image of a small animal trapped by 'hunters | with stick and terriers' (90–94).

[326] See note to 1/1/72.

in my hands of which five per cent for you and five for Tanya Cossey is a very minimum of what I think I owe you.[327]

I am delighted to have this batch of poems (worth a lot more than my minute contribution) and a good deal of interesting discussion.[328] I cant say much about them this chilly day, with my belly misbehaving as it mostly does after a change of temperature. But two points.

Punctuation by stops and commas and so on can help out syntax by hinting how a sentence is put together either grammatically or in speaking. Where the line ends usually shows or hints at the rhythmical structure. Mallarmé (good poet when he didnt let theory get in his way) began spreading his words and lines about the page to indicate some sort of arcane or mystical or otherwise super-punctuation, and Ezra, who didnt usually take much stock in Mallarmé, imitated him rather arbitrarily in English for a while, but forgot about it in the later Cantos days. I cant see what either of them ever got out of it. Somebody else lately has been complaining about sentences of mine starting at the end of a line and getting on with it in the next line, but if you look you will always find that rhythmically, at any rate if you give the full-stop a decent time allowance, such words just complete the line. Of course that looks queer if, like Creeley, you make an exaggerated pause at every line end irrespective of the movement of the sentence. There are exceptions, but in my work generally lines run on, with no pause, or only a tiny pause, much less than half a comma, such as the Persians call a "nim-fatha"[329] and use in other positions too. In most of the Cantos Ezra's long line is "end-stopped," – rarely runs on. But he's not consistent and I daresay I'm not either. The chief puzzle might be Chomei at Toyama, which was first written in very strict quantitative metres, and these of course dictated a line length; but I found I'd let the metres distort my English here and there and also I didnt want disputes with professors about longs and shorts, so I rearranged it, ending the lines where some sort of pause might be wanted in reading it aloud. That wasnt consistent, and no doubt has helped people not to notice that the lines have any steady pattern at all, just, they think, "free verse." I've written very little "free verse." I take my freedoms where I want them, but not too many. Since all the critics hate quantity and distrust anybody who thinks he can discern it, it had better stay the way it is.

[327] BB met Tanya Cossey (b. 1968) and other members of her family while living in Washington, near Sunderland in the late 1970s. She was a friend and correspondent of BB's in his last years.

[328] BB is commenting on poems which fed into Pickard's collection *Custom and Exile*, published by Allison and Busby in 1985.

[329] *Nīm-fatḥa*: device in Persian prosody whereby a short vowel sound is inserted to fill out the metre.

As for what you call an "open-ended epic," no, I always saw the danger which has left all such poems rather shapeless. The Cantos had an excellent shape when they were planned, but the world changed and Ezra changed and all but a fragile wisp of the over-all architecture of the poem vanished as its matter changed. The same thing happened to Spencer's even more carefully planned poem,[330] and though Louis Zukofsky did, in a sense, fulfil his structure as he'd planned it, parts swelled and parts shrank until without being told you'd hardly guess it too had a meticulous shape when it began. As to Olson, he never really tried to have a structure, and his poem degenerated into library notes and became a proper bore. Ezra and Spenser were valiant but not far-seeing.

But a poem regarded as a commentary on the life around you as it alters day by day is a trap anyway. No poet is wise enough or witty enough to keep it going. Wordsworth, writing the Prelude, was not looking on something happening, but on what had happened. His matter was fixed, by the fact that it was past and done with; and even so his view of his own youth altered while he was writing it and took away its planned shape. Like the epic lengths of Ezra and Spencer and Zukofsky, it was presumptuous claiming more insight and wisdom than the author possessed, but it was better because it was restricted by the matter he was using. Dante kept strictly to a scheme, and so did Lucretius, as far as he went, but thought was not changing so fast in their days, not fast enough to destroy the architecture of the poem.

(Suicide saved Lucretius from having to alter his scheme as he surely must have done when Caesar really got going and the notion of Rome was transformed).

So Ezra wrote a poem which was not the one he set out to write. The Alps did happen by chance,[331] or as the mound grows where the labourer chucks his shovelfuls, and the splendours are haphazard. The French, "et l'on entend... le refrain joyeux et leger" – "and one hears the joyous, light refrain," is from a French or Piedmontese Alpine folksong, the singer being a chamois hunter and poacher.[332] One also struggles across the screes of Chinese history etc.

Chaucer is more conversational, yes, but also more verbose.

Love and luck to Joanna. Dont call the baby "Margaret Thatcher Pickard," not even Karl Marx Pickard.

Yrs
B.

[330] I.e. Spenser's *The Faerie Queene*.
[331] See 'On the Flyleaf of Pound's Cantos' (1, 8–9) and *Briggflatts* (Part I, 36–37).
[332] 'On the Flyleaf of Pound's Cantos' (4) references this folksong.

## To Tom Pickard

MS Buffalo

29 May 1984

Corn Close, Dentdale

Dear Tom –

Sorry you were so worn out when I saw you, but I didnt notice it. On the contrary, I thought you were more buoyant than usual.

The London trip tired me very badly, and the drive home was bad – chiefly because Gregory Corso had wished himself on the journey. He is a clot. He lay in a corner of the backseat, looking at nothing all the way, but keeping his windows wide open to blast the rest of the car; and when we paused for a coffee he complained of the ugliness of the English scenery he hadnt looked at. I'd have liked to piss on him.

House? I've just signed the conveyance. It's a fairly old one storey cottage in the car park of the pub at Whitley Chapel, about 8–10 miles s.w. of Hexham. No view, nothing like so good as Greystead, yet a place I'd always have been content to live in. But I cant get in to it before about July!

I'm sorry you've temporarily separated from Joanna and Kuba. I liked your son – so pretty and so friendly.

The vision of your ice-rink flat is grotesque and amusing, but for you it must be rather alarming and distressing. Hope damage is not too severe.

Poet laureate? What a silly notion.

I leave here next weekend, and will be at my daughter's, Farnley Grange West, Corbridge: 971-3279, until I can get into my new cottage at the beginning of July.

Luck be with your stories: and with you

B

## To Kenneth Cox

MS Buffalo

23 June 1984

Fox Cottage, Whitley Chapel, Steel, Hexham, NE47 0HA

Dear Kenneth Cox

There, at last, is a new address, and one I cannot be thrust out of if I pay the mortgage on time – a huge relief after an anxious year. I shall move in about July 4, I believe.

I was so disorganised and harassed that I never found time and energy to thank you for the two Céline books, which have in fact given me a lot of pleasure and are about to be re-read. There is nothing so impressive as the best passages in the three books about the end of the war in Germany, but much, especially in the "London Bridge," which revivifies my recollections of London a few years after the time he describes, and that in spite of careless or wilful inaccuracies which I imagine he considers irrelevant details in his picture.[333] A demonstration for novelists of the sort Pound provided for poets, of where the essence of the art lies. Some are gross – the girl who is 12½ in once scene, 14 shortly after, and "about 15" within two months of the first scene – but it makes no difference at all: it is vivid and moving. (What would Zola or Arnold Bennet have said!) I think I could even find (the site of?) the pub in Tooley Street,[334] though almost every detail is false in my recollection. What a writer!

I'm too thrang, moving house, to write at length. I hope, when you are in the North you will find your way to Fox Cottage: it is not as remote as Greystead was, if less beautiful and, perhaps, less comfortable: still, a nice place.

All my best

B.

## To Sister Victoria Forde

TS Durham

14 July 1984 Fox Cottage, Whitley Chapel, Steel, Hexham, NE47 0HA

Dear Sister Victoria

You have reason to complain of my long silence. All this year until last week, and almost all the year before, I've been so hassled and worried and confused by being turned out of my pretty cottage at Tarset that I've not had either a calm mind or a trace of energy to write letters at all. For a very long time we searched for a new home, I, helped by my daughter and son-in-law, my ex-wife and Colin Simms, but there was nothing even tolerable. Mrs Thatcher revised the law about housing a couple of years ago, and the result is that there are no houses at all to let any more, except a few where kindly landlords protect old tenants;[335] they are all for "summer lets" nowadays, when the landlords can get very large rents for a

[333] Cox had earlier introduced BB to the late work of French writer Louis-Ferdinand Céline (1894–1961), sending him three novels in 1981, which prompted BB to say that he had been 'debauched…good and proper!' (see BB to Kenneth Cox, 7/3/82, Buffalo). The novel mentioned here, *London Bridge: Guignol's Band II* (1964), centres on the protagonist's experiences of the London demi-monde of the 1910s.

[334] Tooley Street: thoroughfare in Southwark, central London.

[335] One of the keynote policies of Thatcher's Conservative administration from 1980 was a largscale sell-off of public housing to private tenants.

few summer months, from townspeople on holiday. They get more that way, and if they let for as much as a year and a day at a time, there are serious penalties. That is so all over the country, and even local councils have been ordered to sell their houses and let no more of them. The Forestry Commission has several villages built to house its foresters, very remote, so that no one but a forester or a shepherd would want to live in them, but it has been ordered to sell all of them, at any loss, and not to let any. Foresters are having to commute from the city, miles away – they cant afford to buy the houses – while the villages are falling to pieces, unrepaired. This is all part of that snatching at ready money, selling off all the country's assets, to avoid taxing the richest section of the people. In the end her policy will restrict the mobility of labour, thus defeating one of her professed aims, and leave England without that foundation of heavy industry on which all prosperity has been and must always be built – electronics (if we can do it at all) is to earn Britain's living, though all these computers are good for big administrations, but very bad for small ones (expensive) and cannot make anything at all – that is done with steel and plastics and aluminum and wood, with coal and oil, or with land. Your country has done some queer things, but hasnt made such gross errors as that yet.

Anyway the upshot is that cottages to let cannot be found. So that after more than a year of searching and disappointment, John, my son-in-law, came up with a plan whereby I might get a mortgage in spite of my age and poverty, and so buy a place of my own. That's what we have done: it's quite a pleasant place, though not a patch on Tarset. I think I will be able to live here comfortably, once it has been paid for, but there were repairs to do before the building society would grant a mortgage, and these have put me badly in debt, which I always dread. So though my worries are much less, they arent over.

Fox Cottage is about eight miles south of Hexham, in a tiny village – no shops at all, but that will be alright once I have a car again, which I expect in a week or so. The cottage stands next door to a well-kept pleasant old pub. It has no immediate outlook, but as soon as I go out of my door I have pretty wide views, still with forest on the horizon – Slaley forest, oak and other deciduous trees, but open and very windy and comparatively high up. It may be cold in winter. I wish it were on the North Tyne, of course, but these parts (Hexhamshire) are also thought beautiful, and the lanes are narrow and twisting. I shall be a little more cramped than I was, but not badly, and when we can finish furnishing it there will be a bed for visitors. The pub's drinkers park their cars all around me, which is noisy at night, but I'll get used to that in the end.

I'm glad you remembered Tanya and her paintings.[336] I'm pleased because she seems to have stood up to her parents, refused to go into a sweatshop factory, and found her way into an art school – the humblest, least efficient of art schools, but a first step towards something better. But I've not seen her for many months, and may have to wait a while yet because I still lack a spare bed.

I've heard nothing from Astley, but I think he told Colin that your book was due soon. You must be very tired of these delays. So many people have to endure them.

I dont think there is much more that I can say. My last trip to London a few months ago tired me beyond reason, so I've no plans of travel even for a few miles (I'll be at this address unless they gaol me for debt until the worms get me). I keep well, free of rheumatism, but in some ways feeble. My utmost walk must be about a mile, and I wont willingly venture on foot more than half a mile.

I've got to apologise for my dreadful typing. I believe it gets worse every day.

Maria wants me to remember her to you. All my family seem well; and though I cant say Tom is flourishing, at least he seems to manage to his own satisfaction. Other friends are pretty cheerful, I think – Montgomery, Henshaw, Tom Pickard, and their various wives and offspring.

I hope you are vigorous, and not overworked, and find your students responsive. And let us have a new Pope please, this one is too conservative.

Love to you dear sister,

B Bunting

Colin Simms sends his love

## To Gael Turnbull

MS Scotland

8 February 1985

Fox Cottage, Whitley Chapel, Steel,
Hexham, NE47 0HA

Dear Gael

Thanks for your friendly letter, but your invitation is one I cant accept. I've no objection to Ed. Morgan,[337] of course, or the other poets you mention, so that two or three years ago I would certainly have said: Yes, please. But by now I am only wreckage – it is weeks since I ventured as far as Hexham. Eating is a chore – cooking an imposition – making my bed is labour. I cant even read for more than about an hour, and only old stuff that spares me the effort of understanding.

[336] See **19/3/83** and note.
[337] Edwin Morgan (1920–1910), major Scottish late-modernist poet.

This may seem very improper to you: and I am ashamed of being so old. Maybe the spring – if there is one – will revivify me a bit, but I have no confidence in it.

Jacques Darras (my French transalator) is to call here early in March. He is a very likable man, a very interesting one, and he hints that he has something special to discuss: but though I'll be as hospitable as I can, I really wish he wasnt coming – the effort will tire me again and leave me with a week or two of exhaustion.

All the best to you, Gael, and to all yours.

B

## To Massimo Bacigalupo[338]

TS Durham

20 March 1985

Fox Cottage, Whitley Chapel, Steel,
Hexham, NE47 0HA

Dear Massimo B.

Yes, it is a long time since I wrote. I was never a good correspondant, and now – any man over seventy or so is a fool and any man over eighty an obscene idiot. Exceptions are exceedingly rare, and I am not one of them. Jonathan Swift understood and pictured the "Strudbrugs" in the third book of Gulliver;[339] and I am reluctant to exhibit myself as something rather similar. So I make little effort to fulfill the usual courtesies of correspondence. My apologies are merely my 85 years.

The same years prohibit me from travelling. Old men are really disgusting to themselves as well as to those who try to put up with them. I shall not revisit Italy, probably not even London. I am even reluctant to cut myself off from the familiar conveniences of my cottage for a whole day.

That does not mean that I disregard my friends. You are at liberty to print anything of mine that has once been in print. I dont regard any published work as private property, though my notions may have changed completely in time.

I dont recognize the bit about Scriabin which you have sent me.[340] It is far too favourable. But I suppose I thought it fairly correct once. As for photographs,

[338] **Massimo Bacigalupo**: Italian Pound scholar and filmmaker, from Rapallo.

[339] The Struldbrugs appear in Swift's *Gulliver's Travels* (1726). Although they are immortal, they are not immune from the ageing process: until the age of thirty they live normal lives, after which their physical and mental health declines, and they are declared legally dead at the age of eighty.

[340] Here and in the following passage BB comments on his contributions to the Rapallo journal *Il Mare* in the early 1930s. Reviewing a performance by pianist Gerhart Münch of works by

nearly all I had vanished when last I moved house. Where they went I cannot guess, but I havent got them any more. There are of course a few recent photos, but you want old ones from Rapallo. I remember a cartoon by Gubi which I think appeared in Il Mare,[341] to which you must have access. It amused me then, and I daresay might seem more characteristic than any mere snapshot.

You ask who Dodsworth was. I can give you very little information. In spite of his name he was an Italian. The family was obviously of British origin, and that made him a useful translator of prose journalism for Ezra and Ezra's friends. He played chess – one of Ezra's regular opponents in the café. I think, though I dont remember, that he had also some connection with Saviotti.[342] But if any translation needed skill, we all turned to Francesco Monotti for it. Dodsworth was the humble labourer in such matters. Very useful, always ready to help. There must be old people in Rapallo who remember him, though he was never conspicuous.

I'm happier to turn to your translation of Homage to Propertius.[343] It seems to me very good. The "Quando, quando e quandunque" seems to have caught the difficult rhythms almost perfectly, and that is no mean feat. So far as modern American poetry is concerned, that poem is (though the poets rarely recognize the fact) the foundation document. In your translation I even imagine I can catch the flavour of Whitman's "Sea Drift,"[344] which is where Ezra caught the hint of it. Thankyou for letting me see it.

Snow and cold winds still imprison me. I survive with whisky's help.

Auguri[345]

B

After a short illness, Basil Bunting died in Hexham General Hospital on 17 April 1985.

Alexander Scriabin (1872–1915) in Rapallo in July 1933, BB commented: 'the Russian composer's defects are less extensive than I thought, and the discoveries of his rich originality are startling even after twenty-five years'. *Il Mare* (June 1933), cutting held in Beinecke (my translation).

341 The caricature of BB appeared in *Il Mare*, 13 August 1931.

342 Gino Saviotti (1891–1980), Italian writer, translator and editor of *L'Indice*, a journal to which Pound regularly contributed.

343 Bacigalupo's Italian translation of Pound's *Homage to Sextus Propertius* was published by San Marco dei Giustiniani in 1984.

344 'Sea Drift': section in Whitman's *Leaves of Grass*, which includes 'Out of the Cradle Endlessly Rocking.'

345 *Auguri*: best wishes (It.).

# ACKNOWLEDGMENTS

The preparation of this edition was far more complex than the actual writing. Over a long decade of research, discussion, negotiation, travel, and recurrent prolonged waiting, I was assisted, encouraged, advised, bucked up, and consoled by far too many people to mention here. The following list acknowledges only the outline of a much further-reaching network of support, collaboration, and friendship.

Foremost thanks are due to Bunting's executor John Halliday, and to Bunting's wider family, without whose support this edition would not have been possible. At OUP, Jacqueline Norton and Aimee Wright deserve great credit for taking on the project and for bearing with it through its long gestation. Thanks also to Saranya Ravi and Christine Ranft for meticulous work at the editing and production stages.

For various forms of often crucial help with the location, collation, preparation, translation, and explication of the correspondence, I am profoundly grateful to Iza Hemelaar, John Challis, James Maynard, Carin Graves, Sarah McElroy Mitchell, Peter Lido, Christine Colburn, Laurie Klein, Maria Elia, Ariel Evens, Lisa A. Macklin, Kathy Shoemaker, Sue Donnelly, Anna Towlson, Will Bowers, Anne-Charlotte Husson, Stephen Ross, Bill Lancaster, Stephen Regan, Ian Davidson, and David Lunn.

In producing this latest addition to Bunting scholarship, I pay tribute to the existence, assistance, and persistence of Don Share, Annabel Haynes, Peter Quartermain, Peter Makin, Richard Burton, Reem Abbas, Paul Batchelor, and Mandana Mashayekhi-Ghoyonloo—fellow strugglers in the desert.

Thanks to Louise Niven (who has shared the whole of my Bunting ordeal) for her love, advice, and good humour. Thanks also to Oswald and Bobby Niven for embodying the Northumbrian future.

Tom Pickard deserves more credit and gratitude from me and from the world of poetry than it is possible to give. My work on this edition is dedicated to him.

AN

# GLOSSARY OF NAMES

Brief biographical summaries of BB's correspondents and major figures in his life and work are included below (with their first mention in the above text in bold). Information about more incidental figures (typically, those mentioned only once or twice in the correspondence) is contained in the annotations above.

**J. J. Adams.** In spite of his prominent place in BB's early writings, John J. Adams is an enigmatic figure. He published a handful of poems in the mid 1920s, notably in several issues of Ford Madox Ford's *The Transatlantic Review* (1924). In 1980 BB related to Carroll Terrell that Adams was 'sort of an Eliot on one side and an animal lover and vegetarian on the other', and that he eventually married 'one of the wealthiest women in England', whose fortune he inherited (see *Basil Bunting: Man and Poet*, 43).

**John Penrose Angold** (*c.*1909–1943). British poet, translator, and member of the circle that gathered around A. R. Orage's *New English Weekly* in the mid 1930s. On Pound's recommendation BB corresponded with Angold in 1936, and met up with him on his return to London from the Canaries later that year.

**George Antheil** (1900–1959), American avant-garde composer and author, perhaps best known for scoring the Dadaist film *Ballet Mécanique* (1923–1924). Pound was an enthusiastic supporter of Antheil's work and introduced him to BB in Rapallo in the late 1920s.

**Massimo Bacigalupo** (b. 1947). Italian filmmaker, translator, and Pound scholar, perhaps best known for his 1980 study *The Forméd Trace: The Later Poetry of Ezra Pound*. A Rapallo native, Bacigalupo corresponded with BB at the end of his life about the Rapallo scene and other matters.

**Bruce Berlind** (1926–2014). American academic based at Colgate University, NY, who hosted a visiting writers' series there in the 1960s.

**Gomer Berry, 1st Viscount Kemsley** (1883–1968). British newspaper magnate, who was variously owner of the major newspapers the *Daily Telegraph* and *Sunday Times*, as well as the Newcastle *Journal* and *Evening Chronicle*, where BB worked in the 1950s and 1960s.

**Eric Bloodaxe** (*c.*885–954). Norwegian warrior king who was possibly ruler of the Kingdom of Northumbria for two short spells in the 940s and 950s (some scholars think the Norwegian and Northumbrian Erics were separate people). He features prominently in *Briggflatts* (especially in parts I and II), where he embodies martial aggression and the controlling impulse, in stark contrast to the Northumbrian spiritual hero Saint Cuthbert (see below). Numerous accounts of Eric's life have survived—as BB's notes to collected editions of his work make clear, he derived his portrait from the *Anglo-Saxon Chronicle*, *Orkneyinga Saga*, and the *Heimskringla*.

**D. G. Bridson** (1910–1980). British radio producer and author. Bridson was a leading figure behind the groundbreaking cultural output of the BBC Third Programme in the years after World War II. A supporter of modernist writing and art more generally, he engineered two broadcasts of BB's work on the Third Programme in the 1950s, at a time when BB was otherwise rather marginalized. BB corresponded with Bridson into the 1960s, giving rise to further collaborations around the time of *Briggflatts*.

**Gordon Brown** (d. 2000). A close friend of Sunderland poet Bill Martin (1925–2010), Brown was involved in the poetry scene that clustered around the Ceolfrith Gallery and Press in Sunderland in the 1970s (Ceolfrith published an edition of Joseph Skipsey's poems edited and with an introduction by BB in 1976). Brown seems to have invited BB to read at a poetry festival in the Sunderland area in 1972, for which BB offered to waive his fee on grounds of Northumbrian solidarity.

**Pete Brown** (b. 1940). British poet and musician perhaps best known for his collaborations with the rock band Cream, especially 'Sunshine of Your Love' (1967) and 'White Room' (1968). Originally from the south-east, Brown came to be associated with the pop poetry of the Liverpool scene, whose leading lights (Adrian Henri, Roger McGough, and Brian Patten) came to widespread attention with *The Mersey Sound*, a Penguin anthology of 1967. Brown was the first reader at Morden Tower, on 16 June 1964 (Bloomsday).

**Annie Bunting** (1876–1968). BB's mother. A significant background presence for much of his life, Annie joined him in Rapallo in the early 1930s and lived with him in Northumberland for much of the period 1939–1968.

**Bourtai Bunting Scudder** (b. 1931). BB's eldest daughter, born in Genoa during the Buntings' final spell in Rapallo.

**Marian Culver Bunting** (1900–1982). BB's first wife, who was from Eau Claire, Wisconsin. BB and Marian met in 1929 in Venice (where Marian was in the middle of a European tour paid for by her parents after she graduated from Columbia University). They married in July 1930.

**Roudaba Bunting Davido** (1934–2018). BB's second daughter, born in the Canaries. After BB's revival in the 1960s, fame and travel to North America put him back in touch with Roudaba, who became one of his chief correspondents in later life.

**Rustam Bunting** (1937–1952). BB's first son. Conceived in the last days of BB's marriage to Marian, Rustam was born after her return to the United States. He died of polio at a New Hampshire boarding school in 1952, aged sixteen, having never met BB.

**Sima Bunting (neé Alladadian)** (b. 1933/1934). BB's second wife. BB met Sima, an Armenian-Kurd, while staying with Ronald Oakshott in Isfahan in late 1947, and they married in December 1948, when Sima was either fourteen or fifteen. Sima moved back to Northumberland with BB in the early 1950s, and they remained married until their separation and divorce in 1977.

**Sima-Maria ('Maria') Bunting** (b. 1950). BB's third daughter, born in Iran while BB was working for the *Times*.

**Tom Bunting** (b. 1952). BB's second son, born after the Buntings had returned to Northumberland in the early 1950s.

**Carolyn Burke** (b. 1940), Australian-American biographer and critic, who corresponded with BB while preparing her 1996 biography *Becoming Modern: The Life of Mina Loy*.

**Samuel Butler** (1835–1902). English novelist and essayist best known for the 1872 novel *Erewhon*, a satire of Victorian England. On the evidence of the early letters, he was one of the most significant literary influences on BB in his formative years.

**William Byrd** (*c.*1540–1623). British renaissance choral composer who was a key aesthetic influence on BB for much of his life. BB witnessed one of the first revival performances of Byrd's 'Great Service', at St Nicholas's Cathedral in Newcastle in 1924.

**John Collier** (1901–1980). British author and acquaintance of BB in the 1920s, who largely abandoned poetry after the publication of his modestly successful novel *His Monkey Wife* in 1930.

**William Cookson** (1939–2003). British poet, writer, and editor of the Poundian journal *Agenda*, which he founded in 1959 partly at the instigation of Pound and Peter Russell. BB was a recurrent presence in *Agenda* (as both subject and contributor) from the mid 1960s onwards.

**Cid Corman** (1924–2004). American poet, translator, and editor. In 1951 he founded the journal *Origin*, which became a major focal point for the publication of late-modernist poetry. He moved to Tokyo in the late 1950s, where he continued to edit *Origin* and began to translate Japanese poetry.

**Gregory Corso** (1930–2001). American Beat poet. BB got to know Corso after he read at Morden Tower in the mid 1960s, and encountered him again several times at readings in Britain and North America.

**Kenneth Cox** (1916–2005). Literary critic, whose career began late in life, with the appearance of the essay 'The Aesthetic of Basil Bunting' in *Agenda* in 1966. He corresponded with BB in the wake of the essay, and returned to his work many times in subsequent pieces. Highlights of his writing are collected in *The Art of Language: Selected Essays*, published by Flood in 2016.

**Robert Creeley** (1926–2005). American poet and a key figure in late-modernist poetry. An erstwhile member of Black Mountain College in North Carolina, Creeley was an important link between the avant-garde scene that developed there in the wake of Charles Olson's 1950 manifesto 'Projective Verse', and the more freewheeling, less academic milieu of Beat poets like Allen Ginsberg. Like Ginsberg, Creeley visited Morden Tower in the mid 1960s, where he became a friend of BB and a profound influence on BB's protégé Tom Pickard.

**Saint Cuthbert** (*c.*634–687). Patron saint of Northumbria. Originally from near Melrose (now in southern Scotland), Cuthbert became a Christian monk and eventually Bishop of Lindisfarne. After his death he was the subject of one of the most popular Anglo-Saxon saint cults (Alfred the Great's struggle against the Danes in the ninth century was reputedly partly inspired by a vision of Cuthbert). Cuthbert features as a (mostly silent) presence in *Briggflatts*, where he embodies self-sacrifice, humility, and surrender to the beauty of nature.

**Edward Dahlberg** (1900–1977). American poet and essayist, who befriended Louis Zukofsky while they were colleagues at Brooklyn Polytechnic Institute in the late 1940s. His name is mentioned several times in BB's letters to Zukofsky of 1951.

**Donald Davie** (1922–1995). British poet and literary critic, who became one of the major scholars of late-twentieth century Anglo-American verse from the 1950s onwards. Davie wrote extensively on Ezra Pound (his 1975 introduction to Pound's work for Fontana occasioned his correspondence with BB), and he placed BB at the centre of his survey of post-war British verse *Under Briggflatts* (1989).

**Mary Dawson** (1903–*c.*2005). Sedbergh resident who BB probably knew from his visits to Brigflatts in the 1910s. She also seems to have been a member of the congregation at Brigflatts, and a friend of Jonathan Williams after he moved to the Sedbergh area in the 1960s.

**Cecil Day-Lewis** (1904–1972). Anglo-Irish poet who was British Poet Laureate 1968–1972. Although Day-Lewis featured in BB's 'English' number of *Poetry* in February 1932, he was more generally a figure associated with the Auden circle of the 1930s, and thereafter with the formally conservative mainstream of English verse. Partly for these reasons, he is a perennial target of BB's ire in the correspondence.

**Margaret De Silver** (1889–1962). Wealthy American socialite and supporter of artistic and political causes, who was BB's patron, sporadically, from 1928 until the 1950s.

**Edmond Dodsworth** (1877–1950). Italian poet and translator, who got to know BB in Rapallo in the early 1930s. He translated some of BB's prose for the local newspaper *Il Mare*.

**C. H. Douglas** (1879–1952). British economist, whose 'Social Credit' theory was enthusiastically taken up by Pound from the late 1910s after a meeting in the

*New Age* office arranged by A. R. Orage (see below). In brief, and at the risk of over-simplification, Douglas's theory highlighted the fact that in many early-twentieth century economies, there was an excess of production and a lack of consumer ability to access goods and services. In response, he recommended the empowerment of consumers through regular distributive interventions by governments, and a corresponding disempowerment of banking institutions and their debt systems. BB apparently met Douglas around 1920, though unlike Pound (an enthusiastic Social Crediter), he was not impressed with his theory.

**John Dowland** (1563–1626). British renaissance composer best known for his secular love songs. Dowland underwent a major revival in the early-twentieth century along with other renaissance composers, and became a favourite of many modernist writers (notably James Joyce). Like his near contemporary William Byrd, Dowland was an important influence on BB throughout his life.

**Karl Drerup** (1904–2000). German artist who began as a painter but achieved widespread acclaim for his work in enamels after he moved to New York in 1937. Prior to his move to the United States, Drerup lived in Tenerife in the Canary Islands, where he became a close friend of BB.

**John Drummond.** American poetry critic with whom Pound corresponded in the 1930s. In 1935 he co-edited a special-issue poetry journal *Bozart-Westminster* (with Pound and T. C. Wilson), which featured contributions by Pound, Lorine Niedecker, BB, and others.

**Ronald Duncan** (1914–1982). British poet and dramatist who founded the journal *Townsman* (1938–1945), partly at Pound's instigation. His poetry was published by Eliot at Faber and Faber from the 1950s on (which was galling for BB given his own rejection by Eliot in this period).

**Ernest Fenellosa** (1853–1908), American academic who specialized in Japanese and Chinese language and culture. After his death, Fenellosa's manuscripts were donated to Pound, who used them to write up the essay 'The Chinese Written Character as a Medium for Poetry'. The basic argument of the essay—that there is a visible correspondence between written character and object in Chinese writing—was hugely influential on Pound's own Imagist practice, and on the subsequent development of modernist poetry more generally.

**Ferdowsi/Firdusi** (*c.*940–1020). Poet who composed the Persian national epic *Shahnameh* in the years around AD 1000. After discovering Ferdowsi's poem in Italy in the early 1930s, BB began an ultimately abortive attempt to translate it, which persisted for the remainder of the decade. More obliquely, BB's engagement with *Shahnameh* led to his move to Iran in the 1940s (where he was posted because of his knowledge of Persian), and to the central, third episode in *Briggflatts*, which is based on an episode from Ferdowsi's poem.

**Roy Fisher** (1930–2017). British poet who played a major part in the British Poetry Revival. Fisher met Gael Turnbull in the mid 1950s and thereafter became central to the transatlantic network of poets and publishers that also included

Robert Creeley, Cid Corman, Stuart Montgomery, and Michael Shayer. After BB's revival he became friends with Fisher and an admirer of his work.

**Dallam Flynn/Simpson.** American poet and publisher, who founded the Texas-based journal *Four Pages* in the late 1940s, to which Pound contributed many times from St Elizabeths. Through the Pound connection, Flynn was made aware of BB, and published his *Poems: 1950*, which collected the majority of BB's works written up to that point.

**Sister Victoria Forde.** American critic and Catholic nun who began corresponding with BB while she was writing a doctoral thesis on his poetry at the University of Notre Dame in the early 1970s. A revised version of Forde's thesis, *The Poetry of Basil Bunting*, appeared via Bloodaxe Books in 1991 (the first monograph on his work).

**Allen Ginsberg** (1926–1997). American Beat poet and the central driving force behind the emergence of a poetic counterculture in the post-war years. Ginsberg befriended BB when he read at Morden Tower in 1965, creating a crucial link between the Newcastle scene and the international counterculture in the months leading up to publication of *Briggflatts*.

**Denis Goacher** (1925–1998). British poet, translator, actor, and broadcaster. Goacher corresponded with Pound in the early 1950s, and was put in touch by Pound with BB, first meeting him in London in 1954. As a producer at the BBC, Goacher was a driving force behind BB's two appearances on the Third Programme (in 1954 and 1957). After BB's meeting with Tom Pickard in 1964, he began a regular correspondence with Goacher which persisted for the next quarter century, and which was especially copious in the late 1960s (perhaps not coincidentally, around the time of BB's estrangement from Louis Zukofsky). Goacher's memoir of his relationship with BB, 'Denis Goacher Talks About Bunting', a conversation with Diana Collecott published in a 1995 special issue of the Durham University Journal, is one of the best (and most opinionated) accounts of BB's later years.

**Robert Graves** (1895–1985). British poet, novelist, and critic. Graves was a near contemporary of BB (and, like him, a figure with a high public profile in post-war Britain).

**Peggy Greenbank** (b. 1904/1905). The dedicatee of *Briggflatts* and inspiration for its central love story. BB met Peggy in 1913, when he visited Brigflatts for the first time with Peggy's elder brother, his schoolmate John Greenbank (BB would spend the next few summers at Brigflatts in Peggy's company). In 1965, while putting the finishing touches to *Briggflatts*, BB was reacquainted with Peggy, and they resumed their relationship. Both phases of BB's connection with Peggy are somewhat unsupported by hard evidence, and it is often difficult to read beyond the highly poeticized depiction of their relationship in *Briggflatts*.

**Roger Guedalla.** British scholar who was managing editor at the poetry journal *Stony Brook* in the late 1960s. Guedalla compiled an important early bibliography of BB for publication in 1973—his research was a key foundation for study of BB's life and work.

**John Halliday.** Executor of BB's estate, who became BB's son-in-law after marrying Maria Bunting in the early 1970s.

**Hafez/Hafiz** (1315–1390). Sufi poet who occupies a central position in Persian culture. BB translated several of his lyrics in the 1930s.

**Richard Hamilton** (1922–2011). British artist credited as a seminal figure in the development of British pop art. Hamilton taught in the Fine Art Department of Kings College/Newcastle University in the 1950s and 1960s, and became an attendee of the Morden Tower readings from 1964. He designed artwork for the pamphlet *King Ida's Watch Chain* and an edition of BB's *The Spoils*, both of which were published by the Morden Tower Book Room in 1965.

**Ian Hamilton Finlay** (1925–2006). Scottish modernist poet who rose to prominence in the 1960s. A proponent of experimental verse practices such as concrete poetry and installations in natural environments, Finlay crossed swords with BB during his long legal dispute in the late 1960s with Fulcrum Press (BB's publisher).

**Nina Hamnett** (1890–1956). Welsh writer and artist, known as the 'Queen of Bohemia' because of her central presence in the London and Paris avant-gardes following World War I. BB befriended her in London in the early 1920s, and also encountered her in Paris in 1923.

**Tony Harrison** (b. 1937). British poet, translator, and playwright born in Leeds, who relocated to Newcastle in 1967 when he became the first Northern Arts Literary Fellow at Durham and Newcastle Universities. On arriving in the city he integrated into the Morden Tower scene and became a friend of BB.

**Michael Henshaw** (1930–2007). BB's London-based accountant in his later years. Henshaw was famous for his militant assertion of the professional rights of artists and poets (especially when it came to taxation). His other clients included Ted Hughes, Alexander Trocchi, Allen Ginsberg, and Monty Python.

**Ted Hughes** (1930–1998). British poet who quickly rose to prominence after his first collection *The Hawk in the Rain* was published in 1957. He was British Poet Laureate 1984–1998. BB and Hughes crossed paths in the late 1960s, and corresponded briefly after spending some time together as judges at the Arvon International Poetry Competition in 1983.

**David Jones** (1895–1974). Anglo-Welsh artist and poet, whose historically inclined late-modernist verse (especially the 1952 long poem *The Anathemata*) bears many similarities with BB's *Briggflatts*. BB and Jones were also united by an interest in forms of British regional and national identity (Northumbrian and Welsh respectively). They became friends in the late 1960s.

**Hugh Kenner** (1923–2003). Canadian critic who became one of the major scholars of modernist literature during its ascendancy as an academic discipline in the post-war years. Kenner wrote extensively on Pound, and was endorsed by BB as the pre-eminent Poundian critic. BB and Kenner met during BB's spell as a visiting fellow at UC Santa Barbara in 1966–1968, where Kenner was a professor.

**Rodger Kingston.** Probably the Seattle-born photographer who opened Photographic Eye Inc, a gallery and bookstore in Cambridge, Massachusetts, in 1975. He corresponded briefly with BB in 1970, apparently floating the idea of writing a critical study of BB's work.

**James Laughlin** (1914–1997). American poet and editor who founded New Directions in 1936 (it subsequently became Pound's American publisher). Laughlin and BB crossed paths in Rapallo in the early 1930s (it was Laughlin who coined the phrase 'Ezuversity' to describe the Rapallo milieu). BB seems to have disliked Laughlin because he neglected to publish him.

**James G. Leippert** (1909–1964). American editor and publisher, best known for publishing major works by Wallace Stevens. Leippert/Latimer ran the literary journal *The Lion and the Crown* in 1932–1933 while he was a student at Columbia College, and later assumed the name by which he is more often known: Ronald Lane Latimer.

**David Lloyd George** (1863–1945). Welsh politician and Liberal Prime Minister of Britain 1916–1922. BB is likely to have met Lloyd George when he served as secretary to the Liberal MP Harry Barnes in the last days of Lloyd George's premiership. Thereafter BB seems to have regarded him as his gatekeeper for the Westminster establishment.

**Mina Loy** (1882–1966). British writer and artist who was at the centre of modernist circles in the early twentieth century. BB met Loy during his stay in Paris in 1923 and owned a copy of her seminal verse collection *Lunar Baedeker* (1923).

**Hugh MacDiarmid** (1892–1978). Poet who wrote mainly in a form of 'synthetic Scots' and dominated the Scottish literary scene for much of the mid-to-late twentieth century. As with David Jones (see above), BB felt a kinship with MacDiarmid on both literary and aesthetic grounds—MacDiarmid's idiosyncratic modernism had loose affinities with BB's own, as did his interest in peripheral British identities (MacDiarmid was an ardent Scottish nationalist). MacDiarmid was an early reader at Morden Tower in the mid 1960s and subsequently visited BB several times (MacDiarmid lived in southern Scotland, not far from the border with Northumberland).

**Archibald MacLeish** (1892–1982). American poet who rose to prominence in the 1920s and 1930s as a figure loosely associated with the modernist scene (like BB, he spent time in Paris in the early 1920s). MacLeish was Librarian of Congress in Washington DC between 1939 to 1944, and helped to secure Pound's release from St Elizabeths in the late 1950s.

**François de Malherbe** (1555–1628). French poet famous for his verbal precision and austere, technical approach to writing. BB cited him as a major influence.

**Robert McAlmon** (1895–1956). American author and publisher, who was part of 1920s modernist circles and helped to publish Pound, William Carlos Williams, Marianne Moore, Hilda Doolittle, and other major figures. BB met McAlmon in New York during his stay there in 1930–1931.

**Thomas ('Tom') Meyer** (b. 1945), American poet, translator, and long-term partner of Jonathan Williams. Meyer assisted Williams with the running of Jargon Press, and got to know BB through him in the 1970s.

**Manuchehri/Minuchihri** (d. 1040). Canonical Persian poet. BB translated several of Manuchehri's lyrics in the late 1940s and early 1950s.

**Harriet Monroe** (1860–1936). American poet and publisher who founded *Poetry* magazine in Chicago in 1912. In the ensuing decades Monroe's journal would become arguably the most important outlet for modernist verse in the world. BB corresponded with Monroe from the late 1920s onwards, and thereafter almost all of his major poems, from 'Villon' (1930) through to *Briggflatts* (1966), were published in *Poetry*.

**Stuart Montgomery** (b. 1938). Psychiatrist and publisher, who founded Fulcrum Press in 1965. Fulcrum became the pre-eminent publisher of Anglo-American modernist verse in the late 1960s, producing editions by almost all the major figures of the transatlantic milieu of which BB was a part (e.g. Allen Ginsberg, Roy Fisher, Tom Pickard, Ed Dorn, Tom Raworth, Gary Snyder, and George Oppen). Fulcrum also published several works by BB in this period, including *Briggflatts* (1966) and his *Collected Poems* (1968). Fulcrum was bankrupted in 1974 after a lengthy legal dispute with Ian Hamilton Finlay, into which BB waded as a friend and supporter of Montgomery.

**Louise Morgan** (1883–1964). American writer, journalist, and wife of Otto Theis (see below), with whom she worked on the *Outlook*, an English political and literary magazine. BB contributed a series of articles to the journal (chiefly as music correspondent) from February 1927 until its closure in 1928.

**Oswald Mosley** (1896–1980). British politician who led the British Union of Fascists (BUF) in the 1930s. Mosley started out as a Conservative MP, but moved to the Labour Party in 1924, where he acquired a reputation for energetic radicalism. After his 'Mosley Memorandum' (a programme for tackling the social and economic crises of the immediate post-1929 period) was rejected by the Labour government in 1930, he resigned to form the interventionist New Party, which morphed into the BUF in 1931–1932.

**Mohammad Mosaddegh/Mossadeq** (1882–1967). Prime Minister of Iran between 1951 and 1953. Mossadegh is generally regarded as an anti-imperialist champion of democratic reform in post-war Iran. However, these qualities put him at odds with British and American interests in the Middle East, and he was removed from power in August 1953 as part of a CIA-backed coup. As a British journalist in Tehran, BB attracted the ire of Mossadegh, who expelled him from the country in May 1952.

**Eric Mottram** (1924–1995). Poet and academic who was a key figure in the British Poetry Revival. As well as championing American late-modernist and Beat poets such as Allen Ginsberg and Robert Duncan, Mottram entered the British literary counterculture as a practitioner from the 1960s onwards, becoming editor of the Poetry Society house journal in the 1970s during a period of struggle between conservative and radical tendencies. He met BB in the late 1960s and they corresponded sporadically over the next decade or so.

**Alexander Nelson.** Presumably someone involved with Sumac Press, for whom the poet George Quasha edited an anthology of experimental verse in the early 1970s. BB wrote to Nelson twice in late 1970, declining to take part in Quasha's anthology in forcible terms.

**Alfred R. Orage** (1873–1934). Political author and founding editor 1907–1922 of seminal left-wing journal the *New Age*, which published major modernist writers such as T. E. Hulme, Katherine Mansfield, and Hugh MacDiarmid. Pound was a major contributor to the *New Age* throughout the 1910s and early 1920s, and it was through Orage that Pound learned of C. H. Douglas's Social Credit theory. BB apparently met Orage in London in the very early 1920s, and later described himself as one of 'Orage's set of likely young men'.

**Connie Pickard (neé Watson).** Co-founder of the Morden Tower poetry readings in Newcastle with her husband at the time, Tom Pickard. She maintained the Tower for many years (often in the face of opposition and indifference from the local authorities and university) until retirement due to ill health in the early 2010s.

**Tom Pickard** (b. 1946). Poet and co-founder with his first wife, Connie, of the Morden Tower as a poetry venue. Pickard met BB in April 1964 and was the driving force behind BB's return to creative activity over the next two years—BB was invited to read at the Tower, and inspired to write *Briggflatts* by the enthusiasm of the young people in its audience. In return, BB became a mentor of sorts for Pickard, writing a preface to his first poetry collection, *High on the Walls*, published by Fulcrum in 1967. BB and Pickard remained friends and correspondents until BB's death in 1985, since when Pickard has published numerous works, most recently the collection *Winter Migrants* (2016) and the memoir *Fiends Fell* (2017).

**Dorothy Pound (neé Shakespear)** (1886–1973). Daughter of novelist Olivia Shakespear and wife of Ezra Pound 1914–1973. Dorothy became good friends with BB (and his mother Annie) during his time in Rapallo, and after Ezra was admitted to St Elizabeths, she was regularly BB's point of contact among the Pounds—sometimes as proxy for Ezra, sometimes not. She visited BB at his Wylam home in the late 1960s.

**Omar Pound** (1926–2010). Scholar of Persian and Islamic history and son of Dorothy and Ezra Pound (though Pound was not his biological father).

**Samuel Putnam** (1892–1950). American writer, editor, and founder (in 1932) of the *New Review*, a journal to which BB contributed.

**Peter Quartermain** (b. 1934). English-born Canadian academic, who became friends with BB during his spell at the University of British Columbia in 1970–1971 (as did his wife Carol). BB and Quartermain remained friends and correspondents over the next decade, and after BB's death Quartermain published 'Basil Bunting: Poet of the North' (1990), the first substantial appraisal of BB's regionalism.

**Kenneth Rexroth** (1905–1982). American poet who rose to prominence as part of the Objectivist grouping (Rexroth featured in the famous February 1931 'Objectivist' issue of *Poetry*) and later played a key part in the post-war San Francisco Renaissance. It is unlikely that BB ever met Rexroth, though his name crops up in the correspondence several times.

**Lionel Robbins** (1898–1984). British economist and academic at the London School of Economics (LSE), who was a key figure in the expansion of British higher education in the 1960s, and a significant influence on the revival of liberal economics in the mid twentieth century. Robbins and BB became friends while they were undergraduates at LSE in 1919–1920.

**John Rodker** (1894–1955). British poet, publisher, and founder of the Cassanova Society, which printed limited editions of modernist works. Rodker was responsible for publishing Pound's *A Draft of the Cantos 17-27* (1928).

**Olga Rudge** (1895–1996). Concert violinist and long-term lover of Ezra Pound from 1923 until his death in 1972. Pound lived with Rudge in Italy following his release from St Elizabeths. During the whole post-war period she seems to have been fairly hostile to BB, apparently blaming him for not helping to secure Pound's release.

**Bertrand Russell** (1872–1970). British intellectual who dominated British philosophy for much of the twentieth century. BB was apparently a long-running admirer of Russell's philosophic liberalism (he owned several of Russell's works, including *Introduction to Mathematical Philosophy* (1919) and *Human Knowledge* (1948)).

**Peter Russell** (1921–3003). British poet and critic (and a cousin of Bertrand Russell). He formed an 'Ezra Pound Circle' in London in the late 1940s, and corresponded briefly with BB in 1950. He also founded the literary journal *Nine* in 1949, which published BB on a couple of occasions in the late 1950s.

**Rumi** (1207–1273) Persian Sufi poet, whose works are hugely popular in Persia, the wider Middle East and indeed throughout the world. BB was lukewarm about Rumi's works (and the prospect of translating them), probably because of their mystical emphasis.

**Sadi/Saadi/Sa'dī** (1210–1292). Major Persian poet, translated by BB on several occasions from the 1930s through the 1970s.

**Domenico Scarlatti** (1685–1757). Italian baroque composer. Scarlatti was a favourite of BB's, and his keyboard sonatas were cited as a key influence on the musical element in *Briggflatts*. At performances of *Briggflatts*, BB regularly arranged for live playing or recordings of Scarlatti to be juxtaposed with his poetry (often during or after Part IV of the poem, which mentions Scarlatti explicitly).

**Tibor Serly** (1901–1978). Hungarian violinist and composer. Serly spent most of his life in New York, where he met Louis Zukofsky and William Carlos Williams. He followed them to Rapallo in the 1930s, where he met BB and helped Pound with his concert organizing. Serly died after being hit by a car in London in 1978, apparently on his way to a reunion with BB.

**Michael Shayer** (b. 1928). Psychologist and poet who—with his schoolfriend Gael Turnbull—ran Migrant, a poetry press of the late 1950s and early 1960s (also briefly a magazine). Migrant published or distributed many of the major Anglo-American modernist figures of the period, notably Roy Fisher, Ian Hamilton Finlay, and Charles Olson. Shayer and Turnbull made contact with BB in the late 1950s, and became close in the mid 1960s, at which point Migrant agreed to distribute the Morden Tower Book Room edition of *The Spoils* (1965).

**Jon Silkin** (1930–1970). British poet and founding editor of the long-running poetry magazine *Stand* 1952–1997. Silkin moved to Newcastle in 1965, where he met BB and encountered the Morden Tower scene.

**Colin Simms** (b. 1939). British poet and naturalist who got to know BB in his revival period, especially during BB's spell at Fox Cottage, Tarset, which was close to Simms's then home.

**Joseph Skipsey** (1832–1903). Northumberland-born 'pitman poet', who wrote many lyric poems on north-east mining subjects in the late-nineteenth century. BB is said to have met Skipsey as a child, and he edited a selected edition of Skipsey's poems for the Sunderland publisher Ceolfrith Press in 1976.

**René Taupin** (1905–1981). French critic, translator, and academic. BB stayed at Taupin's New York apartment for some weeks at the end of 1938, having met him during his earlier 1930–1931 sojourn to New York.

**Otto Theis** (1881–1966). American editor and literary agent. Theis was assistant editor of the *Outlook* in the late 1920s, to which BB contributed music journalism.

**Gael Turnbull** (1928–2004). Scottish doctor and poet who played a major role in kickstarting the British Poetry Revival. Turnbull made contact with the North American modernist scene while living in Pennsylvania in the early 1950s, contributing poems to and guest-editing Cid Corman's *Origin*, and befriending Jonathan Williams (see below). Soon after returning to Britain in 1955, Turnbull founded Migrant Press with Michael Shayer (see above). He started corresponding with BB in late 1956 and, after moving to the English Midlands after another spell in the United States, became a close friend and regular correspondent of BB.

**Joanna Voit.** Polish artist and photographer who married Tom Pickard in 1978. Voit took photos of BB and associated writers in the late 1970s and 1980s.

**Peter Whigham** (1925–1987). British poet and translator, who edited Pound's translation of Sophocles' *Women of Trachis* alongside Denis Goacher in the mid 1950s.

**Jonathan Williams** (1929–2008). American poet, writer, publisher, and photographer. An alumnus of Black Mountain College, Williams founded the Jargon Society in 1951, which became a major publisher of late-modernist verse, including works by Zukofsky, Charles Olson, and Lorine Niedecker. Williams visited BB in 1963 and the two became friends and correspondents. He subsequently bought a cottage in Dentdale, near Brigflatts, which BB visited many times.

**T. C. Wilson** (1912–1950). American poet and critic, who edited the special edition *Bozart-Westminster* poetry anthology in 1935, alongside Pound and James Laughlin.

**Andrew Wylie** (b. 1947). American literary agent (and erstwhile poet), who met BB and took him on a driving tour of Massachusetts when BB read at Harvard University in March 1967. BB returned the favour the following year, taking Wylie on a roadtrip of north-east England.

# INDEX